www.wadsworth.com

wadsworth.com is the World Wide Web site for Wadsworth Publishing Company and is your direct source to dozens of online resources.

At *wadsworth.com* you can find out about supplements, demonstration software, and student resources. You can also send e-mail to many of our authors and preview new publications and exciting new technologies.

wadsworth.com
Changing the way the world learns®

✪

The Wadsworth
Special Educator Series

The following Special Education titles are new for 1998/1999
from Wadsworth Publishing Company:

1998

Benner, *Special Education Issues Within the Context of American Society,*
ISBN 0-534-25230-3

Gersten/Jimenez, *Promoting Learning for Culturally and
Linguistically Diverse Students,*
ISBN 0-534-34417-6

Rusch/Chadsey, *Beyond High School: Transition from School to Work,*
ISBN 0-534-34432-1

1999

Bigge/Stump/Silberman, *Curriculum, Assessment, and
Instruction for Exceptional Learners,*
ISBN 0-534-16770-5

Coutinho/Repp, *Inclusion: The Integration of Students with Disabilities,*
ISBN 0-534-56718-5

Repp/Horner, *Functional Analysis of Problem Behavior:
From Effective Assessment to Effective Support,*
ISBN 0-534-34850-5

Curriculum, Assessment, and Instruction for Students with Disabilities

JUNE LEE BIGGE, ED.D.
San Francisco State University

COLLEEN SHEA STUMP, PH.D.
San Francisco State University

with
Michael Edward Spagna, Ph.D.
California State University, Northridge

Rosanne K. Silberman, Ed.D.
Hunter College of the City University of New York

Wadsworth Publishing Company
I(T)P® An International Thomson Publishing Company

Belmont, CA • Albany, NY • Boston • Cincinnati • Detroit • Johannesburg • London • Madrid • Melbourne
Mexico City • New York • Pacific Grove, CA • Scottsdale, AZ • Singapore • Tokyo • Toronto

Education Editor: Dianne Lindsay
Assistant Editor: Tangelique Williams
Marketing Manager: Becky Tollerson
Project Editor: Jennie Redwitz
Print Buyer: Barbara Britton
Permissions Editor: Susan Walters
Production: Matrix Productions Inc.
Designer: Hespenheide Design

Copy Editor: Patricia Herbst
Illustrator: Asterisk Inc.
Cover Design: Hespenheide Design
Compositor: Thompson Type
Printer: Mazer Corporation

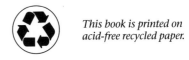

This book is printed on
acid-free recycled paper.

Printed in the United States of America
2 3 4 5 6 7 8 9 10

For more information, contact Wadsworth Publishing Company, 10 Davis Drive, Belmont, CA 94002, or electronically
at http://www.wadsworth.com

International Thomson Publishing Europe
Berkshire House
168-173 High Holborn
London, WC1V 7AA, United Kingdom

Nelson ITP, Australia
102 Dodds Street
South Melbourne
Victoria 3205 Australia

Nelson Canada
1120 Birchmount Road
Scarborough, Ontario
Canada M1K 5G4

International Thomson Editores
Seneca, 53
Colonia Polanco
11560 México D.F. México

International Thomson Publishing Asia
60 Albert Street #15-01
Albert Complex
Singapore 189969

International Thomson Publishing Japan
Hirakawa-cho Kyowa Building, 3F
2-2-1 Hirakawa-cho, Chiyoda-ku
Tokyo 102, Japan

International Thomson Publishing Southern Africa
Building 18, Constantia Square
138 Sixteenth Road, P.O. Box 2459
Halfway House, 1685 South Africa

Library of Congress Cataloging-in-Publication Data
Bigge, June L.
    Curriculum, assessment, and instruction for students
with disabilities / June Lee Bigge . . . [et al.].
        p.   cm.
    Includes bibliographical references and index.
    ISBN 0-534-16770-5
    1. Handicapped children—Education—United States—
Curricula.   2. Handicapped children—Ability testing—
United States.   3. Special education—United States.
I. Title.
LC4031.B46   1999
371.9'0973—dc21   98-34355

Dedication

For my father, Morris L. Bigge, who wrote a landmark book for teaching about learning theories; and for my aunt, Jeanette Bigge, who was everyone's favorite teacher.   —June Bigge

For my grandparents, Bud and Gerry Shea, who taught me to be my own person; and for my husband, Randy, for being my best friend.   —Colleen Stump

BRIEF CONTENTS

CONTENTS

PREFACE

Curriculum, Assessment, and Instruction for Students with Disabilities provides general and special education teachers with foundation information in the workings of special education and describes their roles in designing meaningful programs for students with disabilities. One salient strength of the text is that it is noncategorical. Throughout the text, multiple exhibits addressing a range of disability conditions illustrate ideas and issues. This encourages readers to focus on and understand the unique needs of learners with disabilities rather than interpreting all information through the lens of categorization.

The text is appropriate for both general and special education preservice and general education inservice candidates. It is most appropriate for courses such as Introduction to Special Education, Mainstreaming, Curriculum Foundations, Assessment Methods, and Instruction Methods. *Curriculum, Assessment, and Instruction for Students with Disabilities* also serves as an exceptional text for method courses that integrate curricular, assessment, and instructional issues and practices.

Chapter 1 provides the foundation for understanding the text. In this chapter, special education law, terminology, and professionals are described and defined. Additionally, the three individualized plans for individuals with disabilities are explained and illustrated. Chapter 1 prepares the reader for the information to follow.

Section 1, "Curriculum," consists of Chapters 2–5 and opens with a discussion of the alignment of national, state, and local standards and their relationship to the needs and goals of students with disabilities. The discussion of how to bridge student IEP goals, benchmarks, and objectives to national, state, and local goals, outcomes, and standards reflects the mandate of the IDEA Amendments of 1997 that identifies the general education curriculum as the base for developing a student's special education curriculum as defined in the IEP. Chapters 3–5 in the section present examples of curricular options available to students with disabilities. General education curriculum, general education curriculum with modifications, life skills curriculum, and curriculum in modified means of communication and performance options are illustrated through multiple diverse exhibits representative of the curricular needs of individuals with disabilities.

Section 2, "Assessment," includes Chapters 6–10 and provides a thorough discussion of Stump's model of contextualized assessment (assessment that gathers information across multiple factors and contexts) and methods and tools used in (a) determination of eligibility and development of an initial Individualized Education Program; (b) review of individualized plans; (c) evaluation of instruction; and (d) program evaluation. Prereferral and referral processes, development of individualized plans, attributes of assessment methods and tools and their application with individual students, IEP goal, benchmark, and objective writing, and program evaluation techniques are described through multiple exhibits. A case study chronicles the eligibility assessment process within the context of an individual student's experience.

Section 3, "Instruction," includes Chapters 11–18 and focuses on instructional practices for working with individuals with disabilities. The section begins with a discussion of how to create a context for learning, how to provide quality instruction through planning, and how to select activities when designing instruction for students with disabilities. Chapters delve into lesson planning and the teaching of mathematics, emergent literacy, reading and writing, learning strategies, study skills, and life skills, including education for transitions. A special chapter presents information on the application of technology to teaching.

The final chapter of the book, Chapter 19, provides application activities for each of the preceding chapters. These activities provide readers the opportunity to apply and integrate information gained to create solutions for the challenges that general and special educators encounter when working with individuals with disabilities.

The book offers several features:

Advance Organizers: Each chapter begins with a list of the key topics that are addressed in the chapter. The advance organizer assists the reader in setting a purpose for reading the chapter.

"Theory to Practice": Discussion questions and activities related to each section of a chapter are presented as "Theory to Practice" activities. The questions and activities challenge readers to go beyond the text and apply information to their practice or the practice of others in area schools and other agencies, and to evaluate that practice critically.

"Make It Happen": Ideas presented here provide practitioners with specific strategies and ideas for implementing techniques and practices into their classrooms.

Exhibits, Tables, and Figures: A wealth of illustrative material provides readers with examples of the ideas presented and discussed. These examples may be used in class activities and discussions and can serve as springboards for student practicum experiences and assignments. They may also serve as resources for inservice teachers.

ACKNOWLEDGMENTS

We wish to express appreciation to those people who helped bring this text to fruition. We do this by identifying them and the kinds of help they provided.

Many of the ideas incorporated here emerged from work with graduate students in the Department of Special Education at San Francisco State University. Many of these students are special education teachers by now or teachers who have students with disabilities in their classes. Three provided very specific information for illustrations. They are Eileen Vukicevich, Shana Carol A. Robinson and Shannon Wakeman.

GiGi Whitford, graduate assistant at San Francisco State University and a new special education teacher, made invaluable contributions at all stages of the development of this text. She not only assisted with the technical aspects of a research assistant but also edited some chapters and provided material for illustrations. GiGi and Wandaline Perelli developed charts for organizing the many author requests for photo and other permissions and conducted other helpful computer-based activities. Jennifer Marucheck read some chapters from the point of view of a university student who was unfamiliar with special education. She edited for ease of understanding, readability and also conducted library research.

Professionals who responded to our requests for assistance in obtaining the latest data, examples and viewpoints are William Spady, William Frey, Linda Lynch, Jack Schroeder, Marcia Watson, Carol Allman, Ray O'Connell, Janine Swanson, Jack Hazekamp, Carolyn Compton, Zigfried Engelmann, and Grace Ambrose.

Others provided helpful assistance of different kinds: Gabriella and Keith Holzman, Laura M. Piché, Ginger Woltosz, Larry Gigax, Barry Romich, Amanda Lueck, Phil Hatlen, Jack Hazecamp, and Janine Swanson.

We feel that part of the strength of this text lies in the exhibits, figures, tables, and other illustrations we chose for practical applications of content in each chapter. Many of these came from other teachers, education and related services professionals, and vendors. Please note these specific credits as you read.

University professors who accepted our invitations to author a chapter on computer applications are Vicki Casella and Loretta Giorcelli. Professionals who were invited personally by the authors to review chapters in their particular areas of expertise and to edit or add to the content are Sandra Rosen, Judy Henderson, Ann Corn, Mary Hanlon, Debra Karres, Dorothy Fletcher, Martha Pamperin, and Connie Yannacone. Reviewers invited by the publishers redirected us in several ways. We appreciated their remarks. We hope many will see the results of their reviews in the final product. These reviewers are Charles Atkinson, Woodring College of Education; Sherry Best, California State University—Los Angeles; Carol Burdett, University of Vermont; James Calder, Middle Tennessee State University; Christine Cheney, University of Nevada—Reno; Linda Christensen; Patsy Daly, Ohio Dominican College; Douglas Fisher, San Diego State University; Sheila Fox, Western Washington University; Anne L. Fuller, University of Texas; Susan Glor-Scheib, Indiana University of Pennsylvania; Rena Lewis, San Diego State University; Ben Lignugaris-Kraft, Utah State University; Jeanice Midgett, University of Central Florida; Darcy Miller, Washington State University; Kenneth R. Olsen, University of Kentucky; Paul Thomas, Buffalo State College; Martha Thurlow, University of Minnesota; and John Venn, University of North Florida.

Vicki Knight, Education Editor of Brooks Cole Publishers, gave an inordinate amount of support during the earlier stages of the text. Then, after consolidation of publishing companies and change of staff, Joan Gill, Dianne Lindsay, Valerie Morrison, Jennie Redwitz, Susan Walters, Merrill Peterson, and Pat Herbst played major roles in the development and completion of this text. Wandaline Perelli ably edited all the final page proofs. We appreciated the expertise of each.

Family members and close friends provided encouragement throughout the project. Their patience and support were invaluable. They are Randy Stump, Jeanette Bigge, C. and S. Bigge, Carol Lehnert, Bernard and Henrietta Schwartz, Linda Warner, Winifred Baker, Vi Robinson, and Morris L. Bigge, author of several texts in education, edited some of the manuscript.

These team members—many unknown to each other—worked with us to develop this text to meet the needs of current and future teachers of students with disabilities. We thank each and every one of you on our team.

The Authors

Special Education Foundations

SCENES OF SCHOOLCHILDREN AND YOUTH

As you read each scene, identify what roles you think special education services in the schools played in making the scene possible.

SAMANTHA

When we step into the classroom, we observe Samantha working in a co-operative learning group on a science project. Today's project is to examine how pulleys work to move heavy objects. Samantha and her peers are manipulating the pulleys, discussing and recording their observations in their group laboratory book. The room is buzzing with conversation as these young scientists are at work.

Samantha has some special education needs that make her different from the other children, but these needs do not hamper her participation and learning with her peers. Samantha is in a wheelchair. Because she has limited physical movement and control, she uses a communication aid to share her observations and findings with her classmates. Her group is working with pulleys, and since Samantha has access to modified science equipment, this allows her to pull and move the objects like the other students. Also, through use of a communication aid and its synthesized speech, she can enter her ideas and have them relayed to others. She is integrated into the group and her peers turn to her when discussing their observations and readily include the use of her ideas when writing in their laboratory book.

BENJAMIN

Next, we walk into another classroom to observe a mathematics activity. In this classroom, students are working together in groups to attack the problem of the week. Twenty minutes of each day are devoted to working on the problem of the week. Students use manipulatives, calculators, and other tools in an attempt to find a solution to the problem. All the while, they record their procedures, findings, and questions in a group mathematics log.

Benjamin is one student who receives special education services. He has been diagnosed as having a learning disability and an attention deficit hyperactivity disorder. Benjamin's learning differences are readily observable in the classroom. He has difficulty reading the directions for the problem of the week and he has difficulty writing his ideas into the group's mathematics log. At times, he has an excessively high level of energy, and he seems to be "constantly in motion." However, Benjamin is experiencing success and is learning from the mathematics activity because of some modifications that his general and special education teachers together have designed and implemented in the classroom.

First, there are two forms of the directions for the problem: one is written at the grade level of the average reader in the class; another, a modified direction list that includes simplified syntax and vocabulary and supports the use of specialized terminology through the use of pictures and diagrams. While working through the project, the students in Benjamin's group refer to both sets of directions to aid them in completing the assignment. Benjamin contributes to the group's understanding of procedures by pointing to pictures and diagrams on the modified sheet and drawing his peers' attention to these as tools for learning. When it comes to writing in the group log, students take turns. When it is Benjamin's turn, a buddy in the group assists him with difficult spellings. Furthermore, Benjamin refers to the modified direction sheet for spelling and idea support. As for his energy level, the teacher permits Benjamin to move freely within the work space of his peers as long as his behavior is not distracting to the class. This freedom allows Benjamin the space he needs to learn and interact effectively with his peers.

ROLANDO

Meet Rolando. Rolando is a high school freshman. As part of his IEP/ITP plan, Rolando is exploring career options through participation in a community-based program offered for general and special education students at the school. The purpose of the program is to build stronger links between the community and the school and to allow high school students to experience work in local businesses in order to broaden their awareness of career opportunities within the community.

Today is Rolando's fifteenth day on the job site answering phones. Through assistance from his transition job coach, Rolando has developed basic phone etiquette skills and skills in transferring calls to the appropriate party for the office of five workers. Rolando has a list of the workers and their extensions in front of him and has carefully labeled the phone buttons with the names of these workers to ease the process of connecting callers with the correct party. Rolando also has a script telling him how to answer the phone: "Good afternoon. Thank you for calling Holmes Insurance. How may I direct your call?" He has a card that lists what to do if callers pose questions. For example, all calls concerning home owner's insurance are to be directed to Mr. Williams. If any calls come in for information not listed on the card, he is to transfer them to Ms. Henderson. Because of Rolando's cognitive delay, some difficulty with expressive language, and his difficulties with short-term memory, the script and card are critical job supports.

A coworker who is responsible for filing papers in the central office has also been trained in phone procedures and is there to assist Rolando as needed. Rolando and Ms. Hernandez enjoy working together in the front office and she has helped him make a successful adjustment to the job.

Once a week, Rolando meets with his job coach to discuss how he is doing. In addition, Rolando, his boss, and Ms. Hernandez meet with the job coach to discuss his progress and any concerns. Rolando looks forward to these meetings because he learns new ways to improve his performance on the job.

SERINA

Now let's enter another classroom. Social studies is one of Serina's favorite classes because the class is team-taught by two teachers—Mr. Hasbrow and Ms. Benica. Serina enjoys how the two teachers work together to teach the course and how they help the students. She also greatly appreciates the help that Ms. Benica, the special education teacher, gives her for dealing with her low vision (e.g., providing materials in enlarged print and specialized computer software programs).

The topic of the day is map skills. The sixth grade students are to map out the events of The Westward Movement by drawing major trails onto their map of the United States. In addition, they provide text to describe those trails and the adventures that were experienced by travelers on them, as discussed during the past week in the social studies class.

Ms. Benica welcomes the class and describes to them what they are going to be doing during the class period. While Ms. Benica is speaking, Mr. Hasbrow (the general education teacher) records these directions (steps) on the board for students as a visual reminder. When Ms. Benica has finished giving the directions, she asks if there are any questions, and since there are none, the class begins to work on the assignment.

Serina and her partner move to a computer with specialized software. The computer provides enlarged print on the screen to assist Serina in seeing the map and allows the pair to draw in the trails and input text. When they are finished, they will print out their final product—one copy in enlarged print for Serina's use and two copies in regular-size type for Serina's partner and the teachers.

DEVIN

Devin is a fourth grade student in Mr. Fink's classroom. Today, members of the class are participating in a language arts activity known as Author's Chair. Three students in the class will each have a turn sitting in the Author's Chair and reading their latest work aloud. Classmates will listen to the reading and then ask the author questions. The Author's Chair provides authors with an authentic audience and offers them the opportunity to receive constructive feedback from their peers about how to improve the content of their current piece.

Today, Devin is one of the three authors who will be presenting. When it is Devin's turn, he seats himself in the Author's Chair, remembering to sit tall and to look at his peers. To share his story, he uses a very limited vocabulary and enlarged polaroid photographs that he shot with assistance from others. A peer who understands his speech acts as interpreter and repeats what other peers do not understand. The topic for all the students is "Personal Accounts." Devin uses the photos both as cue cards for himself and as illustrations for his story. He tells his personal account of how he learned to ride the city bus and when he forgot where to get off and got lost.

At the conclusion of his presentation, students ask him questions about the story. Because of concerns about his hearing, the teacher uses simple sign language and gestures to repeat the content of the questions. Devin responds to the questions as best he can—sometimes by gestures and sometimes by role-playing. Peers also comment on his presentation manner, suggest an additional photo that would be helpful, and offer two additional vocabulary words that he might use to describe a specific part of his personal account. Once Devin responds to the questions and suggestions, the audience applauds his work and he takes his seat to practice being a member of an audience—sitting still and listening to his peer who has now assumed the Author's Chair.

As these scenes illustrate, special education has many faces. Special education is not a place but rather services designed to address the individual needs of students identified as having disabilities and being in need of specialized services in order to participate in and benefit from educational programs. Special education has been defined by the Individuals with Disabilities Education Act Amendments of 1997 (P.L. 105-17), or IDEA Amendments of 1997, as:

> *specially designed instruction, at no cost to parents, to meet the unique needs of a child with a disability, including—*
> *(A) instruction conducted in the classroom, in the home, in hospitals and institutions, and in other settings; and*
> *(B) instruction in physical education. (IDEA Amendments of 1997, Sec. 602(25)*

In general, a child with a disability is a child

> *(i) with mental retardation, hearing impairments (including deafness), speech or language impairments, visual impairments (including blindness), serious emotional disturbance (thereinafter referred to as "emotional disturbance"), orthopedic impairments, autism, traumatic brain injury, other health impairments, or specific learning disabilities; and*
> *(ii) who, by reason thereof, needs special education and related services. (IDEA Amendments of 1997, Sec. 602(3)(A))*

For children, ages 3 to 9, the definition of a child with a disability is slightly different. It includes a child

> *(i) experiencing developmental delays, as defined by the State and as measured by appropriate diagnostic instruments and procedures, in one or more of the following areas: physical development, cognitive development, communication development, social or emotional development, or adaptive development; and*
> *(ii) who, by reason thereof, needs special education and related services. (IDEA Amendments of 1997, Sec. 602(3)(B))*

In Chapter 1 of this text we provide a foundation for understanding what special education is and how special education provides needed supports and services to individuals with disabilities. This chapter discusses (a) the federal law that guides the providing of special education programs and services in schools; (b) the categories of special education eligibility; (c) the professionals providing special education and related services; and (d) the three individualized plans that specify goals and objectives and service provisions for individuals with disabilities.

PUBLIC LAW 105-17: THE IDEA AMENDMENTS OF 1997

Federal, state, and local laws guide the structure and delivery of special education and related services. States adhere to federal regulations, policies, and procedures in order to be in compliance and eligible to receive federal funds to support local programs. Decisions concerning implementation of federal laws are made at the state and local levels and determine organization and delivery of special programs and services to individuals with disabilities.

The Education for All Handicapped Children Act (P.L. 94-142) was passed into law in 1975. This landmark act defined special education and established guidelines and policies for special education programs throughout the nation. It was written to ensure that individuals with disabilities receive a free, appropriate public education (FAPE), with emphasis on special education and related services provided at public expense under public supervision and direction.

The Education for All Handicapped Children Act (a) provided definitions for the different categories of disability; (b) established guidelines for special education programs and their delivery to students; and (c) included due-process safeguards for parents, students, and service providers working together to provide services to students eligible for special education services. The law and regulations stipulated that Individualized Education Programs (IEPs) were to be written for every child found eligible for and in need of special education services and that eligible children were to be served in the least restrictive environment (LRE). These practices and concepts were forerunners of the content of each subsequent reauthorization. P.L. 94-142 was historic legislation because it changed the way educators responded to the needs of individuals with disabilities and, for many individuals with disabilities, opened public school doors to them for the first time.

In 1990, the Education for All Handicapped Children Act was reauthorized as the Individuals with Disabilities Education Act (IDEA) (P.L. 101-476). In this reauthorization, IDEA expanded the guidelines established by P.L. 94-142 to embrace both early-childhood special education and the transitional needs of individuals with disabilities. In 1997, IDEA was reauthorized (P.L. 105-17) with changes made in (a) funding provisions; (b) IEP procedures and policies; (c) transitional services, specifically dates and timelines for specification of transition needs; (d) mechanisms and procedures for responding to a child's behavior as related to school discipline codes; and (e) the establishment of a mediation system for addressing due-process procedures. To provide the reader with a basic understanding of the general provisions associated with the law, Table 1.1 lists key components of the IDEA Amendments of 1997 (P.L. 105-17). Familiarity with this information will assist teachers greatly as they serve as members of teams developing individualized plans for students because the development of these plans is dictated by the provisions specified in P.L. 105-17.

TABLE 1.1 KEY COMPONENTS OF THE IDEA AMENDMENTS OF 1997

Free Appropriate Public Education (FAPE)	"(8) . . . means special education and related services that— (A) have been provided at public expense, under public supervision and direction, and without charge; (B) meet the standards of the State educational agency; (C) include an appropriate preschool, elementary, or secondary school education in the State involved; and (D) are provided in conformity with the individualized education program required under section 614(d)." (Sec. 602)
Least Restrictive Environment (LRE)	(A) . . . "To the maximum extent appropriate, children with disabilities, including children in public or private institutions or other care facilities, are educated with children who are not disabled, and special classes, separate schooling, or other removal of children with disabilities from the regular educational environment occurs only when the nature or severity of the disability of a child is such that education in regular classes with the use of supplementary aids and services cannot be achieved satisfactorily." (Sec. 612(a)(5)(A))
Individualized Education Plans	Includes the following plans, all of which are addressed in Chapter 1: • Individualized Family Service Plans (ages 0–3) • Individualized Education Program (ages 3–21) • Individualized Transition Plan (ages 16–21)

Nondiscriminatory Assessment	"(2) Conduct of evaluation.—In conducting the evaluation, the local educational agency shall—
	(A) use a variety of assessment tools and strategies to gather relevant functional and developmental information, including information provided by the parent, that may assist in determining whether the child is a child with a disability and the content of the child's individualized education program, including information related to enabling the child to be involved in and progress in the general curriculum or, for preschool children, to participate in appropriate activities; and
	(B) not use any single procedure as the sole criterion for determining whether a child is a child with a disability or determining an appropriate educational program for the child; and
	(C) use technically sound instruments that may assess the relative contribution of cognitive and behavioral factors, in addition to physical or developmental factors.
	(3) Additional Requirements.—Each local educational agency shall ensure that—
	(A) tests and other evaluation materials used to assess a child under this section—
	    (i) are selected and administered so as not to be discriminatory on a racial or cultural basis; and
	    (ii) are provided and administered in the child's native language or other mode of communication, unless it is clearly not feasible to do so; and
	(B) any standardized tests that are given to the child—
	    (i) have been validated for the specific purpose for which they are used;
	    (ii) are administered by trained and knowledgeable personnel; and
	    (iii) are administered in accordance with any instructions provided by the producer of such tests;
	(C) the child is assessed in all areas of suspected disability; and
	(D) assessment tools and strategies that provide relevant information that directly assists persons in determining the educational needs of the child are provided." (Sec. 614(b))

Procedural Safeguards	"(1) an opportunity for the parents of a child with a disability to examine all records relating to such child and to participate in meetings with respect to the identification, evaluation, and educational placement of the child, and the provision of a free appropriate public education to such child, and to obtain an independent educational evaluation of the child; (2) procedures to protect the rights of the child whenever the parents of the child are not known, the agency cannot, after reasonable efforts, locate the parents, or the child is a ward of the State, including the assignment of an individual . . . to act as a surrogate for the parents; (3) written prior notice to the parents of the child whenever such agency— (A) proposes to initiate or change; or (B) refuses to initiate or change; the identification, evaluation, or educational placement of the child, . . . or the provision of a free appropriate public education to the child; (4) procedures designed to ensure that the notice required by paragraph (3) is in the native language of the parents, unless it clearly is not feasible to do so; (5) an opportunity for mediation . . . ; (6) an opportunity to present complaints with respect to any matter relating to the identification, evaluation, or educational placement of the child, or the provision of a free appropriate public education to such child;

	(7) procedures that require the parent of a child with a disability, or the attorney representing the child, to provide notice (which shall remain confidential)—
	   (A) to the State educational agency or local educational agency, as the case may be, in the complaint filed under paragraph (6); and
	   (B) that shall include—
	     (i) the name of the child, the address of the residence of the child, and the name of the school the child is attending;
	     (ii) a description of the nature of the problem of the child relating to such proposed initiation or change, including facts relating to such problem; and
	     (iii) a proposed resolution of the problem to the extent known and available to the parents at the time; and
	(8) procedures that require the State educational agency to develop a model form to assist parents in filing a complaint in accordance with paragraph (7)." (Sec. 615(b))

Transition Services	"(30) . . . a coordinated set of activities for a student with a disability that—
	   (A) is designed within an outcome-oriented process, which promotes movement from school to post-school activities, including post-secondary education, vocational training, integrated employment (including supported employment), continuing and adult education, adult services, independent living, or community participation;
	   (B) is based upon the individual student's needs, taking into account the student's preferences and interests; and
	   (C) includes instruction, related services, community experiences, the development of employment and other post-school adult living objectives, and, when appropriate, acquisition of daily living skills and functional vocational evaluation." (Sec. 602)

Assistive Technology Devices and Services	(1) Assistive technology device [is] ". . . any item, piece of equipment, or product system, whether acquired commercially off the shelf, modified, or customized, that is used to increase, maintain, or improve functional capabilities of a child with a disability." (2) Assistive technology service [is] ". . . any service that directly assists a child with a disability in the selection, acquisition, or use of an assistive technology device." (Sec. 602).
Early Childhood Education	Services are to be provided for children, ages birth to 5, with Individualized Family Service Plans developed for children ages birth through 3 and their families, and Individualized Education Plans for children ages 3 to 5.
Behavior and Disciplinary Policies	Section deals specifically with the disciplinary actions that may be taken with students with disabilities, on the basis of whether the behavior was or was not a manifestation of the disability. If the behavior is determined not to be a manifestation of the child's disability, disciplinary action may be taken as would be taken with children without disabilities, and the child may be placed in an interim alternative placement to ensure the continuation of educational services.

Participation in District-wide and State Assessments	"(17) Participation in assessments.—
	   (A) . . . Children with disabilities are included in general State and district-wide assessment programs, with appropriate accommodations, where necessary. As appropriate, the State or local educational agency—
	     (i) develops guidelines for the participation of children with disabilities in alternate assessments for those children who cannot participate in State and district-wide assessment programs; and
	     (ii) develops and, beginning not later than July 1, 2000, conducts those alternate assessments." (Sec. 612)

Disproportionality	Data will be gathered to "(1) . . . determine if significant disproportionality based on race is occurring in the State with respect to—
	   (A) the identification of children as children with disabilities, including the identification of children as children with disabilities . . . and
	   (B) the placement in particular educational settings of such children.
	(2) Review and revision of policies, practices, and procedures.—In the case of a determination of significant disproportionality with respect to the identification of children as children with disabilities, or the placement in particular educational settings of such children, in accordance with paragraph (1), the State or the Secretary of the Interior, as the case may be, shall provide for the review and, if appropriate, revision of the policies, procedures, and practices used in such identification or placement to ensure that such policies, procedures, and practices comply with the requirements of this Act." (Sec. 618(c))

➡ Review the key components of the IDEA Amendments of 1997 as identified in Table 1.1, and compare these requirements with practices currently in place in local schools. Are the schools/programs closely adhering not only to the legal mandates but to the spirit of the law as well?

CATEGORIES OF EXCEPTIONALITY

Children are eligible to receive special education services and supports if they meet the eligibility requirements for at least one of the disabling conditions listed in P.L. 105-17 and if it is determined that they are in need of special education services. The proposed regulations in the *Federal Register* (October 22, 1997) provide definitions of 13 disability conditions, separating out deafness from hearing impairments as listed in the law, and including categories of multiple disabilities and deaf-blindness. Students found eligible, or meeting the eligibility requirements for one or more of these categories, are eligible for receiving special education programs and services. Although these definitions, and their associated eligibility requirements as determined by states and local districts, are used to determine eligibility, they do not generally provide specific information about an individual student's needs and strengths. Rather, they serve as overall labels and, as such, allow students to be identified as individuals eligible and in need of receiving special education service. Professionals and parents have long argued the necessity for having and using labels, and moreover, the specific wording of the definitions. In the field of learning disabilities, for example, the debate on the meaning of "basic psychological processes" and how best to describe the impact of learning disabilities across the life span continues. Regardless, these definitions, as stated in the Federal Register, provide us a common language for understanding the disability conditions under which individuals are currently eligible for special education programs and services. These definitions are provided in Exhibit 1.1.

EXHIBIT 1.1

Definitions of Disabling Conditions
(34 CFR §300.7(a)(1–13) pp. 55069–55070) October, 1997

- **Autism** "a developmental disability significantly affecting verbal and nonverbal communication and social interaction, generally evident before age 3, that adversely affects a child's educational performance. Other characteristics often associated with autism are engagement in repetitive activities and stereotyped movements, resistance to environmental change or change in daily routines, and unusual responses to sensory experiences. The term does not apply if a child's educational performance is adversely affected primarily because the child has an emotional disturbance. . . ."
- **Deaf-Blindness** "concomitant hearing and visual impairments, the combination of which causes such severe communication and other developmental and educational problems that they cannot be accommodated in special education programs solely for children with deafness or children with blindness."
- **Deafness** "a hearing impairment that is so severe that the child is impaired in processing linguistic information through hearing, with or without amplification, that adversely affects a child's educational performance."
- **Emotional Disturbance** "a condition exhibiting one or more of the following characteristics over a long period of time and to a marked degree that adversely affects a child's educational performance: (A) An inability to learn that cannot be explained by intellectual, sensory, or health factors. (B) An inability to build or maintain satisfactory interpersonal relationships with peers and teachers. (C) Inappropriate types of behaviors or feelings under normal circumstances. (D) A general pervasive mood of unhappiness or depression. (E) A tendency to develop physical symptoms or fears associated with

personal or school problems. (ii) The term includes schizophrenia. The term does not apply to children who are socially maladjusted, unless it is determined that they have an emotional disturbance."

- **Hearing Impairment** "an impairment in hearing, whether permanent or fluctuating, that adversely affects a child's educational performance but that is not included under the definition of deafness in this section."

- **Mental Retardation** "significantly subaverage general intellectual functioning, existing concurrently with deficits in adaptive behavior and manifested during the developmental period, that adversely affects a child's educational performance."

- **Multiple Disabilities** "concomitant impairments (such as mental retardation–blindness, mental retardation–orthopedic impairment, etc.), the combination of which causes such severe educational problems that the problems cannot be accommodated in special education programs solely for one of the impairments. The term does not include deaf-blindness."

- **Orthopedic Impairment** "a severe orthopedic impairment that adversely affects a child's educational performance. The term includes impairments caused by congenital anomaly (e.g., clubfoot, absence of some member, etc.), impairments caused by disease (e.g., poliomyelitis, bone tuberculosis, etc.), and impairments from other causes (e.g., cerebral palsy, amputations, and fractures or burns that cause contractures)."

- **Other Health Impairment** "having limited strength, vitality, or alertness, due to chronic or acute health problems such as a heart condition, tuberculosis, rheumatic fever, nephritis, asthma, sickle cell anemia, hemophilia, epilepsy, lead poisoning, leukemia, or diabetes that adversely affects a child's educational performance."

- **Specific Learning Disability** "a disorder in one or more of the basic psychological processes involved in understanding or in using language, spoken or written, that may manifest itself in an imperfect ability to listen, think, speak, read, write, spell, or do mathematical calculations, also including such conditions as perceptual disabilities, brain injury, minimal brain dysfunction, dyslexia, and developmental aphasia. . . . The term does not include learning problems that are primarily the result of visual, hearing, or motor disabilities, mental retardation, of emotional disturbance, or of environmental, cultural, or economic disadvantage."

- **Speech or Language Impairment** "a communication disorder, such as stuttering, impaired articulation, a language impairment, or a voice impairment that adversely affects a child's educational performance."

- **Traumatic Brain Injury** "an acquired injury to the brain caused by an external physical force, resulting in total or partial functional disability or psychological impairment, or both, and that adversely affects a child's educational performance. The term applies to open or closed head injuries resulting in impairments in one or more areas, such as cognition; language; memory; attention; reasoning; abstract thinking; judgment; problem-solving; sensory, perceptual and motor abilities; psychosocial behavior; physical functions; information processing; and speech. The term does not apply to brain injuries that are congenital or degenerative, or to brain injuries induced by birth trauma."

- **Visual Impairment Including Blindness** "an impairment in vision that, even with correction, adversely affects a child's educational performance. The term includes both partial sight and blindness."

A student's eligibility for special education services is determined through the administration and analysis of tests and other assessment procedures by a team of qualified professionals and parent(s) of the child. Eligibility is then documented in an evaluation report prepared by a team, and a copy of this report is provided to the parents of the individual. The *Federal Register* (October 22, 1997) further explicates the determination of eligibility and states the following concerning review of gathered assessment information to inform eligibility decision making:

> (a) *In interpreting evaluation data for the purpose of determining if a child is a child with a disability . . . , and the educational needs of the child, each public agency shall—*
>   (1) *Draw upon information from a variety of sources, including aptitude and achievement tests, teacher recommendations, physical condition, social or cultural background, and adaptive behavior; and*
>   (2) *Ensure that information obtained from all of these sources is documented and carefully considered.*
> (b) *If a determination is made that a child has a disability and needs special education and related services, an IEP must be developed for the child in accordance with §§300.340-300.350. (34 CFR §300.535)*

The IDEA Amendments of 1997 include language that cautions teams against the misidentification and/or overidentification of individuals as individuals with disabilities. As stated in the IDEA Amendments of 1997,

> *In making a determination of eligibility . . . a child shall not be determined to be a child with a disability if the determinant factor for such determination is lack of instruction in reading or math or limited English proficiency. (Sec. 614 (b)(5))*

Moreover, the law states:

> *Greater efforts are needed to prevent the intensification of problems connected with the mislabeling and high dropout rates among minority children with disabilities. (IDEA Amendments of 1997, Sec. 601(c)(8)(A))*

The following statistics are cited in the law as examples of this intensification phenomenon:

> (B) *More minority children continue to be served in special education than would be expected from the percentage of minority students in the general school population.*
> (C) *Poor African-American children are 2.3 times more likely to be identified by their teacher as having mental retardation than their white counterpart.*
> (D) *Although African-Americans represent 16 percent of elementary and secondary enrollments, they constitute 21 percent of total enrollments in special education. (IDEA Amendments of 1997, Sec. 601(c)(8))*

The overidentification of individuals of color as being in need of special education services continues to receive local and national attention (e.g., Patton, 1998). School districts are looking for ways to prevent this overidentification. See the "Make It Happen" feature on page 11 for some suggestions on how districts and schools can address the problem of overidentification of students of color as eligible and in need of special education services.

MAKE IT HAPPEN   **Preventing Overidentification and Misidentification of Students of Color**

1. Attempt interventions in the general education setting before referring for special education eligibility testing. Remove teacher tolerance, curriculum selection, and instructional practice variables as causes of the student's difficulties prior to a formal referral for testing.
2. Use a range of assessment tools and approaches when determining eligibility for special education.
   • Include standardized, norm-referenced tools for making peer comparisons.
   • Use informal, curriculum-based assessment and performance-based tools to assess student performance across settings and domains.
   • Collect work samples and other student products to assess performance across settings.
   • Observe students in a variety of settings.
   • Interview individuals familiar with the student, including current and previous teachers, counselors or other support staff, parents and/or caregivers; and where appropriate, interview the student.
3. Ensure test administration adheres to established regulations and guidelines and ensure test administrators are qualified to administer selected tests.
   • This is especially important in situations where special education teachers completing assessments are working under emergency credentials and have not yet completed all requirements for licensure or certification.
   • This is also an issue when an individual at the school site who happens to speak the child's primary language is asked to translate and administer a test but is not trained in test procedures and does not hold the appropriate certification/licensure for test administration.
4. Use caution when interpreting scores of students whose first language or primary language is a language other than English.
   • If a test is not available in the student's primary language and the test is administered in English, a test to determine the student's level of English-language proficiency is needed to interpret scores on the assessment; even with this additional information, caution should still be used when interpreting results.
   • Translating a test into the child's primary language does not resolve all issues because items may be culturally biased or nonsensical in the child's language/culture.
5. Include a diverse group of individuals on the assessment team to achieve a more holistic view of the student. If the child is bilingual, include individuals on the team who speak the child's language and are familiar with the child's culture. Include members of the child's racial and cultural group and support staff and personnel as appropriate.

THEORY TO PRACTICE

➡ Review literature that addresses the overrepresentation of individuals of color in special education programs. What suggestions would you give to district personnel to ensure that students of color are not overidentified for services in their district?

SPECIAL EDUCATION AND RELATED SERVICE PROVIDERS

A number of professionals provide direct and indirect services to individuals with disabilities. Awareness of the diversity of involved personnel and their roles in special education activities can assist parents and teachers in understanding the services these individuals provide. Additionally, this information can lead to better understanding of how individual members of a team can contribute to the development, implementation, and evaluation of special education programs and services. Titles and roles of special education and related service providers include those listed in Exhibit 1.2.

EXHIBIT 1.2

Professionals

- **Special Education Teacher** An educator who is qualified to design and provide instruction to students with disabilities and "has met . . . approved or recognized certification—that apply to the area in which he or she is providing special education" (34 CFR §300.15).
- **Resource Room Teacher** An educator who provides resource room instruction for individuals with disabilities by either pulling students out of a general education class for one or more hours/periods a day to receive this support in a special education resource classroom, or by working in general education classrooms; may also serve as collaborator with general education teachers for arranging modifications in general education classrooms.
- **Itinerant Teacher** "A teacher or resource consultant who travels between schools or homes to teach or [to] provide instructional materials" (Esterson & Bluth, 1987, p. 148) to students with disabilities.
- **Speech-Language Pathologist** "A professional who evaluates and develops programs for individuals with speech or language problems" (Anderson, Chitwood, & Hayden, 1990, p. 220).
- **Occupational Therapist** A professional who delivers "activities focusing on fine motor skills and perceptual abilities that assist in improving physical, social, psychological, and/or other intellectual development; e.g., rolling a ball, finger painting" (Anderson, Chitwood, & Hayden, 1990, p. 218).
- **Augmentative and Alternative Communication Specialist** A specialist who is qualified to meet the needs of individuals who have communication difficulties and who will benefit from special educators and speech-language pathologists providing services that prepare them to use augmentations and alternatives to speaking and writing.
- **Physical Therapist** A professional "primarily concerned with preventing or minimizing [motor] disability, relieving pain, improving sensorimotor function, and assisting an individual to his or her greatest physical potential following injury, disease, loss of body part, or congenital disability" (Esterson & Bluth, 1987, p. 79).
- **Audiologist** "A nonmedical specialist who measures hearing levels and evaluates hearing defects" (Esterson & Bluth, 1987, p. 147).
- **Educational Psychologist** A professional with expertise in test administration and interpretation; may also have expertise in counseling and working with students in crisis situations.
- **District Special Education Administrator or Coordinator** A professional who oversees special education programs in a school district; may assist with assessment, attend IEP/ITP meetings, and provide teacher support.
- **Diagnostician** A professional with expertise in test administration and interpretation; the term may be used interchangeably with *educational psychologist,* although an educational psychologist's role generally requires skills beyond assessment and its interpretation.
- **Inclusion Specialist/Inclusion Facilitator** A professional prepared in a special education field (e.g., learning disabilities) who manages programs of students participating in inclusion programs; responsibilities range from consulting with general education teachers to team planning and co-teaching with general education teachers in inclusion settings.

- **Educational Therapist** A professional who works with individuals who exhibit learning problems and is also skilled in formal and informal assessment procedures, synthesizing assessment findings, developing and implementing remedial programs and strategies for addressing social and emotional aspects of learning problems. The educational therapist also serves as a case manager, and builds and supports communication links among the individual, family, school, and other professionals (Association of Educational Therapists, 1982).
- **Orientation and Mobility Specialist** A specialist who prepares individuals who are visually impaired or blind to "orient themselves to their environments and move about independently" (Hazekamp & Huebner, 1989, p. 113).
- **Adaptive Physical Educator** A person who designs and carries out "a physical education program that has been modified to meet the specific needs" of students with disabilities (Anderson, Chitwood, & Hayden, 1990, p. 211).
- **Social Worker** "In an educational context, a school social worker provides a link between school personnel and the families of . . . children [with disabilities] through activities such as individual pupil evaluation, parent interviews, and contact with community support services" (Anderson, Chitwood, & Hayden, 1990, p. 220).
- **Counselor[s]** "Qualified social workers, psychologists, guidance counselors, or other qualified personnel [who work to] . . . generally . . . improve a child's behavioral adjustment and control skills in order to make the child more available for participation in the educational program" (Esterson & Bluth, 1987, p. 27).
- **Rehabilitation Counselor** An accredited counselor who assists individuals with disabilities in making transitions from school to work.

These individuals work together and with students with disabilities and their parents in multiple ways. Three common modes for working together are coordination, consultation, and teaming. Coordination simply involves working together to ensure programs and services are provided in a systematic and effective way. Although a necessary component of service provision, coordination does not necessarily require service providers to discuss the specifics of their programs, the curriculum and instructional methodologies included, or the means by which the services are evaluated. Coordination may just address such issues as the scheduling of services, but not the goals or objectives of those services or how they compliment or support one another.

Consultation supports team members in their efforts to share information and expertise. One member serves as the consultant and provides support to other team members through the providing of suggestions, modeling of procedures and techniques, or possibly by designing interventions to be implemented by other team members. Although consultation is more collaborative in comparison to coordination and team members share information and expertise, the direction of information is generally *one*-directional: the expert to the novice or the one seeking assistance.

Teaming bridges the two previous modes of working together and builds on their strengths while adding the component of reciprocity and sharing of information among all team members through a more equal exchange. In a teaming model, all team members are viewed as contributing members, each of whom has expertise to share with others that will result in enhanced overall team outcomes. Because of the element of parity, teaming may be the most difficult of the three modes to achieve. Teaming may be set as a goal, with the team beginning their work together by focusing on coordination, and then consultation activities, gradually moving toward teaming. Table 1.2 lists examples of coordination, consultation, and teaming activities. It is assumed throughout that the parents and the child with the disability are involved.

TABLE 1.2 HOW PROFESSIONALS CAN WORK TOGETHER

ACTIVITY	EXAMPLES
Coordination	• special and general education teachers working out class schedules and support schedules for students • therapists and general and special education teachers working out schedules for therapy interventions • general and special education teachers coordinating grading procedures and policies • special education teachers working with job coaches and transition teachers to set community-based experience schedules for students
Consultation	• special education teachers assisting general education teachers • vocational education teachers working with community employers • related service personnel providing support to special education and general education teachers
Teaming	• special and general education teachers, administrators, counselors, support staff, and school psychologists working together on pre-referral teams to design and implement interventions in general education classrooms • special and general education teachers co-teaching in the classroom • paraprofessionals working with general education teachers • special and general education teachers serving together on curriculum-planning teams • team of professionals working together to determine whether a child is eligible for special education services • IEP teams working together to assess the current performance of a student to determine continued eligibility for special education services

THEORY TO PRACTICE

➡ Interview two providers of special education services. What do they identify as their primary responsibilities? What is their typical day like? What do they enjoy most/least about their jobs?

➡ Observe professionals as they work together. What expertise does each bring to the effort? What are the major difficulties they encounter when attempting to work together on a common issue? What do they do to overcome these challenges? What impact does their joint effort seem to have on the educational programs of students with disabilities?

INDIVIDUALIZED PROGRAMS AND PLANS

Individualized programs and plans are at the heart of special education because students found eligible for and in need of special education services receive services through the development and implementation of these programs and plans. The programs/plans take into consideration curricular needs identified through assessment, and they outline educational experiences that address a student's strengths, challenges, needs, and goals.

The IDEA Amendments of 1997 describe three primary individualized programs/plans. *Individualized Family Service Plans (IFSPs)* are developed for infants and toddlers and their families (birth to age 3). *Individualized Education Programs (IEPs)* are developed for children in early intervention programs (ages 3 through 5) and for students ages 6 through 21. *Individualized Transition Plans (ITPs)* focus on transitional planning, with transitional planning beginning at age 14 and transition services at age 16 or earlier. The purpose, essential components, development, implementation, and evaluation of each of these plans are described.

Individualized Family Service Plans

IFSPs are developed for infants and toddlers in need of special education services and supports from birth to age 3. The plan not only targets the needs of the child but also addresses the needs and concerns of the family. It is based on the premise that a child's home environment strongly influences that child's overall experiences and successes; therefore, it includes goals and objectives for the family as a unit, as well as goals and objectives for the individual child. The components of an IFSP include

(1) a statement of the infant's or toddler's present levels of physical development, cognitive development, communication development, social or emotional development, and adaptive development, based on objective criteria;

(2) a statement of the family's resources, priorities, and concerns relating to enhancing the development of the family's infant or toddler with a disability;

(3) a statement of the major outcomes expected to be achieved for the infant or toddler and the family, and the criteria, procedures, and timelines used to determine the degree to which progress toward achieving the outcomes is being made and whether modifications or revisions of the outcomes or services are necessary;

(4) a statement of specific early intervention services necessary to meet the unique needs of the infant or toddler and the family, including the frequency, intensity, and method of delivering services;

(5) a statement of the natural environments in which early intervention services shall appropriately be provided, including a justification of the extent, if any, to which the services will not be provided in a natural environment;

(6) the projected dates for initiation of services and the anticipated duration of the services;

(7) the identification of the service coordinator from the profession most immediately relevant to the infant's or toddler's or family's needs (or who is otherwise qualified to carry out all applicable responsibilities under this part) who will be responsible for the implementation of the plan and coordination with other agencies and persons; and

(8) the steps to be taken to support the transition of the toddler with a disability to preschool or other appropriate services (IDEA Amendments of 1997, Sec. 636(d))

IFSPs are reviewed every 6 months or more often as appropriate. A complete evaluation of the plan is conducted once a year. For a sample of two sections of an IFSP see Exhibit 1.3.

As presented in the exhibit, Lita's needs are in the areas of feeding amd motor function, with her primary needs in health stabilization, weight increase, and body control strengthening. The outcomes for Lita's parents focus on their becoming acquainted with parents of children with special education needs.

EXHIBIT 1.3

Individualized Family Service Plan

Date: _3/8/--_

ASSESSMENT INFORMATION

Child's Name: Lita Mack   **DOB:** _10/2/--_

Instrument (if any):	Date Administered:	By Whom:
Bayley Scales	1/17/--	K. Wollenburg
Clinical Observations	3/10/--	J. Brinckerhoff
Carolina Curriculum for Handicapped Infants	3/17/--	A. Adler
Assessment Log	5/5/--	J. Brinckerhoff

Strengths	Needs
Motor: Despite Lita's rough start, she has symmetrical movements in her arms and legs. For her size, Lita is active. **Communication:** Lita gives her mother clear signals with her facial expressions and uses her gaze to express likes and dislikes. **Social:** Lita is comforted easily by her mother. She smiles reciprocally and distinguishes between her mother and others. **Auditory:** Lita can hear sounds from all directions. **Cognition:** Lita reaches toward objects and bats them with her hands.	Lita's primary need is to stabilize her health, put on weight, and strengthen her head and trunk control. **Feeding:** Use a cylindrical bottle and a premature nipple for bottle feedings. **Motor:** Promote Lita's use of both sides of her body when she moves. Increase functional hand use.

Strengths/Needs Update   Date: _____

Family: Dee - mother; Mark - father; Lita; Jeremy - brother

Present Level of Functioning	Outcomes (Who, What Help, Degree of Success)	Intervention/ Strategies/Materials	Timelines/Person Responsible		
			Initiation	Changed/ Achieved	Review Date/ Comments
Dee and Mark do not know other parents of children with special needs and would like to be matched with other parents.	To link Dee and Mark with other parents of children who have special needs so that they can share ideas, successes, and challenges.	• Identify other parents willing to meet regularly with Mark and Dee. • Share their names and phone numbers with Mark and Dee. • Make the initial contact. • Check back to see how things are working.	4/1/-- by 4/15/-- 4/15/-- 6/1/--		Case Coordinator and other team members Case Coordinator Family by 5/1/-- Case Coordinator monthly

Reprinted with permission of the Association for the Care of Children's Health (ACCH), 19 Mantua Road, Mt. Royal, NJ 08061 from *Guidelines and Recommended Practices for the Individualized Family Service Plan,* 1989, from National Early Childhood Technical Assistance System (NEC-TAS) and ACCH.

Individualized Education Programs

The IDEA Amendments of 1997 state that every eligible infant and toddler, ages 3 through 5, and students ages 6 through 21, have a locally developed Individualized Education Program (IEP). Guidelines for the development, implementation, and evaluation of these programs are guided by IDEA at the federal level with individual states developing specific guidelines for carrying out these mandates. Each district or county within the state develops its own form to be used for writing IEPs.

IEP teams and meetings

Individualized Education Programs are developed by an IEP program team (IEP team) during IEP meetings. The IDEA Amendments of 1997 specify who must be members of the IEP team. The following group of individuals must participate in the development of the IEP:

> (i) *the parents of a child with a disability;*
> (ii) *at least one regular education teacher of such child (if the child is, or may be, participating in the regular education environment);*
> (iii) *at least one special education teacher, or where appropriate, at least one special education provider of such child;*
> (iv) *a representative of the local educational agency who—*
> > (I) *is qualified to provide, or supervise the provision of, specially designed instruction to meet the unique needs of children with disabilities;*
> > (II) *is knowledgeable about the general curriculum; and*
> > (III) *is knowledgeable about the availability of resources of the local educational agency;*
> (v) *an individual who can interpret the instructional implications of evaluation results, who may be a member of the team described in clauses (ii) through (vi);*
> (vi) *at the discretion of the parent or the agency, other individuals who have knowledge or special expertise regarding the child, including related services personnel as appropriate; and*
> (vii) *whenever appropriate, the child with a disability. (IDEA Amendments of 1997, Sec. 614(d)(1)(B))*

The IDEA Amendments of 1997 place emphasis on the role of general education teachers in the development of IEPs. The law states:

> *The regular education teacher of the child, as a member of the IEP team, shall, to the extent appropriate, participate in the development of the IEP of the child, including the determination of appropriate positive behavioral interventions and strategies and the determination of supplementary aids and services, program modifications, and support for school personnel . . . (IDEA Amendments of 1997, Sec. 614(d)(3)(C))*

IEPs are developed *during* IEP meetings attended by a team of individuals. IEPs are not to be developed prior to the meeting. As stated in the *Federal Register* (October 22, 1997):

> 29. *Is it permissible for an agency to have the IEP completed before the IEP meeting begins?*

> *No. Agency staff may come to an IEP meeting prepared with evaluation findings and proposed recommendations regarding IEP content, but the agency must make it clear to the parents at the outset of the meeting that the services proposed by the agency are only recommendations for review and discussion with the parents. Agencies that use this approach must ensure that there is a full discussion with the parents of the child's needs and the services to be provided to meet those needs before the child's IEP is finalized (34 CFR § Appendix C to Part 300— Section IV, Question 29, p. 55129).*

IEP meetings serve as vehicles for communication between all professionals and family members. Meetings enable participants to make decisions jointly about a child's needs; to determine services that are to be provided; to anticipate outcomes related to the provision of those services; and, to give direction to those implementing the program. IEP meetings are occasions for determining goals and objectives, and for planning meaningful educational experiences to meet the unique needs of the child with a disability. During IEP meetings, assessment findings and curricular concerns will be discussed, priorities will be determined, goals and objectives will be defined, and services will be specified.

One major challenge many IEP teams face is how to actively involve parents in IEP decision making. Some parents may be hesitant to voice their opinions, to ask questions, and to contribute to the specification of goals and objectives. They may be uncertain about how the meeting is run or the role they can play in the meeting. The *Federal Register* provides guidelines for parent participation: (a) parents are to be notified early enough to make arrangements to attend; (b) meetings are to be scheduled at a mutually agreed-upon time and place; (c) a notice is to be sent to parents notifying them of the purpose, time, and location of the meeting and who will be attending; (d) steps must be taken to ensure that parents will be able to understand the proceedings of the meeting, and when necessary, an interpreter must be provided for parents; and (e) in cases when parents are unable to attend, individual or conference telephone calls are to be arranged (34 CFR §300.345). When parents, for whatever reasons, do not attend, the *Federal Register* states the following:

> *(d) A meeting may be conducted without a parent in attendance if the public agency is unable to convince the parents that they should attend. In this case the public agency must have a record of its attempts to arrange a mutually agreed on time and place, such as—*
> *(1) Detailed records of telephone calls made or attempted and the results of those calls;*
> *(2) Copies of correspondence sent to the parents and any responses received; and*
> *(3) Detailed records of visits made to the parent's home or place of employment and the results of those visits. (34 CFR §300.345)*

In some instances, parents will need assistance and information about how to participate and contribute. The "Make It Happen" feature on page 19, drawing from the work of Turnbull and Turnbull (1990) and others, presents some suggestions for actively involving parents in IEP meetings. Teachers and other team members, through adoption of these suggestions, can increase parent participation in meetings, and as a result, create a sense of collaboration and teamwork among team members.

Student participation in IEP meetings is also critical because if IEP goals and objectives are to have meaning for them, the students must be allowed and encouraged to participate in their development. However, students' involvement in the development

MAKE IT HAPPEN

Involving Parents in IEP Meetings

Premeeting Activities
- Work with parents to select a convenient time and place for the IEP meeting.
- Inform them of its time and location several weeks prior to the meeting.
- Provide parents with the information about what will be discussed during the meeting.
- If a report is to be discussed, provide parents with a copy of it prior to the meeting.
- Provide parents with a list of the kinds of questions they may want to ask during the meeting.
- Provide a list of the names and titles of individuals planning to attend the meeting.
- Inform parents that they may bring an advocate with them to the meeting.
- If an individualized plan is to be written during the meeting, provide parents with a blank form to assist them in becoming familiar with the format and included information.

Meeting Activities
- Introduce all individuals around the table, indicating their title and role in the meeting.
- Open the meeting by stating the purpose of the meeting and the time allocated for the meeting.
- Notify parents of their rights.
- Continually ask for questions and actively include parents.
- Allow time for reflective thought, rather than setting a pace that sends the message "We need to keep this meeting moving."
- Avoid jargon. If it is used, define it through examples.
- Do not allow any one person to dominate the discussion—all individuals present have something to contribute.
- If conflict arises, address it directly through group problem solving.
- Make goals, objectives, and placement decisions as a team. Do not have these items prepared in writing or determined prior to the meeting.
- Provide specific information related to placement and services. List this information in the plan.
- Close the meeting on a positive note, thank parents for attending and participating, and plan a follow-up meeting or phone call with the parents.

Postmeeting Activities
- Make a follow-up phone call to the parents to check for understanding of meeting events and to clarify any misunderstandings.
- Continue to keep in close contact with the parents.

of their IEPs can be limited, because students may lack basic information about the IEP and the IEP process. Moreover, students may not understand how the IEP relates to their needs and priorities (Lovitt, Cushing, & Stump, 1994). The "Make It Happen" feature on page 20 offers some suggestions for enhancing student participation in IEP meetings, especially for students of high school age.

MAKE IT HAPPEN
Student Participation in IEP Meetings

1. Explain the purpose of the IEP and how students can contribute to its development.
2. When writing IEPs for high school students, develop long-term goals for students that represent what they want to achieve on exiting school. This brings a student's dreams and desires into focus.
3. Indicate success and progress on the IEP document so that the document captures growth. This, over time, results in the creation of a record of student achievement. It also assists in the identification of helpful instructional techniques, strategies, and placements.
4. Write goals and objectives in language that makes sense to all in attendance, including the student. Only include goals and objectives that students understand and can describe to others.
5. Ensure that students understand procedures to be used to determine whether they have met IEP goals and objectives.
6. Ensure that students understand the requirements for graduation and the earning of a diploma. Also make sure that stated IEP goals and objectives lead toward achievement that is appropriate and reasonable.

Source: Lovitt, Cushing, & Stump, 1994.

IEP documents

Consistent with federally mandated procedures, the written statements in the IEP are developed by the IEP team using information from assessments conducted in all areas of a child's suspected disability. The IEP document is a written commitment that the child will receive needed special education and related services, and it will serve as a planning, monitoring, and evaluation tool of student performance. According to the IDEA Amendments of 1997, an Individualized Education Program must contain information about the following topics.

Present levels of educational performance. The statement of present levels of performance provides an overall picture of a student (i.e., what he or she is currently capable of doing, and what areas require additional skill development). According to the law, this statement should include the following:

> (I) *how the child's disability affects the child's involvement and progress in the general education curriculum; or*
>
> (II) *for preschool children, as appropriate, how the disability affects the child's participation in appropriate activities. (IDEA Amendments of 1997, Sec. 614(d)(1)(A)(i))*

The statement presents findings of the assessment efforts of the IEP team and discusses the student's strengths, needs, and challenges across all areas. Academic, social, emotional, behavioral, physical fitness and health status, communicative skills, and self-help skills may all be addressed. Depending on the extent of student need for special education and related services in order to benefit from an educational program, the statement of present levels of performance may be limited or quite comprehensive.

Measurable annual goals including benchmarks and short-term objectives. Goals and benchmarks, or short-term objectives, address the child's needs resulting from his or her disability and (a) enable the child to be involved in the regular, or general education, curriculum and progress within it and (b) meet other educational needs resulting from the child's disability (IDEA Amendments of 1997, Sec. 614(d)). Goals and objectives written in the IEP must relate directly to the information presented in the present-levels-of-performance statement and guide the type of educational experiences and opportunities afforded the student. Goals, benchmarks, and objectives specify what students are to learn and be able to do as a result of their services and instruction. Because of their importance, we devote an entire chapter, Chapter 10, to the writing of IEP goals, benchmarks, and objectives.

Special education and related services, supplementary aids and services, and program modifications or school personnel supports. Some students, as a result of the effect of their disability, require special services beyond services provided to other students, in order to achieve their annual goals, to participate and progress in general curriculum, and to participate in extracurricular and other nonacademic activities with children with and without disabilities. Special education and related services are designed to meet unique needs of these children and to prepare them for independent living and employment (IDEA Amendments of 1997, Sec. 601). Special education services provide instruction specially designed for individual students, or small groups of students, or through collaboration with general education teachers. For example, a teacher certified in visual impairment will assist a student with low vision in using a telescopic visual aid so the material on the chalkboard may be seen while sitting at one's desk.

Related services differ from special education classes and are defined as

> *transportation, and such developmental, corrective, and other supportive services (including speech-language pathology and audiology services, psychological services, physical and occupational therapy, recreation, including therapeutic recreation, social work services, counseling services, including rehabilitation counseling, orientation and mobility services, and medical services, except that such medical services shall be for diagnostic and evaluation purposes only) as may be required to assist a child with a disability to benefit from special education, and includes the early identification and assessment of disabling conditions in children. (IDEA Amendments of 1997, Sec. 602(22))*

Supplementary aids and services, provided as needed, are defined as

> *aids, services, and other supports that are provided in regular education classes or other education-related settings to enable children with disabilities to be educated with nondisabled children to the maximum extent appropriate in accordance with section 612(a)(5). (IDEA Amendments of 1997, Sec. 602(29))*

Examples of auxiliary aids and services include taped texts, brailled materials, assistive listening devices, qualified interpreters, notetakers, paraprofessionals or instructional aides, and modification of equipment.

Child's participation with general education peers in regular classes and activities. The law requires the team to identify when the child will *not* participate with general education peers—not the extent to which the child *will* participate with general education peers. This means that the team must justify any removal or segregation of the child from the experiences provided to his or her general education peers.

Individual modifications for state or district-wide assessment. The law requires that all individuals, including those with disabilities, participate in state and district-wide assessments in order to document progress and growth. For this component of the IEP, the team must specify any modifications necessary for the child's participation in the testing. Or, if the team determines that the child will not participate, the team must state why the assessment is not appropriate and what procedures will be in place for assessing the progress of the child.

Projected dates for the initiation and duration of services. The team must specify the date each special education and related service will begin and the duration of the child's program utilizing these services. This section includes the frequency of services per week and the daily hours for each service (e.g., a weekly session of 40 to 60 minutes; twice/week, 30 minutes each). Services generally start as soon after the IEP meeting as possible; the projected duration is frequently one year but may be less.

Statement of transition needs. The IEP must state the student's need for transition services, beginning at the age of 14, and then with annual updates, be linked with his or her course of study. This means that decisions concerning the child's coursework and experiences must address the child's transitional needs, such as participation in a vocational education program or in an advanced placement program. The IEP must identify the transition services to be provided to the child beginning at the age of 16 (or younger, if determined appropriate by the team) and, where appropriate, specify interagency responsibilities and/or communications and other linkages needed to provide those services to the student (IDEA Amendments of 1997, Sec. 614(d)).

Measurement of the child's progress. This section calls for specification of how the child's progress toward annual goals will be measured and how parents will be regularly informed of their child's progress. These progress reports are to occur at least as often as reports are provided to parents of students without disabilities, and they must include a statement about the likelihood that the student will achieve his or her annual goals given the rate of progress demonstrated to date.

Statement that a student has been informed of one's rights. At least one year before the student reaches the age of majority, under state law, the student must be informed of those rights under the IDEA Amendments of 1997 that will be transferred to him or her upon reaching the age of majority.

Additional considerations. When developing the IEP, the team must also consider

(i) the strengths of the child and the concerns of the parents for enhancing the education of their child; and (ii) the results of the initial evaluation or most recent evaluation of the child. (IDEA Amendments of 1997, Sec. 614(d)(3)(A))

The following list summarizes special factors to be considered when developing an IEP (IDEA Amendments of 1997, Sec. 614)(d)(3)):

1. child's behavioral needs and whether positive behavioral interventions, strategies, and supports are needed

2. the language needs of a child with limited English proficiency

3. provision of instruction in braille, if appropriate for the present or the future, for children who are blind or visually impaired

4. communication needs and modes of students, especially for those who are deaf or hard-of-hearing

5. child's need for assistive technology devices and services.

A sample IEP is presented in Exhibit 1.4. School districts across the country design their IEP formats to reflect local needs and concerns. Regardless of format, all IEPs must include the components previously described.

EXHIBIT 1.4

Individualized Education Program

Date October 10, --	Student: Angela Sanchez	Date of Birth: 2/14/--	Grade: 3

Parent Name: Mario and Maria Sanchez   Home: 999-9999   Work: 888-8888

Purpose of Meeting: Initial _X_   Annual ____   Tri-Annual Review ____

Initiation of Services: October 11, --   Annual Review Date: October 11, --

---

Eligibility Classification: Angela is eligible for special education services as a student with a learning disability in the area of mathematics due to the presence of a severe discrepancy between her potential, as measured by the Wechsler-III, and her performance in mathematics.

Recommended Program (LRE Justification) and Services: Angela will receive all instruction in the general education classroom. The special education teacher will design modifications of classroom mathematics activities and assignments collaboratively with the general education teacher. The special education teacher will provide services in the general education classroom during mathematics instruction two days per week.

Participation in State/District Testing: Angela will participate in all state and district testing and be allowed time-and-a-half when completing any mathematics sections of these tests.

Measurement of Child's Progress: Parents will receive a mid-quarter and quarter report describing Angela's progress toward IEP goals and objectives. Reports will be prepared jointly by Angela's general and special education teachers.

This individualized education program is a statement of the services to be provided to my child. I agree with the goals and objectives, my child's placement and the provision of related services as indicated. I realize this is not a contract, and does not guarantee achievement of stated goals and objectives. I have been given a copy of my rights.

Mrs. Maria Sanchez   *Oct. 10, ---*
_____   _____
Parent Signature   Date

Individuals present at the meeting and serving on the IEP team.

Signature	Position	Agreement/ Disagreement	Date
Mrs. Maria Sanchez	Parent	Agree	Oct. 10, ---
Mrs. Herlinda Gomez	General Education Teacher	Agree	Oct. 10.
Mr. Patrick O'Neil	Special Education Teacher	Agree	Oct. 10
Mr. Donald Taylor	Local Educational Agency Representative	Agree	Oct. 10
Mrs. Karen Holmes	School Psychologist	Agree	Oct. 10
angela Sanchez	student	Agree	Oct. 10

EXHIBIT 1.4

Individualized Education Program *(continued)*

PRESENT LEVELS OF PERFORMANCE

Specific Abilities and Overall Health: Angela's vision, hearing, and motor skills are all in the average range. She is of average weight and height for her age. Angela eagerly engages in physical education activities, joins in games during recess, and plays soccer in the local youth league. Parents report she is in good health.

Cognitive: Performance on the Wechsler-III indicates average performance, with a Verbal IQ of 108, Performance IQ of 93, and a Full Scale IQ of 96. (All reported as standard scores with a mean of 100, SD = 15)

Academic and Related Skills: WJ-R (the assessment used annually for evaluation of special education student progress) outcomes indicate average performance in passage comprehension (SS = 102), dictation (SS = 105), and writing samples (SS = 110), with below average performance in calculation (SS = 82) and applied problems (SS = 75). KeyMath-R overall performance was below average (SS = 79), with greatest difficulty in computation and applications, especially in the areas of time and money. Angela displayed strategies to support her reading of unknown words (e.g., use of context clues) and comprehending text (e.g., skimming the story, looking at the pictures). She did not seem to have parallel strategies for approaching mathematics. She attempted problems quickly and did not seem to call on strategies or to vary her approach across problem types. When asked to respond to problem-solving situations, Angela at times appeared overwhelmed with the amount of information she was given. She was not able to discriminate between necessary and extraneous information. This created extra difficulties for her when working with some of the problems.

Life Skills: Angela gets along well with peers and has many friends. During a personal interview, Angela expressed positive feelings about herself and said that she enjoys school and thinks of herself as a good student. Rating scales completed by the classroom teacher and parent indicate no social concerns. Angela quickly makes decisions when faced with choices in school activities. She is a self-advocate and readily asks questions when she does not understand something. Parents report Angela gets along well with family and community members and demonstrates appropriate life skills for her age.

Transition Needs: Angela demonstrates no specific vocational/transitional curricular needs at this time. Her precareer and vocational skills such as completing assignments, being on time, following through on activities and responsibilities all demonstrate a solid foundation of vocationally and transitionally-related skills.

Behavioral: Classroom and yard observations found Angela displaying behavior appropriate to the setting. Angela did not demonstrate any behavioral concerns. Parents do not report any behavioral concerns at home or when Angela is in the community.

Communication Skills: Performance on the TOLD-1:3 indicated average English communication skills, with an overall percentile rank of 52. Angela is bilingual and speaks fluent Spanish at home and school. The district required assessment of English language proficiency indicates that Angela is a fluent English speaker, reader, and writer.

Goals and Objectives		Person Responsible
Goal	Objective	
Improve computation skills as measured by the annual district assessment	1. Given a teacher-developed quiz of 10 problems involving addition and subtraction of 2- and 3-digit numbers with and without renaming, Angela will write answers to the problems with at least 80% accuracy by February.	General teacher Special teacher
	2. Given a teacher-developed sheet of basic multiplication facts, products to 81, Angela will write solutions at a rate of at least 65 correct digits per minute with no more than 5 errors by June.	General teacher Special teacher
Improve mathematics application and problem solving skills as measured by the annual district assessment	1. Given a manipulative clock and 10 orally dictated times to 5-minute intervals, Angela will set the clock to the stated time and orally state the time correctly for at least 80% of the trials by March.	General teacher Special teacher
	2. Given paper and pencil, Angela will record, in writing, at least 5 of her daily activities, the time she engages in them, and draw a clock face to represent these times, recording and drawing at least 4 out of the 5 times correctly by April.	General teacher Special teacher
	3. Given a set of coins and bills (pennies, nickels, dimes, quarters, ones, fives, and tens) and a newspaper advertisement of items valued up to $20.00, Angela will select 5 items to purchase, will orally state the cost of each item, and will demonstrate that value using coin and bill combinations, demonstrating accuracy for 4 out of the 5 items by June.	General teacher Special teacher Parents
	4. When presented with a mathematical problem to solve, Angela will orally state the procedure she used to solve the problem and two advantages and disadvantages of her approach, 4 out of 5 times by June.	General teacher Special teacher
Improve study skills as measured by teacher-developed formative assessment tools	1. Angela, with assistance from her parents (e.g., nightly sign-off of homework assignment sheet), will complete at least 90% of homework assignments per week.	General teacher Special teacher Parents

Individualized Transition Plans

Students make many important transitions during their school careers. They move from class to class, grade to grade, school to school, and school to postschool experiences. Although all of these transitions require planning, the transition from high school to work/adult living has received the most attention by special education professionals, parents, and students. The IDEA Amendments of 1997 require consideration for this transition that includes identification of needed transition services as linked with courses of study beginning by age 14 and development of Individualized Transition Plan (ITP) specifying transition services by age 16 or earlier as appropriate.

The development of ITPs is based on individual student needs, preferences, and interests. Transition services are defined as

> *a coordinated set of activities for a student with a disability that—*
> (A) *is designed within an outcome-oriented process, which promotes movement from school to post-school activities, including post-secondary education, vocational training, integrated employment (including supported employment), continuing and adult education, adult services, independent living, or community participation;*
> (B) *is based upon the individual student's needs, taking into account the student's preferences and interest; and*
> (C) *includes instruction, related services, community experiences, the development of employment and other post-school adult living objectives, and, when appropriate, acquisition of daily living skills and functional vocational evaluation. (IDEA Amendments of 1997, Sec. 602(30))*

It is essential that students are actively involved in the development of their ITPs. Students' interests and goals must take center stage when the plan is being developed. Without the commitment or interest of the child, the plan is likely to be ineffective (Stump, 1992).

A critical component of ITP development is the linkage with community and adult service agencies. ITP meetings must involve school district personnel and families meeting and interacting with community and adult agency personnel who will begin to assume increased responsibility for students as they approach completion of their school program. As students reach the age of maturity and enter the adult world, they will rely on community and adult agencies for any specialized needs or programs. Exhibit 1.5 presents sample pages of an Individualized Transition Plan. These pages address areas of instruction, community experiences, employment, adult living, daily living skills, and functional vocation evaluation, and together, represent a comprehensive review of Tom's needs and goals. Annual goals for Tom have been established in all areas except for daily living and functional vocation evaluation. An example short-term objective is presented for the employment annual goal.

EXHIBIT 1.5

Individualized Transition Plan

Name: _Tom_   Date: _5/10--_   School: _Central High School_   Age/DOB: _15 years of age/11/9/--_

Student in need of special education: _yes_   Student in need of special education with related

services: _yes_   Soc. Sec. #: _666-77-8888_   Grade Level: _9_   Initial IEP ___

Review IEP _√_   Parent Notification _√_   Student Invitation _√_   Other Agency Invitation _√_

POST SCHOOL OUTCOMES (LONG-RANGE GOALS)

Employment: _Park Ranger_   Community
                                              Participation: _Outdoor activities with friends_

Residential: _Live in own apartment or at home_   Leisure Recreation: _Hunting and fishing_

PRESENT LEVEL OF EDUCATIONAL PERFORMANCE

Tom is a ninth grade student with an emotional disability. He has many hobbies and enjoys being outdoors. He likes to hunt and fish with his family. He enjoys swimming and snowmobiling. On an interest test, Tom shows a high interest in biological science, physical science, and the outdoors. His finger dexterity and manual dexterity skills are high average. Tom has not had any paid jobs. He does not plan on going to college but would be interested in becoming a park ranger. He has basic skills in using money, purchasing, simple cooking and cleaning. He does not have skills in budgeting, money management, banking, meal planning, maintaining a home, or doing laundry. He receives special education in a resource room program one hour per day and has services from the school social worker two hours per month. Tom has average intelligence with a Verbal IQ of 94, Performance IQ of 89, and Full Scale IQ of 98. Tom's Broad Reading score is 6.6, with a Letter-Word Identification of 5.4 and a Passage Comprehension score of 7.6. His Broad Mathematics score is 6.8, with a Calculations score of 5.2 and an Applied Problem score of 8.7. Tom's Dictation score is 2.6. Tom cries easily, is anxious, complains frequently, projects blame onto others, and does not have many friends.

STATEMENT OF NEEDED TRANSITION SERVICES AND COORDINATED ACTIVITIES

Transition Services	Activities	Agency/ Responsibilities	Who Will Provide and/or Pay
Instruction: needed in biology, business, money management, gun safety, and vocational skills. **Services are not needed because:**	1. Enroll in biology with supports. 2. Enroll in courses at high school in basic business or money management and independent living. 3. Enroll in gun safety, hunting, and fishing courses at Izaak Walton League. 4. Possible dual enrollment with Vocational Technical School.	1. School. (see goals and objectives) 2. School. 3. Tom and parents will contact the Izaak Walton League and enroll in courses. 4. School will contact Vocational Technical School about possible courses and dual enrollment.	1. School will provide and pay for cost of biology course and supports. *(continued)*

From Storms, DeStefano, and O'Leary, *Individuals with Disabilities Education Act: Transition Requirements. A Guide for States, Districts, Schools, and Families,* 1996. Available at cost from National Clearinghouse of Rehabilitation Training Materials, Oklahoma State University, 816 W. 6th St., Stillwater, OK 74078, or free from: *http://interact.uoregon.edu/wrrc/wrrc.html.*

EXHIBIT 1.5

Individualized Transition Plan *(continued)*

Transition Services	Activities	Agency/ Responsibilities	Who Will Provide and/or Pay
Community Experiences: needed to explore community resources. **Services are not needed because:**	1. Schedule visits with community service agencies. 2. Schedule visit to the postsecondary Vocational Technical School.	1. School will provide Tom and his family with a listing of community service agencies. Tom and his family will be responsible for scheduling and visiting agencies. 2. Tom and his family will be responsible for scheduling and visiting the Vocational Technical School.	1. Visits scheduled and conducted through the school will be provided by the school. 2. Tom and his family will be responsible for providing all costs for visits to agencies they schedule and the visit to the Vocational Technical School.
Employment: needed to explore potential jobs and training. **Services are not needed because:**	1. Placement in the Experience Based Career Education career exploration program. 2. Placement in Work Study and/or vocational education. 3. Employment through Summer Youth JTPA program. 4. Vocational and post-school employment counseling.	1. School. (see goals and objectives) 2. School. 3. JTPA. 4. Vocational Rehabilitation.	1. & 2. School will provide and pay for the career exploration, Work Study, and/or vocational education program. 3. JTPA will provide and pay for all costs associated with the Summer Youth Employment program. 4. Vocational Rehabilitation will provide and pay for the vocational and post-school employment counseling.
Adult Living: needed in several areas. **Services are not needed because:**	1. Meet with the school social worker and resource teacher regarding behavior, social skills, and building friendships. 2. Group counseling on anger management and conflict resolution. 3. Banking, money management skill development. 4. Cooking and home management skill development. 5. Work toward obtaining driver's license.	1. School. (see goals and objectives) 2. School. 3. Consumer Credit Counseling or local bank. 4. Independent Living Center. 5. School and family.	1. & 2. School will provide counseling and support through the school social worker, resource teacher, and counseling department. 3. Family will contact Consumer Credit Counseling to determine assistance they can provide. Costs and who will pay will be determined. 5. The school will offer driver's education during the summer. The student or parents are responsible for paying for driver's education.

Transition Services	Activities	Agency/ Responsibilities	Who Will Provide and/or Pay
Daily Living Skills: (if appropriate)			
Functional Vocational Evaluation: (if appropriate)	1. Formal and informal vocational assessment.	1. School.	1. The school will provide and pay for the vocational assessments.

OTHER DOCUMENTATION FOR TRANSITION SERVICES

Documentation of the student's preferences and interests in the development of the IEP (Describe): Tom attended his IEP meeting and expressed his postschool goals. Additionally, Tom was given several interest inventories during April [year] to help in beginning to identify employment preferences and interests. The teacher met with Tom to complete questionnaires regarding his postschool interests and preferences in the areas of employment, residential living, community participation, and leisure recreation.

Documentation of other agency(s) participation in planning (Describe): Vocational Rehabilitation and JTPA representatives were present at the IEP meeting and involved in planning. Representatives from Consumer Credit Counseling, the Independent Living Center, and the Vocational Technical School were not in attendance when these activities were discussed at the IEP meeting. They will be contacted to discuss their involvement in planning transition services for Tom and invited to attend the next meeting if they will be providing services.

If any agency fails to provide agreed-upon services in the activities/strategies, a meeting must be held as soon as possible to identify alternative strategies and if necessary revise the IEP. IEP reconvened date: _____

Annual Goals

Annual Goals** Address all activities in the Statement of Needed Transition Services that are the responsibility of special education	Initiation	Completion	Review Date
Instruction: Tom will earn passing grades in biology and basic business.	9/5/		5/1/
Community Experiences: Tom will become familiar with local and regional community service agencies.	9/5/		5/1/
Employment: Tom will enroll in the Experience Based Career Education (EBCE) program to explore two occupational areas.	9/5/		5/1/
Adult Living: Tom will resolve conflicts in an appropriate manner and begin to take responsibility for his actions.	9/5/		5/1/
If Appropriate:			
Daily Living: N A			
Functional Vocation Evaluation:			

*Note: Not all annual goals that are the responsibility of special education are included in this example. Your IEP will need to include all annual goals that correspond to the activities from the Statement of Needed Transition Services that are the responsibility of special education.

EXHIBIT 1.5

**Individualized Transition
Plan** *(continued)*

Short-Term Objectives***

Student Name: <u>Tom</u>

Annual Goal: <u>Employment: Tom will enroll in the Experience Based Career Education (EBCE) program to</u>
<u>explore two occupational areas.</u>

Instructional Objectives	Responsible Parties	Initiation/ Duration	Evaluation Strategies
Given the EBCE assessment inventory for determining career interests and discussion with the Resource Teacher and Work Study Coordinator, Tom will choose two occupational areas to explore during the 19-- - 20-- school year.	Resource Teacher, Work Study Coordinator	9/-- - 6/	Monthly teacher and student conference to determine satisfaction with progress.
Tom will satisfactorily complete weekly EBCE Activity Sheet assignments.	Resource Teacher, Work Study Coordinator, Tom	9/-- - 6/	Teacher review; passing grades or above on weekly assignments.

***Note: These are a few examples for one annual goal. Short-Term Objectives need to be written for each annual goal.

*Note: This IEP prototype does not include all of the requirements for an IEP. The prototype is designed to provide an example of how the information can be presented and how the transition services requirements could fit into an IEP format.

THEORY TO PRACTICE

➡ Interview special education teachers concerning their experiences with IFSP, IEP, and ITP programs and plan development, implementation, and evaluation. Ask them to describe the development process. Does this process comply with the guidelines established in the IDEA Amendments of 1997? What do the teachers identify as the greatest challenges in the process? Do the same with a general education teacher. What are the similarities and differences across their experiences?

➡ After securing parent and school-site permission, sit in on an IFSP, IEP, or ITP meeting. Describe what you see, hear, and feel as the meeting unfolds, taking care to ensure confidentiality of all participants (e.g., include no identifying information). Take the perspective of the parent and critique the experience. Who on the team was most helpful, what information was most relevant, and what decisions were most critical from this perspective? How was the parent included in the process? How included was the student? If you were the parent in this particular meeting, what suggestions would you offer the team for improving the overall process?

➡ With parent and teacher permission, interview a student about his or her experiences in special education. Identify what the student considers most positive and negative about the experience. Assess the student's familiarity with the plan development process and the extent to which he or she was actively involved in the process. Based on this information, what suggestions would you offer the student for becoming more of a self-advocate in his or her special education program? What suggestions would you offer the school/district for involving students more actively in the development, implementation, and evaluation of their special education program?

➡ Meet with the transition special education teacher of a local school district. Discuss with this professional his or her role as a transition teacher and what he or she sees as the greatest positive and negatives of the program. Have the teacher identify some of the common goals and programs students become involved with, and describe his or her role in assisting students in achieving those goals and participating in those programs. Discuss the role that the transition teacher, the student, parents, and community agency representatives play in the development of ITPs.

CHAPTER SUMMARY

This chapter provides a foundation in order for teachers to understand special education and related services. The chapter provides (a) a definition of special education, (b) a brief historical overview of federal law governing the provision of special education services for individuals from birth through the age of 21, (c) a listing of disability categories of eligibility for special education supports and services, (d) descriptions of personnel involved in providing special education and related services, and (e) descriptions of the three individualized programs and plans mandated by the IDEA Amendments of 1997 (P.L. 105-17).

Curriculum

CHAPTER 2

Goals, Outcomes, and Standards

Read to find out the following:

- the meanings of national, state, and local goals, outcomes, and standards and how these concepts may be used in determining a student's curricular program and the development of IEP goals and objectives
- the various influences on the development of national, state, and local goals, outcomes, and standards and their impact on local curriculum
- how curricular decisions are made and the role of teachers in that decision making
- curricular options that are available for students with disabilities

It is second nature for a teacher to adopt a view of curriculum as content taught in specific areas (e.g., mathematics, social studies) and to lose sight of all that a curriculum embraces—that is, the broader meaning and purposes of education. When teaching in classrooms, teachers may become most concerned with the curriculum for which they are held accountable and for their instructional efforts to prepare students to demonstrate content mastery on the tests and assessments required by the school and/or district. Consequently, teachers may lose sight of how what they are teaching connects with (a) what others in the school and community are teaching, (b) what outcomes of significance students are learning, and (c) what has been set as an overall outcome of education—namely, the development of skills and knowledge that students can apply in their daily lives.

To *reinforce* the importance of constantly relating the day-to-day curriculum to overall educational goals, we begin our discussion of curriculum with an exploration of goals, outcomes, and standards. Goals, outcomes, and standards underlie and many times provide structure and cohesiveness for the overall curriculum of schooling and they serve as guideposts for curricular decisions.

Understanding and awareness of goals, outcomes, and standards, and of their influences on curriculum development assist teachers in selecting and designing curriculum that will have broad and positive ramifications for the students they teach. Furthermore, understanding and awareness of goals, outcomes, and standards assists teachers, parents, and students in setting curricular priorities and in developing individual plans that reflect those priorities.

DEFINITIONS

Many states, districts and schools use the concepts *goals, outcomes,* and *standards* interchangeably, neither defining nor differentiating among them. This practice can lead to confusion. Through clearly defining these terms as they will be used in this text, we hope to help readers differentiate terms and apply their meanings in appropriate contexts.

Educational *goals* are based on a shared vision of the kinds of schools and schooling children will need to be prepared for the twenty-first century (Kniep & Martin-Kniep, 1995). Some goals are broad statements of philosophy or mission. One school district's mission is: "To develop life-long learners who value themselves, contribute to their community, and succeed in a changing world" (Boschee & Baron, 1993, p. 39). Other goals may describe school-wide outcomes, such as "Every school will be free of drugs, violence, and the unauthorized presence of firearms and alcohol and will offer a disciplined environment conducive to learning" (Goals 2000: The Educate America Act, P.L. 103-227, 1994). Still others may target specific outcomes for students such as "facility in using the English language," "awareness of acceptable and unacceptable behavior," and "ability to communicate using computer technology" (Posner, 1992, p. 19).

Desired learning *outcomes* derive from and define the goals (Kniep & Martin-Kniep, 1995). "Stated as the desired measurable or observable results, effects, or consequences of schooling, outcomes describe what students must know, be like and be able to do to achieve the stated goals." (Kniep & Martin-Kniep, 1995, p. 88). "Outcomes are the result of interactions between individuals and schooling experiences. Results are what can/ should/does happen when a person has educational experiences. They may be direct or indirect, positive or negative, and intended or unintended" (Ysseldyke & Thurlow, 1993, p. 11). They are "clear learning results that we want students to demonstrate at the end of significant learning experiences . . . actions and performances that embody and reflect learner competence in using content, information, ideas and tools successfully" (Spady, 1994b, p. 2). The learning experience may be for segments of curriculum or for blocks of time or may be an ultimate result sought for the student at or after the end of a student's career in school (Spady, 1994b). "Enabling" or "prerequisite" outcomes enable the student to reach the ultimate outcomes of schooling (Ysseldyke & Thurlow, 1993).

Standards are based on the desired learning outcomes and derive from them (Kniep & Martin-Kniep, 1995). Standards "specify the levels and types of knowledge or performance we expect from students. Standards describe the knowledge, characteristics, and levels of performance embedded in the outcomes" (Kniep & Martin-Kniep, 1995, p. 88). They are generally used as objective bases for appraising student performance and they reflect expectations of uniformity with respect to goals, curriculum, and levels of student achievement (Eisner, 1995). Content standards and performance standards are two common types of standards in education. "*Content standards* (or curriculum standards) . . . describe what teachers are supposed to teach and students are expected to learn . . . *Performance standards* . . . define the degrees or mastery of levels of attainment . . . [they] answer the question 'How good is good enough?'" (Ravitch, 1995, p. 12).

To assist readers in understanding how goals, outcomes, and standards interrelate with each other, we offer an excerpt from the Yonkers (New York) School District Curriculum Guide (Exhibit 2.1.) Yonkers established five overall goals for students. The first goal listed in the first column of the exhibit is for students to be "prepared to live in a world that is characterized by a variety of individual differences and great diversity in social and natural systems." In the middle column, the district identifies outcomes related to the first goal. The third column lists eight standards linked with the first outcome: "Understand value, and act to preserve the great biological and physical diversity of the planet's ecosystems." Review the eight standards to see how they relate to the goal and outcome. Through this process the district goals are put into operation through identification of outcomes, which are further specified by standards of performance.

EXHIBIT 2.1

Yonkers School District Goals, Outcomes, and Standards

GOALS	STUDENT OUTCOMES: GOAL 1	EXIT STANDARDS: GOAL 1, OUTCOME 1
1. **Students completing their education in Yonkers Public Schools will be prepared to live in a world that is characterized by a variety of individual differences and great diversity in social and natural systems.**	1. **Understand, value, and act to preserve the great biological and physical diversity of the planet's ecosystems.**	• **Demonstrate an awareness of the concept of ecosystems.**
2. Students completing their education in Yonkers Public Schools will be prepared to live with the challenges and opportunities of a world that is characterized by interdependence and a variety of interconnections.	2. Understand the historical contributions and contemporary roles of the variety of groups that make up their community, nation, and world.	• **Be familiar with biological and physical characteristics of ecosystems.**
3. Students completing their education in Yonkers Public Schools will be prepared to live in a world that is characterized by accelerating change.	3. Understand that all societies and cultures adopt unique economicic and political systems based on their own histories and circum-stances.	• **Have practical knowledge of how various forces can upset the balance of nature.**
4. Students completing their education in Yonkers Public Schools will achieve their full human potential as individuals and contributing members of society.	4. Appreciate that many diverse cultures have contributed to humankind through unique forms of artistic expression and their histories of ideas.	• **Engage in ongoing ecological activities.**
5. Students completing their education in Yonkers Public Schools will develop a love of learning and will be prepared and committed to be lifelong learners.	5. Interact effectively with a variety of people regardless of individual differences in heredity or culture.	• **Know local, regional, and world topography.**
	6. Respect and be open to the opinions of others in a free exchange of ideas.	• **Be knowledgeable consumers.**
	7. Understand the perspective of others and be able to negotiate and resolve conflicts.	• **Be able to participate in the management of limited natural resources.**
	8. Be aware of the differences in how they see themselves and how others see them.	• **Actively contribute toward preserving and restoring the natural balance of the planet's ecosystems.**

Source: From "Designing Schools and Curriculum for the 21st Century" (p. 95), by W. M. Kniep and G. O. Martin-Kniep, in *Toward a Coherent Curriculum,* ed. J. A. Beane. Alexandria, VA: Association for Supervision and Curriculum Development. Copyright © 1995 ASCD. Reprinted by permission. All rights reserved.

Questions arise for some students with disabilities about the appropriateness of the goals, outcomes, and standards generally established for a student-body-at-large. Teachers have responsibilities, as do parents and other stakeholders (individuals concerned and either directly or indirectly impacted by decisions made) who are interested in the education of children and youth with disabilities, to question the adoption of one set of standards for *all* students. For some students with disabilities, some or all standards as stated by some districts may be inappropriate or be sought at the cost of student achievement in other areas of outcomes important to them (i.e., achievement of skills and understandings needed to survive as independently as possible as adults).

Goals, outcomes and standards form bases of frameworks for curriculum and assessment. They can guide special and general educators in their selection of curriculum and assessments for students with disabilities and in the specification of IEP goals and instruction objectives. Embracing a cohesive framework like this one can benefit the curricular planning for special education students in multiple ways: (a) providing for a more systematic approach for planning a student's curriculum; (b) forcing those planning the curriculum for a student with a disability to consider the general education curriculum as a frame of reference; and (c) providing a common language for general and special education teachers, parents, students, and administrators as they plan curriculum for students with disabilities.

THEORY TO PRACTICE

➡ Secure a copy of either district or state standards for a subject area or other major component of curriculum. Review the standards. What categories are represented? How are the standards organized? Imagine you are a teacher attempting to build a curriculum based on the standards. What standards would your curriculum address? Is it necessary to adapt these standards for students with disabilities, and if so, how would you adapt them? What IEP goals and objectives could you generate using these standards as a base?

SOURCES OF INFLUENCE

Goals, outcomes, and standards are developed by different groups of people for different reasons. For example, one group may be concerned about the mathematical performance of children (e.g., National Council of Teachers of Mathematics) and develop goals, outcomes, and standards to be adopted by states, school districts, and teachers for use when developing a mathematics curriculum. Other groups or individuals may identify other areas of needs (e.g., citizenship, ability to work with others, communication skills) and propose their own goals, outcomes, and standards. Because of the large number of proposed goals, outcomes, and standards, selection of curricular goals, outcomes, and standards may be made by district or school administrators or school boards, or possibly by state or national accreditation bodies; in these and other situations, teachers may have a voice in their selection. Regardless of the selection procedures, teachers need to be aware of the sources of influence on the development and selection of goals, outcomes, and standards so they can make informed decisions when developing curriculum for their students.

We classify sources of influences as being national, state, and local. The influence that each source exercises on the selection and implementation of goals, outcomes, and standards may be top-down, bottom-up, or two-way. Top-down mandates and recommendations from national and state levels dictate, determine, or guide what happens at the lower level (e.g., the districts' schools and classrooms). Bottom-up district and school-level initiatives involve teachers and others working in classrooms and school districts in setting policies and priorities and influencing the selection of state and national policies. Two-way initiatives require the coordination and simultaneous implementing of top-down and bottom-up strategies (Fullan, 1993). To explain more fully how this process works, the following sections describe specific national, state, and local influences and their role in the goals, outcomes, and standards development and/or selection process.

National Influences

Each national political administration plays a major role in establishing or fostering implementation of educational goals, outcomes, and standards for the country. Additionally, citizen groups with special interests in particular student groups (e.g., students whose primary language is not English) or in particular curriculum areas (e.g., science) influence the development and/or selection of national goals, outcomes, and standards.

Perhaps one of the most powerful national influences is the government collection, analysis, and dissemination to local communities of reports such as the SCANS Report from the U.S. Department of Labor (Wagner, 1995). The Secretary's Commission on Achieving Necessary Skills (SCANS) (1991) is one of the primary groups that study job-related skills that high school graduates need to know and be able to do. The job-related skills identified in the SCANS Report are summarized in the "Workplace Know-How" chart presented in Exhibit 2.2. The SCANS Report proposed that these identified competencies be used as a basis for developing and selecting curriculum. As the list of competencies indicates, curriculum implications could be widespread, touching all curriculum areas taught in schools.

The know-how identified by SCANS is made up of five competencies and a three-part foundation of skills and personal qualities needed for solid job performance . . .

EXHIBIT 2.2

Workplace Know-how

COMPETENCIES.

Effective workers can productively use:

- *Resources:* allocating time, money, materials, space, staff;
- *Interpersonal Skills:* working on teams, teaching others, serving customers, leading, negotiating, and working well with people from culturally diverse backgrounds;
- *Information:* acquiring and evaluating data, organizing and maintaining files, interpreting and communicating, and using computers to process information;
- *Systems:* understanding social, organization, and technological systems, monitoring and correcting performance, and designing or improving systems;
- *Technology:* selecting equipment and tools, applying technology to specific tasks, and maintaining and troubleshooting technologies.

THE FOUNDATION.

Competence requires:

- *Basic Skills:* reading, writing, arithmetic and mathematics, speaking and listening;
- *Thinking Skills:* thinking creatively, making decisions, solving problems, seeing things in the mind's eye, knowing how to learn, and reasoning;
- *Personal Qualities:* individual responsibility, self-esteem, sociability, self-management and integrity.

Source: From *Teaching the SCANS Competencies* (p. 6), by Secretary's Commission on Achieving Necessary Skills, 1993, Washington, DC: U.S. Dept. of Labor.

Another prime example of national influence is Goals 2000: The Educate America Act (P.L. 103-227). This act of Congress defined eight national education goals to be met by the year 2000. These goals, as established in 1990 and augmented in 1994, are listed in Exhibit 2.3. Their adoption is optional.

EXHIBIT 2.3	By the year 2000,
Eight National Education Goals from Goals 2000: The Educate America Act	1. All children in America will start school ready to learn. 2. The high school graduation rate will increase to at least 90 percent. 3. All students will leave grades 4, 8, and 12 having demonstrated competency over challenging subject matter including English, mathematics, science, foreign languages, civics and government, economics, arts, history, and geography. 4. U.S. students will be first in the world in science and mathematics achievement. 5. Every adult American will be literate and will possess the knowledge and skills to compete in a global economy. 6. Every school will be free of drugs and violence and the unauthorized presence of firearms and alcohol and will offer a disciplined environment conducive to learning. 7. The teacher force will have access to programs for the continued improvement of their professional skills. 8. Every school will promote partnerships that will increase parental involvement and participation. Source: Adapted from P.L. 103-227, March 31, 1994.

Many stakeholders have concerns that Goals 2000, as stated, seems unrealistic when applied to all children (Olsen & Massanari, 1991; Schrag, 1991). For example, the goal of having all children enter school ready to learn may not be realistic given the economic conditions of inner-city and rural neighborhoods and the diverse preschool experiences of students. For another example, some toddlers participate in academically focused preschools, but other students have limited exposure to school-related curriculum prior to their school enrollment. Moreover, the application of Goals 2000 and its relationship to the needs and abilities of students with disabilities has not been addressed. The importance of these goals for students with disabilities—how they will be achieved, and how they will relate to the development of life skills leading to independent living have yet to be determined.

In contrast to the Goals 2000 approach to goal development, the National Center on Educational Outcomes (NCEO), representing a collaborative effort by the National Association of State Directors of Special Education and the University of Minnesota, developed anticipated outcomes for all students. NCEO *first* identified desired goals and outcomes and indicators for students with disabilities. Then these outcomes were expanded to reflect parallel needs of students without recognized disabilities. Examples of desired educational outcomes for two of the eight identified domains from NCEO for each student completing school are presented in Exhibit 2.4. The other anticipated outcome domains are (a) presence and participation, (b) accommodation and adaptation, (c) physical health, (d) responsibility and independence, (e) contribution, and (f) citizenship and satisfaction. NCEO identifies more specific versions of these outcome domains for different school levels, as well as for the school completion level and a postschool level.

OUTCOMES: Academic and Functional Literacy

- Demonstrates competence in communication
- Demonstrates competence in problem-solving strategies and critical thinking skills
- Demonstrates competence in math, reading and writing skills
- Demonstrates competence in other academic and nonacademic skills
- Demonstrates competence in using technology

OUTCOMES: Personal and Social Adjustment

- Copes effectively with personal challenges, frustrations, and stressors
- Has a good self-image
- Respects cultural and individual differences
- Gets along with other people

Source: From *Educational Outcomes and Indicators for Students Completing School* (pp. 13, 14), by J. E. Ysseldyke, M. L. Thurlow, & C. J. Gilman, January 1993, Minneapolis: National Center on Educational Outcomes.

EXHIBIT 2.4

NCEO Outcomes

National professional organizations, commissions, steering committees, and task forces also influence the setting of national goals, outcomes, and standards. These organizations establish national standards for the various school disciplines, leaving adoption decisions to individual states. One such source to which district and school personnel can refer when constructing their own standards is McREL (Marzano & Kendall, 1995). McREL is a database of standards and benchmarks from 22 national documents organized into nine topics: science, mathematics, U.S. history, geography, communication and information processing, thinking and reasoning, working with others, self-regulation, and life work.

Additionally, there is at least one national organization that recommends standards for each of the different school disciplines. For example, states have the choice to adopt the content standards for mathematics as established by the National Council of Teachers of Mathematics (NCTM). Exhibit 2.5 presents their standard on problem solving, and their listing of skills and understandings that students in grades 5 through 8 should develop in this area.

- use problem-solving approaches to investigate and understand mathematical content;
- formulate problems from situations within and outside mathematics;
- develop and apply a variety of strategies to solve problems, with emphasis on multistep and nonroutine problems;
- verify and interpret results with respect to the original problem situation;
- generalize solutions and strategies to new problem situations;
- acquire confidence in using mathematics meaningfully.

Source: From *Curriculum and Evaluation Standards for School Mathematics* (p. 75), by National Council of Teachers of Mathematics, 1989, Reston: VA: Author. Used with permission.

EXHIBIT 2.5

NCTM Standard 1 for Grades 5 through 8: Mathematics as Problem Solving

Federal government representatives also have a voice in the setting of goals, outcomes, and standards for individuals with disabilities and for special education programs through legislative activities. Two federal laws continue to have a major influence on how the needs of individuals with disabilities are addressed. As mentioned earlier, the IDEA Amendments of 1997 stress the importance of individuals with disabilities receiving their education in the least restrictive environment. In many instances, this has resulted in more and more students with disabilities receiving instruction in the general education curriculum or its modifications. Therefore, P.L. 105-17 has had, and continues to have, influence on the curriculum goals, outcomes, and standards adopted for students with disabilities.

Another highly influential law is the Americans with Disabilities Act (ADA) of 1990 (P.L. 101-336). This law governs the treatment of individuals with disabilities in communities and the private sector. ADA addresses the needs of children and adults as they live, work, and engage in leisure activities in the community. ADA prohibits discrimination against people with disabilities. Hence, it is often referred to as antidiscrimination legislation. Under ADA, people with disabilities are entitled to assistance in the form of "reasonable accommodations" in order to participate in American life and benefit from services available, such as schooling, employment, and a range of public and private services. One prominent example of the impact of ADA is the building of ramps and other access accommodations in the private sector. Unlike IDEA, ADA is not funded legislation; it leaves the local and private sector with the responsibility of financing the provision of reasonable accommodations.

National advisory and special interest groups are vocal about the needs and rights of individuals with disabilities. For example, the National Council on Disability (Washington, D.C.) is a special interest group dedicated to the needs of students with disabilities. The Council for Exceptional Children (Reston, Virginia) is an international group that advocates and lobbies for individuals with disabilities. TASH (The Association for Persons with Severe Handicaps) promotes participation of persons with significant disabilities in all aspects of life. It is an international professional organization that emphasizes advocacy for people with significant disabilities, their families, and individuals who work with this population. The National Parent Network on Disability (Alexandria, Virginia) and the National Information Center for Children and Youth with Disabilities (Washington, D.C.) are also examples of national advisory and special interest groups.

State Influences

The U.S. Constitution leaves the provision of education largely to the states. State departments of education, therefore, are responsible for taking a leading role in establishing goals, outcomes, and standards for the education of schoolchildren within their state. As a result, state-level goals, outcomes, and standards tend to reflect the specific needs of the individual states. For example, states that have a highly diverse student population with a number of the children coming to school speaking a primary language other than English, may establish goals around English-language acquisition and maintenance of the native tongue. States dealing with high unemployment and/or incidence of poverty may place greater emphasis on goals, outcomes, and standards that stress literacy and job-related skills and competencies, and experiences that support health and overall wellness. State education agencies, as specified in the IDEA Amendments of 1997, are required to hold public hearings in order to adopt a plan for implementing federal legislation related to the provision of educational services.

State-determined outcomes

Beyond federally mandated activities and other national influences, states take various approaches for establishing goals, outcomes, and standards. State policy boards generally advocate one of two kinds of outcomes and related accountability systems that affect students with disabilities: unified or differentiated. As defined by McLaughlin and Hopfengardner-Warren (1992), a *unified* system sets one common set of outcomes for all students, although the manner in which competence is demonstrated and assessed may take into consideration unique individual needs. A *differentiated* system, in contrast, sets outcomes based on characteristics and needs of disability groups. More and more we see combinations of unified and differentiated outcomes.

Kentucky uses a *unified* outcome system and identifies outcomes every graduating senior should know and be able to do at a proficient level. Example outcomes include the following: "Students construct meaning from a variety of print materials for a variety of purposes through reading," "Students organize information and communicate ideas by algebraic and geometric reasoning such as relations, patterns, variables, unknown quantities, deductive and inductive processes," and "Students use computers and other electronic technology to gather, organize, manipulate and express information and ideas" (Steffy, 1993b, pp. 27–28).

Michigan uses an option of *differentiated* outcomes and related accountability system. The Michigan Department of Education and Disability Research Systems, Inc. (DRS) collaborated to establish for individuals with disabilities differentiated goals accompanied by performance expectations (i.e., what students within different disability categories are expected to be able to do at the conclusion of their schoolings). For example, categories of outcomes for students with *emotional impairment* include basic academics (e.g., meeting minimum graduation requirements); emotional development (e.g., self-advocacy); prosocial skills and adaptive behavior social skills (e.g., effectively participating in groups); task completion (e.g., being self-directed); lifestyle precautions (e.g., decision-making skills for responding to potentially dangerous behaviors); prevocational, vocational, and career education (e.g., planning for realistic vocational opportunities); and parenting and adult living education (e.g., personal care) (Disability Research Systems, 1992).

Other models combine systems of unified and differentiated outcomes, or expectations. Examples are a collaborative Michigan/DRS model (Disability Research Systems, 1996) and a similar collaborative Florida/DRS model (Florida Commission on Education Reform and Accountability, 1994; Florida State Department of Education, 1995b). We elaborate here on the DRS/Florida model. Performance expectations are the focus of this model, with identification of appropriate educational end targets for students with disabilities based on levels of independence, rather than on a disability category; outcomes are based not on whether students have a learning disability or a physical disability but rather on the level of independence to be achieved in adulthood.

The DRS/Florida model (Florida Commission on Education Reform and Accountability, 1994), identifies four levels of performance expectation representing the levels of independence that the range of students are expected to achieve in major life roles, primarily major adult living roles. The four levels are summarized, each with an example expectation drawn from the DRS/Florida model:

1. **Standards** that are appropriate for most students in the educational system, including students with disabilities who can meet the expectations with some accommodations and modifications (e.g., "Display responsibility, self-esteem, sociability, self-management, integrity, honesty, and healthy decision-making.")

2. **Functional independence**—entails skills and competencies required for independent living (e.g., "Complete routine personal care, health, and fitness activities.")

3. **Supported independence**—entails skills and competencies required for living in a supervised setting (e.g., "Complete domestic activities in personal living environments.")

4. **Participation**—represents the level of participation in age-appropriate tasks and activities required for integration into major life roles (e.g., "Participate in personal care, health, and safety routines.")

Teachers in Florida and other states using the DRS/Florida model have specified outcomes along with more detailed explanatory materials. This whole program is based on standards and performance expectations. This model identifies specific standards or performance expectations by independence level and by grade level or age groups and it provides directly related assessments. Teachers know where they, collectively, should be taking students with disabilities and have consistent means for assessing them along the way.

State assessment systems and curricular frameworks

In those instances where states have not developed specific standards, goals, and outcome models, teachers can look to the state's assessment programs and curricular frameworks or guides as sources for determining and/or selecting goals, outcomes, and standards for students. Through these documented processes, states attempt to provide guidelines for assessing student growth in curriculum and for developing curricula that meet state and national goals, outcomes, and standards (Curry & Temple, 1992).

State assessment programs are helpful sources for determining curriculum. The most common state-level assessment approach is the setting of graduation requirements. Requirements

> range from Carnegie unit requirements (a certain number of class credits earned in specific areas), to successfully passing minimum competency tests, high school exit exams, and/or a series of benchmark exams . . . [or] almost any combination of these. (Thurlow, Ysseldyke, & Anderson, 1995, p. 1)

Although appearing straightforward, graduation requirements vary across and within states, and few states specifically address graduation requirements for students with disabilities. For example, in their review of state department records, Thurlow, Ysseldyke, and Anderson (1995) found that 44 states used Carnegie course units (e.g., a junior English course may be worth two units toward graduation). As the primary determiner of graduation, seventeen states included a minimum competency test or exit exam requirement for graduation. Approximately 15 states set modified diploma requirements for students with disabilities. For many individuals with disabilities, graduation requirements set by type and number of courses can prevent students from earning a high school diploma because students may take courses different from those of their general education peers, and courses different from those required for earning a diploma. Thurlow, Ysseldyke, and Anderson (1995) found that the

> diploma is not the only document that represents successful completion of high school. Among the array of possibilities are diplomas with endorsements, certificates of attendance, and standard diplomas. (p. 1)

Some states are moving to other systems for linking assessment and outcomes. Kentucky is the first state in the nation to fully include *all* its students in its assessment system (Theodore, 1996). Kentucky is using assessment tasks and scoring rubrics to give specificity and clarity to each of the state outcomes while also accommodating existing levels of student proficiency. Scoring rubrics indicate "if a student is scoring at the novice, apprentice, proficient, or distinguished level" (Steffy, 1993a, p. 42) and are used as tools for evaluating students' overall performance and achievement of stated outcomes. Although Kentucky has not differentiated the desired outcomes for students with disabilities, the state has developed a modified portfolio process for students with moderate and severe cognitive disabilities and assesses student progress toward the outcomes (Theodore, 1996). This system addresses the same academic expectations as for typical peers but at different performance levels and performances may be demonstrated through different means. In Kentucky and some other states students with disabilities do not participate in assessment protocols used by the majority of general education students. In Kentucky, mentioned before, they "participate in an alternative portfolio-based assessment to demonstrate their performance on state outcomes" (Shriner, Ysseldyke, Thurlow, & Honetschlager, 1994, p. 39).

State frameworks are another helpful source for determining and/or selecting goals, outcomes, and standards. Such frameworks can play a critical role in the identification of outcomes and standards and the development of curriculum in district classrooms. Teachers may "use the curriculum framework as a vehicle to achieve the desired outcomes students are to attain" (Curry & Temple, 1992, p. 26) and as a starting point for guiding the creation of classroom experiences.

Kniep and Martin-Kniep (1995) identify three main elements of a framework. These are (a) curricular strands that are derived from the outcomes and standards adopted by the state or district, (b) benchmarks selected for age and grade levels that set targets for measuring progress toward standards, and (c) assessment practices. Although some frameworks have a traditional content-driven focus that emphasizes key skills and knowledge in specific content areas (e.g., science), others address school disciplines and related subjects through themes (e.g., poverty) and the linking of concepts and performance outcomes. The latter frameworks focus on highly complex and broad student outcomes to prepare students for the challenges of future life roles. They are not intended to be the specific, prescriptive curricula actually taught in the classroom, but rather they emphasize the variety and reality of future participation in the world outside schools. This type of framework may stress how individuals need skills and understandings to be critical consumers and contributing community members. Skills needed to achieve these outcomes cross all discipline areas and represent a diverse set of understandings from mathematics (e.g., money, budgeting), language arts (e.g., literacy skills), and social skills and competencies (e.g., getting along with others), to name just a few. The outcomes and standards stated in these frameworks cannot be achieved through the completion of a course or two but reflect the generalized learning that occurs across various experiences and content.

The National Council for the Social Studies (1994) proposed such a framework. This framework identifies ten strands ((1) Culture; (2) Time, Continuity, and Change; (3) People, Places, and Environments; (4) Individual Development and Identity; (5) Individuals, Groups, and Institutions; (6) Power, Authority, and Governance; (7) Production, Distribution, and Consumption; (8) Science, Technology, and Society; (9) Global Connections; and (10) Civic Ideals and Practices). The performance expectations are defined for each of these 10 standards. Exhibit 2.6 (p. 46) presents the grade and level of student performance expectations that are associated with the first curricular strand.

Social studies programs should include experiences that provide for the study of *culture and cultural diversity*, so that the learner can:

EARLY GRADES	MIDDLE GRADES	HIGH SCHOOL
a. explore and describe similarities and differences in the ways groups, societies, and cultures address similar human needs and concerns;	a. compare similarities and differences in the ways groups, societies, and cultures meet human needs and concerns;	a. analyze and explain the ways groups, societies, and cultures address human needs and concerns;
b. give examples of how experiences may be interpreted differently by people from diverse cultural perspectives and frames of reference;	b. explain how information and experiences may be interpreted by people from diverse cultural perspectives and frames of reference;	b. predict how data and experiences may be interpreted by people from diverse cultural perspectives and frames of reference;
c. describe ways in which language, stories, folktales, music, and artistic creations serve as expressions of culture and influence behavior of people living in a particular culture;	c. explain and give examples of how language, literature, the arts, architecture, other artifacts, traditions, beliefs, values, and behaviors contribute to the development and transmission of culture;	c. apply an understanding of culture as an integrated whole that explains the functions and interactions of language, literature, the arts, traditions, beliefs and values, and behavior patterns;
d. compare ways in which people from different cultures think about and deal with their physical environment and social conditions;	d. explain why individuals and groups respond differently to their physical and social environments and/or changes to them on the basis of shared assumptions, values, and beliefs;	d. compare and analyze societal patterns for preserving and transmitting culture while adapting to environmental or social change;
e. give examples and describe the importance of cultural unity and diversity within and across groups.	e. articulate the implications of cultural diversity, as well as cohesion, within and across groups.	e. demonstrate the value of cultural diversity, as well as cohesion, within and across groups;
		f. interpret patterns of behavior reflecting values and attitudes that contribute or pose obstacles to cross-cultural understanding;
		g. construct reasoned judgments about specific cultural responses to persistent human issues;
		h. explain and apply ideas, theories, and modes of inquiry drawn from anthropology and sociology in the examination of persistent issues and social problems.

Source: From *Curriculum Standards for Social Studies* (p. 33), by National Council for the Social Studies, 1994, Washington, DC: Author. Used with permission.

Local Influences

Citizens in local communities play major roles in determining and/or selecting goals, outcomes, and standards for children attending their community schools. What the local constituency or individual contributors bring to the decision-making process may reflect national and state influences (top-down) and influence policies and decisions at the national and state levels (bottom-up).

Local stakeholders may identify expected results of schooling by grade level, school subject, and high school graduation requirements. Usually these expectations are consistent with national and state goals. Sometimes they are mandated, such as the outcomes developed for the Aurora, Colorado, School District. The five outcomes are

"Self-Directed Learner . . . Collaborative Worker . . . Complex Thinker . . . Quality Produce . . . and Community Contributor" (Spady, 1994b, pp. 115–116). Each outcome is defined by specific behaviors. For example, the Aurora, Colorado School District defines a self-directed learner as one who:

- Sets priorities and achievable goals
- Evaluates and manages own progress toward goals
- Creates options for self
- Takes responsibility for actions
- Creates a positive vision for self and future (Spady, 1994b, p. 115)

Teachers, parents, students, and school boards play a major role in determining goals, outcomes, standards and resulting curricular emphasis in local schools. Parent-teacher organizations may participate in the development and implementation of curricular initiatives, and teacher groups may express a local voice in curriculum development policies and efforts. For example, a district may consider the adoption of a new reading program for students who are experiencing difficulty gaining literacy skills. Several meetings between parent groups, teachers, students, school administrators, and curricular planners may be held to discuss parents' concerns about their children's lack of reading achievement and to explore various options available to respond to those concerns. Options may include the selection and implementation of new curricular standards, modification of existing standards, and/or the provision of additional resources to assist in the delivery of a modified literacy curriculum for students experiencing difficulties. Results of these grassroots movements may be the development of modified standards, or the development of new programs and service delivery structures to respond to the needs of children within the district and possibly throughout the state. All of this begins with parent, teacher, and student input.

Summary of Influences

This discussion highlights the multifaceted nature of setting goals, outcomes, and standards that influence the education of students, including those with disabilities. Determination may be top-down (i.e., national to classrooms), bottom-up (i.e., starting in classrooms), or two-way. Because of its complexity, the task of determining and/or selecting curriculum for classrooms is a challenging one. The next section provides some suggestions for classroom teachers.

THEORY TO PRACTICE

➡ Contact one of the organizations mentioned in this section. What is its mission? How does it contribute to (a) the understanding of disability, (b) the types of services individuals with disabilities need, and (c) the curricular needs of individuals with disabilities? If the organization has publications, review one or two. Evaluate the quality of those publications, the type of information provided, and the audience the information appears to be most appropriate for. Share your information with classmates. Are there any organizations of which you would like to become a member?

➡ Attend a local school board meeting or parent organization meeting. What issues are being discussed? What concerns are being raised? How do these issues and concerns relate to the provision of services for students with disabilities? What impact do you believe these groups have on the development of curriculum?

➡ Review your state's framework for curriculum and assessment. How do these materials reflect the needs of and issues surrounding individuals with disabilities? Are the needs of students with disabilities addressed in the materials? How helpful are these materials to you as a teacher? What recommendations for additions or revisions would you suggest to the committee(s) that developed these materials?

MAKING CURRICULAR DECISIONS

Given local, state, and national goal, outcome, and standard guidelines, teachers collaborate with parents and students, administrators, curriculum specialists, subject area scholars, and community members to make curricular decisions. The complexity of this task can be overwhelming and it may lead to confusion unless there is some structure for participants to follow when attempting to determine what is most important to include in the curriculum.

One challenge teachers face when designing curriculum is knowing what curricular decisions they are free to make and what decisions are made for them. To assist teachers, some local districts institute specific procedures that clarify their roles. For example, the Westwood Public School District of Westwood, Massachusetts (Monson & Monson, 1993), determined that certain decisions are *centralized* ones (decisions made by administrative offices that all individuals in a system are to follow) whereas other decisions are *decentralized* ones (decisions that teachers make). Also, some decisions are *collective decisions* (decisions made by a group), and others are *individual* ones (decisions made by individual teachers).

Direction of Curriculum Development

Knowing who is making what decisions is a starting point, but teachers also need more information. For example, are outcomes of their curriculum to be based on existing curriculum in textbooks, or is their curriculum to be developed by beginning with the identification of goals, outcomes, and standards for the end of schooling and working backward from there to determine classroom curriculum?

Curriculum may be developed from the bottom up or from the top down. A bottom-up example is designing curriculum goals and outcomes from existing curriculum presented in textbooks and other references and primary sources. This curriculum can be either content dominated or performance based. The development of *content dominated curriculum* starts with existing curriculum organized around traditional school disciplines (e.g., mathematics) and is customarily textbook based. Achievement of outcomes is assessed primarily through quizzes and tests and ultimately through students' earning passing (course) grades.

Performance based curriculum, in this bottom-up orientation, does not rely so heavily on learning the knowledge and skills (content) in textbooks or on performing on tests and quizzes. Instead, it centers on what students do to demonstrate their understanding and/or mastery of the material. It may stem from existing lessons, units, or course curriculum outcomes. Students may be asked to demonstrate competence through demonstrations in specific school disciplines (e.g., oral reports, presentation of research papers) or across disciplines through an integrated approach (e.g., portfolio centered on a theme; dramatic production). Final performance tasks may be specified at the beginning of a major unit or course, and curriculum may be designed backward from there. As a result, teachers use textbooks as reference sources, not as a syllabus outline or for structuring the way in which information will be presented (Kniep & Martin-Kniep, 1995). Each segment of curriculum with a bottom-up orientation, such as a subject-matter course centered around a textbook, builds to its own outcomes, whether they be content-based, performance-based or a combination.

Outcome-based education (OBE) is an example of a top-down curricular development strategy that starts with end-of-schooling outcomes. OBE means

> *clearly focusing and organizing everything in an educational system around what is essential for all students to be able to do successfully at the end of their learning experience. (Spady, 1994b, p. 1)*

Complexity of Learning Demonstrations

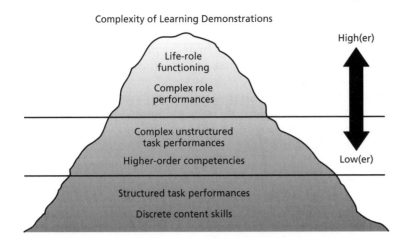

▮ **FIGURE 2.1**
**Spady's
Demonstration Mountain**
Source: Adapted from *Outcome-based Education: Critical Issues and Answers* (p. 62) by W. G. Spady, 1994, Arlington, VA: American Association of School Administrators. Used with permission.

OBE curriculum stems from identified "outcomes of significance" that graduates should know and will be able to do by the culmination of their schooling (Spady, 1994a).

Exit outcomes in OBE differ from other outcomes because they stem from responses to the question: "What is most essential for our students to know, be able to do, and be like in order to be successful once they've graduated?" (Spady & Marshall, 1991, p. 69). Exit, or culminating, outcomes in OBE are "outcomes of significance." Rather than identifying what students should do in each segment of the curriculum to earn a particular grade, outcomes of significance are the

> *development of internalized performance abilities—what students will carry with them throughout and beyond their formal schooling that cannot be developed inside any single segment of curriculum. Designing and carrying out research projects is a case in point; it takes years of study and practice to be able to do it well. (Spady, 1994b, p. 51)*

Typically, the student's demonstrations or performances of their learning reflect

> *(1) what the student knows; (2) what the student can actually do with what he or she knows; and (3) the student's confidence and motivation in carrying out the demonstration. (Spady, Marshall, & Rogers, 1994, p. 29)*

The performance is the goal—content and literacy support the achievement of overarching goals.

Teachers and other stakeholders who want school curriculum to build toward outcomes of student performance abilities that, in the long run, really matter (even after students finish school) may choose to use Spady's framework as a guide for study (Spady, 1994b). This framework directs attention toward the designing of goals, objectives, standards, and resulting curriculum that assist students in accomplishing outcomes such as those represented by the top sections of Spady's "Demonstration Mountain" (Figure 2.1, above).

Spady's Demonstration Mountain "portrays a picture of six major forms that student demonstrations of learning, or competence, may take. These forms range from very simple and discrete skills [bottom of the mountain] to the very complex and challenging performances people carry out within their life responsibilities and roles [top of the mountain]" (Spady, 1994b, p. 61). The lower sectors of the mountain are *content-*dominated. The intermediary sectors are *transitional* because they are forms of demonstrations and competences that provide the way from the bottom to the top forms of demonstrations and competences. The top sectors, then, are considered *context-*dominated because of the need for students to learn complex forms of competence with complex arrays of content for the many different realities and demands required for carrying out one's different roles in different life contexts (Spady, 1994a). This framework "implies that each form of competence serves as a critical enabler for the forms above it . . . [so] the higher one climbs:

- The more complex and significant the demonstrations of learning become.
- The more complex and challenging the settings, circumstances, and contexts [with]in which the demonstration takes place become.
- By implication, the greater the degree of self-direction, motivation, and adaptability required of the learner." (Spady, 1994b, p. 61)

To readers, it may seem most logical for us to begin our description of Spady's framework by starting at the bottom of the mountain with the most simple form of student performances and move upward. This is because most of us are more comfortable with traditional curriculum frameworks that consist of numbers of outcomes that are short-term ends in themselves, unrelated, and each having the characteristics represented by the lower levels of the Mountain. However, the Spady framework is different. Just as mountain climbers have to learn what they need to know and be able to do to survive at the top levels of mountains before they can plan for the journey upward, teachers must analyze what outcomes are expected of their students at the top, or Exit point of schooling, before they can plan for each student's educational journey upward and to the top. Consequently, we start by describing the kinds of more complex student performances portrayed by the top of the mountain to allow readers to appreciate what all is expected as outcomes of schooling and to develop awareness of what kinds of enabling outcomes are necessary to their accomplishment. Then we move down the mountain to allow readers to see how carefully planned curriculum portrayed by each of the lower forms of the mountain both benefit from the enabling functions represented by forms below them and contribute to the critical enabling functions of student performances above them. Therefore, the ultimate outcome of schooling, life-role functioning, takes the lead in our discussion.

Life-role functioning, at the top of the mountain, includes "BEING a citizen, employer, employee, parent, and family member" (Spady, 1994b, p. 190). Life role is "a set of responsibilities and actions that define an individual's position within a society's economic, political, and social relationship" (Spady, 1994b, p. 190). This form of demonstration is a primary aim of education but students frequently do not have opportunities for this form of demonstration while they are still in school. Therefore, during schooling, they are taught to approximate life-role functioning performances through demonstrations of complex role performances described at the form next to the top.

Through *complex role performances,* the next level down the mountain, students demonstrate competence in skills of living and lifelong learning—with responsibilities and actions represented by the top of the mountain. Forms of demonstration of complex role performances sometimes are indistinguishable from life-role functioning. Exhibit 2.7 presents complex role performances and their attributes. Spady (1994b) contends these are cross-disciplinary and essential to most all major life roles students will face once they leave school.

EXHIBIT 2.7

Complex Role Performances

- *Implementers and Performers,* who can apply basic and advanced ideas, information, skills, tools, and technologies as they carry out the responsibilities associated with all life roles. They grasp the demands of a particular situation and use available resources to get things done.
- *Problem Finders and Solvers,* who can anticipate, explore, analyze, and resolve problems, examining underlying causes from a variety of perspectives and developing potential solutions.
- *Planners and Designers,* who develop effective methods and strategies for resolving issues and problems.
- *Creators and Producers,* who seek new possibilities for understanding or doing things and who transform those possibilities into original, workable products or processes that change the operating environment.
- *Learners and Thinkers,* who develop and use cognitive tools and strategies to translate new information and experiences into sound action, and who use their repertoire of knowledge and strategies to extend their capacities for successful action by assimilating, analyzing, and synthesizing new experiences.
- *Listeners and Communicators,* who can grasp and express ideas, information, intention, feeling, and concern for others in ways that are clearly understood and appreciated. They accurately comprehend and use words, pictures, gestures, deeds, styles, symbols, and mannerisms to receive and convey thoughts.
- *Teachers and Mentors,* who can enhance the thinking, skills, performance orientations, and motivation of others through the explanations they provide, the counsel they give, and the example[s] they set. They share the information, time, perspectives, and skills at their disposal.
- *Supporters and Contributors,* who invest time and sources to improve the quality of life of those around them.
- *Team Members and Partners,* who contribute their best efforts to collaborative endeavors and who seek agreement on goals, procedures, responsibilities, and rewards, setting aside personal preferences in order to accomplish mutual aims.
- *Leaders and Organizers,* who can initiate, coordinate, and facilitate the accomplishment of collective tasks by perceiving and designing intended results, determining how they might be accomplished, anticipating roadblocks, and enlisting and supporting the participation of others to achieve the results.

Source: From "Choosing Outcomes of Significance," by W. G. Spady, 1994, *Vocational Leadership, 51* (6), pp. 21–22. Used with permission.

Herein lies the challenge to teachers and others to translate these descriptions of types of complex role performances into student performance during their schooling and in a manner that is authentic as possible. To prepare for this process, districts and teachers need to "identify and define essential components that constitute a particular type of role performer" (Spady, 1994b, p. 67) They must decide what performance with supportive content and literacy skills students need to learn to demonstrate for the responsibilities and actions of being in that role. Complex role performances can be implemented in schools as well as in other authentic life contexts. Such an example follows:

> . . . *students will organize and participate in a community service team that monitors major community issues and problems, develops alternatives—including proposed changes in laws—for addressing them, and explains potential solutions to key community groups. (Spady, 1994a, p. 21)*

Complex role performances such as this one contribute to the form of performance at the top of the mountain (life-role functioning) and reflect student learning of the forms of performance immediately below (complex unstructured task performances) and the forms below that one.

Complex unstructured task performances (see Figure 2.1) call on students to invent or create projects, products, or processes, often integrating knowledge from different disciplines and sources. Students define the parameters of the project as well as the criterion or standards, and mode of execution and evaluation (Spady, 1994a, 1994b). Activities are competency-dominated and there is less emphasis on conducting them in authentic contexts than there is in selecting activities for life-role functioning and complex role performances. An example of a complex, unstructured task performance is as follows:

> . . . *students will design and carry out a project on a major issue or problem that uses data to heighten community awareness and proposes feasible ways to address it by initiating new laws. (Spady, 1994b, p. 20)*

Higher-order competencies, still farther down the mountain, are "a broad group of demonstrable processes requiring the complex manipulation of information, concepts, and language" (Spady, 1994a, p. 20). Forms of demonstration include "analyzing concepts and their interrelations; proposing solutions to multifaceted problems; using complex arrays of data and information to make decisions; planning complex structure, processes, or events; and communicating effectively with public audiences" (Spady, 1994a, p. 20). Demonstrations of higher order competencies may involve different kinds of content over time, and each demonstration may be conducted in a relevant context where students can show the results of their competence in using higher order processes. Here is a specific example of a higher-order task which readers can compare to similar and more complex ones above it and more simple ones below.

> . . . *students will teach an adult civic group how to initiate new laws in the community. (Spady, 1994a, p. 21)*

Structured task performances are tasks highly structured by teachers for students. They include a range of demonstrations that vary substantially depending on the degree of cognitive demand needed to carry out each one (Spady 1994). Forms of demonstration include "writing a paper explaining a specific topic; carrying out a laboratory experiment and comparing its results with established theory; or drawing a map of a region at a specific point in history and contrasting it with a contemporary map of the same region" (Spady, 1994a, p. 20). They usually follow a set of instructions or steps the teacher defines. A structured performance of a task similar to those tasks illustrated above is:

> . . . *students will conduct a research project on methods of initiating new laws at the local level and present their findings to the class and/or to their parents. (Spady, 1994a, p. 20)*

Discrete content skills, at the base of the Demonstration Mountain, are the simplest demonstrations of competence; they cover small segments of the curriculum that are highly structured by teachers. Examples include identifying and labeling the major rivers and lakes of the United States on topographical maps, spelling words dictated, and carrying out certain mathematical operations. One example is:

> ... *students will correctly identify local government procedures for initiating new laws. (Spady, 1994a, p. 20)*

Spady (1994a) explains that these low-level skills tend to call for the kinds of performance commonly stressed in indiscriminate instructional objectives in the American school system. He suggests replacing or deleting any discrete outcomes "that are not significant enabling components for the culminating [exit] outcomes" (p. 19).

Outcome-based education, though responsible for many constructive influences in educational reform, encounters criticism. Many teachers and parents resent OBE's treatment of academic knowledge as a low priority (Gandal, 1995). Others have reservations because of the complex nature of the outcomes and the challenges they present for assessing student performance. Critics fear that some outcomes disguise a politically correct agenda, cheapen the curriculum, lack clarity, and infringe on the rights of parents to teach values (Dykman, 1994–1995; Olsen, 1993). Also under question are (a) assumptions by some that all OBE outcomes are appropriate for all students, (b) adjustments in time and curriculum required to achieve OBE outcomes, (c) provisions of needed services, aids and other supports for successful completion of the outcomes and (d) assessments to determine if OBE outcomes have been accomplished.

Some states and districts prefer not to refer to their programs as being OBE systems, so they substitute terms such as *competency, performance, results* and *standards* for the term *outcomes* (Dykman, 1994–1995). OBE, however, is not dead or dying, although it does face challenges to which openness and a healthy atmosphere of debate can contribute (Dykman, 1994–1995).

All of these considerations—content-dominated curriculum, performance-based curriculum, and outcome-based education curriculum—influence the development and/or selection of curriculum by teachers, districts, and states, and at the national level, and consequently the development of IEP goals and objectives. These influences underscore the complexity of curriculum design and the challenges all educators face when designing programs for students. A structure that integrates all these factors and influences can prove most helpful when teachers and others design curriculum for students with disabilities.

Proposed Curriculum Structure

There are multiple ways to structure curricular factors and influences. Fitzpatrick (1991) emphasizes the importance of aligning curriculum by establishing a scaffold linking the day-to-day planning by teachers to outcomes at the district, state, and national levels. This alignment provides general and special educators with common ground for communicating about curriculum outcomes for students with and without disabilities and for curricular decision making. This notion of alignment serves as the basis of the structure we propose in Exhibit 2.8.

EXHIBIT 2.8	**GOALS AND MISSION STATEMENTS**
Curriculum Structure	

GOALS AND MISSION STATEMENTS

- Aims
- Broad statements of what students are to "be" upon completion of school (e.g., collaborative workers, community contributors, "first in the world" in science)
- Broad statements of what students will demonstrate upon completion of school (e.g., competency in English, mathematics, science, arts, ability to make healthy, lifelong decisions)

EXIT OUTCOMES/PERFORMANCE STANDARDS/PERFORMANCE EXPECTATIONS

- Outcomes students are to demonstrate upon completion of schooling (e.g., Exit outcomes of significance, lists of outcomes/standards; single outcomes/standards from lists) with provisions made for accommodations and modifications
- Outcomes students demonstrate at a level of mastery, attainment, or measure of adequacy expected/ attained
- Life-skill performances expected of students
- Operationalization of goal/mission statements

COURSE OF STUDY OUTCOMES

- What students are to learn and be able to do as a result of completing a series of courses or experiences (e.g., a student's high school transcript may reflect a child's course of study, such as vocational education or college preparation, and a program for life-skill participatory outcomes or participation in advanced-placement courses)
- Outcomes identified in annual or multiyear course/program syllabi, curriculum guidelines, or individualized educational plans (e.g., outcomes descriptions; requirements; ongoing **IEP goals, benchmarks, and objectives**; levels and types of knowledge and forms of performance; learning experiences and context; relation to general education and other curriculum; assessment)

INTERMEDIARY CHECKPOINTS

- Grade-level performance requirements, or desired outcomes
- Benchmarks for measuring student's progress between **annual IEP goals, benchmarks, and objectives** and desired exit outcome

COURSE OUTCOMES

- Outcomes for courses/subjects/major learning experiences/**IEP goals, benchmarks, and objectives** that students complete annually or semiannually (e.g., Natural Science, Language Arts, Mathematics; Accounting I, Functional Social Studies; Transition Education)

UNIT OUTCOMES

- Outcomes for a set of lessons and learning experiences (e.g., a unit on dinosaurs as part of a science curriculum; **a series of lessons on specific IEP goals, benchmarks, and objectives**)

LESSON OUTCOMES

- Outcomes for individual lessons and learning experiences (e.g., the segments of instruction lasting from 15 minutes to several hours during the course of a school day; **specific lesson on an IEP benchmark or objective**)

What is clear from analysis of this type of structure is that decisions at each level influence and are influenced by decisions about curriculum made at other levels. For instance, national guidelines influence what happens at the state and district levels, which in turn affects what occurs at the building level and in teachers' individual classrooms. This influence works in the other direction as well. The structure also stresses the role teachers play in curricular decisions: they have a voice at all levels but may play a more direct role in the development of lesson, unit, course, and course of study outcomes. With minor modifications, teachers can use this structure to determine how the desired outcomes of the curriculum for their students relate to each other and how they relate or should relate to desired outcomes determined at the national, state, and local levels. The structure provides common ground for communications about outcomes for students with and without disabilities.

To illustrate alignments, we incorporate information from the DRS/Florida curriculum. Exhibit 2.9 provides examples for each kind or level of outcome (column one) of (a) one goal and the alignments that are appropriate for most students in the education system (column two) and (b) supported independence outcomes (column three) related to that goal for some students with disabilities when supported independence expectations (see p. 44) are appropriate for them. Take the time to read the information in this exhibit. It illustrates the different levels of the structure within one state in the country. Rarely do teachers have the opportunity to study a coordinated curriculum at all levels between national and state goals, exit outcome and IEPs and daily lessons.

LEVELS OF GOALS/OUTCOMES	ALIGNMENTS WITH ONE STATE LEVEL GOAL: GOAL 3	SUPPORTED INDEPENDENCE EXPECTATIONS OF GOAL 3
National Goals or Mission Statements	["3. Students in Grades 4, 8, and 12 will have demonstrated competency over challenging subject matter including English, mathematics, science, foreign languages, civics and government, economics, arts, history, and geography. 4. U.S. students will be first in the world in science and mathematics achievement" (Goals 2000).]	["3. Students in Grades 4, 8, and 12 will have demonstrated competency over challenging subject matter including English, mathematics, science, foreign languages, civics and government, economics, arts, history, and geography. 4. U.S. students will be first in the world in science and mathematics achievement" (Goals 2000).]
State Level Goal (DRS/Florida)	Goal 3. Student Performance. Students successfully compete at the highest levels nationally and internationally and are prepared to make well-reasoned, thoughtful, and healthy lifelong decisions.	Goal 3. Student Performance. Students successfully compete at the highest levels nationally and internationally and are prepared to make well-reasoned, thoughtful, and healthy lifelong decisions.
Exit Outcomes, Performance Standards, Performance Expectations	Standard 2. Communicate in English and other languages using information, concepts, prose, symbols, reports, audio and video recordings, speeches, graphic displays, and computer-based programs.	Expectation 4. Complete activities requiring transactions in the community.
Course of Study Outcomes	Individuals who express themselves effectively . . . a. correctly follow communication formats and styles when communicating in print. b. use vocabulary, form, spelling, and mechanics correctly. c. organize information in ways that are easy to follow and understand. d. use content and formats that contribute to the achievement of their desired purposes. e. apply techniques that enhance the presentation of information. To demonstrate performance on this standard, student could . . . • give a speech or presentation on a particular topic • participate in a formal or informal debate • prepare a written report on a particular topic • solicit information from others • write a letter or speak on the telephone • develop [ways] to entertain others	Individuals who complete activities requiring transactions in the community . . . a. initiate activities requiring transactions in the community. b. carry out the steps of activities requiring transactions. c. conduct themselves in ways that are safe and appropriate for particular activities and community locations. d. communicate effectively. Individuals are expected to exhibit the behaviors of this expectation while . . . • shopping • completing common service transactions (e.g., banking) • eating out in the community • using leisure and recreational facilities • obtaining a scheduled service (e.g., from a doctor or dentist) • using public transportation

(continued)

EXHIBIT 2.9

**Curriculum Alignment Structure
Applied to the DRS/Florida
Model** *(continued)*

LEVELS OF GOALS/OUTCOMES	ALIGNMENT WITH ONE STATE LEVEL GOAL: GOAL 3	SUPPORTED INDEPENDENCE EXPECTATIONS OF GOAL 3
Intermediary Checkpoints	Performance Requirements for Standard #2 "Grades 1–2 a. use vocabulary, form, spelling, and mechanics correctly in simple sentences. b. use simple sentences (with pictures) to tell stories. c. include information and ideas that contribute to the purpose of their communication. d. present work neatly and speak clearly. Grades 3–5 a. correctly follow assigned formats and styles when communicating in print. b. use vocabulary, form, spelling, and mechanics correctly in simple and complex sentences . . ."	Performance Requirements for Expectation 4 "Ages 10–13 a. initiate activities requiring transactions in the community (. . . arrange for transportation to the movies, go to the barber shop . . .) b. carry out the steps of activities requiring transactions in the community (including locating items; paying for items and services . . .) Performance Contexts • purchasing groceries or personal necessities (toothpaste . . .) • completing common service transactions (cashing a check, depositing money) . . ."
Course Outcomes	Student will complete three major history and language arts projects as specified in the course syllabus.	[Student will demonstrate transitional skills needed for shopping, going to a medical appointment, and participating in leisure activities.]
Unit Outcomes	The students will work independently to complete a research report on the State of Florida. The project will be comprised of the following two parts: 1. A written report following the format given in the direction to the student. 2. Using the material from research as a base, students will participate in an oral presentation in the form of an advertisement persuading people to visit the State of Florida. The report will be assessed in the areas of content, mechanics, and grammar.	[The students will gain transactional skills necessary for going to a medical appointment. Skills will include: a. locating the appropriate phone number in a personal directory b. phoning skills for making an appointment c. riding the bus to the appointment d. attending the appointment e. riding the bus back home]
Lessons Outcomes	[Student will verbally describe the key components of an effective advertisement.]	[Student will verbally state the importance of going to medical appointments and will list the steps involved.]
IEP Outcomes	**[Brenda will meet her annual IEP goal by programming the major points of oral reports on her augmentative communication device.]**	**[Alex will demonstrate those transitional skills needed for successful participation in community services and activities as identified in his IEP.]**

Note: Quoted from segments of the DRS/Florida model with the exception of information bracketed or documented from another source.

Sources: Disability Research System, Inc. & State of Florida Department of Education (1995). *Performance Assessment System for Students with Disabilities (PASSD): Goal 3 student performance standards:* Lansing, MI & Tallahassee, FL. Author; and *Fourth Grade Social Studies Performance Assessment,* (Course of Study Outcomes and Unit Outcomes for Goal 3 by Ann Spurlock and Therese Finigan, teachers) Monroe County Schools, Florida. Used with permission.

Basic understanding of this or a similar structure helps teachers discern patterns, as well as consistencies and inconsistencies with their local, state, and national outcomes, goals, and standards (see Exhibit 2.8). It also helps teachers analyze IEP goals and objectives and their relevance for moving students with disabilities toward attainment of education outcomes at different levels in the structure. Special and general education teachers have major responsibilities and opportunities for collaborating with each other, with families, related service providers and others to change outcomes for individuals with disabilities from "desired" to "achieved"!

Sometimes the need to choose, develop, and implement curriculum content that leads to student achievement of desired outcomes seems like an all-encompassing and overwhelming challenge. The next section on curricular options gives teachers focus and information for this task.

Curricular Options

Familiarity with a structure for determining and selecting desired outcomes and related curriculum for students leads to the next phase of making curricular decisions: choosing from available options. Desired outcomes for students with disabilities can be addressed through content in one or more of four major curricular options: (a) general education curriculum without modifications, (b) general education curriculum with modifications, (c) life skills curriculum, and (d) curriculum in modified means of communication and performance (see Figure 2.2).

General education curriculum without modifications (option 1) is curriculum presented to students with and without identified special education needs and is the primary curriculum offered in schools. This curriculum includes core curriculum traditionally structured by discipline (e.g., English, history), electives (e.g., accounting, drama), basic academic skills (e.g., reading, writing), and perhaps, cross-disciplinary curriculum (e.g., exit outcomes).

General education curriculum with modifications (option 2) includes some areas specified for the general education curriculum, but attention is given to adapting or modifying the curriculum in ways that allow certain students with disabilities and special education needs to gain knowledge, skills, and understandings from it. Adaptations and/or modifications may affect (a) the complexity of the task (e.g., having students work with text written at their reading levels rather than at grade level), (b) the types of demands the task requires (e.g., allowing a student to give a report orally rather than in writing; adaping of physical tasks when in physical education), and (c) the strategies used to support student participation in and mastery of the task (e.g., the teaching of learning strategies and study skills). Many of these modifications are also helpful for students without disabilities; but they are *necessary* to make it possible for certain students with unique needs resulting from their disabilities to benefit from the general education curriculum.

Life skills curriculum (option 3) focuses on the skills that are commonly learned by general education peers through observation and participation in school, home, and community activities and experiences but that require specific and systematic instruction for mastery by some students with disabilities. The life skills curriculum includes functional academic skills (e.g., reading recipes, balancing a personal checkbook), daily and community living skills (e.g., personal grooming, budgeting), and transition skills (e.g., transitioning from middle school to high school).

Curriculum in modified means of communication and performance (option 4) stems from the need for intensive and/or specialized student preparation for communicating and performing that make it possible for students to participate in the other curricular options. It includes skills such as the use of assistive technology and modified means for performing tasks (e.g., using gestures instead of words when making a request).

Figure 2.2 summarizes these four curricular options and their related areas. In Chapters 3 through 5 we discuss these options in detail. The curriculum selected for an individual student with disabilities may reflect one or more of them. For example, a student with a learning disability may participate in (a) general education mathematics curriculum without adaptation or modification; (b) general education curriculum in language arts modified because of difficulties in reading and writing; (c) daily and community living skills curriculum in the area of transition; and (d) modified means of communication and performance in language and speech development. Together, these

FIGURE 2.2
Curricular Options

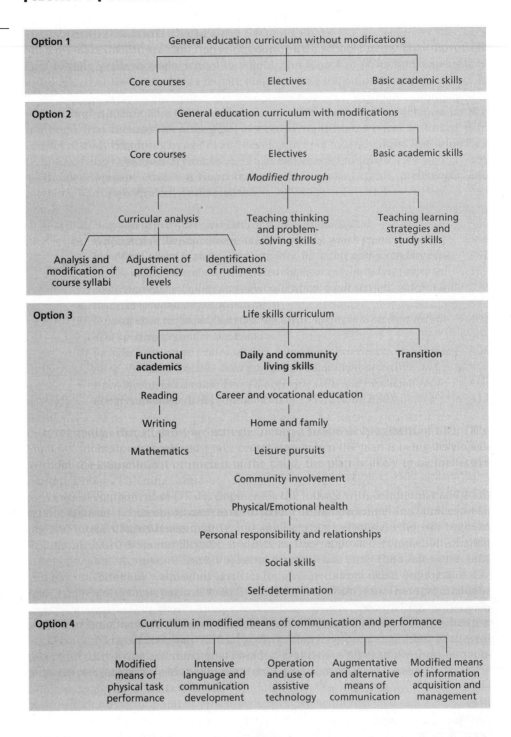

curricular options reflect the types of curricular experiences considered priorities for the student. They may be delivered through a variety of service delivery models, as reflected in a student's course of study. Exhibit 2.10 presents a course of study for this student with learning disabilities. Notice that all curricular areas are addressed in a meaningful way.

EXHIBIT 2.10

**Course of Study Based on
Four Curricular Options**

Student Name _____

Planning Committee Members

Name	Position
_____	_____
_____	_____
_____	_____
_____	_____
_____	_____

Parent Signature	Student Signature

COURSE OF STUDY

	Curricular Options			
	General Education Curriculum	General Education Curriculum with Modifications	Life Skills Curriculum	Curriculum in Modified Means of Communication and Performance
Curricular areas	Mathematics Physical education	Language arts Social studies Science	Transition/Career	Speech and language
Sources of curriculum	General education state curriculum standards	General education state curriculum standards modified to meet student needs	High school transition program curriculum developed by general and special educators in consultation with local businesses	Assessment findings as gathered by the speech-language pathologist
Service delivery	General education classroom	General education classroom with consultation by the special education teacher as specified in the IEP	General education and community-based environments, with instruction provided by the general education vocational education teacher and special education—based job coach as specified in the ITP	Individualized therapy with a speech-language pathologist as specified in the IEP
Extracurricular activities	Student participates in intramural basketball.			

In summary, determining and designing curriculum for individuals with disabilities is a complex task. Understanding curricular and structural options when planning curriculum can assist educators and other team members in making informed decisions about what is most important for students with disabilities to learn and how to organize the curriculum in meaningful and accessible ways.

THEORY TO PRACTICE

➡ Interview a classroom teacher to find out the kinds of curricular decisions she or he is authorized to make and those that are made by others. What process does the teacher use to make her or his curricular decisions? On what are those decisions based? Who is making the other decisions? What is the teacher's opinion and experience with this process of decision making? What recommendations does this teacher have for a new teacher who may have to make curricular decisions?

➡ Return to Spady's mountain (see Figure 2.1). Start at the top and attempt to write some standards, goals, and outcomes of your own. When writing them, consider the needs of a specific special education student, and attempt to respond to his or her needs. Discuss your standards, goals, and outcomes with classmates. What are some commonalities of your work? In what areas do you differ in approach? Revise your standards, goals, and outcomes as you see fit.

CHAPTER SUMMARY

This chapter describes how goals, outcomes, and standards are written to specify and frame curriculum and curricular expectations and how the existence of national, state, and local influences impacts the development of goals, outcomes, and standards, with the direction of influence being top-down, bottom-up, or two-way. Additionally, procedures for making curricular decisions and our proposed curriculum structure are presented as guides for teachers. The chapter ends with an overview of the four curricular options available to students with disabilities and an example of a course of study designed to reflect selected options.

CHAPTER 3

General Education Curriculum with and without Modifications

Read to find out the following:
- components of the general education curriculum
- procedures for determining the appropriateness of the general education curriculum for individual students
- procedures for modifying the general education curriculum to more effectively meet needs of individual students

This chapter is the first of three chapters that address curricular options for students with disabilities. Although curricular decisions are made after the completion of assessments to identify students' needs and strengths, we choose to address curricular options first because we believe an understanding of them will provide readers a context within which to relate assessment focus and related instructional techniques and procedures. It is important to understand the local curriculum, desired outcomes, and curriculum opportunities available in order to know what to assess for and the types of intervention to provide to assist students with disabilities in their gaining of relevant knowledge, skills, and understandings.

As we stated in Chapter 2, at least four curricular options are available for students with disabilities: (a) general education curriculum without modifications, (b) general education curriculum with modifications, (c) life skills curriculum, and (d) curriculum in modified means of communication and performance. We begin with a discussion of general education curriculum with and without modifications because, as stated in the IDEA Amendments of 1997, the general education curriculum serves as the starting point for the planning of curriculum for all students, including those with disabilities.

Starting with a review of the general education curriculum when planning a student's curriculum and developing his or her IEP may be a new approach for many, because team members may not readily see the relevance of this curriculum for some students with disabilities. Teachers, parents, and students may understand how the general education curriculum with and without adaptations may be appropriate for meeting the needs of students with mild disabilities (e.g., learning disabilities), but they may fail to realize that the general education curriculum also has meaning for students with a range of disabilities, including those with severe disabilities. As Giangreco (1997) argues, many of the learning outcomes identified in the general education curriculum are applicable to students with severe disabilities, and teams have a responsibility to

expose them to, and instruct them in, a full range of general education curricular activities to complement more traditional functional life skills. Too often we artificially limit curricular opportunities for students with severe disabilities based on our own preconceived notions. As a student progresses through school, the emphasis placed on various curricular options can be adjusted based on actual experiences rather than speculation. (p. 54)

This same argument applies to other disabling conditions as well. For example, students with visual impairment or those with orthopedic impairment can greatly benefit from participation in general education curriculum experiences while they may also participate in specialized curriculum to address their specific disability needs (e.g., instruction in braille and/or orientation and mobility skills for students with visual impairments, and in uses of adapted equipment in physical education for students with orthopedic impairments). Therefore, regardless of a student's disability, the general education curriculum, as defined by district, state, and/or national goals, outcomes, and standards, should serve as the foundation for the development of a student's curricular plan.

The extent to which students with disabilities participate in and benefit from the general education curriculum will vary, however. Some students with disabilities are able to participate in segments of the general education curriculum without modifications, but other students require modifications of this curriculum in order to understand content, demonstrate achievement, and meet IEP goals. A student may have strengths in the area of mathematics and excel in all mathematics courses without support. But this same student may experience severe difficulties with reading and written language and be in need of extensive modifications in curricular areas such as English, social studies, and science. The types of modifications and other supports needed will be student-specific and identified through eligibility and IEP assessment processes. The following vignette provides one example of how the general education curriculum can be adapted through curricular and instructional modifications to meet the needs of students with disabilities.

JONATHAN

Jonathan is a highly capable student who experiences difficulties gaining information from text and expressing his thoughts in writing. When Jonathan is in his general education science class, he thrives when the class works in cooperative groups to complete science experiments. He is an active participant in classroom discussions and is eager to hear the ideas and perspectives of others. He clearly articulates his hypotheses and ideas and is a highly effective verbal communicator. Peers look to him for assistance when working on class projects. However, in the midst of all this success, Jonathan experiences severe difficulties in reading the textbook, writing up lab reports, responding to chapter questions, and taking tests and quizzes. Without modifications in these areas, Jonathan would be failing the class. Through collaborative planning, the general and special education teachers have implemented the following curricular and instructional modifications to support Jonathan's success in the general education science curriculum:

1. Students work in pairs, reading the book and discussing its content. This arrangement provides Jonathan an opportunity to hear the information in the textbook. At times he listens to the textbook being read by peers or audiotapes from a special playback machine.
2. A partially completed lab report form is available to all groups, and Jonathan is encouraged to use it for his work. This version of the lab report includes all primary categories and key terminology as well as open-ended sentences to be filled in. Additionally, the teacher allows for the use of illustrations to capture key ideas of the experiment.

3. The class has been taught a strategy for answering questions at the end of the chapter. Students are encouraged to read the questions first, and then to look for the answers as they are reading. By working in pairs, reading the questions first, and then reading the textbook, Jonathan is able to answer the questions orally, while his peer captures the responses on paper. At times, Jonathan is required to write his own answers. When this occurs, he is encouraged to use the computer for help with spelling.

4. All members of the class have the option of having tests and quizzes read aloud to them. The special education teacher reads the tests and quizzes to students, moving them to a different setting so as not to disturb students who want to work independently.

With these curricular and instructional modifications, Jonathan is able to achieve success in the general education science curriculum. Without these modifications, he would fail the class although he excels in some of the activities required.

These modifications directly reflect Jonathan's IEP goals and objectives. His goals and objectives address enhancement of reading comprehension skills, development of written language skills, and the use of aids and devices to support his success in both areas.

The general education curriculum may be modified so it becomes accessible, or made available, to students with a range of disabilities. Physical task demands may be modified to take into consideration the needs of individuals with physical disabilities. For example, specially adapted materials may be made available, and alternative means for expressing understanding and for asking questions may be adopted, such as the use of augmentative and alternative communication devices. Materials may be enlarged for students with low vision, and materials may be presented in both auditory and visual formats to better address the needs of individuals who have hearing impairment. The complexity of the curriculum may also be reduced to reflect more closely the needs of a student with a disability. For example, instead of having to write a 10-page report, the student may write a 5-to-7-page report. In this way, the student engages in the general education curriculum and demonstrates competence in that curriculum, but does so in a different way. Other basic accommodations allow students to use word processors, spellchecks, calculators, and other support tools when completing assignments. Letting students work with a peer or an adult when completing assignments is another modification.

Although modifying the general education curriculum opens the curriculum for many students with disabilities, the general education curriculum alone, with or without modifications, may not meet all of their needs. In these cases, student programs may require augmentations, substitutions and integration of curriculum from the remaining two options—life skills curriculum and curriculum in modified means of communication and performance—in order to develop a comprehensive program responsive to a particular student's needs. In most cases, all four options should be considered to ensure the development of a comprehensive and meaningful curriculum as illustrated in the course of study presented in Chapter 2 (Exhibit 2.10).

It is important to understand, moreover, that the selection of curricular options does not in any way limit a student's participation in general education experiences. Students may engage in curriculum from all four curricular options within general education settings and experiences. Curriculum selection does not determine the place in which the student will learn; it determines only what students are taught.

A number of students with disabilities will engage both in general education curriculum without modifications and general education curriculum with modifications.

They will participate in some parts of general education curriculum for which they need no modifications, because they have the skills and knowledge to access the curriculum and demonstrate success. For success in other areas of the general education curriculum, however, students may need modifications and supports.

In this chapter we describe general education curriculum content, structure, and delivery. We then examine procedures for determining (a) the appropriateness of the general education curriculum for individuals with disabilities and (b) modifications of this curriculum that better reflect needs of some individuals with disabilities.

GENERAL EDUCATION CURRICULUM WITHOUT MODIFICATIONS

Most educators have some experience with the general education curriculum, so our descriptions here touch on just the basic principles. We discuss the (a) content, (b) structure, and (c) delivery of the general education curriculum. Then we present procedures for determining whether the general education curriculum needs to be modified to reflect the needs of particular individuals with disabilities, and we present possible modification approaches.

General Education Curriculum Content

General education curriculum content may be presented through three categories: core courses, electives, and basic academic skills.

Core courses

Sometimes referred to as basic academic subjects, core courses are the part of the curriculum planned for all students. They are developed on the premise that a core of common learning ensures that all students have equal opportunities to engage in learning experiences which will be most contributory to their future lives. Typically, the core consists of certain sets of educational learning experiences structured around basic academic subjects and basic academic competencies, or skills. Each grade level, for instance, may have core courses in six areas: American and world civilization, language arts, science, mathematics, fine arts, and physical education. Typically, the core is depicted as composing the major component of students' courses of study. Core subject requirements for some high school programs include the following:

- Language arts
- Life and personal management
- Physical education and health
- Career and employability
- Aesthetics and cultural awareness
- Mathematics and science
- World studies
- Technology education
- Arts

Beyond the core areas represented by specific coursework within disciplines, core curriculum has also come to include various forms of outcome-based curriculum and standards-driven curriculum written within and across disciplines. Recall from Chapter 2 that outcome-based and standards-driven curricula stress the demonstration of significant lifelong learning outcomes rather than simple mastery and/or completion of traditional subject matter organized by school disciplines and courses. This structuring of curriculum calls for the integration, application, and generalization of learning, rather than course completion, as an indicator of learning and achievement.

Electives

The second category of general education curriculum content available to students is electives. This curriculum, selected by students, adds to and enriches their academic and life-long learning outcomes. Electives vary from school to school and from student to student. They may include

- Foreign languages
- Computer skills
- Auto shop
- Visual and performing arts

- Industrial arts
- Music
- Occupational subjects such as business

Extracurricular activities, frequently described as part of the curriculum, are also available to students; and although they may be classified as electives, they may not generate course credits.

Basic academic skills

The third category of general education curriculum content is basic academic skills—skills essential to performance in all school disciplines. Definitions of the basic academic skills or competencies differ according to the goals and philosophies of state and local education agencies. Sometimes they are called "literacy skills," "basic skills," "basic academic competencies," "thinking skills," or "thinking processes." Typically, basic literacy skills are represented by the three R's of decoding and comprehension skills in reading, skills in the mechanics of written expression, and computational skills in mathematics. Some also add the three C's of computing, calculating, and communicating (Bracey, 1983). Other programs include additional basic skills such as speaking, listening, reasoning, and studying.

General Education Curriculum Structure

General education curriculum—core courses, electives, and basic academic skills—can be structured in many ways. Posner (1992) describes four ways to organize curricular content: discrete, hierarchical, linear, and spiral. A *discrete structure* presents "a curriculum in which all content is discrete, unrelated to, or at least independent of, all other content" (p. 129). A *hierarchical curriculum* presents content that is unrelated but is "necessary for learning subsequent concepts or skills" (p. 129). In a *linear structure,* skills are presented in a prescribed order, and mastery of the "immediately previous concept or skill" (Posner, 1992, p. 129) is required. One example of a linear curriculum is courses that occur in a specified sequence and have identified prerequisites. For example, students complete pre-algebra, Algebra I, and Algebra II as a sequence. In addition to affecting the order of courses, linear design may exist within courses, in lessons sequenced to systematically build skills. Within this structure, skills are presented in a prescribed order. Limited time may be spent on revisiting skills once they have been mastered or "covered."

In a *spiral curriculum,* concepts and skills are "taught in different ways at different educational levels" (Posner, 1992, p. 129). This means that concepts and skills are revisited several times throughout a child's school career, each time at a higher level of complexity. One example of a social studies skill taught through a spiral curriculum is the development of map-reading skills. In first grade, students may draw maps of their rooms or homes; in second grade, maps of their neighborhoods. In more advanced grades, they may work with more complicated maps of cities, states, countries, and the world, applying skills for determining distances, differences in time, lines of latitude and longitude, and finding locations. The curriculum spirals, or revisits, the skill area throughout the grades, and the content and challenges increase at each subsequent level. A spiral curriculum may be presented through a scope and sequence chart (*scope* refers to the depth and breadth of the content covered; *sequence,* to the order in which content is presented).

Curriculum may also be structured through strands. *Strands* are areas of learning that are addressed in isolation or through integration with other strands. Strands may be viewed as "continuous threads running throughout the curriculum, each developed at all grade levels" (California Dept. of Education, 1992, p. 80). Curriculum strands many times are directly linked with curriculum goals. Curriculum strands in the history–social studies curriculum used in California classrooms include civic values, rights, and responsibilities, and constitutional heritage and national identity, which together work toward the achievement of the goal of democratic understanding and civic values (California Department of Education, 1992).

General Education Curriculum Delivery

Beyond its content—that is, core courses, electives, and basic academic skills—and structure (e.g., linear or spiral), curriculum may be delivered in many ways. Adapting from the work of Jacobs (1991) and later Kline (1995) and, where indicated, from Giangreco and Putnam (1991), we summarize eight options that teachers may adopt for organizing and delivering curriculum to their students.

CURRICULUM ORGANIZATION	EXAMPLE
Discipline-based curriculum: Subjects are taught individually, during separate times of the school day.	High school students move from period to period, and each period represents instruction in a different discipline.
Parallel disciplines: Two or more teachers from two or more related subject areas teach related material simultaneously.	A social studies teacher teaches a unit on the California gold rush at the same time an English teacher is working with students writing research reports on a historical event—in this case, the California gold rush.
Multidisciplinary approach: Two or three subject areas are integrated and presented as a single course or unit that focuses on a theme, issue, problem, topic, or concept.	A social studies teacher and a science teacher work together to present a unit on recycling—the social studies teacher focuses on the social ramifications of recycling, the science teacher on the process of recycling.
Interdisciplinary approach: All subject areas are integrated; information is structured around a theme or unit; students learn and use information from all areas to solve problems, create products, or explore new ideas.	An integrated theme on poverty challenges students to gather and read narrative and statistical information related to poverty, to devise a means for addressing poverty in their community, and to present their proposal to an authentic audience. Students apply reading, mathematical, and written language skills while being exposed to social studies and science concepts (e.g., citizenship, nutrition) related to poverty.
Integrated day: The day begins with a question, problem, or issue that students are to resolve during the day.	Students turn to various resources and draw on various skills to arrive at a response to the question.

CURRICULUM ORGANIZATION	EXAMPLE
Field-based approach: Students develop knowledge and skills in community-based settings.	Students visit members of their community to learn how the various disciplines they are learning about in school come together in the face of real-world tasks and challenges.
Multilevel curriculum/instruction (Giangreco & Putnam, 1991): Students work in the same curricular areas, but curricular outcomes vary from student to student.	When a small group of students is discussing a story, some students may demonstrate comprehension of the story through character analysis, while others focus on identifying the names of the primary characters in the story.
Curriculum overlapping (Giangreco & Putnam, 1991): Students work and learn together but have their own learning outcomes that represent different curricular areas.	In a small group, the goal for three students is to comprehend a written passage and the goal for the fourth group member is to respond to the others by maintaining eye contact and participating in turn-taking.

Teachers may participate in one or several of these curricular delivery systems, singularly or in combination. For example, a teacher working with a group of special education students with cognitive delays may select the field-based approach as the most appropriate method for teaching job skills. This teacher may also be working with a general education teacher on an interdisciplinary unit of instruction focused on participation in service-learning activities. The interdisciplinary unit may be classroom and community based. Therefore this teacher is delivering curriculum to students through both a field-based and an interdisciplinary approach.

These approaches to curriculum can open the door of general education classrooms to students with special education needs because they acknowledge and embrace the need to select, design, and deliver the general education curriculum in ways that are meaningful to all students. For example, many middle schools embrace an interdisciplinary teaming approach to curriculum selection and delivery. In this approach, special education teachers become members of the general education teams and, together with general education teachers, they select curriculum and develop units of instruction that address the needs of all students, including students with disabilities. As stated by Clark and Clark (1994), this interdisciplinary teaming

> *facilitates cooperative efforts between regular and special education teachers, provides an excellent opportunity for special education students to be "mainstreamed" into the regular classroom settings and for students in the regular classrooms to benefit from the special skills and training of the special education teachers.*
> *(p. 128)*

When students with disabilities are included in general education classrooms, the task of selecting, structuring, and delivering the general education curriculum must be broadened to include the identification of means for meeting the needs of students with disabilities. For some of these students, there may be a need to modify the general education curriculum or to introduce alternative curricular options to meet their curricular needs. In the next section, we describe approaches for making curriculum selection decisions.

THEORY TO PRACTICE

➡ Meet with a special education teacher to discuss the program of a selected special education student. What components of the general education curriculum does this student participate in? What components of the general education curriculum are not addressed? How were the decisions concerning general education curriculum made for this particular student? What assessment information were these decisions based on?

➡ Meet with a general education teacher to discuss how he or she develops curriculum for students. Attempt to determine the type of curriculum structure the teacher has adopted. On what information are you basing your classification? What are the implications of this curriculum structure on the way in which the curriculum is presented to students?

➡ Observe a teacher at work who uses one of the curricular organizations listed above. Analyze this arrangement. What are the possible benefits for students? What are possible drawbacks? Consider the needs of individuals with disabilities. How does this curricular organization support their learning, and what types of barriers does it present for them?

DETERMINING MODIFICATION NEEDS

Without modification, the content of general education curriculum may fail to meet the needs of many students with disabilities, as well as many without identified disabilities. This shortcoming is partially due to the great diversity in classrooms. Reading skills may range over as many grade levels as the grade level of the classroom—that is, in a typical third grade classroom, student reading levels may vary from preprimer to sixth grade reading level or beyond. And the possibility is great that a number of languages other than English are spoken by the students. Because of this diversity, there is no one best way to deliver curriculum. All students can benefit from adaptations that take into consideration their prior knowledge, culture and experience, approaches to learning, language and English language proficiency, and other abilities.

Finding the match between what the general education curriculum has to offer and students' needs is one of the greatest challenges that teachers face. Special education teachers and other educators often ask, "How can we avoid denying students with special needs the right to study, understand, and appreciate what they can from a variety of school subjects that other students typically study?" To answer this question, educators need to know when to consider or maintain the general education curriculum, when and how best to modify it so that it is more meaningful and beneficial for students, and when it may be best to substitute curriculum that more directly meets identified needs.

These curricular decisions for students with special education needs are generally discussed and agreement is reached during IEP and ITP meetings. Team members, including teachers, administrators, parents, and the student, as well as others, discuss the needs and goals of the student and the curricular options available and most appropriate for meeting those needs. In the next section we describe three approaches that may be used to make these curricular decisions: (a) question and analysis, (b) question and choice, and (c) objective evaluation.

Question and Analysis Approach

Westling and Fox (1995), drawing from the work of Snell (1993) and focusing on the needs of students with severe disabilities, propose the following five questions (quoted from Westling and Fox, 1995, pp. 134–135) for determining the appropriateness of traditional academic curriculum for students with disabilities. These questions, with paraphrased comments following each, serve as a beginning step in evaluating the appropriateness of the general education curriculum, with and without modifications, for students with disabilities.

1. **What is the age of the student and how much time does he or she have remaining in school?** The more traditional curriculum may be appropriate for a younger student, but as the student ages, the functionality and applicability of those skills to the child's development of skills for independence may decrease. Continued focus on these traditional academic skills may not be in the best interest of the child.

2. **What amount of success has the student had thus far in learning academic skills?** If the child has experienced success and the skills being taught are functional and important to the child's overall development, continued emphasis in these areas may be appropriate. But if the child has failed to make progress or achieve success following instruction in these areas, it may be most appropriate to reexamine the curricular focus for this student.

3. **What type of academic skills are needed for functioning in relevant environments and also for leisure and recreational activities?** Analyzing to determine the type of academic skills needed can lead to decisions about the skills to be taught. The academic skills most necessary for success in life activities should receive priority. Examples include counting money needed to ride the bus and basic writing skills needed to write a grocery list.

4. **What is the relative value or significance of academic skills when compared to other skills? Are there other skills that will reduce dependence or increase independence?** What is important here is to weigh the value of traditional academic skills against the value of other basic skills the child needs to function independently and be accepted by others. As Westling and Fox (1995) observe, "If a student cannot brush his teeth, pull up his pants, or use appropriate social responses and also lacks basic academic skills, which is more important to teach"? (p. 135).

5. **What are the wishes of the student and the student's parents regarding instruction in academic skills?**

Question and Choice Approach

Falvey and Grenot-Scheyer (1995) propose another approach for determining curriculum: analyzing the general education curriculum by asking three questions:

1. What do students need to learn?

2. How do students need to learn?

3. What modifications or adaptations are necessary for student learning? (p. 153)

The choices for the question about modification or adaptation necessary for student learning include (a) leaving the curriculum as it is, with no modifications; (b) providing physical assistance to students as they participate in the same activities as their peers; (c) providing adapted materials that students use when participating in the same activities as their peers; (d) providing a multilevel curriculum, as described by Giangreco and Putnam (1991); (e) providing for curriculum overlapping, as described by Giangreco and Putnam (1991); and (f) providing a substitute curriculum. Some, such as Falvey and Grenot-Scheyer (1995), consider a substitute curriculum the choice of "last resort," because students with disabilities will engage in activities different from the activities of their peers part of the time. This choice, however, does not necessarily mean that the student will participate in this substitute curriculum outside the general education experience. General education peers may assist students in meeting the objectives of the substitute curriculum.

Objective Evaluation Approach

Another, more complex approach for determining the appropriateness of the general education curriculum, with and without modification, is to evaluate general education curriculum objectives systematically and determine their value for individuals with disabilities. Through systematic evaluation, teams can determine whether to adopt, modify, or totally replace general education curriculum to meet the needs of specific individuals with disabilities.

Exhibit 3.1 provides a framework for undertaking this evaluation. The framework, originating from a California Department of Education model (1978), has merit for educational practices today. Steps for deriving differential proficiencies in this model were adapted by Bigge (1987) for use in describing differential instructional objectives and curriculum content for students with disabilities. Recent uses in a special education teacher preparation program resulted in further adaptations and refinements. The procedures listed in the exhibit are described and illustrated in the rest of this section.

EXHIBIT 3.1
Procedures for Determining Student Needs for Modification of General Education Curriculum and Alternatives to It

Procedure A: Identify instructional objective(s) for those areas of the general education curriculum in which individual students may need modifications in complexity.

Procedure B: Create a checklist of competencies enroute to accomplishment of the objective and highlight those that are considered CRITICAL to accomplishment of the objective at any level of complexity.

Procedure C: Use the checklists to assess student possession of each of the competencies.

Procedure D: Use information about student possession of those competencies considered CRITICAL to determine whether to keep, modify, or change the objective and related content.

Procedure E: Develop appropriate objectives tailored to the needs of specific students, keeping the general education curriculum in mind as a point of reference.

Procedure F: Plan curriculum to help students attain or advance toward meeting the objectives.

Source: Adapted from "Steps in Devising Differential Standards," California Dept. of Education, 1978, in *Developing Proficiency Standards for Pupils in Special Education Programs: Workshop Outline and Agenda,* Sacramento: Author.

Procedure A: Identify instructional objective(s) for those areas of the general education curriculum in which individual students may need modifications in complexity.

Decisions about modifications of general education (GE) curriculum for students with disabilities start with the identification and recording of existing, original general education objectives. In collaboration with general education teachers, special educators identify grade-level and other expected outcomes. This information, representing grade- and age-appropriate curriculum content and subcontent, comes from sources such as course syllabi, curriculum guides, teacher handbooks, board-adopted courses of study, state guidelines, curriculum frameworks, comprehensive curriculum packages, teachers' editions of textbooks, and curriculum developed by the teachers themselves. Teachers identify the original general education instructional objectives, which state the intended outcome of instruction in terms of specific and observable student performance. These objectives are then recorded. Here is an example of a general education instructional objective taken from a unit in paragraph writing: *Given a topic sentence and a series of up to 4 related sentences containing time-order words, students will first locate the topic sentence, write it down, then continue to write the detail sentences in logical order in paragraph form. Students meet the criteria when they sequence the sentences correctly into a written paragraph.*

Procedure B: Create a checklist of competencies enroute to accomplishment of the objective and highlight those that are considered CRITICAL to accomplishment of the objective at any level of complexity.

Procedure B provides the groundwork for determining whether modifications of curriculum are needed and, if they are, the type of modifications most appropriate for a particular student. The procedure begins with the drafting of a checklist of the literacy, skills, and knowledge that a student will likely need to complete a targeted objective. The format of Exhibit 3.2 guides teachers through this procedure for the paragraph writing objective identified through the use of the step before this, Procedure A.

Objective: *Given a topic sentence and a series of up to 4 related sentences containing time-order words, students will first locate the topic sentence, write it down, then continue to write the detail sentences in logical order in paragraph form. Students meet the criteria when they sequence the sentences correctly into a written paragraph.*

EXHIBIT 3.2

Checklist of Enroute Competencies (Procedure B)

LITERACY (BASIC SCHOLASTIC MECHANICS)	+ – C	SKILLS ("KNOWING HOW TO"— PERFORMANCE)	+ – C	KNOWLEDGE ("KNOWING THAT"— CONTENT)	+ – C
Reading—can read lesson paragraphs of at least 5 sentences		Summarize the main idea of a group of related sentences		• knows that a paragraph is a group of related sentences, all dealing with a particular idea	
		Identify the topic sentence in a group of related sentences	C		
Vocabulary—has adequate vocabulary and concepts to understand the meaning of the material	C	Identify the detail sentences in a group of related sentences		• knows that a topic sentence expresses the main idea of a paragraph	C
		Select and copy the topic sentence from a group of sentences		• knows that each paragraph has a topic sentence	
Writing—can copy material/ information into specified format		Scan for time-order words in a group of related sentences		• knows that most paragraphs begin with a topic sentence	
		Select detail sentences and write them in logical order under the topic sentence		• knows that detail, or supporting, sentences tell about the main idea	
		Write the topic and related sentences in paragraph form		• knows that paragraphs include detail sentences	
				• knows the meanings of time-order words (e.g. first, second, last) can indicate sequence	C
				• knows that detail sentences frequently can be arranged in logical order through use of time-order words	
				• knows proper paragraph form involves indentation and punctuation	

Teachers will find the format of Exhibit 3.2 useful for their efforts to try to analyze the specific nature of student strengths and problems in curriculum. It helps teachers assess student competencies or abilities in three areas—literacy, skills, and knowledge—that contribute to the achievement of a target objective. *Literacy,* the first column of Exhibit 3.2, directs the teacher's analysis to the basic literacy skills needed for accomplishing the specified objective. These literacy skills may include specific reading, vocabulary, and writing skills. To begin to gather information for an analysis of a student's performance in relation to a targeted objective, teachers may ask themselves questions about the student's literacy: "What reading, vocabulary, and writing skills does the student *need* to be able to perform the targeted objective?" The second column directs the teacher's analysis to those *skills,* or performance abilities, that a student needs to accomplish the objective. Teachers can ask themselves one key question to determine this information. This question is "What all does a person need to be able to *do* in order to accomplish this objective?" Simultaneously, teachers can direct attention to the third column to analyze what student *knowledge* (content knowledge) is necessary for accomplishment of the objective. To determine this information, teachers can ask this question: "What all does a person need to *know* in order to accomplish this objective?"

Answers to each of these questions create checklists of enroute, or contributing, competencies that students need to accomplish the targeted objective as stated. The entries represent enroute competencies in each of three categories that, integrated with each other, lead to the achievement of a more advanced skill or objective.

Once teachers complete the checklist they can go back through the listed items to determine which are the most critical to student accomplishment of the original objective at any level of complexity. Teachers can code these *CRITICAL* skill(s) with a "C." It may the presence or absence of CRITICAL skills that help determine the student's ability to accomplish the objective. If a student is not able to identify the topic sentence of a paragraph and does not know that time-order words indicate a specific sequence of information, then the student may be unable to organize sentences into a logical paragraph order. Without those skills considered to be most critical, the accomplishment of the objective at any level of complexity may be jeopardized.

Procedure C: Use the checklists to assess student possession of each of the competencies.

Procedure C involves going through the newly developed checklist to assess whether the student has the enroute competencies necessary for achieving the original objective. A plus (+) or minus (−) sign may be used to notate the student's ability to perform each area identified in the checklist. Teachers should pay particular attention to those entries presumed to be CRITICAL (C) to the accomplishment of the objective. Those items are key in making decisions about whether the original objective at the original level of complexity is an appropriate target at the present time. This analysis and rating allows for the answering of questions such as these: "Is the student missing some of the enroute skills or performances?" "Are any of the missing skills assumed to be *critical* to accomplishment of the objective at any level of complexity?" "Does the individual student possess the necessary skills, but cannot use them here because he or she does not have the higher level of literacy and knowledge required to accomplish the targeted objective?" Exhibit 3.3 presents a notated checklist.

LITERACY (BASIC SCHOLASTIC MECHANICS)	+ – C	SKILLS ("KNOWING HOW TO"— PERFORMANCE)	+ – C	KNOWLEDGE ("KNOWING THAT"— CONTENT)	+ – C
Reading—can read lesson paragraphs of at least 5 sentences	+	Summarize the main idea of a group of related sentences	+	• A paragraph is a group of related sentences, all dealing with a particular idea	
		Identify the topic sentence in a group of related sentences	– C	• A topic sentence expresses the main idea of a paragraph	C
Vocabulary—has adequate vocabulary and concepts to understand the meaning of the material	– C	Identify the detail sentences in a group of related sentences	–	• Each paragraph has a topic sentence	+
Writing—can copy material/ information into specified format	+	Select and copy the topic sentence from a group of sentences	–	• Most paragraphs begin with a topic sentence	+
		Scan for time-order words in a group of related sentences	–	• Detail, or supporting, sentences tell about the main idea	–
		Select detail sentences and write them in logical order under the topic sentence	–	• Paragraphs include detail sentences	–
		Write topic and detail sentences in proper paragraph form	–	• Meanings of time-order words (e.g. first, second, last) can indicate sequence	– C
				• Detail sentences frequently can be arranged in logical order through use of time-order words	–
				• Proper paragraph form involves indentation and punctuation	

Procedure D: Use information about student possession of those competencies considered CRITICAL to determine whether to keep, modify, or change the objective and related content.

Determining whether to (a) keep the original general education objectives, (b) modify the objectives, (c) select different but related objectives, or (d) create alternative or entirely different objectives, becomes the focus of teacher efforts at this point. To make this decision, teachers combine information about the student's *literacy* level with what CRITICAL *knowledge* and *skills* the student does and does not currently possess. Using this information, teachers make judgments about (a) the likelihood that the student could learn the skills and knowledge in a reasonable time or in the time the student has left in school, (b) the importance of accomplishing the objective in relation to accomplishing other important learning outcomes, (c) the overall importance of the accomplishment of the skill to the student's life, and (d) the relative importance of other material the student could be learning in the amount of time it would take to accomplish this learning outcome. The moment of truth is here. This process is designed to help teachers make these decisions with confidence. Exhibit 3.4, the IF. . . THEN Decision-Making Chart, presents guidelines for making these decisions and represents the next step in the process.

EXHIBIT 3.4

IF . . . THEN Decision-Making
Chart (Procedure D)

IF	THEN
IF a student possesses the CRITICAL competencie(s) . . .	**THEN** follow general education standards by keeping the original objective(s) and content and maintaining their complexities.
IF a student possesses some CRITICAL competencie(s) but still has difficulty meeting the objective, or **IF** a student possesses some but not all of the enroute competencie(s) with the probability that the student can learn the rest of the crucial and other enroute competencie(s) in a reasonable amount of time . . .	**THEN** follow Option E1 for keeping the original objective(s) and content and reducing the complexity.
IF a student does not possess the CRITICAL competencie(s), and **IF** there is some probability that the student can learn one or more enroute competencie(s) in a reasonable amount of time and those competencie(s) would be useful to the student . . .	**THEN** follow Option E2 for substituting different but related objective(s) and content.
IF a student does not possess the CRITICAL competencie(s), and **IF** totally different objectives would be more useful to the student . . .	**THEN** follow Option E3 and incorporate alternative objectives that involve the student's participation in alternative curriculum components that reflect the student's unique needs (e.g., objectives for life skill outcomes; objectives for modified means of communication and performance).

Source: Adapted from "Steps in Devising Differential Standards," California Dept. of Education, 1978, in *Developing Proficiency Standards for Pupils in Special Education Programs: Workshop Outline and Agenda,* Sacramento: Author.

Procedure E: Develop appropriate objectives tailored to the needs of specific students, keeping the general education curriculum in mind as a point of reference.

This procedure allows three levels of modification of general education objectives. Each option is described and illustrated separately.

Option E1: Keeping the original objectives and content but reducing their complexity. A teacher may determine that a student is not able to accomplish the general education objective as written. Still, the teacher finds that the student does in fact possess the CRITICAL skills and knowledge, or is close to mastering the CRITICAL skills and knowledge required. With this information, the teacher has reason to modify the complexity of the objectives and/or the related content, allowing the child to work toward the original general education objective, with slight modifications. Material for the modification of complexity may be inspired by or taken directly from a lower-grade-level curriculum. In this situation, content is parallel and age appropriate and relies on general education standards; the difference is that the materials and objectives are reduced in difficulty.

Option E1 would be appropriate for students who may not currently demonstrate the same level of proficiency as their peers yet are able to perform or learn the critical skills. For example, Shanti, who is not able to sequence 5 sentences into paragraph form but is able to sequence 3 sentences into paragraph form, could benefit from continued lessons in the original objective and content, at a modified complexity. The teacher modifies the objective by reducing the number of sentences required for sequencing. Additionally, the content can be modified by reducing the complexity of the sentence structure and vocabulary. This may be achieved by using materials written at a lower grade level more appropriate to Shanti's reading level. In this case Shanti, a fourth grade student, uses a modified second grade curriculum to meet expected outcomes and completes the activity alongside her peers in the same classroom. This example shows that it is possible to establish specifications to allow students to complete an activity at a reduced level of complexity without inventing different objectives. Exhibit 3.5 demonstrates how this modification option may be carried out for the written language objective. Compare the information in Column 2: (a) modified objective, (b) specifications for generating modified activities and assessments, and (c) modified activities and assessments material with the same kinds of information for the original objective (Column 1).

EXHIBIT 3.5

Examples Resulting from Option E1—Modified Objective

ORIGINAL OBJECTIVE	E1: MODIFIED OBJECTIVE
Given a topic sentence and series of up to 4 related sentences containing time-order words, students will first locate the topic sentence, write it down, then continue to write the detail sentences in logical order in paragraph form. Students meet the criteria when they sequence the sentences correctly into a written paragraph.	Given a topic sentence and 2 related sentences containing time-order words, students will first locate the topic sentence, write it down, then continue to write the detail sentences in logical order in paragraph form. Students meet the criteria when they sequence the sentences correctly into paragraph order.
SPECIFICATIONS OF ORIGINAL OBJECTIVE	**SPECIFICATIONS OF MODIFIED OBJECTIVE**
1. Each group of sentences consists of 5 or more sentences, one of which is the topic sentence. 2. All detail sentences begin with a time-order word. 3. Each sentence has between 5 and 10 words. 4. Vocabulary is at grade level (approx. 4th). 5. Sentence construction is according to grade reading level.	1. Each group of sentences consists of no more than 3 sentences, one of which is the topic sentence. 2. All detail sentences begin with a time-order word. 3. Each sentence has no more than 8 words. 4. Vocabulary is at lower grade level (approx. 2nd). 5. Sentence structure is kept to simple, not compound, sentences.
ORIGINAL ACTIVITY AND ASSESSMENT MATERIAL	**MODIFIED ACTIVITY AND ASSESSMENT MATERIAL**
Then, she searched her entire house. Finally, Sarah found him sleeping under her bed. Sarah lost her dog, Mr. Buster. Second, Sarah looked in her neighbor's yard. First, she looked in her backyard.	First, she looked in her yard. Then she found the dog under her bed. Sarah lost her dog, Mr. Buster.

Option E2: Substituting different but related objectives and content. For a student who does not possess the CRITICAL skills or knowledge required to complete the original activity, teachers may choose to change the original performance objective, yet maintain a direct relationship to the original content. Again, a student does not lose her or his relationship or position in the classroom but has her or his educational needs met through modification of the curriculum. Option E2 would be appropriate for students who could benefit from the accomplishment of an enroute skill on a competence checklist. Although students may not be able to accomplish the original objective in an allotted amount of time even if it is modified, they may be able to accomplish an important subskill (enroute skill) derived from the original objective. When a teacher selects a subskill from the competence checklist and then defines that particular subskill as the new objective, a different but related objective has been devised. A student may, for example, learn about topic sentences and learn to identify them.

This student, Marquez, is able to read each sentence and knows that a main topic or idea expresses the main idea of a paragraph, but he is not currently able to continue on to the next level which requires him to locate the topic sentence (and write it down on paper). Because Marquez cannot meet this competency CRITICAL to the accomplishment of the original objective, he cannot complete the original objective at this time. However, because he can perform two of the enroute skills (reads sentences, knows a topic sentence expresses the main idea of a paragraph), the teacher decides that he is likely to benefit from continued work in this area. The teacher decides to substitute an unaccomplished enroute skill—Identify the topic sentence—for the original objective, creating a different, but related, objective:

> Given a topic sentence and a series of up to 3 related sentences containing time-order words, the student will identify the topic sentence from the series. The student meets the criteria when he correctly locates the topic sentence and writes it down.

Sample sentences that could be used in the task are the following:

(a) First, she put him in the tub.

(b) Then, she started to wash Rex.

(c) Next she turned on the water.

(d) Tanita's dog, Rex, needed a bath.

Option E3: Incorporating alternative objectives for student participation in alterfjnative curriculum. If a student is unable to demonstrate the CRITICAL skills and knowledge and also is unable to perform and benefit from an enroute competency, the student may be able to benefit from a different objective and content design. Totally different objectives and content may be more useful to the student now and in the future. It may be more important for the student to concentrate on skills for working in a community business rather than working to achieve the objective set in the general education curriculum. When selecting Option E3, the teacher embraces totally different (alternative) curriculum and objectives which are frequently incorporated into the GE classroom.

It is determined that a student is not currently able to perform any of the CRITICAL skills required for the original objective nor is its performance seen to be in the student's best interest. So the teacher forgoes the original objective and/or enroute competencies for the student and instead, creates a totally new and different objective. The objective may or may not be in the same academic discipline as the original objective. For example, the original language arts objective may be changed to the functional academic objective (in language arts) of addressing envelopes:

> Given verbal instructions, written information to copy, and lined envelopes to accommodate the information, the student will address envelopes to the addressee and write his or her own name and address as sender. The student meets the criteria when he or she correctly completes a stack of 20 envelopes.

Procedure F: Plan curriculum to help students attain or advance toward meeting the objectives.

The final step is to plan learning experiences to assist students in achieving the selected objectives. Strategies for planning and designing learning experiences are described later in this text in Section 2, on assessment, and in Section 3, on instruction.

In summary, this process for evaluating different general education objectives assists in determining whether the general education curriculum is appropriate, whether general education curriculum with modifications is appropriate, or whether a different curriculum is most appropriate for a particular student. Options E1 and E2 are modifications of general education curriculum; E3 is the adoption of different, or alternative, curriculum content to meet those particularly unique needs of a student.

THEORY TO PRACTICE

➡ With a particular student in mind, select one of the three approaches to determining curricular modification. Apply the approach. How helpful is your selected approach in helping you make curricular decisions? What are the advantages and disadvantages of the approach? Present your findings to a peer for feedback. Reflect on the possible outcomes, both positive and negative, that the approach may have on the curriculum development process as applied to students with special needs.

GENERAL EDUCATION CURRICULUM WITH MODIFICATIONS

Once it is determined that modification of general education curriculum is most appropriate for meeting the needs of the student and the learning goals and objectives have been identified, specific strategies for modifying that curriculum and supporting student success in it become the focus. We now present some global approaches for modifying the curriculum.

Modification through Curricular Analysis

One way to modify the general education curriculum for students with disabilities is to analyze the curriculum to identify underlying concepts, skills, and knowledge. This modification strategy is similar to the objective evaluation approach because it involves a detailed analysis of the general education curriculum to determine what is most important for teachers to teach and students to learn. Understanding the underlying concepts, skills, and knowledge of the curriculum allows teachers to make decisions about what is most important to teach and how it can be presented to students in meaningful ways. We identify three ways to identify these underlying concepts, skills, and knowledge.

Analysis and modification of course syllabi

One way to begin curriculum analysis is with an examination of existing course and unit syllabi. Syllabi are summaries or outlines of school courses and units of study that contain course descriptions and information about course objectives and competencies and required activities. They are a summary of the results of planning the local curriculum. They serve as a public record of what content is, will be, and was covered in particular courses and units of study. Teachers can formally adapt plans for curriculum for students by modifying and/or editing these original syllabi or by writing syllabi.

A modified syllabus adjusts what is to be taught, how it is to be taught, and the type of learning demonstrations required so those students with disabilities and in need of curriculum modification have access to the general education curriculum. Implementation of modified syllabi allows teachers to devise ways to make it possible for these students to learn, study, and discuss material along with general education peers. Teachers may find that groups of students not identified as having disabilities also benefit from the modifications designed to assist special education students and, therefore, they implement these syllabi with these students as well. Exhibit 3.6 presents a unit syllabus that has been modified to reflect the needs of students with disabilities.

EXHIBIT 3.6	NINTH GRADE OVERVIEW

Example of the Modification of a Syllabus for a Unit of Study

Objectives

The students will ~~as a disease you can catch.~~

1. define AIDS ~~and know the meaning of the words represented by each letter.~~

2. describe the ~~prognosis of AIDS.~~ *results of getting AIDS.*

3. describe how the HIV affects the immune system and causes AIDS. [optional]

   discuss eight common symptoms of AIDS.

4. ~~identify eight common symptoms of AIDS.~~

5. list the four major ways in which AIDS is spread. [optional]

6. identify high-risk behaviors associated with AIDS.

7. distinguish between myths and facts about AIDS.

   contraction

8. list methods to prevent and minimize the ~~spread~~ of AIDS.

9. discuss the social implications relating to AIDS.

Source: "9th Grade Overview" from *9th–12th Grade AIDS Curriculum*, Baldwin Park Unified School District, Baldwin Park, CA. Used with permission.

Teachers generally like the idea of a modified syllabus because it allows them to remain focused on a systematic rather than random plan for students. The syllabus provides a blueprint for implementing the curriculum in a prescribed way. As a result of this approach, special education students may receive a more coherent and sequential curriculum than they would if their teachers invented modifications on a daily basis.

Adjustment of proficiency levels

Another way to modify the general education curriculum is to modify expected proficiency levels—that is, the level of performance to be demonstrated for skills to be considered mastered. As with the students-at-large, some students with disabilities may be required to pass proficiency tests in school subjects in order to graduate from high school with a diploma. The level of required proficiency for students with disabilities may be adjusted from what is required of general education students as a result of an IEP team decision and based on an individual's unique need for that type of modification.

The National Assessment of Education Progress (NAEP) in Washington, D.C. is a congressionally mandated organization that assesses student proficiency in several academic subjects on a national scale. Using common measures that trace growth in achievement across and within grade levels, this organization has established proficiency levels to describe and categorize student performance (National Assessment Governing Board, 1991, 1996). NAEP data illustrate that in a particular content or skill area, some students will develop more specialized expertise than others, as reflected by different levels of proficiency achieved. Exhibit 3.7 provides a description of the three achievement, or proficiency levels in science—basic, proficient, and advanced—used by the NAEP. Here,

> Basic *denotes partial mastery of the knowledge and thinking skills, but performance that is fundamental for adequate work in grades 4, 8, and 12.* Proficient *represents solid academic performance and competency over challenging subject matter. If a majority of students performed at the* Proficient *level on this assessment, the consensus committees believe they would have learned enough science to be competent students and productive citizens.* Advanced *performance on this assessment represents performance that is equal to that expected of top students in other industrialized nations—the ability to think critically about scientific issues and be able to integrate knowledge and skills into problem solving situations (National Assessment Governing Board, 1996, p. 36).*

Achievement or proficiency level descriptions guide the curriculum goals and objectives for students expected to achieve at different levels. See Exhibit 3.7 for differentiation of proficiency levels in fourth-grade science. Differentiations guide curriculum modification.

> **EXHIBIT 3.7**
>
> **Achievement, or Proficiency, Level Descriptions in Science for Grade 4**

- **4th-Grade Basic.** Students at the basic level should be able to make simple measurements. For example, they should be able to use a thermometer, fill a container to a specified point, and weigh an object using a balance. Students at this level should be able to make comparative statements about the physical properties of objects and be able to estimate length, weight, volume, and temperature. Students should be able to describe and classify familiar objects and/or organisms and be able to describe their properties using the five senses. They should be able to distinguish most living things from those that are not living, and distinguish plants from animals. Students should be able to identify major features of the Earth's surface and about the Earth in space, and identify Earth resources used in everyday life. Given clear, sequential directions, students should be able to perform simple science tasks.

- **4th-Grade Proficient.** Students at the proficient levels should be able to conduct accurate measurements of temperature, volume, length, and weight. When students classify, they should be able to offer a reasonable justification for whatever system they use. Proficient skills and understandings should be demonstrated through written summaries of descriptive investigations of the natural world. While the proficient student should be able to conduct tests for properties that cannot be directly observed with the five senses (e.g. solubility, magnetic properties, conductivity), they should be able to apply concrete procedures to solve abstract problems. Proficient students should be able to understand various concepts, such as the water cycle, the relationship of seasonal changes to weather conditions and the motion of the Earth in space.

- **4th-Grade Advanced.** Students at this level should be able to select appropriate measures and measuring devices in the design of an investigation. They should be able to propose multiple systems of classification that rely on observable and appropriate criteria. Advanced students should be able to appreciate the application of classification in their daily lives and recognize the advantages and disadvantages of classification systems (Which one is the best, [and] why?). When testing reasonable hypotheses, they should be able to justify their conclusions using observable evidence. Students should be able to relate structure and function in living things and be able to cite advantages for the observed structure/function relationship. Advanced students should be able to describe ways to measure various natural phenomena, such as weather changes, and to identify tools used to gather information about space. They should be able to describe some relationships between and among the Sun, Moon, and Earth in the solar system.

(National Assessment Governing Board, 1996, pp. 36–37).

Identification of rudiments

Besides working with course syllabi and modifying proficiency levels, teachers may turn to a variety of sources and approaches to identify the rudiments of the general education curriculum. In this context, rudiments are the fundamentals of a subject, other areas of knowledge, or a task performance. There is no simple or single approach for finding rudiments, but here are five time-tested tactics identified by Bigge (1988).

Find patterns of emphasis in different resources. This tactic is based on looking for patterns or repetitions in the information emphasized in different curriculum resources. For example, regardless of whether a person is a preschooler or an adult learning about the field of *sports,* certain content patterns are evident: teams, scoring, rules, penalties for rule infractions, time limits, equipment, boundaries, and so on. What is altered in the curriculum is the depth and complexity of the information. Progressively more sophisticated or complex information is presented as students move through their school career.

Find longitudinal progressions. The second tactic is to find longitudinal progressions and benchmarks leading to desired outcomes. Teachers of academic subjects may refer to scope and sequence charts to determine which subskills to teach prior to others. Scope and sequence charts indicate the whole longitudinal progression of skills across the grades, from the very simple to more complex within one subject area.

When evaluating a scope and sequence chart, look for increasingly complex progressions within each subskill area. This progression, or strand, may be traced by moving from basic concepts, knowledge, and skills to more complex understandings. This sequence can guide teachers as they develop curriculum for students.

Note key vocabularies. The third tactic is to note key vocabularies. Terms and definitions can be extremely important for learning content area information. The key here is to analyze an array of vocabularies to identify those likely to be most useful for individuals with learning difficulties—namely, vocabularies that have important or frequent use in life activities, those that appear frequently in an area of study, those that can be used at various levels of difficulty, and those that are of particular interest to the individual student.

For example, consider a music appreciation class and all the terminology students study. From this array, a teacher might select certain terms and concepts because they can be taught at a basic level, are used frequently in the class, and have implications for use in the community—such as beat, rhythm, melody, harmony, tempo, pitch, and intensity. Teachers may decide to use a more basic vocabulary (e.g., "fast" and "slow" instead of "tempo") when introducing fundamental concepts to students, throughout instruction, and/or some students gradually move to more advanced levels as they become familiar with the content.

Analyze concepts. In concept analysis, teachers look for meaning rather than key vocabulary. Students need to find meaning in their learning materials and learning experiences and, based on that information and understandings, learn to construct new knowledge.

Identification of the concepts students already possess and the concepts they need to be able to recognize, label (or define), or apply in varieties of tasks is a good place to start. Analysis comes from three basic sources when teachers are preparing for instruction: (a) students' existing and developing concepts in relation to needed concepts, (b) students' anticipated and future needs in major life areas, and (c) curriculum materials for the different school disciplines.

Concept analysis by teachers and parents frequently starts with analysis of concepts that children and youth already possess and the depth and breadth to which these concepts are developed. When teachers assess concepts, for example, a student may be asked to group a number of objects which could be classified in any of several ways, while the teacher notes the strategies and procedures and language the student uses when sorting objects. At the conclusion of the activity, the student may be asked to label the groups of objects and describe how he or she arrived at the groupings, or categories. The student's descriptions reveal his or her concepts or generalized ideas about the things in the groups.

Teachers may also identify the concepts they believe are most important for students to learn and generalize. When teaching these concepts, teachers may first identify the concept (e.g., vehicles), define it (vehicles take you places), and then discriminate examples from nonexamples or counterexamples (house, chair, tree). Finally, students may be asked to generate their own examples and nonexamples of the concept.

Conduct a task or activity analysis. The fifth tactic for identifying the rudiments of a curriculum is to conduct a task or activity analysis. Task analysis breaks down skills, understandings, or activities into their component parts and sequences those parts to represent the order in which the skills, understandings, and activities are to be presented to and/or performed by students. Exhibit 3.8 presents a task analysis for the daily living skill of packing a lunch.

Pack lunch (e.g., make sandwich, select dessert/salty snack, select fruit, select drink, wrap food items, pack in bag, refrigerate lunch when appropriate)

EXHIBIT 3.8

Task Analysis: Packing a Lunch

PERFORMANCE SKILLS
1. Select sandwich type
2. Get needed items
3. Make sandwich
4. Wrap sandwich
5. Select dessert/snack
6. Select fruit
7. Select drink
8. Wrap items
9. Bag items
10. Clean up
11. Identify whether lunch needs refrigeration (e.g., meat)

Key: − = incorrect; + = correct; A = Attempted

Source: *Instruction of Students with Severe Disabilities* by Snell, 1993, p. 490. Reprinted by permission of Prentice-Hall, Inc., Upper Saddle River, NJ.

When the teacher completes an activity analysis, the components or requirements of an activity are specified, and the student's ability to engage in those activities is evaluated. It may be that the student is able to engage independently in some of the activity components, but will need some components adapted to reflect her or his needs, will need assistance in other components, or will need to have other individuals complete those components for her or him.

Exhibit 3.9 presents an activity analysis for a student who does not communicate verbally. The student, Angel, is participating in a reciprocal teaching group. Reciprocal teaching (Palincsar & Brown, 1984) is a group reading strategy in which students assume the role of teacher and take turns in the teacher role, moving the group through the following sequence of activities: (a) reading a short passage or paragraph, (b) clarifying for understanding, (c) summarizing what was read, (d) asking questions about what was read, and (e) predicting what will happen next. The task requirements for this activity are described in the lefthand column of the exhibit, and the means by which Angel responds to those tasks—whether independently, through modifications, or with assistance—are described in the righthand column. Rudiments of the task performance suggest how curriculum can be modified to allow physical access by students with unique means of communication and performance.

TASK	STUDENT RESPONSE
1. Move to the group and gather necessary materials	Angel completes the task independently
2. Select who will be the first teacher	Angel completes the task independently

3. When another student is the teacher:
  a. If Angel is called on to read the passage . . .
  b. If Angel is called on to clarify information . . .
  c. If Angel is called on to summarize information . . .
  d. If Angel is called on to answer questions . . .
  e. If Angel is called on to predict . . .
	a peer reads the passage for Angel
	Angel uses her augmentative communication device to reply with one or two key words for each response; Angel then answers with *yes, no,* and *I don't know* gestures to others who try to gain more information about what she meant by the key words

4. When Angel is the teacher:
  a. To ask another student to read the story . . .
  b. To ask another student to clarify information . . .
  c. To ask another student to summarize information . . .
  d. To ask another student to predict . . .
	Angel points to a peer
	Angel points to a peer and chooses appropriate requests preprogrammed on her augmentative communication device
	Angel points to a peer

Modification through Teaching Thinking and Problem-Solving Skills

General education curriculum requires students to be critical thinkers and problem solvers. Some students develop these skills naturally. When these students are presented unique challenges, they easily integrate new and old information, draw generalizations, and demonstrate their understanding. However, for other students, including those with disabilities, the development of these essential skills can be extremely difficult. Moreover, these students may lack confidence in their critical thinking and problem-solving skills. Therefore, in order to perform general education tasks calling for critical thinking and problem solving, students may require direct and intensive instruction in these areas to support their participation in general education curriculum.

The *Dimensions of Learning* thinking skills curriculum (Marzano, 1992) is an example of representative content for the development of thinking and problem-solving skills. It addresses five types of thinking that Marzano (1992) and Marzano, Pickering and McTighe (1993) call dimensions of learning:

1. **Positive attitudes and perceptions about learning:** assisting students in seeing themselves as learners and in adopting positive attitudes about their abilities in school.

2. **Thinking involved in acquiring and integrating knowledge:** assisting students in skills for making connections between what they know and what they are learning. Students are taught differences between procedural knowledge (knowledge needed to do something) and declarative knowledge (knowledge needed to understand and explain concepts and ideas).

3. **Thinking involved in extending and refining knowledge:** teaching students to extend and refine knowledge through activities that involve "comparing, classifying, making inductions, making deductions, analyzing errors, creating and analyzing support[ing information], analyzing perspectives, and abstracting" (Marzano, Pickering, & McTighe, 1993, p. 2).

4. **Thinking involved in using knowledge meaningfully:** teaching students to use "decision making, investigation, experimental inquiry, problem solving, and invention" (Marzano, Pickering, & McTighe, 1993, p. 2) and to apply knowledge in meaningful ways in different types of tasks.

5. **Productive habits of mind:** teaching students skills that allow them to continue to learn on their own. Habits of mind include being clear and seeking clarity, being open-minded, restraining impulsivity, being aware of one's own thinking, evaluating the effectiveness of one's actions, pushing the limits of one's knowledge and abilities, and engaging intensely in tasks even when answers or solutions are not immediately apparent" (Marzano, Pickering, & McTighe, 1993, p. 3).

To help students master these thinking or cognitive skills, teachers choose activities that meet unique needs of students and that "fit naturally with the curriculum content, so as to fully integrate the teaching of cognitive skills and the teaching of content" (Marzano, Pickering, & McTighe, 1993, p. 2). Teachers who use the *Dimensions of Learning* approach come to view learning as the product of the five types of thinking identified in the model. Developers and users of this curriculum suggest that teachers plan units of instruction that address all five dimensions (Marzano, Pickering, & McTighe, 1993).

Modification through Teaching Learning Strategies and Study Skills

Schools strive to ensure that children and youth will, as students and future citizens, be lifelong learners and individuals who have "learned how to learn" (Collett, 1990). According to Mercer (1997), the

> *goal of strategy development is to identify strategies that are optimally effective (i.e., help students meet the demands of both current and future tasks) and efficient (i.e., help students meet the demands of a task in a manner that is appropriate, timely, resourceful, and judicious). (p. 380)*

Curriculum in learning skills and study strategies assists students in acquiring information from written materials (e.g., scanning, use of visual aids), and it guides them in identifying and remembering important information (e.g., textbook usage and notetaking) (Wood & Lazarus, 1991). It includes skills for accessing information, processing (interpreting) information, reporting and sharing information, and using information to plan activities in home, community, and work. Study skills support students in their efforts to learn and demonstrate understanding of concepts and skills.

Deshler and colleagues working at the University of Kansas Center for Research on Learning have developed a *Learning Strategies Curriculum* for students with learning disabilities. The curriculum includes strategies for dealing with unfamiliar words when reading, for applying self-questioning when reading, and for writing sentences and paragraphs. A complete description of this curriculum is available in Mercer (1997).

An example of a study skills program is *Skills for School Success,* developed by Archer and Gleason (1994). This four-level program is designed to teach critical organization and study skills systematically to students in the elementary and middle school grades (Books 3, 4, 5, and 6). *Skills for School Success* is a teacher-directed program that expands in a spiral fashion with a scope and sequence chart of skills identified as Introduced (I), Extended (E), and Reviewed (R). Exhibit 3.10 presents the scope and sequence for the series.

EXHIBIT 3.10

Scope and Sequence of *Skills for School Success*

	Book			
	3	4	5	6
School Behaviors and Organization Skills				
Using Appropriate Before-Class Behaviors	I	E	R	R
Using Appropriate During-Class Behaviors	I	E	R	R
Organizing and Using Notebooks	I	R	R	R
Writing Entries on an Assignment Calendar	I	E	R	R
Using a Calendar to Plan Homework	I	E	E	E
Getting Ready to Do Homework	I	E	R	R
Completing Homework	I	E	E	R
Organizing Assignments on Papers (HOW)	I	R	R	R
Organizing Desks and Other Materials	I	R	R	R
Learning Strategies				
Strategies for Gaining Information and Responding in Class				
• Completing Assignments with Directions	I	E	R	R
• Memorizing/Studying Information (RCRC)	I	E	R	R
• Answering Chapter Questions	I	E	E	E
• Proofreading Written Assignments	I	E	E	R
• Previewing Chapter Content (Warm-Up)		I	R	R
• Reading Expository Chapters (Active Reading)		I	E	R
• Taking Notes on Written Material			I	E
• Taking Notes on Lectures				I
Strategies for Studying for and Taking Tests				
• Multiple-Choice Tests	I	E	R	R
• True-False Tests		I	E	R
• Short-Answer Tests			I	E
• Content-Area Tests			I	E
• Skill-Based Tests			I	E
Textbook Reference Skills				
Using the Table of Contents	I	E	R	R
Using the Glossary	I	E	R	R
Using the Index	I	E	E	R
Selecting the Appropriate Reference Source	I	E	E	R
Locating Information on the Title Page			I	R
Using the Copyright Page			I	R
Using Other Reference Lists				I
Graphics				
Reading and Interpreting Graphics				
• Pictographs	I	E	E	E
• Pie Graphs	I	E	E	E
• Vertical Bar Graphs	I	E	E	E
• Line Graphs		I	E	E
• Horizontal Bar Graphs			I	E
• Tables			I	E
Comparing Information on Graphs of Same Type			I	E
Interpreting and Comparing Information from Different Types of Graphs				I

	Book			
	3	4	5	6
Reference Books				
Alphabetizing	I	R		
Locating Words Quickly in a Dictionary	I	R	R	R
Reading and Interpreting Dictionary Entries	I	E	E	E
Locating Entries in an Encyclopedia			I	E
Locating Information in Encyclopedia Entries			I	E

I = INTRODUCED The skill or strategy is introduced at this level.
E = EXTENDED   The skill, strategy, and/or instructional examples are extended and therefore are more difficult.
R = REVIEWED   The skill or strategy is systematically reviewed and maintained.

Source: *Skills for School Success (Book 6): Teacher Guide* and *Student Book* (back cover), by A. Archer and M. Gleason, 1994, North Billerica, MA: Curriculum Associates, Inc. Reprinted by permission.

Modification through Natural Supports

Planning for the use of the natural supports of peers and others to help attain success of students with disabilities in the mainstream is another means by which the general education curriculum can be modified to reflect student needs and IEP/ITP goals. The use of natural supports may be combined with other curricular modification procedures to provide students additional means by which to engage in the curriculum.

The concept *natural supports* refers to "assistance provided by people, procedures, equipment in a given workplace or group that (a) leads to desired personal and work outcomes, (b) is typically available or culturally appropriate . . . , and (c) is supported by resources within the work place [including school], facilitated to the degree necessary by human service consultation [e.g., peers, fellow employees]." (Butterworth et al., 1996, p. 106).

Ryan and Paterna (1997) describe one example of how natural supports in combination with cooperative learning assisted Steven, a middle school student with severe disabilities, in participating in general education curriculum and experiences. Natural supports were identified through the use of a natural support matrix and cooperative learning planning system. The first step was to complete the natural supports matrix. Exhibit 3.11 provides an example of Steven's matrix. Objectives and supports were identified for his participation in general education activities. Teachers then developed a cooperative learning plan, specifying group size, how students would be assigned to groups, how the room would be arranged for cooperative group work, materials to be used, and the roles individual group members would play in the cooperative activity. Ryan and Paterna consider this cooperative activity plan critical to the overall success for inclusion of students with disabilities in general education, because it is through cooperative activities that the natural supports are implemented in the classroom.

EXHIBIT 3.11

Sample Natural Supports Matrix: Steven in the Eighth Grade Iditarod Multidisciplinary Unit

SUBJECT/ PERIOD	GENERAL GOALS AND ACTIVITIES	STEVEN'S GENERAL OBJECTIVES	SUPPORTS
Period 1 Language Arts 8:15–9:15	**Creative Writing:** Cooperative Group Iditarod Unit: Musher interviews. Interview musher at checkpoint. Students ask musher questions, record answers, and take pictures of musher and dog team.	Ask the musher two questions, in order to work on expressive language skills; hold tape recorder's microphone; use camera to take two pictures of musher and dogs.	Speech therapist will prompt him to ask musher prewritten questions on his board. Julie, Sam, and Fred verbally cue him to use microphone and take pictures.
Period 5 Lunch 12:20–12:50	Students go to the cafeteria and move through the line to choose food and pay for it. Sit at tables and eat with friends.	Steven will go with students to cafeteria, walk through line, and choose food. Will give money for lunch and collect change. Will eat with students and socialize.	Sam and Fred will cue Steven in line to choose his food. At the table, they will practice communication with pictures and smiles and other nonverbal communication.
Period 6 Orchestra 12:55–1:45	**Alaskan Native Music:** Iditarod Unit. Native Music along the Iditarod Trail. Athabascan and Eskimo folk music recital practice. Students will learn an Athabascan love song in E major.	Steven will listen with class to tape recording of music. Steven will beat an Athabascan drum with Harry. Each will practice their parts together and then with group.	Harry will initiate drum music. Steven will set up and put drum away.
Period 7 Social Studies 1:50–2:35	**History of Alaska:** Iditarod Unit. History of the villages on the Iditatod Trail. Each group will finish reports about the villages they chose. Cooperatively, make outline of report notes and use computer to type them.	Steven will help type the report on the computer. He will proofread the typing of the group and help edit.	Sam, Mary, and Julie will take turns assisting Steven as he types two paragraphs and will help him as he edits.

Note: The Iditarod is an internationally acclaimed dog sled race in Alaska from Anchorage to Nome, held in February of each year.

Source: From "Junior High Can Be Inclusive: Using Natural Supports and Cooperative Learning," by S. Ryan and L. Paterna, 1997, *Teaching Exceptional Children, 30*(2), p. 37. Reprinted with permission.

THEORY TO PRACTICE

➡ Considering the curriculum requirements in a targeted subject area, establish basic, proficient, and advanced levels of proficiency for key content. Present your system to a teacher in this content area for feedback. How could this information be used to adapt/modify the general education curriculum and performance expectations for students with disabilities?

➡ Imagine that you are responsible for teaching a unit in science and are somewhat unfamiliar with the material. Using the process of identifying rudiments of the curriculum, work to identify the concepts and skills that you would include in the teaching of this unit. Also address how you would modify this curriculum to ensure access to the curriculum for students with disabilities.

➡ Observe in a general education classroom. Look specifically at students in different activities. Select one of these activities and complete an activity analysis. What are the demands/tasks of the activity? How would you ensure the participation of students with disabilities in this activity?

➡ Read further on the topic of modifying curriculum through teaching thinking and problem-solving skills. How would you apply this approach to your teaching in the classroom?

➡ Meet with a special education teacher to discuss how he or she includes the teaching of learning strategies and study skills in the curriculum as one means for modifying the general education curriculum for students with disabilities. What procedures, techniques, and materials does the teacher use? How does he or she ensure student application of these skills and understandings to experiences in the general education curriculum?

CHAPTER SUMMARY

This chapter introduces the basic content, structure, and delivery of the general education curriculum and provides three approaches for determining the appropriateness of this curriculum for individual students with disabilities. Through application of these procedures, teachers can select or modify objectives and related curriculum that are meaningful for individual students who have a disability. The chapter also describes how to modify curriculum through curricular analysis, the teaching of thinking and problem-solving skills, the teaching of learning strategies and study skills, and the use of natural supports.

CHAPTER 4

Life Skills Curriculum

Read to find out the following:
- what content is represented by life skills curriculum and how this curricular option can serve to modify, augment, or substitute for parts of general education curriculum with and without modifications
- the meaning of functional academics and when it is an appropriate curricular option for students
- the multiple categories of daily and community living skills and how these categories can contribute to a student's overall curriculum
- the importance of transition and the components of a transition curriculum

General education curriculum with and without modifications will not address all the curricular needs of some students with disabilities. Some students will need additional, specifically designed, and intensive instruction in life skills curriculum in order to achieve a degree of independence and participation at school, work, home, and in the community. We have clustered life skills curriculum into three areas: (a) functional academics (e.g., academic skills that support independence); (b) daily and community living skills (e.g., household maintenance); and (c) transition (i.e., moving from one learning experience and/or site to another).

Life skills curriculum should be taught across the grades and from early childhood—not from just a couple of years prior to a student's exit from school. For example, skills in self-help areas such as eating, dressing, and brushing teeth can be developed at a young age. Skills related to vocational preparation such as being on time, completing assigned work, and getting along with others can be introduced and reinforced across the grades. In Exhibit 4.1, Wehman (1996) provides examples of some categories of life skills curriculum and curricular activities that students may engage in across the grades.

EXHIBIT 4.1

**Life Skills Curriculum
Across the Grades**

STUDENT	DOMESTIC	COMMUNITY	LEISURE	VOCATIONAL
Tim (elementary age)	—Picking up toys —Washing dishes —Making bed —Dressing —Grooming —Practicing eating skills —Practicing toileting skills —Sorting clothes —Vacuuming	—Eating meals in a restaurant —Using restroom in a local restaurant —Putting trash into container —Choosing correct change to ride city bus —Giving the clerk money for an item he wants to purchase —Recognizing and reading pedestrian safety signs —Participating in local scout troop —Going to a neighbor's house for lunch	—Climbing on swing set —Playing board games —Playing tag with neighbors —Tumbling activities —Running —Playing kickball —Playing croquet —Riding bicycles —Playing with age-appropriate toys	—Picking up plate, silverware, and glass after a meal —Returning toys to appropriate storage spaces —Cleaning the room at the end of the day —Working on a task for a designated period (15–30 minutes) —Wiping tables after meals —Following two- to four-step instructions —Answering the telephone —Emptying trash —Taking messages to people
Mary (junior high age)	—Washing clothes —Preparing simple meals (e.g., soup, salad, sandwich) —Keeping bedroom clean —Making snacks —Mowing lawn —Raking leaves —Making grocery lists —Purchasing items from a list —Vacuuming and dusting living room	—Crossing streets safely —Purchasing an item from a department store —Purchasing a meal at a restaurant —Using local transportation system to get to and from recreational facilities —Participating in local scout troop —Going to a neighbor's house for lunch on Saturday	—Playing volleyball —Taking aerobics classes —Playing checkers with a friend —Playing miniature golf —Cycling —Attending high school or local basketball games —Playing softball —Swimming —Attending craft class at city recreation center	—Waxing floors —Cleaning windows —Filling lawn mower with gas —Hanging and bagging clothes —Busing tables —Working for 1–2 hours —Operating machinery (e.g., dishwasher, buffer) —Cleaning sinks, bath tubs, and fixtures —Following a job sequence

(continued)

**Life Skills Curriculum
Across the Grades** (continued)

STUDENT	DOMESTIC	COMMUNITY	LEISURE	VOCATIONAL
Sandy (high school age)	—Cleaning all rooms in place of residence —Developing a weekly budget —Cooking meals —Operating thermostat to regulate heat and air conditioning —Doing yard maintenance —Maintaining personal needs —Caring for and maintaining clothing	—Utilizing bus system to move about the community —Depositing checks into bank account —Using community department stores —Using community restaurants —Using community grocery stores —Using community health facilities (e.g., physician, pharmacist)	—Jogging —Archery —Boating —Watching college basketball games —Playing video games —Playing card games (e.g., UNO) —Attending athletic club swimming class —Gardening —Going on a vacation trip	—Performing required janitorial duties at J.C. Penney —Performing housekeeping duties at Days Inn —Performing groundskeeping duties at college campus —Performing food service at K Street cafeteria —Performing laundry duties at Moon's Laundromat —Performing photocopying at Virginia National Bank headquarters —Performing food stocking duties at Farm Fresh —Performing clerical duties at electrical company —Performing job duties at company standards

Source: From *Life Beyond the Classroom: Transition Strategies for Young People with Disabilities,* 2nd ed. (pp. 144–145), by P. Wehman, 1996, Baltimore: Paul H. Brookes Publishing, P.O. Box 10624, Baltimore, MD 21285-0624. Used with permission.

As Clark (1994) points out, both general and special education teachers may be responsible for the delivery of life skills curriculum for students. The life skills curriculum may be taught through general education curricular experiences, through modified general education curricular experiences, or through additional curricular experiences designed for a particular child with a disability. One example of a life skill that can be taught through general education curriculum (drawing from Clark, 1994) is the IEP goal of "speaking in front of a group," which can be addressed in general education language arts, social studies, music, and science activities. Similarly, the IEP goal to "improve functional reading skills" can be addressed during language arts, social studies, reading, science, photography, math, and library activities. Clearly, participation in life skills curriculum does not necessarily exclude children from participating in instructional opportunities in the mainstream.

FUNCTIONAL ACADEMICS

Study in a specially planned functional academics curriculum in a comprehensive and cumulative way enables students to learn practical academic skills and fundamental knowledge that will help them participate meaningfully in activities of their daily lives. Functional academic content includes money and budgeting skills and reading survival words such as *poison* and *entrance*. According to Ford and colleagues (1989), achievement of functional academic outcomes allows individuals to experience a greater degree of participation in an independent and enjoyable lifestyle.

A functional academics curriculum may overlap the topics covered in the general education curriculum, but it is not a repackaging of the general education curriculum. Consistent with concepts described by Ford and colleagues (1989), functional academic curriculum is not a watered-down or slower-paced version of the general education curriculum. Nor is it a lesson-by-lesson modification of the general education curriculum or a curriculum that results in student acquisition of nonuseful, splinter skills. Rather, functional academics come from a comprehensive and ongoing course of study designed specially for students with special needs. The goal of a functional academic curriculum is to provide students with the skills and understandings they will need to become as independent as possible as adults.

Previously discussed questions for determining the appropriateness of general education academic curriculum presented in Chapter 3 (questions proposed by Westling and Fox, 1995) are helpful in determining whether a functional academic curriculum is appropriate for a student. Once it is determined that a functional academic curriculum is appropriate, several approaches are available for delivering that curriculum. Browder and Snell (1993) identify two approaches. One is the *generalized approach.* The goal of this approach is to teach students academic skills they can apply across different contexts, people, time, and tasks. One functional academic skill of this type is learning to write personal information (e.g., signature, address, phone number). This skill can be applied when filling out job applications, opening bank accounts, applying for charge cards, and writing letters to friends. The skill can be generalized for many different purposes.

The second approach to teaching functional academics is the *specific, embedded academic skills approach:*

> In this approach, teachers first consider the activities of daily living that are priorities for instruction and then target academic skills that are **embedded** within these activities. (Browder & Snell, 1993, p. 444)

Exhibit 4.2 presents some specific, embedded functional academic skills. In this matrix developed by Cronin and Patton (1993), functional skills are identified in six adult domains.

Specific, Embedded Functional Academic Skills

	EMPLOYMENT/ EDUCATION	HOME AND FAMILY	LEISURE PURSUITS	COMMUNITY INVOLVEMENT	EMOTIONAL/ PHYSICAL HEALTH	PERSONAL RESPONSIBILITY/ RELATIONSHIPS
Reading	Read library books on various occupations	Read directions to prepare brownies from a mix	Look for ads in the newspaper for toys	Read road signs and understand what they mean	Locate poison control numbers in the phone book	Read a story to a younger child
Writing	Write to the school board about a pothole in the school driveway	Make a list of items needed from the grocery store	Fill out a magazine order form completely	Complete an application to play little league	Keep a daily diary of food you eat in each food group	Write a thank-you note to a relative for a gift
Listening	Listen to a lecture by a bank official on savings accounts	Listen to a lecture on babysitting tips	Listen to radio/TV to see if a ball game is rained out	Listen to a lecture on how children can recycle	Listen to the school nurse explain the annual eye exam for your class	Listen to a friend describe their family vacation
Speaking	Discuss reasons we work	Ask parents for permission to stay at a friend's house	Invite friends over to play Monopoly	Discuss park and playground improvements with the mayor	Ask the school nurse how to care for mosquito bites	Discuss honesty, trust, and promise. Define them.
Math Applications	Calculate how much you would make babysitting at $1.25 an hour for 3 hours	Compute the cost of a box of cereal using a coupon	Compute the cost of going to the movies	Compute tax on a video game	Calculate and compare the cost of different types of Band-Aids. Include tax.	Ask a friend to share a candy bar. Calculate your part of the cost.
Problem-Solving	Decide which environment you work best in: out or in; quiet or noisy; active or at a desk, etc.	Decide how to share TV time with a sibling	Given $15 for the afternoon which would you do: go to the movies, go bowling, or play videos?	Role-play the times you would use the 911 emergency number	Decide how many hours of sleep you need per night	Decide if you have enough coins to purchase a vending-machine soda for you and your friend
Survival Skills	Keep homework assignments in a special notebook	Develop a checklist of what to do before and after school	Use a map to find the best way to the mall	Draw a map of the way you go to/ from school	Mark the calendar for your next dental appointment	Identify important table manners
Personal/ Social	Ask a classmate to assist you with a job	Settle a dispute with a sibling	Call a video store to see if they have a specific movie	Role-play asking a police officer for help if you're lost	Ask a friend to go bicycling with you	Role-play appropriate behavior for various places (movies, church, restaurant, ballpark)

Source: From *Life Skills Instruction for All Students with Special Needs: A Practical Guide for Integrating Real-Life Content into the Curriculum* (p. 32), by M. E. Cronin and J. R. Patton, 1993, Austin, TX: ProEd. Used with permission.

A third approach to a functional academic curriculum is an *interdisciplinary approach*. One example of this approach to teaching functional academic skills to students with mild to moderate disabilities is the development of a unit focused on life skills associated with getting a job and managing a budget. Miller (1994) describes a unit of instruction called "On Your Own," which targets life skills and their underlying functional academic skills. Exhibit 4.3 presents an example of the skills associated with the interdisciplinary unit. Cognitive levels of the different activities are also highlighted (e.g., knowledge, comprehension, etc.).

EXHIBIT 4.3

Interdisciplinary Functional Academic Skills

COGNITIVE LEVELS	PHASE 1 CHOOSING A CAREER	PHASE 2 FINDING AN APARTMENT	PHASE 3 FURNISHING THE APARTMENT	PHASE 4 LEARNING TO BUDGET
Knowledge	List career options Identify career preferences	Read ads Record measurements Write results	Draw blueprint and items Document purchases List needed items	Indicate costs of living in an apartment
Comprehension	Compare wages Contrast wages Discuss wages Differentiate between annual and monthly wages Estimate benefits Relate reasons for career choices	Differentiate north, south, east, west Translate ad abbreviations Compare ads Explain choices Contrast choices Discuss choices Locate apartment information	Compare items needed Contrast items bought Discuss item choices Distinguish between needs and wants Compare items in catalogs, newspapers Distinguish between needed and luxury items	Discuss options Differentiate between costs Estimate savings and expenditures Give examples of budget options Predict budget shortfalls or savings
Application	Calculate hourly wage Calculate percentages Apply math skills Indicate differences in benefit packages	Utilize budget information Employ listening skills Apply newspaper ad skills Choose apartment to view Test the feasibility of choice Measure apartment and appliances	Apply math skills Calculate interest Plan a list of needed items	Apply math skills Calculate interest Consider budget alternatives
Analysis	Analyze value of time/work Categorize differences in wages Describe differential benefits	Describe possible apartment choices Analyze apartment options Explain apartments of choice	Describe a furniture budget Transform drawing and measurements to scale	Categorize new information in budget Plan a financial strategy Produce new budgets
Synthesis	Make up career plans Suggest other career options Plan career paths Synthesize career information	Put together a list of living requirements Develop a strategy for viewing apartments Formulate a list of questions for manager	Propose a plan for furniture arrangement Formulate a revised furniture budget Make up a future furniture plan	Think of ways to budget for needs and wants Propose alternate budgets Create plans for coping with unforeseen expenses
Evaluation	Evaluate salary and benefits Choose career to match personality Judge career feasibility	Check all apartment options Select questions for apartment manager Evaluate apartment information Choose an apartment	Decide on most appropriate furnishings Check on availability of appliances Select appropriate furnishings and appliances	Select appropriate budget options Evaluate purchases Assess financial stability Judge the budget alternatives against given criteria

Source: From "On Your Own: A Functional Skills Activity for Adolescents with Mild Disabilities," by D. R. Miller, 1994, *Teaching Exceptional Children, 26*(3), p. 32. Used with permission.

Representative Content

Representative content in functional academics follows familiar classifications. Browder and Snell (1993), Westling and Fox (1995), and others identify curricular topics for students with special needs in reading, math, and writing. Topics in reading include reading signs on restrooms, vending machines, and streets; reading job notices in newspapers; and reading for school, for pleasure, for information, and for improving reading skills. In mathematics they include putting the correct number of utensils on the dinner table, telling time and staying on schedule, and selecting proper coins for vending machines, parking meters, and videogame machines. In the area of writing they include writing signatures, communicating through writing, and using writing shortcuts. The *Syracuse Community-Referenced Curriculum Guide* (Ford et al., 1989) can be a useful resource for teachers working with a functional academic curriculum.

Beakley and Yoder (1998) developed an example of teaching functional academic skills to middle school students with moderate disabilities through a community-based, embedded-approach curriculum. Students developed functional academic skills in the following ways:

- We enhance *reading recognition and comprehension skills* by using shopping lists, reading directions, reading product information, and enjoying magazines and library books.
- Students improve their *math skills* by adding cost totals, using a calculator, and handling money. Students use a classroom banking program to learn banking skills, as well as managing the money the students bring to make purchases on shopping trips.
- Students use *writing skills* by applying for an identification card, using the card for completing personal information, and writing letters to complement a postal unit. (Beakley & Yoder, 1998, p. 18)

THEORY TO PRACTICE

➡ Meet with a special education teacher to discuss how he or she addresses students' functional academic skills. Which of the three approaches described in this section most closely resembles this teacher's approach? How much importance does the teacher place on this curriculum? How does he or she monitor student achievement in this curricular option and the students' possible needs to move into the academic structure of the general education curriculum, with and without modifications?

➡ Observe a teacher's lesson addressing functional academic skills. What skills, understandings, and knowledge does the lesson target? What type of approach to the teaching of functional academics did the teacher take? How did students respond to the lesson? How did the teacher address the issue of generalization? How does this lesson relate to general education curriculum with and without modifications? What impact might the lesson have on a student's life outside of school?

DAILY AND COMMUNITY LIVING SKILLS

Daily and community living skills are life skills that allow students to deal with current and future adult day-to-day demands and responsibilities. Usually, general education peers readily learn these skills as they participate in home and community activities. In contrast, students with disabilities many times require direct and intensive instruction in order to acquire and generalize these skills to school, family, and community contexts. According to Mercer (1997), a functional, life skills–based curriculum is appropriate for those secondary-age students who demonstrate very low academic skills, defined by Mercer to be below the fourth grade level. We suggest that this curriculum applies to special education students of other ages and performance levels as well.

Representative Content

We have selected the "Domains of Adulthood" model proposed by Cronin and Patton (1993) to explain and describe this curriculum. Cronin and Patton (1993) identify six key curriculum domains that come under the umbrella of daily and community living skills. Exhibit 4.4 highlights these domains and their subdomains and life demands. For example, the subdomains of employment/education are (a) general job skills, (b) general education/training considerations, (c) employment setting, and (d) career refinement and reevaluation. Working with this model and a model developed by Loyd and Brolin (1997), we choose to address seven domains within the daily and community living skills curriculum: (a) career and vocational education, (b) home and family, (c) leisure pursuits, (d) community involvement, (e) physical/emotional health, (f) self-determination, and (g) social skills. In the remainder of this next section we describe each of them.

EXHIBIT 4.4

Domains of Adulthood

DOMAIN	SUBDOMAIN	LIFE DEMANDS
EMPLOYMENT/ EDUCATION	*General Job Skills*	seeking and securing a job learning job skills maintaining one's job understanding fundamental and legal issues
	General Education/ Training Considerations	knowing about education/training options gaining entry to post-secondary education/training settings (higher education, adult education, community education, trade/technical schools, military service) finding financial support utilizing academic and system survival skills (e.g., study skills, organizational skills, and time management) requesting employment services when needed (e.g., Department of [Vocational Rehabilitation], unemployment) accessing support services of training setting
	Employment Setting	recognizing job duties and responsibilities exhibiting appropriate work habits/behavior getting along with employer and co-workers understanding company policies (e.g., fringe benefits, wages, sick/personal leave, advancement procedures) understanding take-home pay/deductions managing employment-related expenses (travel, clothes, dues) understanding OSHA regulations
	Career Refinement and Reevaluation	revitalizing career choice exploring alternative career options pursuing career change

(continued)

EXHIBIT 4.4

Domains of Adulthood
(continued)

DOMAIN	SUBDOMAIN	LIFE DEMANDS
HOME AND FAMILY	*Home Management*	setting up household operations (e.g., initiating utilities) arranging furniture and equipment identifying and implementing security provisions and safety procedures cleaning dwelling maintaining and landscaping a yard laundering and maintaining clothes and household items performing/contracting for home repairs/improvements and regular maintenance storing household items maintaining automobile(s) and equipment, appliances, etc. reacting to environmental dangers (e.g., pollution, extreme weather conditions)
	Financial Management	creating a general financial plan (e.g., savings, investments, retirement) maintaining a budget using banking services paying bills establishing a good credit rating purchasing day-to-day items (clothes, food, etc.) renting an apartment selecting and buying a house (building new/purchasing existing) making major purchases (e.g., auto, computer) determining payment options for major purchases (cash, credit, layaway, debit card, finance plan, etc.) preparing and paying taxes buying insurance purchasing specialty items throughout the year (e.g., birthday gifts, Christmas gifts, etc.) planning for long-term financial needs (e.g., major purchases, children's education) obtaining government assistance when needed (e.g., Medicare, food stamps, student loans)
	Family Life	preparing for marriage, family maintaining physical/emotional health of family members maintaining family harmony scheduling and managing daily, weekly, monthly, yearly family events (e.g., appointments, social events, leisure/recreational pursuits) planning and preparing meals (menu, buying food, ordering take-out food, dining out) arranging for/providing day care (children or older relatives) managing incoming/outgoing mail
	Child Rearing	acquiring realistic information about raising children preparing for pregnancy and childbirth understanding childhood development (physical, emotional, cognitive, language) managing children's behavior preparing for out-of-home experiences (e.g., day care, school) helping children with school-related needs hiring and training in-home babysitter
LEISURE PURSUITS	*Indoor Activities*	playing table/electronic games (e.g., cards, board games, puzzles, Nintendo, arcades, etc.) performing individual physical activities (e.g., weight training, aerobics, dance, swimming, martial arts) participating in group physical activities (e.g., racquetball, basketball) engaging in individual hobbies and crafts (e.g., reading, handicrafts, sewing, collecting)
	Outdoor Activities	performing individual physical activities (e.g., jogging, golf, bicycling, swimming, hiking, backpacking, fishing) participating in group physical activities (e.g., softball, football, basketball, tennis) engaging in general recreational activities (e.g., camping, sightseeing, picnicking)

DOMAIN	SUBDOMAIN	LIFE DEMANDS
	Community/ Neighborhood Activities	going to various ongoing neighborhood events (e.g., garage sales, block parties, BBQs) attending special events (e.g., fairs, trade shows, carnivals, parades, festivals)
	Travel	preparing to go on a trip (e.g., destination, transportation arrangements, hotel/motel arrangements, packing, preparations for leaving home) dealing with the realities of travel via air, ground, or water
	Entertainment	engaging in in-home activities (e.g., TV, videos, music) attending out-of-home events (e.g., theaters, spectator sports, concerts, performances, art shows) going to socially oriented events (e.g., restaurants, parties, nightclubs) and other social events
COMMUNITY INVOLVEMENT	*Citizenship*	understanding legal rights exhibiting civic responsibility voting in elections understanding tax obligations obeying laws and ordinances serving on a jury understanding judicial procedures (e.g., due process, criminal/civil courts, legal documents) attending public hearings creating change in the community (e.g., petition drives)
	Community Awareness	being aware of social issues affecting community knowing major events at the local, regional, national, world levels using mass media (TV, radio, newspaper) understanding all sides of public opinion on community issues recognizing and acting on fraudulent practices
	Services/ Resources	knowing about the wide range of services available in a specific community using all levels of government agencies (tax office, drivers license [DMV], permits, consumer agencies [BBB]) accessing public transportation (trains, buses, subways, ferries, etc.) accessing private services (humane society, cable services, utilities [phone, water, electric, sewage, garbage]) accessing emergency services/resources (police, EMS, hospital, fire, civil defense, [911]) accessing agencies that provide special services (advocacy centers) securing legal representation (e.g., lawyer reference service)
PHYSICAL/ EMOTIONAL HEALTH	*Physical*	living a healthy lifestyle planning a nutritional diet exercising regularly as part of lifestyle having regular physical/dental checkups understanding illnesses and medical/dental needs across age levels using proper dental hygiene/dental care preventing illness and accidents recognizing health risks recognizing signs of medical/dental problems reacting to medical emergencies administering simple first aid using medications providing treatment for chronic health problems recognizing and accommodating physical changes associated with aging recognizing and dealing with substance use/abuse

(continued)

EXHIBIT 4.4

Domains of Adulthood
(continued)

DOMAIN	SUBDOMAIN	LIFE DEMANDS
PHYSICAL/ EMOTIONAL HEALTH *(continued)*	*Emotional*	understanding emotional needs across age levels recognizing signs of emotional needs managing life changes managing stress dealing with adversity and depression dealing with anxiety coping with separation/death of family members and friends understanding emotional dimensions of sexuality seeking personal counseling
PERSONAL RESPONSIBILITY AND RELATIONSHIPS	*Personal Confidence/ Understanding*	recognizing one's strengths and weaknesses appreciating one's accomplishments identifying ways to maintain or achieve a positive self-concept reacting appropriately to the positive or negative feedback of others using appropriate communication skills following one's religious beliefs
	Goal Setting	evaluating one's values identifying and achieving personal goals and aspirations exercising problem-solving/decision-making skills becoming independent and self-directed
	Self-Improvement	pursuing personal interests conducting self-evaluation seeking continuing education improving scholastic abilities displaying appropriate personal interaction skills maintaining personal appearance
	Relationships	getting along with others establishing and maintaining friendships developing intimate relations deciding upon potential spouse or partner being sensitive to the needs of others communicating praise or criticism to others being socially perceptive (e.g., recognizing contextual clues) dealing with conflict nurturing healthy child/parent interactions solving marital problems
	Personal Expression	sharing personal feelings, experiences, concerns, desires with other people writing personal correspondence (e.g., letters, notes, greeting cards)

Source: From *Life Skills Instruction for All Students with Special Needs: A Practical Guide for Integrating Real-Life Content into the Curriculum* (pp. 16–19), by M. E. Cronin and J. R. Patton, 1993, Austin, TX: ProEd. Used with permission.

Career and vocational education

This is the domain where students develop skills for preparing for, seeking, and maintaining work. This includes career education as well as vocational preparation for transition to the world of employment. The Federal Register (October 22, 1997) defines vocational education as:

> organized educational programs that are directly related to the preparation of individuals for paid or unpaid employment, or for additional preparation for a career requiring other than a baccalaureate or advanced degree (34 CFR §300.24(b)(4) p. 55073)

The SCANS Report from the U.S. Department of Labor identifies five competencies and a three-part foundation of skills and personal qualities needed for solid job performance (Secretary's Commission on Achieving Necessary Skills (hereafter cited as SCANS, 1991)). The competencies "span the chasm between school and the work place" (SCANS, 1994, p. 4), and the foundations that "lie at the heart of job performance" (p. 3). Exhibit 4.5 provides an example of one SCANS competency. The key dimensions of the competency are defined, and examples of tasks or performances that illustrate the use of the interpersonal skill are given (Copple et al., 1993) (see the work by Copple and others for details about teaching this and other SCANS competencies in the schools).

EXHIBIT 4.5

Example of a SCANS Interpersonal Competency

Participates as a Member of a Team. Works cooperatively with others and contributes to group with ideas, suggestions, and effort.
Examples: • collaborate with group members to solve a problem;
  • develop strategies for accomplishing team objectives; or
  • work through a group conflict situation.

Teaches Others. Helps others learn.
Examples: • train a colleague on-the-job; or
  • explore possible solutions to a problem in a formal group situation.

Serves Clients/Customers. Works and communicates with clients and customers to satisfy their expectations.
Examples: • demonstrate an understanding of who the customer is in a work situation;
  • deal with a dissatisfied customer in person; or
  • respond to a telephone complaint about a product.

Exercises Leadership. Communicates thoughts, feelings, and ideas to justify a position; and encourages, persuades, convinces, or otherwise motivates an individual or group, including responsibly challenging existing procedures, policies, or authority.
Examples: • use specific team-building concepts to develop a work group;
  • select and use appropriate leadership styles for different situations; or
  • use effective delegation techniques.

Negotiates. Works toward an agreement that may involve exchanging specific resources or resolving divergent interests.
Examples: • develop an action plan for negotiating;
  • write strategies for negotiation; or
  • conduct an individual and a team negotiation.

Works with Cultural Diversity. Works well with men and women and with a variety of ethnic, social, or educational backgrounds.
Examples: • demonstrate an understanding of how people with differing cultural/ethnic backgrounds behave in various situations (work, public places, social gatherings); or
  • demonstrate the use of positive techniques for resolving cultural/ethnic problem situations.

Source: From Copple, C. E., Kane, M., Matheson, N. S., Meltzer, A. S., Packer, A., & White, T. G. SCANS in the Schools. In Secretary's Commission on Achieving Necessary Skills, *Teaching the SCANS Competencies* (pp. 10–11), 1993, Washington, DC: U.S. Dept. of Labor.

As Exhibit 4.5 demonstrates, identified competencies needed in the workforce can be easily translated to similar ones needed by students for school and a variety of community-based activities. Therefore, employment skills do not have to be postponed until the student is seeking employment or working at a job site.

Teachers may want to examine some existing curriculum before determining on-going careers and vocational education programming for their students. Razeghi (1998) identifies four phases of career education, similar to those that Bronlin (1991) describes (see Table 4.1). Razeghi suggests that career awareness begin in preschool and be extended through the elementary grades. Like other content within a life skills curriculum, skills, understandings, and knowledge do not have to be developed separately from the general education curriculum. In many instances, career and vocational education skills may be embedded in general education curriculum or presented through an overlapping curricular arrangement. Razeghi (1998) illustrates how career and vocational education goals can be related to general education objectives. For example, if the general education objective is "Given a list of 10 words, student will alphabetize them with 90% accuracy using first and second letters," a related career objective could be "Student will identify six careers in which alphabetization is used" (p. 153).

TABLE 4.1 PHASES OF CAREER EDUCATION

PHASES	PURPOSE	TECHNIQUES
Career awareness Begins in preschool and can extend through sixth grade. Covers all aspects of the world of work and provides foundation for all further career education. Numerous careers introduced.	To stimulate the student's interest in work as it relates to self, home, family, and the community.	Infusion of career education concepts into all instructional areas, small-group discussions, games, projects, role plays and skits, simulations, interviews, guest speakers, field trips, career learning centers, cooperative learning.
Career orientation Can begin in elementary grades, in conjunction with awareness activities. Provides link between the awareness and exploration phases. Builds on the occupational knowledge and self-awareness acquired during the previous phase, but changes focus of instruction so that students look at occupations in terms of "what do I want to be."	To provide students with occupational knowledge, self-knowledge, and decision-making skills that will help them to begin narrowing their career choices.	Infusion of career education concepts into all instructional areas, small-group discussions, games, projects, role plays and skits, simulations, interviews, guest speakers, field trips, career learning centers, cooperative learning, competency-based instruction.
Career exploration Intended for implementation in seventh through ninth grade. Can include prevocational education for those who want and need it. Introduction of various tools, terminology, and basic skills prepares students for vocational education and other types of career preparation.	To provide students with more information, knowledge, and skills necessary for making a tentative career decision in order to complete viable career and transition plans.	Infusion of career education concepts into all instructional areas, projects, games, role plays and skits, simulations, hands-on activities, interviews, guest speakers, field trips, career learning centers, cooperative learning, competency-based instruction, prevocational education, individual and group counseling, career interest inventory, volunteer work, job shadowing, prevocational courses, part-time job.
Career preparation Can begin in 10th grade and extend into college, university, community college, technical school, or other settings. Upon completion of this phase, student should possess necessary competencies and skills to successfully enter job market. Can include vocational education and professional technical training. Not all students with disabilities require or want such training, but it should be available to those who need it.	To provide opportunities for the development of skills needed to effectively function in a selected career area.	Vocational (career) assessment, vocational education, individual and group counseling, job placement and work experience, job coach, on-the-job training, community college, college or university, professional technical school, apprenticeship, military.

Source: From "A First Step Toward Solving the Problem of Special Education Dropouts: Infusing Career Education into the Curriculum," by J. A. Razeghi, 1998, *Intervention in School and Clinic, 33*(3), p. 151. Copyright 1998 by PRO-ED, Inc. Reprinted by permission.

Because of the significance of career and vocational education curricular topics, we have chosen to present this content as a separate component of life skills curriculum: transition. We present information about transition in the final section of this chapter.

Home and family

As indicated in Exhibit 4.4, this is the domain of the daily and community living skills curriculum where students develop the skills and understandings they need to function independently and participate in activities occurring within the home and with family members. Again, the majority of students without disabilities will not require direct instruction in this domain at such a basic level, but instead will gain these skills through interactions with family members and, possibly, through participation in the general education social science, home economics, and health sciences curriculum. In contrast, many students with disabilities will develop these basic foundation skills only through specialized instructional programs taught at school and carried over to the home by parents and other caregivers.

Leisure pursuits

This is the domain of the daily and community life skills curriculum that addresses how individuals spend time outside work and school. Identification of its content is only limited by teachers' or parents' imaginations. Recreational activities identified by Westling and Fox (1995) include games (e.g., board and card games), sports, camping and being in the outdoors, studying nature, hobbies, arts and crafts activities, and participation in cultural and entertainment opportunities. Participation in leisure pursuits offers multiple benefits to students. Among these benefits are:

> developing friendships, exploring interests, and learning skills. Students also learn
> to budget and use money, to identify and use transportation and community re-
> sources, and to prioritize time. (Johnson, Bullock, & Ashton-Schaeffer, 1997, p. 30)

Skills that are introduced at school and included in IEPs may be developed, reinforced, and generalized through student participation in leisure pursuits (Johnson, Bullock, & Ashton-Schaeffer, 1997).

Although many leisure activities are available to individuals with disabilities, their participation may not be as easily gained as the participation of their nondisabled peers, because of possible needs for modifications and adaptations. For example, a student with a physical disability may want to participate on a soccer team but be unable to run the length of the field several times during the game. That student, however, can learn to play a certain position on the field, and when the ball comes to that area of the field, the child is able to participate. Because of their need for modifications or adaptations, individuals with disabilities may not feel comfortable or confident in pursuing leisure activities. They may need adapted physical education in school and other special strategies, techniques, or equipment and extra encouragement from parents, siblings, and others in order to participate. Thus it is important to plan a leisure pursuits curriculum systematically so students with disabilities learn to engage in and enjoy leisure pursuits throughout life.

Community involvement

This is the domain where individuals learn to become active members of their community by participating in community events and fulfilling their roles as citizens (e.g., following community rules, recycling, volunteering, joining PTA or church, voting). They develop community awareness by reading the paper, listening to the radio, or watching television to learn of community events, and they learn about community agencies (e.g., Social Security, Public Health, SPCA, Social Services, YMCA, and Mental Health)—the services they provide and how to gain access to those services.

Development of citizenship skills could occur within the general education curriculum, with modifications as needed. A multilevel curriculum approach may be most helpful. For instance, when learning and teaching about local laws and ordinances, general education peers may be required to demonstrate understanding of how local laws and ordinances come into existence, and the role they as citizens play in influencing laws and ordinances. At the same time, those students with disabilities who benefit from modifications may be required to demonstrate their understanding of the existence of laws and ordinances and specify their role as a citizen in following them.

Developing awareness of and gaining access to community resources may be a very worthwhile challenge for individuals with disabilities. While students are in the school system, IEP and ITP meetings assist students, parents, teachers, and administrators in coordinating necessary resources. In many cases, these services are provided directly at the site or through coordination efforts by someone at the school site. However, once a child transitions out of school the responsibility for acquiring knowledge of and access to these resources transfers to the student and/or the parent/caregiver. The purpose of an Individualized Transition Plan (ITP) is to ease this transition and to provide a link between the services available at the school site and those the individual needs as an adult. Providing explicit information about and preparation for accessing these resources and services and monitoring their delivery can greatly help individuals with disabilities to maintain independence in their adult years.

Physical/emotional health

This is the domain of the daily and community living skills curriculum where students focus on both physical and emotional health issues. Physical needs are related to the self-help skills of the home and family domain but extend also to the ability to plan and prepare nutritious meals; to participate in exercise programs to maintain health; to address first-aid and medication concerns; and to participate in medical checkups. Because individuals with disabilities may have many complex physical and health-related needs, a curriculum aimed at managing those needs may be necessary. With instruction, some students will be able to manage their physical and health-related needs on their own; other students will need to be able to inform other people or rely on others to attend to their needs. For example, some students will be on regimens that require them to take medications at prescribed times. Some individuals with disabilities will be able to manage this drug therapy schedule; others may need reminders (e.g., photographs showing the time and medication to be taken posted in a prominent place); still others will need the help of a caregiver to follow through with the drug regimen. Some individuals with disabilities will be able to learn nutritious meal planning with and without supports (e.g., cue cards, prepared foods, or having someone make the meals of their choice); others will need to have others plan and prepare their meals.

Emotional needs deal with the students' ability to handle the ups and downs of life. This is the primary area of disability for some students. They may require mental health supports (e.g., extensive counseling for several years or throughout their life span). They may also need to manage drug regimens in order to manage their mental health. In other cases, individuals with disabilities may need to develop coping strategies and skills for responding appropriately to and the handling of personal crises such as a death in the family, the loss of a friendship, or feelings of isolation or depression. Mental health services may be delivered at the school site in conjunction with the academic program. In other instances, mental health services are provided outside the school environment.

Regardless of service delivery—whether in or outside school—it is important for teachers, parents, students, therapists, counselors, and other mental health personnel to communicate and work together for the benefit of the individual student. Common goals and consistent use of reinforcers or other behavioral/emotional intervention plan components (e.g., helping a student self-monitor and self-regulate behaviors) should be in place across environments to provide a sense of security for the child (e.g., the child knows what will happen across different environments and situations and will feel supported by those around him or her). These intervention plans assist the child in generalizing across therapeutic, academic, and home and community settings.

Self-determination

As defined by Serna and Lau-Smith (1995, p. 144),

> *Self-determination refers to an individual's awareness of personal strengths and weaknesses, the ability to set goals and make choices, to be assertive at appropriate times, and to interact with others in a socially competent manner. A self-determined person is able to make independent decisions based on his or her ability to use resources, which includes collaborating and networking with others. The outcome for a self-determined person is the ability to realize his or her own potential, to become a productive member of a community, and to obtain his or her goals without infringing on the rights, responsibilities, and goals of others.*
> [With modification in the use of italic type and print.]

Martin and Marshall (1995, p. 149) identify seven self-determination concepts: (a) self-awareness (e.g., identifying one's own needs, interests, and values; identifying and understanding one's own strengths and limitations); (b) self-advocacy (e.g., assertively stating one's own wants, needs, and rights; determining, pursuing, obtaining, and evaluating needed supports; conducting one's own affairs); (c) self-efficacy (e.g., expecting to achieve personal goals); (d) decision making (e.g., setting goals and developing a plan to achieve those goals); (e) independent performance (e.g., completing tasks and employing self-management strategies); (f) self-evaluation (e.g., comparing work performance to a standard); and (g) adjustment (e.g., changing goals, strategies, and plans as needed).

Different programs have been and continue to be developed to respond to the emergence of a self-determination curriculum. One example is the *Take Charge* program. The *Take Charge* (1994) program, developed by Dr. Laurie Powers and colleagues at Dartmouth University (Powers et al. 1996a; Powers et al. 1996b), provides adolescents who are physically challenged with opportunities to experience and incorporate self-determination skills into their lives. Because the ultimate goal of the program is independence, the information presented easily transfers across a variety of student populations. The *Take Charge* program helps students to develop self-determination skills across the major domains of their lives of work, daily life, school/college, and recreation/friendship.

Take Charge identifies four elements integral to self-determination. Specifically, a student must be given the (a) information needed to make choices, plans, and decisions, (b) opportunity to perform the chosen activity in an authentic situation, (c) skills required to be successful at the activity, and (d) support from facilitators and parents to carry out their plans. Exhibit 4.6 presents a summarization of the program.

The *Take Charge* approach uses a five-step sequential process. The five steps are (a) Dream, (b) Set Goals, (c) Problem-Solve, (d) Plan, and (e) Do It. the steps can be linked to a first-letter mnemonic memory device for ease, which translates to: (1) Dream . . . *Domino's,* (2) Set Goals . . . *Serves,* (3) Problem-Solve . . . *Pepperoni,* (4) Prepare . . . *Pizza,* and (5) Do It . . . *Daily.*

The first step, DREAM, takes the student on a journey to his or her future. The facilitator encourages the student to imagine the options for his or her life a few years down the line. The student responds to questions about the four major domains of his or her life: (a) work, (b) daily life, (c) school/college, and (d) recreation/friendship.

The second step is to SET GOALS. The student selects one main goal and an additional back-up goal that are meaningful in the context of his or her life. The student then makes a commitment to reach his or her goal.

The third step, in which the student begins to make the goal a reality, is to PROBLEM-SOLVE. Considering what needs to be done to accomplish the goal, what will be difficult to accomplish, and the easiest way to conquer the difficulties, the student attacks each part of the activity to identify the best possible Game Plan. The facilitator can incorporate a traditional task analysis to uncover potential snags, have the student do a guided-practice/dry run, and then, together with the student, devise new strategies that promote student independence. The best practices, in a guided order, will be performed by the student.

The student assigns deadlines to all tasks needed to be completed before carrying out the plan, in the fourth step, PREPARE.

The fifth and final step, in which the dream becomes a reality, is DO IT. After completing the activity, the student will document the difficulties he or she encountered and the successes he or she achieved.

Source: From *Take Charge* A Program for Self-Determination for adolescents with physical disabilities. Presentation materials for conference, California Educators of Physically handicapped, Los Angeles, February, 1995. Also see Powers, et al, 1996. Used by permission. Summary by Gigi Whitford, teacher.

Self-determination implies making decisions according to one's own will. It involves the right of people to consider options, make choices, and have some control over their lives. Results of the National Consumer Survey of self-determination by people with mental retardation (Wehmeyer & Metzler, 1995) raises concern about what schools, families, and societies are doing and need to be doing to aid students in the development of their self-determination competencies. The study gathered data about self-determination as measured by individuals making choices about and taking control of very personal aspects of their lives. It revealed that most choices were not self-determined. A very large percentage of these adults did not choose where they live, most did not choose their roommates even with assistance, and many did not have a chance to decide what clothes they would wear each day. Such decisions are basic choices that many of us take for granted; they indicate the importance of the domain of self-determination in the daily and community living skills curriculum.

Social skills

Many students struggle with interpersonal relationships and the development of appropriate social interaction skills. But teachers, peers, and parents perceive children and youth with disabilities to be especially deficient in essential social process competencies (Hazel & Schumaker, 1987; Walker, Colvin, & Ramsey, 1995) and identify this curricular domain as a major concern for many individuals with disabilities. Students with a range of disabilities can experience difficulties in this area: students with visual impairment may need to be taught to approach others in social situations; students with learning, behavioral, and communication disabilities may need to learn how to read and respond appropriately to the social cues of others; and students with physical disabilities may need to develop alternative means for interacting socially with others especially if they are unable to communicate verbally. The presence or lack of social skills has profound implications for nearly every facet of the lives of students, whether at home, in school, or in the community (Morgan & Jenson, 1988). Getting along with classmates and teachers, with coworkers and bosses, and with family and community friends and acquaintances can greatly enrich an individual's life. Ongoing difficulties in this domain may leave individuals isolated and segregated from others and limit their potential to become independent, contributing, and productive members of a community.

Walker and colleagues (1983), cited in Walker, Colvin, and Ramsey (1995), define social skills as a

> *set of competencies that (1) allow an individual to imitate and maintain positive social relationships, (2) contribute to peer acceptance and to a satisfactory school adjustment, and (3) allow an individual to cope effectively and adaptively with the larger social environment. This definition encompasses the following three essential elements of social competence: (1) to recruit social-support networks and friendships, (2) to meet the demands of teachers who control classrooms and peers who control playgrounds, and (3) to adapt to changing and difficult conditions in one's social environment. (p. 227)*

Social skills content may focus on the development of prosocial skills or the replacement of inappropriate behaviors with prosocial responses. Development of initial and increasingly sophisticated prosocial behaviors is a starting point for social skills content. Learning how to exchange greetings and learning strategies for forming and maintaining interpersonal relationships are examples. Many times, students with disabilities do not possess the social skills to act or respond appropriately in certain situations. Some individuals may require instruction in how to join in a game they see on the playground; how to join a group of people at a lunch table; and how to participate in but not dominate a conversation. The teaching of prosocial skills and strategies can greatly ease student acceptance into the school and community. For instance, learning how to take turns during a conversation; how to introduce a peer to a friend, and a parent to an adult at the school; and learning how to resolve conflicts in positive, nonthreatening ways can aid a child in becoming a more positively received and sought-after member of the classroom, family, or neighborhood community.

Prosocial skill development has received increased attention in the curriculum development for students with behavior disorders or emotional disturbance as well as students with other disabilities. One example of a curriculum that develops these skills is *Skillstreaming,* developed by Goldstein and colleagues. For example, in *Skillstreaming the Adolescent* (Goldstein & McGinnis, 1997), skills such as asking a question, giving a compliment, asking for help, apologizing, understanding the feelings of others, standing up for one's rights, responding to teasing, and dealing with embarrassment are developed. *Skillstreaming* curriculum guides are also available for preschool and elementary-age children.

Students may be taught positive replacement behaviors as another approach to social skills curriculum. For example, when teased by others, the child may act out, yell at the teasers, or become physically aggressive toward them. These behaviors could be replaced with more positive behaviors such as learning to walk away from the situation, using I-statements ("I don't like it when you tease me because . . ."), and applying conflict management strategies (e.g., Schrumpf, Crawford, & Bodine, 1997). The learning of replacement behaviors results in the child's behavior becoming more socially acceptable, and many times the replacement behaviors serve as a natural reinforcer. In response to one of the new behaviors, those around the child may stop the teasing because they no longer get the response they want of seeing the child become angry and frustrated and possibly punished for his or her actions.

One way to describe social skills curriculum is to categorize social skills by the functions they serve. One function of social behavior, for instance, is to initiate. The *Syracuse Curriculum* (Ford et al., 1989), using the work by Meyer and colleagues (1985), identifies the social functions of skills. These can easily be translated into instructional objectives for students. Exhibit 4.7 from the *Syracuse Curriculum* provides examples of social skills functions at various school levels.

EXHIBIT 4.7	SOCIAL FUNCTION	AS PERFORMED BY A NONDISABLED CHILD	AS PERFORMED BY A CHILD WITH DISABILITIES
Syracuse Social Skills Curriculum	Initiate	Gets attention by approaching another person	Gets attention by pressing buzzer on wheelchair
	Self-regulate	Follows written directions	Follows directions by using picture prompt booklet
	Follow rules	Locates own school locker by its number	Locates own school locker by using color-coded symbol
	Request assistance	Verbally asks store clerk for location of desired item	Asks store clerk for location of desired item by showing picture card or coupon
	Indicate preference	Chooses to play with certain video games during leisure time	Communicates choice of leisure activity by using eye gaze

Source: From *The Syracuse Community-Referenced Curriculum Guide for Students with Moderate and Severe Disabilities* (p. 179), by A. Ford et al., 1989, Baltimore: Paul H. Brookes Publishing. Used with permission.

Other critical areas in the domain of social skills are friendship and a sense of belonging. Friendships are essential to any student's overall curriculum. Having friends at school to interact with, share ideas with, and to participate in events with (e.g., assemblies, trips, dances) adds a satisfying component to the school experience and allows for the development of interpersonal skills for future participation at work and work-related events and family and community-based leisure activities. Lutfiyya (1988), as cited in Falvey and Rosenberg (1995), identifies six conditions essential for the formation of friendships: (a) *opportunity*—having access to and being close to others; (b) *support*—having assistance in and opportunities to develop relationships (e.g., transportation to and from events); (c) *diversity*—having access to individuals who are different from oneself (e.g., students without disabilities, students from different cultures or racial backgrounds); (d) *continuity*—having opportunities to see and interact with the same people on a frequent basis (e.g., students with disabilities going to the same school as the other children in their neighborhood); (e) *freely given and chosen*—having opportunities to be involved in a reciprocal friendship, not one that is forced through artificial interactions or proximity.

The selection of social skills curriculum must include consideration of the sociocultural aspects of the curriculum to ensure that it reflects the norms and expectations of the community as well as the values and beliefs of the child and the child's family. Concerns with a mismatch between the school curriculum and family beliefs may be pronounced when working with children and parents from cultural and linguistic backgrounds different from the mainstream. Rivera and Rogers-Adkinson (1997) identify a set of social behaviors and describe how various ethnic and cultural groups may perceive those behaviors (see Table 4.2). As with all information of this type, readers must be careful not to generalize the behavior of individuals to what is listed as group characteristics—individuals within groups may have their own unique values and beliefs. The key here, and our reason for including this information, is to raise readers' awareness of differences and to encourage readers to consider those unique differences when planning a social skills curriculum.

TABLE 4.2 SOCIOCULTURAL ASPECTS OF SELECTING SOCIAL SKILLS CURRICULUM

SOCIAL BEHAVIOR	HISPANIC AMERICAN	AFRICAN AMERICAN	ASIAN AMERICAN	NATIVE AMERICAN
Behavioral and emotional expressiveness	restraint of feelings, particularly anger and frustration	high-context, rely on nonverbals	control of emotions and feelings, self-effacing, modest	introverted
Verbal expressiveness	limited verbal expressions toward authority figures	affective, emotional, interpersonal	formal one-way communication from authority figure to individual	indirect gaze when listening or speaking
Nonverbal expressiveness	preference for closer personal space avoidance of eye contact when listening or speaking to authority figures	preference for closer personal space importance placed on nonverbal behavior	preference for distance between speaker and listener	preference for closer personal space
Family orientation	deference and respect strongly emphasized patriarchal family structure pronounced extended family systems	respect for elderly emphasized, but taught not to trust all authority unquestioningly kinship and extended family bonds authoritarian childrearing practices	family is primary unit family solidarity, responsibility, and harmony dependence on family is fostered one-way communication with authority figures strong deference and respect emphasized loyalty to authority	obedience and respect for elders, experts, and those with spiritual powers is strongly emphasized emphasis on family responsibility supportive nonfamily or other helpers are incorporated into family network development of independence and autonomy emphasized
Concept of time	present time perspective relaxed about time, punctuality immediate short-term goals	oriented more to situation than time concrete, tangible, immediate goals	tradition, living with the past immediate short-term goals	time and place viewed as permanent, settled immediate short-term goals
Social orientation	collective, group identity interdependence cooperative rather than competitive emphasis on interpersonal relations	sense of "peoplehood" collective	mutual interdependence collective responsibility cooperative rather than competitive	group centered cooperative rather than competitive
Philosophy	spiritual/magical belief orientation conformity	religious, spiritual orientation	spiritualism, detachment conformity	spiritualism, seeks harmony
Control over environment	resides outside the individual	control is external	fatalism	harmony with the environment

Source: From "Culturally Sensitive Interventions: Social Skills Training with Children and Parents from Culturally and Linguistically Diverse Backgrounds," by B. D. Rivera and D. Rogers-Adkinson, 1997, *Intervention in School and Clinic, 33*(2), p. 77. Copyright 1997 by PRO-ED, Inc. Reprinted by permission.

THEORY TO PRACTICE

➡ Secure a copy of the Cronin and Patton (1993) and Loyd and Brolin (1997) curricular models for daily and community living skills. Compare and contrast the models. What are their differences and similarities? Select one domain within each of the models to study (e.g., personal responsibility and relationships) and examine it across the two models. From there, identify what you consider to be most critical to include in a student's curriculum. List these topics, and think about how these topics could be presented systematically to students for the year and simultaneously over the next few years, if necessary. Develop a plan for providing instruction in these skills and understandings through the general education curriculum. What modifications and adaptations would be necessary to make this curriculum available through general education learning experiences?

➡ Meet with a special education teacher to discuss how he or she presents daily and community living skills to his or her students. What topics within this curriculum does he or she consider to be most important? How are these topics represented in the students' overall curriculum? How are they represented in the students' IEPs and ITPs?

➡ Meet with a general education teacher to discuss the role of daily and community living skills curriculum in the general education curriculum. How familiar is this teacher with this curricular content? How important does he or she believe this curriculum is for all students and, specifically, for students with disabilities? Is this teacher currently integrating this curricular content into his or her curriculum? If yes, how is he or she doing that? If not, would the teacher consider its integration? If so, how would he or she go about it?

TRANSITION

Although Cronin and Patton (1993) and Loyd and Brolin (1997) include employment and occupational preparation as part of their models for daily and community skills, we believe that an additional area—transition—deserves specific attention and focus and that for some students it is a vital area of their overall curriculum. Transition addresses changes that children experience during all levels of schooling, not just when they exit high school.

For certain students—in particular, many with disabilities—major transitions can be defeating if the students do not have advance preparation as well as special assistance in making the transitions. Several points of transition occurring during school careers merit teacher attention. We identify three important types of transitions:

- *transition from one major school level to another,* such as from preschool to kindergarten, elementary to middle/junior high, and from middle/junior high to high school
- *daily transitions between service delivery situations,* such as from general to special education experiences, special to general education experiences, and school to community-based experiences
- *transitions from school to young adult roles and responsibilities,* such as from school to employment, school to postsecondary experiences, and school to the military.

Representative Content

There are general considerations for transition curriculum that go across those different types of transitions. Exhibit 4.8 presents a beginning list of common core topics of transition education curriculum. As the exhibit indicates, transition skills are needed in other areas of the life skills curriculum, including the domains of social skills and self-determination. Transition education curricular needs are reflected in general education curriculum options as well as in virtually all components of the life skills curriculum.

EXHIBIT 4.8

**Transition Skills Content:
Working Across All Transitions**

SELF-ADVOCACY
- ability to ask for needed accommodations
- ability to ask for assistance when needed
- ability to ask questions and seek out support of others

CURRICULAR PREPARATION
- awareness of what skills and understandings will be needed to be successful in the new learning experience
- mastery of prerequisite skills as a foundation for success in new learning experiences

BEHAVIORAL PREPARATION
- understanding of behavioral expectations of the new setting
- mastery of prerequisite behavioral skills and techniques to be successful in the new learning experience
- development of additional behavioral responses reflective of the new learning experience

SITUATION OBSERVATION AND PARTICIPATION
- ability to join a group
- knowing how and when to participate and when to be an observer

SOCIAL SKILLS
- demonstration of skills for interacting with others in positive and acceptable ways
- ability to make new acquaintances and friends
- ability to read social cues and respond appropriately
- awareness of who is in charge and ways to respond to them
- understanding of situational roles and responding appropriately

SELF-MANAGEMENT SKILLS
- ability to monitor own behavior
- ability to monitor work completed and to work/participate at an acceptable rate/degree

SELF-DETERMINATION
- ability to determine what needs to be done next and to take the initiative for doing it
- demonstration of confidence in ability to succeed in the new learning experience

Transition from one major school level to another

Transitions between school levels present major challenges for all students and, possibly, additional challenges for students with disabilities because of their unique disability needs (e.g., need for specialized support services, curricular adaptations and modifications, behavioral interventions, and mental health needs). One of the first transitions for many students is from preschool or the home environment to kindergarten. At this stage, the focus is generally on the readiness of the children for the social and behavioral demands of the kindergarten environment. One example of essential skills for a successful transition into kindergarten from preschool or home was developed by Chandler (1993) and is presented in Exhibit 4.9.

EXHIBIT 4.9	Recognizes when a problem exists.
Kindergarten Transition Skills: Self-Help Behaviors	Locates and cares for personal belongings.
	Avoids dangers and responds to warning words.
	Takes outer clothing off and puts it on in a reasonable amount of time.
	Tries strategies to solve problems.
	Feeds self independently.
	Cares for own toileting needs.

Source: From "Steps in Preparing for Transition: Preschool to Kindergarten," by L. K. Chandler, 1993, *Teaching Exceptional Children, 25*(4), p. 54.

As with other curricular options, adaptations and modifications may be necessary for the inclusion of students with disabilities to ensure their successful transition from one environment to another. A child with a physical disability may require assistance with removing her outer clothing, with feeding, and with toileting, yet be ready to participate in kindergarten. Such transition considerations must be made so as not to exclude students with disabilities and to ensure that children are prepared to make a smooth transition into their new learning environment.

Daily transitions between service delivery situations

Many students with disabilities move among multiple settings during their school day. These transitions require them to make adjustments, to be aware of expectations and routines within each environment, and to respond appropriately in order to be accepted. For example, Santos, a high school student with a learning disability, may participate in the general education curriculum with and without modifications for history, mathematics, and a business course in accounting, and may also participate in a special education–based curriculum for literature to receive specialized instruction in functional reading and writing skills. Santos may participate in a community-based career/vocational education exploration program, volunteering five hours per week at a local business and earn school credit for his service to the community. Each of these learning environments is likely to have unique expectations for behavior, social skills, and academic performance, as well as unique routines. Some students are able to discern these differences and make necessary adjustments; others need assistance, through a transition education curriculum, to achieve success and make transitions smoothly across these environments.

Design of this curriculum could begin with identifying the expectations and routines of each environment, and then move to identifying the skills and knowledge that the child will need to be successful. Santos, for example, may have need for developing skills in self-management and organization, working in small groups or independently, and taking notes in class. He may also need to participate in a self-advocacy and self-determination curriculum to prepare for work in the community.

Transitions from school to young adult roles and responsibilities

Wehman (1996) identifies seven areas in which students will make transitions when exiting high school. These seven are presented in Exhibit 4.10. Exhibit 4.11 presents one approach for planning these transitions. The plan lists multiple options in each category of desired postsecondary outcomes.

Employment	• working in competitive employment allows for the earning of a wage • working builds self-esteem and dignity • working assists individuals in making friends and developing networks of social support	**EXHIBIT 4.10** **Transitioning Out of High School**
Living Arrangements	• living at home • living independently • living in supported living environments (e.g., group homes)	
Getting Around the Community	• using public transportation, if available • having friends who drive • accessing other mobility supports (e.g., community vans for individuals with disabilities)	
Financial Independence	• planning savings and expenditure of money • understanding bills, budgeting • gaining enough awareness so as not to be susceptible to financial scams	
Making Friends	• needing to make social connections independently and form friendships with others • having the skills needed to seek out others • taking part in and initiating social interactions and activities with others	
Sexuality and Self-Esteem	• expressing sexuality • establishing own values	
Having Fun	• seeking out and participating in leisure activities • securing necessary equipment and adaptations to participate in family and community leisure activities	

Source: Adapted from Wehman (1996).

EXHIBIT 4.11

Transition Services Planning Guide

Based on _____ (student's name) _____ interests, aptitudes, and needs, the following desired postsecondary transition outcomes have been identified to date _____:

DESIRED POSTSECONDARY EDUCATION OUTCOME(S)	DESIRED POSTSECONDARY EMPLOYMENT OUTCOME(S)	DESIRED POSTSECONDARY COMMUNITY LIVING OUTCOME(S)
Adult Education _____	Full-Time Competitive Employment _____	Living alone, with Friends or Partner _____
Vocational Training _____	Part-Time Competitive Employment _____	Living with Family _____
Community College _____	Full-Time Supported Employment _____	Transportation Independently _____
College or University _____	Part-Time Supported Employment _____	Transportation Support _____
Tech Prep _____	Apprenticeship _____	Independent Living Support _____
Other _____	Sheltered Workshop _____	Community Participation _____
	Other _____	Other _____
Specialized transition services or planning needed in this area? Yes _____ No _____	Specialized transition services or planning needed in this area? Yes _____ No _____	Specialized transition services or planning needed in this area? Yes _____ No _____

STATEMENT OF NEEDED TRANSITION SERVICES:

Based on _____ (student's name) _____ interests, needs and desired postsecondary outcomes identified, this IEP team has determined that _____ is in need of specialized transition services and/or support in the following areas:

Desired Long-Range Outcome: _____

_____

_____

Annual Goal: _____

_____

_____

Annual Objective(s): _____

_____

_____

Activities/Resources: _____

_____

Time Line(s): _____ Review Date: _____

Person(s)/Agencies Responsible: _____

From "Transition for Youths with Learning Disabilities: A Focus on Developing Independence," by H. B. Reiff and S. deFur, 1992, *Learning Disability Quarterly, 15,* p. 243. Used with permission.

Although the primary focus of transition has been from school to work, more individuals with disabilities are now electing to go on to postsecondary education prior to entering the workforce full-time. Students with disabilities are choosing to attend vocational training schools, community colleges, and four-year colleges and universities. This transition raises different concerns for students and their parents as well as for service providers. Common concerns for this type of transition as highlighted by Kravets (1996) and Burke (1996) among others are presented in Exhibit 4.12. Students with disabilities may encounter numerous challenges once they are in these educational

AREA	CHALLENGES AND CONCERNS
Exploration	• determining goals and type(s) of school to address those goals • identifying schools that offer special programs and support services for individuals with disabilities
Admission Policies	• meeting grade-point expectations • meeting curricular expectations, especially if student was enrolled in special education curriculum for core courses (e.g., mathematics) • meeting testing requirements (e.g., gaining needed testing accommodations, ensuring school's acceptance of scores derived through modified testing situations)
Application Procedures	• securing and filling out forms
Transportation	• getting to and from school and classes: providing one's own personal transportation (e.g., driving), taking public transportation, having a friend or parent drive the student to school, going through a community agency that transports individuals with disabilities
Living Arrangements	• determining where to live while going to school: at home, on campus, with friends, independently, in a supported environment
Financial Considerations	• working: finding a job and setting realistic work hours • not working: securing financial aid, taking out a loan, making other arrangements

EXHIBIT 4.12

Common Postsecondary Education Transition Concerns

environments. Wehman (1996) identifies some of the challenges and barriers students may face when enrolled in these postsecondary institutions:

- Misunderstanding, distrust, and unwillingness to make accommodations from instructors, professors, and other school staff
- Discrimination on the part of faculty, staff, and students as a result of modification in course requirements or procedures requested by students with disabilities
- Poor access within and between buildings
- Limited parking areas designated as handicapped only; noncompliance with handicapped parking regulations by other students, faculty, staff, or state personnel; and lack of enforcement of handicapped parking
- Unavailability of tutors, readers, and other assistants, as well as limited special equipment and aids such as tape recorders and texts in alternative media (p. 65)

THEORY TO PRACTICE

➡ With parent permission, meet with a student with a disability to talk about his or her ITP and transitioning to young adult roles and responsibilities. How familiar is the student with his or her ITP? How active has the student been in planning for his or her transition? What are the student's primary goals? How are they reflected in the ITP? What is being done to support the student in achieving his or her goals? To what extent does it appear that local businesses and agencies are involved in supporting this student's transition to post–high school roles? What suggestions would you have for strengthening this student's transition?

➡ Make an appointment to meet with a representative of the disabled student services agency on your campus. What types of services and supports do they provide? How many students take advantage of these supports and services? What are the most common uses of the agency? What are the biggest challenges this agency faces in helping students with disabilities to transition and be successful on the college campus? What recommendations do you have for improving the program and services at your school?

CHAPTER SUMMARY

This chapter presents the third curricular option available to students with disabilities: life skills curriculum. A life skills curriculum consists of education in functional academics, daily and community living skills, and transition. It may be taught through the general education program or modifications of it, through additional curriculum taught in the general education classroom or separately from it or through different curricular combinations.

Curriculum in Modified Means of Communication and Performance

Read to find out the following:

■ what curricular options and interventions are available in these areas:
— modified means of physical task performance
— speech and language
— access, operation, and use of assistive technology
— augmentative and alternative means of communication
— modified means of information acquisition and management

■ the importance of curriculum in modified means of communication and performance for students with disabilities

All students need to develop communication and performance methods that enable them to participate in learning and other life activities. Some students with disabilities need other-than-typical means to do so. For example, some students with disabilities do not speak as a means of communication; they may sign, indicate requests through body movement, or communicate with others through conversation books or communication boards and other specialized communication methods. Curriculum in modified means of communication and performance provides students with personally efficient ways to show what they think, feel, know, and can do, and it prepares them with personally effective ways to obtain information from printed materials, places, and events, as well as from other people. Without this organized and structured curriculum, students will be left unnecessarily with insufficient skills to communicate and perform personally as fully as possible in school and other major life activities.

In this chapter we introduce five components of curriculum in modified means of communication and performance. Teachers who are qualified professionals prepared to teach in the area of a child's disability provide special education services in this curriculum. Standards adopted by professional organizations (e.g., Council for Exceptional Children, 1995) define minimum core and exceptionality-specific (disability-specific) knowledge and skills for special educators who teach students with particular exceptional needs. The five components requiring supplementary aids and services for students are (a) modified means of physical task performance; (b) speech and language; (c) access, operation, and use of assistive technology; (d) augmentative and alternative means of communication; and (e) modified means of information acquisition and management.

Assessment, planning, and implementation in these five areas often involve the participation of members of an interdisciplinary team whose members bring their specialized knowledge and skills into play. For example, educators providing special education services to students with visual impairments have expertise in teaching reading and writing in braille, and in using computer equipment with braille, enlarged screen displays, and speech output. Teachers with expertise in deaf education teach communication and language skills in special ways. Special educators serving students with orthopedic and health impairments have expertise in assessment and instructional interventions that require modifications and special conditions to meet these students' unique motor, health, alternative communication, and learning needs. Physical and occupational therapists have expertise in positioning and motor control recommendations and solutions. Speech-language specialists have unique expertise in providing intervention and services in speech, language, as well as augmentative and alternative communication. These educators and related service professionals, alongside general educators, parents, and students, will plan content and interventions based on knowledge about each child, the child's particular disability, the child's personal preferences, and the family's preferences.

Generally, content in modified means of communication and performance is taught to students with disabilities as they learn to perform tasks in naturally occurring situations and activities. However, students sometimes need extra time and specialized instruction for learning the modified content. Consequently, these curricular components may be treated in different ways: as an expansion to the core curriculum (Hatlen, 1996), a substitution for certain core curriculum, or a different curriculum which is taught separately or integrated into general education curriculum and its modifications.

COMPONENT 1: MODIFIED MEANS OF PHYSICAL TASK PERFORMANCE

In the sixth grade class today, several students will be giving oral reports as classmates take notes. The name of each student who will be giving a report is written on the chalkboard. The teacher calls the name of the first student on the list. The student picks up the handwritten copy of his report from his desktop, moves from his seat, and goes to the front of the class. He writes his report topic on the board next to his name, reads the report aloud, asks for questions, calls on students who raise their hands, and then responds to their questions. Before returning to his seat, he turns in his written report putting it in the basket provided for that purpose.

In this example, the student uses a complex set of physical tasks in order to respond to the oral report assignment: the student refers to his handwritten notes, speaks, writes, manipulates paper, and moves from one place to another. In the course of the report, the student may also draw on the chalkboard and respond to the gesture of a raised hand by pointing. Typically, students are able to perform all of these basic physical tasks with little difficulty, so that the focus of the activity is on the quality of the report itself, not on the student's performance of the physical acts associated with the presentation of the report. The physical tasks required to produce and deliver the report are part of the background, noticed only when the student has trouble doing one or more of the tasks.

What about students who are not able to do one or more of the physical tasks that are expected and a normal part of classroom and other life activities?

Those activities, among others, all fall under the component of physical task performance. One system for identifying and classifying these physical tasks was developed by Bigge (1988). To anticipate where students with physical impairments may have difficulties, Bigge and teacher candidates sought answers to the question: "What physical tasks are typically required of students in school subjects, in life skills curriculum, and authentic role performances?" Together they identified six means of physical task performance frequently required, separately or in combination, irrespective of content. These six means of physical task performance are: (1) gesturing, (2) speaking, (3) drawing, (4) handwriting, (5) showing dexterity, and (6) mobilizing.

Assessment of students' needs for intervention in the area of physical task performance may be accomplished through administration of the Bigge Inventory of Means of Task Performance (MTP) (see Chapter 8 on assessment methods and tools) or through use of similar tools. Based on assessment results, team members work collaboratively to prepare students with disabilities to use the typical means of physical task performance, to learn adaptive means of physical task performance, and/or to learn alternative means of physical task performance. The primary goal is to help students with disabilities demonstrate their abilities and to function meaningfully in natural environments. Each of these six means of physical task performance is next described.

Representative Content

Gesturing

Typically, people use gestures alone or with other actions to communicate to others. A nod affirms, a shake of the head says "no," a raised hand asks for attention, pointing indicates something wanted or indicates the correct answer, and a stare can direct someone's attention to something important. A significant look, a shrug, thumbs down, and a thousand other gestures compose a silent language of the body without which a major part of communication is lost.

Some factors may interfere with one's ability to learn or perform gestures. Cerebral palsy may limit control of muscles needed to make gestures. Health impairments may limit muscle control or strength. Blindness or low vision may eradicate or limit the ability to see the gestures of others and thus limit an individual's opportunity to learn gestures through observation and imitation. Needs for interventions become apparent. Students with physical disabilities may require instruction in how to perform functional physical movements or in how to perform alternative gestures, such as different eye movements, to communicate *yes, no,* and *I don't know*. Intensive instruction in the use of gestures may be required for students with visual impairments because they are unable to observe these gestures as they occur naturally as people interact with one another.

Speaking

Speech impairment is one of the largest categories of disability in special education. Students with a range of disabilities receive speech-language intervention. Students with learning disabilities, as well as individuals with low incidence and/or severe disabilities (e.g., hearing impairments, severe cognitive disabilities), may receive services. Intervention, including individual and small group speech-language therapy sessions outside the classroom as well as in-classroom and in-community programming, helps students improve their production of speech and development of expressive language. This intervention may be provided by specially prepared teachers (e.g., teachers of students who are deaf or hard-of-hearing) and by speech-language pathologists. Since speaking is so widely used by students in their communication and performance, we treat speech and language later in the chapter as a separate component of curriculum in modified means of communication and performance.

Drawing

From early childhood, children draw for personal pleasure or to communicate ideas. In school, drawing and related activities take on academic skill functions such as drawing straight lines to connect words with their definitions, underlining correct words and phrases, circling correct responses, and making *x*'s and filling in ovals on test forms with number 2 pencils. Students who for some reason have trouble physically making the required lines and other drawing marks may be at a disadvantage in daily lessons, testing, and other situations unless modifications are made.

Some possible factors that interfere with the ability to draw include poor control of shoulders, arms, and hands; poor hand-eye coordination; perceptual orientation difficulties; cognitive impairment; and an inability to see the product of their drawing. For example, students with cerebral palsy may lack the muscle control needed to manipulate a standard pen or pencil, a student with a learning disability may have an impairment in visual-motor integration (i.e., difficulty in reproducing, through drawing, what is seen), and students with low vision may have difficulty seeing the writing surface and the marks they make on that surface.

Curricular intervention in this area includes modification of posture to stabilize the student when drawing; use of drawing tools modified to accommodate motor impairment (e.g., a pencil with a specialized grip or the use of a different part of the body, such as teeth, to manipulate specialized pens and other marking tools); modification of the work space (e.g., allowing more work space to accommodate wider arm movements); development of techniques to direct others what to draw rather than drawing it oneself; and the use of computers for drawing.

Handwriting

Handwriting is connected with these basic drawing tasks but requires a different type of skill. Writing a personal signature, jotting down something to remember in school, writing checks, taking notes in school, writing thank-you letters, writing school assignments, and writing for personal pleasure are occasions when handwriting serves our needs. Handwriting allows us to preserve information and ideas so we can handily refer to them later. Moreover, handwriting is part of one's identity and is extensively required in school to demonstrate knowledge and competence.

Some factors that can interfere with the ability to write by hand include poor hand-eye coordination, perceptual orientation difficulties, directionality confusions, inability to control required muscles, low stamina or poor muscle tone, and inability to see the results of one's writing. For example, students with learning disabilities sometimes have perceptual trouble forming letters, positioning them on the lines of writing paper, and/or writing in an organized fashion on blank paper. These students benefit from learning strategies such as writing on raised-line paper, which provides them with kinesthetic cues, and using color coding to cue them where to start and stop when writing individual letters. As a prerequisite to independent writing, some students may be taught to write through writing in clay or sand to accentuate the feeling associated with letter formation. Others may learn mnemonic devices to aid memory of the features of certain letters. Still others benefit from learning verbal cues to remind them how to form letters. Students with orthopedic impairments may learn to write with adaptive writing tools such as pencils with built-up shafts and pencils in holders that clip onto the hand. Even with these tools, however, writing can be slow for those with physical impairments. When handwriting is not functional for some students, they can learn to use alternatives such as Braille and computer writing. We introduce curriculum in technology alternatives to handwriting later in the chapter.

Showing Dexterity

Holding, manipulating, and maneuvering objects are all variations of dexterity—primarily manual dexterity. Try to think of how the lack of ability to hold, manipulate, or maneuver things would affect your activities for the next 24 hours. Most of us give little or no thought to manual dexterity challenges such as managing our personal self-care needs; doing school and work tasks; entertaining oneself when alone; participating in sports, extracurricular, and leisure activities; and participating in various community activities.

Some possible factors that interfere with dexterity include movement impairments such as those resulting from cerebral palsy or muscular dystrophy; difficulties with fine motor control of hands and fingers; paralysis of the upper extremities; limp deficiency; and inability to observe others performing manipulative tasks to learn how they are done. Intervention involves the preparation of students to use adaptations within the curriculum and to request physical assistance from others so that they can accomplish fine motor tasks (e.g., holding, manipulating, maneuvering).

Students with severe dexterity limitations learn to use special remote control devices and procedures to control their personal environment: to operate the TV, VCR, and CD player, and to turn on lights, open doors, use the telephone, and operate kitchen appliances. Becoming a competent user of environmental control technology devices is frequently a significant outcome for many students with severe dexterity limitations. For instance, students with dexterity problems can learn to use only a single switch or an eye blink to conduct scientific experiments as they access specially designed access and simulation software on computers.

Curriculum that targets dexterity for students with visual impairments can be deliberately planned to teach tasks that sighted students learn incidentally. Exhibit 5.1 presents an example of procedures that a teacher of students with visual impairments may apply when teaching a young student to complete an every-day classroom activity.

EXHIBIT 5.1

Representation of Content for Teaching Students Who Are Blind to Do Tasks They Have Never Observed

Thomas seems to be lost when the class is asked to put their books back on the reference bookshelf. The teacher does the following to assist Thomas in gaining this physical behavior required in the classroom. The teacher says,

"Come over here and I'll show you a trick about putting books on the shelf. We need to put your book on the bookshelf in front of you. We need to push these books to the left. I'll put my hand on the nearest book on the shelf. Check out where my hand is."

The teacher taps on the book cover so Thomas can find it.

Then the teacher instructs, "Push on my hand so we can move these books out of the way."

Thomas pushes so that the books on the shelf are pushed aside, making more room on the shelf.

The teacher states, "Now keep your hand there on the shelf in the empty space we just cleared. Pick up your book by the binding edge with your other hand. Hold it so the binding is up and down. Now put the book onto the shelf in the space you made."

The teacher reaches around the student's back and guides the book as the student pushes it onto the shelf.

"There it is. We did it together."

Next time, Thomas will not need so much help. Soon he will be able to do the task alone.

Source: Martha Pamperin, teacher of students with visual impairment, Davis, California.

Mobilizing

Try visualizing your typical daily activities, but visualize yourself as a wheelchair user who always requires assistance to move the chair. What immediately comes to mind about your mobility, comfort, and control over your life? Now think about physically moving from place to place in rooms, buildings, and playgrounds and on city streets without sight or hearing. How would your experience be different from that of individuals with sight and hearing? What would your challenges be? How would you achieve independence and be safe and efficient as you move about in these different environments? These experiences and challenges encountered by individuals with disabilities make self-mobility difficult and, at times, impossible. Factors that may limit an individual's mobility include disabilities affecting (a) muscles; (b) stamina and strength; (c) ability to see obstacles and destinations; (d) ability to hear voices, cars, and other sounds in the environment; (e) ability to determine position in space and in relation to desired destination; (f) a sense of direction; and (g) planning body movements.

Specialized curriculum in orientation and mobility (O & M) for students with visual impairments, which may also be generalized to other individuals with disabilities as well, prepares students to travel independently (or interdependently) to or through various types of environments (e.g., classroom, playground, residential and downtown areas) using various mobility strategies (on foot or as an aware and self-sufficient passenger). The outcomes of O & M instruction for students include developing the necessary skills for independent travel, taking and accepting responsibility for their actions, solving problems if/when the students become disoriented, and reorienting themselves with little or no help from others.

Related service providers often have major responsibilities for orientation and mobility skill development. O & M specialists, for instance, are authorized to teach skills of independent travel to children and adults who are blind or visually impaired (including those with any additional impairments). The ultimate goals of orientation and mobility training are to enhance orientation and promote independent mobility that is safe and efficient (Hill & Ponder, 1976). Exhibit 5.2 identifies some highly specialized content that O & M specialists teach.

Qualified teachers of students with visual impairments (VI teachers) also teach some of this content (e.g., noncane mobility skills, spatial concepts, and uses of landmark clues within classroom environments). VI teachers and, when appropriate, family members reinforce student learning of other content as guided by O & M instructors.

EXHIBIT 5.2 **Orientation and Mobility Content for Students with Visual Impairments**	1. Use of a long cane to detect obstacles, hazards, and drop-offs (e.g., curbs) in the path 2. Use of low-vision aids in travel (e.g. telescopic device) 3. Development of spatial concepts in travel (e.g. up-down; through-under; far-near) 4. Development of environmental awareness (e.g., What is a curb?) and community awareness (What is a post office and how does one use it?) 5. Development of orientation skills (e.g., use of environmental landmarks and clues; mental mapping of environments; planning efficient travel routes) 6. Development of noncane mobility skills (e.g., walking with a human guide) 7. Development of use of electronic travel devices (e.g., Mowat Sensor, a handheld device that vibrates when chest-high obstacles are in the travel path) 8. Development of community travel skills (e.g., crossing streets and using public transportation systems such as buses, subways, and trains) Source: Dr. Sandra Rosen, professor, O & M, San Francisco State University.

Examples of specific outcomes associated with orientation and mobility curriculum for sighted students include

- mobility with power chairs and other power mobility aids
- basic safety practices as a mobility aid user (use of safety belt; regulation of speed; regulation of travel directions and turns)
- directing wheelchair pushers and dissuading inappropriate pushers
- troubleshooting architectural and environmental barriers
- troubleshooting mechanical problems
- adaptive driver's training using modified car controls

In addition to O & M specialists, physical and occupational therapists, rehabilitation engineers, and special educators with expertise in the area of a student's disability assist in the development of similar kinds of skills (e.g., mobility with power and manual wheelchairs, mobility with crutches or other ambulatory aids). Additionally, teachers and parents provide opportunities for functional development and practice of orientation skills in home, school, and community environments.

THEORY TO PRACTICE

➡ Shadow a student with a physical disability through a typical day at school. Log the types of physical task demands the student encounters and what he or she does to respond to those demands. Identify natural supports found in the environment to assist the individual in meeting these demands. Identify barriers in the environment and instructional programs that interfere with the student's ability to demonstrate orientation and mobility skills safely. Develop a list of recommendations for modifying and adapting the environment to remove physical task barriers for the shadowed student. Discuss these recommendations with the student, parent, and teacher.

➡ Sit in on a general education classroom and observe and record all the physical task demands you see. Come up with an alternative way in which students with different disabilities might carry out each task. Consider the feasibility of your suggestions for implementation in general education classroom settings.

COMPONENT 2: SPEECH AND LANGUAGE

In the second grade class today, the students are participating in writing and illustrating a story. The class has decided that the story will be about their latest trip to the art museum and that each student will tell about his or her favorite piece of art by describing the piece and explaining through writing why they like it and then drawing it. Students are to work in small cooperative groups and each student will contribute to the story. Each group member will then tell about his or her favorite piece, show a drawing of it to others in the group, and read to the group what he or she has written about the piece. The written/oral work is to include complete sentences, incorporate specialized art vocabulary introduced in the unit, present ideas in a logical sequence, and support ideas through multiple details and examples. Each, in turn, will listen and learn from his or her peers.

In this example, students are required to demonstrate competence in a range of expressive and receptive language skills. The telling and writing about the trip assumes language skills in grammar, semantics, syntax, phonology, and morphology. Additionally, the social aspects of working in a group require students to demonstrate pragmatic skills, or the application of language skills within social contexts and responsiveness to context-related variables such as turn-taking, appropriate sharing of information, and ability to respond appropriately to the subtle verbal and nonverbal cues of group members. Students are also expected to listen to and process orally presented information effectively. The majority of these skills are part of the background of the activity, with the emphasis on shared learning and dialogue about the field trip.

What about students who are not able to perform all of these skills or who are just developing these skills? What if students have speech impairments that impede their ability to communicate with others? How will they perform in this situation, to what degree can they be contributing members of their groups, and—perhaps most important—what can these students gain from participation in this activity?

Students with almost any disability may have language difficulties. Speech-language services may focus on speech needs (i.e., articulation, fluency, voice) or language (e.g., semantics, syntax) and a combination of the two. When an individual receives services for speech therapy, the intervention focuses on the production of sounds, the fluency of speech, and the correct use of the voice. Language services focus on the functional uses of language, both verbal and nonverbal, to communicate with others.

Speech impairments are associated with the physical task of speaking. Speech impairments often result in difficulties in three areas: articulation, fluency, and voice. Conditions that can cause these disorders include cerebral palsy (which frequently results in poor control of the muscles involved in speech production), hearing loss, cognitive impairment, autism, and head trauma. *Articulation disorders* are primarily phonetic—affecting soundmaking, especially sounds used in speech (Crystal, 1992). Difficulties with the speech mechanism frequently impact students' abilities to produce sounds and sound combinations of the language. *Fluency disorders* include repeated interruptions, hesitations, or repetitions that seriously interfere with the flow of communication (Hardman, Drew, & Egan, 1996). *Voice disorders* include disorders of pitch (high to low), intensity (too soft or too loud), and quality (hoarseness, nasality, breathiness).

Interventions for articulation disorders aim to reduce or eliminate sound substitutions (e.g., the sound *w* for *r* as in *wadiation* instead of *radiation*), omissions (e.g., *mos* for *most*), as well as distortions and additions of certain sounds in speech. Interventions for fluency disorders aim at intelligibility through improvement in flow of speech in conditions such as cluttering and stuttering. Cluttering is speech that is rapid, disorganized, and filled with unnecessary words. Stuttering occurs when the speech flow is abnormally interrupted by repetitions, blocking, or prolongations of sounds, syllables, words, or phrases (Hardman, Drew, & Egan, 1996). Interventions for voice disorders help individuals relearn (or learn) speech production that is not so sufficiently different that it diverts attention away from the message to the voice (Hardman, Drew, & Egan, 1996). Intervention for voice disorders focuses on learning the correct usage of the voice box through such activities as breathing and use of the diaphragm. In some instances, it is necessary for students to learn augmentative communication and alternatives to speech such as manual signs, communication boards, and computerized devices. (Later in this chapter we introduce curriculum in the area of augmentative and alternative means of communication.)

Language skills are developed over time and with maturation. Typically developing language skills are marked by the achievement of language milestones. These milestones are highlighted in Table 5.1. Individuals with language disabilities may develop these skills at different times or may be unable to develop these skills as a result of their disability. We present this list of language milestones to provide readers with a sense of what is considered to be a typical, developmental sequence of language development. At times it may be helpful to refer to this table when one is interpreting the assessment findings of a student with an identified language disorder; the table may be less helpful when one is determining interventions for addressing a child's needs.

TABLE 5.1 LANGUAGE MILESTONES

AGE	PHONOLOGY	MORPHOLOGY AND SEMANTICS	SYNTAX	PRAGMATICS
Birth	Crying			
1 month	Attends and responds to speaking voice			
2 months	Cooing, distinguishes phoneme features			
3 months	Vocalizes to social stimulus			
4 months	Chuckles			Pointing and gestures
6 months	Babbling			
9 months	Echolalia	Understands a few words		Understands gestures: responds to "bye-bye"
12 months	Repeated syllables, jabbers expressively	First word		Waves "bye-bye"
18 months		Comprehends simple questions, points to nose, eyes, and hair, vocabulary of 22 words	Two-word utterances, telegraphic speech	Uses words to make wants known
24 months		Vocabulary of 272 words	Uses pronouns and prepositions; uses simple sentences and phrases	Conversational turn-taking

Source: From the manual of the *Bayley Scales of Infant Development.* Copyright © 1969 by The Psychological Corporation. Reproduced by permission. All rights reserved.

Representative Content

The primary components of language are described in Table 5.2. When working with students with speech and language disorders, speech-language pathologists or teachers may address all components listed in the table or they may focus upon specific ones identified as problematic through assessment. For example, if a student is having difficulty understanding the meaning of words spoken to him and is using a limited vocabulary when writing, the speech-language pathologist will most likely work on semantics to build the child's receptive and expressive vocabulary systematically. If a child is having difficulty in pragmatics, the pathologist, working in conjunction with the classroom teacher, may provide instruction in this skill area through role-play. During role-play, the student's attention will be directed to the speaker's use of nonverbal signals and other gestures used to communicate to others, and to the demonstration of the need to match language to the social context of the situation.

TABLE 5.2 COMPONENTS OF LANGUAGE

COMPONENT	DEFINITION	RECEPTIVE LEVEL	EXPRESSIVE LEVEL
Phonology	The sound system of a language and the linguistic rules that govern the sound combinations	Discrimination of speech sounds	Articulation of speech sounds
Morphology	The linguistic rule system that governs the structure of words and the construction of word forms from the basic elements of meaning	Understanding of grammatical structure of words	Use of grammar in words
Syntax	The linguistic rule system governing the order and combination of words to form sentences, and the relationships among the elements within a sentence	Understanding of phrases and sentences	Use of grammar in phrases and sentences
Semantics	The psycholinguistic system that patterns the content of an utterance, intent, and meanings of words and sentences	Understanding of word meanings and word relationships	Use of word meanings and word relationships
Pragmatics	The sociolinguistic system that patterns the use of language in communication, which may be expressed motorically, vocally, or verbally	Understanding of contextual language cues	Use of language in context

Source: From *Students with Learning Disabilities,* 5th ed. (p. 422), by C. D. Mercer, 1997. Reprinted by permission of Prentice-Hall, Inc., Upper Saddle River, NJ.

Students who are either deaf or hard-of-hearing may receive intensive curricular intervention in language development. As early as possible, children are given amplification and intensive intervention in language. It is the child's success in learning language that is a major determiner of how successful he or she will be in accessing the curriculum. It is not necessarily the deafness itself but how deafness is handled that is important for giving the child a strong language background. Special interventions and programming for these students may be instituted to counteract delayed language acquisition, information missed in the spoken language of others, inarticulate speech, and limited auditory perceptive skills caused by the hearing impairment. Exhibit 5.3 lists representative topics in language programming for students who are deaf or hard-of-hearing (Taylor, Sternberg, & Richards, 1995; Disability Research Systems, 1993).

EXHIBIT 5.3

Interventions in Language for Learners Who Are Deaf or Hard-of-Hearing

- Speech perception and production
- Utilization of visual, spatial, sequential, auditory, and language capabilities for concept development
- Language comprehension and production
- Vocabulary development
- Syntax and morphology development (structure and form of words as in grammar)
- Use of equipment such as amplification devices
- Strategies to avoid word omissions, inappropriate vocabulary, grammatical errors, and unnatural pauses

THEORY TO PRACTICE

➡ Observe a speech-language pathologist at work with an individual or a small group of students. What interventions/strategies are used to support students' acquisition of language development? How do the students respond to these interventions/strategies?

➡ Interview a special education teacher working with students who are deaf or hard-of-hearing to find out how he or she assists students in developing language concepts. What does the teacher identify as the students' biggest hurdles to language development? What has the teacher identified as key strategies, approaches, or curricular interventions for assisting students in this area?

➡ Observe a language arts or English class at any grade level, K–12. Identify the activities and tasks the teacher models and assigns that support student development of language skills. What language skills are being specifically targeted through each of these activities and tasks? How does the teacher introduce these skills and understandings to students?

COMPONENT 3: ACCESS, OPERATION, AND USE OF ASSISTIVE TECHNOLOGY

In the ninth grade physics class, students are required to use the computer for writing lab reports and for completing complex scientific calculations. Six computers in the lab are available for students as they work in lab teams to complete calculations and produce reports of their findings. These computer stations provide all the software and hardware (e.g., encyclopedias, printers, scanners, etc.) that the teams need to complete assignments. At the end of each lab session, team members move to the computers and enter data, analyze findings, and write up the final report.

This situation requires that all students have the skills necessary to use the lab equipment and to access, operate, and use the computers available for completing complex calculations and for generating reports. Requirements include being able to secure and manipulate the lab equipment—to turn on the computer, operate the specially developed software programs, and use this technology for solving programs and generating lab reports.

What about students who are not able to perform all of these skills or who, because of their disability, do not have access to needed tools and equipment and/ or are unable to manipulate or operate them? How can their situation be remedied in order to complete the assigned tasks and gain knowledge and skills?

Students who use assistive technology devices, or aids, and accompanying services can gain access to activities that otherwise would be inaccessible to them. An assistive technology device is

any item, piece of equipment, or product system, whether acquired commercially off the shelf, modified, or customized, that is used to increase, maintain, or improve functional capabilities of a child with a disability. (IDEA Amendments of 1997, Sec. 602(1))

Assistive technology may be nonelectronic and simple to learn to use, such as a book holder or a goose-neck microscope, or it may be technologically advanced, such as a customized computer. Assistive technologies are used to (a) augment a sense or movement, (b) circumvent a sense or movement, (c) provide alternatives or adaptation for means of communication and information expressed and received, and (d) provide means of performance in learning demonstrations and in varieties of educational and life activities (34 CFR §300.5).

Representative Content

In this section we introduce three areas of assistive technology: (a) access, (b) operation, and (c) functional use. These areas are not necessarily developed in this order, in a hierarchical fashion; they can be cyclical, as individuals' skills and needs demand. Illustrations of assistive devices are found in Figure 5.1, pages 132–136.

Access

Whenever possible, potential users should be physically able to set up and activate their assistive technology devices. People operate most standard equipment by using their hands directly to select and activate the parts desired (e.g., press keys, push buttons, pull levers). This may prove difficult for some students with motor, visual, and other disabilities. These students may require adapted methods and equipment to activate their devices (e.g., to turn them on, select and/or activate specific keys).

Three methods of accessing assistive devices are taught in the curriculum: (a) direct selection and direct selection with modifications, (b) use of single switches and (c) voice recognition. The needs of individual students determine which method or methods are taught. Each method is described briefly.

Direct selection is the most common means of accessing most technologies. Using their hands and fingers, students directly select the operating components of the device itself, pushing a button to start the device or selecting keys. Marking "home" keys and labeling switches with braille or with large-print labels are simple ways for many students with visual impairments to meet the direct selection challenges. Instead of using their hands and fingers to activate the keys, students with certain disabilities can learn to make direct selections with modifications, using other body parts, procedures or aids. For example, Chris, who has an orthopedic impairment that involves his hands, is taught to access the computer by directly selecting keys on the keyboard with a pointing stick, or wand, mounted to a helmet on his head. Another student may use a light sensor on a headband to select icons and combinations of them on his communication aid and, in this way, to activate different speech output messages. (See Figure 5.1f, p. 135.) Specially designed alternative keyboards provide another direct selection modification. They are typically flat, rectangular palates, usually larger than a standard keyboard, which can be customized in one or more of several ways to meet the user's need. Alternative keyboards take the place of standard computer keyboards, as in Figure 5.1h, bottom. They may have the same functions and offer the same choices as a standard keyboard but with larger, smaller or rearranged keys, or they may be customized to accommodate visual, communication, or cognitive needs of users (e.g., customized content on keys; enlarged labeling of content on switch or keys; reduced number of keys).

Certain students learn to use *single switches* (sometimes referred to as microswitches) or other mechanisms to access computers and other assistive devices when a direct selection method, even with modification, is not functional for them. Activating one or two switches with some body part (e.g., hand, elbow, foot, tongue) provides an alternative way to control a moving cursor to scan computer key choices shown on the screen and then to select from them the needed keys in sequence. Matthew is a beginning switch user. Learning the motor act of reliably activating a switch with his elbow took many months because of his severe motor impairment (see Figure 5.1b, p. 133). He and his family hope that some day he will learn to use his single switch as functionally as his idol, Stephen Hawking. This well-known scientist uses one switch and his very complex, computer-based communication device for all personal communication, university lectures, professional writing, and lectures he gives around the world.

A *voice recognition system* that accesses a computer is perhaps one of the most recent assistive technologies to be developed. Speech recognition is primarily a hands-free access method. Users "teach" computers to "recognize" their unique speech input when they say different letters, words, and computer functions, so the computer can respond to their voice input. The computer treats the information just as it would treat information coming from a standard keyboard. J.R. has an orthopedic impairment that affects his arm and hand use. Using special software, Dragon Dictate (Dragon Systems Products, Newton, MA), he is learning strategies to "dictate" words into a microphone and other special strategies required to access computers in a modified way. J.R.'s words are converted into text by the computer and displayed on the monitor.

Operation

As students gain access to aids and devices, they need to learn procedures to operate different features of them. Computers, communication aids, and other assistive devices and specialized software come with basic operations and additional options for users. Each has its own user's guide. Teachers refer to these guides, knowing that procedures may need to be customized for users with particular impairments.

Exhibit 5.4 provides information related to the use of special screen reading software to assist users in the operation of computers. This exhibit focuses on the needs of individuals with visual impairments who cannot see clearly what is on the computer screen. A synthesizer physically produces speech and a software program directs the synthesizer to say (read) the information appearing on the computer screen. This system also tells users what they are inputting from the keyboard (Espinola & Croft, 1992). Curriculum on how to use these technologies may be beneficial for students with other disabilities, such as those with learning disabilities, who benefit from operating a computer with screen reading capabilities.

EXHIBIT 5.4

Examples of Advanced Content in Assistive Technology Operation for Students Who Have Visual Impairments

READING ON COMMAND
Screen reading programs let you read the current, previous, and next character, word, or line. Some let you read by sentence and paragraph, as well.

KNOWING THE CONDITION OF TEXT
The screen reading program lets you control the announcement of punctuation, capitalization, color, or other attributes of the text you are reading. You can instruct the speech system to read or not to read punctuation, depending on whether you wish to skim the document or actually check for punctuation.

KNOWING WHERE THINGS ARE
Screen reading programs help you locate pockets of information on the screen. You can interrogate the program about the column and row location of the active cursor, text, or special characters (like smiley faces).

MOVING AROUND THE SCREEN
You can navigate around the screen by moving the arrow keys (up/down, right/left) as the application permits, and hear the text under the cursor read as you move the cursor through the text.

CONTROLLING THE SPEECH
You are in charge of how much of the screen you read, how fast, and at what volume and pitch. You should be able to interrupt speech instantaneously. Some or all of these parameters depend on the synthesizer you are using.

FINDING SPECIAL ATTRIBUTES
The screen reading program lets you search for attributes (inverse video, blinking text, graphic characters, color, and highlighted text).

MONITORING SCREEN CHANGES
Screen reading programs alert you to changes—either unexpected or recurring—in specified areas of the screen, such as error, status, and help messages. . . .

Source: Adapted from *Solutions: Access Technologies for People Who Are Blind* (pp. 49–50), by O. Espinola and D. Croft, 1992, Boston: National Braille Press. Used with permission.

Functional use

The goal of assistive technology access and operation is for one's independent or self-directed functional use of it—in other words, functional competence. Functional competence is the ability to use devices for communication and other purposes in contexts where and when communication and other functions occur naturally (Buzolich & Higginbotham, 1985). Functional competence is demonstrated when a student with low vision can use a large-print book or optical reading device and participate in a reading group with sighted classmates. Another example is a student with a learning disability using a word processing program to write a letter to a pen pal, take a spelling test, or respond to a variety of writing assignments. Functional competence is demonstrated because the individual is capable of using the device to perform a needed task in an authentic context.

Whether students with unique needs are functional users of their assistive technologies largely depends on the support they receive from others. Learning to use technology through structured lessons with teachers and service providers is vital but not enough. Its generalized use with a variety of people in natural situations where it is functionally useful also becomes important. As a result, teachers find themselves focusing on ways in which they and others—such as families, peers, and employers—can provide the support that results in effective and satisfied users of this technology. The "Make It Happen" feature provides examples of how members of a student's school, home, and community can support a student's use of assistive technology devices.

MAKE IT HAPPEN **Strategies to Support the Use of Assistive Technology by Students with Disabilities**

Strategies for Family Members
- Develop skills in operation of the assistive technology used by their child so they can troubleshoot problems their child may have while using the technologies at home and in the community.
- Demonstrate interest and pride in the child's accomplishments.
- Give the child plenty of time to access and operate his or her technologies.
- Provide meaningful opportunities for the child to use assistive technologies in various natural environments and with various people, including cultural or religious ceremonies.

Strategies for Peers
- Interact with users as they would with their other friends.
- Ask users to show them how the technologies work.
- Encourage users to engage in activities that require use of their technologies.
- Wait extra time for users to use technologies in activities, if necessary.
- Compliment users, if appropriate.
- Help others appreciate the opportunities made possible with assistive technologies.

Strategies for Employers
- Structure the job environment with needed furniture (e.g., raised desk for wheelchair user, larger table for specialized computer equipment).
- Explore the types of accommodations that would allow individual job seekers or employees to experience success on the job.
- Provide accommodations to ameliorate the functional limitations of job seekers.

- Provide users with opportunities to teach others about the technologies they use.

Strategies for Teachers

- Help families, peers, and employers implement supportive activities such as those listed above.
- Apply many of the same kinds of supports in the educational program as are listed above.
- Ensure that the student has technologies that match his or her needs, abilities, and technology preferences.
- Prepare the student with knowledge and skills needed for technical and functional uses of technologies.
- Procure needed repairs, replacements, or personal assistance with expedience to avoid a waste of time.
- Ensure that the school and other environments support and reward use.
- Engage students in curriculum that helps them learn to advocate for themselves and to solve problems related to their personal technology needs and preferences.

When selecting assistive devices for students, teachers must be sure to consider parents' needs and wishes as well as their cultural perspectives on the use of these devices. Hourcade, Parette, and Huer (1997, p. 40) identify a number of issues to consider when assistive devices are introduced to families:

- When we fail to involve the family in decisions about possible uses of assistive technology devices, assistive technology abandonment can result.
- Informal information-collection strategies require from special education teachers a high level of sensitivity to families and their needs.
- Parents need information, and how that information is provided can be as important as what is provided.
- The introduction of any technology device into a child's life is likely to have unanticipated effects on both the child and the family.
- Some families prefer to blend in and feel that an assistive technology device makes the child (and the family) more noticeable.
- Families and teachers may have very different perceptions and values, based in part on the differing cultural backgrounds they bring to the IEP table.
- A family's values will affect the nature and extent of family participation in assistive technology decision making.

THEORY TO PRACTICE

➡ Interview and observe a student who uses an assistive device. Ask the student how the device assists in accessing activities and what he or she finds easy or difficult about using the device. Ask for recommendations about how the device may be used across multiple settings and what advice the student would give general and special education teachers for working with students who use assistive devices. Ask how the student's schooling is affected when the device is not in working order. When observing, notice how the child uses the device in multiple situations and how other people respond to his or her use of the device.

➡ With the assistance of someone knowledgeable about a student's device or a student who uses a device, learn how a device works. Gain information about the symbols that are used in the device and the commands and operation skills necessary for accessing, operating, and using the device. Identify ways to support individual students' access, operation, and functional uses of assistive devices.

COMPONENT 4: AUGMENTATIVE AND ALTERNATIVE MEANS OF COMMUNICATION

It is recess time. All the students are out on the playground, hanging out with their friends—talking, playing kick-ball, or playing tether-ball. Some students are engaged in serious conversations; others are telling jokes or talking about something funny that happened over the weekend; others are very serious about the game they are playing, as they yell directions and suggestions to other teammates.

This normal interaction on the playground is most readily accessible for students who communicate through speech or other standard means (e.g., gestures used during sporting events to signal actions to be taken). This can be difficult for those students who do not communicate through speech or those who are unable to gain information through sight and observation. For example, a student who is hard-of-hearing and who signs or speech-reads to gain information from the speech of others, may have difficulty understanding all the communication that occurs during a game on the field (e.g., a shout from another fielder). This difficulty also arises if students are standing together talking.

If a student does not use speech as one's primary means of communication, what kind of communication can be used to include the student in an activity? What tools and/or approaches can be implemented to assist such individuals in highly interactive, social environments?

Some students require modes other than speech, writing, or gesturing as their primary means of expressive communication. Augmentative and alternative communication (AAC) offers modes through which such students may meaningfully and effectively communicate with others. In this book, *augmentative* communication refers to ways to augment or supplement partially intelligible speech. *Alternative* communication refers to means of communication other than by speech and writing. Representative curricular areas within the augmentative and alternative curriculum taught by special educators or related service providers include: (a) aid and symbol use, (b) braille, and (c) AAC systems for students who are deaf or hard-of-hearing.

Representative Content

Aid and symbol use

Curriculum in uses of communication aids or devices and communication symbols on them prepares students to develop and use modes other than speech and writing for expressive communication. Communication aids, or devices, take several forms. These forms of aids can be seen in Figure 5.1. At any time in their schooling, AAC users with speech intelligibility difficulties are likely to learn to use, and perfect their use of, one or more of these forms of AAC aids: (a) low-tech, nonelectronic aids; (b) aids specially designed for AAC users; and (c) computer-based communication systems. *Low-tech, nonelectronic aids* include communication or vocabulary boards (e.g., Figure 5.1c and e, pp. 133 and 134). *Aids specially designed for AAC users* generally have speech output of complete messages or message units chosen by the user (e.g., Figure 5.1f, p. 135). Some of these aids are particularly helpful to beginner AAC users because someone can speak into them and record different messages in the different locations on the aid depending on the users' anticipated needs. Different messages can be placed in the different locations as needed (see Figure 5.1 b and d, pp. 133 and 134). Many specially designed AAC aids have computerized speech output. *Computer-based communication systems* consist of a standard computer, special software that transforms the computer screen into one or more displays of symbols that represent full or partial content of potential communications (e.g., Figure 5.1 h, p. 136, top) and speech output of those communications selected.

The selection of aids for a certain child depends on which device best matches the child's needs and preferences. Factors to consider when selecting devices (adapted from Galvin & Schere, 1996) include

- *communication needs of the child*—goals; activities to be accomplished; degree of need for a device
- *personal preferences*—comfort in using the device; feeling of success and lack of frustration in using the device; contribution to quality of life
- *functional capabilities of the user*—physical and mental abilities; changes in functional abilities
- *environment, psychosocial setting, or situation of aid use*—support in the environment for the technology; use in home, school, community; availability of training in device use
- *technical features of the device*—durability; reliability; method of input or access to device; output options; rate of communication
- *language*—method for representing vocabulary; arrangement of symbols on the display; how language is stored and retrieved

Symbols are the representations of language that individuals use to express thoughts, ideas and concepts. Symbols used in AAC can be auditory (e.g., synthesized or recorded speech output), visual (e.g., pictures, printed words), and tactile (e.g., actual objects, braille symbols). The majority of symbols used with augmentative communication aids are visual and include (a) pictures that represent single concepts (see Figure 5.1a, p. 132); (b) letters, including printed words and phrases (see Figure 5.1e, p. 134); and (c) pictures or icons that have an obvious primary meaning and several secondary meanings when combined with other icons (see Figure 5.1f, p. 135).

To express their thoughts, students learn to select the appropriate symbol or combination of symbols on communication aids and devices. Beginning students learn to develop a repertoire of single symbols to make requests (e.g., making association between a picture of grape juice and the request, "Grape juice, please.") These associations do not come easily to some and heavy curricular intervention is required. Eventually, many AAC users learn to use advanced language access systems such as Minspeak (Prentke Romich Company, Wooster, OH). Minspeak is based on just one overlay (display) containing multimeaning icons (see Figure 5.1f) that can be used individually for more obvious meanings or in combinations with other icons to gain secondary meanings, and therefore it meets many communication needs. But even with the most sophisticated language representation system such as Minspeak, students are not always able to relay exactly what they want to say. The reliance on printed words, pictures, and icons alone on AAC aids and devices leaves room for misunderstandings between the sender and the receiver. The addition of spelling, therefore, becomes extremely important. The ability of the sender to be able to spell for the receiver allows the sender to say exactly what he would say if he or she could speak (see Figure 5.1e, p. 134). Many AAC aids "speak" or visually display the words users spell on them (see Figure 5.1h, p. 136, bottom right). Spelling, often used on some devices in combination with symbols that represent specific words, phrases or sentences, eliminates guesswork by the receiver. Spelling thus becomes another major curriculum goal for students—however, spelling is often difficult because, as a result of their disability, some cannot pronounce the words themselves to analyze the components and the sequences.

Curriculum should prepare students who do not speak intelligibly to use one or more communication aids or devices and symbols sets that match their personal communication needs and to continue to develop their functional, as well as their operational, competence in augmentative and alternative communication. Figure 5.1 gives eight examples of typical personal communication needs of these students (as well as illustrating features of aids and symbol uses that we discussed earlier in the chapter).

Review the **bold** captions under the graphics in Figure 5.1. Consider these as some functional competencies that many of these students might lack or need to refine in order to communicate effectively in all of these natural situations with teachers and peers. From there think about the implications for content of instuction in functional competence. Then, read the points below to see what functional outcomes and intermediary annual goals might be set for many of these students in the area of communicative interactive behaviors alone. Buzolich and Higginbotham (1985, p. 3) suggest these:

1. Ability to initiate and maintain interaction.

2. Ability to use the system to perform a variety of academic and communicative functions across contexts and individuals.

3. Ability to contribute to conversations and achieve reciprocity.

4. Ability to obtain turns 80% of the time.

5. Ability to use the system to manage conversational interactions.

6. Ability to resolve communicative breakdowns using a wide variety of accompanying nonverbal, verbal (linguistic), and vocal strategies.

7. Ability to make oneself understood using a particular system with familiar and unfamiliar conversational partners.

8. Ability to interrupt others and give input, if so desired.

9. Ability to communicate affective meaning to a partner given the constraints of the system.

❚ **FIGURE 5.1**
AAC Aids and Symbol Uses to Meet Communication Needs

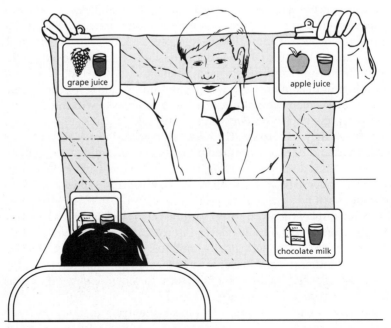

Figure 5.1a. **Expressing need and wants.** Tina Marie uses eye gaze to indicate what she wants to drink with her lunch. From Bigge, 1991. Used by permission of Prentice Hall.

Figure 5.1b. **Participating in special events.** Matthew uses his elbow to press a switch (and move a moving indicator light) to select what he wants his communication aid to say "aloud" for him. The messages can be changed easily for different needs. Drawing adapted with permission from *Book of Possibilities,* 1996, by ABLENET, Minneapolis, MN.

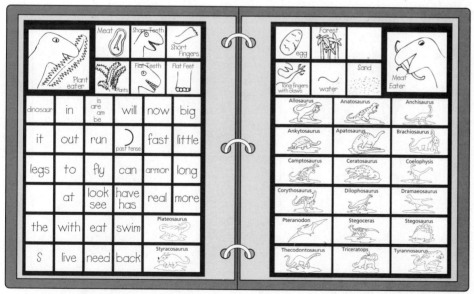

Figure 5.1c. **Using lesson-specific vocabularies.** Suk Mi points to lesson-specific vocabularies and graphics instead of using speech to comment and answer questions. Courtesy of Jane Kelly, teacher.

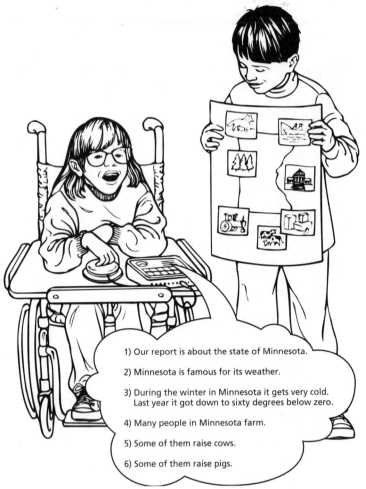

1) Our report is about the state of Minnesota.

2) Minnesota is famous for its weather.

3) During the winter in Minnesota it gets very cold.
   Last year it got down to sixty degrees below zero.

4) Many people in Minnesota farm.

5) Some of them raise cows.

6) Some of them raise pigs.

Figure 5.1d. **Giving reports.** Julianna and Robby give a joint report and answer questions. They collaborated on content of the report and organization of its presentation. Drawing adapted with permission from *Book of Possibilities,* 1996, by ABLENET, Minneapolis, MN.

Figure 5.1e. **Engaging in personal interactions with peers.** Peter points to his communication board to tell jokes, debate, and interact with classmates in different high-school classes.

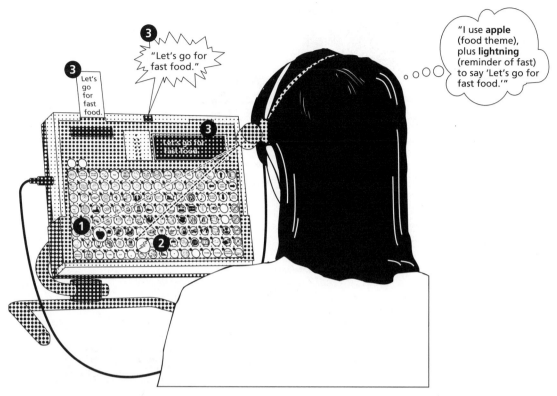

Figure 5.1f. **Instigating ideas and activities.** Using an infrared pointer and a communication aid with speech output, Heather instigates ideas for an afterschool activity. Images courtesy of: Prentke Romich, Wooster, OH and Prentice-Hall, Upper Saddle River, NJ.

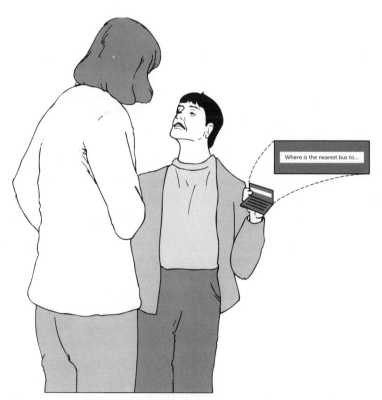

Figure 5.1g. **Communicating with strangers in the community.** Ron asks for directions from strangers by pointing to questions that he wrote in advance and put in a card holder.

Standard keyboard
and mouse; special
communication software

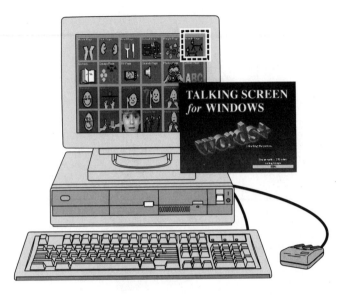

Alternative keyboards; special communication software

Figure 5.1h. **Combining AAC uses with other personal uses of a standard computer.** Several students in the school use computers in different ways to assist them with augmentative and alternative communication. Top photo courtesy of Words +; bottom photo courtesy of IntelliTools, Inc., Novato, CA.

Braille

Individuals with visual impairments can use braille as a tactile mode of expression when they are unable to see to handwrite legibly or easily. They might produce materials in braille for their own use or to share with another braille reader, or to be translated later into print for print readers. Students learn to write and read braille when a recommendation for braille use follows a **learning media assessment** (LMA) that takes into consideration student preferences. In some situations, for instance, individuals with visual impairment may choose to handwrite or type in print even though braille is their main mode of written expression.

Curriculum in braille prepares students with knowledge and skills for reading and writing. In Grade I Braille (uncontracted), words are spelled out; in Grade II Braille (the most commonly used form of braille), words are written in contraction form. Writing (and reading) braille involves memory and synthesizing multiple uses of 63 available braille characters or configurations. Each braille character is formed by combinations of from one to six embossed dots arranged within a braille cell consisting of two vertical columns of three dots each. The dots on the left side from top to bottom are 1, 2, and 3. The dots on the right side from top to bottom are 4, 5, and 6.

Basic literacy in writing (and reading) braille is an initial focus of braille curriculum (see Figure 5.2). Students learn, among other things, that the letter *a* is made by one raised dot in the top left position (dot 1). The letter *b* is made with the top and middle dots on the left (dots 1 and 2). Other letters, punctuation marks, and other symbols are represented by other patterns of raised dots in the cell. Some configurations, called contractions, represent more than one letter. The contraction *er* is made with just one braille cell. Some letter groups are represented by two or more braille cells. The letter group *ness,* for instance, is made with the middle and bottom dots on the right in one cell followed by the letter *s* in the next cell. Some words are represented in braille by shortened forms. The word *mother* is written in braille with the middle dot on the right and then the braille letter *m.* The word *knowledge* is written as the letter *k* by itself. The word *receive* is written *rcv.* These contractions and other short forms reduce the space needed by braille words. Even so, braille is a very bulky reading medium.

Students learn different braille codes for reading literary materials, mathematics, music, foreign languages, and computer language. The interpretation of the configuration

▮ FIGURE 5.2
English Braille Symbols.
These symbols form the basis of literacy in writing and reading braille.

Courtesy of Victor S. Hemphill.

varies with the specific code in which it is used. For instance, the braille symbol used for the dollar sign (dots 2, 5, and 6) is interpreted differently in literary, math, and computer codes. Students must learn the codes in the context in which they are being used.

Devices that students can use to learn to write braille characters include (a) a braille-writer, (b) a slate and stylus, and (c) a computer using a braille software program. Pictures of the first two are shown in Figure 5.3. Students require different curriculum to learn to write braille with the different devices. The braillewriter and computers with software that allows certain computer keys to be used to produce braille both use a spacebar and six keys corresponding to the braille cell. All dots in a cell are produced at

▌ **FIGURE 5.3**
Braillewriter (top) and Slate and Stylus
Photos courtesy of American Printing House to the Blind, Inc.

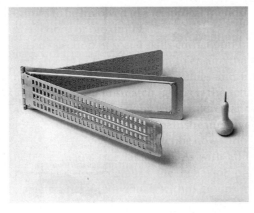

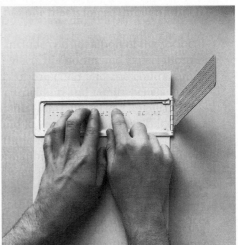

once and are read the way they are produced. When a slate and stylus are used, dots are produced one at a time in a cell. The embossing (raising of the dot) appears on the underside of the paper; thus, students must learn to produce braille from right to left, so that when the page is turned over, it can be read from left to right (Mangold, 1985).

AAC systems for students who are deaf or hard-of-hearing

A variety of communication systems and philosophies are available to meet the needs of students who are deaf or hard-of-hearing. Some systems and philosophies that meet language and communication needs are described in Exhibit 5.5. Depending on the child's primary language and communication mode (e.g., use of sign language to send and receive messages; use of spoken language, with or without visual signs or cues; a combination of the two), these systems and philosophies are the bases of highly specialized curricular content and instruction.

		EXHIBIT 5.5
Oral/Aural Systems	• Students use their voices (spoken language) as the primary mode of face-to-face communication. • Students may use speech-reading to gain information from someone else's speech. • Students may use cued speech to supplement speech-reading—hand shapes represent the sounds letters make (visual cues) and thus allow recipients to "see-hear" spoken syllables (Schwartz, 1996). • Students depend on their residual hearing, with and without amplification, in order to listen, to learn to talk, and to understand speech.	**Communication Systems and Philosophies for Deaf or Hard-of-Hearing Students**

Manual Systems	• Students use visual-gestural symbols, including symbolic representations of words and finger spelling (e.g., spelling words letter-by-letter)
	 • *American Sign Language* (ASL)
	   ⇒ is a language with unique syntactical and grammatical features
	   ⇒ does not follow standard English
	 • *Signing Exact English* (SEE)
	   ⇒ is not a language but a system to represent standard English using signs and finger spelling—it is a verbatim translation of English into sign, with signs used according to the rules of English, including prefixes, suffixes, tense markers, and plurals
	   ⇒ may be used for instruction
	   ⇒ corresponds to spoken English
	 • *Finger spelling*
	   ⇒ is a manual system used for parts of conversation (e.g., names and technical terms and for words for which there are no signs)
	   ⇒ uses 26 hand configurations to spell (see Figure 5.4)
	 • *Pidgin Sign English*
	   ⇒ American Sign Language vocabulary and fingerspelling in English word order
	   ⇒ signs chosen according to their meanings
	   ⇒ can be signed alone or simultaneously with spoken English	

Total Communication	• This philosophy combines different communication approaches to provide linguistic input to people who are deaf: sign (English-based), speech, gestures, facial expressions, amplification, finger spelling, speech-reading, and printed words. • Users combine communication approaches as needed in different situations. • Often, Signing Exact English is used simultaneously in combination with speech and amplification to provide a complete model of English (SEE + speech). • This is not only a philosophy; it is used also as another "method."	

Historically, two camps—the manualists and the oralists—have disagreed about how to educate children who are deaf. However, in this controversial field there is a trend to

▌**FIGURE 5.4**

Signs for Finger Spelling

Source: From *Curriculum Based Instruction for Special Education Students,* by J. Bigge, 1988, Mountain View, CA: Mayfield.

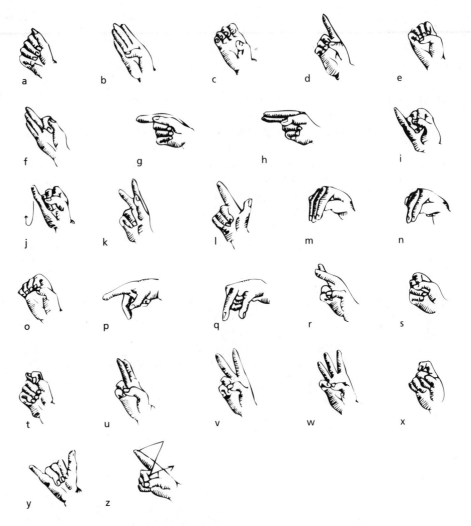

provide parents and their children with informed choices about several communication options, presented with pros and cons and without bias (Schwartz, 1996). We encourage readers to study the different communication options for children who are deaf and to investigate the personal experiences of those children and their parents as a result of choosing among these very disparate options. Readers should also develop awareness of trends to think of curriculum in some of these communication systems as bilingual-bicultural education within Deaf Culture, rather than as augmentative and alternative communication.

THEORY TO PRACTICE

➡ Research the latest information on AAC devices. What types of devices are available for students? What research and data are available to support the use of these devices by students with disabilities? What does the literature suggest are the best practices associated with the use of AAC devices by individuals with disabilities?

➡ Interview and observe a student who uses an AAC device. Ask how the device assists the student in accessing activities and what the student finds easy or difficult about using the device. Ask for recommendations about how these devices could be used across multiple settings to support individuals with disabilities and for any advice the student could give general and special education teachers working with students who use AAC devices. When observing, notice how the child uses the device in multiple situations and how others respond to his or her use of it.

➡ Meet with a teacher of students with visual impairments or with an individual with visual impairments who is familiar with braille. Have him or her demonstrate the use of a slate and stylus and/or a braillewriter. Ask him or her to identify the advantages and disadvantages of it and what teachers can do to support its use in the classroom.

➡ Interview a teacher specializing in education of individuals who are deaf or hard-of-hearing. Explore his or her perceptions and beliefs about the best means for developing the language skills of individuals who are deaf or hard-of-hearing. Also, inquire about his or her beliefs about Deaf Culture.

COMPONENT 5: MODIFIED MEANS OF INFORMATION ACQUISITION AND MANAGEMENT

Today the third grade class is conducting a science experiment exploring the cells of plants. The students have read about cells; have interacted with computer software that models how cells live, grow, and reproduce; and have drawn models of cells based on gathered information. Today, they will be looking under a microscope at slides of cells taken from plants found in the classroom. Students are to look at the slides and determine how these cells are the same as or different from those they have studied and drawn. They are to create a poster that illustrates and describes the plant cells they see under the microscope and that incorporates key vocabulary and concepts developed throughout the unit.

This task requires students to visually observe, record, and compare/contrast visual images and to use specialized science equipment. To gain understanding and achieve goals as the activity is presently described, students must be able to see the specimen under the microscope, to visually compare and contrast it to previous illustrations and to ideas previously presented through text, and to visually present what has been learned, incorporating key vocabulary and concepts.

What about students who are not able to gain information through text? What about those students who are not able to gain information visually, including those with blindness and low vision, as well as students with learning disabilities who struggle with the visual processing of information? What about students who experience difficulty in sharing ideas through visuals and graphics, including students with visual impairments; those who have difficulty organizing information visually; and those experiencing motor difficulties that interfere with their ability to draw and manipulate common writing tools? How will they perform in this situation, and what could these students gain from participation in this activity?

Learning personally effective means of acquiring and managing information is basic to communication and performance. Methods for acquiring and managing information include reading, speaking, listening, touching, moving the body, and observing. When disabilities prevent use of these prevalent means of acquiring, managing, and relaying information, individuals may require curricular intervention to learn how to use modified means to perform these tasks. Information acquisition and management curriculum meet the needs of these students in the areas of: (a) information acquisition, (b) adaptive means of information storage and retrieval, and (c) communication of information to others.

Representative Content

Information acquisition

Most people rely on their eyesight to acquire visually presented information, on hearing for aurally presented information, and on touch for tactually presented information. Students who have visual and/or auditory acuity difficulties, or motor difficulties, do not have full or perhaps any use of these channels for acquiring information. Teachers and others can accommodate these students and assist them in information acquisition by making lessons and lesson materials available to them in modified forms.

A variety of print media can be used to assist students with low vision to acquire information. Large-print books can be valuable for students. However, teachers sometimes provide students with large print without actually documenting that it is valuable or efficient (Koenig, 1996). The overuse or exclusive use of large print can prevent students from gaining access to the majority of available printed materials, so other options must be considered as well.

Devices that make it possible for students with low vision to read regular-print materials along with their peers include closed-circuit television (CCTV) (see Figure 5.5) and optical devices such as magnifiers, telescopes, and field-expansion devices, which use lenses or prisms that are placed between the eye and the object being viewed to enhance visual functioning (Levack, 1991). These devices provide access to a variety of reading opportunities that are not available in large print. Magnifiers assist with tasks such as reading telephone directories, directions on food packages and medicine bottles, menus, and numbers on paper money. Telescopes assist with tasks such as reading a street sign or the words on a chalkboard in the classroom and viewing sporting events. It is important for teachers to provide direct instruction in the use of these devices and provide sufficient opportunities for practice in using them in natural contexts (Koenig & Rex, 1996). Exhibit 5.6 lists examples of curriculum to provide specific training in the use of specialized optical devices.

▌ **FIGURE 5.5**
Closed Circuit Television with Video Magnification. This technology helps students with low vision to see print and other materials.
Source: Optelec of Westford, MA, (800) 828-1056.

- Use of bar, handheld, illuminated, and stand magnifiers (Zimmerman, 1996)
- Use of computer software with different sizes and types of fonts, enlarged monitors, and screen magnifiers (Zimmerman, 1996)
- Use of handheld monocular telescope designed for intermediate and distance tasks such as:
  - (a) finding toys hidden around the room
  - (b) meaningful copying from charts in the classroom
  - (c) identifying signs in stores and malls (Cowan & Shepler, 1990)
- Use of closed-circuit television that provides electronic magnification by using a video camera to project images onto a television monitor (Corn & Koenig, 1996):
  - (a) focusing the camera on the visual display (e.g., printed page of book or worksheet, train schedule, handwritten report)
  - (b) selecting appropriate degree of magnification (can enlarge up to approximately 60 times)
  - (c) selecting colors for figures and background for optimal contrast (black on white, white on black, yellow on black)
  - (d) developing tracking and scanning skills to access the information on the television monitor

EXHIBIT 5.6

Curriculum in Uses of Specialized Optical Devices to Access Information

Students acquire knowledge and skills for using many other kinds of specialized materials and equipment to acquire information. Examples include aids and devices with synthesized speech (e.g., talking clocks), computers, and large-print calculator software such as CALC-TALK (G. W. Micro, Inc., Fort Wayne, IN). Teachers help students develop skill in the use of tactile graphics, adapted science equipment, and adapted math equipment such as the Cranmer abacus (American Printing House for the Blind, Louisville, KY) as means of acquiring information usually presented visually.

Specialized curriculum can also prepare individuals with visual impairments to gain information through tactile means of communication (e.g., braille). Students will require content in braille reading if reading is an appropriate objective for them or if they prefer to use braille instead of print for some purposes. Braille can give individuals with visual impairments the ability to access a wide range of materials—not only educational and recreational reading and practical manuals but also labels on objects used in daily life, such as elevators, restroom doors, and ATM keypads. See Exhibit 5.7 for curriculum topics that teach efficient skills for reading braille.

DEVELOPMENT OF EFFICIENT MECHANICAL SKILLS

- (a) coordinated use of both hands
- (b) use of index fingers and the next several fingers to contact dots
- (c) tracking skills
- (d) light and even pressure applied to braille dots
- (e) continuous left-to-right movements across braille cells
- (f) efficient techniques for handling pages (Heinze, 1986)

BUILDING OF SKILL LEVELS

- (a) braille character recognition training
- (b) spelling skills to accompany learning of braille contractions
- (c) use of contractions
- (d) use of peripheral cues such as spatial position of characters (e.g., placed together or separated by one space) to change the meaning
- (e) word attack skills
- (f) comprehension skills
- (g) improved synthesizing of letters into words, and words into complete messages (Heinze, 1986)

BUILDING BRAILLE READING SPEED

- (a) repeated reading of passages to reach criterion of efficient and fluent reading
- (b) paired reading, with a braille-using model reading the passage first and patterning his or her reading to that of the model braille reader
- (c) frequent practices from early childhood to get rhythm and sound of efficient reading (Olson, 1981)

EXHIBIT 5.7

Curriculum in Reading Braille as an Alternative to Print

Not only students with visual impairments but students with other disabilities also may benefit from curriculum that prepares them to access information generally presented in print when print is not a medium they can readily use. For example, those with physical impairments may use alternatives to print when their physical disabilities limit their ability to hold a book and turn pages. Some students may use aurally presented information to augment or replace their reading of print. Books on tape are an example of this adaptation, which can be used by students with a range of disabilities and are becoming commonplace in the classroom and at home. They are helpful as long as they do not undermine literacy in reading print or braille (see Chapter 17 for more information on books on tape). Also, specialized computer software that transcribes print into spoken symbols allows students who experience difficulties working with print to hear the information rather than visually read it. For students who have difficulty gaining information from print, Exhibit 5.8 lists possible curriculum in the use of these and other alternatives.

EXHIBIT 5.8
Curriculum in Modified Access to Print and Other Visually Presented Information

- Making requests from school personnel for recordings of needed textbooks
- Studying and learning from audiotapes of textbooks and other print materials
- Using specially designed playback equipment and accessories
  - (a) operating audio playback machines with two- and four-track discs and cassettes
  - (b) using special indexing systems to locate and mark different information in various locations on audiotapes
  - (c) selecting appropriate playback speeds for audio discs
  - (d) locating and ordering playback machines and audiotapes for personal enjoyment and hobbies outside of school (e.g., from the National Library Service for the Blind and Physically Handicapped, Library of Congress, Washington, DC; and from cooperating local libraries)
  - (e) requesting and using special accessories (e.g., headphones, amplifiers, remote control units, special switches and levers) for playback machines, when needed
- Using or explaining to others one or more processes to transfer print from textbooks to computer disks (e.g., with scanner and optical character recognition software)
- Using or explaining to others the processes of conversion of print on the computer disk to an individually accessible medium (e.g., from text to speech, large print, and braille)
- Using or explaining processes to control access to speech output and to locate what should be read on the screen in speech output and to determine when it should be read
- Using sighted readers when material is not available in an accessible medium such as braille, recorded cassette tape, or computer disk

Just as students with visual impairments require adaptations and alternatives to printed material to acquire and manage information, students with hearing impairments require adaptations and alternatives to aurally presented information. Many have difficulty relying on their residual hearing for aurally presented information, including the speech of others. Curriculum needs to be designed to teach them how to gain access to sounds in the environment, to verbal communications, and to orally presented instructions so that they have opportunities to gain information and learn along with their peers.

Adaptations for students who have enough functional (residual) hearing to use the auditory mode for some or all of their learning include amplification systems (e.g., hearing aids, auditory trainers, cochlear implants) (Taylor, Sternberg, & Richards, 1995). Even with amplification, many have difficulty relying on residual hearing and require curriculum to help them. An alternative for gaining aurally presented information is

having someone interpret the information into sign language (see Figure 5.6). Exhibit 5.9 summarizes some specialized curriculum.

- Use of accommodations made by teachers and others:
  (a) written materials
  (b) assistive listening devices
  (c) manual signs
  (d) video displays
  (e) speech-reading (lip-reading and attention to nonverbal components of speech)
- Use of interpreter translations of "auditory information into word-for-word visual representation (speech read/sign language) . . ." (Waldron, Diebold, & Rose, 1985, p. 39)
- Use of assistive devices and services for everyday functional activities (e.g., electronic aids for the telephone, such as TTY and relay services, and captions or subtitles for television)
- Use of visual information (pictures, concrete examples, video, drama, pantomime) to teach aurally presented language

Adaptive means of information storage and retrieval

Many times, students who are not able to use handwriting readily as the primary mode for recording information for later retrieval require curricular intervention. Laptop computers, portable keyboards, and notetakers especially designed for braille users are among the most exciting advances in tools for helping these students learn to store and retrieve information in a personally useful medium. We consider the personal use of laptop computers adaptive because they are not yet prevalent personal tools for every student in school and because they are frequently loaded with specialized software to meet an individual's needs resulting from disability. Laptops are available in both Macintosh and PC formats.

Portable keyboards, such as the LINK Keyboard (Assistive Technology, Inc., Chestnut Hill, MA), are notebook-size keyboards that are easy to carry from class to class and

▌**FIGURE 5.7**
Braille 'n Speak
Photo courtesy of Blazie Engineering, Inc.

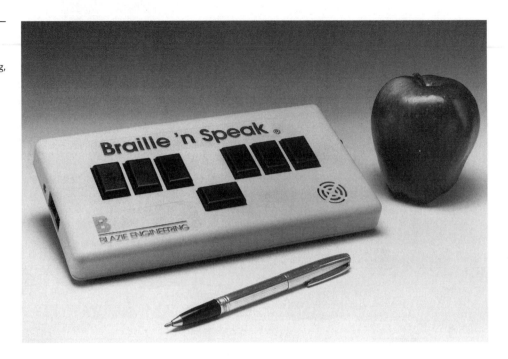

between home and school. They are not computers, but students can save information in them and later transfer that information into print or auditory output through the use of a classroom or home computer and print system.

Computerized notetakers can make notetaking and retrieval possible for those who read and write braille. The Braille 'n Speak and the Braille Lite are examples. The Braille 'n Speak (see Figure 5.7) is a portable computer with a braille keyboard. It has six keys representing the dots in a braille cell plus a spacebar and a small speech synthesizer for speech output. Users learn to "key in" braille to signal the function they want to work with (e.g., the word processor; the calendar) and then braille in their notes or other information. They then can access their input by entering commands to cause the speech synthesizer to read a desired portion of the text. The Braille Lite (Figure 5.8) is a similar device with an added, refreshable braille display (instead of speech output) that gives the feedback to the user. This display is a strip in which a line of braille characters—made by small, pop-up pins—displays information to be read through the fingers.

Communication of information to others

Part of one's managing information is sharing it and using it collaboratively with others. Students must have the ability to provide information to peers, teachers, employers and others in lessons, demonstrations, reports, and during social situations. Besides using the Braille 'n Speak and Braille Lite to store and retrieve information, students can learn to use them to translate their input into synthesized speech output or in hard copy of braille or standard print for use by others.

Other approaches for relaying information are available as well. For example, scientist Stephen Hawking exemplifies the ultimate in producing information in modified means and sharing it in whatever medium is appropriate for the audience. Hawking has no natural speech and only slight movement in one hand. He uses the slight hand movement to activate a switch to scan and access special software that allows him to select letters, words, phrases, and sentences from a computer screen to compose his messages and lectures. Sometimes he uses his switch and computer to translate this information into print for his scientific papers, for his university students, and for the readers of his famous book, *Journey Through Time*. When lecturing and giving presenta-

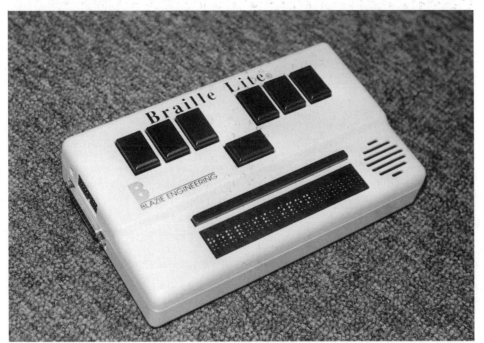

FIGURE 5.8
Braille Lite
Photo courtesy of Blazie Engineering, Inc.

tions to various audiences around the world, and when talking to family and friends, he uses voice output from his computer.

The possibilities for modified means of communication and performance truly are amazing during these years of technological advancements.

CHAPTER SUMMARY

This chapter features curriculum in modified means of communication and performance. It highlights the importance of providing curriculum, time, and instruction to prepare students unable to communicate and/or physically perform typical school or other major life activities with skills in modified means of communication and performance. Subcomponents of this curriculum are (1) modified means of physical task performance, (2) speech and language, (3) access, operation, and use of assistive technology, (4) augmentative and alternative means of communication, and (5) modified means of information acquisition and management. This chapter carries a reminder that teachers with exceptionality-specific expertise and certification have many of the primary instruction responsibilities for curriculum in this component. They collaborate with general education teachers, related service providers, and others in the child's different environments to move each child toward meeting IEP objectives and other significant outcomes of schooling. Although this curriculum specifically addresses the needs of individuals with sensory and motor disabilities, it has application for students with other disabilities as well.

Assessment

CHAPTER 6

Purposes of Assessment: Part I

Read to find out the following:

- the four main reasons for special education assessment
- steps and procedures involved in determining eligibility for special education services
- the differences between ecological and contextualized assessment and the unique benefits to be gained from contextualized assessment

When you think of assessment, perhaps you think of students spending hours hunched over test papers, carefully filling in bubbles on answer sheets, circling or checking their selection, or writing out short answers. But testing is only a small part of assessment. Observations of students in classrooms and evaluations of student work products and performances, and interviews with teachers, parents, and students are also part of assessment. Assessment is much more than administering tests and achieving scores. It is gathering information to make decisions. Assessment is

> *an additional occasion for learning—a tool for students, as much as for teachers, parents, and administrators to discover strengths, possibilities, and future directions in students' work. (Zessoules & Gardner, 1991, p. 63)*

Gearheart and Gearheart (1990) define assessment as

> *a process that involves the systematic collection and interpretation of a wide variety of information on which to base instructional/intervention decisions and, when appropriate, classification or placement decisions. Assessment is primarily a problem-solving process. (pp. 3–4)*

In special education, we assess for four primary reasons. These are: (a) determination of eligibility for special education services through prereferral and referral activities and development of an initial IEP, if appropriate; (b) review of individualized plans; (c) evaluation of instruction; and (d) program evaluation. In this chapter we discuss the first of these; in Chapter 7 we discuss the remaining three.

CONTEXTUALIZED ASSESSMENT

When assessing, you need to cast a wide net to gather information that collectively will provide a holistic understanding of the child—the individual's successes and challenges in the environments in which he or she lives, plays, works and learns—if you are to design meaningful educational programs. Some suggest this information gathering be accomplished through the application of an ecological assessment approach, defined

❙ **FIGURE 6.1**
The Contextualized
Assessment Model

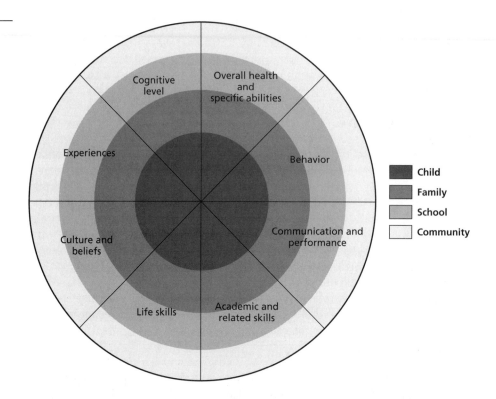

by Overton (1996) as analyzing "a student's total learning environment" (p. 276). According to Overton (1996), ecological assessment includes the following elements: (a) interactions between students, teachers, and others in the classroom and in other school environments; (b) presentation of materials and ideas; (c) selection and use of materials for instruction; (d) physical arrangement and environment of the classroom or target setting; and (e) students' interactions in other environments. Ecological assessment can also draw on (a) the culture and beliefs of individuals the child comes in contact with and how these influence the child; (b) the teacher's teaching style and instructional repertoire; (c) the way time is used in the classroom; (d) academic, behavioral, and social expectations within the learning environment; and (e) the overall tone of the classroom. In effect, ecological assessment aims to develop understanding of the multiple factors at play within a particular environment.

Although ecological assessment can be broad in scope, it generally has been used in selected environments for specific purposes, and many times it fails to assess the abilities and skills of a specific child across contexts (e.g., home, school, work). For example, ecological assessment may be used in a prevocational education program to analyze the performance demands required in a cafeteria setting. Information gathered may be used to design a program to prepare a student with a severe cognitive impairment to assume a job as a cafeteria worker. However, the findings from one environment are not always readily generalizable to other situations that the individual encounters. Therefore, we suggest that ecological assessment be expanded more broadly to embrace all environments in which a child learns, works, plays, and lives, as well as the child's specific experiences, abilities, and skills within and across those environments. We call this approach to assessment "contextualized assessment" (Stump, 1995).

A contextualized assessment gathers information about a child's experiences, skills, and abilities across a variety of contexts and factors to answer multiple assessment questions (Stump, 1995). As Figure 6.1 indicates, the child is at the center of contextualized assessment, and branching out from the center are the three contexts in which the **CHILD** lives, works, learns, and plays: the **family**, the **school**, and the **community**.

Gathering information about a child's performance across these three contexts to gain an understanding of the characteristics of those contexts results in an in-depth, multi-perspective database from which a team may make decisions when (1) determining a child's eligibility for special education services and (2) designing educational programs for students with identified special education needs.

Cutting across these contexts are essential factors for investigation. These factors are drawn from the literature and represent categories of learning and performance. They assist teams in determining what is important for students to learn and to be able to do, as well as what is important for teams to assess in order to select curriculum and design meaningful learning experiences for the students. The factors are (a) *culture and beliefs* of the child, his or her family, and community; (b) *experiences* that the child's family, school, and community provide and that the child brings to learning; (c) *cognitive level* of the child, as indicated by testing instruments; (d) *overall health and specific abilities* of the child, abilities that McLoughlin and Lewis (1994) identify as perception, vision, hearing, motor, memory, and attention; (e) *behavior*, meaning responses of the child to his or her environment and his or her acceptance by others; (f) *communication and performance*, meaning how the child communicates and performs routine tasks when typical routes are not available or feasible; (g) *academic and related skills*, meaning curricular areas such as reading, mathematics, learning strategies, and problem-solving skills; and (h) *life skills*, including functional academics, daily and community living skills, and transition. The multiple contexts and factors of contextualized assessment illustrate the advantages of approaching assessment in a holistic fashion and the importance of such an approach when making decisions about a student's educational needs. Approaching assessment in a contextualized problem-solving manner readily assists educators and makes the assessment process especially meaningful.

Contextualized assessment begins with the articulation of concerns in the form of questions. Questions frame what the assessment team wants to know and the type of information members need to make informed decisions about a specific child's program. The selection of questions depends on the purpose of the assessment. When a child is initially referred for determination of eligibility for special education services, questions will lead to assessment of the child's performance in all areas of suspected disability. For annual reviews and reevaluations, questions may address areas identified by previous IEP goals and objectives. When generating questions, teams may refer to factors (e.g., academic and related skills) and contexts (e.g., community) of contextualized assessment to develop a comprehensive assessment plan. Table 6.1 presents several kinds of questions that team members may find useful when planning a contextualized assessment for an individual student. Questions are presented by context and would be addressed to appropriate individuals within that context.

TABLE 6.1 CONTEXTUALIZED ASSESSMENT: GUIDING QUESTIONS

FACTOR	QUESTIONS
Culture and Beliefs	*Child/Family* 1. What do you value most in life? 2. What do you think is most important to know and be able to do? *Family* 1. What are your beliefs about education? 2. What are your attitudes and beliefs about disability? 3. What are your beliefs about behavior in and outside school? *School/Community* 1. What characteristics best describe the school and community culture? What roles do individuals play in these cultures (e.g., children, teachers, paraprofessionals, parents, business leaders)? 2. How aware and accepting of students with disabilities and their needs are individuals at the school and in the community?

(continued)

TABLE 6.1 CONTEXTUALIZED ASSESSMENT: GUIDING QUESTIONS *(continued)*

FACTOR	QUESTIONS
Experiences	*Child/Family/School/Community* 1. What prior experiences does the child bring to learning, and what types of learning experiences do the family, school, and community create for the child? 2. Through what kinds of home, school, and community learning experiences do the children learn best?
Cognitive Levels	*Child* 1. What is the student's overall functioning level? 2. Is the student performing at a level commensurate with his or her ability? 3. Is the child experiencing significant difficulties in processing information (e.g., auditory processing)?
Overall Health and Specific Abilities	*Child* *Overall Health* 1. How is the child's overall health? 2. Does the child have any special health-care needs? *Vision, Hearing, and Motor* 1. What, if any, vision, hearing, or motor difficulties could be interfering with the child's learning and performance? 2. What are the signs that the child has or may have a vision, hearing, or motor problem? 3. How does the child use any existing vision, hearing, or motor skills in different situations and conditions? 4. How does the child try to compensate for any vision, hearing, and/or motor problems? 5. Does the child have physical limitations due to his or her disability? What are they? What coping and/or compensatory skills does the child have? What assistive aids does the child need to be more independent? 6. How developed are the child's gross and fine motor skills? Are there any areas of difficulty? *Perception* 1. When presented information orally, visually, tactilely or kinesthetically, how does the student show that he understands and can respond to the information? What types of information presentation are the easiest/most difficult for the student to process? *Memory* 1. Does the child have any difficulties in the area of short- or long-term memory? What strategies does the child use to help himself or herself with short- and long-term memory tasks? *Attention* 1. Does the child demonstrate difficulties attending to tasks? 2. Under what circumstances does the child exhibit difficulty attending? 3. What strategies does the child use to help himself or herself attend?
Behavior	*Child/Family/School/Community* 1. What types of behavior does the child exhibit at home, at school, and in the community? 2. Under what family, school, and community situations does the child exhibit appropriate behaviors? Under what family, school, and community situations does the child seem to have the greatest difficulty exhibiting appropriate behavior? 3. What strategies does the child use for controlling and regulating his or her behavior when in school, at home, or in the community? 4. What behaviors are of greatest concern? What does the child hope to gain by engaging in these behaviors? 5. What expectations do the family, school, and community have for the child's behavior? 6. What information does the child have about family, school, and community rules and expectations? 7. What is done to assist the child in controlling and coping with his or her behavior? *School* 1. What are the school rules and the procedures for handling behavior difficulties? 2. What types of behavior does the child exhibit in the classroom? In less-structured school environments and activities, such as lunch and recess? 3. What types of work habits does the child demonstrate? What work habits does the child need to develop in order to experience greater success in the school environment? 4. What is the child's attendance pattern?
Communication and Performance	*Child/Family/School/Community* 1. How do the child's speech and language skills compare to those of peers? 2. How does the student communicate with others in the home, at school, and in the community? 3. How do other family members or those in school and community settings respond to the student's attempts to communicate? Does the student experience any speech-related difficulties?

FACTOR	QUESTIONS
	4. What does the student communicate to others?
	5. With whom does the student communicate? When and how often do these communications occur? Where do they occur?
	6. During what family, school, and community circumstances does the student seem to find communication easy? Difficult?
	7. To what extent is the child able to read and understand the nonverbal aspects of communication?
	8. What home, school, and community environmental factors serve as barriers to and/or facilitators of the student's communication?
	9. How does the child communicate his or her needs in the home, at school, and in the community?
	10. What is the child's primary language? What language is spoken in the home, at school, and in the community?
	11. Are the child's difficulties linked with his or her limited English proficiency skills?
	12. What opportunities does the child have at home, at school, and in the community to develop communication skills in the primary language and in English?
	13. What home, school, or community communicative supports are available or needed? What factors serve as barriers or facilitators to the child's communication development?
	14. If the child uses augmentative/alternative communication supports, how capable is the child in using these tools? What additional skills does the child need to use these tools to their full advantage?
	15. Does the child use modified means to acquire, record, and manage information? If so, what are these means? Does the child need additional assistance in developing skills in these areas?
	16. Does the child use modified means for performing physical tasks? If so, what are these means? Does the child need additional assistance in developing skills in this area?
Academic and Related Skills	*Child/Family/School/Community*
	1. What are the barriers and facilitators to the child's participation in home, school, and community learning opportunities?
	2. What academic skills and understandings are most important for the student?
	3. What expectations do family, school, and community members have for the child's academic performance?
	4. What types of school, home, and community supports are available to assist the child in completing homework and school projects?
	5. What types of academic learning opportunities are available in the home, at school, and in the community?
	6. When given a choice, how does the child prefer information to be presented?
	7. When given a choice, how does the child prefer to demonstrate understanding of ideas and concepts?
	8. What types of activities or tasks does the child find most difficult to respond to? easiest?
	9. What types of activities or tasks does the child find most challenging and interesting?
	10. How does the child feel about his or her performance in the school curriculum?
	11. How do family members, school personnel, and community members judge the child's academic performance? Is the child making adequate progress? Why or why not?
	12. What materials are available or needed in the home, school, and community to support the child's academic development?
	Related Skills: Learning Strategies and Study Skills
	1. What learning strategies and study skills does the child exhibit in the home, at school, and in the community? What learning strategies and study skills does the child need to develop?
	2. To what extent is the child aware of the need to learn and apply learning strategies and study skills?
	Related Skills: Thinking and Problem Solving Skills
	1. What problem solving strategies does the child employ when faced with challenges at home, in school, and in the community? What other strategies are needed?
	2. To what extent is the child able to analyze, synthesize, and evaluate information?
	3. To what extent is the child able to explain his or her thinking processes?
	Family
	1. What academic skills and understandings are most important for your child?
	2. What skills do you need or have to assist your child in completing homework and school projects?
	3. What type of learning supports and opportunities are available in the home?
	School
	1. What is the child's overall academic skill profile?
	2. In what areas of the school curriculum is the child experiencing success? What strategies does the child employ when working in those areas?
	3. In what areas is the child experiencing difficulties? What specific skills and understandings does the child have? What specific skills and understandings does the child not yet demonstrate? What strategies does the child employ or need when working in these difficult areas?
	4. What types of instructional activities or manner of presentation does the child best respond to?

(continued)

TABLE 6.1 CONTEXTUALIZED ASSESSMENT: GUIDING QUESTIONS *(continued)*

FACTOR	QUESTIONS
Academic and Related Skills *(continued)*	5. How is the child doing in the general education curriculum? What accommodations or adaptations are used to support student acquisition of academic skills and understandings? What else is needed? What curriculum options are available to and accessed by the student? To what extent does this curriculum address student's needs? What other curricular options should be considered? 6. What instructional strategies do teachers employ in the classroom? What accommodations in instructional practices are needed, if any? 7. In what ways are classroom materials used to support student learning? What else is needed? 8. In what ways do evaluation practices support student learning and inform instructional practice? What changes need to be made?
Life Skills	***Child/Family/School/Community*** *Functional Academics* (see Academics and Related Skills) *Daily and Community Living Skills* CAREER AND VOCATIONAL EDUCATION (see Academics and Related Skills; Life Skills) HOME AND FAMILY 1. How well is the student able to function in the home environment? What skills does the child exhibit when in the home? What skills to be taught in the home, school, or community are needed for this student to function more effectively in the home environment? 2. Does the child face barriers to participation in family life and activities? What compensatory or adaptive skills or equipment supports does the student use or need to overcome these barriers? What additional skills does the student need to participate more actively? LEISURE PURSUITS 1. To what extent does the child engage in leisure pursuits with or without family members? What needs to be done to encourage greater involvement? 2. What leisure pursuits does the child enjoy most? 3. What leisure pursuits would the child like to try? 4. What skills are needed to be taught in the home, school, or community to support the child's engagement in leisure pursuits? 5. What value do family members place on leisure and recreational activities? What types of activities are available to family members at home, at school, and in the community? In what activities does the family participate? Is the child included? If so, how? If not, what are the reasons for not including the child? COMMUNITY INVOLVEMENT 1. What does the family do to support and encourage the child's involvement in community activities? What needs to be done to further enhance participation? 2. What kinds of community activities does the child participate in with and without family members? 3. Does the child have a circle of friends? What types of activities do they do together? If not, what could be done to assist the child in developing friendships in the community? 4. To what extent are family members involved in their community and what experiences do they provide for their child's community involvement? 5. What community services and agencies are available to support the student and family? How are these supports accessed? Are there any barriers to accessing them? PHYSICAL/EMOTIONAL HEALTH 1. What types of supports are available in the home, school, and community for the child's physical and emotional needs? 2. What are the barriers to student wellness and his/her development in these areas? What can be done at home, at school, and in the community to overcome these barriers? SELF-DETERMINATION 1. How does the child go about making choices and decisions? 2. Is the child a self-advocate or do others (e.g., classmates, family members, community members) serve as his or her advocate? 3. To what extent is the child able to identify and express his or her needs, interests, and values? 4. To what extent does the child understand his or her strengths, weaknesses, and disability? 5. What information does the child have about his or her disability and his or her unique needs (e.g., medical, diet, learning)? 6. What initiative does the child demonstrate for improving things for himself or herself and for others?

FACTOR	QUESTIONS
	SOCIAL SKILLS
	1. How does the child respond to social situations at school, home, and in the community?
	2. What social skills does the child possess and/or need to develop?
	3. What strategies does the child have for responding to situations?
	4. How does the child respond to his or her peers? to authority figures? to family members? to community members?
	5. How does the child respond to the feelings and needs of others?
	6. How effective is the child in communicating with others in social situations? Under what situations does the child appear to have little difficulty? What situations seem to cause the child to experience difficulty?
	Transition
	1. What are the long-term goals of the student? What are the child's career/employment/educational aspirations?
	2. What skills and/or strategies does the child have to make successful transitions from (a) class to class, (b) grade to grade, and/or (c) school to postsecondary school or work? What skills and/or strategies are needed? What are the child's vocational education/career/transition curricular needs?
	3. What supports are available within the home and family structure and the community to assist the student in making transitions and developing job-related skills? What is needed?
	4. What community/job related skills does the student have? need to develop?
	5. What are the child's preferences and interests for postsecondary activities?
	6. What type of school and community career/vocational counseling and educational opportunities are available to the student? Do these services meet the needs of the student? What else is needed?
	7. What opportunities are available at the school and in the community for exploring career and vocational education experiences? Do they reflect the student's needs? Are they readily accessible to the student?
	8. What community supports are available and/or needed to assist the child in transitioning successfully from home to community situations and from community to community situations?
	9. What community-based experiences has the student been involved in? What level of success has he or she experienced? What are the next steps?

As Table 6.1 suggests, structuring questioning within a contextualized assessment framework results in the casting of a wide net across contexts and factors and results, too, in a thorough, holistic evaluation of a child's needs. Contextualized assessment does not limit the gathering of information on how a child performs within one context. The underlying belief is that what is happening in all contexts significantly impacts the child's performance and learning in any context.

Contextualized assessment can be used to achieve the four main purposes of education assessment. In the remainder of this chapter we address the first purpose of assessment—determination of eligibility—and link it with contextualized assessment and the generation of questions.

THEORY TO PRACTICE

➡ Interview a general education teacher who has served on an evaluation and/or IEP team. Ask the teacher what kinds of questions she or he wanted answered through the evaluation procedure. Categorize those questions using contextualized assessment contexts and factors. What areas are being primarily addressed? What areas are being overlooked? If you were to serve on this particular team, what additional questions would you pose, and what contexts and factors would your questions address?

➡ Interview a school psychologist or diagnostician. Ask him or her to define the purposes of assessment and the types of information gathered through assessment activities. Analyze this information in terms of contextualized assessment. What areas are given the most attention? What areas are being overlooked? What, if anything, would you recommend to the school psychologist or diagnostician to broaden the type of information gained through the evaluation process?

ASSESSMENT PURPOSE 1: DETERMINATION OF ELIGIBILITY AND DEVELOPMENT OF AN INITIAL IEP

Determination of eligibility for special education services is the first step toward providing special education programs and services. For the majority of students, the eligibility process begins with *prereferral*. The purpose of prereferral is to identify, implement, and evaluate specially designed interventions in general education settings to determine whether these interventions can support student success in the general education environment. If the prereferral interventions are found to be ineffective or only minimally effective, or if the teacher continues to suspect that the student has a disability, the child moves to the next phases—screening and referral. The purpose of *screening* is to gain a quick assessment of the child's overall performance levels. The purpose of *referral* is to determine, in a comprehensive way, whether the child is eligible for and in need of special education services.

Although the general sequence for determining eligibility moves from prereferral to screening to referral, prereferral is not always appropriate or necessary. For children whose needs for special education services are readily apparent, such as children with visual impairments or physical disabilities that impact school performance, a formal referral is made directly and the prereferral and screening stages are sidestepped. For example, a student may have a hearing loss that goes undetected until the first hearing screening is done at the school. At that point, it is important for the child to be referred for assessment quickly in order to receive necessary services and supports; going through the prereferral and screening processes would only delay the student's access to needed services. Being able to expedite the process is important if schools are to be responsive to the needs of students who clearly have disabilities, even if the disability has not been formally diagnosed.

Although prereferral, screening, and referral procedures vary within districts and states, the purposes of the various procedures are similar across states and districts. Each of these stages in the eligibility process is described.

Prereferral

Prereferral is an example of team problem solving that can result in the development, implementation, and evaluation of interventions to help children achieve success in general education classrooms. The prereferral stage emerged out of concern for the over-referral and/or inappropriate referral of students for special education testing (Graden, 1989). It offers an opportunity to look at concerns and possible solutions before a student is referred for testing for special education eligibility. Prereferral serves a critical function at the school site because it creates opportunities for teachers, support staff, and parents to work together addressing concerns they have about a particular child's performance at school, in the family, and in the community.

Limited research is available concerning the effectiveness of prereferral teams and the specific tasks they undertake, but a study by Simpson, Ormsbee, and Myles (1997) provides some understanding of how general and special educators view the prereferral process. Simpson, Ormsbee, and Myles (1997) surveyed general and special education teachers and found that the teachers agreed that the prereferral teams' primary responsibilities were to "(a) clarify student referral problems, (b) design general curriculum interventions, and (c) review student records" (p. 162). Less frequent activities included "(a) providing documentation of team-designed interventions, team-suggested interventions, or both, to general educators; (b) writing interventions as measurable objectives; (c) interviewing parents; and (d) interviewing students" (p. 162). The authors conclude that although additional research is needed, it is encouraging that general and special educators shared common views of prereferral.

Structures for providing prereferral intervention

Prereferral is not a mandated step in determining the eligibility of students for special education services and, because prereferral is not federally mandated, it is carried out several ways. The most common structure for prereferral is teacher-assistance teams. Many schools establish teacher-assistance teams to meet with teachers who are concerned with the performance of students in their classrooms. The purpose of these teams, sometimes referred to as "student study teams" or "child guidance teams," is to work with referring teachers to develop action plans that respond to identified student needs in general education classrooms. There is no prescribed membership on the team. Teams may consist of general educators, special educators, psychologists, nurses, counselors, administrators, and speech and language therapists. In some cases, the parent of the child under discussion may be an active participant in team activities. In other instances, a parent representative may serve on the team in a permanent capacity.

Although team membership is generally open, some considerations need to be addressed. For example, participation by school administrators may enhance or impede the work of the team. Administrators may assist teams in designing and implementing plans because of their ability to provide immediate administrative support, but their presence may also impede the work of the team if they dominate the meetings or their presence makes some members of the team hesitant to raise concerns or offer suggestions. Additionally, since the administrator at the site is generally responsible for the evaluation of teachers' instructional effectiveness, teachers experiencing difficulty with a student or group of students may be reluctant to discuss challenges and problems in front of an administrator for fear that those discussions will color the administrator's perception of their effectiveness as teachers. A similar challenge may arise when a school psychologist attends prereferral meetings. The school psychologist may dominate the meeting or team members may look to him or her for solutions. This dynamic may interfere with team members' willingness to participate in an open discussion and may limit the suggestion of types of interventions that could be implemented in classrooms.

Parent involvement, either by the parent of the child being discussed and/or by a parent who is elected to serve on the committee as an on-going committee member, also requires special consideration. The inclusion of the parent of the student being discussed is critical to the team efforts because parents can bring a wealth of information to the problem-solving task by providing insight into their child's behavior at home as well as at school. Election of a parent representative to serve on the team presents special considerations. Because the parent representative may, through community activities, be familiar with the child being discussed and/or with the child's family, care must be taken to ensure confidentiality of information learned through personal contact outside of school. This information should not be shared with the team without the permission of the parent of the child being discussed. Additionally, the parent representative, along with all other members of the team, must be informed that information discussed at the meeting must remain confidential.

A related issue is the role of special educators on prereferral teams. Although special education personnel may serve on the team, it is generally best if the majority of team members are general education teachers. If special education personnel dominate team membership, the tone of the meetings may shift away from group problem solving, as special educators fall into the role of prescribing what general education teachers need to do to assist children in general education classrooms. This prescriptive tone and acceleration to interventions without group discussion and problem solving could reduce the likelihood that general education teachers will seek assistance from the team. They believe that going to the team may be perceived as an admission of their failure to reach students and/or their inability to create solutions to the challenges their students face.

Therefore, creating a team composed mostly of general education teachers and allowing team members to work jointly toward solutions to challenges may invite greater general education teacher participation in prereferral activities.

The membership of the prereferral team is the first critical consideration when forming prereferral teams. Team goals, student population needs, teacher personalities, teaching styles, and teacher needs, and the strengths and weaknesses of potential team members must all be considered if a well-functioning, productive team is to be established.

Prereferral activities

Prereferral involves several activities. Each activity is described below.

1. Gathering premeeting information. Prior to the prereferral meeting, referring teachers and/or parents may be asked to complete forms that ask questions aimed at identifying specific concerns and the interventions that have already been attempted to address those concerns. This information is then shared with others at the first prereferral meeting.

2. Identifying and specifying the concern. Following the completion of a prereferral form a meeting is held. At this meeting, team members and the referring teacher and/or parent discuss information reported on the form to pinpoint the primary concern. This fact-finding stage is critical. Teachers and parents are likely to have many concerns about the student or to be quite frustrated with the difficulty they are having in finding ways to support the child in the general education classroom. Unless time is spent discussing what is occurring and when and how often it is occurring, the real problem may go unidentified. In fact, a discussion aimed at identifying and specifying the concern may reveal that what it was first thought to be represents only the surface of what is actually occurring.

Identification of the problem can be especially important when the team is focused on the needs of a child whose first language is not English or whose cultural or ethnic background is different from the teacher's. In such a case, the language of instruction, the style of instruction, or the learning opportunities provided in the classroom may not meet the child's needs. For example, if a child is not fluent in English and all instruction in the classroom is in English with little or no support for second-language learners, the child's academic performance may be jeopardized and the child may act out his or her frustration through inappropriate behavior. The same result may occur due to different teaching and learning styles within the classrooms. If a child's classroom calls for all independent work with little or no attention given to the social nature of learning (as demonstrated through discussions and paired/cooperative learning circles) and the child learns best when working with others, the mismatch between the child's needs, strengths, and learning styles and the opportunities present in the classroom may lead to depressed overall performance. In these situations, the underlying problem is most likely not a disability, but rather a need for a learning environment more responsive to the student's learning needs.

3. Collecting data around the identified problem. At this point, team members may determine that they need more information and will generate a list of questions they want answered. They may want to expand their discussion and fact finding to encompass factors identified in the contextualized assessment model. One of the first actions of the team may be to request vision, hearing, and motor screenings in order to rule out problems in these areas. This is a critical step because if, for example, the child's difficulty is related to a vision problem, the vision concern must be addressed first.

Students and parents may be interviewed as part of the fact-finding process. A team member may talk with the student about how things are going at school. Many times the student can pinpoint what he or she perceives as the source of the difficulty. Regardless of whether this perception is accurate, understanding it is extremely important in order to design meaningful interventions.

Parents' role in fact finding is equally as important. They can provide information about a multitude of factors, including their child's educational and medical history, behavior at home, language use at school and in the home, as well as their perceptions of their child's school experiences. Moreover, parents can offer information about what interventions have worked at home or at school in the past. Refer again to Table 6.1 for questions that may be asked during a parent interview.

Observation of students across multiple settings is also essential at this stage of fact finding. Observing the child in the classroom, on the playing field, during passing periods, during electives, during lunch, and when participating in after-school programs; and if possible in home and community settings, provides a wealth of information. The child may be experiencing difficulties in only one environment or that may be generalized across multiple environments. Without observational data, the team will not be able to discern the environments in which the child is succeeding or in which he or she is experiencing difficulties and the factors in those environments that may contribute to the child's success or difficulty.

4. Brainstorming interventions. Once team members have clearly specified the problem, have observed the pupil in multiple settings, have screened out vision, hearing, and motor functions as the primary concern, and have collected supporting information, another meeting is convened to discuss findings and to brainstorm possible interventions to be implemented in the general education setting. The goal of this meeting is to generate several intervention strategies designed to address the student's needs. As with all brainstorming sessions, all ideas are accepted without judgment. Teams may find it helpful to record these ideas on poster paper or on a board for future reference.

5. Selecting an intervention. After brainstorming, the team reviews suggestions and identifies one or two interventions that appear most reasonable and feasible for the student, the teacher, the learning environment and where appropriate, the parent. The team then develops an action plan that clearly explains the intervention, specifies who is to do what, describes how the intervention will be evaluated, and sets timelines for carrying out the action plan.

One consideration in designing an action plan is to clearly define the intervention to be implemented. Identifying the various facets of the intervention—when these intervention procedures will be implemented, what type of preparation is required, and what needs to be done to carry out the intervention—assists in ensuring not only that the intervention is implemented, but that its effectiveness is evaluated. Statements like "individualizing instruction," "providing additional materials," and "changing seat assignment" do not provide this needed information.

Another key consideration in the selection of prereferral interventions is the intrusiveness of the intervention—that is, the degree to which the intervention requires the teacher or others in the classroom to do something different or unique to meet the needs of an individual student. For example, when the concern is a child's inability to complete tasks, having the child work with a peer or in a cooperative group may be a simple step in assisting the child. If the teacher is already using some paired learning and cooperative group work in the classroom, the intervention will be a natural part of what is already occurring. What will be new is the teacher's pairing of the student with a peer or a group that will support the student's task completion. This contrasts with a highly intrusive intervention, such as having this same child meet individually with the teacher after each instructional period to discuss work completed. Individual conferences may require the teacher to stop instruction and/or work with the class in order to check in with the one student. These individual conferences place additional demands on the teacher, which may reduce the likelihood that the teacher will consistently follow-through with the intervention. As a general rule, in order to provide maximum benefit to the student in the general education classroom while at the same time calling the least amount of attention to him or her, the least intrusive interventions should be attempted first.

Another key consideration is the extent to which the proposed intervention matches the child's linguistic needs and is responsive to the child's cultural and ethnic needs as well. Providing language-learning supports and infusing culturally appropriate and diverse materials into the curriculum might be all the intervention that is needed to enhance the success of some students within the general education environment. At a minimum, their consideration and inclusion in instructional practice within the classroom creates a learning environment more supportive and responsive to the needs of the students.

6. Implementing the intervention. In some cases, the referring teacher is responsible for implementing the plan; however, a greater degree of success may be achieved when team members assist in implementation. For the intervention suggestion to implement paired or group reading with a student who is having difficulty comprehending text, the classroom teacher, though understanding the basic principles of paired and group reading activities, may require assistance in setting up the reading activities in her classroom. It may be helpful for this teacher to observe a fellow teacher who uses these activities or to ask a teacher experienced in the techniques to come into her classroom to provide assistance in setting up the reading activity. In this way, intervention becomes a team effort and not the sole responsibility of the referring teacher.

7. Monitoring and evaluating the intervention. Team members may also assist the referring teacher in monitoring and evaluating the intervention. This monitoring and evaluation can be carried out through classroom observations; discussions with the teacher, student, and parent; and/or review of student work samples. Monitoring and evaluating interventions can be very demanding. Approaching them as a team effort may enhance the likelihood of careful monitoring and evaluation.

The intervention plan depicted in Exhibit 6.1 includes elements necessary for the design, implementation, and evaluation of a prereferral plan. The plan lists the dates intervention activities will begin and end as well as procedures for monitoring the student's progress toward goals. Currently, Angelica, the student, and her teacher are working on step 4 of the plan. Note how the special education teacher works with the general education teacher in the development of the assignment monitoring sheet.

Student Name __Angelica__   Grade __6__   Teacher __Jordon__   Date __10/3__

Concern: Student fails to complete and turn in assignments

Goal: By the end of 3 weeks, student will complete and turn in 80% of assignments by their due date.

Date initiated __10/4__   Meeting date to discuss outcome __11/4__

Intervention activities	Evaluation Procedures	Who Is Responsible	Date and Outcome
1. Develop assignment monitoring sheet.	sheet will be shared with team	General and special teachers Parent	10/4 sheet developed
2. Meet with student to discuss concern. Refer to gradebook to highlight number of missing assignments.	student debriefing of the session	General education teacher	10/6 student was receptive—indicated an awareness of the concern
3. Introduce assignment monitoring sheet and demonstrate how it is to be used.	student debriefing of the session	General education teacher	10/6 student seemed to understand the process
4. Have student use assignment monitoring sheet and match it with the teacher every day for one week to ensure it is being completed and all procedures followed. Teacher and student will match recordings and make any necessary changes.	chart maintained by the student and general education teacher to record the degree of match between teacher and student	General education teacher Parent	10/7 student did not record all assignments and their due dates 10/8 student did record all assignments and due dates but did not turn work in 10/9 student recorded and turned in all assignments
5. Student and teacher will meet two days a week for one week to monitor progress and sheet use.	chart maintained by the student and general education teacher	General education teacher Parent	
6. Student and teacher will meet once a week for one week to monitor progress and sheet use.	chart maintained by the student and general education teacher	General education teacher Parent	

EXHIBIT 6.1

Prereferral Intervention Plan for a Sixth Grade Student

Following the timeline set in the intervention plan, the team will meet on November 4 to determine the overall effectiveness of the plan, and to clarify the next steps to be taken. At that time team members may find that the intervention is having a positive effect and should be continued; they may find that the intervention is not effective and decide that something else should be tried or more information should be gathered; or they may decide that the difficulties Angelica is experiencing go beyond what they can reasonably address as a team and the child should be referred for special education testing. If the team determines that the child should be tested for eligibility for special education services, the team moves on to the screening and referral stages of the eligibility process.

The assignment monitoring sheet mentioned in the plan (see Exhibit 6.1) may show that the problem has been remedied since Angelica has begun to turn in completed assignments on a regular basis. Or, the monitoring sheet may reveal previously unknown problems or factors impacting the student's ability to complete and submit work. Through close monitoring, the teacher may learn that assigned work is too difficult or too easy for Angelica, that she experiences significant difficulties processing information, has great difficulty attending to task, or does not have the self-management skills necessary for monitoring her own behavior. These insights could lead to the development and implementation of new interventions or the referral of Angelica for special education testing.

Screening

Some school districts require a screening of the child during or immediately after prereferral if the prereferral was not found to ameliorate the child's difficulties in the general education classroom; others do not. The purpose of screening is to determine whether the child is likely to be found eligible for special education services and should be referred for special education testing.

One common approach to screening is testing the child. Screening tests generally assess a wide range of skill areas in a quick fashion. Standardized tests may be used.

Informal reading inventories, behavior rating scales, classroom observation, and interviews with teachers and parents may also be used during screening. Vision, hearing, and motor screening, if not included as part of the prereferral process, are completed as well. If screening involves assessments, parents must be informed and must give their consent.

If the child's performance on screening instruments does not suggest a significant concern, the child may be referred back to the prereferral team for further consideration. However, if the child's screening outcomes reveal a performance profile similar to that of students with a disabling condition, the child is likely to be referred for special education testing.

Referral and Development of an Initial IEP

If the evaluation of prereferral interventions suggests that the interventions have not significantly remediated the concern, and if screening outcomes indicate the need for more testing, the team may decide to refer the student for an initial special education evaluation. As stated in the IDEA Amendments of 1997, the purpose of this initial evaluation is

> (i) to determine whether a child is a child with a disability . . . ; and
> (ii) to determine the educational needs of such child. (IDEA Amendments of 1997, Sec. 614(a)(I)(B))

A team is formed to carry out this initial evaluation. This team consists of experts representing various disciplines who work together with the parents to gather information about the child's strengths, challenges, and needs. Team members may include a school psychologist, a district special education representative, general and special education teachers, support personnel such as speech-language pathologists and occupational therapists who are specially skilled to assess particular disabilities, as well as including the parents, and when appropriate, the student.

Make a referral for an initial evaluation

The referral for testing is generally initiated by the general education classroom teacher but may be requested by parents and other school personnel familiar with the student. The referring individual fills out a form requesting the referral and states the reason for the referral and the activities and outcomes of prereferral and screening, as appropriate. In some districts, a letter of intent is sent to the parents to inform them of the team's decision to refer the student for special education testing.

Develop an assessment plan for the initial evaluation

Next, the team develops an assessment plan based on information gathered and evaluated during prereferral and/or screening activities. The type of questions being asked and the type of information wanted help to structure the plan. The assessment plan lists the tests and procedures to be used as well as a rationale for their selection. The plan may also indicate who will be responsible for specific components of the plan.

The types of assessments and procedures included in the assessment plan must conform with federal law. IDEA Amendments of 1997 provide specific guidelines for conducting assessments. Primarily, the law addresses issues of nondiscriminatory assessment—providing a fair assessment so information gathered truly represents the skills and needs of the student being tested and is not biased in any way. Federal guidelines for assessment practices specified in the IDEA Amendments of 1997 are as follows:

> (2) (A) use a variety of assessment tools and strategies to gather relevant functional and developmental information, including information provided by the parent, that may assist in determining whether the child is a child with a disability and the content of the child's individualized education program, including information related to enabling the child to be involved in and progress in the general curriculum or, for preschool children, to participate in appropriate activities;
>
> (B) not use any single procedure as the sole criterion for determining whether a child is a child with a disability or determining an appropriate educational program for the child; and
>
> (C) use technically sound instruments that may assess the relative contribution of cognitive and behavioral factors, in addition to physical or developmental factors.
>
> (3) Additional requirements. Each local educational agency shall ensure that—
>
> (A) tests and other evaluation materials used to assess a child under this section—
>
> > (i) are selected and administered so as not to be discriminatory on a racial or cultural basis; and
> >
> > (ii) are provided and administered in the child's native language or other mode of communication, unless it is clearly not feasible to do so; and
>
> (B) any standardized tests that are given to the child—
>
> > (i) have been validated for the specific purpose for which they are used;
> >
> > (ii) are administered by trained and knowledgeable personnel; and
> >
> > (iii) are administered in accordance with any instructions provided by the producer of such tests;
>
> (C) the child is assessed in all areas of suspected disability; and
>
> (D) assessment tools and strategies that provide relevant information that directly assists persons in determining the educational needs of the child are provided. (IDEA Amendments of 1997, Sec. 614(b))

Careful attention to these procedures, however, does not guarantee that all issues of bias are removed. For example, the guidelines state that all testing should be done in a child's native language or mode of communication unless doing so is not feasible. In many cases, it is not feasible to assess a child in his or her native language because testing instruments are not available in that language. According to the Council for Exceptional Children (1997, p. 1), "Currently, educators have no measurement tool that will produce an accurate assessment of a CLD [culturally and linguistically diverse] student's abilities." In districts and states serving highly diverse populations of students who speak languages other than English, the challenge to conduct all evaluations in the children's native language has generally gone unmet. These districts must grapple with how to accurately determine whether a child has a disability and whether the testing procedures that are used capture the child's true ability and performance. Many professionals argue that the lack of available instruments and the adoption of faulty evaluation procedures place students whose primary language is not English at a disadvantage and, moreover, is one of the primary reasons for the overrepresentation of individuals of color in special education.

Issues of bias are present in all types of assessment, including life skills assessments, which evaluate student skills in such areas as daily and community living (Lim & Browder, 1994). An individual's engagement in daily and community living skills such as shopping, hygiene, and communication varies across cultures and many times is governed by cultural beliefs and expectations. For example, some students may not be provided opportunities to develop some daily living skills (e.g., use of a knife and fork when eating) because they are not common practices in their family, community, or cultural group. Another example is found in the assessment of the adaptive behavior of African-American children. In comparisons of the adaptive behavior of African-American children against European-American standards, many times the children were reported to be immature or delayed in their social development (van Keulen, Weddington, & De Bose, 1998). But, according to these authors, when the same behaviors were viewed by members of the African-American community, the children were viewed as simply enjoying being children—meeting a cultural expectation. Lim and Browder (1994) offer several steps to make life skills assessment more responsive to and reflective of a multicultural perspective. These are presented in Exhibit 6.2.

EXHIBIT 6.2 **Multicultural Life Skills Assessment**	**GAIN CULTURAL AWARENESS** Recognize the importance and influence of culture Learn about the influence of culture Clarify personal values about multiculturalism Utilize books, courses, or inservice on multicultural education Learn about the culture of students to be taught Get to know students and their families as well **IMPROVE COMPETENCE TO WORK WITH FAMILIES** Consider family's priorities, needs, and strengths from the perspective of their own values and culture Invite the family to participate in the assessment and to help define what life skills will be assessed Avoid making generalizations about a family based on culture. Remember diversity *within* cultures. **RETAIN AN OUTCOME-BASED FOCUS** Ask the student and family to set priorities for the assessment and IEP to aid the teacher in achieving a bicultural balance Ask the student and family to help set criteria for mastery that are sensitive to cultural standards **CONSIDER LEARNING STYLE WHEN CONDUCTING ASSESSMENT** Be aware of field-sensitive and field-independent learning styles **CONSIDER CONTEXT WHEN CONDUCTING ASSESSMENT** Assess across contexts to define the environment in which competence is, or is not present Explore discrepancies in performance between home and school with the family to determine if these are adaptive (e.g., bicultural strengths) or reflect skill needs **APPLY THESE STEPS TO** Planning the assessment Conducting the assessment Analyzing and summarizing the assessment From Table 1, "Steps to Make Life Skills Assessment More Multicultural," in Lim and Browder, "Multicultural Life Skills Assessment...," *Journal of the Association of Persons with Severe Handicaps* 19(2) 1994:133. Title adapted and material reprinted by permission from the copyright holder.

Exhibit 6.3 presents an example assessment plan. Guiding questions and related contextualized assessment factors are identified, followed by a list of selected assessment tools and approaches and the professionals responsible for their administration. In this case, prereferral activities identified difficulties in reading and written language. Factors and questions included in the plan are drawn from contextualized assessment questions provided in Table 6.1. Some districts may not present such a detailed plan. Some districts may use a checklist assessment plan that allows for the checking off the types of tests to be administered.

EXHIBIT 6.3

Assessment Plan

Student Name ___Jimmy___   Grade __4__   Teacher ___Rodriguez___

Reason for Referral: Jimmy is experiencing difficulty in reading and writing, especially in the areas of vocabulary, reading comprehension, spelling, and writing mechanics.

Proposed Assessment Plan

Guiding Questions	Tool	Who
Overall Health and Specific Abilities • How is the child's overall health? • Does the child have any special health-care needs? • What, if any, vision, hearing, or motor difficulties could be interfering with this child's learning and performance?	• Satisfactory as evaluated on December 2 • Health history interview	Nurse or school psychologist
Communication and Performance • How do the child's speech and language skills compare to those of peers?	• Test of Language Development-3 Intermediate	Speech-language pathologist
Cognitive • What is the student's overall functioning level? • Does the child appear to have a processing disorder that is impacting his performance?	• Wechsler Intelligence Scale for Children-III	School psychologist
Academics and Related Skills • What is the child's overall academic skill profile? • In what areas of the school curriculum is the child experiencing success and difficulty? What strategies does the child employ when working in easy/difficult areas? • What types of instructional activities or manner of instructional presentation does the child most respond to? • What accommodations or adaptations are provided in general education settings? • What learning strategies and study skills does the child exhibit?	• Woodcock-Johnson Psycho-educational Battery-Revised • Woodcock Reading Mastery Tests-Revised • Informal reading inventory • Test of Written Language-2 • Teacher interview • Parent interview • Student interview • Observation • Paragraph writing checklist	Special and general education teachers School psychologist
Life Skills • How does the child respond to social situations? • What strategies does the child have for responding to situations? • How does the child go about making choices and decisions? • Is the child a self-advocate or do others serve as his advocate?	• Observation • Student and parent interviews	School psychologist Special and general education teachers Physical therapist

Complete informed parental consent

The referral request and assessment plan, along with a copy of parent rights, are presented to the parents, who decide whether to consent to the proposed assessment. Parents indicate their agreement by signing a statement of consent. If parents give consent, a local plan agency, the child's school district, or regional special education personnel then conduct a comprehensive assessment in all areas of suspected disability and, if the child is found eligible and in need of special education services, develop an Individualized Education Program (IEP). If parents do not provide their written consent for the assessment, the assessment is not initiated and the eligibility determination process comes to a halt unless school district personnel choose to go through mediation and/or due-process procedures.

This parental consent is referred to as *informed* consent. In order for consent to be informed, information concerning the referral must be provided in a language understood by the general public and, if necessary, translated into the parent's primary language or primary mode of communication (e.g., sign), or given orally if written notification is not feasible. Additionally, consent can be considered informed only if parents understand their rights. Among the rights to be discussed with the parent are that they have the right to refuse testing and can revoke their permission for testing at any time, and that the results of the testing will indicate whether their child is eligible for special education services.

Involving parents is not just a legal requirement—it is essential to the overall success of the process. Communicating to parents what is going to occur, how it is going to occur, and what the possible ramifications of proposed actions are, can build a strong communication link and sense of trust between parents and school personnel and should prevent future problems and disagreements. For example, a parent who is told only that the testing is being done to "help your child" may fail to realize that one possible outcome of the testing is the placement of the child in a special education program. Having a clear understanding at the beginning of the assessment process will help parents make informed decisions along the way.

Conduct the assessment

Once the parent has agreed in writing to the assessment, individual members of the team set out to complete their part of the assessment plan. School psychologists may be responsible for conducting psychoeducational cognitive assessment batteries (tests that measure general intelligence and adaptive behavior). Special education teachers may administer achievement tests (tests that assess skills in curriculum content areas such as reading, mathematics, and written language) and performance evaluations (e.g., sign language, social skills in the community).

Specialists, such as speech and language pathologists, may be asked to complete specialized assessments. General education teachers may be asked to collect and analyze student work samples and to record classroom observations. A parent may be interviewed to provide additional family and medical history and insight into the child's learning difficulties. The child may be interviewed about his or her opinions regarding difficulties, personal goals, and other topics. Parents, teachers, and the child may be asked to describe and/or demonstrate what the child can and cannot do and to complete rating scales concerning behavior.

If the student's primary language is not English, a bilingual specialist also should be included on the team to assist in the assessment of the child's language in both the primary language and in English. This expert also should observe in the classroom and other settings (a) to determine how the child is accessing and using language to learn and (b) to identify the greatest barriers to language development and learning through language that the child encounters during the day.

Report results

After the assessment has been completed, a report detailing outcomes is written. The report should present a holistic view of the child across contextualized assessment factors and contexts and avoid reducing the child's profile to a listing of assessment scores and identification of deficits. The report should provide the following information: (a) whether the student is recommended for special education and support services; (b) the basis for making such a determination; (c) all relevant observed behavior noted by the team; (d) the relationship between observed behavior and the current academic and social functioning of the student; (e) all relevant health, developmental, and medical findings; and (f) consideration of environmental, cultural, or economic effects on learning.

Parents receive written notification when the report is completed and information telling them how they may request a written copy of the report. This written notification also contains information about the IEP team conference, including the scheduling of the conference. The notification should encourage parent participation in the conference.

Determine eligibility and develop an initial IEP as appropriate

The team, including the parent and, when appropriate, the student, meet to discuss the findings of the evaluation. At this meeting the team determines the child's eligibility for special education services. To aid in the determination of eligibility for special education services as an individual with a disability, each state, guided by the definitions provided in federal law, specifies eligibility criteria for each area of disability. Teams refer to these criteria when determining a child's eligibility.

A child who is found ineligible may be referred back to the prereferral team, whose job then is to develop interventions to support the child's learning in the general education classroom. Moreover, a child who is found ineligible for special education services may be eligible for accommodations under Section 504 of the Rehabilitation Act of 1973 (P.L. 99-506). Section 504 is a civil rights law that stipulates that institutions receiving federal funds cannot discriminate against individuals with disabilities. Section 504 responds to the needs of individuals with functional disabilities that limit their engagement and participation in major life activities, such as schooling. Section 504 defines an individual with a disability as someone who "(a) has physical or mental impairment that substantially limits or restricts one or more major life activities, (b) has a record or history of such a physical or mental impairment, or (c) is regarded as having such an impairment." Individuals who meet this definition of disability but fail to meet the requirements specified for the categories of disability recognized under the IDEA Amendments of 1997 receive services and accommodations in general education settings under Section 504.

Examples of accommodations provided under Section 504 include the use of modified textbooks (e.g., textbooks written at different grade levels to reflect student reading levels) and the tailoring of assignments to reflect individual students' needs and abilities (e.g., presenting fewer problems per page for a child experiencing difficulties with processing a great deal of information at one time) (Conderman & Katsiyannis, 1995; Reid & Katsiyannis, 1995). These accommodations are generally outlined in a plan collaboratively developed by general and special education teachers and parents. Exhibit 6.4 is an example of a Section 504 accommodation plan. This plan specifies the child's areas of need and outlines accommodations to be made to address those needs. The purpose of the plan is to outline specific procedures to be followed in order to support the child's success in the learning environment.

EXHIBIT 6.4

Section 504 Accommodation Plan for a Second Grade Student

Name _Samantha Sojourn_   Age _7_   Grade _2_   Teacher _Ms. Page_   Date _December 3_

Referral and Assessment Data Summary

Reason for Referral

Samantha has great difficulty attending in class. During story time, she is unable to stay in her space on the rug, touches other children, and makes it difficult for those around her to pay attention to the story. She struggles with independent and group work, and fails to turn in assignments.

Assessment Data Summary

Samantha performed in the above-average range in all academic areas tested (reading, written language, mathematics). Classroom observations revealed that, in comparison to peers, Samantha experiences great difficulty organizing her materials and starting and maintaining interest in an activity. She moves from activity to activity, many times starting but not finishing. During an interview, Samantha commented that "school has too many rules" and that she wants to do things her way. Parent interviews indicated that these behavior patterns are also evident in the home. Rating scales completed by the classroom teacher and parent identified organization skills and task persistence as primary areas of concern.

Accommodation Plan   Date of Initiation _December 5_   Review Date _February 25_

Target Areas and Goals	Intervention	Evaluation Procedures	Person Responsible
ORGANIZATION SKILLS			
1. Student will keep all personal supplies not in use in a designated box on top of her work space.	Student will keep personal supplies in a box stored on the table-top of her work space.	Teacher periodic check	General education teacher
2. Homework folder will go home, the work completed, and assignment sheet signed off by parents at least 4 out of 5 weekdays.	Homework folder will be used each evening. Parent will sign off that the folder got home and the homework was completed, and then place completed homework in the folder to be brought back to school.	Review of parent sign-off sheet	General education teacher Parent
TASK PERSISTENCE			
1. Student will turn in at least 90% of in-class assignments.	Daily assignment completion sheet will be taped to the top of the student's work space. Each time an assignment is completed and turned in, student will draw a star on the chart.	Teacher will compare student chart to work turned in for accuracy. Teacher will chart and evaluate daily assignment completion rate.	General education teacher Counselor
2. Student will remain with the group for the entire story time activity at least 4 out of 5 weekdays.	During story time, student will be given three off-task disruptive chances indicated by color strips pulled from a folder kept near the teacher and in clear view of the student. On the fourth occurrence, the student will be asked to leave the group and return to her individual work space.	Teacher will record the number of chances remaining at the conclusion of each story time session or if the student was asked to return to her seat.	General education teacher Counselor

Plan Participants

Monique Sojourn	✓			_Ms. Page_	✓	
Parent	Agree	Disagree		General Education Teacher	Agree	Disagree
Tsai Hsia	✓			_Samantha_	✓	
Special Education Teacher	Agree	Disagree		Other	Agree	Disagree

A child who *is* found eligible and in need of special education services receives a *label* that reflects the disability category for which he or she is eligible (the categories of disabilities are listed in Chapter 1). This label provides minimal information about the child's unique educational needs but serves as the means through which the child receives services. Once eligibility has been determined through prereferral or directly, for those with obvious disabilities and need for special education services, an individualized program is developed, implemented, and monitored on an annual basis. The development of these individualized plans is discussed in Chapter 1 and should be reviewed at this time. If appropriate, an initial IEP can be developed.

THEORY TO PRACTICE

➡ Arrange with a local school to sit in on a prereferral meeting. Who is present at the meeting? Who contributes what types of information? Who participates the most and least? What types of questions are asked? What issues are of primary concern? How does the team arrive at a plan of action? If you were a member of this team, what recommendations would you have for the team process?

➡ Interview a general education teacher who has referred a child for special education evaluation. What was the experience like? What did the teacher like most and least about the experience? What suggestions does the teacher have for improving the process?

➡ Secure copies of prereferral, screening, and referral forms used by area school districts (e.g., prereferral form for individual referring the student, prereferral intervention form, assessment plan, statement of parent rights, IEP meeting announcement). Evaluate these forms. What type of language is used on them? Is the language appropriate for parents and other family members? Are the forms clear in their purpose and intent? What information appears to be missing from the forms? What are the positive features of the forms? What suggestions do you have for improvement?

➡ Read additional literature about the evaluation of students of color for special education eligibility. Identify the strategies proposed, and the strengths and weaknesses of each strategy. Summarize and present your information to a member of an evaluation team for feedback.

➡ Contact a local school to find out how the staff is designing and implementing Section 504 plans. What types of students have Section 504 plans, and what is the staff's overall impression of these plans and their ability to support the individual's success at that particular school site?

CHAPTER SUMMARY

This chapter describes contextualized assessment and discusses the first purpose of special education assessment: determination of eligibility for special education services and development of an initial IEP. The process generally consists of three steps: prereferral, screening, and referral. At each step assessment teams, with parent involvement, engage in a series of unique tasks. Through this process, students may be identified as eligible or ineligible for and in need of special education services. An IEP is developed for students found eligible; those found ineligible may be referred back to the prereferral team, or if appropriate, a Section 504 plan may be developed to address their unique needs.

CHAPTER 7

Purposes of Assessment: Part II

Read to find out the following:
- assessment procedures for annual reviews and reevaluations
- assessment procedures for evaluating instruction
- assessment considerations and procedures for program evaluation
- terminology associated with assessment classification systems and the shortcomings of these systems
- features of a proposed model for analyzing assessment methods and tools

Following the previous chapter's discussion of assessments for (a) referral and initial IEP development, this chapter continues the discussion of assessment purposes. We address the remaining three purposes of educational assessment: (b) review of individualized plans; (c) evaluation of instruction; and (d) program evaluation. In the final section of the chapter we introduce classification systems available for understanding the range of available assessment methods and tools.

ASSESSMENT PURPOSE 2: REVIEW OF INDIVIDUALIZED PLANS

The second purpose of assessment is to review individualized plans—IFSPs, IEPs, and ITPs—mandated by the IDEA Amendments of 1997 and developed for students receiving special education and related services. The purpose of the review is to determine the degree to which (a) goals and objectives are achieved, (b) the educational environments are supportive of student growth, and (c) services are meeting the child's needs as specified in the plan. Mandated reviews include six-month reviews of IFSPs and annual reviews of IEPs and ITPs, as well as reevaluations of all individualized plans.

Annual reviews generally are not as in-depth as the initial evaluation and at least every three years reevaluations may be in-depth if that level of detail is deemed appropriate by the team or parents. Using the factors and contexts identified through contextualized assessment and information contained in the existing individualized plan, the IEP team develops an assessment plan to evaluate student performance and progress toward goals and objectives included in the most recent individualized plan. An example of an assessment plan for the annual review of an IEP is provided in Exhibit 7.1. The purpose of the plan presented in Exhibit 7.1 is to compare Brenda's present levels of performance to existing IEP goals and objectives. It is also to determine her needs in academic, social, transition, and communication and performance domains.

Student Name <u>Brenda</u>   Age <u>14</u>   Grade <u>9</u>   Teacher <u>McMillan</u>

Eligibility: Orthopedic Impairment

Previous Goal and Objective Areas: Life Skills and Modified Means of Communication and Performance

Proposed Assessment Plan

Guiding Questions	Tool	Who
Current IEP • What goals and objectives did Brenda achieve? • What goals and objectives did Brenda fail to achieve? Is she making adequate progress toward their achievement? Are the goals and objectives still appropriate?	• "Inventory of Means of Task Performance" • IEP checklist of current goals and objectives • Observation	• General education teachers • Special education teacher • Specialist in augmentative and alternative communication • Parents • School psychologist

• What are Brenda's long-term goals? What are her career/employment aspirations?
• What family and community supports are available to assist Brenda in making the transition to work and community situations?
• What community-based experiences has Brenda been involved in? What community/job-related skills does she have? need to develop?
• How is Brenda getting along with others in school and community settings? To what extent and how does she advocate for herself and her needs?
	• Rating Scale
	• Inventory
	• Observation
	• Interview:
	  Teacher
	  Parent
	  Community support
		• Special education teacher
		• School psychologist
		• Vocational education coordinator
		• Parents

• How is Brenda doing in the general education curriculum? What accommodations or adaptations are used to support her success in general education settings? What else is needed?
• What learning strategies does she use when faced with new tasks? What study skills does she employ while completing school and job tasks?
	• Woodcock-Johnson Psycho-Education Battery-Revised: Tests of Achievement
	• Interviews:
	  Teacher
	  Parent
	  Community support
		• Special education teacher
		• General education teachers
		• School psychologist

• What modified means for acquiring and managing information does Brenda use? Does she need additional assistance in developing skills in this area?
• What modified means for performing physical tasks does Brenda use? Does she need additional assistance in developing skills in this area?
	• Observation
	• Interviews:
	  Teachers
	  Parents
		• Special education teacher
		• General education teachers

EXHIBIT 7.1

Assessment Plan for the Annual Review of an IEP

Reevaluations of individualized plans are conducted "if conditions warrant a reevaluation or if the child's parent or teacher requests a reevaluation, but at least once every 3 years" (IDEA Amendments of 1997, Sec. 614(a)(2)(A)). During a reevaluation, the IEP team must do the following:

(A) *review existing evaluation data on the child, including evaluations and information provided by the parents of the child, current classroom-based assessments and observations, and teacher and related services providers observations; and*

(B) *on the basis of that review, and input from the child's parents, identify what additional data, if any, are needed to determine—*

 (i) *. . . whether the child continues to have such a disability;*

 (ii) *the present levels of performance and educational needs of the child;*

(iii) . . . *whether the child continues to need special education and related services;* . . . *and*

(iv) *whether any additions or modifications to the special education and related services are needed to enable the child to meet the measurable annual goals set out in the individualized education program of the child and to participate, as appropriate, in the general curriculum. (IDEA Amendments of 1997, Sec. 614(c)(1))*

When conducting a reevaluation, the team must consider information from the most recent evaluation and any new information gathered to determine if the child continues to have a disability and, if so, to determine his or her educational needs. If the team decides no assessment is needed to determine whether the child continues to be a child with a disability, the school or school district

(A) *shall notify the child's parents of—*
  (i) *that determination and the reasons for it; and*
  (ii) *the right of such parents to request an assessment to determine whether the child continues to be a child with a disability; and*
(B) *shall not be required to conduct such an assessment unless requested to by the child's parents. (IDEA Amendments of 1997, Section 614(c)(4))*

Thus, reevaluations of plans vary according to student needs. A complete contextualized assessment may be conducted if deemed necessary by the district or parents, or an abbreviated review based on information gathered through on-going assessment may be held.

THEORY TO PRACTICE

➡ Meet with a special education teacher to learn how she or he manages annual reviews and reevaluations. What type of information does the teacher believe is most important to collect? How extensive is the testing for annual reviews and reevaluations? How does the teacher involve other professionals, the parents, and the student in the process?

➡ Interview a parent of a student with a disability concerning annual reviews and reevaluations. What does the parent consider to be most important about these reviews? What does the parent find least valuable? What recommendations does the parent have to make annual reviews and reevaluations more meaningful for herself or himself and for the child?

ASSESSMENT PURPOSE 3: EVALUATION OF INSTRUCTION

The third purpose of assessment is evaluating instruction. Once individualized programs are developed, teachers and other team members work together to design instructional plans to present curriculum to students. This instructional planning is implemented through daily lessons. It is the job of the teacher—along with the student, parent, and others responsible for working with the student—to evaluate the success of this instructional planning.

There are many ways in which instructional evaluation is carried out. Some teachers may adopt portfolio assessment as their primary approach. Portfolio assessment (discussed in Chapter 8) involves the collection and evaluation of student work samples—works that represent drafts or steps toward a final product, as well as final products selected by students and teachers. The evaluation of the portfolio is carried out by both the teacher and the student. Students reflect on their own work and discuss what they believe the work demonstrates about them as learners, and both students and teachers can use rubrics and checklists and other tools to assess the work included in the portfolio.

Teachers may also adopt procedures such as curriculum-based measurement (Fuchs & Deno, 1992) and running records (Clay, 1993) to monitor the ongoing performance of students. Both approaches address fluency (the rate at which students complete tasks) and, through close observation of students' skills when performing tasks, determine whether children are making adequate progress or whether a change in curriculum or instructional approach is warranted.

Still other methods that may be adopted are the use of checklists, rating scales, reading retells, and observation. In Chapter 8 we describe these and other ways teachers and students can assess the effectiveness of instructional planning.

THEORY TO PRACTICE

➡ Meet with a special education teacher to learn how she or he monitors student performance throughout the year. Ask the type of information each method provides and how the teacher manages it in the classroom. What methods does the teacher find most valuable?

➡ Meet with a general education teacher who has students with special education needs in her or his classroom. How does the teacher monitor the students' performance on a daily, weekly, monthly, and quarterly basis? Who is responsible for the monitoring? What type of information does the monitoring provide? What additional information does this general education teacher believe is needed?

➡ Interview a special education teacher about her or his monitoring of student IEPs. What mechanisms does this teacher have in place for determining ongoing progress toward IEP goals? What does the teacher find most challenging in monitoring students' performance throughout the school year? What mechanisms does the teacher have for informing parents of this ongoing information?

➡ Interview parents about the monitoring of their child's performance at school. What type of information does the teacher provide the parents concerning the child's ongoing performance? How is this information relayed to them and how often? How valuable do the parents consider this information? What other additional information would they like to receive?

ASSESSMENT PURPOSE 4: PROGRAM EVALUATION

Program evaluation is the fourth main purpose of special education assessment. Program evaluation is broad in scope and embraces not only the assessment of individualized programs (Assessment Purpose 2) and evaluation of instruction (Assessment Purpose 3) but also the evaluation of overall programs and services. Educational evaluation, by definition, is a systematic investigative process by which an individual or group makes a judgment to determine the worth and merits of a curriculum and the system through which it is delivered (Joint Committee on Standards for Educational Evaluation, 1994). According to Ysseldyke and Thurlow (1993),

> *Knowing to what degree students, schools, and systems achieve desired outcomes is an essential component in the evaluation of instructional practices and resources. (p. 8)*

Because of their complexity and comprehensive nature, program evaluations require the expertise of many individuals and generally are carried out by teams of individuals. Administrators, school psychologists, program coordinators and supervisors, teachers, support personnel, students, and parents may all serve as members of evaluation teams.

Conducting the Evaluation

Like other forms of assessment, program evaluation begins with the articulation of questions that serve to clarify the purpose of the evaluation and assist in determining how results will be used and disseminated. These questions can be framed by the two major purposes of program evaluation identified by the Joint Committee on Standards for Educational Evaluation (1994): (a) program quality and (b) program improvement. Program quality addresses the overall effectiveness of the program; program improvement addresses how the program could be changed to bring about desired results.

Once the purpose(s) for the evaluation are determined by the team and questions are posed, team efforts turn to identifying sources of information that will provide answers to proposed questions and will provide evidence of outcomes. Table 7.1 provides a beginning list of information sources and the types of evidence they can provide, as drawn from work of the Joint Committee on Standards for Educational Evaluation (1994).

TABLE 7.1 SOURCES OF INFORMATION AND EVIDENCE FOR PROGRAM EVALUATION

SOURCE	EVIDENCE
Individual Student Files (including K–12 and post-12 files)	• academic achievement profiles (e.g., performance on proficiency and achievement tests) • courses taken, course credits earned, course grades • activity involvement • employment records, job supervisor ratings • health histories/records
Student Portfolios	• specific work samples and projects • student self-reflection and -evaluation statements • employment opportunities and experiences
Teacher, Building, District, State, and National Databases	• graduation and dropout rates • incarceration levels • postsecondary education enrollment, employment and housing statistics, voter and driver registration

Once information sources are identified, team members work together to develop an evaluation plan. The plan serves as a blueprint of the effort through specification of team members' roles and responsibilities, information to be gathered and information-gathering procedures to be used, and analysis and presentation procedures. Exhibit 7.2 presents an evaluation plan used by a team of teachers evaluating a lunchtime tutoring program. The plan lists the purpose of the evaluation, how the results of the evaluation will be used, the questions to be addressed, sources to be tapped, methods and tools for data gathering, individuals responsible for each activity, and the timeline for the completion of those activities.

Purpose: To evaluate the effectiveness of the lunch tutoring program in assisting students in completing and turning in assignments.

Use of Results: To develop specific plans for improving the program for the next academic year

EXHIBIT 7.2

Sixth Grade Tutoring Program Evaluation Plan

QUESTIONS	INFORMATION SOURCES AND EVIDENCE	METHODS/TOOLS	PERSON RESPONSIBLE	TIMELINE
Program Quality To what extent do students participate in or take advantage of the program?	Daily sign-in sheet: students' names and frequency of their participation	• Tallying how many students use the program and their frequency of use	• Team 1 will tally outcomes	Week 1
Program Quality What type of students participate in the program?	Daily sign-in sheet: students' names and their program affiliation	• Tallying which students use the program and their current course of study	• Team 1 will complete the tallying	Week 2
Program Improvement What influences students' participation?	Students: opinions and perceptions of the program	• Interviews with students who participate in the program	• Team 2 will individually interview 10 randomly selected students who participated in the program on a consistent basis and 10 who participated in the program in the past but are no longer participants	Weeks 3–5
Program Quality In what areas do students participating in the program demonstrate the greatest gains in completing and submitting assignments? In what areas do students demonstrate the fewest gains?	Teacher grade books: student assignment completion histories by subject area	• Tallying assignment completion rates by subject areas for all students participating in the program, and calculating percentage of assignments completed per week	• All sixth grade teachers, given a list of students participating in the program, will calculate the percentage of assignments completed by these students on a weekly basis and submit copies of this information to Team 1 • Team 1 will summarize the weekly assignment completion rates of participating students • Team 3 will work together to evaluate the weekly assignment completion rates of participating students	Week 6
Program Improvement What are some of the barriers to program effectiveness? What is being done/needs to be done to overcome these barriers?	Students, teachers, parents, and administrators: perceptions and opinions	• Interviews with students • Surveys for teachers, parents, and administrators	• Team 2 will interview students • Team 4 will develop, disseminate, and analyze the survey	Weeks 7 and 8

Analyzing Findings

Once information is collected, it must be analyzed. Analysis can be completed in several ways. In this section we describe four approaches to the analysis of evaluation data.

Discrepancy analysis

One commonly used procedure for analyzing evaluation data is discrepancy analysis as reported by Disability Research Systems (1994) and based on the work of Provus (1971). This discrepancy evaluation model identifies individual student or program needs through a simple comparison of "What do we observe?" to a standard of "What do we expect?" which leads to the identification of discrepancies. When discrepancies are positive—that is, when "what is" exceeds "what should be"—the information suggests that teachers and schools are achieving or surpassing program goals. When discrepancies are negative—that is, when observed performance falls below expected standards—the program may be in need of modification, or standards of "what should be" may need to be revisited and adjusted. An example of this type of analysis is presented in Exhibit 7.3.

EXHIBIT 7.3	**Purpose:** To evaluate the effectiveness of community field trips on ten students' awareness of and participation in community recreational experiences.
Discrepancy Analysis	**Use of Information:** Revision of current program structures to more strongly support student participation in community recreational opportunities.

QUESTIONS	WHAT DO WE EXPECT?	WHAT DO WE OBSERVE?	DISCREPANCIES
Program Quality: In what areas did students participating in the program demonstrate the greatest gain and achievement?	• students will exhibit greater ease and comfort while in the community • students will self-select activities to participate in • students will become actively involved in at least one community activity	• students were eager to try new things, were willing to attend events • 8 students self-selected activities they wanted to participate in • 5 students are actively involved in a community activity	• 2 students failed to self-select activities • 5 students failed to actively participate in a community activity
Program Quality: To what extent did student gains within the program generalize to activities outside the program?	• students will seek out new programs on their own • students will self-select other activities and become involved on their own	• 3 students have discovered new programs on their own • 1 student has become involved in a community activity she discovered on her own	• 7 students have not discovered additional programs or activities on their own • 9 students have not become involved in additional, self-selected activities

Comparison of group performance

A traditional form of evaluative comparison is the comparison of the performance of one group of students to that of another. This can be completed through administration of achievement tests that compare student performance to a norm group. Information about student performance on these tests may be used to compare schools within a district to one another, or districts or regions within a state may use this information to compare performances.

Comparison to a criterion or standard

A different type of comparison involves the use of criterion standards that specify performance levels students are expected to achieve to demonstrate competence in a given area. District and/or school proficiency tests in reading and writing are one example. In many schools, students are required to pass proficiency tests—that is, achieve or exceed a specified performance level or score—in order to be eligible to earn a diploma on school exit.

Another type of analysis is comparing outcomes of one program to a similar program regarded as highly effective. For example, a school may want to evaluate a program in which general education peers serve as buddies for students with severe disabilities. The program at the school may be compared to an existing program at another school rated as being highly effective. The comparison of the two programs can provide valuable information for enhancement of the newly developed buddy program.

Longitudinal analysis

Analysis may also be longitudinal. At the program level, data may be collected across several years of a district, state, or national program and analyzed to identify trends. For example, job placement statistics of vocational education program graduates could be charted and compared over several years to determine whether the program is effective in helping graduates to secure employment.

IEP annual reviews and reevaluations and district and state assessment programs are other examples of longitudinal analysis. Annual IEP reviews capture and evaluate student performance over the course of the academic year; reevaluations evaluate student performance over three years. District and state assessment programs call for student completion of standardized achievement testing each year or on a cycle such as every third year in school, and allow for longitudinal evaluation of student performance as well. Until recently, students with disabilities generally were excluded from this type of testing because of the belief that the tests were inappropriate in content or format to assess their skills and understandings meaningfully. However, the IDEA Amendments of 1997 changed this practice, mandating:

> *Children with disabilities are included in general State and district-wide assessment programs, with appropriate accommodations, where necessary. (IDEA Amendments of 1997, Sec. 612(a)(17)(A))*

Specifically, the amendments state that the state or local agency

> (i) *develops guidelines for the participation of children with disabilities in alternative assessment for those children who cannot participate in State and district-wide assessment programs; and*
> (ii) *develops and, beginning not later than July 1, 2000, conducts those alternate assessments. (IDEA Amendments of 1997, Sec. 612)(a)(17)(A))*

Using Evaluation Findings

Educators and politicians use evaluation results for accountability, program modification, public information, and policy formation. Table 7.2 lists some uses of evaluation findings.

TABLE 7.2 USE OF EVALUATION FINDINGS

LEVEL OF INFLUENCE	USE
National	• setting policy and priorities • passing legislation to respond to identified needs • establishing programs to address identified needs • developing curriculum frameworks and suggestions
State	• identifying teacher inservice and preservice needs • setting certification/licensure standards for teachers
District	• identifying teacher inservice and preservice needs • setting teacher and support staff hiring standards • appraising personnel considerations (e.g., need for new hires, need to reduce program size)
Building	• developing curriculum guidelines • developing teacher-support programs within the school (e.g., pre-referral teams) • identifying teacher inservice needs • setting teacher and support staff hiring standards
Teachers	• modifying instructional procedures for better matching of student needs • collaboratively developing curriculum guidelines and interdisciplinary curricular opportunities • developing collaborative efforts among teachers in order to address student needs better • attending inservice programs

THEORY TO PRACTICE

➡ Meet with district personnel involved in a special program (e.g., an after-school tutoring program for students) or the director of special education. Interview them about how they evaluate their program. Critique their evaluation procedure in terms of information provided here. If no official evaluation component is in place, draft an evaluation plan based on the information you are able to gather concerning the program. Present your plan to project personnel for consideration.

➡ Imagine you are a special education teacher working in a newly developed, full-inclusion program. How will you evaluate the effectiveness of the program? What questions will you ask, what information sources will you tap to respond to questions, how will you analyze collected data, and how will you use findings to inform program policies and procedures?

CLASSIFYING ASSESSMENT METHODS AND TOOLS

In order to achieve the four purposes of special education assessment, team members need to be familiar with and have access to a variety of assessment methods and tools. Traditionally, assessment methods and tools have been described as belonging to discrete categories based on their characteristics (e.g., how they are administered). Today many classification systems are available for describing assessment methods and tools. This section describes the most commonly used classification systems and highlights their uses and limitations by describing the range of tools and methods available to teams.

Formal and Informal Tests

McLoughlin and Lewis (1994) divide assessment methods and tools into two broad categories: *formal* and *informal*. Formal tests have set procedures for administration, scoring, and interpretation, and they generally report outcomes in terms of how students perform in relation to a comparison group (a norm group). These tests report technical adequacy—that is, reliability and validity.

Formal tests generally include a protocol for recording student responses and a book or easel that includes all test items. The easel contains information for the examiner and cues, prompts, items, and visuals for the student to refer to when responding to items. The easel is placed between the student and the examiner; the examiner reads directions or items and the student responds. The examiner records either the student's exact response or a mark that indicates the correctness of the response (e.g., 0 for incorrect and 1 for correct).

Formal tests include basals and ceilings to prevent the examiner from having to administer all items within each test. A basal indicates a starting point; all the easier items are not administered but are assumed to be answered correctly. For example, when testing a fifth grade student, the examiner may begin on item 20 of a test, the starting point indicated for fifth graders. This starting point is selected because items 1 through 19 are generally answered correctly by students who are in the fifth grade. Once a basal is established, the examiner administers items until the student achieves a ceiling— point at which the student has made a predetermined number of errors and the examiner assumes that the student's answers to all the more difficult items will be incorrect. For example, on the KeyMath-Revised (Connolly, 1988), a diagnostic test that assesses students' mathematical performance, three incorrect responses in a row represent a ceiling. As you can see from this brief description, administration procedures are detailed and precise in formal assessment tools.

Results gained from formal tests are reported as standard scores, percentiles, stanines, normal curve equivalents, and other such scores. These allow examiners and team members to determine whether the child's performance is average, above or below average, or significantly below or above average (these scores are more specifically described in an upcoming section on test results).

Examples of formal tests include IQ tests and standardized achievement tests such as the Woodcock Reading Mastery Tests-Revised (Woodcock, 1987) and the Peabody Individual Achievement Test-Revised (Markwardt, 1989). These tests are not curriculum specific but rather assess a wide range of skills within academic domains. This means that the tests may or may not reflect the curriculum taught in a particular school; there may be a mismatch between what is taught and what is tested because the curriculum in the school focuses on one set of skills and understandings and the test assesses other skills and understandings. Because of this possible discrepancy, testing outcomes derived from formal tests generally provide a broad picture of student performance, rather than inform classroom practice and curriculum selection. (Formal tests are also discussed in Chapter 8, in the section "Peer-Comparison Tests.")

In contrast, informal tests take many forms and are commonly associated with curriculum-based assessment. As defined by King-Sears (1994), curriculum-based assessment is

a data collection procedure that is a direct measure of student progress within a curriculum, with the data serving as a basis for confirmation of adequate and expected progress as well as determination that effective teaching and learning is occurring. (p. 9)

Examples of informal, curriculum-based assessments include teacher-made quizzes; analysis of student writing samples using checklists, rating scales, and rubrics; and interviews with students, parents, caregivers, and teachers. In most cases, informal tests do not follow predetermined administration, scoring, and interpretation procedures but rather leave decisions about these matters to the classroom teacher or examiner. For example, when analyzing student writing samples, a teacher may use a rubric or a checklist or choose to write a narrative highlighting strengths and weaknesses. Additionally, the teacher or examiner may have students use self-evaluation checklists, rate their own writing by using a rubric, or evaluate their writing through peer feedback. All of these methods fall under the category of informal assessment. Because of these varied formats and purposes, the types of scores derived from these assessments vary greatly (e.g., percentage correct, oral reading rate, narrative description).

Although on the surface this classification of assessment tools and methods as either formal or informal appears to group tools into two distinct categories, in reality not all tools fall neatly into one or the other category. Observation, for example, is generally considered informal, but some observation tools have predetermined administration, scoring, and interpretation procedures and report findings in comparison to a norm group (group of same age/grade peers) and thus share characteristics with both formal and informal tools and break down this classification system.

Norm-Referenced and Criterion-Referenced Tests

Norm-referenced tests compare a student's performance to a norm group (a representative sample of students of the same age and grade as the student taking the test) and indicate whether the child is performing at, above, or below the average expected for his or her grade and/or age. The term *norm-referenced* can be used interchangeably with *formal;* norm-referenced assessment has all the characteristics described above for formal assessment.

Criterion-referenced tests are considered one form of informal assessment. They compare student performance to an established criterion or standard of performance. Criteria reflect specific curricular and skill levels (e.g., reading at the third grade level; solving addition problems with renaming at 80 percent correct accuracy; tracking a moving object with one's eyes 4 out of 5 trials). These tests indicate whether students are performing at the established levels.

This classification system, too, is limited in its ability to classify assessment tools and methods meaningfully. The same concerns highlighted in the discussion of informal and formal tests apply here, and there is another key drawback: not all of the tools and methods that are not norm-referenced are criterion-referenced. This system does not address tools and methods such as observation, interviews, and questionnaires, among others, that may be neither norm-referenced nor criterion-referenced.

Summative and Formative Assessment

Assessment practices may be classified as *summative* or *formative*. Summative means that the findings gained from the tools or methods summarize student performance—that is, they tell what a student has learned as a result of instruction. Examples of summative tools are tests or quizzes that teachers administer at the end of a unit of instruction; proficiency tests administered at the end of the year or at a set time such as at the end of the junior year of high school; and academic achievement tests administered annually or on a predetermined cycle (e.g., students taking achievement tests every year or every four years—in grades 4, 8, and 12).

In contrast, formative assessments are ongoing and are used to inform instructional practice. They provide information about how a student is doing as instruction is delivered, and they inform teachers about needed instructional modifications. For example, a teacher may give mini-quizzes or probes throughout an instructional unit, rather than just at the end. She can then use this information to modify instructional approaches, to reteach concepts with which students are having difficulty, and to reinforce concepts in which students are demonstrating some understanding but lack proficiency or mastery. Examples of formative assessments include curriculum-based assessment, curriculum-based measurement, assessment portfolios, and checklists (all discussed further in Chapter 8).

It may appear that summative tests may also be classified as formal and norm-referenced and that formative tests may also be classified as informal and criterion-referenced, but again there are exceptions. Some informal tests may be used as summative measures, others as formative measures. Nevertheless, this classification system, if taken alone, without reference to the formal and informal or norm- and criterion-referenced categories, is somewhat stronger than the two other systems we described. Tools and methods generally do fall into either the summative or the formative category. The primary limitation of this classification system is that it fails to explain all of the other important characteristics that examiners and teams need to know about assessment methods and tools—administration, scoring, and interpretation procedures, technical adequacy, and performance indicators.

Static and Dynamic Assessment

According to Campione (1989), assessment may be viewed as falling into the two categories of *static* and *dynamic*. Static assessment is concerned with outcomes and products and places emphasis on what students can and cannot do. Many static measures can also be classified as formal, norm-referenced, and summative. In comparison, dynamic assessment is concerned with the processes involved in learning and change, not just the outcome or product (Campione & Brown, 1987). Dynamic assessment may be framed as a constructivist approach to assessment.

As specified by Meltzer and Reid (1994), the goal of a constructivist approach to assessment is to "determine what the students *do, can do, and can do with help*" (p. 339), and to devote less attention to comparing student performance to set standards or to norm-group performance in an attempt to identify deficiencies. Assessment is focused on student learning and performance over time, and comparisons are made between a student's current and past performance. Additionally, dynamic assessment is concerned with learning what a student is able to do when provided supports in the form of prompts, cues, or physical supports, some of which naturally exist within environments in which the student lives, works, learns, and plays. For example, the examiner asks the student a question and the student is unable to respond. In dynamic assessment, the examiner would not mark the item as incorrect and move to the next item; the examiner would restate the item, providing the item in language more familiar to the student and possibly defining unfamiliar terms. If the student is still unable to answer the question, the examiner may ask the student to respond to a different question, a question that reflects an understanding of an underlying concept needed to respond to the original question. This sequence of scaffolding is continued until the student is able to respond. Information is analyzed to determine what the student knows and can do in this area, and the types of supports he or she needs to be successful. When conducting constructivist-based assessment, examiners are more interested in revealing how a student learns and what strategies the student applies when approaching tasks or problems.

Currently most forms of assessment fall into the category of static assessment. Rarely do examiners alter formats and provide prompts or other supports as students complete assessment activities. The provision of prompts and supports is not the same as modifying test formats to take into consideration the unique needs of learners with disabilities (e.g., allowing the student to point to an answer rather than having to state it aloud). Prompts and supports are provided as the student is responding and are delivered in such a way as to allow for the determination of the type and extent of support a student needs in order to respond correctly. Therefore, this classification system does not provide a great deal of information in light of current assessment practices. However, it does challenge examiners to question the type of information that static assessments fail to provide—information that could be gained through dynamic assessment approaches.

Naturalistic, Alternative, Authentic, and Performance-Based Assessment

Currently, there is a growing movement to embrace a different form of assessment referred to as *naturalistic, alternative, authentic,* and/or *performance-based* assessment. Although several terms are suggested to describe this new breed of assessment, the common purpose of these approaches is to provide alternatives to traditional formal, norm-referenced testing. This group of assessment methods and tools does not form a classification system, like the others previously described, but provides a label for describing emerging forms of assessment.

Herman, Aschbacher, and Winters (1992) use the terms *alternative, authentic,* and *performance-based* interchangeably to describe various forms of performance assessment. They define performance assessment as something that

> *requires students to actively accomplish complex and significant tasks, while bringing to bear prior knowledge, recent learning, and relevant skills to solve realistic or authentic problems. (p. 2)*

Moreover, they identify the following characteristics as being common to these assessment approaches:

- Ask students to perform, create, produce, or do something.
- Tap higher-level thinking and problem-solving skills.
- Use tasks that represent meaningful instructional activities.
- Invoke real-world applications.
- People, not machines, do the scoring, using human judgment.
- Require new instructional and assessment roles for teachers. (p. 6)

Examples of assessment formats include (a) constructed-response items, such as fill-in-the-answer and short-answer formats; (b) writing; (c) oral discourse, including interviews and defense of work completed; (d) exhibitions, including demonstrations and/or live performances before an audience; (e) demonstrations in employment and other community situations; (f) experiments—namely, activities involving the application of the scientific method; and (g) portfolios, defined as "collections of student's work assembled over time" (Feuer & Fulton, 1993, p. 478).

This category of assessment is evolving—new methods and tools are continually being developed. Because of this constant change, agreement on terminology to be used to describe this new breed of assessment is still to come.

Shortcomings of the Current Classification Systems

Although those systems of classification may help our understanding of assessment in a general way, they also may restrict our thinking about assessment and contribute to the confusion surrounding assessment practice, because many assessment tools and methods do not fall neatly into discrete categories.

In actuality, all forms of assessment vary along several dimensions, and those dimensions can vary along a continuum. One way to overcome the shortcomings of the classifications described above is to identify the dimensions of tools and methods and analyze them in terms of their characteristics. By analyzing tools and methods in this way we do not focus on labeling the method or tool as belonging to one category or another thus avoiding possible problems with overlapping among categories; instead, we focus on thoroughly understanding the specific characteristics of a method or tool based on identified dimensions. This system, the Assessment Dimension System (Stump, 1995), identifies seven dimensions, six of them seen as being on a continuum (see Figure 7.1). This notion of a continuum is drawn from the work of Elliott (1994) who presented continua related to task demands and authenticity. By evaluating an assessment method or tool along these seven dimensions, team members may select or design a tool or method that most effectively addresses the assessment questions raised. If multiple questions are being asked, identifying the dimensions of primary concern can assist in making determinations about which methods and tools to include in the assessment battery. In the remainder of this chapter we examine the Assessment Dimension System.

THEORY TO PRACTICE

➡ Select and review a standardized achievement test. What does the test test? What types of items are included and in what format(s) are these items presented to students? How is the test administered, scored, and interpreted? Who was included in the norm group?

➡ Meet with a general education teacher to discuss the types of assessment methods and tools he or she uses in the classroom. What do the teacher's choices of testing instruments suggest about his or her assessment questions? What type of information is the teacher most interested in gathering? Does the teacher have a well-rounded plan for assessing the students? If you were this teacher, what other considerations would you have for assessing ongoing student performance?

➡ Meet with a special education teacher to discuss the types of informal, curriculum-based, authentic assessment approaches he or she uses for assessing student performance. How does the teacher use these tools in the classroom, and what type of information do they provide? What does the teacher identify as the strengths and weaknesses of these testing approaches?

ASSESSMENT DIMENSION SYSTEM

The Assessment Dimension System (ADS) (Stump, 1995) describes assessment methods and tools along seven dimensions: (a) information uses, (b) administration procedures, (c) assessment findings, (d) technical adequacy, (e) performance demands, (f) authenticity, and (g) alignment with curriculum content. *Information uses* is the first decision made when selecting an assessment method or tool, and provides the foundation of the system. The remaining six dimensions are viewed as having their own continuum. For example, the continuum for the dimension of administration procedures ranges from standardized (having preset procedures that must be strictly followed) to varied (see Figure 7.1).

Dimension 1: Information Uses
The first dimension, information uses, is not found on a continuum, but rather, identifies three primary ways assessment information can be used (see the base of Figure 7.1). These three ways are:

1. To make peer comparisons: compare a student's performance to that of his or her same age/grade peers to determine if the student is performing in the average, above or below, or significantly above or below the average range.

2. To make criterion comparisons: compare a student's performance to a set standard or criterion to determine if the student's performance meets or exceeds the standard, or falls below the minimum level set for performance. Comparisons include (a) curricular (how students perform in the school curriculum), (b) outcome (what students know and are able to do at the conclusion of instruction), and (c) life performances (how students respond to tasks and challenges faced in job-related and community settings).

FIGURE 7.1
The Assessment Dimension System

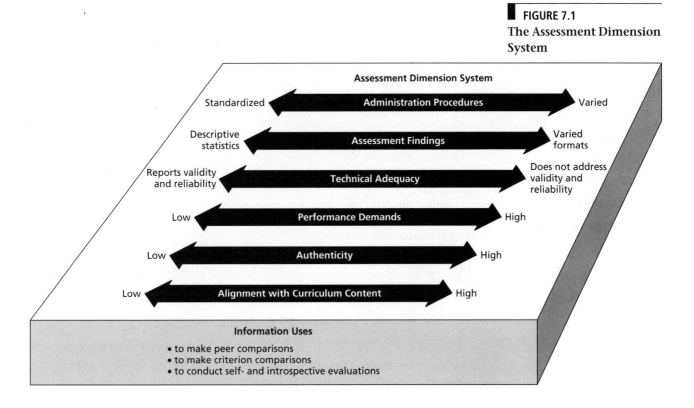

3. To conduct self- and introspective evaluations: have students reflect and evaluate their performance and growth over time. Evaluation includes students' perceptions, attitudes, and experiences toward learning and themselves as individuals and their thinking processes and strategies for approaching tasks.

Dimension 2: Administration Procedures

The design of and procedures for administering specific assessment tools and methods constitute the second dimension to consider when assessment methods and tools are selected. This dimension is framed by the two extremes of *standardized* and *varied*. Standardized procedures mean that regardless of who administers the test—a teacher in Washington or a teacher in Maine—the test will be given in exactly the same way, in accordance with predetermined rules and procedures. Evaluators everywhere will use the same directions and words when asking questions and giving directions, and all students will respond in a specified manner (e.g., orally responding, pointing to responses, or filling in answers on a protocol sheet). Examples include achievement tests and tests for vision and hearing.

At the other extreme, administration procedures can vary by administrator and setting. This variability allows flexibility in administration and response methods. The teacher may assist students with directions, explain unfamiliar words, provide cues or alter administration procedures to reflect student needs.

Dimension 3: Assessment Findings

Some assessment methods and tools report scores in a descriptive statistic format; others report findings in varied formats. Each is described.

Descriptive statistics

Descriptive statistics include grade and age equivalents, standard scores, and percentiles, as well as stanines and normal-curve equivalents. These scores are derived through statistical procedures and compare a child's performance to a norm group. Grade equivalents (e.g., 4.5, meaning the fifth month of the fourth year of school) represent how an average child at a specific grade level would respond to the test. For example, a third grader who earns a grade equivalent of 4.5 answered, on average, as many items correctly as an average fourth grader in the fifth month of the school year would answer. Age equivalents (e.g., 7-9, meaning seven years, nine months) work similarly. A child of age 8-9 who scores an age equivalent of 7-9 answered correctly as many items on average as an average child of age 7 years, 9 months.

Although these scores may appear straightforward, they are commonly misinterpreted (McLoughlin & Lewis, 1994) and thus should be avoided when testing outcomes are reported. Suppose a second grade boy earns a grade-equivalent score of 9.9 on a standardized reading test administered to all second graders in the school district. Upon receiving this news, the boy's parents are elated because they believe their son is reading like a ninth grader. This interpretation is flawed, however, because it is likely that if the child were asked to read a ninth grade history book, he would have great difficulty reading and understanding the text.

Standard scores are more useful scores because they are much easier to interpret. Figure 7.2 presents a bell curve which aids in understanding these scores. Standard scores are generally based on a mean (arithmetic average) of 100 and a standard deviation (how far away a score is from the mean) of 15 or 16. A child earning a standard score of 100 is considered to have displayed average performance on a test. A child who scores 120 is considered to have performed above average, because he scored more than one standard deviation above the mean (100 + 15 = 115). A child who scores 140 is considered to have performed significantly above average, because the score is more than two standard deviations above the mean (100 + 15 + 15 = 130).

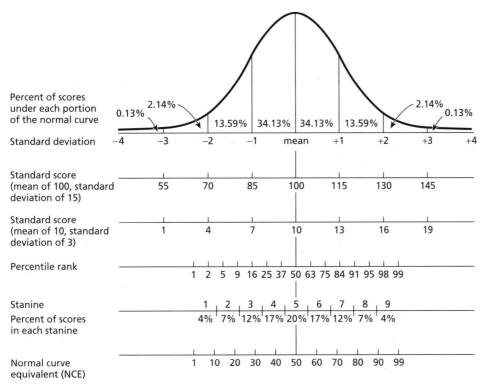

Similarly, a student with a standard score of 78 is considered to be performing below average, scoring more than one standard deviation below the mean (100 − 15 = 85); and a child with a standard score of 55 is considered to have scored significantly below average because the score is more than two standard deviations below the mean (100 − 15 − 15 = 70). These scores and their classifications are illustrated in Figure 7.2.

Once you have determined a student's standard scores on a test, you are able to make multiple comparisons of how the child performed in relation to the norm group and across test subcategories, and you can base educational decisions on those comparisons. For example, look at Benjamin's profile on the Woodcock Reading Mastery Tests-Revised (Woodcock, 1987), presented in Exhibit 7.4. If Benjamin has an average IQ (mean = 100), in what areas is he performing at an average level? (See "Standard score (mean of 100, standard deviation of 15)" in Figure 7.2.) In what areas is he performing below average? Above average? If you were going to work with Benjamin what would be some areas you would want to develop? (Of course, you would need more information to make educational decisions concerning his overall needs and educational plan.)

SUBTEST	STANDARD SCORE	PERCENTILE
Word Identification	99	47
Word Attack	96	39
Word Comprehension	80	9
Passage Comprehension	76	5

EXHIBIT 7.4

Benjamin's Profile on the Woodcock Reading Mastery Tests-Revised

Benjamin's percentiles are also presented in Exhibit 7.4. Percentiles are another type of score that can be interpreted through the analysis of their location on the bell curve.

As indicated in Figure 7.2, percentiles have a mean of 50—that is, a child who scores at the 50th percentile has scored in the average range. Scoring at the 50th percentile does not mean that students answered half of the questions—50 percent—on a test correctly. Getting 50 percent of the answers correct is very different from scoring in the 50th percentile. What the latter means is that 50 percent of the students who took the test scored at the same level as or below the student who scored at the 50th percentile, and 50 percent of the students who took the test scored at the same level as or above the student's performance.

Here is a way to visualize percentiles. Imagine that your feet, as you are standing, represent the 1st percentile and that your hands, extended above your head as high as you can reach, indicate the 99th percentile. When you place your hands on your hips, they mark the 50th percentile—the midpoint at which 50 percent of the students scored higher and 50 percent scored lower. When you place your hands on your shoulders, they mark the 75th percentile. When a student scores at the 75th percentile, this means that 75 percent of the students in the norm group who took the test scored at or below this student's level of performance and 25 percent of the group scored at or above this student's level of performance. And when you place your hands on your knees, they mark the 25th percentile.

Although percentile ranks may appear to be easily interpreted, comparisons of percentiles can be difficult. If a child scores at the 50th percentile, how well did the child do? How well did a child who scores at the 25th percentile do? Your first instinct may be to say that the child scoring at the 25th percentile did poorly, but look again at the bell curve (Figure 7.2). According to the bell curve, the child's score is in the average range of performance. In summary, percentiles may be easily misinterpreted.

Returning to Benjamin's scores (Exhibit 7.4), assess how Benjamin performed on the test by reviewing his percentile ranks. Notice that examination of the percentile ranks provides the same information as derived through analysis of the standard scores. This is because both types of scores represent different ways for expressing performance on the bell curve. In fact, by using a conversion chart, you can easily convert standard scores into percentiles, and all other types of scores listed in Figure 7.2 as well.

Varied formats

There are several other ways in which to report assessment findings besides descriptive statistics. Findings may be reported as a percentage of correct answers—for example, if a child correctly answers 8 out of 10 questions, the child achieves 80 percent accuracy. Frequency of performance—for example, a student performs an activity correctly 3 out of 4 trials—and holistic ratings or marks on a checklist may be used. Findings may also be reported in narrative form. For example, students may reflect and comment on their own work or present their work to others who then comment on it either orally or in writing. Teachers may write statements to describe behavioral incidents. Other methods count and graph student data, which are then visually inspected. (These varied formats are described in detail in Chapter 8.)

Dimension 4: Technical Adequacy

Technical adequacy indicates the appropriateness and consistency of assessment methods and tools. Technical adequacy is generally indicated through the reporting of validity and reliability. Not all assessment methods and tools report validity and reliability coefficients; therefore, understanding the type of information that validity and reliability provide can help team members determine what level of validity and reliability is needed for an assessment method or tool, or whether validity and reliability are critical considerations in selection.

Validity

As defined by McLoughlin and Lewis (1994), validity is "the degree to which a test measures what it purports to measure" (p. 604). For example, if a test is identified as a reading test but assesses word attack skills only, the test would most likely not be considered a strong indicator of overall reading skill because it does not assess the critical skill of comprehension. Therefore, you would not select this test as a valid indicator of overall reading performance, but you could select it to measure a child's word attack skills. As Overton (1996) argues, to be valid, a test must provide evidence of a student's ability in the target area. In this example, the test would provide evidence of (would be considered a valid indicator of) word attack skills but would not provide evidence of (would not be considered a valid indicator of) reading comprehension skills.

Reliability

Reliability is a measure of the consistency of a method or tool. For example, test-retest reliability, one form of reliability, is concerned with how a student performs on a test if given it multiple times, with *no* instruction delivered between test administrations. For the test to be considered reliable, a student would have to perform at similar levels each time the test is given, demonstrating consistent performance. If the student earned very different scores each time the test was given, you would not know which score was a true representation of the student's understanding or what was causing the student's performance to be so erratic. If a test is unreliable, it is difficult, if not impossible, to interpret a student's performance and to make decisions based on test findings.

Another form of reliability is interrater reliability. This form of reliability is concerned with the consistency in scoring when two or more people (raters) score the same test or paper. For example, two teachers independently score a student's essay and then compare their scores to determine whether they are consistent, or reliable. If the two teachers report very different scores, there are concerns about consistency. Consistency among raters is critical when you are assessing student performance because you want to ensure decisions are not unduly influenced by the perceptions of only one individual.

Considerations

Some assessment methods and tools report reliability and validity figures; others do not. For example, tests that report findings as norm-referenced scores report both reliability and validity, whereas teacher-created instruments (e.g., quizzes, interviews) generally are not assessed for technical adequacy. Some individuals are concerned with the failure of informal methods and tools to report validity and reliability figures and suggest that, in the absence of these figures, findings derived from these informal methods and tools are uninterpretable or at least must be interpreted with great reservation and caution. Others are less concerned about whether methods and tools meet the traditional rigors of validity and reliability standards. They argue that "Clarifying the purposes for which scores are needed and requiring only sufficient rigor for those needs would increase the variety of ways in which assessment information is reported" (Mitchell, 1992, p. 189). They maintain that collecting information across multiple sources may make the need to meet traditional validity and reliability requirements no longer necessary or an appropriate concern (Chittenden, 1991). As stated by Herman, Aschbacher, and Winters (1992), "The higher the stakes associated with an assessment, the greater the need to document its quality—its validity and reliability" (p. 100).

Dimension 5: Performance Demands

Performance demands describe what an individual does in response to a task or problem. As defined by Poteet, Choate, and Stewart (1993), performance tests

> *require that the student* do *(produce, demonstrate, perform, create, construct, apply, build, solve, plan, show, illustrate, convince, persuade, or explain) some task.*
> (p. 5)

Elliott (1994) describes tasks as being on a performance continuum ranging from low to high. Circling a correct item is an example of a low-level performance demand; conducting a science experiment represents a higher performance demand.

Understanding the performance demands of specific assessment methods and tools aids teams in selecting those appropriate for assessment. For example, a low performance demand response format (e.g., point to a correct response) may be an appropriate means for assessing the reading comprehension skills of a student with a physical disability, but a test format requiring the same student to write out responses to comprehension questions may be inappropriate and may place the child at a disadvantage for scoring well on the test.

Assessment tools and methods vary greatly in their performance demands. Most tests that are standardized and have a descriptive statistic format for reporting performance generally make low performance demands. Students fill in bubbles on testing sheets, write or orally state one-word answers, or point to an answer. This is in contrast with methods and tools that require students to demonstrate what they know and can do through portfolio entries, exhibits, and presentations. For these assessment methods and tools, students must actively engage in an activity and demonstrate their skills to an audience. For example, portfolio entries may include written pieces, both final products and all drafts that led up to the final piece. Exhibits may require students to build a diorama or model and be able to explain its purpose and how it works to others. Presentations may take multiple formats as well, including oral presentations, video and audiotape presentations, and use of multimedia. In these cases, the student must produce something and be actively involved—a much greater performance demand than providing one-word answers.

Dimension 6: Authenticity

Authenticity refers to the degree to which a task is related to or representative of a real-life activity or skill demonstration. As Poteet, Choate, and Stewart (1993) observe, "any type of assessment can be authentic if it focuses on application of knowledge to real-life, real-world settings" (p. 6). Elliott (1994) describes authenticity as falling on a continuum ranging from high to low. For example, answering multiple-choice questions about the components of a business letter would be rated as low, and writing a business letter to a state legislator would be rated as high. Authenticity concerns are reflective of the movement toward more authentic, performance-based assessment approaches.

Concerns with authenticity and the push toward more authentic tasks are evident in the national movement toward standards (discussed in Chapter 2). Standards identify desired understandings and skills of graduates of our educational system and reflect skills and understandings that individuals need to be productive and contributing members of society. Many standards reflect concerns with student performance in authentic tasks (e.g., students are able to communicate effectively with others). The push toward greater authenticity challenges the current and sometimes exclusive use of peer-comparison testing regimens by many schools—tests that students take once a year or in cycles to demonstrate learning—and supports the adoption of more performance-based measures (as described above under "performance demands").

Teachers and school-site administrators are also expressing greater interest in the adoption of more authentic testing methods and tools because information gathered through authentic testing can be used to inform curriculum and instructional decisions. Authentic tasks (e.g., having students write letters to community leaders and analyzing those letters for needed writing skills enhancement; having students participate in presentations that demonstrate skill acquisition) provide teachers with a more in-depth analysis of student understanding and skill level than does a score achieved through a peer-comparison test. The information gained through more authentic tasks tends to be more specific and curriculum related when compared to tools that are low in terms of authenticity.

Adoption of a balanced approach to testing (e.g., selecting tools that vary in terms of authenticity), allows for the gathering of information to learn how a child performs in relation to peers (generally through low-authenticity tools) and to inform teachers' instructional planning (generally through high-authenticity tools).

Dimension 7: Alignment with Curriculum Content

The final assessment dimension represents the degree of match between what is being assessed and the curriculum being taught. Some assessment methods and tools may be commercially developed and not highly aligned with what is being taught in the classroom. This commonly occurs with the use of peer-comparison tests. These tests are used across the nation, and the content of a test may not reflect the particular curriculum offered at a school site.

Generally, informal assessment tools and methods are more closely aligned with curriculum than peer-comparison and, possibly, criterion-comparison tests. This is due to the nature of these tools and methods—they are generally developed by teachers and are based on current curriculum. Tools and methods closely aligned with the curriculum help teachers and district members make informed curricular and instructional decisions. Methods and tools that differ somewhat from the curriculum offered at the site provide more of an overview of performance, and this information may not be as helpful for curricular and instructional site decisions.

Again, a balanced approach may be best in terms of curriculum alignment. Peer-comparison tests, which are generally not highly curriculum aligned, present a portrait of how a specific school population is performing in relation to peers across the nation. Assessment approaches and tools that are highly curriculum aligned can complement this information by capturing information about students' performance as specifically related to key curriculum areas and targets and can be used for program and instructional planning.

Summary of the Assessment Dimension System

ADS is a system for evaluating assessment methods and tools on seven dimensions in order to make informed decisions about the most appropriate approach for addressing specific assessment questions. The system does not require the classification of methods and tools into discrete categories, but it allows for a more thorough understanding of individual approaches and an analysis of each method and tool along the seven dimensions.

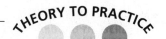

THEORY TO PRACTICE

➡ Secure a copy of a peer-comparison test. Evaluate it in terms of the Assessment Dimension System. Where does it fall on each of the continua? If an IEP team were to use this tool, what type of information would it provide and how could that information be used? What additional information would the team need for making informed decisions about the child's educational needs?

➡ Gather two informal tools that a teacher is currently using in the classroom. Evaluate these tools in terms of the Assessment Dimension System. Where do the tools fall on each of the continua? If an IEP team were to use these tools as part of a contextualized assessment, what type of information would the tools provide and how could that information be used?

CHAPTER SUMMARY

The first chapter on assessment purposes addressed the first purpose: to determine eligibility for special education services and the development of initial IEPs. This chapter explores three of the four purposes of assessment: (a) review of individualized plans, (b) evaluation of instruction, and (c) program evaluation. Additionally, the chapter highlights the terminology commonly used to classify assessment methods and tools and also the strengths and weaknesses of those classification systems. The Assessment Dimension System is presented as an alternative system for understanding available assessment methods and tools. It prepares teachers with understandings about how to analyze assessment methods and tools they will consider for use with their students.

CHAPTER 8

Assessment Methods and Tools

Read this chapter to find out the following:
- characteristics of specific assessment methods and tools
- development and implementation of these assessment methods and tools
- the types of findings generated by these different assessment methods and tools

In this chapter we describe assessment methods and tools available to teams responsible for evaluating student performance and the overall effectiveness of programs. These tools may be used to address the four main purposes of assessment: (a) determination of eligibility for special education services and the development of initial IEPs; (b) review of individualized plans; (c) evaluation of instruction; and (d) program evaluation. These methods and tools align themselves to many regions on the Assessment Dimension System (ADS) model. They vary in how information will be used, in administration procedures, in assessment findings reported, in the extent to which technical adequacy is determined and reported, and in performance demands, authenticity, and alignment with curriculum. Because of their variety, assessment methods and tools can be selected specifically to address the contexts and factors of contextualized assessment of greatest interest to the team.

The tools and methods are discussed in three categories: individual methods and tools, combined methods and tools, and special cases of specific ability tests. Individual methods and tools stand alone. Combined methods and tools bring together several of the individual methods. For example, portfolio assessment may include the use of interviews, rubrics, and rating scales, all of which are individual methods that when combined provide the information needed to assess portfolios. In the final category are special cases such as ability tests in the areas of vision, hearing, perception, motor, memory, attention, and language development.

INDIVIDUAL METHODS AND TOOLS

Peer-Comparison Tests
Peer-comparison tests compare a student's performance level to that of a norm group (e.g., a representative sample of same-age and same-grade peers). They are administered, scored, and interpreted in prescribed ways. Findings are reported as standard scores, percentiles, and grade and age equivalents. The tests may be administered to groups or individuals. Two examples are intelligence tests and achievement tests.

Intelligence tests
Intelligence tests (IQ) are one example of a peer-comparison test. Intelligence tests may be conducted as part of the team's activities to gain a sense of a student's overall ability.

Individually administered IQ tests report performance in both verbal and nonverbal reasoning and provide a full scale IQ score. Verbal items require students to respond orally to questions; nonverbal activities are visual-motor tasks.

The use of IQ tests in general, and specifically for determining eligibility for special education services, continues to be debated (e.g., Singham, 1995). The debate over the meaning of IQ testing and outcomes was refueled by the publication of *The Bell Curve* (Herrnstein & Murray, 1994). It has been suggested that the use of IQ tests for determining eligibility for special education results in the overidentification of students of color as being in need of special education. For example, *Diana v. State Board of Education* (1970) challenged the use of an IQ test administered in English to a student whose primary language was Spanish, and *Larry P. v. Riles* (1984) challenged the use of IQ tests with children of African-American descent. These challenges were based on the concern that these tests had not been standardized on students of color and that some of the test items were biased, although overall the tests were not found to be discriminatory (Overton, 1996). Districts and states have adopted measures for addressing the appropriate use of IQ tests as part of the eligibility process and follow federal guidelines that require that more than one test be used to determine whether a child has a disability and is in need of special education services. To learn more about IQ tests, refer to McLoughlin and Lewis (1994) and Overton (1996).

Achievement tests

Achievement tests are another example of peer-comparison tests. These tests are standardized, norm-referenced instruments that measure ability in core curricular areas such as reading, written language, mathematics, social studies, and science.

There are two categories of achievement testing: *screening* and *diagnostic*. If the posed assessment question calls for a better understanding of a student's performance across curriculum content, a *screening* achievement test is as an appropriate tool. If the team wants to gain a better understanding of the difficulties and strengths within a child's performance in a specific curricular area, such as reading, a *diagnostic* achievement test specifically designed to assess reading skills is more appropriate.

Screening tests may be administered to a group or to an individual. Many school districts conduct group screening achievement testing on a three- or four-year cycle. This testing may last over the course of a week with students filling in computer-bubble sheets to indicate their response. Historically, some districts include students with disabilities in these testing cycles; others do not. This practice of exclusion, however, has changed. As we explained in Chapter 1, the IDEA Amendments of 1997 require students with disabilities to be included in these testing cycles; and if a test, as is, is not appropriate for a particular child with a disability, testing adaptations must be made to include the child, or alternative means of assessing the child must be developed and administered.

When testing for eligibility for special education, screening tests are administered individually. An example of an individually administered achievement screening test is the Woodcock-Johnson Psycho-Educational Battery-Revised: Tests of Achievement (Woodcock & Johnson, 1989). The tool is extensive and assesses skills in letter-word identification, passage comprehension, calculation, applied problems, dictation, writing samples, science, social studies, and humanities. Another common screening test is the Wide Range Achievement Test 3 (Wilkinson, 1993). This test is brief (administration requires approximately 20 minutes) and assesses a limited number of areas—spelling, arithmetic, and word recognition. Selection of the appropriate screening tool depends on the type of information wanted—a quick overview of student performance or a more in-depth look at student skills across a range of areas—and the time available for testing.

Diagnostic tests measure performance in one curricular area or domain and provide specific information that can be used to inform instructional practice. One example of a diagnostic test is the KeyMath-Revised (Connolly, 1988). This test measures a student's ability in the area of mathematics only. It consists of three content areas, with several subtests in each: (a) Basic Concepts, including numeration, fractions, geometry, and symbols; (b) Operations, including addition, subtraction, multiplication, division, mental computation, and numerical reasoning; and (c) Applications, including word problems, missing elements, money, measurement, and time.

Exhibit 8.1 presents a list of commonly used screening and diagnostic achievement tests. Compton's *Guide to 100 Tests for Special Education* (1996) is an comprehensive reference for learning more about these individual tests. The author discusses the purpose and content of the tests, the types of scores obtained, and approximate administration time requirements. Additionally she identifies strengths and limitations of each test.

EXHIBIT 8.1
Common Achievement Tests

SCREENING

TOOLS	AREAS ASSESSED
Peabody Individual Achievment Test-R (Markwardt, 1989)	General knowledge, reading, mathematics, spelling, and written expression
Wide Range Achievement Test3 (Wilkinson, 1993)	Spelling, arithmetic, reading recognition
Woodcock-Johnson Psycho-Educational Battery-R: Tests of Achievement (Woodcock & Johnson, 1989)	Reading, mathematics, written language, and knowledge (science, social studies, and humanities)
Wechsler Individual Achievement Test-III (Wechsler, 1991)	Reading, mathematics, spelling, written expression, listening comprehension, and oral expression
Kaufman Test of Educational Achievement (Kauffman & Kaufman, 1985)	Mathematics, reading, and spelling

DIAGNOSTIC

TOOLS	AREAS ASSESSED
Woodcock Reading Mastery Tests-R (Woodcock, 1987)	Reading readiness, basic reading skills (word identification and word attack), word and passage comprehension
Gray Oral Reading Tests (3rd ed.) (Wiederholt & Bryant, 1992)	Oral reading rate, accuracy, and comprehension
KeyMath-Revised: A Diagnostic Inventory of Essential Mathematics (Connolly, 1988)	Basic concepts, operations, and applications
Test of Mathematical Abilities, Second Edition (Brown, Cronin, & McEntire, 1994)	Attitude toward math, vocabulary, computation, general information, story problems
Test of Written Spelling-3 (Larsen & Hammill, 1994)	Spelling predictable and unpredictable words
Test of Written Language-2 (Hammill & Larsen, 1988)	Conventional, linguistic, and conceptual components of written language

Some students may need to have the test formats of these screening and diagnostic achievement tests modified in order to demonstrate their level of skill and understanding. Administering the test without modifications can greatly limit the type of information gained about some students. For example, a student with a physical disability that affects speech may have a clear understanding of the concept he is being tested on but have difficulty stating the answer orally as the test requires. Having the child point to the answer or write the answer on paper may be a more direct route to learn what this child knows and understands. It is important to note that if a test has been modified in any way, those modifications must be noted when the findings are reported. Written comments contained in the report must indicate that standardized test administration procedures were not followed and that test outcomes are invalid or at least must be interpreted with caution. The "Make It Happen" feature presents ways for modifying tests to reflect student needs. Some of these suggestions modify the way in which the test is administered and the student responds. Other modifications alter the questions asked, as is suggested in dynamic assessment.

MAKE IT HAPPEN
Test Modification

- *Modality.* Adapt the way items are presented and students respond.
  - For a student who is unable to hear questions, present questions visually.
  - For a student who is unable to write a response, have the student dictate the response.
  - For a student who is unable to give a verbal response, have the student point to the answer.
- *Language.* Reword items, using language the student is familiar with and understands.
  - Restate directions in simplified language (e.g., syntax, vocabulary).
- *Complexity.* Reduce the level of complexity of the item so the student is able to demonstrate what she or he understands.
  - If the item asks the student to identify the theme of the story and the child is unclear about what a theme is or has difficulty identifying themes, the item may be changed to ask for an explanation of what happened in the story.
  - If the item presents a chart and asks the student to answer a question using the information on the chart and the child is unable to perform that task, the examiner may ask the child to describe the various parts of the chart and the information they provide.
- *Space.* Check for student understanding of the meaning of words such as *over, under,* and *between.*
  - If directions require a student to put an X *underneath* the correct response, ensure that the child understands what *underneath* means and how to indicate her or his response.
- *Time.* Allow enough time for students to respond to items and complete tasks.
  - Extend response time when appropriate.

Source: Gearheart & Gearheart (1990).

Modifications are also necessary when assessing skills of English-language learners. One tactic for responding to the challenge of assessing non-native English-speakers has been to translate tests written in English into the primary language of the child. This can be done as the test is administered—someone fluent in the child's primary language translates items as testing proceeds. At other times, items may be rewritten in the primary language prior to a testing session. However, translation from one language to another does not ensure that the meaning or intent of an item is conveyed in a culturally appropriate or meaningful way. Items presented in the child's primary language may be foreign to the culture or experiences of the child and may make no sense to the child.

Because of all these concerns, it is critical that several methods (e.g., observation, interviews, language samples, testing) be used when assessing the skills of students whose primary language is not English.

ADS Analysis: *Peer-Comparison Tests*

Information uses: To make comparisons
Administration procedures: Standardized
Assessment findings: Descriptive statistics
Technical adequacy: Report validity and reliability
Performance demands: Varied, but generally low
Authenticity: Varied, but generally low
Alignment with curriculum content: Varied, but generally low

Criterion-Comparison Tests

Criterion-comparison tests, also referred to as criterion-referenced tests, compare a student's performance to a standard or criterion. Criteria are predetermined levels of performance that must be achieved to demonstrate accuracy and competence. Criterion-comparison tests are generally curriculum related and outline skills and competencies students are to master over time.

The *Brigance Diagnostic Inventories* are examples of criterion-comparison instruments, although they may provide standardized scores as well. The Brigance Diagnostic Inventories address a wide range of skills, establishing criteria of performance in each area, ranging from early development (birth to age 7) to life skills for vocational education at the high school level. Brigance inventories may be used as a quick means to determine students' skills in identified areas and may be repeated throughout the year to provide formative assessment information for curricular and instructional planning decision making. Brigance inventories may also be used in determining whether students have met IEP goals and objectives. Because of their ease of use and the limited time demands associated with administration, Brigance inventories are very helpful to classroom teachers.

Informal reading inventories (IRIs) are another example of a criterion-comparison test. Informal reading inventories generally include two main sections: word recognition and passage reading. The interpretation of an IRI is based on criteria, or levels of performance, and identifies three reading levels: independent, instructional, and frustration. According to Lipson and Wixson (1997), the *independent* reading level is the level at which a student reads fluently and for pleasure (word recognition of 96 to 99% correct paired with correct comprehension of 75 to 90%). The *instructional* reading level is the level at which the student can experience success with assistance (word recognition of 92 to 95% correct paired with correct comprehension of 60 to 75%). The *frustration* level is the level at which the reading process breaks down for the student (word recognition of 90 to 92% or less paired with correct comprehension of 60 to 75% or less), as demonstrated by depressed comprehension and difficulties with word recognition.

ADS Analysis: *Criterion-Comparison Tests*

Information uses: To make criterion comparisons
Administration procedures: Generally varied, although some require standardized procedures
Assessment findings: Varied formats
Technical adequacy: Generally do not report validity and reliability
Performance demands: Varied, but generally low
Authenticity: Varied
Alignment with curriculum content: Varied, but generally midline to high

---

Quizzes

Teachers may develop quizzes to evaluate student knowledge, skills, and understanding of what is being taught in the classroom. Quizzes take various forms—multiple choice, fill-in-the-blank, short answer, essay—and may be employed as summative and formative measures. Quizzes may present challenging problems that require students to apply knowledge to arrive at conclusions, or they may ask students simply to recall information presented in class.

Many times quizzes are an indirect means for assessing student understanding. For example, when monitoring a student's development of capitalization skills, the teacher may devise a written language quiz with sentences requiring students to circle or underline all words requiring capitalization. This is an indirect measure of the student's skills because the student is not generating his or her own sentences and using capital letters as needed; the student is simply reading a list of sentences and indicating where capital letters are required.

The development of quizzes, though a common practice in schools, is challenging. Writing good questions that are worded appropriately and clearly and require students to apply, analyze, and synthesize knowledge, and not just repeat it, is not easy. Having a peer review a quiz and offer suggestions for revision, having a student group complete a quiz as a pilot test, and/or adapting and modifying commercially developed quizzes may help teachers fine-tune their quiz development skills.

ADS Analysis: *Quizzes*

Information uses: To make criterion comparisons

Administration procedures: Generally varied

Assessment findings: Varied formats

Technical adequacy: Do not report validity and reliability

Performance demands: Varied, but generally low

Authenticity: Varied, but generally low

Alignment with curriculum content: Generally high

Curriculum-Based Measurement

Curriculum-based measurement (CBM) is a measurement approach involving timed tests and the charting of student performance. CBM measures are concerned with fluency—the rate at which students are able to perform tasks. Researchers (e.g., Lindsley, 1990) have argued that fluency data are (a) more sensitive to learning patterns than is percentage correct, (b) indicative of the quality of performance (White, 1986), and (c) informative about the efficiency of responding (West, Young, & Spooner, 1990). CBM has been applied across all basic skills areas. Examples of CBM measures include students orally reading from text and the number of correct words per minute recorded and charted; students completing computation problems and the number of correct problems completed during a predetermined time period (generally 2 to 3 minutes) charted; students spelling dictated words at a predetermined rate and the number of correct words charted; and students writing stories for a predetermined time period and the counting and charting of the number of words written (Shinn & Hubbard, 1992). Student performance is charted on equal-interval graph paper and is compared to an aim line—a line drawn from the student's initial performance (or baseline performance) to the goal level beginning with the first session and extended across the chart to the last session of the year—to determine whether adequate progress is being made or instructional modifications are needed.

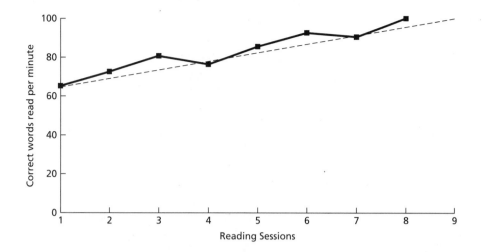

As described by Fuchs and Deno (1992), CBM focuses on long-term instructional goals and students' performance on goal-level materials (materials that represent learning to be demonstrated at the completion of a set time period, generally an academic school year). This approach is unique because the testing includes skills and concepts not yet taught. For example, for a mathematics CBM measure, students attempt computation problems they will encounter during the year-long curriculum. Thus at any given time during the year, students will be familiar with some of the problems, are learning procedures for completing others, and have not been introduced to others included in the measure. CBM tests students' skills on curriculum that represents what will be learned throughout the school year, not just skill based on what has been taught or is being taught.

Figure 8.1 presents a CBM graph of a second grade student's oral reading performance. The aim line—the dashed line on the graph drawn from 65 to 100 correct words per minute—represents the level of performance and rate of progress the child will need to demonstrate in order to achieve the goal of 100 words read correctly by the end of the school year. The student's correct reading performance is indicated by the line connecting the boxes. Each box represents a reading session, one session per month, for the nine months of school. During sessions, the student reads orally for one minute from passages written at the end of the second grade level. These passages represent the goal-level material for the student—end of second grade. Although this student's performance bounces slightly, overall the performance fluctuates around the aim line, indicating the child is making adequate progress and will, most likely, achieve the goal by the end of the school year.

ADS Analysis: *Curriculum-Based Measurement*

Information uses: To make criterion comparisons

Administration procedures: Standardized

Assessment findings: Varied formats; graphs of performance

Technical adequacy: Report validity and reliability

Performance demands: Varied, but generally low

Authenticity: High (e.g., writing passages/stories) to low (e.g., writing answers to addition facts)

Alignment with curriculum content: High

▌**FIGURE 8.2**
Precision Teaching:
On-Task Behavior

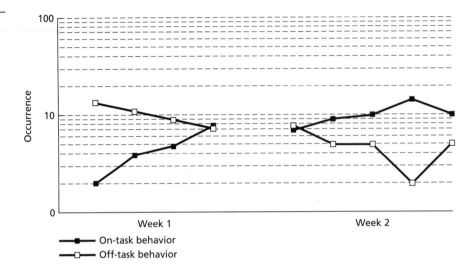

▌**FIGURE 8.2**
Precision Teaching:
On-Task Behavior

Precision Teaching

Though similar in approach to CBM, precision teaching has a different curricular focus. Whereas CBM assesses student ability on an identified universe of skills or problems (performance on goal-level curriculum content), precision teaching assesses students' mastery of subskills as they are taught or skills that were taught in the past.

Precision teaching has been used to monitor academic, behavior, and social skills, and on-the-job performance. It can be applied across a variety of contexts and provides ongoing information about performance. For example, an oral reading rate (described in the section on CBM) may be gathered through precision teaching. In precision teaching, however, the student would read not from goal-level material but from material that she or he is currently reading or read previously.

Data are generally charted on semilogarithmic graph paper. The boxes in Figure 8.2 represent the on-task and off-task behavior of a child during a 30-minute instructional period measured in two-minute intervals using time sampling procedures (time sampling procedures are explained below the section on observation). As the chart indicates, in the first week the child engaged in more off-task than on-task behavior; in the second week, the child demonstrated more on-task than off-task behavior.

Teachers can introduce students to the charting components of precision teaching and make students responsible for charting their own behavior. This activity increases students' interest in their work and accountability for their progress, and it can boost motivation as students attempt to improve their performance on a daily or weekly basis.

ADS Analysis: *Precision Teaching*

Information uses: To make curriculum comparisons

Administration procedures: Standardized

Assessment findings: Varied formats; graphs of performance

Technical adequacy: Do not report validity and reliability

Performance demands: High (e.g., performing job skills) to low (e.g., writing answers to addition facts)

Authenticity: High (e.g., performing behaviors in social settings) to low (e.g., orally reading a list of words)

Alignment with curriculum content: High

Running Records

Running records capture and assess how students approach and interact with text. According to Clay (1993), running records may be used to make decisions about the following:

- The evaluation of text difficulty
- the grouping of children
- the acceleration of a child
- monitoring progress of children
- allowing different children to move through different books at different speeds while keeping track of (and records of) individual progress
- observing particular difficulties in particular children (Clay, 1993, pp. 22–23).

As with CBM and precision teaching, the child is given text to read and reads that text orally to the examiner. Fluency, however, is not the primary concern. In running records, emphasis is on evaluating the types of errors the child is making in order to assess his or her reading behavior. A mark is made for every word the child reads correctly, and every error is recorded. Additionally, the teacher checks for directional movement by having the student read a section of text by moving his finger under the text as he is reading. Error rate is calculated as the percentage of errors. A child whose reading included one error in every 5 words is considered to be experiencing difficulty with the text. An acceptable error rate is one error in 20 running words. The text is considered hard for a child if the error rate is more than 10% of the overall record.

Error analysis can reveal information about a student's (a) oral language skills, (b) speed of reading (e.g., pauses), (c) kinds of information the child uses when interacting with text (e.g., meaning, structure, visual cues), and (d) cross-check strategies (e.g., checking information with other information found in the text).

More information concerning running records can be found in Clay's "An Observation Survey of Early Literacy Achievement" (1993).

ADS Analysis: *Running Records*

Information uses: To make interpersonal comparisons
Administration procedures: Standardized
Assessment findings: Varied formats; graphs of performance
Technical adequacy: Do not report validity and reliability
Performance demands: High
Authenticity: High
Alignment with curriculum content: High

Observation

According to Merrell (1994), "Direct observation of behavior is a cornerstone of the assessment of behavioral, social, and emotional problems exhibited by children and adolescents" (p. 44). An examiner or teacher may observe a child working in cooperative groups, eating lunch in the cafeteria, and participating in life skill development activities at a job site. Observation is a critical component of many initial, annual, and reevaluation processes.

Observational data may be gathered in several ways. *Event recording* is a basic observational method. A teacher records the number of times an event occurs during a specific time period. Data can be charted over weeks and analyzed. *Interval recording* and *time sampling* are more complex than event recording and, at times, may be confused with one another. Both involve taking a specified block of time (e.g., reading time, recess) and dividing that time block into intervals of, let's say, 5 minutes each. For *interval recording,* the observer watches the student throughout each of the intervals or until the child engages in the target behavior. If she engages in the behavior at any time during the interval, the observer places a check or plus sign in that interval and stops watching the child until the start of the next interval. Only one occurrence of the behavior is recorded per interval. If the child does not engage in the behavior during the entire interval, a minus sign or zero is recorded.

In contrast, *time sampling* requires the observer to note the child's behavior only at the end of the interval. At the end of the interval, the observer glances at the child to determine whether he is engaged in the behavior. If he is, a plus sign or check is placed on the observation grid; if he was not, a zero or minus sign is recorded. In this case it does not matter whether the child engaged in the behavior during the interval; the behavior is recorded as occurring only if it is observed at the end of the interval.

Latency recording and *duration recording* are behavior-specific methods. The former is used when there is a concern about students getting started with activities; the latter, when there is a concern about how long a child engages in a behavior. When using *latency recording*, the teacher may give directions, ask for questions, or tell students to begin working. A stopwatch is started and the number of minutes and/or seconds it takes the student to begin the task is calculated and recorded. *Duration recording* is done by starting a stopwatch as soon as the child begins the behavior and turning it off once the behavior stops. The duration of behavior may be important when a student's physical condition or health is being monitored (e.g., epileptic seizure activity) or when the goal is to increase a student's engagement time with activities.

Another form of observation is the use of *anecdotal recordings*. When anecdotal recordings are used, objective and descriptive language is recorded to describe exactly what happened before, during, and after a behavioral incident. Review of anecdotal recordings collected over time assists teachers and teams in identifying factors that may be instigating behavioral incidents or reinforcing behaviors. Anecdotal recordings may use the ABC method (A = antecedent, B = behavior, and C = consequence). The teacher records what occurred prior to the behavior (A), a description of the behavior (B), and the consequence of the behavior (C). Analysis of all three can lead to the identification of behavior triggers (A) or events or reactions (C) that are serving to reinforce the behavior.

ADS Analysis: *Observations*

Information uses: To make criterion comparisons and to conduct self- and introspective-evaluations

Administration procedures: Standardized to varied

Assessment findings: Varied formats

Technical adequacy: May or may not report validity and reliability

Performance demands: Varied, but generally high

Authenticity: Varied, but generally high

Alignment with curriculum content: Varied, but generally high

---

Interviews

Interviews allow for the gathering of a range of information about a child's performance across several factors and contexts. Interviews come in many formats. In a *highly structured* interview, the interviewer asks predetermined questions and records responses. In a *semistructured* interview, the questions may be listed but not necessarily asked in the specified order or language, and allowances are made for additions and deletions as the interview proceeds. In an *unstructured* interview, the conversation is free flowing, with topics discussed as they surface.

Students may be interviewed about their preferences, learning styles, and strategy use. They also may be asked to describe their interactions with peers and adults at school, at home, and in their community. Their responses provide valuable information about their social and interpersonal skills. Also, asking students what their goals are and what is most important to them can greatly assist a team in designing plans and instructional activities, and in creating environments conducive to learning. Student interviews may also prepare students for participation in IEP meetings.

Stenmark (1989) suggests using student interviews to assess understanding of mathematical problem solving. This interview could be used after a problem-solving activity or as a culminating assessment of an intensive unit on problem-solving techniques. Questions to be included in the interview could include the following: (a) Tell me what the problem is about in your own words. (b) What strategy did you use to solve the problem? (c) How did your strategy work? Did you experience any problems in applying that strategy, and if so, what did you do?

Teacher and parent interviews can also be valuable means for gathering information. Choate, Enright, Miller, Poteet, and Rakes (1995) identify several purposes for teacher interviews. They allow evaluators to (a) assess what teachers identify as essential curriculum content, (b) gain teachers' perspectives on how students are performing in subject areas, (c) gain insight into how teachers perceive students' learning styles and preferences, and (d) gather information on how teachers perceive students' adjustment to the learning environment. Interviewing parents broadens the database by bringing in information about the culture and beliefs of the family, parents' expectations for the child, their lifestyle and its impact on the child, as well as revealing other factors included in contextualized assessment (Figure 6.1). Having a broad understanding of how the child performs and acts across several contexts and with different people can assist teams greatly in designing programs for him or her.

Another form of interview is a *group interview,* exemplified by the Making Action Plans (MAPs) approach. As discussed in Gage and Falvey (1995), MAPs is a process through which team members—the student, his or her peers, family members, friends, teachers, and service providers—work together to explore the needs, goals, and wishes of the student. During the MAPs activity, team members work together informally to address seven key questions:

1. What is the student's history?

2. What is your dream for the student?

3. What is your nightmare for the student?

4. Who is the student?

5. What are the student's strengths, gifts, and abilities?

6. What are the student's needs?

7. What would the student's ideal day look like, and what must be done to make it happen? (Gage & Falvey, 1995, p. 68)

Responses to the questions are written on large poster paper or on a chalkboard or whiteboard so that all responses are visible to all participants as the meeting unfolds. Information gathered is then used when the student's IEP is developed.

A similar group interview process identified by Gage and Falvey (1995) is PATH (Planning Alternative Tomorrows with Hope), developed by Pearpoint, O'Brien, and Forest (1992). As presented by Gage and Falvey (1995), PATH questions address these issues: (a) dreams for the individual, (b) what group members would like to see the person doing one year from now, (c) the individual's present situation, (d) who can help the person achieve these dreams, (e) strategies needed to assist the individual in moving from the present state to achieve one-year aspirations, (f) actions that are priorities to be accomplished during the next three months, (g) who will do what during the next month and when those actions will be completed, and (h) what each participant will do to assist the individual in achieving his or her dreams. Information gathered through the PATH process is used much in the same way as information gathered through MAPs.

ADS Analysis: *Interviews*
Information uses: To conduct self- and introspective-evaluations
Administration procedures: Standardized to varied
Assessment findings: Varied formats
Technical adequacy: Generally do not address validity and reliability
Performance demands: Generally low
Authenticity: Midline to low
Alignment with curriculum content: Varied

Checklists

As defined by Herman, Aschbacher, and Winters (1992),

> *A checklist is a list of dimensions, characteristics, or behaviors that are essentially scored as "yes-no" ratings. A check indicates that either the characteristic or behavior was present or absent. (p. 64)*

Checklists list items, and an informant checks the behaviors that represent the student (in the case of a behavior checklist) or the items that the student has mastered (in the case of an academic skill checklist). Checklists may be completed by the student, his or her classmates, parents, teachers, and others who are familiar with him or her. Teachers may develop their own checklists, use those developed by districts, or use those commercially available. Students may use them to monitor and evaluate their own performance. Parents may complete checklists to describe and monitor their child's behavior.

ADS Analysis: *Checklists*
Information uses: To make criterion comparisons and to conduct self- and introspective-evaluations
Administration procedures: Standardized to varied
Assessment findings: Varied formats
Technical adequacy: Generally do not address validity and reliability
Performance demands: Generally low
Authenticity: Midline to low
Alignment with curriculum content: Generally high

Rating Scales

Rating scales are similar to checklists in that they list items and ask students and their classmates, teachers, parents, and other informants familiar with the child to evaluate the child's performance on each item. However, instead of checking *yes* or *no*, the informant rates a child's performance using a scale. Exhibit 8.2 is an example of a rating scale for evaluating student writing. It can be used by students to evaluate their own writing and by pairs for peer feedback. The rating scale could be attached to the writing product and included in a student's assessment portfolio. Other rating scales may assess behavioral and adaptive skills, and job performance.

EXHIBIT 8.2

Rating Scale for Evaluating Student Writing

Student Name _____   Date _____

Key: O = Outstanding   S = Satisfactory   NW = Needs Work

Area	O	S	NW	Comments
Legibility				
Message • has a clear purpose or theme • develops ideas through details and examples • is well organized				
Spelling				
Punctuation				
Capitalization				
Sentence Structure • incorporates complete sentences • incorporates complex sentences				
Paragraph Structure • includes a topic sentence • includes supporting sentences • includes a concluding sentence				
Word Choice • uses descriptive language • incorporates variety in word choice				
Other				

Source: Stump, C. S. (1998). Data-based decision making. *Unpublished manuscript, San Francisco State University.*

ADS Analysis: *Rating Scales*

Information uses: To make peer and criterion comparisons and to conduct self- and introspective-evaluations

Administration procedures: Standardized to varied

Assessment findings: Varied formats

Technical adequacy: Varied

Performance demands: Generally low

Authenticity: Midline to low

Alignment with curriculum content: Varied, but generally high

Questionnaires

Questionnaires are interviews in written form. Questions are written on paper, and informants are asked to write responses. Questionnaires may be used to assess a student's self-concept, awareness of strategy use, and motivation (Meltzer & Reid, 1994). Questionnaires may be completed by students and their classmates, teachers, parents, and others familiar with the student. They generally are quick and easy to administer and can address a wide range of areas and skills.

Questionnaires may include open-ended items for which respondents write answers in sentence form. They also may include checklists or rating scales to decrease the amount of writing required of a respondent. Exhibit 8.3 presents a questionnaire for general education teachers working with fully included high school special education students. The special education teacher could use this questionnaire as an ongoing monitoring tool.

EXHIBIT 8.3

Questionnaire for General Education Teachers Working with Fully Included Special Education Students

Student: _____   Date: _____

Course(s): _____

1. Overall, the student's academic performance in the class is:
   ___ outstanding
   ___ satisfactory
   ___ in need of improvement
   If in need of improvement, the primary areas of concern are:

   _____

   _____

2. The child's current grade is: ___ A ___ B ___ C ___ D ___ failing.

3. The child's current test/quiz performance is: ___ A ___ B ___ C ___ D ___ failing.

4. The child turns in:
   ___ all assignments
   ___ the majority of assignments
   ___ relatively few assignments
   ___ no assignments

5. The student has failed to turn in the following assignments:

   _____

   _____

6. Overall, the student's behavioral performance in the classroom is:
   ___ appropriate
   ___ in need of improvement
   If in need of improvement, the primary areas of concern are:

   _____

   _____

7. I recommend the following be done to support the student in my class:

   _____

8. I would like assistance in:

   _____

Source: Stump, C. S. (1998). Data-based decision making. *Unpublished manuscript, San Francisco State University.*

Findings derived from questionnaires must be interpreted with caution. For example, when students respond to questionnaires designed to assess how they see themselves as learners, they may provide answers that reflect how they would like to be or how they would like others to see them, rather than writing about themselves as they are. Meltzer and Reid (1994) suggest that to overcome these concerns, questionnaires should be supported with observations.

Information uses: To conduct self- and introspective-evaluation

Administration procedures: Standardized to varied

Assessment findings: Varied formats

Technical adequacy: Generally does not address validity and reliability

Performance demands: Generally low

Authenticity: Midline to low

Alignment with curriculum content: Varied

Rubrics

Hart (1994) defines a rubric as "an established set of criteria used for scoring or rating students' tests, portfolios, or performances" (p. 70). Rubrics list descriptors that describe a performance and "tell the evaluator what characteristics or signs to look for in a student's work and then how to place that work on a predetermined scale" (p. 70). The Conejo Valley School District, Thousand Oaks, CA (1994) developed a problem-solving rubric to be used by students. Exhibit 8.4 displays the rubric.

EXHIBIT 8.4

Kid Friendly Math Rubric

	UNDERSTANDING	SUPPORT FOR THINKING	COMMUNICATION
6 exceptional awesome goes beyond	• finds *all* important parts of problem • has *full* understanding of math needed • uses unusual, creative thinking	• finds more than one way to solve problem • uses many ways to show thinking like diagrams, charts, graphs, etc. • experiments, designs, analyzes • does *more* than problem asks	• writes a clear, convincing, thoughtful answer • writes to an audience • diagrams very clear
5 very good clear strong	• finds *most* of the important parts of problem • has good understanding of math needed	• finds one or more ways to solve problem • uses several ways to show thinking like diagrams, charts, graphs, etc. • may experiment, design, analyze • may compare problem to another, predict	• writes clearly • makes sense • writes to an audience • diagrams clear
4 pretty good gets the job done	• finds *most* of the important parts of problem—some less important are missing • understands most of the math needed	• uses one way to solve problem • some ways to show thinking may be missing • may experiment, design, or analyze	• addresses all parts of the problem • writes to an audience • writing may be unclear
3 O.K. good try unclear	• finds a *few* of the important parts of problem • understands *some* of math needed • thinking gets mixed up • might miss the big idea	• may or may not solve the problem • mathematical thinking is unclear or limited • chooses wrong ways to solve problem	• has trouble writing ideas • may or may not write to an audience • diagrams or charts not clear
2 incomplete confusing	• little understanding of problem • finds less important parts of problem • understands bits and pieces of math needed	• doesn't explain thinking • uses ways to solve problem which don't fit the problem	• writes in a confusing way • may or may not write to an audience
1 may or may not make an effort no understanding	• doesn't understand problem	• answer difficult to understand • makes little or no attempt to explain results	• writes in a way that is very hard to understand

Source: Conejo Valley School District, Thousand Oaks, California, May, 1994. Used by permission.

Rubrics are similar to holistic scales and result in an overall appraisal of student performance. They may be used in evaluating writing samples, problem-solving activities, and other tasks for which there are varying levels of performance, rather than right or wrong responses.

ADS Analysis: *Rubrics*

Information uses: To make criterion comparisons and to conduct self- and introspective-evaluations
Administration procedures: Varied
Assessment findings: Varied formats
Technical adequacy: Generally do not address validity and reliability
Performance demands: Varied
Authenticity: Midline to high
Alignment to curriculum content: High

Reading Retells

Reading retells require students to retell in their own words what they have read. Upon finishing a story or section of text, students are asked to recall the material in their own words. Reading retells allow evaluators "to get a view of the quantity, quality, and organization of information constructed during reading" (Lipson & Wixson, 1997, p. 284). According to Lipson and Wixson (1997), retells should begin with the student's free recall of the text—the examiner does not provide questions or prompts. If, however, the student is hesitant to respond or is unsure of how to respond, the examiner may use broad prompts such as "Tell me what happened in your own words." After this free recall, the examiner may use probes, such as "Tell me more," and structured questions. Questions may ask for information about characters, setting, main events, conflict, and resolution of conflict.

Although a powerful strategy for assessing comprehension, Anderson and Roit (1998) caution that if a retell requires students merely to retell the story verbatim, it may not be an indicator of the story comprehension of students who are English-language learners. They argue that students who are learning English may be good at retelling stories but fail to comprehend the meaning of those stories, and they suggest that teachers ask students to explain what a passage means and to explain it in their own words. Anderson and Roit refer to this strategy as "text explaining" and suggest that it "not only improves comprehension but also increases verbal elaboration and language flexibility" (p. 49).

Analysis of student retells may be completed in multiple ways. One way is to use a checklist of a retell that lists all elements to be included. Students receive a check for each element they mention. The checklist could include items such as:

(a) Named main characters

(b) Mentioned setting, including time and place

(c) Named major events in the story in sequence

(d) Identified the primary conflict in the story

(e) Stated how the conflict was resolved

(f) Explained how the story ended

The same key elements may be organized into a rubric to go beyond indicating (*yes* or *no*) whether the child included an element of a story, to a rating of the extent to which the child addressed each story element. For example, a retelling earning the top score on a rubric may be described as including the following:

Names main characters and describes their qualities and the role(s) they played in the story. Describes the time and place using descriptive words and details included in the story. Describes the major events in the story, in sequence, highlighting the role of the characters and using details and descriptions found in the story. Identifies the primary conflict in the story and discusses the feelings and emotions of the main characters in relation to this conflict. Describes in detail, with examples and descriptive words, how the conflict was resolved and how the characters participated in and felt about this resolution. Describes in detail how the story ends.

ADS Analysis: *Reading Retells*

Information uses: To make criterion comparisons and to conduct self- and interpersonal-evaluations
Administration procedures: Varies
Assessment findings: Varied formats
Technical adequacy: Does not address validity and reliability
Performance demands: Midline to high
Authenticity: Midline to high
Alignment to curriculum content: High

Inventories

As defined by McLoughlin and Lewis (1994), inventories "examine how a student performs within a specific curriculum or with instructional material" (p. 9). Inventories assess a wide range of skills by including sample items for each skill that students are expected to master. Students work through and respond to as many of the items as they can. Information gathered through inventories can provide an overall view of the skills the student possesses and those that are yet to be developed.

A different type of inventory is presented in Exhibit 8.5. Bigge's Inventory of Means of Task Performance (1988; 1991) uses a rating scale and narrative to record how a student performs in relation to physical performance demands of the curriculum. Listed in the first column are typical task requirements in school and life activities (e.g., "Points to indicate, looks to indicate: people, places and things"), grouped by typical means of performing them (e.g., "Gesturing"). In the second column the rater uses

EXHIBIT 8.5

Inventory of Means of Task Performance

Name: _____ Age/Grade _____ Date _____

Typical Task Requirements by Typical Means of Task Performance	Numerical Descriptions of Present Means of Performance	Observations and Explanations (e.g., can speak but chooses not to)	Action Plan Ideas (e.g., individualized or additional instruction; further assessment to identify needs)
GESTURING			
1. Points to indicate, looks to indicate: people, places, and things			
2. Gives a sign to direct attention to something: boys in a fight; an example of the concept "hard"			
3. Makes movements of body to express or emphasize ideas, emotions: dramatizes			
SPEAKING			
4. Replies *yes, no, I don't know,* etc.			
5. Names personal needs and wants, people, places, and things			
6. Reads aloud			
7. Initiates and replies using short phrases			
8. Engages in basic conversational dialogues			
9. Expresses thoughts, questions, feelings, etc.			
10. Makes oral presentations, reports, debates, etc.			
DRAWING AND RELATED MEANS			
11. Draws lines to connect, to underline, etc.			
12. Marks choices, marks to eliminate items, etc.			
13. Draws shapes			
14. Creates artistic works			
15. Colors or paints			
HANDWRITING			
16. Writes letters of the alphabet			
17. Writes own signature			
18. Writes short exercises: answers, lists, note taking, stories, etc.			
19. Writes long exercises: formal reports, compositions, letters, etc.			
20. Writes numerals, math problems, calculations, and answers			

Typical Task Requirements by Typical Means of Task Performance	Numerical Descriptions of Present Means of Performance	Observations and Explanations (e.g., can speak but chooses not to)	Action Plan Ideas (e.g., individualized or additional instruction; further assessment to identify needs)
HOLDING, MANIPULATING, AND MANEUVERING			
21. Holds and steadies objects			
22. Manipulates common school and work tools: scissors, measuring devices, staplers, papers			
23. Handles equipment in sports and recreation activities: game pieces, balls, ropes			
24. Manages common household items: brooms, silverware, trash cans			
25. Manages common educational, vocational, domestic tasks: clearing desktop, uses the phone, washes dishes, etc.			
26. Runs common electrical appliances: household, vocational, personal care, etc.			
27. Sets up and operates aids and devices: communication aids, TTY telephone units for deaf			
28. Operates machines: car, washing machine, vending machines			
29. Makes things: exhibits, displays, crafts			
30. Maneuvers things: carries, pushes, pulls, lifts			
MOBILIZING SELF			
31. Maneuvers self: from one position or posture to another, etc.			
32. Moves about safely in a variety of environments: school, home, work place, shopping center, etc.			
33. Uses transportation systems: car, bus, train, plane			
34. Completes physical routines: washing dishes			
35. Uses steps, elevators and escalators			
OTHER			
36. Other:			

Source: Adapted from Curriculum Based Instruction for Special Education Students *(p. 75), by J. Bigge, 1988, Mountain View, CA: Mayfield.*

the following rating scale to analyze the student's performance of the task requirements when they are needed in a variety of school and other life activities:

5 = Satisfactorily uses means typically used by peers

4 = Needs individualized/additional instruction in use of typical means

3 = Satisfactorily uses modified means for performance (e.g., adaptations, alternatives, or augmentations to the typical means)

2 = Needs individualized/additional instruction in uses of modified means of performance

1 = Needs assessment to determine best means of performance in different school and life activities

0 = Not applicable

The third column provides room for observational notes and explanations about physical performance methods of individuals and targets any needs for immediate intervention. The fourth column, "Action Plan Ideas," is for recording any considerations and recommendations for (a) individualized or additional instruction in uses of typical or adaptive means and activities of performance or (b) assessments to determine the best means of performance of curriculum and other life activities when one or more task requirements is problematic for the student. Functional and efficient participation in schools and other types of activities is the desired outcome.

This inventory guides assessment of current performance and identifies needs for any additional special education and related services. These needs then become targets of IEP goals, benchmarks, and objectives. This inventory may be used to represent student physical task performance across curriculum in multiple school years, to track student skill development, and to identify the need for transition from grade to grade and from setting to setting.

ADS Analysis: *Inventories*

Information uses: To make criterion comparisons and to conduct self- and introspective-evaluations
Administration procedures: Standardized to varied
Assessment findings: Varied formats
Technical adequacy: Do not address validity and reliability
Performance demands: Generally low, although varies
Authenticity: Midline to low
Alignment with curriculum content: Midline to high

THEORY TO PRACTICE

➡ Select one of the screening and diagnostic assessment tools listed in Exhibit 8.1 to evaluate. Begin by reading the manual. How was the test normed? How were reliability and validity determined? What does the test test? How comprehensive is the test? How is the test administered? Approximately how long does administration take? What are the rules for establishing basals and ceilings? What types of scores does the test provide? Look at the easel of actual items. What item formats are used? How current are the items? Do you encounter any items you consider to be culturally, racially, or gender biased? Overall, what is your rating of this specific tool?

➡ Collect examples of rubrics, checklists, questionnaires, and interviews that special and general education teachers use in their programs. Assess the type of information these tools provide, the areas they target, and the ease with which the tools may be administered and the results interpreted. From these tools, develop one of your own that you could use in the classroom.

COMBINED METHODS AND TOOLS

Combined methods make use of several of the individual methods. Ecological assessment, for example, may utilize checklists, observation, interviews, and rating scales. We present three combined methods and tools: functional assessment, portfolio assessment, and ecological assessment.

Functional Assessment

Functional assessment (not to be confused with functional curriculum and functional performance) is a form of assessment that challenges the examiner to collect information about the student's behavior as well as about environmental factors possibly influencing that behavior, in order to form hypotheses to explain why a student is engaging in a specific behavior. In this context, the term *function* means "purpose"—what is the child's purpose for engaging in the behavior? By having an understanding of the setting in which behavior occurs (e.g., home, school, community) and the functions the behavior plays (e.g., to get something or to escape from something), an examiner can make adjustments more effectively in the environment, develop appropriate interventions, and/or provide instruction in needed social skills to help the student develop more socially appropriate responses to behaviorally challenging situations. As defined by Dunlap and colleagues (1993), functional assessment is "a process of identifying functional relationships between environmental events and the occurrence and nonoccurrence of a target behavior" (p. 275).

Foster-Johnson and Dunlap (1993) describe two phases of functional assessment: (a) conducting the functional assessment and (b) developing an intervention based on information collected. To conduct the functional assessment, the examiner collects information and develops hypothesis statements about the behavior. The collection of information may be completed through observation, interviews, rating scales and other methods that allow for the gathering of descriptions of student behavior in different contexts and situations. Then, based on this information, a plan for teaching replacement behaviors and/or modifying events or circumstances associated with the behavior can be implemented. Functional assessment may be used to decrease inappropriate behaviors and increase prosocial behaviors through environmental manipulation and social skills instruction. It may also serve as a vehicle for integrating and supporting students with severe and other disabilities in community placements (e.g., Redmond, Bennett, Wiggert, & McLean, 1993).

An example of a functional assessment is data collection to determine why a child is aggressive toward others during cooperative art activities. Observations of the student in the classroom might be completed by the special education teacher with interviews, rating scales, and checklists completed by the classroom teacher, the parent, and the student. They may reveal that the student is hesitant to show others his artwork, is unwilling to share materials because of his need for secrecy around the product he is producing, and becomes defensive about his abilities in art class. This reluctance to collaborate and participate with others during cooperative art activities is manifested in his calling out, grabbing materials from peers, and shouting at group members when things do not go his way. Understanding that the underlying reason for these behaviors is possibly linked with the child's uncertainty about his ability in art and fears of public humiliation will possibly lead to different intervention selections than would have been chosen if this information had not been collected. Without this additional information, the teacher may have assumed that the behavior modification technique of providing reinforcement of positive peer interaction behaviors would help to turn the behavior around. The additional information about the possible function of the behavior (the reason why the child engages in the behavior) will focus the intervention on discussions around the child's art ability, the development of strategies for dealing with feelings of uncertainty, and so forth. The result is a behavior intervention plan that directly attacks the underlying problem, not just the behaviors that appear on the surface.

Profile: *Functional Assessment*	
Tools and Methods Menu	
Peer-comparisons tests	Criterion-comparison tests
Curriculum-based measurement	Precision teaching
Observation	Interviews
Questionnaires	Checklists
Rating scales	Rubrics
Inventories	

Portfolios

According to Paulson, Paulson, and Meyer (1993) a portfolio

> is a portfolio when it provides a complex and comprehensive view of student performance in context. It is a portfolio when the student is a participant in, rather than the object of, assessment. Above all, a portfolio is a portfolio when it provides a forum that encourages students to develop the abilities needed to become independent, self-directed learners. (p. 63)

As defined by Valencia (1990), portfolio assessment "is an expanded definition of assessment in which a wide variety of indicators of learning are gathered across many situations before, during, and after instruction" (p. 340).

Batzle (1992) states that portfolio assessment (a) is ongoing, with information gathered over time; (b) celebrates differing developmental levels; (c) mirrors and guides instructional practice; (d) captures the uniqueness of each child; (e) places emphasis on what students know; (f) brings teachers and students together through conferencing and evaluation activities; and (g) provides a variety of evidence through both process and product samples. Consequently, Hart (1994) points out that portfolios allow teachers to assess student progress more closely over time, aid teachers and parents in communicating about a student's performance, assist in program evaluation efforts, and provide a means through which students can actively participate with their teachers in the assessment process. Graves (1994) identifies five essentials in the use of portfolios: (a) all students maintain a portfolio; (b) students are allowed to choose what will go into their portfolio; (c) students must justify why they have included something in their portfolio; (d) teachers and peers critique and respond to the student's portfolio collection; and (e) teachers maintain their own portfolio and through it demonstrate how they, too, reflect and judge their own work over time.

Types

Portfolios may be housed in manila folders, expanding folder cases, boxes, or stored on laser disks and CD-ROMs. Although there are several ways in which portfolios may be developed and maintained, Batzle (1992) identifies three general types of portfolios:

1. *Working portfolio*—Teacher, student, and parents all contribute to the portfolio. Both works-in-progress and final product pieces are included.

2. *Showcase portfolio*—The portfolio houses only the student's best work and generally does not include works-in-progress. The student manages the portfolio and decides what to place in it.

3. *Record-keeping or teacher portfolio*—The portfolio houses student test papers and work samples maintained by the teacher. It contains work *not* selected by the student for inclusion in the showcase portfolio.

Another form of portfolio is a *video portfolio*. Video may be used to capture student skills in all areas and viewed to evaluate performance gains over time. Light, Dunlap, and Stecker (1993) used video to create video résumés for students with severe disabilities. Students were videotaped as they engaged in job-related tasks, and the videotapes were shown to prospective employers. The use of videotape helped these students with severe disabilities to portray their skills and talents accurately to prospective employers—strengths and abilities that may be overlooked or overshadowed when students engage in traditional, face-to-face interviews.

Swicegood (1994) describes another type of portfolio—*assessment portfolio*. Although other portfolio types are used for assessment, this type of assessment portfolio identified by Swicegood (1994) is unique because it is used in the evaluation of a student's performance and for evaluating the effectiveness of his/her special education program. Included in this type of portfolio are (a) artifacts of behavior and adaptive functioning (e.g., behavior checklists, videotapes of student behaviors); (b) indicators of academic and literacy growth (e.g., criterion-comparison methods and tools, curriculum-based assessments, reading and writing samples); (c) indicators of strategic learning and self-regulation (e.g., student think alouds, ratings of study skills); and (d) indicators of language and culture (e.g., primary language sample, observations of the student in various settings). Members of a team, including the parents and classmates, contribute to this portfolio, which is reviewed during IEP meetings and other parent-teacher conferences.

Contents

The types of portfolios created determine portfolio contents. For example, the Arts PROPEL writing-portfolio project (Wolf, 1989) carried out in Pittsburgh public schools identified three types of works for inclusion in portfolios: biographies of works, range of works, and reflections. A *biography of works* catalogs and documents the various stages that precede the creation of the final product. In the case of a written piece, notes, semantic webs, and drafts leading to the final version of a piece would be included in the biography of works. The *range of works* is a diverse array of works, such as letters, poems, short stories, and notes that represent the student as a writer. *Reflections* are activities that require students to revisit and appraise their own work. While reviewing past and present works, students may write comments that capture their personal reactions to the work and express what the pieces suggest about their development as a writer, or they may record their reflections on audiotape.

Batzle (1992) suggests the following items be included in a portfolio: (a) testing materials, including standardized tests and chapter or unit tests; (b) samples of curriculum-based work in language arts, mathematics, fine arts, science, and social studies; (c) teacher observations and measures, including running records, process checks, and conference records; (d) inventories and other forms, such as informal reading inventories, parent surveys, and records of student participation in community-based activities; and (e) items such as cassettes or photos of drama productions. Wesson and King (1996) provide examples of special education portfolios and describe the contents of a behavior portfolio of a sixth grade student identified as seriously emotionally disturbed. This portfolio included (a) videotapes of the student working with peers in the classroom, (b) ongoing log of the student's social events and activities and descriptions of how he feels about his participation in these activities, (c) narrative descriptions of the student's actions in social situations, (d) observations of the student in school settings that focus on target behaviors, and (e) copies of the parent survey completed monthly to rate the parents' perceptions of their child's behavior. Wesson and King (1996) also list these items included in the portfolio of a high school student with severe disabilities: (a) videotape of the student working in different environments (e.g., school, community job sites), (b) transcript of an interview with the student concerning her hopes and goals, (c) vocational checklists of skills the student has mastered, and (d) a list of the student's friends and the role they play in her life.

Implementation

One way to implement portfolios is illustrated by the Arts PROPEL project (Eresh, 1990). First, students were told that all the writing they did—finished and unfinished pieces— would be maintained in a folder. Second, they were told that they would be provided many opportunities to review and reflect on their writing, individually and with peers. Third, they were told that they would be asked later in the year to select pieces to include in their portfolio in order to help them learn about their own writing and to gain understanding of themselves as emerging writers. They would also be keeping a record of the major readings they did throughout the year to determine whether and how their reading influenced their writing. Throughout the year, teachers were asked to evaluate students' writing on two dimensions: strengths in the writing and goals for future writing. The Arts PROPEL questions to guide students' self-evaluation and peer evaluation activities are listed in Exhibit 8.6.

EXHIBIT 8.6
Arts PROPEL Portfolio Self-Evaluation Questions

SELECTING AND EVALUATING WRITING PIECES AT AN EARLY TIME OF THE SCHOOL YEAR:

1. What in these pieces of writing is like what you see in other pieces of your writing?
2. What do these pieces show about yourself as a writer? . . .
3. Where did you get your idea for this piece?
4. How did you do it? Describe the stages the writing went through, when and where you wrote, and roughly how long each stage took. . . .
5. What did you find out about writing or what you do as a writer that you did not know before you wrote this piece? (p. 7)

SELECTING AND EVALUATING WRITING PIECES AT THE CONCLUSION OF THE SCHOOL YEAR:

1. What do you notice when you look at your earlier work?
2. How do you think your writing has changed?
3. What do you know you didn't know before?
4. At what points did you discover something new about writing?
5. How do the changes you see in writing affect the way you see yourself as a writer?
6. Are there any pieces you have changed your mind about over time—any that you liked before but don't like now, or any that you didn't like before that you do like now? If so, which ones?
7. What made you change your mind about these pieces?
8. In what ways do you think your reading has influenced your writing? (p. 8)

Source: From *Portfolio Assessment as a Means of Self-Directed Learning* (pp. 7; 8), by J. T. Eresh, April 1990, Paper presented at the meeting of the American Educational Research Association, Boston.

Evaluation

According to Herman, Aschbacher, and Winters (1992), assembling a portfolio is not portfolio assessment. Portfolio assessment occurs when the contents of a portfolio are appraised and evaluated. Portfolios may be evaluated to monitor ongoing student skill development, or evaluation may be used as a summative tool to document student growth.

There is general agreement that portfolios must be evaluated in order to serve as tools for assessing student performance. But how to evaluate them is an issue fraught with conflict and controversy. What tools and approaches will be used? Will student self-evaluations be considered part of the evaluation? Are the most appropriate tools checklists, rating scales, and rubrics, or would evaluation of students' presentations of their portfolios be better if made by a panel of parents, students, and teachers? Who should be responsible for evaluating the portfolios—teachers, students engaged in self-evaluation and peer evaluation, parents, others?

Other questions relate directly to the content of portfolios. How does one evaluate and compare student portfolios, especially when students choose to include different types of pieces? If students decide what to include in their own portfolios, how can evaluators make fair and equitable comparisons and evaluations across students? If portfolios are being used to evaluate student performance, is there a need for standardization—that is, should students be required to include certain pieces for judging? Moreover, how do you achieve interrater reliability (agreement between two raters who rate the same portfolio independently)? If students are encouraged to include not just their best pieces but works-in-progress, or pieces that represent earlier work, how will those pieces be evaluated?

Profile: *Portfolios*	
Tools and Methods Menu	
Peer-comparisons tests	Criterion-comparison tests
Quizzes	Curriculum-based measurement
Precision teaching	Observation
Interviews	Questionnaires
Checklists	Rating scales
Rubrics	Inventories

Ecological Assessment

One approach to ecological assessment has two parts: an ecological inventory (EI) and a student repertoire inventory (SRI) (Gage & Falvey, 1995). The purpose of this form of ecological assessment is to identify the current and anticipated future performance needs of students with disabilities in different settings (school, work). This is done by conducting an *ecological inventory* (EI) of performances typical of peers in the same kinds of activities in the same kinds of settings. The steps of this process, as specified by Gage and Falvey (1995, p. 72), are as follows:

1. Divide the curriculum into subjects or curriculum domains such as vocational.

2. Delineate the environments that are available to peers without disabilities.

3. Delineate the subenvironments within each environment.

4. Delineate the activities within each subenvironment.

5. Delineate the specific skills expected or required in order to participate in each activity.

A *student repertoire inventory* follows an ecological inventory. Exhibit 8.7 shows a sample student repertoire inventory with information from steps 1–4 of the ecological inventory recorded at the top. The first step in the student repertoire inventory is the same as the last one (Step 5) in the ecological inventory. Listed in the first column of the student repertoire inventory, therefore, are the skills required of peers without disabilities. The observer, or recorder, indicates in the second column whether the student with a disability performs the listed skills while participating in the activity and in the third column "conducts a discrepancy analysis of the student's performance against the performance of peers without disabilities" (p. 73). Once these three columns are completed, individual teachers or IEP team members hypothesize possible adaptations or accommodations needed by the student on any skills not performed (fourth column) and they plan instruction (fifth column). If the student does not perform any of the skills, three options may be considered: teaching the skill, developing an adaptation and teaching the student to use it, or teaching the student to perform a different but related skill (Gage & Falvey, 1995). It is from this combination of inventories that IEP objectives and curriculum specifics are determined.

EXHIBIT 8.7

Student Repertoire Inventory

Name: Courtnee

Domain: Vocational

Environment: Cafeteria

Subenvironment: Lunch line and counter

Activities: 1) Locate lunch line

2) Secure lunch tray

3) Locate seat

Date: 9/5

Recorder: STG

Inventory for Student without Disabilities	Inventory for Student with Disabilities	Discrepancy Analysis	Adaptation Hypothesis	What to Do?
1. Locate end of lunch line				
Enter cafeteria	+			
Scan for end of line	−	Looks around	Pair with peer	
Go to end of line	−	Walks to middle of line		Teach skill
2. Secure lunch tray				
Scan for lunch tray	+			
Pick up tray	+			
Place it on lunch counter	−	Holds to side		Teach skill
Push it along counter	−	Waits for others to push		Teach skill
Scan selections	+			
State choice	−	Grabs for items	Point to item	Teach to point and state choice
Pick up tray at end of line	−	Waits for someone to do it		Teach to pick up
3. Locate seat				
Scan for empty table/seat	+			
Locate empty seat	−	Walks around	Sit with peer	Teach to find peer
Set tray down	−	Stands at seat		Teach to set it down
Sit at empty bench	+			

From: Inclusive and Heterogeneous Schooling: Assessment, Curriculum and Instruction, Mary A. Falvey, ed., pp. 92–93. Copyright © 1995 by Paul H. Brookes Publishing Co., Inc., P.O. Box 10624, Baltimore, MD 21285-0624.

The model that Evans, Evans, and Gable (1989) propose for ecological assessment takes a broad view and surveys a student's abilities and skills as demonstrated in a variety of environments: (a) biophysical, (b) physical, (c) psychological, and (d) social.

Within the *biophysical environment* are elements such as health factors, physical impairments, and drugs and/or other medications the student is receiving under the supervision of a physician. These elements may significantly impact the student's ability to perform and achieve within a learning environment. Interviews, checklists, and questionnaires are some of the methods that can be used to collect this type of information.

Within the *physical environment* are two main areas of concern: (a) conditions present in the home and community and (b) conditions present in the classroom and school. Factors such as adequate housing, parental supervision, home routine, methods of discipline, the death of one or both parents, divorce, sibling rivalry, potential psychological and/or sexual abuse, and parental expectations all might affect a youngster's classroom performance. Information about the home and community can be gained through interviews, questionnaires, and rating scales. Classroom and school conditions of interest to the evaluator include classroom arrangement (e.g., seating arrangements and the use of classroom space), lighting, noise level, and architectural accessibility.

Psychological factors are usually assessed by the school psychologist or by other licensed personnel at the school site trained in the administration of psychoeducational instruments designed to determine whether emotional or learning problems might be contributing to the academic difficulties of a student. However, teachers, parents, and students can also provide insight into these factors through discussion and identification of teaching and learning styles. This exploration can shed light on whether these styles are working in concert or are at odds. Among the many assessment methods and tools available for gathering this information are peer-comparison tests, criterion-comparison tests, interviews, and rating scales.

Finally, to understand classroom behaviors, it is important to examine factors found in the youngster's *social environment.* These factors, generally referred to as interpersonal factors, are the social interactions the student has with classmates, parents, teachers, and community merchants and service workers, as well as with others in the student's learning and living environments. Observations, interviews, rating scales, questionnaires, and inventories may be helpful tools in gathering this type of information.

Together, this information creates a profile of the student and the successes and difficulties he or she is experiencing. This information can be used to develop interventions and modifications that support the student's continued development.

Profile: *Ecological Assessment*

Tools and Methods Menu

Precision teaching	Checklists
Observation	Rating scales
Interviews	Rubrics
Questionnaires	Inventories

➡ Meet with a district behavioral intervention specialist who is responsible for conducting functional assessments for the district or who prepares others to conduct functional assessments. Ask the specialist to describe the procedures she or he goes through when conducting a functional assessment. What does the specialist consider the most challenging aspects of conducting functional assessments? What types of information gained through functional assessment does the specialist consider most valuable?

➡ Visit an area school that is requiring students to develop portfolios. With permission, meet with some students to discuss their portfolios. Ask them to explain how they created their portfolios and what the different pieces mean to them. Reflect on this experience. If you were to include portfolios in your classroom, what essential processes and procedures would you put into place to make the development and evaluation of student portfolios meaningful for students, teachers, and parents?

➡ Using one of the ecological assessment models, conduct an ecological assessment of a selected environment with a peer. Outline what you are most interested in learning, how you will go about data collection, and list the procedures you will use to analyze gathered data. When you have finished, debrief about the process. What type of information did you gain? What kinds of curricular and instructional decisions could you make based on your gathered data? What could you do next time to enhance the type of data gathered?

SPECIAL CASES: SPECIFIC ABILITY TESTS

Specific ability tests (McLoughlin & Lewis, 1994) are used to assess vision, hearing, perception, motor, memory, attention, and language development and the acquisition of a second language. Tests used to assess these areas are unique because they utilize all of the tools and methods already described.

Vision

Checking students' vision is an essential first step of the contextualized assessment process and is done to rule out vision difficulties. Vision screenings are regularly conducted in schools. Generally all children have their vision checked during the elementary and middle school grades, once every two or three years. A Snellen chart (known as the "E" chart) is the standard vehicle for checking a child's visual acuity. An alternative vision chart, the "Lighthouse Flashcard Test for Children," uses symbols (e.g., apples, houses, hearts) rather than letters and can be used with young children and those with cognitive disabilities. A child who fails the vision screening is referred to an optometrist or ophthalmologist for a more thorough vision test. As a teacher, if you notice a child squinting, rubbing his or her eyes, or complaining about scratchy or tired eyes, you should have the child's vision tested.

When a visual impairment is present or suspected, additional vision assessments are necessary. Visual impairments are considered conditions in which eyesight cannot be corrected to what is considered "normal" (Holbrook, 1996). Professionals such as ophthalmologists and optometrists determine whether a child has a visual impairment. They measure, among other things, how clearly a child sees (visual acuity) and what the child can and cannot see without moving the head (visual field). Visual impairments can be described by degrees of vision loss and through assessments of how a child functionally uses vision. Two broad categories are used to classify visual impairments. Compiled by Silberman (1996), these are:

Blind	A person who is blind has only light perception without projection or is totally without the sense of vision (Faye, 1984). Educationally, a child who is blind learns through tactile and sensory channels other than vision (Scholl, 1986).
Low vision	A person with low vision has a significant visual impairment but also has significant usable vision. This person is educationally still severely visually impaired after correction, but his or her visual functioning may be improved through the use of optical aids, nonoptical aids, and environmental modification and techniques (Corn, 1980). The low-vision population must not be treated as "blind" (Barrage & Erin, 1992).

Koenig (1996) describes assessment practices for the purpose of selecting learning and literacy media for children and youth with low vision. Assessment, usually conducted by the teacher of students with visual impairments, targets the areas identified by Koenig with a series of questions such as those presented in Exhibit 8.8. Information also comes from interviews with parents, general education teachers, diagnostic specialists, and physical and occupational therapists.

Use of Sensory Channels	Which sensory channels are primary sources of sensory information in which kinds of situations?
Visual Functioning	What is the current condition of the eye(s) and is the current condition stable? Will optical devices other than glasses improve visual functioning?
Reading Efficiency	What is the child's oral reading rate with comprehension on different modes of materials (e.g., regular print; large-print closed captioned TV)?
Handwriting	What are the child's primary modes of expressive writing (e.g., keyboarding; dictation; limited handwriting in math)?
Literacy Tools	What literacy tools are in the child's repertoire for accomplishing reading tasks (e.g., reading large print; using live readers)?
	What literary tools are in a child's repertoire for accomplishing writing tasks (e.g., keyboarding, dictation)?
	What expanded literacy tools for reading should be considered by the educational team (e.g., use of textbooks on tape; use of CCTV; use of synthetic speech and large print on the computer)?
	Source: Adapted from Koenig (1996), pp. 273–278.

EXHIBIT 8.8

Areas of Assessment and Representative Questions to Determine Learning and Literacy Media for Individual Students Who Have Visual Impairments

Hearing

Checking a child's hearing is another essential early step of the contextualized assessment process. The team needs to determine whether the child's difficulty is the result of a hearing loss. Like vision screenings, hearing screenings are commonly conducted in schools. As a teacher you will want to keep your eyes open for a child who is possibly having difficulties with hearing. If you see a child turning her head to one side, looking at others for cues about what to do, rubbing her ears, frequently asking for information to be repeated, or complaining of earaches, you will want to have the child's hearing tested.

A pure-tone audiometer is used by a specially trained assessor to test hearing in schools. The student will hear sounds of different frequencies (pitch) and intensities (loudness) and will raise a hand to indicate when a sound is heard. If the student experiences difficulties, an audiologist will administer a pure-tone threshold test. This test yields more specific information about the child's hearing. If there are still concerns, or if it is suspected that the child has a hearing loss, the child will be referred to a audiologist or to an otologist for a more thorough hearing examination (McLoughlin & Lewis, 1994).

For students with existing or suspected hearing impairment, functional assessments are likely to accompany doctors' and audiologists' examinations that measure hearing and check for physical causes of hearing problems. The type of hearing loss a child has—*sensorineural loss,* involving nerves that carry sound to the brain; or *conductive loss,* involving the passage of sound through the ear canal or structures of the middle and inner ear—determines how the loss can be lessened or compensated for (Holbrook, 1996). Functional examinations provide information about how students react to sound frequencies and intensities, among other things. For example, does a child notice the stereo but ignore running water? Does the child notice men's voices more than women's? In what situations is noise most helpful? Most confusing and distracting? Where in the room does the child learn best? And, most important, how does the child learn and communicate best?

In addition to acquiring information about the types and degree of hearing loss and the conducting of functional assessments, experts in hearing impairment try to assess what influence the hearing loss is likely to have on language learning and educational progress. According to Lowenbraun and Thompson (1994),

> the extent of the effect [of hearing impairment on language learning and the influence on educational progress] will depend on (1) the type of loss (conductive or sensorineural), (2) the degree of loss, (3) the age of onset, (4) the time of detection, (5) the time of intervention, (6) the age at which hearing aids are fitted and consistently worn, (7) the home environment, and (8) the presence of other disabilities. (p. 387)

Perception

Perception tests assess how students process information received through the senses. The two most common kinds of perception tests are visual and auditory.

Tests of *visual perception* may take several forms. They may measure visual-motor skills (looking at a shape or figure and reproducing it through drawing) or visual memory (seeing an object and then reproducing it by drawing it from memory). For example, the Developmental Test of Visual-Motor Integration (3rd revision) (Beery, 1989) tests a child's ability to reproduce, through drawing, visually presented shapes that increase in complexity. The test measures how the child perceives the visual stimulus (the shape) and is able to translate that image into motor skills by drawing the shape on paper with a pencil.

Tests of *auditory perception* also take several forms. A common test measures auditory discrimination of sounds. For this test, the administrator says two words, such as *bag* and *bat,* and asks the student whether the words are the same or different. The test measures the degree to which the student is able to differentiate among speech sounds.

Although perception tests are usually a component of a comprehensive assessment, the overall technical soundness of the instruments (e.g., Venn, 1994), the importance of measurements of perceptual skills, and the tests' link with instructional practice have drawn questions, and the importance of such testing and intervention continues to be questioned.

Motor

Two major areas of concern in motor development are fine and gross motor skills. *Fine motor skills* include writing and drawing, buttoning and zipping. *Gross motor skills* involve the large muscles involved in running and jumping. Other motor skills include balance and body awareness.

The Bruininks-Oseretsky Test of Motor Proficiency (Bruininks, 1978) is one example of a motor test that assesses both fine motor and gross motor development. The test is divided into three sections, with subtests in each: (a) gross motor development includes running speed and agility, balance, bilateral coordination, and strength; (b) gross and fine motor development includes upper-limb coordination; and (c) fine motor skills include response speed, visual-motor control, and upper-limb speed and dexterity.

An assessment conducted in a variety of a child's natural environments with familiar activities, natural materials, and familiar cues can provide a more comprehensive picture of a student's functional motor abilities than will an assessment conducted in a clinical setting (Falvey, 1995). Specific motor abilities and disabilities are also determined by observing a child's physical task performance attempts and omissions in his or her overall daily functioning. Teachers with special education preparation in the education of students with physical and health impairments most frequently have the opportunity to conduct such assessment. The Means of Task Performance Inventory (see Exhibit 8.5) described earlier in this chapter is often useful.

For students with more severe motor impairments, assessments focus on mobility, upright positioning, range of motion, reflexive involvement, structural disorders, and tonal qualities (Falvey, 1995). *Physical therapists* conduct formal assessments leading to their intervention and consultation with others to prevent or minimize disability, relieve pain, improve sensorimotor function, and assist individuals to reach their motor potentials in life activities. *Occupational therapists* concentrate on fine motor and perceptual skills that assist in improvement of physical and other types of development (e.g., intellectual, social) and that lead to functional outcomes in life activities such as handling balls in games and using fine motor skills in managing tools.

Therapy assessments should be conducted in conjunction with teacher and parent assessments of students in ongoing activities in home, school, and community (Falvey, 1995). For example, head control may be assessed while a child is having lunch in the cafeteria, or twisting and turning skills may be assessed as a child turns faucets on and off. Very detailed assessment occurs when a student is being evaluated for solutions to technology access problems (Williams, Sternach, Wolfe, & Stanger, 1993). Steps to improve motor function in overall daily functioning is a responsibility shared by therapists, teachers, parents, and the student.

Memory

According to McLoughlin and Lewis (1994), memory may be described in terms of four factors:

1. **Type of information to be recalled.** It is believed that the more meaningful information is, the easier it is to recall.

2. **Time since original learning.** This category includes short-term and long-term memory.

3. **Type of memory.** A differentiation is made between recognition memory (the individual recognizes that the information was presented at another time) and recall memory (the individual must produce the information from memory).

4. **Organization of recall.** This category includes free recall (information that can be remembered in any order), serial recall (information that must be remembered in a specific order), and paired-associative recall (the individual pairs a stimulus with a response, as when seeing a letter and saying its name).

Memory assessment generally focuses on serial recall and short-term memory. For example, the examiner may say a list of numbers and ask the student to repeat them in the same order. Some tests measure visual memory by presenting pictures of objects in a series, then removing and shuffling the pictures and having the student place the pictures back in the original order (McLoughlin & Lewis, 1994).

Attention

Attention, the ability to focus on specific stimuli for a set period of time, is difficult to assess. The student must attend to a task in order for his or her attention to be measured. If the task is of great interest to the student, the student may demonstrate an enhanced ability or desire to attend. But if the task is of limited or no interest, the student may choose not to attend. As a result, it is not always possible to get a true measure of a child's attention ability. The assessment may be measuring only the child's response to selected tasks.

Many suggest that observations, interviews, questionnaires, and rating scales offer the most promising ways to gain information about a student's attention (Garber, Garber, & Spizman, 1990). A child could be observed over several days in several different situations to gain insight into his or her true attention abilities. Teachers, parents, and the child could be interviewed and asked to respond to questionnaires and/or rating scales to describe attending behavior. It appears that gathering data across a variety of sources is extremely important for measuring attention. Such a practice is critical when a team is faced with the question of whether a student has attention deficit hyperactivity disorder.

Language Development and Second-Language Acquisition

Several different methods are available for assessing language development and second-language acquisition. Language assessment measures both verbal and nonverbal behavior, and involves both speech (articulation, fluency, voice) and language (semantics, syntax, phonology, morphology, and pragmatics). Generally, a speech-language pathologist conducts the language development assessment, and a bilingual or ESL (English as a second language) teacher or other specialist assists if the student's home language is a language other than English.

One essential component of a language assessment is observation. Observing the child in the classroom, on the playground, and in settings outside school is imperative if a full understanding of the child's understanding and use of language is to be achieved. Samples of a child's language may also be gathered and analyzed. A speech-language pathologist may visit with a student and talk about the child's favorite activity or some other topic in which the child has expressed interest. The session is tape-recorded, and the tape is transcribed word for word for analysis. Turn-taking skills, staying on topic, and more specific skills such as use of word endings and subject/verb agreement may be analyzed. The language sample of English-learners—individuals learning the English language—may be analyzed to evaluate their vocabulary level and syntax skills.

Interviewing the student, school personnel, and family and community members is another means for gaining insight into a child's communicative competence. Information about language use at home is essential, especially to assess language development of students learning English as a second language. Also, an understanding of speaking patterns and family communication structures can be important for developing intervention plans. Other methods are available as well. Peer-comparison tests may be used to compare a child's language development to that of peers, and criterion-referenced tests may be used to identify a student's language level or proficiency in English.

THEORY TO PRACTICE

➡ Interview a school psychologist or diagnostician to find out how she or he tests students in these identified areas of specific skills. How often are these assessments administered and what type of information is gained? What value does the school psychologist or diagnostician place on this category of assessment? What is this professional's position on testing and training in perceptual areas?

➡ Observe a child who is identified by his or her teacher as having difficulty in school. Formulate contextualized assessment questions that can be answered through the application of assessment methods and tools described in this chapter. Choose and justify these methods and tools in terms of their ability to provide needed information for answering target questions.

CHAPTER SUMMARY

This chapter explores a variety of assessment tools and methods. Tools and methods are divided into three categories: individual methods and tools, combined methods and tools, and methods for special cases of specific abilities. Each method is described in terms of the Assessment Dimension System.

CHAPTER 9

Making Sense
of Assessment Results

Read to find out the following:

- how assessment results are interpreted and lead to the development of IEP present levels of performance statements
- how IEP teams can prioritize curricular options for students with disabilities

Conducting contextualized assessments to determine eligibility for special education services or for annual reviews and other reevaluations leading to the development of IEPs results in the gathering of great quantities of information. Making sense of that information, writing reports and describing present levels of performance, and based on that information, writing goals and objectives for inclusion in the IEP, constitute a formidable task. In this chapter, by focusing on the interpretation of findings and their use for the writing of present levels of performance statements, we provide guidelines and examples for carrying out this task. In the final section of the chapter we discuss the next step—setting priorities for a student's curriculum.

Contextualized assessment (see Figure 6.1) provides a context within which to analyze collected data. Remember, contextualized assessment results in the casting of a wide net. Information across contexts (school, family, and community) and across factors (culture and beliefs, experiences, cognitive level, overall health and specific abilities, behavior, communication and performance, academics and related skills, and life skills) is gathered to make possible a holistic understanding of a child's strengths, needs, challenges, and goals. This holistic view should not be lost when assessment findings are reported—emphasis should remain on the goal of presenting a broad understanding of the student that includes specific and supportive information. Emerging from this process is identification of specific special education and related needs.

STARTING POINT: THE ASSESSMENT PLAN

A logical starting point for analyzing assessment findings is the original statement of the purpose of the assessment and the list of guiding questions. The sample assessment plan presented in Chapter 6 (Exhibit 6.2) is presented again in Exhibit 9.1. We will use it to organize and interpret assessment findings. The purpose of this assessment plan is to determine whether Jimmy is eligible for special education programs and services, and, if found eligible, to develop an IEP to address his needs.

EXHIBIT 9.1

Assessment Plan

Student Name _Jimmy_   Grade _4_   Teacher _Rodriquez_

Reason for Referral: Jimmy is having difficulty in reading and writing, especially in the areas of vocabulary, reading comprehension, spelling, and writing mechanics.

Proposed Assessment Plan

Guiding Questions	Tool	Who
Overall Health and Specific Abilities • How is the child's overall health? • Does the child have any special health-care needs? • What, if any, vision, hearing, or motor difficulties could be interfering with this child's learning and performance?	• Satisfactory as evaluated on December 2 • Health history interview	Nurse or school psychologist
Communication and Performance • How do the child's speech and language skills compare to those of peers?	• Test of Language Development-3 Intermediate	Speech-language pathologist
Cognitive • What is the student's overall functioning level? • Does the child appear to have a processing disorder?	• Wechsler Intelligence Scale for Children-III	School psychologist
Academics and Related Skills • What is the child's overall academic skill profile? • In what areas of the school curriculum is the child experiencing success and difficulty? What strategies does the child employ when working in easy/difficult areas? • What types of instructional activities or manner of instructional presentation does the child mostly respond to? • What accommodations or adaptations are provided in general education settings? • What learning strategies and study skills does the child exhibit?	• Woodcock-Johnson Psycho-Educational Battery-Revised • Woodcock Reading Mastery Tests-Revised • Informal reading inventory • Test of Written Language-2 • Teacher interview • Parent interview • Student interview • Observation • Paragraph writing checklist	Special and general education teachers School psychologist
Life Skills • How does the child respond to social situations? • What strategies does the child have for responding to social situations? • How does the child go about making choices and decisions? • Is the child a self-advocate or do others serve as his advocate?	• Observation • Student and parent interviews	School psychologist Special and general education teachers Physical therapist

As the plan indicates, Jimmy was initially referred because of his difficulties in "reading and writing, especially in the areas of vocabulary, reading comprehension, spelling, and writing mechanics." These areas are our focal point when we analyze the assessment findings. The guiding questions listed in Exhibit 9.1 will help us to pinpoint exactly what tools to use and will aid in the structuring of our analysis of assessment findings.

THE GUIDING QUESTIONS AND WHAT WAS LEARNED

The process of interpreting gathered information begins with the return to the guiding questions and the assessment tools that were administered to provide answers. These questions can be used to structure the information about Jimmy that was gathered and to interpret outcomes.

In this section of Chapter 9 we return to each question listed in the assessment plan and describe the information gathered from the various sources. Before you read the analysis section for each set of questions, challenge yourself to respond to the questions in order to practice and sharpen your interpretation skills. Please keep in mind that there are multiple ways to complete this analysis and to interpret results. We demonstrate only one way through this example. Also, remember that analysis and interpretation should be a team effort. Therefore, diverse views should be brought to bear on information gathered and on its significance to a particular student and its part in the development of the student's individualized plan.

Overall Health and Specific Abilities

The questions in this section of the assessment plan for Jimmy are as follows:

- How is the child's overall health?
- Does the child have any special health-care needs?
- What, if any, vision, hearing, or motor difficulties could be interfering with this child's learning and performance?

The school nurse visited with Jimmy's mother over a 30-minute period, gathering information about the boy's developmental and health history. The parent said that Jimmy reached milestones at expected ages and experienced no major health problems or concerns. As a result of the interview, the school nurse rated Jimmy's health to be within the normal range. Moreover, information gathered by a visiting nurse found Jimmy to have no vision, hearing, or motor difficulties. Therefore, problems in these areas were ruled out at this time.

> Given that information, how would you answer the questions about overall health and specific abilities?

We have already answered three primary questions and have ruled out any physical or health-related concerns. This suggests that Jimmy's difficulties are not due to visual, hearing, motor, or health difficulties.

Communication and Performance

The assessment plan poses this question:

- How do the child's speech and language skills compare to those of peers?

The speech-language pathologist met with Jimmy on two occasions. During that time she administered the Test of Language Development-Intermediate:3 (TOLD-I:3) (Hammill & Newcomer, 1997). This test assesses:

1. sentence combining: constructing sentences

2. picture vocabulary: understanding word relationships

3. word ordering: constructing sentences

4. generals: knowing abstract relationships

5. grammatic comprehension: recognizing grammatical sentences

6. malapropisms: correcting ridiculous sentences

Subtest scores are reported in standard scores and percentile ranks. Jimmy performed in the average range on all subtests.

> Based on this information, how would you answer the question about communication?

Jimmy's performance on the TOLD-I:3 indicates his overall language skills are age appropriate and there are no apparent concerns with vocabulary development or language use. Jimmy does not appear in need of speech-language intervention.

Cognitive

Here is the question listed in the assessment plan:

- What is the student's overall functioning level?

The school psychologist administered the Wechsler Intelligence Scale for Children-III (Wechsler, 1991). Jimmy was found to perform in the average range, with a Verbal IQ standard score of 92, a Performance IQ standard score of 107, and a Full Scale IQ of 102.

> Based on this information, how would you answer the question about cognitive level?

Jimmy's overall functioning level is in the average range for his age and grade. This suggests that his difficulties are not due to a cognitive impairment, but rather may possibly be associated with a learning disability. Additionally, the gap between the verbal and performance standard scores suggests possible processing difficulties, such as auditory processing, which should be investigated by the school psychologist or diagnostician.

Academics

The following four questions pertain to Jimmy's academic skills:

- What is the child's overall academic skill profile?
- In what areas of the school curriculum is the child experiencing success or difficulty? What strategies does the child employ when working in easy/difficult areas?
- What types of instructional activities or manner of instructional presentation does the child most respond to?
- What accommodations or adaptations are provided in general education settings?

Several tools were used to assess Jimmy's academic abilities.

Woodcock-Johnson Psycho-Educational Battery-Revised: Tests of Achievement

The Woodcock-Johnson Psycho-Educational Battery-Revised: Tests of Achievement (WJ-R) (Woodcock & Johnson, 1989) was the first test the special education teacher administered. The WJ-R, a screening achievement test, provides peer-comparison data reported through standard scores, percentiles, and age and grade equivalents. Jimmy was administered the following subtests and achieved the listed scores:

SUBTEST	STANDARD SCORE	PERCENTILE
Letter-Word Identification (naming letters and reading words)	75	5
Passage Comprehension (cloze procedure)	73	4
Dictation (spelling, mechanics, endings)	76	5
Writing Samples (writing word and sentence responses)	76	5
Calculation (computation problems)	106	66
Applied Problems (story problems)	102	55

Woodcock Reading Mastery Tests-Revised

Because Jimmy displayed low performance on the reading sections of the WJ-R, the special education teacher next administered the Woodcock Reading Mastery Tests-Revised (WRMT-R) (Woodcock, 1987). The following subtests were administered, and Jimmy achieved the scores listed:

SUBTEST	STANDARD SCORE	PERCENTILE
Word Identification (reading isolated words)	74	4
Word Attack (reading nonsense words)	72	3
Word Comprehension (antonyms, synonyms, and analogies)	89	23
Passage Comprehension (cloze procedure)	75	5
Basic Skills Cluster (word identification and word attack)	73	5
Reading Comprehension Cluster (word and passage comprehension)	83	13

Informal reading inventory

The general education teacher administered an informal reading inventory to determine how Jimmy performed when presented with grade-level passages. The informal inventory indicated that Jimmy's independent reading level was at the end-of-first-grade level and his instructional level was at the beginning-of-third-grade reading. Fourth grade material was at his frustration level.

Test of Written Language-2

This test, known as TOWL-2, has two sections: (a) a *contrived subtest,* involving vocabulary, spelling, style, logical sentences, and sentence combining, and (b) a *spontaneous subtest,* including thematic maturity, contextual vocabulary, syntactic maturity, contextual spelling, and contextual style (use of punctuation and capitalization skills). Jimmy completed only the *spontaneous subtest.* For this test, he was presented with a picture and was asked to write about that picture. He was allowed 15 minutes to write the story. Outcomes are reported in standard scores with a mean of 10. Jimmy's scores were as follows:

AREA	STANDARD SCORE (MEAN = 10)
Thematic Maturity	9
Contextual Vocabulary	4
Syntactic Maturity	7
Contextual Spelling	1
Contextual Style	1

Parent, teacher, and student interviews

During separate interviews, the school psychologist asked Jimmy's teacher, Ms. Rodriquez, Jimmy's parents, and Jimmy himself to describe the type of reading and writing activities Jimmy engages in at school and home; the type of reading materials available and used for instruction; and the interventions and strategies that have been used to support Jimmy's reading and writing. Parent and teacher questions included in the academic portion of interviews are listed in Exhibit 9.2. Interview questions for addressing these issues were drawn from the guiding questions presented in Chapter 6 (see Table 6.1).

EXHIBIT 9.2

Guiding Questions for Parent and Teacher Interviews About a Student's Academic Skills

PARENT INTERVIEW

- What academic skills and understandings do you think are most important for your child?
- What expectations do you have for your child?
- What types of supports are available to assist your child in completing homework and school projects?
- What skills do you have or need to assist your child in completing homework and school projects?
- What materials are available, or needed, in the home and community to support your child's academic development?

TEACHER INTERVIEW

- What curriculum is selected and provided? To what extent does this curriculum address the student's needs?
- What academic expectations do you have for the student?
- What types of activities or manner of presentation does the child respond to most?
- What are the barriers and facilitators to the student's participation in learning opportunities?
- What instructional strategies do you employ in the classroom?
- What accommodations in instructional practice are needed by this student, if any?
- What materials are available, or needed, in the classroom to support the student's academic development?
- How is the student's academic performance evaluated?
- In what ways do your evaluation practices support student learning and inform instructional practice? What changes need to be made?

Parent interview. Jimmy's mother indicated that Jimmy does not enjoy reading and seldom picks up a book or magazine at home. His father reported that when Jimmy was younger, they went to the public library once every couple of weeks to check out books. At first Jimmy was interested and selected many books to read, but as he progressed in school, he expressed less and less interest. Mother noted that Jimmy's interest started to drop when he entered second grade. At that time, the classroom teacher was starting to call and send notes home about Jimmy's minimal progress in reading. Currently Jimmy reads at home only when he has to, although the parents subscribe to special magazines just for Jimmy. Both parents indicate they enjoy reading but seldom have time for it. When asked whether Jimmy ever sees them reading, Father commented that most evenings Jimmy sees him reading the newspaper. The parents were also asked about Jimmy's writing abilities and writing activities carried out in the home. They paused for a moment, somewhat stumped by the question. They concluded that, except for homework, Jimmy does very little writing at home.

As for interventions and strategies to help Jimmy with his reading, Mother commented that having Jimmy read with a partner was very helpful last year but said that this year Jimmy is embarrassed to read aloud or to have others read to him. He thinks it is "babyish" and gets embarrassed when he has to read in front of the class. Allowing Jimmy to tell stories and ideas orally, rather than in writing, is helpful. Jimmy enjoys telling stories.

The thing that seems to be helping Jimmy most in both areas is the computer. The family has just purchased a home computer and has bought some software for Jimmy to use. He has expressed some interest in using a word processing program for writing assignments, but what he really likes most is surfing the World Wide Web. Several times he has asked one of his parents to help him read and understand something he has found on the Web. The parents are encouraged by this, although they are also vigilant about monitoring his Web use. The parents were not aware of any computer use by Jimmy at the school—they think this might be something that could be tried.

When asked about Jimmy's overall attitude toward school, both parents commented that he continues to be positive, although lately he has become more frustrated. Homework time has become a major battleground, especially when there are reading and writing assignments. Social studies and science are becoming more difficult. Jimmy struggles to read and understand his textbooks and to write answers to the end-of-chapter questions. Father comments that when Jimmy really gets stuck, Jimmy asks him for help. They read the pages, answer the questions together, and work together to get ideas down on paper. When they read the information together, Jimmy comprehends; when he reads independently, he does not seem to understand what he has read. When they "write" together (Jimmy dictates, and the parent writes it down), writing assignments are more quickly finished.

Overall, the parents are pleased with what is going on in the classroom but are worried about Jimmy's reading and writing progress. They are hopeful that this assessment will help identify what can be done to help Jimmy in these areas.

Teacher interview. The interview with Ms. Rodriquez revealed that Jimmy has been involved in a variety of reading and writing activities. Students read in pairs at least two days a week for approximately 15 minutes each time. Ms. Rodriquez commented that Jimmy seems to enjoy this, although he does get frustrated at times. Students also work in cooperative groups for some reading and writing activities. When in cooperative groups, students engage in reciprocal teaching: they take turns reading, summarizing, clarifying, asking questions, and making predictions. When it is Jimmy's turn to be the teacher, instead of reading the text aloud, he calls on someone in the group to do the reading, and instead of summarizing and clarifying, he calls on students to do that as well. Jimmy does seem to enjoy asking peers questions and making predictions. Ms. Rodriquez suspects that having other students read, summarize, and clarify information helps Jimmy to understand the material and gives him the confidence to ask a question and make a prediction. As for writing, students work in pairs and cooperative groups to discuss their topics and ideas and ask each other for suggestions. Jimmy enjoys this stage of the writing process. It is the actual putting of ideas on paper that causes him great frustration.

The teacher provides small-group mini-lessons as needed. Last week, Jimmy participated in group lessons on finding the main idea and locating details. When in the group, he was able to identify main ideas and supporting details; but when he was independently completing a worksheet on the same skill, he was able to complete only 7 of the 10 items accurately. Jimmy's overall reading and writing skills are below those of his classmates—including those attending this small-group lesson.

Also last week, Jimmy participated in a mini-lesson on the use of capital letters and periods. The group worked on a paragraph written by a classmate from which all capitalization and punctuation had been removed. When discussing the rules of capitalization and punctuation, Jimmy participated and was highly successful. But when asked to provide the capitalization and punctuation for the student-written paragraph, he became agitated and did not finish the assignment during the allocated time.

When asked about word attack skills, the teacher commented that they are taught in context, meaning that when students have difficulties with a word, she supports them in applying decoding skills. No isolated instruction in word attack or word analysis skills is provided. The teacher believes teaching those skills in isolation is not helpful to students' reading or spelling skill development.

Students in the class read literature books rather than basal textbooks. At times, students are allowed to select their own reading materials; at other times, material is assigned. Moreover, at times, all students are reading the same materials, and at other times, they are reading different texts. Jimmy seems to do best when he is reading from teacher-selected materials and when he is the only one reading that material. The teacher believes that she is better able to select materials that reflect Jimmy's reading level than he is (he tends to select material that is too hard for him), and she thinks that he feels less pressured when he is the only one reading a particular book.

No spelling or language textbook is used in the classroom. Spelling words are identified through student writing activities and products. The written language curriculum is based on the application of the writing process. Students write every day in their journals, and every week they write a new story. They also maintain a personal spelling dictionary into which they enter the words they are learning to spell.

As for reading strategies, Ms. Rodriquez has introduced story mapping to the class and the use of semantic webs. She has each child develop a personal reading log of best-loved stories and a vocabulary treasure chest, in which students are to keep records of the new words they are learning. Although Jimmy has identified a few favorite stories, his vocabulary treasure chest is virtually empty—he has not made a new vocabulary entry for the past three weeks.

When asked whether Jimmy uses the computer for reading or writing assignments, the teacher commented that the computer is generally used as a reward for work completed. Consequently, Jimmy rarely works on the computer during classtime.

Reading and writing instruction have been integrated in the classroom as well. Students read and then write stories, or they write their own stories and then share them with the class. Ms. Rodriquez notes that Jimmy seems to enjoy telling but not writing his own stories. He struggles with spelling, but when he uses a word card (a reference card on which he records words that give him spelling difficulty), he does much better. He tends to ask peers and the teacher for spelling assistance. Mechanical skills (e.g., capitalization and punctuation) continue to be troublesome. Jimmy turns in many writing products without capitalization and punctuation or with words used incorrectly.

The teacher reports that Jimmy has a positive attitude toward school, although his reading and writing difficulties are starting to make it hard for him to achieve overall school success. He is struggling with the science and social studies textbooks and consequently does poorly on assignments for those subjects. Ms. Rodriguez is using many of the same techniques she uses in reading and writing instruction to assist Jimmy with the reading and writing components of his social studies and science instruction. Jimmy is doing fine in mathematics, although the reading requirements of solving problems is becoming more challenging.

Student interview. The interview with Jimmy revealed that he is well aware of his difficulties in reading and writing. When asked what he likes most and least about school, he mentioned recess and physical education as "most" and reading and writing as "least." He thinks he is a good student—works hard and does his best—but reading and writing really slow him down. He hates having to read in front of others and is starting to worry that his peers are going to think he is "dumb" if they find out the extent to which he struggles with reading. Jimmy said he likes math class. He also likes the information the class is learning in social studies and science but really hates having to read the book and answer questions. He likes telling stories—not writing them.

When asked specifically about reading and writing, he said he likes being read to and he likes reciprocal teaching, especially when it is his turn to be the teacher. Jimmy did not feel intimidated during reciprocal teaching because most students in the group enjoy reading the passage when it is his turn to be the teacher—that lets him off the hook. Once it is read aloud, he said, he has no problem understanding it.

Jimmy sometimes likes working in pairs, depending on whom he is working with. He said some students are nicer than others and help him more; some are impatient and tell him to "Hurry up."

When asked what the teacher does to make reading and writing easier for him, he said the teacher reads the story aloud or has someone else read it aloud. He also finds discussing stories and information in the social studies and science books helpful—discussing helps him to understand. As for writing, he likes it when he is allowed to dictate stories rather than write them. He expressed frustration with mini-lessons on capitalization and punctuation. He commented that they are boring and that he just "didn't understand that stuff." For the most part, he likes it when the teacher selects books for him to read. He thought he did better with those books than with the books he selected for himself. He commented that just when he thought he had found the perfect book, he would start reading it and find it was too hard.

When asked what the teacher does sometimes to make reading hard for him, he said reading is especially hard when she requires him to do the work all on his own. He said he has a hard time concentrating and figuring out all the words and getting his ideas down on paper. He offered that when he has to do it all on his own, it takes him way too long.

When asked whether he reads outside school, he said "sometimes." He expressed real interest in using the computer and surfing the World Wide Web. He said reading that information is fun—lots of graphics and material written by someone living far away in another part of the world. He found that intriguing.

Observation

The school psychologist visited Ms. Rodriquez's room on two occasions to observe reading and writing instruction. During the first session, the school psychologist maintained a narrative record of ongoing events. She did this so that she could get an overall sense of what went on in the classroom.

During the first 10 minutes of the session, Jimmy was reading with a partner. Although they seemed to get along well, when it was Jimmy's turn to read aloud, he read a sentence or two and then asked his partner to take over. His partner then completed the page, reading for the majority of the time. Jimmy kept his eye on the page as his partner read, but it was difficult to tell whether he was following along or was just resting his eyes on the page.

Following this activity, students returned to their desks to write answers to comprehension questions derived from the story. Jimmy began the work immediately but five minutes into the activity he seemed to lose interest. He approached his partner for help, but when his partner said Jimmy needed to complete the work on his own, Jimmy returned to his seat and spent the remainder of the period looking through the pages for answers to the questions. Jimmy did not finish the assignment.

During the second visit, the school psychologist collected information about Jimmy's level of participation during reading and writing instruction. Participation was defined as reading text, answering questions, listening to someone else read, and sharing ideas for writing. A time sampling method was used. The one-hour instructional time period was divided into five-minute intervals. The school psychologist observed Jimmy at the conclusion of each interval, noting whether he was participating. Jimmy was found to participate for 50 percent of the intervals. He spent the remaining time daydreaming, walking around the class, and asking to leave the room. Jimmy did not finish the reading assignment for that day.

Paragraph writing checklist

The general education teacher evaluated Jimmy's paragraph writing skills through use of a curriculum-based checklist. Writing samples to be analyzed were selected from Jimmy's portfolio. The checklist included the following skills: follows correct format (indentation) and includes (a) a topic sentence, (b) at least three related supporting sentences, (c) a closing sentence, (d) descriptions and examples, (e) accurate spelling, (f) accurate application of capitalization conventions, and (g) accurate application of punctuation conventions.

Four writing samples were evaluated. In all, Jimmy used correct format and included a topic sentence but did not include supporting sentences or a closing sentence. Each sample included some description and examples; greater inclusion would have strengthened the writing. Multiple spelling errors were found in each writing sample. Capitalization and punctuation skills were virtually nonexistent in the samples analyzed.

> Based on this information, how would you answer the questions related to academics in the areas of reading, written language, and mathematics?

This information suggests that Jimmy is experiencing significant reading difficulties in the areas of vocabulary, word attack, and comprehension. Standard scores of 75 (WJ-R—letter-word identification) and 74 and 72 (WRMT-R—word identification and word attack) indicate that Jimmy is performing below average in reading isolated words and applying word attack skills. Comprehension, for both words (standard score of 89 on WRMT-R—word comprehension) and connected text (standard score of 73 on WJ-R—passage comprehension and standard score of 75 on WRMT-R—passage comprehension) indicate Jimmy is performing below average for his age and grade. This is supported by the informal reading inventory outcomes. Jimmy's independent reading level is at the end-of-first-grade level, and his instructional level is at the beginning of third grade. As indicated on the TOLD-I:3, Jimmy experiences great difficulties with applying capitalization and punctuation conventions (standard score of 1 on contextual style). Spelling was also a major concern, as indicated by a standard score of 1 for contextual spelling.

Interview and observation data also assist in identifying the types of difficulties Jimmy is experiencing. Although he appears positive and attempts tasks, he becomes frustrated and pulls away from activities. He seeks peer assistance but also wants to be independent. He has developed mechanisms for covering up his difficulties (e.g., having others do the reading for him), suggesting that he is aware of the difficulties he is encountering in reading and writing, something he revealed during his interview. Jimmy does not appear to be interested in reading and writing but does appear interested in the computer.

We now have answers to the team's academic questions:

1. Jimmy's current reading level is below or significantly below average.

2. Jimmy is experiencing difficulties in the three reading areas of decoding, comprehension, and vocabulary. As for written language, he is experiencing difficulties in capitalization, punctuation, and spelling.

3. Successful interventions and strategies include using the computer and, to some extent, peer supports. Requiring Jimmy to demonstrate skills in front of peers or requiring him to work independently appear to be less successful strategies.

4. Teacher-selected materials appear to be most helpful, and the computer is a possible avenue for enhancing Jimmy's interest and success in reading and writing.

5. During reading and writing, Jimmy is exposed to small- and large-group instruction, peer and independent activities, and some skill-based instruction. Peer activities, if structured in ways that do not require Jimmy to reveal his difficulties, appear to be helpful.

6. Jimmy does not do much reading or writing at home but does enjoy surfing the World Wide Web and reading the information he finds there.

7. Jimmy appears to be performing in the average range in mathematics.

8. Jimmy, his parents, and his teacher are aware of his reading and writing difficulties. Jimmy considers himself to be a good and hardworking student.

Related Academic Skills

This is the final question in the section of the assessment plan called "Academics and Related Skills":

- What learning strategies and study skills does the child exhibit?

Observation and interviews are helpful tools for answering this question. Interview questions for addressing learning strategies and study skills, presented in Exhibit 9.3, may be drawn from the guiding questions presented in Chapter 6. Student questions may be developed through adaptation of parent and teacher questions. These questions lead to contextualized assessment—the gathering of information across a variety of contexts and factors.

EXHIBIT 9.3

Guiding Questions for Parent and Teacher Interviews About a Student's Learning Strategies and Study Skills

PARENT INTERVIEW
- What learning strategies and study skills does your child exhibit at home? To what extent are you able to assist your child in developing learning strategies and study skills?
- What problem-solving strategies does your child use in the home?
- To what extent is your child able to analyze, synthesize, and evaluate information?

TEACHER INTERVIEW
- What learning strategies does the child apply when learning new material, completing tasks, and solving problems?
- What study skills does the child use to support school success?
- Does the student experience success when presented with problem-solving activities? What strategies does the student employ?
- To what extent is the student able to analyze, synthesize, and evaluate information?

Learning strategies and study skills

Interviews and observations indicated that Jimmy is not currently aware of the strategies he uses when approaching reading and writing tasks. When asked what he does when he reads a story, he said, "I just read it. I just try to read all the words." When asked what he does when he comes to a difficult word or a word he does not know, he responded that he guesses what the word is or asks a peer or the teacher for help. The teacher interview also revealed Jimmy's lack of reading strategies. The teacher commented that although activities of story grammar and story mapping were introduced and practiced in class, Jimmy did not apply those strategies to his reading, nor did he seem to understand how the strategies would help him comprehend. The most successful written language intervention to date is having Jimmy discuss and brainstorm ideas with classmates, followed by his dictating a story to the teacher or a peer.

As for study skills, when asked how he studies for social studies and science tests, Jimmy said that he reads the chapter and his class notes. When asked what he does after reading that information, he said he reads it again if there is time.

Jimmy's parents indicated that sometimes they help Jimmy study for social studies and science tests. They ask him to define key words and to answer questions. Sometimes these strategies are helpful; at other times, Jimmy becomes too frustrated and just wants to read the material again. At that point, they help him read the chapter.

The teacher said that she provides study guides for the students to use for test preparation but Jimmy rarely completes the study guide. Class notes, orally and visually presented through graphic organizers on overheads, are used with all students but Jimmy rarely takes complete notes or captures completed graphic organizers in his notebook.

> Based on this information, how would you answer the questions about related academic skills?

Jimmy does not appear to apply learning strategies or study skills systematically to his reading and writing tasks. He is not able to describe the strategies he does use. He also does not seem to make connections between (a) the strategies and study skill supports taught and used in the classroom and (b) his learning.

Life Skills

The assessment plan raises four questions about Jimmy's life skills:

- How does the child respond to social situations?
- What strategies does the child have for responding to social situations?
- How does the child go about making choices and decisions?
- Is the child a self-advocate or do others serve as his advocate?

Again, observations and interviews are helpful tools. Exhibit 9.4 presents interview questions for addressing these areas.

EXHIBIT 9.4

Guiding Questions for Parent and Teacher Interviews About a Student's Life Skills

PARENT INTERVIEW
- How does your child respond to social situations that occur with other family members?
- What social skills does your child possess and/or need to develop?
- How does your child go about making choices and decisions?
- Is your child a self-advocate or do you or other members of the family serve as his or her advocate?
- What community situations seem to present the most difficulty for your child? How does the child respond to these situations?

TEACHER INTERVIEW
- How does the child respond to social situations? to peers? to authority figures?
- What social skills and strategies does the child possess and/or need to develop?
- What school situations seem to present the most difficulty for the student? How does the child respond to these situations?
- How effective is the child in communicating with others? What situations appear to be more/less difficult? What strategies does the child have for communicating across a variety of school situations?
- How does the child go about making choices and decisions?
- Is the child a self-advocate?

Although many informative rating scales for assessing behavior and social skills are available, the team determined it was not necessary to include them in the assessment because Jimmy did not appear to have significant difficulties in those areas.

Social skills

Observational data, collected through use of anecdotal recording, indicate that Jimmy gets along well with others. During reading and writing instruction, he interacted with others, asked questions, and worked independently. He did not interfere with others' learning or call unneeded attention to himself. On the playground he joined in games and was sought out by peers. In the community, he blended in with peers except in his avoidance of choosing from menus when his Saturday baseball team goes to lunch after a game.

Teacher, parent, and student interviews also indicated no concerns about his social skills. Jimmy has many friends, both in and outside school. He plays basketball through his church league and is a Boy Scout. During his interview, Jimmy said how much he likes going camping with his friends. He enjoys hikes, swimming, and talking late into the night. He reads what he can of the information on the baseball cards he trades and the flavors listed in the local ice cream store.

Self-determination

Observation revealed that Jimmy is starting to self-advocate through manipulation of the environment. He does not always come out directly and ask for assistance, but he changes what is going on around him to support his reading and writing. For example, during paired reading, he encouraged his peer to do a great deal of the reading—in fact, to do a major portion of the reading for him. During reciprocal teaching activities, the student in the role of teacher is generally the one who reads the passage and summarizes and clarifies information. When Jimmy is the teacher, however, he calls on other students to do these tasks. In this way, he eliminates the need to read in front of his peers and, in a way, creates a learning environment more responsive to his needs.

> Based on this information, how would you answer the questions related to life skills?

Social Skills: Jimmy gets along well with others. He appears to avoid purposefully most practical writing tasks in the community.

Self-determination: Although Jimmy appears to be manipulating the environment to better meet his needs and at times asks for assistance, he does not appear able to specify yet what he needs in different situations to support his reading and writing skill development or task completion.

Summary of Data Analysis and Interpretation

This section presented data gathered through the carrying out of a contextualized assessment plan structured by questions presented in an assessment plan. Interpretation of findings led to the identification of student strengths, needs, and challenges. This information, when combined with the report of the school psychologist, is included in the present levels of performance statement of the IEP if Jimmy is found eligible for special education services. The next section describes the process for writing IEP statements of present levels of performance.

WRITING A STATEMENT OF PRESENT LEVELS OF PERFORMANCE

The statement of present levels of performance is a key component of an Individualized Education Program (IEP). As stated in the law, the present levels of educational performance statement should include the following:

> *(I) how the child's disability affects the child's involvement and progress in the general education curriculum; or*
> *(II) for preschool children, as appropriate, how the disability affects the child's participation in appropriate activities. (IDEA Amendments of 1997, Sec. 614(d)(1)(A)(i))*

The present levels of performance statement records findings of the assessment efforts of the IEP team and discusses students' strengths, needs, and challenges across all areas. Academic, social, emotional, behavioral, physical fitness and health status, communicative skills, and self-help skills may all be addressed. Depending on the extent of student need for special education and related services in order to benefit from an educational program, the statement of present levels of performance may be limited or quite comprehensive.

When students are initially referred for eligibility testing, the school psychologist writes a psychological report. This report organizes and highlights findings and can be extremely helpful for writing the IEP present levels of performance statement. A psychological report may also be produced for reevaluations. This type of support, however, is generally not provided for annual reviews. Therefore, teachers need skills in analyzing, synthesizing, and evaluating findings so that whether or not a psychological report is provided, they are able to make informed decisions about what needs to be stated in the IEP present levels of performance statement.

In Jimmy's case, a psychological report was available because Jimmy's referral was an initial referral to determine eligibility. The team determined that Jimmy is eligible under the disability category of learning disability because of a severe discrepancy between his achievement in reading and writing and other academic areas, as well as a discrepancy between his reading and writing achievement and performance on the cognitive measure. He also has an auditory processing deficit that interferes with his ability to decode and spell words.

Jimmy's statement of present levels of performance draws on information gathered through the analysis and interpretation of assessment findings presented in a psychological report as well as information gathered by other team members. A sample statement, based on Jimmy's information, is provided in Exhibit 9.5. There are multiple ways in which this statement can be written. This is just one example to get you started in writing IEP statements. You will need to follow your district and building-level guidelines when writing statements of present levels of performance for IEPs for your students.

EXHIBIT 9.5

**Statement of a Student's
Present Levels of Performance**

OVERALL HEALTH AND SPECIFIC ABILITIES

Jimmy does not appear to have any difficulties in vision, hearing, or motor areas. He is of average weight and height for his age. He participates in a church basketball league and is a Boy Scout. He was observed playing with peers during recess. Parents report he is in good health.

COGNITIVE

Performance on the Wechsler-III indicates average performance, with a Verbal IQ of 92, Performance IQ of 107, and a Full Scale IQ of 102.

ACADEMIC AND RELATED SKILLS

WJ-R outcomes indicate average performance in calculation (standard score, SS = 106) and applied problems (SS = 102), with below-average performance in letter-word identification (SS = 75), passage comprehension (SS = 73), dictation (SS = 76), and writing samples (SS = 76). Further assessment in reading using the WRMT-R revealed similar reading-level performance with a SS of 73 for the Basic Skills Cluster and SS of 83 in the Reading Comprehension Cluster. Performance on an IRI indicated an independent reading level of end-of-first-grade, an instructional level of beginning third grade, and a frustration level at the beginning of fourth grade. Performance on the TOWL-2 (a language development test) also indicated significant difficulties in mechanical and spelling skills, with standard scores of 1 (mean of 10) earned. All information indicates Jimmy is experiencing difficulties in decoding (word attack), vocabulary, reading comprehension, application of capitalization and punctuation rules, and spelling. Interviews with the classroom teacher, parents, and student all reveal an awareness of Jimmy's reading and writing difficulties. Classroom observations found Jimmy to be a hard worker during instruction, but one who shied away from having to read in front of a group and one who needed assistance in successfully completing writing tasks in school and in the community.

As for related skills, Jimmy did not demonstrate awareness or application of learning strategies or study skills that would support his reading and writing activities.

LIFE SKILLS

Observations and interviews found Jimmy to get along well with peers and to have many friends. Jimmy thought he was a good student, although he had difficulties in reading. For the most part, he enjoys school. Parents and teachers also commented that Jimmy gets along well with others and is involved in a variety of peer-related activities (e.g., Boy Scouts, basketball league). Although Jimmy was observed to structure the environment to assist himself in reading and writing and on occasion to request assistance, he did not appear to have skills in or understanding of what he needed to be more successful with his reading and writing tasks.

BEHAVIOR

Classroom and playground observations found Jimmy displaying behavior appropriate to the setting. Jimmy joined in games and was sought out by peers. During instruction, Jimmy did not call undue attention to himself, although during one observation period he was found to be off-task 50 percent of the time. He spent this time daydreaming, walking around the class, and asking to leave the room. His interview indicated that he engaged in those behaviors when he was frustrated or unable to complete a task. Although not displaying any behavioral concerns at this time, this area should be monitored.

COMMUNICATION

Performance on the TOLD-I:3 indicated average communication skills, with subscale standard scores (mean = 10) ranging between 9 and 11. This indicates that at this time, Jimmy is performing in the average range in terms of communication skills.

THEORY TO PRACTICE

➡ Meet with a special education teacher to discuss how he or she goes about the interpretation process. With parental permission, have the special education teacher share the testing protocols of a student with you, going over the scores and interpreting their meaning for designing a program for the student with disabilities. Reflect on this experience. How can you use this information in your practice?

SETTING PRIORITIES: THE MULTIYEAR MATRIX

The statement of present levels of performance serves as the primary basis for selecting curriculum and setting priorities through development of IEP goals and short-term objectives. For example, Jimmy's present levels of performance statement (Exhibit 9.5) highlights his difficulties in reading and written expression. Using gathered information, Jimmy's IEP team will write goals and objectives in the areas of reading and writing for him.

Prioritizing student needs from information reported in the present levels of performance statement can be an arduous task for teachers, families, the student, and other team members because the process requires that they work collaboratively to identify areas of need and to prioritize goals and objectives in light of these needs and preferences (Turnbull, Turnbull, Shank, & Leal, 1995). The decision making process can be facilitated by the application of a multiyear matrix (Bigge, 1988; 1991). The value of the model lies in the mind-set it provides team members when they are extracting priorities for individual children during IEP meetings.

The multiyear matrix provides a framework in which IEP teams can determine priorities for particular students. Through application of this model, IEP teams can share information and values as they (a) identify and chart desirable and meaningful present major life activities of an individual student, (b) predict and chart meaningful and seemingly feasible major life activities for three years from now, (c) predict participation in life activities one year from the present, and (d) use this information to identify potentially powerful annual goals and objectives for the coming year that will also contribute to desired outcomes farther in the future. Instead of being limited to one-year projections for their derivation, goals and objectives developed by means of this matrix have the advantage of being based on three-year projections.

Acting as group facilitator, a special education teacher introduces the concept of organizing into three matrices the information reported in the present levels of performance statement. The matrices are identical in format but represent different time periods in the target student's life. Part I is for recording information about present student performance in life activities. Part II is for recording projections of desired student participation in activities three years in the future. Part III is for determining new or expanded activities for a given student by the same time next year—a one-year cycle. Based on the content of matrices I and II, information in matrix III is used for current development of powerful annual goals and objectives that are unique to the individual student.

Each matrix breaks down information into the three contexts of home, school, and community and into life activities likely to be most affected by a child's difficulties as determined by the contextualized assessment. These contexts and life activities are reflective of the contexts and factors included in contextualized assessment. For students with mild and moderate disabilities, factors addressed may be communication, behavior, and academics and related skills. For a child with more severe difficulties, contextualized assessment factors of life skills and communication and performance may be most appropriate. Exhibit 9.6 presents a matrix for a student with more severe disabilities. In the remainder of this section we examine this matrix concept part by part.

We encourage readers to role play IEP team members in a meeting to develop an IEP for Jimmy, the child studied throughout this chapter. Decide who will represent different people who would be involved in his IEP, including Jimmy and his parents. Drawing from the information in this chapter, collaborate with other team members to complete three matrices similar to those in Exhibit 9.6. (We suggest you put each matrix on large chart paper so all participants can see and contribute.)

Start the role play by reviewing and synthesizing key pieces of information about Jimmy's present levels of performance in various kinds of activities and recording this information into your Part I. After identifying and charting current activities (Part I), predict and chart life activities for three years from the present (Part II). Realize that this is a role play and that some ideas may come directly from information in the chapter, some from observations of peers, some from board-adopted outcomes in the hypothetical district, and some from creative thinking on the part of team members. Then, continue the role play and identify desires for Jimmy's participation in life activities one year from the present (Part III). Finally, make a choice of what to do with that information.

EXHIBIT 9.6

Sample Multiyear Matrix for Students with Suspected Disability in Several Areas

**PART I
CURRENT
ACTIVITIES**

	Home	School	Community
Self-Help			
Work			
Leisure Use and Social Interaction			
Application of Academic Learning			

**PART II
ACTIVITIES
3 YEARS
FROM PRESENT**

	Home	School	Community
Self-Help			
Work			
Leisure Use and Social Interaction			
Application of Academic Learning			

**PART III
ACTIVITIES
1 YEAR
FROM PRESENT**

	Home	School	Community
Self-Help			
Work			
Leisure Use and Social Interaction			
Application of Academic Learning			

Source: From Curriculum Based Instruction for Special Education Students *(p. 318), by J. Bigge, 1988, Mountain View, CA: Mayfield.*

Identifying and Charting Current Activities

Part I, describing the student's present performance levels and participation activities, involves recording information from various members of the team. Teachers might include a brief school history and summary of present levels of performance based on assessment and other data. Parents might include information about the student's special interests, characteristics, and performance in the home situation, and their own concerns.

This initial recording step does not require team members to make choices or decisions, yet it is a potentially valuable communication process. It provides common background information about the child. As individuals listen to each other, they learn more about the child and may even notice that the child is capable of doing things they did not realize he or she could do. Parents can learn, for example, that their child, who does not dress himself at home, gets dressed independently for swimming during physical education. They can learn that their child does assignments with little or no help at school but requires significant help on similar assignments at home. Teachers can learn that a student talks spontaneously on many subjects at home but not at school. Gathering information about the student's performance and participation in different contexts and situations is vital to proposing and evaluating future objectives and extracting top-priority annual goals and objectives.

Predicting and Charting Life Activities for Three Years into the Future

Three-year projections are used to expand everyone's view of the student. This jump from present to more distant functioning makes planning for the immediate year more relevant and effective. It guides plans for transitions between school levels and programs and from school to postschool activities. It is particularly valuable for parents to participate in this long-range planning, for it helps them confront the reality of their situation—which they might easily be tempted to avoid—and plan a practical future for their child.

To guide the planning of future activities, team members ask such questions as these: "What kinds of activities will same-age peers be doing three years from the present?" "What roles do they demonstrate?" "What recommendations do we have for this particular student three years from the present?"

Identifying Desired Participation in Life Activities One Year from the Present

Members of the IEP team, including the student when appropriate, refer to the information in Parts I and II and the statement of present levels of performance when they begin to work on Part III of the matrix. They may begin this part of the matrix by asking: "Knowing what the child does at the present time, what do we want the child to accomplish a year from now?" and "What does this student need to learn this next year that would contribute to accomplishing the projected three-year activities?" Answers to these questions are recorded in Part III and become the basis for generating annual goals and objectives.

At this point, IEP team members have three choices. They may select the most important activities listed in Part III of the matrix and, with very little change, make them the goal and/or objective. Or, team members can use the information to write a goal and/or objective for a priority that will result in the child's performance of the activity but in more than one context. Or, even more exciting is the choice to use the information to determine priorities that result in goals and objectives that generalize across activities, contexts, and people. Through activities such as these, the team follows a time-consuming but constructive process for setting priorities. Team members work together to identify activities that (a) are or will be personally meaningful to the child; (b) will empower the child to perform a variety of personally meaningful activities in different contexts (and with different people); and (c) will contribute to the child's accomplishment of outcomes that are desired beyond a one-year time period.

➡ Work through the curriculum prioritization process, identifying a student with a disability. What contexts and factors will you include in your matrix? What activities do you identify as being most important for this student? How do you address all the curricular options described in Section I of this text? What assessment tools and methods will you need to access in order to obtain the information you need to complete this prioritization of curriculum? How will you convert these ideas into IEP goals and objectives?

CHAPTER SUMMARY

This chapter presents the case study of a student named Jimmy. The chapter began with the presentation of the contextualized assessment plan developed by the team. Questions were presented and responded to through the application of assessment tools and methods. Findings were reported and analyzed. The process culminated in the writing of the present levels of performance statement to be included in Jimmy's IEP. This statement highlights Jimmy's strengths, needs, and challenges. The final section of the chapter modeled one procedure for setting IEP goal and objective priorities for students based on assessment findings reported in the present levels of performance statement included in the IEP. The next chapter takes this process one step further—writing IEP goals and objectives.

CHAPTER 10

Writing IEP Goals, Benchmarks, and Objectives

Read to find out the following:
- how to write measurable IEP goals, benchmarks, and objectives
- how to include required components of IEP objectives in multiple formats
- how to write objectives for different purposes
- how to evaluate objectives

After a child's present levels of educational performance are specified and curricular priorities are set, the next task involved in writing IEPs is writing

> *(ii) a statement of measurable annual goals, including benchmarks or short-term objectives related to—*
> > *(I) meeting the child's needs that result from the child's disability to enable the child to be involved in and progress in the general curriculum; and*
> > *(II) meeting each of the child's other educational needs that result from the child's disability. (IDEA Amendments of 1997, Sec. 614(d)(1)(A))*

Goals, benchmarks, and short-term objectives provide the focus for the various formalized plans and programs for children and youth with disabilities: Individualized Family Service Plans, Individualized Education Programs, and Individualized Transition Plans. They are developed from information gathered through contextualized assessment, and they guide the type and focus of services selected for individual students and their families.

In this chapter we walk you through the process of designing goals, benchmarks, and objectives for individualized plans to offset or reduce the problems resulting from a child's disability that interferes with learning and educational performance. Although we focus on the writing of goals, benchmarks, and objectives for IEPs, similar procedures apply to IFSPs and ITPs.

To formulate curriculum content and identify goals, benchmarks, and objectives for students with disabilities without considering information gained from assessment would be like building a house without assessing the specifications of the foundation on which it will sit. Assessment findings serve as the foundation on which the team cooperatively develops a blueprint of desired performance outcomes and periodically evaluates progress toward those outcomes. Just as members of a construction crew begin with the foundation and refer to the blueprint as the plan for their building effort, so must team members base a child's plan on information gathered through assessment.

Teams should consider assessment findings in light of district, state, and/or national standards, goals, and outcomes, and use these curricular guidelines when developing goals and objectives for students' individualized plans. As we stated in Chapter 2, the development of goals, benchmarks, and objectives from a standard, goal, and/or outcome base that can (a) provide a more systematic approach for planning a student's curriculum, (b) force a team planning the curriculum for a student with a disability to consider the general education curriculum as a frame of reference as required by the IDEA Amendments of 1997, and (c) provide a common language for general and special education teachers, parents, students, and administrators as they plan curriculum for students with disabilities.

DEFINITIONS

Annual Goals

IEP annual goal statements describe what the individual with a disability can reasonably be expected to accomplish within a year as a result of special education services and interventions. Goal statements are broad statements of aims that are measurable. Exhibit 10.1 lists some representative goal statements for IEPs.

EXHIBIT 10.1
Examples of Annual IEP Goals

- Increase scores on achievement tests in mathematics.
- Improve reading comprehension as measured by an informal reading inventory.
- Increase computer use to complete schoolwork as monitored by a teacher-developed checklist.
- Increase participation in age-appropriate activities in the community as measured by a student-maintained activity log.
- Increase the speed of handwriting as measured by the charting of fluency over the course of the year.
- Increase initiative in making choices as assessed through student and parent interviews and parent and teacher observation of the child in school, family, and community settings.
- Reduce disruptive behavior as monitored through weekly behavioral charts.
- Increase independence in community activities as assessed through parent and student interviews and observations of the student in these environments.
- Travel within the local community as assessed through student-maintained travel logs.
- Develop good work habits as measured through punctuality to class and completed and turned-in homework as measured by teacher-developed weekly checklist.
- Use appropriate social skills on the job as measured by a rating scale completed by a job coach.
- Move about the community using public transportation in a safe and socially acceptable manner as measured through community-based observations.
- Facilitate care and use of adaptive devices in a work setting as evaluated by a job coach using a rating scale skill inventory.

Benchmarks

Benchmarks are "performance samples that serve as a concrete standard against which other samples may be judged" (Hart, 1994, p. 71). They provide points of reference for measuring or judging the quality, level, or other characteristics of student performance. For selected age or grade levels, benchmarks "set targets for measuring students' progress toward meeting [certain] standards." Those standards "specify the levels and types of knowledge [expected] from students." (Kniep & Martin-Kniep, 1995, p. 88) Benchmarks can be used to assess students in performance-based curriculum and instruction. They provide teachers with information about present levels of student performance in relation to some absolute standards established in a formal, standard-setting process. They also provide direction in facilitating the next step in a student's learning and individualized education program.

Special educators provide benchmarks to accompany annual goals for students who receive special education and related services. Child development information about stages of learning and development provides benchmarks or standards "based upon research evidence by which changes in children's development and learning are noted or marked" (Puckett, 1994, p. 277). Benchmarks may also be "provided for each achievement level in a scoring rubric" (Hart, 1994, p. 71). Different levels of descriptors and related performance samples represent the range of student performances in specified tasks.

Exhibit 10.2 presents two related benchmarks for this annual goal: "to create and write mathematical story problems as evaluated by the district third grade level mathematics assessment program." The benchmarks were selected from five levels of benchmarks stated in the district assessment program. The IEP team determined that benchmark Level 3 was the most appropriate target for this particular student to achieve by October, and Level 5 by the conclusion of the school year. Exhibit 10.2 presents the Level 3 and Level 5 benchmarks. The students will be presented with a picture of six dogs and asked to create and write a story problem; students did not have to solve the problem.

EXHIBIT 10.2	
Examples of IEP Benchmarks	

Level Five: The student writes a multi-step problem that involves more than one mathematical operation. The story problem is logical and creative, realistically relates to the picture, and allows a numerical solution. If units (e.g. dollars) are worked into the story, they are appropriately chosen and used. The student's control of standard written English does not interfere with reading the problem.

Benchmark paper illustrating story problem creation and writing that exhibits Level 5 descriptors

Level Five
there were 6 dogs 2 are pregnent each dog is having nine babies how many dogs (inclouding the six others.) are there all together

Level Three: The student writes a one-step story problem that can be solved easily. One-digit numbers are usually used. The student may present the information and various elements of the problem without properly stating a mathematical problem. The student's control of standard English may interfere with reading the problem.

Benchmark paper illustrating story problem creation and writing that exhibits Level 3 descriptors

Level Three
there are 6 dogs and one of them walked away how meny are left?

Source: "Elementary Mathematics Example Benchmarks: Standards of Student Achievement," Toronto Board of Education as printed in *Authentic Assessment: A Handbook for Educators* (p. 72), by D. Hart, 1994, Menlo Park, CA: Addison-Wesley.

Objectives

Objectives (IEP objectives) are written statements, formulated by IEP teams, that specify what a student is expected to accomplish in a particular area as a result of special education and related services. IEP objectives serve as milestones for evaluating a child's progress toward those expected accomplishments. Objectives also serve to focus instruction and other interventions toward helping students to meet goals set for them and to accomplish performances against benchmarks. Objectives may become ends in themselves or contribute to longer range outcomes intended for students. IEP objectives also inform students about what they will be learning and what they have accomplished.

An IEP objective may include several kinds of information. The basis is a statement of the *student behavior or performance* expected. In addition, an IEP objective should include *criterion, evaluation procedures,* and an *evaluation schedule* for determining whether the objective has been achieved and, when appropriate, include the *condition* under which the objective will be achieved.

Behavior or performance

A student's behavior or performance is "any measurable or observable student response that is a result of learning" (Gronlund, 1995, p. 9). (In this text, we use the two terms behavior and student performance interchangeably.) In an IEP, the statement of student behavior/performance tells what the student will do as a result of instruction. Each objective states the type of behavior or performance that the IEP team expects the student to demonstrate by the timeline written into the objective. Example verbs for describing the student's behavior or performance include *write, read orally, analyze and orally state, underline, label with text, build, verbally hypothesize, orally generate (e.g. creative solutions), organize (time), negotiate (free time),* and *physically operate (technology device).* Verbs, such as *comprehend* and *understand,* that do not clearly describe the expected behavior or performance, require additional statements to tell what observable evidence will be accepted. Consider this objective: "The student will *demonstrate understanding* of nutrition when planning meals." What exactly must the student do to demonstrate this understanding? If the verb *demonstrate* is used in an objective, it needs to be accompanied by an example of observable behavior or performance that will be accepted as evidence. By mentioning evidence—such as (a) ability to list all elements from the food pyramid in their proper amounts, (b) ability to orally state at least two facts about the nutritional quality of the meal being planned, or (c) ability to point to the location of a selected food on the food pyramid—teachers and evaluators facilitate the evaluation of student efforts to achieve the objective. Using verbs that describe observable activity can simplify evaluation.

Criterion

A criterion (*criteria* is the plural form) is a standard against which a judgment about performance can be based. Criteria are the measures or guideposts that team members use to determine whether a student accomplishes the desired learning outcomes or meets the criterion, or standard, of performance. The selection of a criterion is influenced by: (a) present levels of student performance at the time the objective is written; (b) the behavior or performance being taught; (c) the kind and amount of instruction or other intervention needed; (d) the rate of learning expected from the student, and (e) information that will be accepted as evidence the student accomplished the objective. Here are some examples of criteria:

duration (how long)	• at least 30 seconds • no longer than 1 minute • for two hours without stopping
rate/frequency (speed and how often)	• at least 100 correct words per minute • half the rate of employees • at the rate of at least 15 per minute • at least 4 out of 5 trials • at least 4 out of 5 days
count (how many)	• at least 3 sentences • at least 25 items
accuracy (correctness)	• with 80% accuracy
level	• to a 4.5 grade level • 40% level of independence in the performance

A criterion may also be described in checklists and rubrics. These tools list qualities or characteristics that a student is to display in order for a behavior to be rated as achieved. Checklists move beyond traditional measures, allow for a more in-depth and more authentic assessment of student performance, and can be used to inform instruction.

Evaluation procedures

Procedures and assessment methods and tools for evaluating objectives take into consideration (a) the behavior or performance to be assessed; (b) the time needed to assess and monitor performance, and (c) any accommodations or special conditions needed to evaluate student progress meaningfully. Most importantly, the selection of evaluation procedures depends on the type of outcome that is wanted and the nature of the criterion established to measure that outcome. Assessment methods and tools described in Chapter 8 can all be used as evaluation procedures.

Evaluation schedule

An evaluation schedule establishes dates by which objectives are expected to be achieved and/or student progress toward objective achievement will be evaluated. Examples include:

- in one year [from date of IEP]
- by February of [year]
- six months from [day of IEP]

Conditions

Conditions tell under what circumstances the student must demonstrate the behavior. A statement of conditions can spell out any unique circumstances or setups that are important to student accomplishment of the objective. Conditions may include one or more pieces of information such as those shown in Exhibit 10.3.

EXHIBIT 10.3

Examples of IEP Conditions

LEVEL OF ASSISTANCE NEEDED (INDIVIDUALIZED AND TEMPORARY)

- full physical assistance
- with physical guidance
- given modeling
- with a verbal cue
- from gestural cues
- from natural cues

One model moving from most to least level of assistance.

ACCOMMODATIONS NEEDED (INDIVIDUALIZED AND LONG TERM)

- presented with 3-inch-high letters on flashcards of questions from the *Department of Motor Vehicle Study Guide*
- with software selected by the special education teacher
- when shown pictures that match vocabulary words
- with a spellchecker in a word processing software program
- given extra time for completing examinations
- given braille book
- provided a notetaker

ASSISTIVE DEVICES NEEDED

- with a modified slide rule
- with a tape recorder that is voice activated
- with a voice output communication device
- using a wheelchair
- with a calculator with large keys and large display

CONTEXT

- in school
- on the bus to and from school
- in the lunchroom
- in the home
- at work
- in the community

STIMULI ACCOMPANYING THE BEHAVIOR OR PERFORMANCE

- under controlled conditions of using prompting procedures to correct errors
- under natural conditions in the community, using nothing more than what similar-age peers would use or experience
- given age-appropriate reinforcers
- given opportunities to order own food in a restaurant
- given natural cues such as a supervisor saying, "Next"
- presented mathematics problems with operation signs highlighted

THE CONFIGURATION OF IEP OBJECTIVES

The configuration of IEP objectives is generally determined by an IEP team or by the IEP form itself. A single statement of a behavior or performance may be supported by specifications of criterion, evaluation procedure, an evaluation schedule, and a list of the conditions under which the objective is to be demonstrated, or all components may be written as one statement. Exhibit 10.4 presents four formats that you may encounter.

EXHIBIT 10.4

**Representative
Configurations of IEP
Objectives**

A. Behavior or performance statement stands alone and is supported with criterion, evaluation procedure, evaluation schedule, and condition indicators.

Format: **Student will** _____
                                    (behavior/performance)

Example: Student will write the sums of 2-digit + 2-digit addition problems with renaming.
    Criterion: 80% accuracy
    Evaluation Procedure: Teacher-developed 10-item quiz
    Evaluation Schedule: Three weeks from _____
    Condition: Calculator may be used

B. Behavior or performance statement is combined with condition and criterion and supported with evaluation procedure and schedule indicators.

Format: **Given** _____ **, student will** _____ **with** _____ **.**
                (condition)   **(behavior/performance)**   **(criterion)**

Example: Given a calculator, and 10 addition problems involving 2-digit + 2-digit numbers with renaming, student will write the sums with 80% accuracy.
    Evaluation Procedure: Teacher-developed 10-item quiz
    Evaluation Schedule: Three weeks from _____

C. All elements are included in one statement.

Format: **Given** _____ **, student will** _____
                        (condition)(evaluation procedure)   **(behavior/performance)**
                with _____ **by** _____ **.**
                        (criterion)   **(evaluation schedule)**

Example: Given a calculator and a 10-item teacher-developed quiz of problems involving 2-digit + 2-digit numbers with renaming, student will write the sums with 80% accuracy three weeks from _____ .

D. Components are listed in a table.
Format:

Behavior or Performance and Condition	Evaluation of Objective		
	Criterion	Evaluation Procedure and Conditions	Evaluation Schedule

Example:

Behavior or Performance and Condition	Evaluation of Objective		
	Criterion	Evaluation Procedure	Evaluation Schedule
1. Given a calculator, student will write sums of 2-digit + 2-digit addition problems with renaming.	• 80% accuracy	• 10-item teacher-developed quiz	• three weeks from _____

Some teams may prefer to write the minimum of two objectives per goal. Other teams may choose to list several objectives per goal. Multiple objectives may be arranged in an instructional hierarchy, in which the first objective to be met is listed first. In other cases, all objectives may be worked on simultaneously, and their order of appearance in the IEP is of little or no consequence. Exhibit 10.5 shows objectives listed in hierarchical order.

EXHIBIT 10.5

Objectives Arranged in a Hierarchy

Goal: Student will enhance paragraph writing skills as measured by a teacher-developed checklist.

OBJECTIVE	EVALUATION OF OBJECTIVE		
Behavior or Performance and Condition	Criterion	Evaluation Procedure	Evaluation Schedule
1. Student will write four sentences.	• Each sentence will begin with a capital letter and end with the appropriate punctuation.	• teacher-developed checklist	• by September
2. Student will write four supporting sentences pertaining to a self-selected topic.	• Each sentence will begin with a capital letter and end with the appropriate punctuation. • All sentences will be related to the selected topic.	• teacher-developed checklist	• by October
3. Given two supporting sentences on the same topic, student will write a topic sentence.	• Each sentence will begin with a capital letter and end with the appropriate punctuation. • Sentence will reflect the topic of the two provided sentences.	• teacher-developed checklist	• by November
4. Given two supporting sentences on the same topic, student will write a topic sentence and a concluding sentence.	• Each sentence will begin with a capital letter and end with the appropriate punctuation. • Topic sentence will reflect the topic of the two provided sentences. • Concluding sentence will tie together ideas presented.	• teacher-developed checklist	• by December
5. Student will write a paragraph that includes a topic sentence, two supporting sentences, and a concluding sentence.	• Each sentence will begin with a capital letter and end with the appropriate punctuation. • Topic sentence will represent the topic of the paragraph. • Two supporting sentences will add details about the topic. • Concluding sentence will tie together ideas presented.	• teacher-developed checklist	• by February

➡ Meet with a special education teacher to discuss the types of goals, benchmarks, and objectives she or he includes in student IEPs. Are the goals measurable? Are the benchmarks representative of skills and knowledge to be developed? Do the objectives include all necessary components? Are these goals, benchmarks, and objectives reflective of district, state, and/or national goals, outcomes, and standards? If not, why not? How meaningful do you believe these goals, benchmarks, and objectives are for students' development of needed skills and understanding? To what extent do the students and parents participate in the development of goals, benchmarks, and objectives? To what extent are students' general education teachers involved in goal, benchmark, and objective development?

DEVELOPING IEP GOALS AND OBJECTIVES FROM DISTRICT, STATE, AND NATIONAL STANDARDS, GOALS, AND OUTCOMES

One approach for writing goals, benchmarks, and objectives based on contextualized assessment findings is to begin with the consideration of district, state, and/or national goals, outcomes, and standards, because they represent broad goals and outcomes for all students, including those with disabilities. Beginning with this frame of reference broadens one's view of IEP goals and objectives and helps teachers to make connections between a student's needs and the general education curriculum and to use a common language for describing goals for students. Beginning with this frame of reference also prevents teams from developing IEP goals and objectives that have no relationship to the general education curriculum and to what peers are learning, and that fail to help a student develop needed skills because of the inconsistent and isolated manner in which they were developed. Teams that do not have a long-term frame within which to develop goals and objectives may lack a vision of what the child should know and be able to do one year from now, three years from now, and upon exit from school. As we discussed in Chapter 2, many times teams develop students' IEP goals and objectives in a special education vacuum—without considering what general education peers are learning and doing. Beginning with a broader frame of reference should assist teams in three ways: *first,* in including students more actively in the general education curriculum, as appropriate; *second,* in identifying the types of modifications needed to engage students in that curriculum; and *third,* in developing means and ways for curriculum outside the traditional general education curriculum (e.g., life skills; modified means of communication and performance) to be addressed within the general education program as well as through special education support services and interventions. Exhibit 10.6 presents a sample of one state's reading standards and possible IEP goals and objectives that are consistent with these standards.

EXHIBIT 10.6

IEP Goals Based on California Reading Standards

STANDARD 2.2 RESPOND TO *WHO, WHAT, WHEN, WHERE,* AND *HOW* QUESTIONS

Goal: Improve reading comprehension as measured by an informal reading inventory.

Objectives: After being read a story at the student's grade level, the student will orally respond to questions concerning *who, what, when, where,* and *how,* achieving 100% accuracy in four out of five trials. Given passages written at the student's instructional level, the student will orally respond to questions concerning *who, what, when, where,* and *how,* achieving 100% accuracy in four out of five trials.

STANDARD 2.7 RETELL THE CENTRAL IDEAS OF SIMPLE EXPOSITORY OR NARRATIVE PASSAGES

Goal: Improve reading comprehension as measured by an informal reading inventory.

Objectives: After listening to passages from grade-level social studies and science texts read by a peer, the student will orally restate the main idea of the passages for 3 out of the 4 passages. Given passages written at the student's instructional level, the student will orally or silently read the story and then orally retell the story, achieving a rating of at least 80% comprehension as assessed using a teacher-developed story retelling rubric.

Source: State of California Academic Standards Commission, Spring, 1998, *http:www.ca.gove/goldstandards/Drafts/Language Objectives*

THEORY TO PRACTICE

➡ Select a curricular area and, with a particular student in mind, examine district, state, or national goals, outcomes, and/or standards. Identify which goals, outcomes, and/or standards are most appropriate for the student (match needed areas identified through assessment). Using these goals, outcomes, and/or standards as guidelines, write an IEP goal and two objectives to reflect the child's needs in this curricular area. Write each of the objectives in the four configurations shown in Exhibit 10.4. Present your goal and objectives to a peer for feedback.

TYPES OF OBJECTIVES

Gronlund's Classification

We selected and modified Gronlund's (1995) model and approach to objective writing for several reasons. Gronlund supports the writing of objectives for different kinds of learning outcomes and shows the value of identifying what kinds of things will be accepted as evidence, or indicators, of the accomplishment of different kinds of objectives. In addition, he shows how to keep the same objective for students while varying the level of instruction. Gronlund (1995) identifies five types, or categories, of objectives: (a) knowledge, (b) understanding, (c) higher-level thinking, (d) affective, and (e) performance. Definitions and examples of each are provided in Exhibit 10.7. Here we draw heavily from Gronlund's types and definitions of objectives and we generate practical examples for our readers.

EXHIBIT 10.7

Gronlund's Classification of Objectives

Knowledge	• recall of previously learned material: names of persons, places or things, terms, facts, concepts, principles, procedures, or theories

Presented pictures of 15 common household items (e.g., sink, stove, bath towel), student will verbally identify them by name with 100% accuracy by December _____ .

Evaluation Procedures: teacher-developed checklist individually administered

Understanding	• comprehension—understanding material; interpreting information • application—using information learned; transferring and applying that information to other situations; stating new examples; solving a new problem

(continued)

EXHIBIT 10.7

Gronlund's Classification of Objectives *(continued)*

Comprehension

After observing a videotape of a social encounter in which one participant responds in socially inappropriate ways, the student will orally describe what occurred during the incident and identify the actions of the individual that were socially inappropriate.

Criterion: student description will reflect what occurred on the tape and identify at least 5 of the inappropriate behaviors exhibited by the individual in the videotape

Evaluation Procedures: observation and tallying of inappropriate behaviors identified by the student

Evaluation Schedule: end of the unit on handling conflict

Application

After observing a videotape of a social encounter in which one participant responds in socially inappropriate ways, the student will write ways in which the individual may respond more appropriately the next time she is faced with a similar situation.

Criterion: written document will include at least three suggestions of how the individual could respond more appropriately, with each suggestion clearly explained through the use of an example

Evaluation Procedures: peer review of student work sample using a student-developed rubric

Evaluation Schedule: end of the unit on handling conflict

Condition: Using ESL and interpreter

Higher-Level Thinking	• analysis—taking information apart; analyzing a problem as in critical thinking • synthesis—finding relationships among information and putting information together in new and meaningful ways • evaluation—judging the quality or value of information and supporting his or her judgments

Analysis

When presented information that includes both fact and fiction, the student will identify and classify the information as facts and fiction by creating a graphic that represents these ideas and their classifications.

Criterion: student will accurately classify as fact or fiction at least 80% of the items

Evaluation Procedures: appraisal of student work sample for level of accuracy

Evaluation Schedule: at end of a unit on differentiating fact from fiction

Synthesis

After listening to several accounts of a famous person's life, the student will create a collage of the person's contributions through use of a computer graphics/painting program.

Criterion: collage will include at least three major contributions of the individual

Evaluation Procedures: appraisal of student work sample for inclusion of contributions

Evaluation Schedule: by June _____

Evaluation

At the completion of performing a task at a community work site, the student will evaluate his performance by viewing a videotape of himself in action.

Criterion: successful demonstration of at least 4 out of the 5 steps listed on an evaluation task checklist

Evaluation Procedures: observation scored through the use of a checklist that includes the steps of the evaluation task

Evaluation Schedule: at the completion of each four-week period until April _____

Familiarity with these different types of objectives may assist teams in writing goals and objectives across curriculum options (e.g., general education with and without modifications, life skills, and modified means of communication and performance). In Exhibit 10.8 we again apply the classification proposed by Gronlund (1995) and present objectives developed for each of the curricular options identified in Section I of this text (see Figure 2.2). We selected transition as the representative area for life skills curriculum.

Affective	• attitudes—responding to information
	• interests—engaging in behavior that indicates interest in a topic or skill
	• appreciations—demonstrating ability to differentiate between works of high and poor quality and desire to learn more about a topic or skill
	• adjustments—demonstrating ability to work cooperatively and get along with others

With continuation of a point system for desired behavior, student will demonstrate a positive attitude toward learning mathematics by completing at least three of five predetermined indicators each day for the six-week grading period during mathematics class as measured by a student-completed self-monitoring checklist by December _____ .

Indicators are:

1.1 Listens attentively when problems are explained.

1.2 Follows directions when solving problems.

1.3 Works independently when solving problems.

1.4 Asks questions when a procedure is not clear.

1.5 Completes class assignments on time and submits them for grading.

Performance	• process—evaluating the procedure or process one goes through to create a final product or perform an activity
	• product—evaluating what is produced as a result of efforts or resulting from a performance
	• combination—evaluating both the process and the product

Process-Focused

Student will use the "calculator system for determining affordability" to purchase more than one item and avoid spending more money than he has in his pocket. His performance will be satisfactory when he completes the procedures described in the *Syracuse Curriculum* (1989) for three consecutive days with no assistance in each context of school and community.

Procedures:

"(1) count the money to be spent;

(2) enter amount into calculator, disregarding decimals;

(3) press the minus sign and [enter] the price of the item; and

(4) repeat step three unless the display shows a minus sign, which means that there is 'not enough' money to purchase the last item subtracted" (p. 135).

Product Outcomes

By January, student will assemble at least 50 earphones per workday for Delta Airlines. The earphones will meet the standard of the industry as evaluated by the job coach every two weeks the student is on the job.

Combined

Student will follow class procedures to develop a videotape contribution for his senior year portfolio. Student will satisfy all checklist components as assessed through a student-teacher conference to be held at least two weeks prior to submission of the portfolio.

Checklist of Procedures:

___ (1) follow the steps listed in the project plan for all class members;

___ (2) choose a personal project to show progress in independence at school in activities identified in the IEP;

___ (3) use personal communication system to relay personal decisions about the project;

___ (4) invite someone to provide physical assistance with the videotape project;

___ (5) indicate to the chosen assistant which activities, as the student attempts them, should be videotaped for the portfolio;

___ (6) plan the taping sessions so that they do not waste time; and

___ (7) plan the taping sessions so that editing will not be necessary.

Source: *How to Write and Use Instructional Objectives* by Gronlund. © 1994. Adapted by permission of Prentice-Hall, Inc., Upper Saddle River, NJ.

EXHIBIT 10.8

Examples of IEP Objectives for the Four Curricular Options

	GENERAL EDUCATION CURRICULUM WITH AND WITHOUT MODIFICATIONS	LIFESKILLS CURRICULUM: TRANSITION	CURRICULUM FOR MODIFIED MEANS OF COMMUNICATION AND PERFORMANCE
Knowledge	After listening to each of 5 stories read aloud, Sean will orally state the names of 3 of the central characters and will list at least 1 characteristic of each by January.	Ven will indicate which 3 pictures out of 10 represent three different things people do to make sure they are on time at school and on the job. She will make the correct choices 5 of 6 times she is asked when she reports to her once-a-week job assignment in the cafeteria.	By the end of the school year, Mario will demonstrate knowledge of all parts of his assistive devices by correctly pointing to them when someone names them.
Understanding	Following an instructional unit on the reproduction cycle of the butterfly, Amber will draw the stages of the butterfly and write at least 2 sentences that accurately describe each phase in sequence, to demonstrate her ability to identify, sequence, and describe the stages.	During each weekly career education experience in the community, Peter will observe 2 different workers and record on a checklist at least 3 good work habits of each (e.g., cleans the work space, follows directions). He will meet criterion when he records appropriately good work habits observed and expands the checklist to include at least 5 additional good work habits observed.	By June, Scotty will apply knowledge of at least 10 basic manual signs (e.g., food, bathroom, and drink) by using the sign appropriately for requests at school, at home, and in the community, as charted by family and school personnel.
Higher-Level Thinking	Using self-selected resource materials on a self-selected issue, Marcel will (a) read material, (b) identify main themes and ideas expressed in the material, (c) compare and contrast these ideas, and (d) present findings in poster format, including the following components: (1) title, (2) overall issue addressed, (3) at least three major findings and related sources, and (4) recommendations and rationale for resolving the issue as evaluated by a teacher-developed rubric by June.	Given an evaluation tool of correct work habits with workscale ratings of 1–5 (5 is the highest), G.W. will rate herself independently and plan a video to synthesize her findings. In it she will illustrate her strengths and areas requiring change. The video will be shown to her class and evaluated by her teacher.	By May 1—Susan will evaluate arguments for and against moving into her own apartment off campus vs living in a dorm when she goes away to college. She will give special consideration to the implication of her blindness.
Affective	Given a piece of paper and art supplies, Anne will draw a sketch of how she feels about herself as a student and dictate at least four adjectives that describe her feelings by March.	Caitlin will express her feelings (e.g., loneliness, confusion, satisfaction, or happiness) when talking to people in school or in the community and reasons for the feelings at least one time each day for 20 days in the next 8 weeks as evidenced by what she self-reports in a journal as read to the special education teacher.	During Circle of Friends, Kakov will express interest in peers and their families by using her interpreter to ask questions (e.g., What makes you happy? What do you like best to do?) at recess for at least two Fridays per month for 3 months.
Performance	Using a graphics software program and a computer, Juan will create and explain to his teachers and peers a graphic that illustrates the relationship between supply and demand. His performance must meet benchmarks established for class presentations of creative works.	Before dismissal time at the end of each day, when the teacher says, "It's time to clean up," Michael will organize his materials (e.g., notebooks, pencils, pens) on top of and inside his desk by putting things in an orderly, neat manner independently for at least 4 days a week for 5 weeks, as evaluated by the teacher and classmates.	As part of a schoolwide Exit Outcome, Kim will independently use his augmentative communication device with voice output to prepare and give a 5-minute presentation during a special Senior Day event. The speech performance will meet criteria set in his IEP.

Quality Objectives for Functional Outcomes in Natural Settings

Teachers and other IEP team members sometimes find it more difficult to develop IEP objectives for functional outcomes from community-based experiences than for school-based ones. We direct readers to the original work of Hunt, Goetz and Anderson (1986). Hunt and associates developed a valid and reliable (and relevant) IEP evaluation instrument that measured the quality of IEP objectives for students with intellectual disabilities. Student IEPs were evaluated on the degree to which they contained seven "indicators of best practices." The greater number of indicators up to seven, the higher the quality of the objective. The quality indicators of best practices were "associated with functional, community-based education models" (p. 203) [as opposed to traditional academic objectives]. The seven indicators of best practices fell into three categories: *age-appropriateness, functionality,* and *potential for generalization to a variety of environments.* Exhibit 10.9 identifies these seven indicators of best practice in their three categories. Across from each indicator is its definition. These indicators from the original IEP evaluation instrument can serve as guidelines for the development of similar kinds of IEP objectives for students with other disabilities as well.

EXHIBIT 10.9

IEP Evaluation: Indicators of Best Practice

INDICATORS OF BEST PRACTICE	DEFINITION
Age Appropriate	
1. Materials	It would be appropriate for a peer of the same chronological age without disabilities to use the materials.
2. Task	It would be appropriate for a peer of the same chronological age without disabilities to perform the task.
Functional	
3. Basic skill	The skill is based on needs identified in 1 of 5 areas: communication, social, behavior, motor, and academic.
4. Critical activity	The task must be performed for the student if he or she cannot do it for himself or herself.
5. Interaction activity	The activity necessitates the mutual participation of a person with disabilities and a person without.
Will Generalize to a Variety of Environments	
6. Taught across settings and materials	The skill facilitates the student's ability to function in a variety of environments; specifically, a basic skill taught within and across critical activities or a critical activity trained across settings and materials.
7. Taught in the natural setting	The skill is taught in a way that reflects the manner in which the skill will be used in the natural environment.

Source: Hunt, P., Farron-Davis, F., Beckstead, S., Curtis, D., & Goetz, L. (1994). "Evaluating the effects of placement of students with severe disabilities in general education versus special classes." *JASH,* 19(3) 200–214.

A rating sheet for scoring these IEP objectives directs evaluators to give each indicator of best practice contained in the objective a score of one (1) for a possible total of seven (7) (Hunt et. al., 1986). Our readers can use the information in Exhibit 10.9 to evaluate informally the quality of existing objectives and to improve the quality of new ones. Teachers, for instance, might urge IEP team members to review newly developed IEP objectives and to consider increasing the number of best practice indicators. It is highly possible that, as a result, each of the students would receive increased benefits from their education because of improvement in the quality of their IEP objectives.

Objectives for Participation in General Education Experiences

By law, IEPs are to specify the **l**east **r**estrictive **e**nvironment (LRE) for each student, defined as

> *(A) In general—To the maximum extent appropriate, children with disabilities, including children in public or private institutions or other care facilities, are educated with children who are not disabled, and special classes, separate schooling, or other removal of children with disabilities from the regular educational environment occurs only when the nature or severity of the disability of a child is such that education in regular classes with the use of supplementary aids and services cannot be achieved satisfactorily. (IDEA Amendments of 1997, Sec. 612(a)(5)(A))*

This information may be listed on the IEP form as a statement of LRE and in the form of objectives. Here is an example of a general education participation objective:

> Sue Ming will attend English, Social Studies, and Science for a total of 20 hours a week and Art and Music 2 hours a week in a general education program, arrive to class on time, bring necessary materials, and submit at least 80% of the assignments on time.
> *Evaluation Procedures:* student self-monitoring checklist to be signed by teachers and reviewed by the special education teacher and student
> *Evaluation Schedule:* end of the first semester

Sometimes teams develop comprehensive objectives for student achievement anticipated as a result of participation in general education activities and experiences. Here is an example of such an objective:

> Using a variety of assistive technology devices described in the IEP and a 1-to-1 aide (one paraprofessional to help one student) for physical assistance and changes in positions as recommended by the physical therapist, Ashton will complete all academic class assignments earning a grade of C or better.
> *Evaluation Procedures:* review of teacher's grade book
> *Evaluation Schedule:* end of the third quarter

THEORY TO PRACTICE

➡ Try your hand at writing objectives for each curricular option described in Section I of this text (see Figure 2.2). When writing these objectives, relate their content to district, state, and/or national standards.

➡ Thinking of a particular student, write objectives for the child's participation in community-based activities as well as for general education experiences. Evaluate your objectives using the system developed by Hunt et al. (1986; 1994). Make any necessary changes. Present your objectives to peers for feedback.

➡ Meet with a general education teacher who has special education students in his or her class. What types of objectives does this teacher believe are important for these students, in terms of their participation in general education experiences? Working with this teacher, write objectives for participation in general education experiences. Present these objectives to a special education teacher for review and comment.

MODIFICATION OF OBJECTIVES

Gronlund (1995) indicates that objectives can be written to reflect different levels of difficulty or instruction. Exhibit 10.10 indicates how each of the five types of objectives that Gronlund identified may be written to vary the difficulty or complexity of the behavior or performance.

EXHIBIT 10.10

Adaptation of Objectives
to Reflect Appropriate
Instructional Level

TYPE OF OBJECTIVE	LOWER-LEVEL DIFFICULTY	HIGHER-LEVEL DIFFICULTY
Knowledge	• points out an object, symbol, or fact from given objects, symbols, or fact statements	• identifies information as representative of an idea or concept
Understanding	• describes story events • provides explanation for a character's actions	• describes story theme • provides possible motivations for characters' actions
Higher-Level Thinking Skills	• describes events leading up to a historical event • evaluates arguments for and against staying up late on weekends	• describes how events leading up to a historical event may have contributed to or influenced the event and its outcome • evaluates arguments for and against participating in a disability demonstration
Affective	• willingly expresses own ideas • expresses feelings	• listens to the ideas of others, evaluates how they "fit" with their own ideas, and expresses this "fit" in a positive manner • classifies feelings of self and others
Performance	• gathers and organizes equipment listed on a problem-solving activity sheet (process) • produces a paragraph that includes all components identified on a checklist (product) • uses scissors and other school tools properly	• reads a problem, determines equipment needs, and gathers that equipment (process) • produces a 5-paragraph essay using classmates' examples as guides (product) • uses science laboratory equipment properly

Source: *How to Write and Use Instructional Objectives* by Gronlund. © 1994. Adapted by permission of Prentice-Hall, Inc., Upper Saddle River, NJ.

Writing objectives that vary the difficulty of the behavior or performance to reflect needs for different levels of instruction can be a great challenge, but allows for differentiating not only by type of objective but by difficulty within type as well. It is helpful also to know how to vary the other four components of IEP objectives. Exhibit 10.11 presents objectives written for lower and higher levels of a comprehensive objective and demonstrates how the level of complexity of criteria and evaluation procedures can also be customized.

EXHIBIT 10.11	OBJECTIVE	COMPONENT OF OBJECTIVE		
Comprehension Objectives at Different Levels of Difficulty		**CRITERION**	**EVALUATION PROCEDURE**	**EVALUATION SCHEDULE**
	Lower-Level Comprehension After listening to a story read orally by a peer, the student, working with a partner, will identify two main characters, draw pictures of these characters, and explain the drawings orally to the group, highlighting the personal characteristics of these characters.	• each character is represented in the drawing • oral explanation includes discussion of at least 3 characteristics of each character	• appraisal of student work sample • observation and tallying of the number of characteristics mentioned for each character	(The evaluation schedules do not need to be modified)
	Upper-Level Comprehension After listening to a story read orally by a peer, the student, working with a peer, will compare and contrast the characteristics of the two primary characters and present those findings using a Venn diagram.	• Venn diagram will include at least 3 separate and 3 common characteristics for each character recorded in the appropriate regions of the diagram	• review of student work sample • observation and tallying of the number of characteristics mentioned for each character	(The evaluation schedules do not need to be modified)

THEORY TO PRACTICE

➡ Begin by writing an objective for a particular student. Then modify the objective to reflect a different level of difficulty and complexity. Compare these objectives to those provided in this section of the chapter. How are they the same? How are they different? What can be gained through the modification of the difficulty and complexity and the various components of objectives?

EVALUATION OF ACHIEVEMENT OF OBJECTIVES

Annual review of progress toward achieving annual goals and objectives is a minimal schedule of evaluation because the IDEA Amendments of 1997 require that parents be informed of their child's progress on IEP goals and objectives at least as often as parents of general education students are informed of their children's performance. This means that IEP updates must be presented to parents at report card time and, possibly, at other report periods established by the school.

If ongoing monitoring of IEP goals and objectives reveals that a student is not making adequate progress toward meeting a particular objective, the teacher should request an interim meeting of the IEP team to determine the need for revising the objective and perhaps even the goal. Delay in progress may be caused by a change in medication, recent illness, crisis in the family, or other circumstances. If the delay is temporary, change probably will not be necessary. If conditions interfering with accomplishment of the objective persist, adjustments may be necessary. At times, teams may conclude that the objective itself, the criterion, or specific conditions are not appropriate for the individual even in the best of circumstances.

If adjustments are indicated, IEP teams have several options. Before changing the goal or objective, team members should review the present situation. They may begin by discussing the characteristics of the student and any changes in these characteristics. They may also review the assessment tools being used as well as the appropriateness of the annual goals and objectives. Then they should consider whether the lack of student progress is due to inconsistent implementation of the intervention procedures across teaching and learning situations (DePaepe, Reichle, Doss, & Shriner, 1994). The effectiveness of the intervention procedures is another area to inspect (DePaepe, Reichle, Doss, & Shriner, 1994). When intervention procedures are suspect, teachers should look for indications that changes are needed in the elements of curriculum used as part of the procedures: the subject matter, the learning experiences, the instructional procedures, and the materials. It may be that the selected learning experience is not responsive to student needs or that adjustments need to be made to maximize student opportunity for success.

The next set of options the team may consider is whether to change some part of the original objectives (see the previous section on modification of objectives). The objective may be too broad given the amount of time the student has to accomplish it. The objective as stated may not be leading to the kind of changes desired. The criteria may need revision, or the conditions may not be adequate to accommodate the child's disability. If these factors are considered troublesome, the team may rewrite the objective or generate new ones.

THEORY TO PRACTICE

➡ Meet with a special education teacher to discuss how he or she monitors student achievement of IEP goals and objectives. What policies or practices does this teacher have in place? How effective are they in assisting the teacher in monitoring student performance? What additional steps could this teacher take to monitor a student's progress toward IEP goal and objective mastery more closely?

➡ Develop a plan for how you, as a special or general education teacher, will monitor student achievement of IEP goals and objectives. For the procedure that will be evaluated, be specific in your plan, identifying who will do what, when, and how. Present this plan to a general and special teacher team for review. What recommendations do team members have for improving your plan and making your plan feasible for the workplace?

➡ Meet with a parent to discuss how the school monitors her or his child's progress toward IEP goal and objective mastery. How familiar is the parent with the procedures? How are the parents informed of their child's progress and how often? What suggestions do the parents have for improving the monitoring of their child's performance toward IEP goal and objective mastery and for communicating that progress to them?

CHAPTER SUMMARY

This chapter provides examples of the types of goals, benchmarks, and objectives that may be included in student IEPs. Classification of types of objectives and some of the examples were drawn from the work of Gronlund (1995). Objectives may be written to reflect desired levels of understanding, functional outcomes, and participation in general education experiences. They may be modified to increase or lessen their complexity and difficulty. The importance of ongoing monitoring of student progress toward the achievement of IEP goals and objectives is stressed.

Instruction

Creating a Context for Learning

Read to find out the following:
- how teacher and student attributes, such as culture and beliefs and learning and teaching styles influence the context in which teachers and students learn
- how management interventions and approaches can be implemented to support student success in the classroom
- how grouping arrangements can be devised to respond to individual student needs and interests

Once an individualized educational program has been developed, including goals, benchmarks, and objectives, attention turns to instruction. Instructional considerations begin with the development of a learning context that supports teaching and learning. Identifying factors that influence the development of a context for learning and the understanding of how they support or detract from teaching and learning can assist teachers in designing effective and meaningful instructional learning environments and experiences for students. In this chapter we introduce these factors and discuss their importance.

BUILDING BLOCKS

A number of factors affect the climate for learning. In Figure 11.1 these factors are presented as the building blocks of classroom climate, and each is described in Table 11.1. Such factors can be especially critical when students with special education needs are included in instructional environments so that these students do experience success and not become isolated from others or be limited in their participation. For example, clear expectations, not only for academic tasks but for behavioral and social interactions, can help students accept and work with one another in cooperative and supportive fashions. This atmosphere of acceptance can also be built through the creation of a learning climate that requires mutual respect. When students are working and learning in environments in which they know they are considered valuable and contributing members, they are more likely to participate, succeed, and learn.

┃ **FIGURE 11.1**
Factors That Shape the Context of Learning

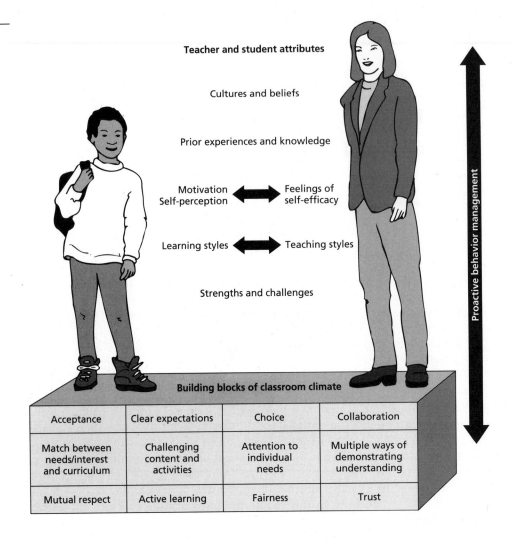

Teacher and student attributes

Cultures and beliefs

Prior experiences and knowledge

Motivation Self-perception ⟷ Feelings of self-efficacy

Learning styles ⟷ Teaching styles

Strengths and challenges

Proactive behavior management

Building blocks of classroom climate

Acceptance	Clear expectations	Choice	Collaboration
Match between needs/interest and curriculum	Challenging content and activities	Attention to individual needs	Multiple ways of demonstrating understanding
Mutual respect	Active learning	Fairness	Trust

TABLE 11.1 BUILDING BLOCKS OF CLASSROOM CLIMATE

FACTOR	CLASSROOM PRACTICES
Acceptance	• Discuss differences and the richness these differences bring to the classroom, and model acceptance of differences. • Move beyond tolerance of differences to the celebration of differences.
Clear Expectations	• Before beginning an activity, state your expectations for both academic and behavioral performance, and when appropriate, have students determine behavioral expectations for activities. • Demonstrate behavioral expectations through modeling and role-play. • Provide explanations in writing as well as orally stating them to the group. • Provide students with examples, rubrics, or checklists to clarify academic expectations.
Choice	• Begin with simple choices (e.g., working with a red pencil or a blue pencil, reading this book or that book), and support students in their choices. • Once choices are offered, do not pull back. Follow through with whatever was originally offered as a choice. • As students become more sophisticated in making choices, increase the significance of the choices offered. • Debrief students about their choices, the consequences associated with their choices, and strategies they may apply when making choices.

FACTOR	CLASSROOM PRACTICES
Collaboration	• Model compromise and ability to work with others. • Inservice all adults working in the classroom as to classroom procedures and rules, and jointly determine how you will work together. • Provide students many opportunities to work with one another, starting with informal activities requiring brief amounts of time, and gradually extend that time to longer activities that require more negotiation and compromise among participants.
Match Between Needs/Interests and Curriculum	• Include materials in the classroom that are reflective of the community and the students' cultures and interests. • When teaching, incorporate examples drawn from the students' experiences and from their culture, and design activities and units that build on student interest. • Allow students some voice in selecting topics to study and materials to be used.
Challenging Content and Activities	• Select activities that are neither too easy nor too hard, so students will feel successful while also being challenged. • Provide a range of activities for students to engage in. • Differentiate activities in order to respond to students' skills and needs.
Attention to Individual Needs	• Interact with each student on an individual basis every day, or at least several days per week, and take a personal interest in each student. • Provide time for individualized activities tailored to students' needs and interests. • Build in reflection activities in order to gain some insight into student thinking and attitudes toward learning in the classroom.
Multiple Ways of Demonstrating Understanding	• Vary the way in which assignments are to be completed—in groups, individually, in writing, through oral reports, through drawing. • Ensure all students are challenged to demonstrate their understanding in multiple ways (e.g., writing, oral reports, illustrations) to expose them to multiple formats and also to raise their awareness of the differences in their abilities in these formats (this raises awareness of different learning styles and needs).
Mutual Respect	• Model respect for all members of the classroom through day-to-day interactions. • Pay attention to both verbal and nonverbal communication signals when interacting with members of the classroom community. • Engage students in problem-solving activities around respect issues in order to assist them in developing strategies for getting along with others and for respecting the views and wishes of others.
Active Learning	• Provide learning through multiple channels (e.g., auditory, visual, motor) and allow students to learn through hands-on experiences. • Chunk class time between listening activities and activities that require active participation to allow for a higher level of engagement.
Fairness	• Model fairness in all your dealings with members of the classroom community. • Discuss conflicts concerning fairness as a class, and highlight how the "same" is not always indicative of fairness.
Trust	• Support students in their decision making. • Keep confidences and respect privacy. • Follow through with promises made.

THEORY TO PRACTICE

➡ Meet with a classroom teacher to discuss how she or he creates a context for learning. What actions does the teacher take in the beginning of the year, in the middle of the year, and at the end of the year? What actions and factors does she or he consider most important?

➡ Observe in a general education classroom. Keeping in mind the building blocks of classroom climate, identify factors in this learning context that support the inclusion of students with disabilities. What factors in this classroom, or missing from this classroom, support the inclusion of students with disabilities?

TEACHER AND STUDENT ATTRIBUTES

Teachers and students bring unique characteristics and needs to the learning environment. These attributes interact to create the classroom climate and influence the degree to which teachers and students experience success. In this section we describe five pairs of teacher and student attributes (see Figure 11.1).

Culture and Beliefs

Every individual in a learning environment views the environment and his or her role in it through the lens of his or her own culture and beliefs. The values that teachers and students place on activities, the level of motivation and dedication they bring to tasks, and the ways in which they interact with others are all influenced by their culture and beliefs, which, to a great extent, determine what goes on in classrooms and other learning environments. Because of this strong influence, teachers need to be aware of possible conflicts between their cultures and beliefs and those of their students and their students' families. More than tolerance of differences is needed; efforts must be made to acknowledge, accept, and accommodate differences. According to Delpit (1995),

> *When a significant difference exists between the students' culture and the school's culture, teachers can easily misread students' aptitudes, intent, or abilities as a result of the difference in styles of language use and interactional patterns. Secondly, when such cultural differences exist, teachers may utilize styles of instruction and/or discipline that are at odds with community norms. (p. 167)*

To overcome or prevent cultural conflict in the classroom, teachers and students need to work together to create environments in which the culture and learning styles of all individuals are recognized and valued. This can be accomplished by attending to the building blocks of classroom climate and through selection of materials and activities that reflect students' cultures and community experiences.

Prior Experience and Knowledge

Both teachers and students bring to the learning environment a range of prior experience and knowledge about teaching and learning. Accessing this rich reservoir can enhance instruction. Therefore, it is important to identify and understand experiential and knowledge-based differences among both teachers and students.

Teachers have a range of experiences and go through various career stages, from novice to veteran. During these stages, they develop different perspectives on and insights into teaching and learning, and these perspectives and insights influence what goes on in their classrooms. New teachers (0 to 2 years of experience) may be open to ideas, may seek the advice and support of others, or may isolate themselves due to fear of letting others know they are experiencing difficulties. Practiced teachers (3 to 10 years of experience) may be open to suggestions and new approaches but have a more critical consumer approach to suggestions; they may also be getting set in their ways and no longer eager to try new ideas. Veteran teachers (10 or more years of experience) may be highly effective or possibly too comfortable in their practice and unwilling to make changes. They may also be positive role models and mentors to new teachers. These different experiences and stages can significantly influence what goes on in classrooms.

Students, too, bring different experiences to the learning task. Students' prior experiences and knowledge include what they have learned about "doing school," what curriculum content they have learned through instructional experience, and what they have learned through family and community experiences. Awareness of these prior experiences and acknowledgment of their impact on current behavior and performance help teachers see beyond troubling behavior or lack of motivation to the possible root of a problem. Students' experiences and knowledge related to curriculum content can be drawn on to help students make connections between what they learned through previous instruction and what they are currently learning in school, and what they are experiencing and learning in their lives outside school.

Making connections between experiences and prior knowledge is not easy. Not all students come to school with the same experiences and knowledge. Some students may have a great deal of knowledge about a particular topic while others have limited or no knowledge of it. The same holds true for experiences. It is the teacher's job to assist all students in making connections between what they know and are comfortable with, and what they are expected to learn and do in the current learning environment. Ladson-Billings (1994) suggests that teachers, "Rather than expecting students to demonstrate prior knowledge and skills . . . help students develop that knowledge by building bridges and scaffolding for learning" (p. 25).

This building of bridges and scaffolding can be especially important for teachers working with individuals with disabilities who are included in general education learning environments, because the discrepancies between the students' experiences and those of their nondisabled peers may be great. For example, special education curriculum may focus on daily and community living skills, rather than on the traditional curriculum content emphasized in general education programs. As a result, students may not have the prior knowledge or experiences to draw on when they participate for the first time in general education curriculum with their nondisabled peers. If students are to be successful, teachers need to bridge students' understanding from what they know to what is being presented, thereby filling in the gap between what students bring to the learning situation and what is being learned and practiced.

Additionally, expectations and curriculum may need to be modified for students with disabilities in order for them to benefit from general education experiences. Students may not be familiar with having to raise a hand before speaking, because in special education learning environments the smaller number of students or the emphasis on the development and practice of communication skills may have encouraged free expression and participation. In academics, students may not initially have the skills to participate meaningfully in cooperative learning groups. They may require instruction in social skills as well as in academic skills associated with working and learning in groups if they are to be successful in those situations. The "Make It Happen" feature highlights some strategies for building these bridges for student success.

MAKE IT HAPPEN

Building Bridges to Prior Knowledge and Experiences

- Assess what students know and bring to the learning experience.
- Meet and talk with teachers who have worked with the students in the past to learn about their skills and needs.
- Meet and discuss the student's curriculum (e.g., IEP review, discussion with the special education teacher and the child's parents).
- Talk with students about knowledge and familiarity with topics covered in the curriculum.
- Ask students to bring in artifacts of prior experiences.
- Have students work in groups and share their expertise and experiences with each other.

(continued)

**Building Bridges to Prior Knowledge
and Experiences** *(continued)*

- Ask questions when presenting new ideas to draw in students.
- Encourage students to express their ideas and previous knowledge.
- Employ the K-W-L (Ogle, 1986) strategy: What do students Know about a topic? What do they Want to know? What did they Learn as a result of instruction?
- Before beginning a new unit, have students write, orally present, or draw what they know about the topics and present this information to peers.

Motivation, Self-Perception, and Feelings of Self-Efficacy

Although the terms vary for teachers and students, this cluster of attributes represents constructs of how individuals feel about themselves and their ability to be successful. When talking about students, we generally use the terms *motivation* and *self-perception;* when talking about teachers, *feelings of self-efficacy.*

Motivation refers to students' desire to participate in activities and learn. Some students come to school eager to learn; others are unwilling or hesitant to try. Lack of motivation may manifest itself in the adoption of a passive learning style (e.g., students resist new activities, are hesitant to begin their work, give up before starting), deviant behavior, or withdrawal. Motivating students can be a daunting task for teachers. One suggestion is to allow students to select what they want to learn and the ways in which they will demonstrate that learning. Fulk and Montgomery-Grymes (1994) offer other suggestions for enhancing student motivation. A number of their suggestions are presented in the "Make It Happen" feature.

| MAKE IT HAPPEN

        Motivation Tips

- Offer a menu of assignment options that lead to mastery of an objective and allow students to select the ones they will complete.
- Allow students to determine the sequence in which they will complete tasks.
- Allow students to set due dates for projects.
- Allow students to correct and/or grade their own work by providing them with answer keys.
- Allow students opportunities to self-correct their work with assistance from peers or adults.
- Vary the length of assignments so that if the criterion for mastery is demonstrated at a set point in the assignment, the remainder of the assignment does not have to be completed.
- Provide students opportunities and assistance in setting their own short-term goals.
- Have students self-evaluate their performance through graphing or charting.
- Provide instruction at a challenging level.
- When introducing a lesson or unit of instruction, demonstrate enthusiasm for the topic and inform students what they will be learning and how this information can be of value to them.
- Vary the way in which information is presented during instruction.
- Vary the types of activities students engage in.
- Provide clear directions and explanations.
- Always connect what students are learning to their daily lives in school and outside.

- Present learning experiences and content in authentic contexts.
- Provide frequent feedback that is specific (e.g., state exactly what was done well, not just that the student did a good job).
- Return graded assignments in a timely fashion.
- Display student work throughout the room—even older students are motivated by seeing their projects displayed.
- Help students understand connections between their efforts and outcomes (e.g., attribution training).

Source: Fulk & Montgomery-Grymes (1994).

Students' level of motivation may be influenced by how they view themselves as learners. Understanding attribution theory, student self-advocacy, and self-determination may help you as a teacher to motivate students. Definitions and examples of these considerations and related interventions are presented in Exhibit 11.1.

EXHIBIT 11.1

Students' Perceptions of Themselves as Learners

AREA OF CONSIDERATION	DEFINITION	EXAMPLES	INTERVENTIONS
Attribution Theory	• "The way people explain to themselves the causes of their success" (Lerner, 1997, p. 553)	• Students who are successful approach tasks positively and with enthusiasm because they know if they apply themselves, they will succeed • Students who tend to be unsuccessful attribute their successes to luck or forces outside of their control	• Provide short-term activities through which students directly observe the connection between their efforts and achieved outcomes (e.g., drama productions, art displays and exhibits, writing of reports) • Have students formally self-reflect and analyze their work on a frequent basis • Have students share their successes with others • Have students describe their approaches to tasks • Have students debrief after an activity to identify what went well and what they could do next time to increase the likelihood of success
Self-Advocacy	• The ability to advocate for yourself and to ask for what you need	• Requesting additional time to complete assignments • Requesting permission to tackle topics, problems, issues, or performance of personal issues • Telling a prospective employer why you should be hired	• Through role-play, provide students opportunities to practice making requests • Help students become aware of their strengths and needs and how they can use their strengths to address needs • Assist students in developing a sense of responsibility for their own well-being
Self-Determination	• The ability to make your own choices	• Choosing what to wear and eat • Choosing leisure-time activities • Selecting friends	• Have students practice making choices in authentic situations • Assist students in analyzing the consequences of their choices and developing alternative responses to situations • Help students evaluate their own behavior to learn what they may be doing that encourages others to make choices for them and removes opportunities to advocate for themselves

The term *self-efficacy* is used to describe how teachers view themselves as instructors. According to DiBella-McCarthy, McDaniel, and Miller (1995), "A sense of personal teaching efficacy is the teacher's perception of his or her own teaching capabilities and the belief that one can employ these capabilities to bring about student learning" (p. 68). The construct of self-efficacy originated with Bandura (1982) and may be divided into two categories: personal teaching efficacy and teaching efficacy. Gibson and Dembo (1984) defined personal teacher efficacy as the "belief that one has the skills and abilities to bring about student learning" (p. 573), and they define teaching efficacy as the "belief that any teacher's ability to bring about change is significantly limited by factors external to the teacher, such as the home environment, family background, and parental influences" (p. 574). *Personal teaching efficacy* is exemplified by this statement: "If a student masters a new math concept quickly, this might be because I knew the necessary steps in teaching that concept" (p. 573). *Teaching efficacy* is exemplified by this statement: "A teacher is very limited in what he/she can achieve because a student's home environment is a large influence on his/her achievement" (p. 573). Teachers with a strong sense of personal teaching efficacy believe in their students and believe that all students are capable of learning (DiBella-McCarthy, McDaniel, & Miller, 1995). Teachers with a weak sense of personal teaching efficacy may see many barriers to student learning and are less confident that all students will achieve.

Enhancing your sense of self-efficacy can be a great challenge. Begin by (a) developing a positive mind-set—believe in yourself and your students; (b) believing in the potential of your students—believe all students will be successful even though they may face great challenges; (c) setting realistic and achievable, though demanding, goals for yourself and for your students; (d) adapting teaching skills and instructional approaches to meet student needs; (e) monitoring student performance on an ongoing basis; and (f) seeking parent and school support (McDaniel & DiBella-McCarthy, 1989). Moreover, as a special educator, (a) achieve a close match between teaching approaches and environmental conditions, and students' specific and special needs; (b) provide direct instruction to groups and ensure active student involvement; (c) maintain an ongoing assessment plan for monitoring student performance to capture small but meaningful changes; (d) watch out for trouble spots through ongoing assessment, classroom management techniques, and reflecting on activities and student responses; (e) refer to present levels of performance to set high but realistic goals, and constantly evaluate the progress toward goals through data evaluation; and (f) establish support networks with colleagues and parents (DiBella-McCarthy, McDaniel, & Miller, 1995).

Learning and Teaching Styles

Another attribute both students and teachers bring to the learning environment is learning and teaching styles. Learning styles may be defined as

> *the way that students of every age are affected by their* (a) immediate environment, (b) own emotionality, (c) sociological needs, (d) physical characteristics, and (e) psychological inclinations *when concentrating and trying to master and remember new or difficult information or skills. (Carbo, Dunn, & Dunn, 1986, p. 2, original emphasis)*

The "immediate environment" has to do with sound, light, temperature, the noise level and formal/informal style of a learning environment and its effects on learners. "Own emotionality" includes motivation, persistence, responsibility, and structure and is based on the belief that if students enjoy what they are learning, they will exhibit longer attention spans and assume greater responsibility for what they are learning.

"Sociological needs" are concerned with how students interact with those around them—some students work best independently, and others work best when working cooperatively with others. "Physical characteristics" include perception, intake, time, and mobility and have to do with auditory, visual, tactual, and kinesthetic learners. "Psychological inclinations" represent how some students learn best when presented with small steps leading to the whole, whereas others learn best when first presented with the overall picture.

Butler (1986) offers a different conceptual understanding of learning styles. She identifies four learning styles: (a) concrete sequential, (b) abstract sequential, (c) abstract random, and (d) concrete random. *Concrete sequential learners* learn best when information is presented in an orderly, step-by-step fashion. They enjoy working on group projects and do best in situations where procedures and expectations have been set and hands-on learning experiences are provided. *Abstract sequential learners* learn best when focusing on ideas and engaging in discussion of those ideas. They enjoy reading about ideas, rather than engaging in hands-on activities. *Abstract random learners* learn best when challenged with problems that involve people. They enjoy gaining information through reading, discussion, and lecture. They enjoy discussing a topic, rather than working on projects. *Concrete random learners* learn best when using a problem-solving approach. They do best in environments that support investigation and the trying out of ideas.

Others discuss the issue of learning styles by distinguishing between field-sensitive and field-independent students. According to Gollnick and Chinn (1990), students who are field-sensitive are especially sensitive to the social aspects of the learning environment. They like to work with others and are concerned with developing a relationship with the teacher. Field-independent learners, in contrast, are independent individuals who are more analytical and enjoy a discovery approach to learning.

These proposed systems for understanding learning styles and for taking those styles into consideration when planning instruction for students must be interpreted and applied with caution. In a discussion of the relationship between culture and learning styles, Nieto (1996) points out the many shortcomings of attempting to classify students by learning style and plans her instruction accordingly. She comments that research attempting to identify the learning styles of groups of students, though identifying differences among groups, "also runs the risk of oversimplification and stereotyping and can be used as rationale for poor or inequitable teaching" (p. 139). For example, the field-sensitive/field-independent dichotomy has been used to classify Euro-Americans as field-independent and students of color as field-sensitive. However, not all individuals of color are field-sensitive and not all Euro-Americans are field-independent. The overgeneralization overshadows the needs and learning styles of individual students. Indeed, as Guild (1994) asserts,

> *Although people connected by culture do exhibit a characteristic pattern of style preferences, it is a serious error to conclude that all members of the group have the same style traits as the group taken as a whole. (p. 16)*

Guild (1994) goes on to say that often these classifications have been used to explain learning difficulties:

> *A second source of controversy is the understandable sensitivity surrounding attempts to explain the persistent achievement differences between minority and nonminority students—it is all too easy to confuse descriptions of differences with explanations for deficits. (p. 16)*

Guild (1994), through a review of the research surrounding culture and ways of learning, identified five commonly agreed-upon conclusions about the relationship between culture and learning styles:

1. students of any particular age will differ in their ways of learning,

2. learning styles are a function of both nature and nurture,

3. learning styles are neutral,

4. within a group, the variations among individuals are as great as their commonalties, and

5. [there exists a] cultural conflict between some students and the typical learning experiences in schools. (pp. 18–19)

One theory of instruction that considers learning styles without limiting students by classification is Gardner's (1983) theory of multiple intelligences. Gardner challenges traditional ways of thinking about how students learn and express themselves and their understandings. His theory allows for diversity of learning and demonstrations of knowledge and accentuates the positive while challenging teachers to orchestrate instructional factors for the maximum benefit of students. His research supports the theory that there are unknown numbers of human competencies—and at least eight intelligences—each having its own distinctive mode of thinking to approach problems and create products.

Armstrong (1994), building on Gardner's work, offers a checklist for assessing multiple intelligences to determine students' intelligence strengths and challenges. This checklist, presented in Exhibit 11.2, also helps to define seven of the eight intelligences that Gardner describes (it does not address what Gardner calls "naturalist intelligence").

EXHIBIT 11.2	
Checklist for Assessing Students' Multiple Intelligences	

Name of Student: _____

Check items that apply:

LINGUISTIC INTELLIGENCE
_____ writes better than average for age
_____ spins tall tales or tells jokes and stories
_____ has a good memory for names, places, dates, or trivia
_____ enjoys word games
_____ enjoys reading books
_____ spells words accurately (or if preschool, does developmental spelling that is advanced for age)
_____ appreciates nonsense rhymes, puns, tongue twisters, etc.
_____ enjoys listening to the spoken word (stories, commentary on the radio, talking books, etc.)
_____ has a good vocabulary for age
_____ communicates to others in a highly verbal way

Other Linguistic Strengths:

LOGICAL-MATHEMATICAL INTELLIGENCE

_____ asks a lot of questions about how things work

_____ computes arithmetic problems in his/her head quickly (or if preschool, math concepts are advanced for age)

_____ enjoys math class (or if preschool, enjoys counting and doing other things with numbers)

_____ finds math computer games interesting (or if no exposure to computers, enjoys other math or counting games)

_____ enjoys playing chess, checkers, or other strategy games (or if preschool, board games requiring counting squares)

_____ enjoys working on logic puzzles or brainteasers (or if preschool, enjoys hearing logical nonsense such as in _Alice's Adventures in Wonderland_)

_____ enjoys putting things in categories or hierarchies

_____ likes to experiment in a way that shows higher order cognitive thinking processes

_____ thinks on a more abstract or conceptual level than peers

_____ has a good sense of cause-effect for age

Other Logical-Mathematical Strengths:

SPATIAL INTELLIGENCE

_____ reports clear visual images

_____ reads maps, charts, and diagrams more easily than text (or if preschool, enjoys looking at more than text)

_____ daydreams more than peers

_____ enjoys art activities

_____ draws figures that are advanced for age

_____ likes to view movies, slides, or other visual presentations

_____ enjoys doing puzzles, mazes, "Where's Waldo?" or similar visual activities

_____ builds interesting three-dimensional constructions for age (e.g., LEGO buildings)

_____ gets more out of pictures than words while reading

_____ doodles on workbooks, worksheets, or other materials

Other Spatial Strengths:

BODILY-KINESTHETIC INTELLIGENCE

_____ excels in one or more sports (or if preschool, shows physical prowess advanced for age)

_____ moves, twitches, taps, or fidgets while seated for a long time in one spot

_____ cleverly mimics other people's gestures or mannerisms

_____ loves to take things apart and put them back together again

_____ puts his/her hands all over something he/she's just seen

_____ enjoys running, jumping, wrestling, or similar activities (or if older, will show these interests in a more "restrained" way—e.g., punching a friend, running to class, jumping over a chair)

_____ shows skill in a craft (e.g., woodworking, sewing, mechanics) or good fine-motor coordination in other ways

_____ has a dramatic way of expressing herself/himself

_____ reports different physical sensations while thinking or working

_____ enjoys working with clay or other tactile experiences (e.g., fingerpainting)

Other Bodily-Kinesthetic Strengths:

(continued)

EXHIBIT 11.2

Checklist for Assessing Students' Multiple Intelligences
(continued)

MUSICAL INTELLIGENCE

_____ tells you when music sounds off-key or disturbing in some other way

_____ remembers melodies of songs

_____ has a good singing voice

_____ plays a musical instrument or sings in a choir or other group (or if preschool, enjoys playing percussion instruments and/or singing in a group)

_____ has a rhythmic way of speaking and/or moving

_____ unconsciously hums to himself/herself

_____ taps rhythmically on the table or desk as he/she works

_____ sensitive to environmental noises (e.g., rain on the roof)

_____ responds favorably when a piece of music is put on

_____ sing songs that he/she has learned outside of the classroom

Other Musical Strengths:

INTERPERSONAL INTELLIGENCE

_____ enjoys socializing with peers

_____ seems to be a natural leader

_____ gives advice to friends who have problems

_____ seems to be street-smart

_____ belongs to clubs, committees, or other organizations (or if preschool, seems to be part of a regular social group)

_____ enjoys informally teaching other kids

_____ likes to play games with other kids

_____ has two or more close friends

_____ has a good sense of empathy or concern for others

_____ others seek out his/her company

Other Interpersonal Strengths:

INTRAPERSONAL INTELLIGENCE

_____ displays a sense of independence or a strong will

_____ has a realistic sense of his/her strengths and weaknesses

_____ does well when left alone to play or study

_____ marches to the beat of a different drummer in his/her style of living and learning

_____ has an interest or hobby that he/she doesn't talk much about

_____ has a good sense of self-direction

_____ prefers working alone to working with others

_____ accurately expresses how he/she is feeling

_____ is able to learn from his/her failures and successes in life

_____ has high self-esteem.

Other Intrapersonal Strengths:

According to Nieto (1996)

> *The implications of the theory of multiple intelligences for multicultural education may be significant because the theory goes beyond the limited definition of intelligence valued in the school. (p. 140)*

However, she continues on to caution that "The danger, as always, lies in extrapolating from individual cases to the entire group" (p. 140), echoing the cautions associated with the practice of classifying cultural groups and students by learning style.

Teachers have teaching styles as well as learning styles. Butler (1986) defines teaching style as

> *a set of attitudes and actions that open a formal and informal world of learning to students. It is a subtle force that influences student access to learning and teaching by establishing perimeters around acceptable learning procedures, processes, and products. The powerful force of the teacher's attitude toward students as well as the instructional activities used by the teacher shape the learning/teaching experience and require of the teacher and student certain mediation abilities and capacities. Thus, the manner in which a teacher presents himself or herself as a human being and receives learners as human beings is as influential upon the students' lives and learning as the daily activities in the classroom. (p. 52)*

Butler identifies four teaching styles:

1. *concrete sequential:* use of hands-on learning experiences and materials; emphasis on development of specific skills through worksheets and skill builders; use of teacher-directed/teacher-centered instructional practices; highly task oriented

2. *abstract sequential:* emphasis on ideas and concept development and on gaining information through reading and lecture; encourages student engagement in finding out "why"; wants students to be challenged and enjoy learning for learning's sake

3. *abstract random:* emphasis on development of self-esteem and students' self-concept; use of cooperative learning; celebrates individual achievement and individuality; develops curriculum based on student needs and interest

4. *concrete random:* uses investigation and encourages student exploration and investigation of ideas; values student development of skills for working with others and with divergent ideas

These four teaching-style profiles may be used as a framework from which teachers analyze their own behavior, reflect on their practice, and create learning opportunities for students.

Even though information related to styles may help teachers make instructional decisions, understanding learning and teaching styles involves much more than assigning children or teachers to one category or another or as one type of learner/teacher. Awareness of a range of styles challenges teachers to broaden their thinking to incorporate a variety of learning experiences and instructional strategies in the classroom. As offered by Guild (1994),

> *Ideas about culture and learning styles can be of great help to teachers as they pursue such intentional instructional diversity. A teacher who truly understands culture and learning styles and who believes that all students can learn, one way or another, can offer opportunities for success to all students. (p. 21)*

Strengths and Challenges

Both teachers and students bring strengths and challenges to teaching and learning. Teachers and students may have expertise and skills in certain areas and be greatly challenged in others. When designing learning experiences, teachers need to attend to their own strengths and challenges and to those of their students.

Because a student's disability may present unique challenges in the classroom, teachers first need to identify those challenges and then identify the means for modifying and/or adjusting experiences so the student gains maximum access to and experiences success in curriculum and learning. Table 11.2 surveys some areas teachers may want to address when working with students with disabilities and provides suggestions for enhancing student success in each.

TABLE 11.2 SUGGESTIONS FOR ADDRESSING STRENGTHS AND CHALLENGES

CONCERN	OPTIONS
Reading social situations and responding appropriately	• Discuss and analyze social situations and practice appropriate responses.
Making friends	• Include strategy instruction in how to make and keep friends—how to be a friend. • Provide multiple opportunities for students to interact with one another to encourage friendships and the forming of relationships.
Attending to and obtaining information from the environment	• Assist students in developing skills to differentiate between important and unimportant stimuli in the environment. • Provide strategy instruction in how to seek and gather information available in the environment.
Gaining information from printed material	• Provide means for students to gain information presented through auditory modes (e.g., working with a partner; books on tape). • Present information in both written and auditory form.
Expressing ideas through speech	• Implement speech therapy recommendations, augmentative/alternative communication, and related interventions across all environments.
Generalizing ideas to new situations and people	• Provide opportunities to teach for generalization. • Teach skills in multiple authentic contexts.
Developing organizational skills	• Teach and monitor application of organizational skills. • Teach self-management skills.
Enhancing motivation	• Provide students with activities in which they will experience success. • Allow students to make choices and decisions. • Give students responsibilities and make them accountable for following through.
Experiencing success	• Present tasks at a level and in ways that will guarantee success. • Draw students' attention to success. • Give students jobs and responsibilities that they can carry out successfully and provide them strategies for carrying them out.
Reacting to the feelings and needs of others	• Draw students' attention to verbal and nonverbal communication patterns. • Provide opportunities for students to assume a facilitative role. • Discuss emotions. • Provide multiple opportunities for students to interact with others in authentic contexts, followed by debriefing sessions to discuss outcomes.
Developing self-control	• Provide behavior management interventions. • Teach students to self-manage their behavior. • Teach students problem-solving skills.

CONCERN	OPTIONS
Accepting responsibility for their own behavior	• Teach self-management skills. • Teach problem-solving skills and provide opportunities for students to apply them in authentic contexts. • Engage students in discussions of their behavioral responses to situations and related consequences.
Building basic academic skills	• Focus on development of functional academics. • Provide students with activities that assist them in associating skill development with their current and future life needs. • Provide systematic instruction in areas of need.
Addressing issues of stamina or strength	• Teach use of adaptive and support materials and equipment. • Develop flexible schedules that reflect student patterns of strength and stamina. • Provide opportunities to develop or strengthen existing physical abilities.
Developing self-reliance	• Teach students how to manage their own care. • Teach students how to work with care providers. • Teach self-determination skills.

Challenges linked with disability are different for every individual. Conferencing with parents, talking with the student, and meeting with teachers and support personnel familiar with the student can provide invaluable insight into what can be done to fully support the children and include them in learning environments and activities.

THEORY TO PRACTICE

➡ Reflect on your own culture and experiences as a student. What classroom practices did you most enjoy, and what made learning easier for you? What classroom practices did you find uncomfortable/disturbing, and what made learning difficult for you? Compare your list of ideas with classmates'. What are the similarities? What are the differences? If you were to be the teacher of these other students, what types of cultural and learning preferences would you want to put into place in order to create a classroom climate responsive to their interests and needs?

➡ Observe in a classroom to identify ways in which the teacher builds on students' prior knowledge. Analyze these practices. How are they supportive of student learning? How and to what extent would they support the inclusion of students with disabilities in instruction? What else could be done to assist students in bridging their prior knowledge and experiences to the current content being taught in the classroom?

➡ Using the tools and information provided in this chapter section, analyze your own learning and teaching styles. What types of teaching and learning practices and activities are you most comfortable with in the classroom? Identify those you find uncomfortable or challenging. Next, analyze how your styles could match or mismatch with students' needs. List strategies you would use to overcome any mismatches between your styles and those of your students.

PROACTIVE BEHAVIOR SUPPORTS

An additional consideration for the creation of a positive and supportive learning environment for students is the manner in which the teacher manages student behavior and works with students in the management of their own behavior. A teacher who is a proactive classroom manager analyzes the environment, instructional practices, and expectations to identify ways to prevent the occurrence of inappropriate or challenging behaviors. This type of teacher is always thinking ahead, identifying what she or he can do and what the children can do to ensure a smoothly running operation, one with minimal conflict and few behavioral outbursts or challenges. Exhibit 11.3 lists examples of what a proactive classroom manager does.

EXHIBIT 11.3 **Examples of Proactive Classroom Management**	• teaching classroom routines early in the year (e.g., sharpening pencils, using the restroom, getting a drink, and turning in completed assignments) • teaching students to be independent learners • using praise effectively to maintain productive behavior • holding students accountable • minimizing interruptions • maintaining a positive feeling tone • eliminating "dead time" • encouraging cooperation • teaching the rules to make their meaning clear • constantly monitoring students' behavior • planning transitions • reducing time spent in transitions • treating everyone with respect and dignity	• planning ahead to prevent problems • making sure all necessary materials are ready and available • arranging the room to match procedures • arranging the room so all students can be seen at all times and planning for traffic patterns • planning procedures for distributing materials • planning activities for those students who finish early • planning how to start and end lessons • providing clear directions: (a) getting students' attention, (b) giving directions and demonstrating what to do, (c) checking for understanding, and, if directions are complex, (d) presenting directions in steps and through visual and auditory channels • establishing a cooperative, democratic, and friendly classroom environment

Rules

A proactive manager begins the year by determining rules for the classroom and teaching these rules to the students. The teacher may determine the rules and present them to the students, or the students may be involved in their generation. Regardless, the rules should be kept to a minimum (three to five) and the most important behaviors expected in the classroom should be spelled out. The rules should be written in positive language (e.g., "Students will raise their hands before speaking") and posted in the room.

It is not enough just to read the rules to students. The meaning of the rules should be discussed until all students understand them. It may be necessary for students to act out or role-play the rules before they truly understand the differences between appropriate and inappropriate behavior. Time spent on discussing and practicing rules is time well spent—it can prevent misunderstandings and incidents later.

Routines

A proactive manager identifies and teaches classroom routines, such as sharpening pencils, getting a drink of water, leaving the room to use the restroom, and getting and returning supplies. A beginning list of routines that teachers should consider is presented in Exhibit 11.4. As the exhibit indicates, there are multiple routines that occur in the classroom and numerous ways in which individual teachers may handle these routines. The proactive teacher does not assume that students will automatically pick up on these routines just by being in the classroom, but rather teaches these routines directly to all students as one way to prevent misunderstandings that can lead to misbehavior.

EXHIBIT 11.4

Classroom Routines

- Knowing how to come and go from the classroom
  - need to line up
  - may leave as a group without having to line up
  - need a hall pass from the teacher in order to leave the room
  - may self-select when to leave the room and pick up the hall pass by the door upon leaving
- Knowing where assignments will be listed
  - assignments written on the board each day
  - assignments listed in a three-ring binder found on the teacher's desk
- Knowing expectations during independent seatwork
  - must work independently
  - may ask peers for assistance
  - must work as a cooperative group
- Knowing how work is graded
  - students self-correct assignment
  - student papers are graded by peers
  - all work is graded by the teacher
  - teacher randomly selects one assignment per week to count toward the grade
  - the lowest test score during the term may be deleted before the calculation of the final grade
- Knowing how to seek help with tasks and assignments
  - raise hand and wait patiently
  - ask three peers for assistance before asking the teacher

- Knowing what to do when work is completed
  - turn the work in to an assignment basket
  - turn the work in to an assignment binder
  - hand the work to the teacher
- Knowing how to complete make-up work
  - ask the teacher for assignments missed
  - ask a peer for assignments missed
  - complete the work by the next day for complete credit
  - turn the work in to the absent basket
- Knowing how to participate in classroom discussions
  - need to raise hand
  - may talk out without raising hand
- Knowing how the class period begins
  - begin journal writing upon entering the classroom
  - visit with friends until teacher calls the class to order
- Knowing when it is all right to get out of seat
  - need permission from the teacher to leave the seat
  - may get up and move about the room as needed
- Knowing how to return materials
  - all materials are to be left on top of desks
  - all materials are to be returned to shelves in the back of the room

The teaching of routines to students through practice can be paramount to a child's success in a learning environment. This can be especially true for individuals with disabilities, because many times they move among many different types of learning environments (e.g., general education classroom, gym for physical therapy) and routines vary from one setting to another. For example, in one setting students may be encouraged to call out as needed, whereas in another, students are expected to raise their hands before speaking. Students who move among different learning environments may confuse the routines and thus fail to follow them. Instead of seeing this mistake as misbehavior, the teacher should explain the routine to the student and provide an opportunity for the student to practice it.

Systems for Supporting Positive Behavior

A proactive manager puts into place some type of system for supporting positive behavior. Systems may be highly complex (e.g., level systems) or simple (e.g., use of praise).

Token economies

Many teachers find it helpful to begin the school year with some system of reinforcement for positive behavior. They may implement a token economy. They assign point values to certain behaviors, and students accumulate points that they can cash in for reinforcers. For example, students may earn points for participating in discussions, for working well as a group during a cooperative learning activity, or for completing assignments. Reinforcers may be tangible reinforcers (e.g., small piece of candy, a pencil), social reinforcers (e.g., social praise, a positive note sent home), or privileges (e.g., homework pass to be excused from one homework assignment, taking a note to the office). Other reinforcers include stickers, tutoring or one-on-one time with the teacher or a peer, being the first person in line, computer time, free time, opportunity to lead the class in an activity, and reading time. Students earn points for their individual behaviors in this type of token economy.

Another type of token economy is based on the use of table points or class points. In a table-point system, the teacher awards points to tables (groups of children working at a table or at desks pushed together to form a tablelike work area) when they exhibit appropriate and desired behavior. Teachers award points to tables that appear ready to begin a new task, those ready to line up for lunch, or those that have put away supplies. These points may then be turned in for group reinforcers at the conclusion of the day, the week, or some longer period of time.

Class points may be earned in similar ways. A common approach to class points is the use of a marble jar. Each time the class is engaged in appropriate behavior, a marble is tossed into a glass jar. Students work to fill the jar and when it is filled receive a group reinforcer, such as having a pizza or popcorn party or viewing a movie.

Level systems

Another reinforcement system common to some special education classrooms is the level system. A level system consists of a number of levels (generally between 3 and 5) that students move through. Each successive level requires more positive behavior, which is paired with more student privileges. For example, the first level may highly restrict students' interactions with others. Students are greeted by the teacher or paraprofessional once they arrive at school; they are escorted to the classroom, where they remain for the entire day; their lunch is delivered to them; their trips to the restroom are chaperoned; and at the end of the day, they are escorted back to the bus. In order to move from this most restrictive level to the next level, which provides some privileges or freedom (e.g., students walk unescorted from the bus to the classroom), students must demonstrate certain types of behavior. For example, students are expected to turn in all classroom assignments and to have no more than one "blowup" during a school day. Once a child meets the criteria set for a particular level, the child advances to the next level. At the final level, the one offering the most privileges, the child is allowed to move freely about the school and participate in a wide range of classes and activities. Along with these privileges comes a set of high behavioral expectations.

Level systems are most commonly used in classrooms with individuals with emotional disturbance and/or behavioral disorders. Although level systems are quite restrictive in their early stages, they are highly effective for some of these students.

Self-management

Another approach to support positive behavior in the classroom is to teach students how to manage their own behavior. Self-management can involve students in charting their own behavior, rating their own behavior, and reflecting on their own behavior. For example, students may be asked to chart the number of times they call out and the number of times they raise their hands during a class activity. At the conclusion of the activity, students count their tallies, chart their totals for the two behaviors, and reflect on their overall behavior. Are they improving in controlling their classroom outbursts and raising their hands to request a chance to speak?

Figure 11.2 presents a countoon used by a third grade boy who was having difficulties with calling out during class. The child tallied his behaviors during class and then met with the teacher after class to discuss his behavior and the data he had collected. The child was rewarded for improving his hand-raising behavior over time.

Talking in class

▍ **FIGURE 11.2**
A Countoon Used to Support Positive Behavior

Your Name _____

Date _____   Class _____

This boy raises his hand
before he talks out.

This boy does not raise
his hand before he talks out.

Total [   ]   Total [   ]

Another strategy for self-management is the use of a checklist. Exhibit 11.5 is an example of a checklist for students to use as a reminder to bring supplies to class. Students complete the checklist upon arrival to class each day, and on Friday they review their overall performance during the week. They can tally the number of supplies they remembered each day or tally the total for the week, comparing their performance to the previous week's. Through use of the self-management checklist, students begin to take ownership of their behavior and take responsibility for bringing the necessary supplies to class.

Student Name _____   Week of _____

SUPPLIES	MONDAY	TUESDAY	WEDNESDAY	THURSDAY	FRIDAY
pencil					
paper					
binder					
textbook					

EXHIBIT 11.5

Self-Management Checklist

A very common self-management approach is the use of an assignment sheet or an assignment binder. The assignment sheet can be organized by subject or class period. Students write in their assignments on a daily basis. A more sophisticated format for older students may be needed to capture long-term assignments, in addition to daily assignments.

Some schools use assignment binders, sometimes called "reminder-binders." The binder is a calendar provided to each student at the beginning of the year. The binder provides spaces for recording daily and long-term assignments. Teachers generally agree among themselves on procedures for using these binders. They ask students to write in their assignments at the end of each period, and they check students' binders on a daily or weekly basis. Some binders also have space to include important school dates and events, as well as studying and testing-taking tips.

Another common self-management technique is to have students rate their own behavior. The teacher may ask the children to rate their behavior at the completion of an activity. The teacher may prompt students to consider to what extent they participated in the activity; the extent to which they contributed to the activity and advanced their own learning and the learning of others; and the manner in which they responded to the questions, ideas, and needs of others. This rating of behavior may also be done at the end of the day and/or at the end of the week. The self-ratings, along with teacher reports, may be sent home to parents daily, weekly, or once in each six- or nine-week grading period. Not only do these self-ratings raise students' awareness of their own behavior, but they serve as a formative tool for the teacher and parent.

We mentioned only a few of the proactive behavior supports available to teachers. All have their advantages and disadvantages. It is the teacher's responsibility to design and implement the behavioral approach that is most appropriate for his or her students. These strategies may be changed as the school year progresses and as students assume more responsibility for controlling their own behavior. Remember that a proactive manager plans ahead and establishes rules, routines, and systems that will support students' positive behavior in the classroom.

THEORY TO PRACTICE

➡ Observe the behavior support techniques employed by a classroom teacher. What seem to be the classroom routines? What is the teacher's behavior support system? How do the students respond to this system? What impact does this system have on the climate within the classroom?

➡ Interview a special education teacher about her or his way of providing positive behavior supports within the classroom. What does the teacher find most challenging? What practices does the teacher find most important to the overall running of the classroom? What recommendations does the teacher have for a new teacher trying to establish a classroom environment with positive behavior supports?

➡ As a teacher what do you consider most important when it comes to supporting positive student behavior in the classroom? What routines do you identify as essential to teach students? What rules will you have in your classroom? What type of behavior system will you put in place? How will you account for student differences and needs when setting up your plan?

GROUPING ARRANGEMENTS

Another consideration for creating a positive and supportive context for learning is the type of grouping arrangements students experience when learning. Grouping arrangements include individualized instruction, dyads, cooperative learning groups, and large groups.

Individualized Instruction

One type of individualized instruction occurs when curriculum and activities are specifically designed to meet the individual student's needs. This requires the custom designing of assignments for individual students. Another form of individualized instruction occurs when students complete tasks alone. The task itself may be required of all students in the setting, but individuals complete it on their own, without the assistance of others. Working independently gives students opportunities to assess their own learning and understanding and gives teachers opportunities to gain insight into the strategies students are applying to accomplish a task, into the effectiveness of those strategies, and insight into new strategies that are needed for further skill development.

The inclusion of some form of individualized instruction is essential to providing a balanced program. Some students excel when working individually and become frustrated or bored if they must complete all activities in pairs or in small or large groups. Additionally, requiring students to complete some tasks on their own serves as a formative assessment for teachers—allowing them to determine the extent to which an individual student is grasping concepts and applying skills. If all work is done in pairs or groups, it is much more difficult for a teacher to determine the progress individual students are making and to identify areas needing additional instruction or practice.

Dyads

A dyad consists of two individuals working together. Tutoring is a common dyad arrangement. One form of tutoring is *reciprocal tutoring*. In their study of reciprocal tutoring, Gartner and Riessman (1994) recruited high school students to serve as tutors who would help newly arrived students become acclimated to the school and school policies and routines and assist them in completing homework assignments. The following semester, several of the tutees were asked to serve as tutors for newly incoming students. Gartner and Riessman (1994) discovered that as students prepared to become tutors, they became more open to receiving assistance and more motivated to learn. Further, the opportunity to help someone else made them feel that they were contributing and valuable members of the school community, served to reduce the stigma associated with needing and receiving assistance, and resulted in the development of positive attitudes among the students at the school.

Classwide peer tutoring is another form of tutoring. Students work in pairs and during their time together take turns serving as both tutor and tutee. A common example in reading is to assign the role of tutee to one student who reads a selected passage aloud and then answers questions posed by the other student, the tutor. At the end of 15 minutes or so, the students switch roles: the tutee becomes the tutor, listening to his or her partner read and answering questions.

Classwide peer tutoring can be applied across multiple grades and subjects. For example, high school students may assist one another in preparing for an upcoming test through classwide peer tutoring. Students take turns quizzing each other on the material, using a study guide and class notes. Classwide peer tutoring can also be used to practice procedures for solving problems. When assuming the role of tutor, the student is required to verbalize the steps of the problem-solving process as the pair works through a problem. Students then switch roles, allowing the partner an opportunity to assume role of tutor, verbalizing and applying his or her strategy to a new problem.

Another form of tutoring is *cross-age tutoring*. Two students of different ages work together in a tutoring dyad. Like peer and classwide tutoring, cross-age tutoring can be arranged to assist students in gaining academic and behavioral skills. For example, Cochran, Feng, Cartledge, and Hamilton (1993) arranged for fourth and fifth graders with behavioral disorders to tutor second grade low-achieving students in sight word recognition. Tutors participated in a five-day training program and then tutored low-achieving second graders over an eight-week period. At the conclusion of the tutoring, both tutees and tutors demonstrated enhanced sight word recognition, exhibited positive social interactions during tutoring sessions, and were rated by their teachers as demonstrating more favorable social behavior.

The *buddy system* offers students another way to work in dyads. A new student in a school or class may be assigned a buddy who will show the newcomer where things are in the classroom and where the lunchroom is and inform the newcomer of school rules. The buddy system may also be used to enhance students' interpersonal and communicative skills. In a high school buddy program in Washington state, general education juniors and seniors volunteered to serve as buddies to peers with severe disabilities. The buddies received training in how to be a buddy and then worked with the students two or three times a week. As a result, students with severe disabilities were more included in the school environment, ate in the cafeteria with their buddies, participated in breaks, and attended school events such as assemblies. The buddy system allowed these students to become part of the overall school community.

Creating effective dyads can be challenging. The "Make It Happen" feature provides some suggestions for getting started.

MAKE IT HAPPEN
Creating Effective Dyads

- Prepare students for dyad work (e.g., develop their social skills such as how to give a partner support or how to respond to conflicts).
- Set clear expectations of what is to occur in dyad work.
- When first starting dyad work, limit the amount of time students work together. This time can be gradually increased as they become more comfortable working with one another.
- Consider students' strengths and challenges when forming pairs.
- Pairing very high with very low achievers may result in conflict and students may experience difficulties in developing an equally beneficial relationship. Individuals may benefit more when paired with peers whose levels of proficiency are similar to or only slightly different from their own.
- Periodically change pairs so students have opportunities to work with other peers.
- Include debriefing sessions during which dyads discuss how things are going and what individuals can do to improve their time together.
- When conflict breaks out within a dyad, have the students attempt to resolve the issue. The teacher should be the last resort for conflict resolution.

Cooperative Learning Groups

Cooperative learning groups is another grouping arrangement. Johnson, Johnson, and Holubec (1994) define cooperative learning as "the instructional use of small groups that allows students to work together to maximize their own and each other's learning" (p. 3). Numerous studies document the positive relationship between cooperative learning and student academic achievement (e.g., Jenkins, Jewell, Leicester, O'Connor, Jenkins, & Troutner, 1994), and a small number of studies address the effect of cooperative learning activities on student behavior (Battistich, Solomon, & Delucchi, 1993).

Johnson, Johnson, and Holubec (1994) identify five essential components of cooperative learning. These components and related interventions, drawn from the work of Johnson, Johnson, and Holubec (1994) and others, are described in Table 11.3.

TABLE 11.3 FIVE ESSENTIAL COMPONENTS OF COOPERATIVE LEARNING

COMPONENT	DEFINITION	INTERVENTIONS
Positive Interdependence	Each member of the group is responsible for learning the information and responsible for ensuring all other group members learn the information as well.	• Define different criteria for group members (Stainback & Stainback, 1992). • Vary amounts of material to be learned by group members (Stainback & Stainback, 1992). • Establish a common goal for the group. • Provide materials that must be shared among group members. • Assign different tasks to group members (Stainback & Stainback, 1992).
Face-to-Face Promotive Interaction	Students work to help each other learn and be successful.	• Teach students to provide assistance to one another. • Encourage students to encourage each other and to act in trusting ways toward one another. • Encourage students to exchange and share needed resources. • Provide feedback to groups as they work.
Individual Accountability and Personal Responsibility	Each group member contributes his or her fair share, doing his or her part in assisting the group in achieving goals and completing tasks.	• Keep cooperative groups small. • Give individual tests to measure the learning of each group member. • Observe and record how often each group member contributes to the group. • Ask individual group members to explain what is happening and what is being learned. • Tailor what students are to learn that will reflect their skill levels and goals. • Provide for a variety of ways to demonstrate understanding (e.g., writing, orally telling, drawing, use of an augmentative device).
Interpersonal and Small-Group Skills	Students develop social skills needed to work together and respond to the needs and feelings of each other.	• Prior to having students work in cooperative groups, provide training in pro-social skills in the following four areas: 　forming—moving together as a group, using quiet voices while working as a group 　functioning—stating the purpose of the assignment, asking questions, providing assistance 　formulating—assigning roles such as summarizer, elaboration seeker, and explainer 　fermenting—asking for justification of an idea, extending a group member's idea
Group Processing	Group members analyze and reflect on what happened as they worked together as a group.	• At the conclusion of an activity or session, ask the group, either individually or as a whole, to identify what went well and what was difficult for the group. • If a group had difficulties getting along or completing an assignment, have group members problem-solve what they could do next time to prevent the problem from recurring. • Have group members problem-solve what they could do next time to include everyone more actively in the activity (e.g., adapting materials for a student with a visual impairment).

Primary Source: Johnson, Johnson, and Holubec (1994).

Many adaptations and modifications may be necessary to achieve these five components when working with a diverse group of students. Stainback and Stainback (1992) describe how a cooperative learning activity was adapted to meet the needs of junior high students without disabilities and their collaborative group member with multiple disabilities. One goal of the student with multiple disabilities was to increase the frequency of vocalizations. As the group worked together on a frog dissection activity, the students implemented a program to engage the student in vocalizing his ideas. In this way, the general education students completed the dissection activity (their goal) while the student with the multiple disabilities worked toward increased vocalization (his goal).

As students work in cooperative groups, teachers assume the role of facilitator, not the provider of information. Teachers facilitate groups as they work and do not intercede and interject their ideas into the group process. When first working with cooperative learning groups, teachers may find it difficult to take a back seat when students are in conflict, are unable to arrive at a conclusion, or do not seem to understand concepts or skills. However, for cooperative learning to be effective, students need ample opportunities to solve problems as a group first and then, and only then, resort to asking the teacher for assistance. Of course, the structuring of the task and the setting up of the groups are paramount to the creation of successful cooperative learning group situations—and the teacher's greatest contribution is in these areas.

Teachers may need to intercede when students with disabilities are included in cooperative groups for the first time. Many times, students find supportive and productive ways of including students with disabilities, and many students with disabilities find ways for their own participation. But sometimes teacher guidance is needed to assist groups in including students with disabilities in group discussions and activities. Students may need to be made aware of how to communicate with the student and how the student will communicate ideas to them. The student may communicate needs and ideas through gestures (e.g., head movements, blinking of the eyes) or through the use of a communication device. Students in the group will need to become familiar with this system of communication in order to respond to it. Students may also need assistance in including a student who has limited reading and writing skills. Discussions of differences and the importance of ensuring that each group member contributes to the group and is held accountable for learning can lead children to come up with ways to include everyone.

When forming groups, teachers may consider friendships, behavioral patterns, and levels of understanding, sometimes forming heterogeneous groups or more homogeneous groups, depending on the purpose of the task. It is also helpful to alter the group membership periodically. Some group members may work very well together and want to remain as a group, whereas other groups may experience great difficulty in getting along with one another. Although one of the purposes of cooperative learning is to provide students opportunities to resolve conflicts and learn to work with others toward common goals, it is also good to change group membership so groupings do not become stale and students become too frustrated or too comfortable with the workings of their group.

Large Groups

Although we tend to think of large groups only in traditional lecture formats, large groups may engage in topic discussions, view videos and discuss their content, and view multimedia presentations of course content. Successfully carrying out large-group activities, however, can be especially challenging. If students are at different readiness levels for the material being presented, some students are likely to become frustrated and others bored because the information is either too advanced or too elementary. Also, large-group instruction places increased demands on student motivation and attention; students must be able to self-regulate and find ways to remain attentive to what is being presented.

One approach for increasing students' participation and their accountability for learning and engagement is to use response cards. Heward and colleagues (1996) define response cards as "cards, signs, or items (such as felt boards) that are simultaneously held up by all students in the class to display their responses to questions or problems presented by the teacher" (p. 5). These authors identify several benefits offered by response cards. They allow all students to respond to all questions raised in the class. They help students learn from each other by watching the responses peers make to questions. And teachers can evaluate students' understanding quickly by reviewing their responses.

Another approach for managing large-group instruction is the numbered-heads-together strategy (Kagan, 1989–1990). Students are organized into heterogeneous learning groups of four students and each member of the group is assigned a number from 1 through 4. The teacher presents information to the entire group and then pauses to ask a question. The group members turn to each other, discuss the question and their proposed response, and ensure that each member has the response for the question. The teacher then summons the class back together as a single group and calls out a number from 1 through 4. Students with the number called are responsible for presenting their group answer to the entire class. The "Make It Happen" feature provides some more suggestions for working with large groups.

MAKE IT HAPPEN
Large-Group Instruction

- Provide clear expectations at the beginning of the session.
- Encourage active participation through group responses, choral responses, and student voting.
- Require students to be accountable for their participation and learning through use of shared pairs (turning to a peer and discussing what was learned and what questions the peer has), quizzes, and questioning.
- Break up long, large-group activities into short blocks, allowing for breaks and time to move about the room.
- Alternate between teacher-dominated and student-dominated activities during large-group activities (e.g., after presenting information using the overhead projector, have students take a moment to write questions they have about the content, then let students ask and answer questions among themselves, with the teacher as facilitator).

In summary, there are multiple grouping arrangements available for instruction. Regardless of the type of grouping arrangement selected, teachers must ensure that all students are presented avenues through which to participate and that grouping structures are responsive to students' needs. For example, a student with a hearing loss may have difficulty hearing the comments of group members if several groups work close to one another. Finding additional space for groups to meet, strictly enforcing volume levels, or using augmentative devices to aid the student's hearing (e.g., FM systems that amplify sounds) may be necessary for this student to be able to benefit fully from the learning experience.

Attending to behavioral, social, and attention needs is also critical. If students are asked to work individually or in groups for long periods of time, some students may need accommodations if they are to be successful. Allowing them to break tasks into small segments and allowing for movement (e.g., getting out of their seats) between segments may assist students in being successful in this grouping situation. Also, as emphasized in the discussion of cooperative learning, students need to be prepared to work effectively as group members. Teaching students how to get along with one another, how to ask for help, and how to resolve conflicts is imperative if students are to benefit from group work.

THEORY TO PRACTICE

➡ Observe cooperative groups at work. Select one group of students to focus on during your observation. Analyze how they are demonstrating or failing to demonstrate the five elements of cooperative learning identified by Johnson, Johnson, and Holubec (1994) (see Table 11.3). What recommendations would you make for supporting students in this group to demonstrate the five elements of cooperative learning?

➡ Observe a pair of students working together on an assignment. Capture in field notes the types of questions they ask one another, the comments they make to one another, and the overall tone of their interaction. Analyze your notes to determine the overall effectiveness of the pair's work together. In what areas did the pair work extremely well to support each other's learning and success? In what areas did the pair struggle? If you were the teacher of this classroom and were going to have students work in pairs on an activity, how would you prepare the students for their pair work in order to build on the strengths you identified and to help them overcome some of the challenges you observed in your pair?

CHAPTER SUMMARY

This chapter introduces the importance of creating a context for learning and all the factors that go into the creation of this learning environment, including teacher and student attributes. Included in this discussion is an overview of the strategies and techniques a proactive manager uses in the classroom and an explanation of grouping arrangements available for instruction.

CHAPTER 12

Providing Quality Instruction through Planning

Read to find out the following:
- features of quality instruction
- how planning leads to quality instruction
- written formats that may be used to plan instruction

Establishing a positive context for learning (the subject of Chapter 11) is the first step in designing meaningful and effective instruction. The next step is to consider elements essential to quality instruction—instruction that is responsive to students' needs and interests; takes into consideration their learning styles, prior knowledge, strengths, and challenges; and that results in student development in cognitive, affective, behavior, and language domains—and foremost, incorporates those essential elements into instructional planning. In this chapter we address both of these issues: the elements of quality instruction and procedures and written formats for instruction planning.

QUALITY INSTRUCTION

Quality instruction takes into consideration all of the elements identified in Chapter 11 and brings them to life in the classroom through the application of meaningful and effective teaching behaviors. A teacher who considers carefully the factors of an instructional context conducive to learning begins by responding to those factors through the adoption of teaching behaviors that support students' active engagement in learning.

Lists of teaching behaviors have been developed to describe what constitutes quality instruction. Rosenshine and Stevens (1986), through review of process-product research on effective teaching practices, identify six specific instructional functions exhibited by effective teachers: (a) reviewing and reteaching information previously taught; (b) presenting new information clearly; (c) combining supervised practice activities and checking for understanding; (d) providing immediate positive and corrective feedback, combined with reteaching as necessary; (e) providing independent practice opportunities; and (f) incorporating weekly and monthly reviews of concepts and skills.

Haberman (1991) has a different view of what constitutes effective teaching behaviors. Haberman begins by describing something he calls the pedagogy of poverty. According to Haberman, certain teaching practices, when "Taken together and performed to the systematic exclusion of other acts" (p. 291), become the "pedagogy of poverty."

These practices include "giving information, asking questions, giving directions, making assignments, monitoring seatwork, reviewing assignments, giving tests, reviewing tests, assigning homework, reviewing homework, settling disputes, punishing noncompliance, marking papers, and giving grades" (p. 291). The list includes practices commonly found in classrooms—practices adopted by both good and weak teachers. Haberman's point in listing these elements and labeling them as a unit the "pedagogy of poverty" is to emphasize that if these are the primary practices occurring in classrooms, together they create an instructional situation that fails to lead students to critical thinking and application of knowledge (among other skills), and limits what students learn and can learn through instruction.

Knapp and Shields (1992) have similar concerns about instructional practices taking place in schools and suggested in the literature. Their work focuses primarily on the needs of students they identify as disadvantaged and those at risk for academic failure. They argue that these students are continually shortchanged by the type of instruction they receive. In their argument for the need to reconceptualize instructional approaches for teaching students identified as disadvantaged, or as children of poverty, Knapp and Shields call for a reevaluation of the following tenets of instruction: (a) heavy reliance on teacher-directed learning, (b) rapid pacing of instruction, (c) frequent feedback, (d) multiple opportunities for review and practice, and (e) homogeneous grouping of students. Knapp and Shields (1992) argue that these approaches

> *may limit the learning of children by not encouraging analytical or conceptual skills, by failing to nurture the ability to express oneself orally or in writing, by repetitively exposing children to the same material, or by failing to provide a larger meaning or purpose to learning.* (p. 5)

Both Haberman (1991) and Knapp and Shields (1992) offer suggestions for improving instructional practice in school and for moving beyond what they refer to as a limited view of instructional practice. Knapp and Shield identify the following principles as essential ingredients for instruction when working with disadvantaged students: (a) maximized time on task, (b) high expectations and a school climate that supports academic learning, and (c) strengthened parent involvement in supporting instruction. Haberman (1991) proposes good teaching as students (a) dealing with issues important to them; (b) addressing issues dealing with differences among people; (c) working with "big ideas," not just isolated facts; (d) planning activities; (e) "applying ideals such as fairness, equity, or justice to their world" (p. 293); (f) being actively involved in learning; (g) working in heterogeneous learning groups; (h) analyzing, synthesizing, and evaluating ideas; (i) revising and rethinking their work; (j) using technology to gather information; and (k) reflecting on their own beliefs and actions. Implied in both sets of suggestions is the importance of students working with each other, dialoguing about their experiences, and sharing their thinking and problem-solving processes.

Review of these different proposals of elements of quality instruction reveals two different philosophies toward instruction. One is more teacher directed and focused on the transmission of ideas and skills from teacher to student. The other calls for increased student-to-student learning, that is, students' ownership of their own learning and learning experiences, and increased emphasis on the social nature of learning.

The first view places the teacher at the center of the instructional experience. The teacher is the provider of information and the person who continually monitors for student understanding. Many of Rosenshine and Stevens's (1986) suggestions seem to apply to this model: opening lessons with a goal statement, reviewing prerequisite skills, introducing information in small steps, and so on. This model of instruction may be labeled by some as the transmission model or as a skills or mastery approach. Transmission models break down understandings and demonstrations into subskills or tasks through task analysis. Students are then introduced to these skills in a systematic, pre-determined order (Au, 1993).

One well-documented transmission model of instruction is Direct Instruction, initially developed by Bereister and Englemann (1966). According to Englemann (1996) in Direct Instruction, (a) lessons are carefully designed to be completed within a specified time period; (b) lessons are scripted (scripts provide the exact language and examples the teacher is to use during instruction and inform the teacher how she or he is to respond to various student responses); (c) multiple skills and topics are presented during each lesson; (d) students are highly engaged in responses, and their responses are considered "tests" of their understanding; and (e) periodic testing of students is completed to ensure effective teaching.

As detailed by Englemann (1996), teaching with Direct Instruction consists of mechanical and interactive details. Mechanical details have to do with organizing for instruction, including beginning lessons on time, pacing instruction at a rate appropriate to students' needs, precisely following the script provided, and projecting a positive attitude throughout. Interactive details include the following: (a) forming very homogeneous groups, (b) specifying expectations to students, (c) using praise, and (d) using positive reinforcement.

Although at first Direct Instruction may seem too highly structured and somewhat offensive to teachers (e.g., the use of scripts), the systematic procedures employed in this instructional program have proven to be effective in over 50 research studies (Englemann, 1996). Additionally, more than 35 studies have compared Direct Instruction with other approaches and found it to be superior in student outcomes (Englemann, 1996). Moreover, Donahue (1996) has identified the empirical truths about Direct Instruction, including that Direct Instruction is effective at teaching both higher-order problem solving as well as basic academic skills and strategies, has a positive effect on students' self-concepts and affective learning, has long-lasting effects, and is challenging and rewarding for teachers. However, this type of instructional model raises the concerns identified by Knapp and Shields (1992) and Haberman (1991)—hence, the presentation of an alternative approach.

In contrast to the teacher-centered and teacher-directed approach, this second approach places the student at the center of instruction as the individual constructing knowledge and making connections. In this model, the teacher assumes a more facilitative role, referred to as scaffolding, and guides and supports students as they learn. This second view is reflective of the social constructivist approach. The constructivist approach places emphasis on students constructing knowledge by building on their prior knowledge and experiences while being supported by teachers who serve as facilitators and guides. Reflecting these beliefs and drawing from the work of Vygotsky (1978), Au (1993) defines this approach to instruction in this way:

> *helping the student to become interested and involved in a meaningful activity, then providing the student with the support needed to complete the activity successfully. (p. 40)*

Within this model, learning is a social process in which students construct knowledge through interactions and work with capable and knowledgeable peers and others in the learning environment (Vygotsky, 1978). Students learn from one another, as well as from the teacher. Scaffolding is used to support students as they engage in learning. Scaffolding is defined by Au (1993) as

> *help provided while the child is engaged in a meaningful task. The child does everything he can, and the adult provides the assistance needed so that the child can complete the task successfully. (p. 41)*

The type and extent of scaffolding provided are determined by the needs of the student and thus the student is responsible for the majority of the work and learning required for task completion.

Au (1993) identifies many advantages of the constructivist model as compared to the transmission model. One advantage she cites is that a constructivist approach to instruction places all learning within a social context. This means that skills are not taught in isolation but rather are presented within authentic tasks. For example, students learn how to add and subtract decimals when purchasing supplies for a class science project, instead of learning to perform the skills by completing worksheets of problems. Another advantage cited by Au (1993) is that a constructivist model is "student-centered rather than skill-driven" (p. 45). This is one of the primary concerns raised by Knapp and Shields (1992)—namely, that for many students identified as at risk for academic failure, the curriculum places too much emphasis on the mastery of isolated, discrete skills. As Knapp and Shield (1992) argue, many students identified as at risk for academic failure may become bored with such a curriculum because they see no relevance in what they are learning—the curriculum does not appear to connect with their current or future lives or is not personally meaningful.

Brooks and Brooks (1993) compare the transmission model with the more recently emphasized model of the constructivist classroom. This comparison, presented in Exhibit 12.1, highlights the differences between the transmission model (called "traditional classrooms" in the exhibit) and the constructivist model ("constructivist classrooms").

EXHIBIT 12.1 **Brooks and Brooks's Comparison of Traditional and Constructivist Classrooms**	TRADITIONAL CLASSROOMS	CONSTRUCTIVIST CLASSROOMS
	Curriculum is presented part to whole, with emphasis on basic skills.	Curriculum is presented whole to part, with emphasis on big concepts.
	Strict adherence to fixed curriculum is highly valued.	Pursuit of student questions is highly valued.
	Curricular activities rely heavily on textbooks and workbooks.	Curricular activities rely heavily on primary sources of data and manipulative materials.
	Students are viewed as "blank slates" onto which information is etched by the teacher.	Students are viewed as thinkers with emerging theories about the world.
	Teachers generally behave in a didactic manner, disseminating information to students.	Teachers generally behave in an interactive manner, mediating the environment for students.
	Teachers seek the correct answer to validate student learning.	Teachers seek the students' points of view in order to understand students' present conceptions for use in subsequent lessons.
	Assessment of student learning is viewed as separate from teaching and occurs almost entirely through testing.	Assessment of student learning is interwoven with teaching and occurs through teacher observations of students at work and through student exhibitions and portfolios.
	Students primarily work alone.	Students primarily work in groups.

Source: From *In Search of Understanding: The Case of Constructivist Classrooms* (p. 17), by J. G. Brooks and M. G. Brooks, 1993, Alexandria, VA: Association for Supervision and Curriculum Development. Copyright © 1994 ASCD. Used by permission. All rights reserved.

As with all models, many times extremes are used to demonstrate differences. However, there are similarities across these two instructional models, and, further, both have a place in special education instructional practice together because they offer varied and

FIGURE 12.1
Quality Instruction Pyramid

• adopt formative
assessment techniques
• engage students in self- and peer-assessment
activities
**FREQUENTLY AND CONSISTENTLY ASSESS STU-
DENT LEARNING AND ACHIEVEMENT**

• incorporate activities and experiences that embrace multiple intelligences • incorporate and respond to students' needs
when designing instruction
ALLOW FOR MULTIPLE EXPRESSIONS OF UNDERSTANDING

• provide students opportunities to dialogue with one another and with the
teacher through shared pairs, cooperative learning, paired learning • encourage
students to ask and answer questions • avoid public criticism • create leadership
roles for students
ENSURE ACTIVE STUDENT INVOLVEMENT AND ACCOUNTABILITY

• provide multiple practice opportunities when attempting new skills • attend to students'
challenges, especially those due to disability, and modify as needed • connect students' prior
knowledge and experience with content • consider clarity, complexity, and format when giving instruction • provide immediate and specific feedback
INCORPORATE PROMPTING, CUING, AND SCAFFOLDING INTO INSTRUCTION

• select materials that reflect student, family, and community cultures • select materials that represent a range of
ability, talents, and interests • place community materials in locations where they are accessible to all students
MAKE A VARIETY OF MATERIALS FOR LEARNING AVAILABLE AND ACCESSIBLE TO STUDENTS

• engage students in metacognitive activities • provide a balance between teacher-centered and student-centered instruction,
highly structured and open-ended activities • encourage students to articulate their thinking processes and problem-solving
strategies • provide students opportunities to apply ideas and understandings to authentic tasks • teach students strategies and
problem-solving approaches
FOCUS ON PROBLEM SOLVING AND CRITICAL THINKING

• determine whether to move from whole to part or to start with task analysis of isolated skills based on curricular demands and students'
strengths, needs, challenges, and interests • arrange curriculum and experiences in ways that capitalize on students' interests, needs, strengths,
challenges, and readiness • build students' skills over time
PROVIDE SYSTEMATIC LEARNING OPPORTUNITIES

• prepare students and plan for transitions • be organized • make students accountable for learning and using their free time effectively • plan for instruction
USE CLASS TIME WISELY

• select curriculum and activities that reflect student interests and abilities • help students make links between what they are learning and what they need to know
and be able to do in their lives outside school • include community-based activities
SELECT CURRICULUM AND RELATED ACTIVITIES THAT ARE MEANINGFUL TO STUDENTS' CURRENT AND FUTURE LIFE ROLES

• revisit building blocks in Chapter 11
CREATE A SUPPORTIVE, NURTURING, SAFE ENVIRONMENT

• develop a collaborative spirit among adults • share ideas openly and honestly • deal with conflict and resolve issues • recognize each other's expertise • celebrate successes
WORK COLLABORATIVELY WITH PARENTS, ADMINISTRATORS, AND SUPPORT STAFF

needed ways to meet the unique needs of individuals. When it comes to instruction, there is more than one answer as to what is the best approach. This is especially true when we consider the heterogeneity of today's student population. Being prepared to teach in only one way, or with only one approach, limits what teachers can offer students. Therefore, it is imperative for teachers to embrace a wide variety of approaches and become familiar with their own strengths and weaknesses in order to be able to make informed decisions about their instructional approach to their teaching selected topics to select groups of students.

In an effort to synthesize this information and present an overall frame of what constitutes quality instruction, we have developed a quality instruction pyramid of suggested practices, incorporating the best from both of these models (see Figure 12.1). The practices presented at the bottom of the pyramid provide the foundation from which quality instruction is built. This list of best practices is not exhaustive but rather serves as a starting point for identifying practices that constitute what we consider quality instruction.

PLANNING FOR INSTRUCTION

Planning for instruction is one of the most important responsibilities of teachers. Reys, Suydam, and Lindquist (1995) identify six reasons for careful and systematic planning: it (a) leads to the establishment of goals and objectives; (b) allows for allocation of time for achieving goals and objectives, and for sequencing content and skills; (c) results in lessons that gain students' attention, move at a good pace, and end satisfactorily; (d) holds the attention of students; (e) controls repetition—avoids unnecessary repetition while providing opportunities for systematic and needed review; and (f) assists teachers in gaining confidence in their instruction. Additional reasons for planning exist for teachers of students with disabilities. Perhaps the most important is the clarification of who will plan the actual instruction (e.g., special and general education teachers together or separately); who will record performance data (e.g., special and general education teachers); and who will make instructional decisions (e.g., special and general education teachers together or separately) (Disability Assessment Systems, 1996). In this section of the chapter we focus on the writing of instructional objectives and plans.

Writing Instructional Objectives

The starting point for writing instructional plans is to specify instructional objectives. Instructional objectives specify what students are to know and be able to do as a result of instruction. Instructional objectives lead to the achievement of IEP goals, benchmarks, and objectives, and district, state, and national goals and standards. Therefore, instructional objectives are intimately linked to the broader goals of schooling.

Like IEP objectives, instructional objectives are based on assessment findings and the specification of appropriate curriculum. When students with disabilities engage in instructional activities, the objectives of those activities should assist them in achieving their IEP benchmarks and objectives as derived through assessment of their strengths, challenges, and present and future needs and goals, as well as the objectives in curricular areas outside their IEP but essential to their overall course of study. Making links between IEP goals, benchmarks, and objectives and instructional objectives is the primary responsibility of general and special education teachers working with students with disabilities. Linking these sets of objectives requires systematic planning.

We return to the IEP for Angela presented in Chapter 1 (see Exhibit 1.2) to illustrate the development of instructional objectives from IEP goals and objectives by selecting one goal and one objective from Angela's IEP. Remember, Angela was found eligible for special education services as a student with a learning disability in the area of mathematics. As indicated on her IEP, she is to receive all instruction in the general education classroom. According to the plan, the special education teacher will design modifications of classroom mathematics activities and assignments collaboratively with the general education teacher and provide services in the general education classroom during mathematics instruction two days per week. The selected goal and objective are:

Goal: Improve money skills as measured by the annual district assessment.
Objective: Given a set of coins and bills (pennies, nickels, dimes, quarters, ones, fives, and tens) and a newspaper advertisement of items valued up to $20.00, Angela will select 5 items to purchase, will state the cost of each item orally, and will demonstrate that value using coin and bill combinations, demonstrating accuracy for 4 out of the 5 items by June.

Exhibit 12.2 provides examples of instructional objectives based on this IEP goal and objective. The general education teacher could design lessons, based on these objectives, for the entire class, for small groups, or for students working in pairs. With the assistance of the special education teacher, the general education teacher could design and deliver lessons that assist Angela in meeting these objectives as peers work on related objectives. The general and special education teacher could also decide that the special education teacher will develop lessons for Angela tailored to her specific needs and also be primarily responsible for providing these lessons to Angela and any of her classmates who could benefit from instruction in these areas.

EXHIBIT 12.2

Instructional Objectives Developed from an IEP Objective

OBJECTIVE

Given a set of coins and bills (pennies, nickels, dimes, quarters, ones, fives, and tens) and a newspaper advertisement of items valued up to $20.00, Angela will select 5 items to purchase, will state the cost of each item orally, and will demonstrate that value using coin and bill combinations, demonstrating accuracy for 4 out of the 5 items by June.

INSTRUCTIONAL OBJECTIVES

1. Presented a penny, nickel, dime, quarter, one-dollar bill, five-dollar bill, and a ten-dollar bill in random order, Angela will state the name of each coin or bill and its value orally with 100 percent accuracy.
2. Given 5 sets of at least 5 coins and 2 bills valued to $5.00, Angela will count the value of the set, state the value orally, and write the value on paper with 100 percent accuracy.
3. Given a set of at least 5 coins and 2 bills valued to $5.00 and a newspaper advertisement of items valued under $5.00, Angela will select 5 items to purchase, will state the cost of each item orally, and will demonstrate that value using coin and bill combinations, demonstrating accuracy for 4 out of the 5 items.
4. Given 5 sets of at least 5 coins and 2 bills valued to $15.00, Angela will count the value of the set, state the value orally, and write the value on paper with 100 percent accuracy.
5. Given a set of coins and bills valued to $15.00 and a newspaper advertisement of items valued under $15.00, Angela will select 5 items to purchase, will state the cost of each item orally, and will demonstrate that value using coin and bill combinations, demonstrating accuracy for 4 out of the 5 items.
6. Given 5 sets of at least 5 coins and 2 bills valued to $20.00, Angela will count the value of the set, state the value orally, and write the value on paper with 100 percent accuracy.
7. The final instructional objective may be the same as the IEP objective.

As with IEP objectives, there are many ways in which instructional objectives may be written. As this exhibit demonstrates, instructional objectives may be written in the same format as IEP objectives. We suggest that when writing instructional objectives, teachers include the components that we identified in Chapter 10 as essential for IEP objectives—behavior or performance, criterion, evaluation procedures, evaluation schedule, and conditions—because inclusion of them results in more clearly stated objectives. (The evaluation schedule may not be clearly stated in instructional plans as in IEP objectives (e.g., will be achieved by December), but be implied to be at the completion of the lesson or activity.)

The sample set of instructional objectives in Exhibit 12.2 is very linear and is based on a task analysis of what Angela will need to be able to do in order to achieve the final objective. This is not the only way in which instructional objectives can be derived for lesson planning, however. Exhibit 12.3 presents another set of instructional objectives for the same IEP objective. These instructional objectives represent a sequence of tasks Angela will work through to achieve the final objective, but each objective reflects her participation in the authentic task of using coins and bills to purchase items.

EXHIBIT 12.3

Instructional Objectives: The Big Picture

IEP OBJECTIVE

Given a set of coins and bills (pennies, nickels, dimes, quarters, ones, fives, and tens) and a newspaper advertisement of items valued up to $20.00, Angela will select 5 items to purchase, will orally state the cost of each item, and will demonstrate that value using coin and bill combinations, demonstrating accuracy for 4 out of the 5 items by June.

INSTRUCTIONAL OBJECTIVES

1. Given a newspaper article of items valued up to $5.00 and working in cooperative groups, students will identify at least 5 items they wish to purchase, will list those items on a piece of paper, and will write the amount that each item costs with 100 percent accuracy.
2. Referring to their list of items they want to purchase, students will write the items in order, with the item costing the most listed first, onto a money matrix grid with 100 percent accuracy.
3. Using their money matrix and a set of coins and bills, students will work in pairs to create at least two different coin and bill combinations they could use to purchase each of the 5 items, with at least 8 of the 10 combinations representing possible combinations that do not include excessive coins or bills.
4. Given a newspaper article of items valued up to $15.00 and working in cooperative groups, students will identify at least 5 items they wish to purchase, will list those items on a piece of paper, and will record the amount that each item costs with 100 percent accuracy.
5. Referring to their list of items they want to purchase, students will write the items in order, with the item costing the most listed first, onto a money matrix grid with 100 percent accuracy.
6. Using their money matrix and a set of coins and bills, students will work in pairs to create at least two different coin and bill combinations they could use to purchase each of the 5 items, with at least 8 of the 10 combinations representing possible combinations and combinations that do not include excessive coins or bills.
7. Using a money matrix and a set of coins and bills, and working independently, Angela will work to create at least two different coin and bill combinations she could use to purchase each of the 5 items, each valued up to $15.00, with at least 8 of the 10 combinations representing possible combinations that do not include excessive coins or bills.
8. The final objective may be the same as the IEP objective.

These two sets of instructional objectives can be interpreted as representing the two approaches to quality instruction discussed earlier. The objectives listed in Exhibit 12.2 are based on task analysis and the mastery of subskills and are appropriately linked with the transmission model. The objectives listed in Exhibit 12.3 are more reflective of a holistic, constructivist approach: students work on the authentic goal or task from the start—only the complexity of the task is sequenced to reflect greater understanding over time. The constructivist approach may also have Angela begin working with the $20.00 objective and, aided by supports in the form of scaffolding, develop the strategies she needs to solve the problem.

Once instructional objectives are written, teachers are challenged to write plans that assist students in achieving those objectives. There are a number of ways in which instructional plans may be written.

Writing Instructional Plans

A primary component of designing meaningful lessons is the actual writing of those lessons based on instructional objectives and selected activities. All teachers, regardless of their years of experience, need to plan systematically for instruction. Plans may represent what is to be learned in instructional units during an academic year, during a semester or a quarter of instruction. An instructional unit is a set of lessons and/or experiences focused on a particular theme that lasts one to several weeks.

Year, quarter, and unit plans

Exhibit 12.4 presents a plan that reflects year, quarter, and instructional unit planning. This plan is an example of what a special education teacher may develop when working from a curriculum designed by Archer and Gleason (1994) in their *Skills for School Success* program. The skills outlined in this plan directly follow the curriculum proposed by the *Skills for School Success* program. This instructional plan is developed for a group of eighth grade students receiving resource room instruction in study skills. The plan focuses on three curricular areas: completing assignments, gaining information, and test-taking skills. It is very general and serves as a map for the entire year of instruction.

EXHIBIT 12.4

Planning Schematic: Year, Quarter, and Unit Plans

QUARTER 1: UNIT 1	QUARTER 2: UNIT 2	QUARTER 3: UNIT 3	QUARTER 4: UNIT 4
COMPLETING ASSIGNMENTS	**GAINING INFORMATION**	**TAKING TESTS**	**SUCCESS**
Unit 1 Objective: Applying introduced assignment completion strategies, students will complete and turn in 90% of class assignments for all class periods.	*Unit 2 Objective:* Applying strategies for gaining information from text and lecture, students will achieve at least 75% accuracy or a letter grade of C+ or better on at least 80% of their classroom assignments. Maintenance of goal of Unit 1.	*Unit 3 Objective:* Applying test-taking skills, students will achieve at least 75% accuracy on at least 80% of the test/quizzes taken during the quarter in all classes. Maintenance of goals of Units 1 and 2.	*Unit 4 Objective:* Maintenance of goals of Units 1, 2, and 3.
Activities: • strategy instruction in using an assignment sheet • instruction in organizational strategies • reteach skills/strategies as needed • instruction in self-monitoring and charting of assignments completed and turned in and matching with teachers' gradebooks on a weekly basis	*Activities:* • strategy instruction in taking notes from lectures • strategy instruction in taking notes when reading text • strategy instruction in how to self-monitor reading comprehension • strategy instruction in how to use notes and active reading strategies when completing assignments • weekly self-evaluation of lecture and reading notes taken in other classes and revision of notes as needed • reteach skills/strategies as needed • student self-monitoring and charting of assignments completed and turned in and grades earned on those assignments matched with teachers' gradebooks on a weekly basis	*Activities:* • strategy instruction for handling different tests and test question formats • practice quizzes/tests in these formats • self-evaluation of tests/quizzes completed in classes to identify areas of difficulty and develop strategies to overcome them • reteach skills/strategies as needed • student self-monitoring and charting of assignments completed, grades earned on those assignments, and grades earned on quizzes and tests	*Activities:* • student self-monitoring and charting of assignments completed, grades earned on those assignments, and grades earned on quizzes and tests • reteach skills/strategies as needed

Weekly plans

Exhibit 12.5 presents a weekly plan based on the plan presented in Exhibit 12.4. This plan serves to introduce the "Completing Assignments" unit. Weekly plans, too, are very general, though more specific than the year, semester, quarter, and unit plans. The weekly plan outlined in Exhibit 12.5 may be enough to guide instruction by practiced teachers. However, for beginning teachers, one more step may be necessary for effective planning and instruction—the writing of detailed daily lesson plans.

EXHIBIT 12.5

The First Weekly Plan for Unit 1: "Completing Assignments"

MONDAY	TUESDAY	WEDNESDAY	THURSDAY	FRIDAY
Objective: • Given an assignment sheet for recording assignments for all classes, students will orally define the components of the assignment sheet, write the three steps for completing the sheet, and write a personal goal specifying the number of assignments he/she will turn in by the end of the week. *Activities:* • introduce assignment sheet • identify/explain the purpose of each component of the sheet • write out the steps for completing the assignment sheet • model the setting of a personal goal for completing assignments and the assignment sheet	*Objective:* • Students will self-evaluate the use of the assignment sheet and chart the number of assignments due so far this week and the number of assignments completed and turned in, charting with 100% accuracy. *Activities:* • review assignment sheet process • discuss any problems and brainstorm solutions • model how assignments given and completed are charted • have students chart their assignment completion rates • have students evaluate their assignment completion rates and compare those rates with their personal goals	*Objective:* • Students will self-evaluate the use of the assignment sheet, chart the number of assignments due so far this week and the number of assignments completed and turned in, charting with 100% accuracy. • Students will develop a four-item organizational checklist for their binder. *Activities:* • review assignment sheet process and chart performance • discuss any problems and brainstorm solutions • discuss the importance of organization • have students generate a list of things they could do to have organized work binders • working in pairs, have students develop a four-item checklist of essential characteristics of an organized binder	*Objective:* • Students will organize his/her binder and present it to a peer who will evaluate it using the organizational checklist. • Students will chart assignment completion rate for the day with 100% accuracy. *Activities:* • review assignment sheet process and chart performance • discuss problems and brainstorm solutions • have students organize their binders according to their checklists • have students present their binders to others in the room for peer comment • debrief • allow students to revise their binders' organization based on peer feedback	*Objective:* • Students will chart assignment completion rate for the day with 100% accuracy. • Students will review their performance for the week, determine if they met the personal goal they had established on Monday, and write a goal for next week on a new assignment sheet. • Students will brainstorm at least 5 ways they can improve their assignment completion rates next week. *Activities:* • review assignment sheet process and chart performance • discuss problems and brainstorm solutions • review and evaluate binder organization skills using checklists • compare performance to goals • write goal for next week • brainstorm ways to improve assignment completion rates

Daily lesson plans

Regardless of curriculum content or the purpose of a lesson, effective daily lesson plans (hereafter referred to simply as lesson plans) have some common ingredients. Among the common ingredients are (a) objectives or a purpose for the lesson and their evaluation, (b) identification of what the teacher and students will be doing, (c) identification of materials and equipment needed for the lesson, and (d) organization of lesson activities. The manner in which these ingredients are organized and referred to in lesson plans may vary, but all should be included in written plans.

Reys, Suydam, and Lindquist (1995), referring to the National Council of Teachers of Mathematics (NCTM) professional standards, identify six essential lesson plan components. These components are listed in Exhibit 12.6.

- Specify the objective or objectives.
  – What are students to learn?
  – What is the purpose of the lesson?
  – Are there any prerequisites students need to know or be able to do?
- Determine class organization.
  – Will students be working in pairs, small groups, individually, or as an entire class?
- Specify procedures.
  – What teaching strategies will you use?
  – How will you gain and maintain student interest throughout the lesson?
  – What will you be doing? What will the students be doing?
  – What questions will you ask?
  – What materials will you need?
  – How will you accommodate individual needs?
  – Will there be a practice activity? Homework?
- Determine how much time will be spent on each part of the lesson.
- Identify procedures you will use to evaluate student learning throughout and at the close of the lesson.
- Write the lesson plan.

Source: Paraphrased from Reys, Suydam, & Lindquist (1995), p. 43.

> **EXHIBIT 12.6**
>
> **Essential Lesson Plan Components**

Exhibit 12.7 presents a basic lesson plan. This plan is based on a reading comprehension strategy involving the use of story grammar. Story grammar focuses attention on the overall organization of a story and calls for the identification of story elements: characters, setting, sequence of major story events, and actions of the characters. Story grammar may be very sophisticated or simple in form.

LESSON OBJECTIVE

After listening to a story read orally by the teacher, students will write the names of the three principal characters of the story, where the story took place, and what occurred at the beginning, middle, and end of the story, including each component of the story grammar and accurately reporting story information.

ORGANIZATION

- Students will complete the writing assignment working in pairs. One grade will be assigned to the pair based on the joint product.
- Students will remain at their seats during the oral reading. They will push their desks together when completing the written assignment.

(continued)

> **EXHIBIT 12.7**
>
> **A Basic Lesson Plan Format**

EXHIBIT 12.7

A Basic Lesson Plan Format
(continued)

PROCEDURES

- Review the basic story grammar introduced yesterday. Refer to a poster of the story grammar when discussing story components. (10 minutes)
- Shared pairs—following the discussion, have students turn to their partner and discuss the story grammar components. Answer questions. (3 minutes)
- Inform students that today you will be reading a story aloud and then they will work in pairs to write its story grammar.
- Introduce the story by playing one of the characters in the story—the grandmother. Change voice and become the character; have the character describe what is going to be happening in the story. (2 minutes)
- Begin reading the story, showing the pictures and using a different voice for each character. Stop and answer questions as needed. (5 minutes)
- Halfway through the story, stop and use shared pairs. Have students turn to their partners to discuss what has happened so far in the story and to discuss the story grammar components. Answer questions. (3 minutes)
- Finish reading the story. (5 minutes)
- Give directions for how the story grammar is to be written. Model the writing of the story grammar on the blackboard. Answer any questions. (5 minutes)
- Have students begin work and monitor progress. Answer questions as needed. (20 minutes)

ACCOMMODATIONS

- Make an outline grid of the story grammar available for those pairs who choose to use it.
- Allow students to draw ideas as well as write them.
- Provide copies of key illustrations students may paste into their story grammar (e.g., pictures of the three characters, picture of what occurs in the middle of the story).

MATERIALS

- Story grammar outline grid
- Photocopies of story illustrations
- Poster of story grammar
- Storybook
- General drawing supplies, scissors, and glue

EVALUATION

- Evaluate work samples to ensure that all story grammar components are included and that the information presented matches that of the story.

Exhibit 12.8 presents a lesson plan in a different format that is more detailed in design than the previous plan though consisting of the same basic components. The key components of this lesson are the *rationale* (to determine why the lesson is important); *objectives* (to specify what students are to learn and are expected to do as a result of the lesson); *motivator* (to gain students' attention and interest for the lesson); *advanced organizer* (to inform students of what is going to occur during the lesson and to specify expectations); *demonstration/modeling* (to describe the activities the teacher models and students observe and the interactions teachers and students have with one another and with lesson materials); *guided practice* (to provide students opportunities to attempt the skills on their own while receiving teacher supervision/assistance as needed); *independent practice* (to provide students opportunities to practice skills on their own with minimal teacher support); *closure* (to provide students opportunities to review lesson activities, and skills and understandings learned); and *evaluation* (to determine the extent to which students achieved the lesson objective). This lesson is similar to the seven-step plan developed by Hunter (1995). The lesson plan presented in Exhibit 12.8 is designed for three students receiving special education instructional support in language arts.

EXHIBIT 12.8

Alternative Lesson Plan Format

Subject: <u>Language Arts</u> Topic: <u>Writing a friendly letter</u> Date: <u>February 14</u>

Students: Rebecca, Nathan, and Matthew

RATIONALE
Writing friendly letters is an authentic means for practicing spelling, capitalization, and punctuation skills.

OBJECTIVE(S)
Given paper and pencil and an outline of a friendly letter, students will write a friendly letter including all of the following components, each with correct capitalization and punctuation: date, greeting, body (including at least two sentences), closing, and signature.

MATERIALS
friendly letter poster • overhead stencil of a friendly letter/overhead pen • copies of letter outline

PROCEDURES
Motivator and Advanced Organizer

- Have you ever received a letter in the mail? Who was it from? How did you feel about getting the letter? Have you ever written a letter to a friend? Why? What did you say?
- Today we are going to learn how to write a letter to a friend. We will first write letters together, and then you will have a chance to write the first draft of a letter you will send to a friend.

Demonstration/Modeling

- Show students the large poster of a sample friendly letter. Read the letter to the class.
- How many parts does a friendly letter have? What can you tell me about the parts of the letter? Why is each important? Point to each component of the letter; discuss its purpose and how it is written.
- Place a stencil of a friendly letter (graphic outline of the components) on the overhead projector. Tell students that this outline will help us write a friendly letter today.
- Tell students about Martha (friend) in Texas. Tell the class she is a teacher, too, and would enjoy learning more about them. Tell the class you would like their help in writing a letter to Martha.
- Begin with the date. Point to the date on the sample friendly letter. What is this part of the friendly letter called? Why do we include it in our letter? How do we write the date? Where does it go? Write the date on the overhead, thinking aloud through the process.
- Follow the same process for the greeting. Brainstorm greetings and write ideas on the board. Think aloud while writing the greeting on the overhead, discussing capitalization and punctuation.
- Define the purpose of the body of the letter—it is where the message is written. Go back to the sample letter and discuss what was included in the body of the sample letter.
- Brainstorm things they could include in the body of the letter they are writing to Martha. Write these in the body of the letter. While writing, discuss spelling, capitalization, and punctuation.
- Go back to the sample letter, and discuss the purpose of the closing, and brainstorm ways to close a letter. Write suggestions on the board. Write a student-selected closing on the overhead letter, using think-alouds for position, capitalization, and punctuation.
- Return to the sample letter and talk about the importance of the signature and the ways people sign their names. Ask students when it may be important to include both first and last names or when a first name is all that is needed.

(continued)

EXHIBIT 12.8

Alternative Lesson Plan Format
(continued)

- Go back to the overhead outline and sign the sample letter.
- Read the letter aloud to the students. Ask them whether there are any changes they would like to make. Make those changes using a different overhead pen.
- Go back and review the parts of the letter on the overhead, pointing to the parts and asking students to name and explain the parts.

GUIDED PRACTICE

- Provide each student with an outline of a friendly letter (the same as used on the overhead). Tell them that you would like to write one more letter with them, this time to a classmate who moved away two weeks ago.
- Place a new, empty letter outline on the overhead. Ask students what they need to do first to write the letter. Have students write the date on their letter outlines. When finished, ask one of the students to come to the overhead and write the date as she/he did on her/his paper. Have the other students compare their letter to the one on the overhead. Discuss any differences. Using this same process, work through the writing of the other components of the letter. Refer students to brainstormed lists for ideas.

INDEPENDENT PRACTICE

Provide students with a new friendly letter outline. Tell them that now they will write a first draft of a letter on their own. They should first think of whom they want to write to. Then they can begin writing the letter. Refer them to the written ideas. Assist as needed.

CLOSURE

Ask students to identify the parts of a friendly letter, referring to the poster sample letter. Ask students to tell the purpose of each part and to explain how it is written. Have students read the letter they have started to write to a friend. Discuss how they are doing with their letters and what they need to do tomorrow to finish the first draft of their letter to a friend.

EVALUATION

- Evaluate students' letters written from guided practice to ensure all parts were included and correctly written.
- Provide feedback on students' first draft of their letter to ensure they have a good start.

Not all lesson plans will be so extensive or include all of these components. For example, when working with a new concept or skill that will take several days to introduce to students, the teacher may focus the majority of a lesson on the presentation of information and spend limited or no time on guided or independent practice. Or student needs and challenges may lead the teacher to spend the entire first lesson on modeling/demonstration—the group writing of the first letter in Exhibit 12.8. Then, during the next lesson, time may be spent on the guided practice activities. Not until the third or fourth day of instruction would students take on the independent practice writing activity.

Other lessons may have more of a student focus. In these lessons, students may be discovering ideas/concepts on their own or in cooperative groups or dyads. Exhibit 12.9 provides a lesson plan for this type of lesson.

Subject: Mathematics   Topic: Nonstandard units of measurement   Date: March 1

EXHIBIT 12.9

A Student-Centered Lesson Plan

RATIONALE

Prior to working with standard units of measurement, students need to develop an understanding of why standard units are needed for accurate measurement.

OBJECTIVE(S)

Given beans and paper clips, and using outlines of one foot, each student will measure at least 6 team-selected objects in the classroom, record their measurements on a grid, and compare the measurements with teammates. Students will identify similarities and differences among measurement tools and findings, and will discuss the advantages and disadvantages of each tool. Finally, students will write at least 3 sentences in their math journals that describe the differences in these measurement tools, which one they think is best for which task, and why. (The student with a physical disability and the student with a cognitive impairment will draw pictures in their journals to represent their ideas.)

MATERIALS

beans, paper clips, paper for tracing an outline of a foot, scissors, and measurement grid for recording results

PROCEDURES

Motivator and Advanced Organizer

- Show students the beans, paper clips, and construction paper for making foot outlines. Inform students they will be using these tools to become measurement wizards.
- "Today we are going to measure objects in the room using these measurement tools. This will help you develop your skills as a measurement wizard."

Cooperative Group Activity

- Inform students they will be working in their math groups today.
- Bring out the measurement grid. Explain the different columns of the grid and what needs to be done to complete the grid. Highlight that, as a group, they will select six objects in the room to measure, will measure each one using the three measuring tools, and record their findings on the measurement grid.
- Demonstrate how to make a foot outline and to use it as a measurement tool.
- Inform students they will be writing about the experiences in their math journals when they are finished.
- On the board, list what is to be included in the journal entry. Encourage students to work together on developing ideas to write in the journal. Answer any questions. Tell students you will let them know when they should begin writing in their journals.
- Have students begin working in groups. Monitor and facilitate as needed. (Check to be sure group members are assisting peers as needed with measuring and recording.)

CLOSURE

- Ask representatives from each group to describe what their group measured and what they found.
- Ask individuals to share ideas from their journals.

EVALUATION

- Collect and review measurement grids. Check that all students measured at least 6 objects using the measurement tools.
- Collect and review math journal entries for criteria—at least three sentences that describe differences in the tools, which tool they think is best, and why—or three drawings to represent ideas.

Other plans may be written to describe how a student with a disability is to be included in general education classrooms and experiences. Exhibit 12.10 presents a plan outline describing how a student with multiple disabilities is included in a reading activity in a general education setting. The student, Stacy, is a 6-year-old functioning in the moderate to severe range of cognitive ability; she has some paralysis and has low vision. Adaptations made in the classroom include the following: (a) use of a cardboard box to house Stacy's supplies, (b) rubber stamps for her first name and date, (c) attachment of colorful pompoms to her mailbox, coathook, lunch ticket, and desk for easy identification, (d) looped scissors for whole-hand grasping to ease cutting, (e) use of a holder for crayons, pencil, and name/date stamp on top of her desk for quick retrieval, (f) use of 0 through 9 math number stamps to ease writing demands during math, (g) attachment of a folder holder on top of her desk, and (h) use of a glue stick.

EXHIBIT 12.10

A Lesson Plan for Including a Student with Disabilities in General Education Reading Activities

ACTIVITY	STACY	PEERS
1. Listen to the book *Hot Fudge Pickles* read by the teacher.	Sits quietly on floor in assigned spot; directs her attention to the teacher.	Sit quietly on floor in assigned spots; face teacher; appear to be listening.
2. Color and cut out pickle-shaped cover for story by the student.	Is handed her green marker by the student seated next to her; is instructed to color both sides green and indicate completion by verbally informing peer. Peer cuts out the pickle cover because curved sides make it too difficult for Stacy.	Choose various green crayons and/or markers to color pickle covers; when finished, cut out the cover.
3. Write story about class activities from previous day: finger painting with chocolate pudding and dipping dill pickles in hot fudge.	On her own, quietly scribbles in her book. With integration facilitator present, is asked to generate ideas based on the activities. Integration facilitator writes two sentences based on Stacy's responses: "We finger painted with chocolate pudding. It was yummy."	Write down ideas based on their activities. Frequently leave their desks to ask the teacher or integration facilitator to spell words.
4. Illustrate student books based on the content of their story.	Is prompted by integration facilitator to ask her neighbor (Laurie) to draw her picture. Together they decide that Laurie will draw the picture in black marker and Stacy will color it in. Laurie will provide appropriate crayon.	On the blank pages of their books, draw pictures of themselves finger painting with chocolate pudding and eating hot fudge pickles.
5. Two reading groups share their stories on the floor in the front of the room.	Opens book. Student seated next to her prompts her by making the initial sounds of several words.	Take turns around the circle, opening their books and sharing their stories with the group.

Source: From "Enhancing Participation of a Student with Multiple Disabilities in Regular Education," by S. Hamre-Nietupski, J. McDonald, and J. Nietupski, 1994, *Teaching Exceptional Children,* 26(3), pp. 60–63.

THEORY TO PRACTICE

➡ Analyze one of the lesson plan examples. Evaluate it in terms of its response to factors associated with a supportive context for learning, as well as the elements of quality instruction. How would you improve the plan?

➡ Meet with a classroom teacher and gather instructional materials for teaching a mini-unit (3 to 5 lessons) to a group of students. Using the materials and the information you have gained from Chapters 11 and 12, develop 3 to 5 lesson plans that you could provide for the identified group of students. Follow the lesson plan formats provided here or develop a format of your own. Present these plans to the teacher for review.

CHAPTER SUMMARY

This chapter opens with a discussion of quality instruction and two different approaches to instruction generally found in today's schools. The advantages and disadvantages of these approaches, as well as the need for a balanced instructional approach, are highlighted. The chapter concludes with examples of written instructional plans.

CHAPTER 13

Selecting Instructional Activities

Read to find out the following:
- the range of activities available to include in instructional planning
- the advantages and disadvantages of activities and how to modify them to meet the needs of individual students
- approaches for identifying appropriate activities to include in lessons

Being aware of the variety of activities that are available for presenting instruction and having a strategy for determining which ones are most appropriate to a specific instructional objective are the next steps in designing quality instruction. This chapter opens with a discussion of the wide range of activity options available to teachers and closes with a description of two ways in which teachers can identify activities to include in their instructional plans.

ACTIVITY OPTIONS

Discussions

According to Good and Brophy (1991), discussions are "designed to stimulate students to respond diversely and at higher cognitive levels to what they have been learning" (p. 474). During discussions, "teachers and students, working as a group, share opinions in order to clarify issues, relate new knowledge to their prior knowledge or experience, or attempt to answer a question or solve a problem" (p. 486).

Discussions can be used in situations where differences of opinion, responses to content, or development of positions are identified as instructional goals. Discussions are helpful in developing students' public speaking skills and skills in presenting ideas to others. Moreover, discussions can lead to the development of social skills because they require listening and responding to another person in positive and constructive ways.

Discussions are more than everyone talking at once or students stating their ideas without taking into consideration the ideas and feelings of others. They require teachers to be facilitators who set boundaries and keep the exchange on topic. Throughout discussions, teachers

> *point out connections between ideas, identify similarities or contrasts, request clarification or elaboration, invite students to respond to one another, summarize progress achieved so far, or suggest and test for possible consensus as it develops.*
> *(Good & Brophy, 1991, p. 487)*

Student-to-student exchange, including that between aided and natural speakers, is a critical element of discussions. Students' ability to challenge one another's ideas and to keep the discussion going is an indicator of significant student engagement in thinking and in responding to the ideas and views of others.

Teacher and student attributes, as well as other variables within the learning environment, influence the quality of discussions. Foremost, for discussions to be meaningful and engaging, they must occur within an environment of trust and respect, patience and support. If students do not believe their classmates will wait for them, listen to them, or take their comments seriously, they are not likely to participate. Teachers' and students' cultural beliefs and attitudes concerning sharing opinions and their views of their ability to contribute, influence the degree to which individuals will participate and profit from the discussions. The "Make It Happen" feature suggests ways to orchestrate discussions that encourage student participation, take into consideration individual needs and characteristics, and support and encourage higher-level thinking skills.

▌ **MAKE IT HAPPEN**

   Discussions

- Articulate clearly what is going to be discussed.
- Specify behavioral expectations before beginning the discussion.
- Start with short discussion periods, gradually increasing their length.
- Practice strategies for voicing agreement and disagreement among peers.
- Provide time for students to reflect and form their thoughts before speaking.
- Use preferential seating for those who have difficulty hearing their peers and ask speakers to face them when speaking.
- Schedule breaks during discussions to allow students to get up and move around.
- If a student needs extra time to form his or her thoughts, tell that individual that you will come back to him or her; call on someone else; then when that person finishes, return to the first student.
- Allow students to pass if asked to contribute or to respond to a peer's comments.
- If a student has difficulties understanding the content of the discussion, have a peer or support person quietly explain the ideas being discussed or answer the student's questions.
- Do not allow any one person to dominate the discussion.
- Do not dominate the discussion yourself.
- Tell a student using a communication device what kinds of contributions you will be wanting to hear from her or him shortly; go on with the discussion; and then return to the student to receive her or his input.

When students with disabilities are included in discussions, it may be necessary to modify and adjust the types and levels of questions asked. Some students may be able to participate and contribute better if asked recall and specific-information questions rather than questions requiring the analysis of presented information. But keep in mind that if students with disabilities are to develop skills of critical thinking and problem solving, they need experiences that allow them to develop and apply those skills. A teacher may modify the manner in which these higher-level thinking questions are asked of some students with disabilities but continue to pose them. One way to accomplish this is through shared pairs: the teacher poses the question, students, in pairs, talk over their ideas with a neighbor, and then the group returns to discuss responses to the question. In this way, every child is held accountable for the information and should be able to contribute—during the shared paired and/or the large-group interaction.

Discussions have advantages and disadvantages. Advantages include (a) providing a forum for students to present their opinions and to respond to those of their classmates, (b) challenging students to make connections between content and their personal experiences, and (c) shifting curricular focus to what is most important to students. Disadvantages include: (a) some students will not participate, (b) some students will have difficulties hearing or concentrating on what others have to say and may miss out on a great deal of content, and (c) not all students will be willing to make contributions in front of a large group.

Presentations

This activity option offers ways to communicate information to individual students, dyads, cooperative groups, and large groups. Teachers, students, and community members may take on the role of presenter through individual lectures and presentations, panel discussions, demonstrations, reports, and exhibits.

Because of the listening demands associated with presentations, it is critical to match presentation formats carefully to student characteristics and needs. For example, lecturing to a group of students who have short attention spans, have difficulty taking notes, and/or struggle with the content being presented may not be the best way to support learning. Having students make presentations or demonstrate what they have learned may be much more effective. Table 13.1 lists advantages and disadvantages associated with presentations. Overcoming the disadvantages requires planning and organization. The "Make It Happen" feature provides suggestions for organizing presentations.

TABLE 13.1 ADVANTAGES AND DISADVANTAGES OF SOME PRESENTATION FORMATS

FORMAT	ADVANTAGES	DISADVANTAGES
Lectures	• quick way to present a great deal of information to a group of students • everyone hears the same message at the same time	• students may have difficulty attending and monitoring their own learning • students may have difficulty taking notes • students may not understand content being presented
Speakers and Panel Discussions	• brings the community into the classroom • helps students make connections between curricular content and life outside school • students can serve as speakers or panelists, sharing their ideas and learning with peers	• speaker's message may not match students' understanding • speaker may not have the skills to actively engage students or know how to respond to student behavior • speaker's pace may be too rapid for comprehension for some students
Demonstrations and Oral Reports	• students share their learning with peers • community members share their expertise with students • demonstrations are "doing" something so they may hold students' attention • students can choose their personal best means of demonstration	• students may have difficulty seeing and hearing • students may need extensive amount of rehearsal before they are ready to present • activity may have unique equipment needs
Exhibitions	• all students can display their work and view the work of others	• great deal of organization required • space requirements

---

MAKE IT HAPPEN

Presentations Formats: Overcoming Disadvantages

Format	Suggestions
Lectures	• Use visuals to support ideas (e.g., overheads, posters). • Provide outlines, guidelines, or vocabulary lists to support student notetaking and/or provide notetakers. • Tailor the level of complexity of questions and answers for individuals. • Stop periodically to check for understanding and to allow students to talk to one another about content. • Check with interpreters about the pacing of lectures.
Speakers and Panel Discussions	• Prepare students by exploring the topic and discussing behavioral expectations. • Inform speakers about what the scope of their presentation should be, what has been covered in class, the level of student understanding of the topic, and any special needs. • Secure copies of handouts prior to the presentation and go over them with students. • Ensure all students can see and hear the presenters. • Allow students to ask questions privately and to meet with the speaker following the presentation. • Make arrangements for follow-up conversations with speakers.
Demonstrations and Oral Reports	• Secure all equipment prior to the event and arrange seating so all students can see and hear. • Consider photographing or videotaping demonstrations for viewing at a later date. • If students are making presentations, teach presentation skills and provide rehearsal time. • Allow for multiple ways to demonstrate and present reports (e.g., use of augmentative communication devices and alternative presentation modes).
Exhibits	• Allow ample time for students to create products and ways for displaying them at the exhibit. • Begin early to make arrangements for space and equipment (e.g., tables, chairs, easels). • Create a schedule for setting up and taking down the exhibit and assign jobs to students and volunteers. • Plan multiple ways to inform others about the exhibit.

Another way to overcome disadvantages associated with presentations is to require students to self-manage their behavior and attention during the presentations. Students may be asked to chart each time they make a contribution, each time they catch themselves listening, or each time the teacher signals to them to evaluate and record their behavior. Students may also evaluate their behavior at the conclusion of the presentation, indicating the degree to which they attended to the speaker and the extent to which they understood the speaker's message and gained new information.

Experiments and Laboratory Experiences

Experiments challenge students to develop hypotheses and investigate them to determine whether they are true or will hold under differing situations. They challenge students to employ the scientific method, to act as scientists, and to observe and investigate phenomena carefully and systematically. They require students to observe, collect and analyze data, communicate their ideas to others, classify information and findings, and measure, compute, and predict (Gurganus, Janas, & Schmitt, 1995).

Experiments and labs are powerful learning tools when content lends itself to discovering new information or the reasons something acts or behaves as it does. They provide highly motivating experiences for students to try out their ideas and to test their thinking skills. Because of these challenges, experiments and labs require teachers to set the stage carefully for learning and to examine what needs to be done to accommodate student needs and differences. Part of this planning involves taking into consideration students' prior experiences in conducting experiments, their learning styles (e.g., how they respond to group learning activities), and their motivation to participate. The "Make It Happen" list highlights some of the difficulties teachers will encounter implementing experiments and labs and offers suggestions for overcoming these difficulties. Other implementation considerations include (a) securing all materials prior to the start of the lab, (b) determining how materials will be disseminated and returned, (c) making a list of group members' jobs to be carried out during the lab, and (d) making any special arrangements to include a student with a disability in the lab.

❚ **MAKE IT HAPPEN**

Experiments and Labs

Challenges	Suggestions
Demands a safe learning environment as students work with equipment	• Supervise student groups closely by moving about the room and monitoring. • Assign one person per group to be in charge of safety. • Discuss safety concerns prior to each lab and have students practice safety procedures prior to working with equipment.
Calls for tools that accommodate student needs	• Obtain equipment or tools specially designed for individuals with disabilities if possible. • Adapt existing equipment to meet student needs. • Have peers manipulate the tools for a student with a disability, or assign a paraprofessional to work with the group and provide assistance.
Requires close observation and recording of observations	• Provide lab outlines or study guides for students who have difficulty with reading and writing. • Use technology (e.g., cameras, computers, camcorders, audiotape recorders) to record observations and impressions.
Requires explaining directions carefully	• Provide audiotaped or written copies of directions. • Provide short forms of directions that include simplified vocabulary, drawings, and symbols. • Have students work with partners to read and process directions. • Break down tasks into small steps.

Involves teaching critical thinking and the forming of hypotheses	• Discuss activities and possible outcomes prior to beginning the lab. • Record student predictions on the board, and discuss what would have to happen for the predictions to come true. • Have students identify which parts of the experiment may be most difficult and discuss those sections.
Generally requires teamwork	• Discuss behavioral expectations. • Practice social skills for working together.
Requires encouraging students to participate and contribute actively	• Explain what will occur during the experiment and what students will be asked to do. • Answer any questions about what is expected, and clarify lab procedures. • Structure activities so all students feel they can be successful (e.g., provide outlines and simplified directions, provide assistance as needed).

Simulations

Through simulations, students gain "almost first-hand experience" of what it would be like to be involved intimately with the concepts, ideas, and performances being discussed. Simulations may be used when access to authentic contexts is unavailable, although it is known that learning skills in authentic contexts helps to ensure greater generalization and maintenance of understanding.

One common simulation activity is used in driver's education. Soon-to-be drivers sit behind the wheel of a simulated car and maneuver the car as they view a videotape. The simulation requires individuals to brake and turn and make split-second decisions, and it provides feedback about their performance. This simulation is generally used in the beginning stages of driver education and gives students a "behind the wheel" experience before they actually drive a car on local streets.

Another example of simulation involves changing the classroom into a restaurant setting and having students prepare menus and meals to serve to invited guests. This simulation can be used to teach food preparation skills, social skills, written and oral language skills, and mathematics skills.

Simulations may also be used to raise awareness of disability. For example, teachers and school staff may want to prepare general education students for the inclusion of their peers who have disabilities. A common example used to simulate a visual impairment is to cover students' eyes with blindfolds and, with the assistance of sighted peers, have them move about the school campus. To simulate a communicative disorder, students may be forbidden to express their ideas and needs verbally over an extended period of time in order to gain some awareness of what it is like to have difficulty expressing oneself verbally. To simulate some of the difficulties associated with learning disabilities, students may be asked to write with their nondominant hand and to read scrambled sentences.

Although these activities may raise students' awareness of the unique challenges experienced by individuals with disabilities, great caution must be observed prior to, during, and following these simulations. If the simulation is of short duration, students may see the activity as "fun" and not gain any understanding of what a person with a disability truly experiences on a day-to-day basis. These activities may also result in feelings of sympathy, not empathy. Students may leave the experience feeling sorry for individuals with disabilities, and this attitude may lead them to respond in nonproductive ways to individuals with disabilities (e.g., providing excessive help that prevents students with disabilities from achieving independence). Also, these activities may have a discomforting effect on students in the classroom who have disabilities; they may feel self-conscious with simulation activities. If these activities are to be used, a balance must be struck between "living in someone else's shoes" and just playing a game, and all activities must be designed and carried out with respect and sensitivity.

Implementation of simulations can be especially challenging. The attempt to convert a classroom into a setting similar to a targeted setting (e.g., a job site) can fall short and fail to help students generalize skills to actual environments. Also, real-world problems generally generate some sense of urgency or provide strong motivation for individuals. That sense of urgency is hard to create in simulations, and at times students will need to be convinced of the importance of the activity or problem before they become truly engaged. Consequently, whenever possible, teaching skills and concepts within authentic environments and situations is best, but when doing that is not possible, simulations may be a valuable alternative. The "Make It Happen" feature provides suggestions for implementing simulation activities.

MAKE IT HAPPEN
Simulations

- Do your research—find out as much as you can about the authentic setting and problem parameters and incorporate that information into the simulation.
- Collect materials from the authentic situation (e.g., if you are working on developing students' job application and interview skills, gather job application materials from different community businesses, and interview employers to develop a list of interview questions).
- Require students to dress and act the part (e.g., if the experience being simulated is going to a job interview, have students dress appropriately).
- If students do not have the opportunity to go to a community setting to observe the activity or event as it naturally occurs, videotape the setting and view the tape with students.
- Take a field trip to community sites where the activities/skills are being performed. Discuss with students what is occurring.

Learning Centers

Good and Brophy (1991) describe learning centers as places "where students can go to work independently or in cooperation with peers on various learning projects" (p. 357). Learning centers are places where all the materials and equipment needed for a particular task are provided and where students can go to complete those tasks. Learning centers may be stations about the classroom where students go to work independently on projects or to use specialized equipment. At learning centers, students may listen to tapes or view filmstrips, videocassettes, or laserdisks, or work with computer programs. Learning centers can also be places where students go to write, paint, sculpt, or read. Setting up learning centers can be very time-consuming initially, but the benefits afforded students generally outweigh the time investment. The "Make It Happen" feature provides suggestions for creating and implementing learning centers.

MAKE IT HAPPEN
Learning Centers

Creating

1. Establish goals and objectives of the center.
2. Identify activities and gather materials.
3. Design means for storing these materials. Boxes, files, and other storage containers may be needed.
4. Specify and display center directions. For younger students and students with reading challenges, pictures and audiotapes may be used.
5. Develop means for managing student work. Make individual folders, cubbies, storage bins, or shelves available and accessible for the housing of student work.
6. Make the learning center inviting to students.
7. Develop a system for managing and recording who will be using the center, how many students can work at the center at one time, when students are able to use the center, how long they may work at the center, and when student work will be evaluated.

Introducing

1. Discuss rules and guidelines for working at the center.
2. Describe the types of activities available, what is to be done, and what can be learned by working at the center.
   Options:
   * Explain the center to the entire class.
   * Introduce the center to two or three students who may then serve as guides and mentors to others. As a consequence of being a center leader, students develop leadership and collaborative skills.

Learning centers offer many advantages. First, they provide opportunities for independent study and add flexibility to the classroom because they expand the range of learning opportunities available (Good & Brophy, 1991). For example, books, videos, and other media related to a topic under study may be provided in a learning center to expand student knowledge and exploration of the topic. Second, they encourage students to become independent learners who monitor their own progress. Students select what they are going to do and motivate themselves to stay with and complete selected tasks. Centers may also allow students to check their own work and chart their performance.

Third, centers allow teachers to individualize instruction. For example, students may have individual folders of work to be completed at the center. Upon arriving at the center, they pick up their folders, read what they are to do, and get started. For students who need help in physical management of folders and books, instructions and lessons may be on computer with voice output. In a reading center, students may be reading different books and practicing different reading skills. By working at the center, each student is working on activities specifically tailored to his or her needs.

Fourth, learning centers allow teachers to broaden the scope of the curriculum. Center activities may include review and practice of previously presented skills or extensions of concepts covered in class. Students who are experiencing difficulty learning a skill can be provided additional opportunities to work with that skill at a learning center through worksheets or other support materials. Fifth, centers may be designed to address the unique needs of individuals with disabilities. For example, students may go to a center to practice their signing skills or braille skills. Other students may go to a center to work with activities that build their physical strength. Centers can also present activities that stress a more functional curriculum. Activities involving money, safety, and/or other daily living skills may be housed in centers.

Some care must be taken, however, when centers are used in a classroom. First, center activities must represent things that students can do independently or with the help of a peer. Centers should not add to the instructional load of the teacher or provide "busy-work" for students; they should open doors for teachers to work more closely with individual students on specific skills. Centers should allow students to move to areas and begin independent work on projects, thus freeing the teacher to work with individuals who are having difficulty with the core curriculum. Second, all students must be encouraged to work at all centers, even though some centers may target skills needed by some and already mastered by others. If it becomes apparent to students that some centers are for the "top dog" individuals and other centers are for those who do not do so well in school, centers will serve to divide or stratify students. If all centers are available to everyone and the students are encouraged to work at all of the centers, centers will be viewed as having something for everyone.

Exhibit 13.1 provides an example of a center that may be developed for a middle school science/health classroom. This particular learning center is designed to reinforce and expand students' understanding of nutritious eating habits. Students may access the center when they have completed other classwork or on days that are strictly set aside for work at centers. The center described in the exhibit would be only one of many centers in the classroom.

| **EXHIBIT 13.1** | **Purpose:** to reinforce and extend students' understanding of meal planning and good eating habits |

Learning Center on Nutritious Eating Habits

Projects available:
a. making a food pyramid poster, including favorite foods in each of the categories
b. planning a meal for the class that meets the requirements of the food pyramid
c. tracking and evaluating personal eating habits
d. tracking and evaluating the quality of food served in the school cafeteria
e. making a self-help tape for others wanting to learn more about the food pyramid

Materials Available
- art and writing materials: crayons, markers, paints, drawing paper, writing paper, colored paper, string, yarn, sticks, glue, cloth swatches, buttons
- graph paper for charting
- food magazines for cutting out pictures
- computer with CD-ROM, Internet access, and graphics and word processing programs (synthesized speech)
- CD-ROMs discussing the food pyramid and good nutritional practices
- list of World Wide Web sites that deal with nutritional issues and meal planning
- books on nutrition and meal planning
- audio- and videotapes on nutrition and meal planning
- posters dealing with nutrition and the food pyramid
- audiotape recorder, blank tapes, and earphones

Organization
The directions and requirements for each project are provided in individual folders. Information is provided in written form along with illustrations for clarification, and on audiotape as well as on the computer with access to screen reading software. Each folder also contains a checklist that students are to use to monitor their progress on projects. Each checklist lists the steps to be followed for completing a project. Students are to check off items as they progress through to project completion.

Folders are provided for the students' work and checklists. For students unable to manipulate paper materials physically, this material is also provided on the computer. These students, along with any other students who prefer this mode, may access information via the computer and store their work in a file on the computer as well.

Management

No more than three students may work at the center at any one time. All work done at the center is to remain at the center; all center materials must remain at the center. The teacher will review student progress once a week and will meet with students one-on-one during scheduled classroom conferences to discuss the progress of their projects.

Packets

Packets are collections of activities that students complete individually. Packets may contain a set of worksheets, a list of directions and supplies needed for completing tasks. In many instances, packets reflect individualized instruction, containing activities that target students' specific needs and skills. Packets may be in the form of individual folders, three-ring binders, files on the computer, or activity lists posted in learning centers. Teachers place assignments and/or a schedule for the week in the packet, along with all task materials. Students pick up their materials and begin their packet work. Because of the individualized nature of packets, teachers are able to address a variety of curricular concerns and to tailor activities to a student's needs and challenges.

In a general education classroom, teachers may develop individual packets that include both review and fun activities students may do when they have finished other assignments. Packet materials can be tailored to individual students' needs and provide another means for students, teachers, and parents to monitor skill development in targeted areas. They allow for individualization in the general education classroom.

The initial implementation of packets can be very time consuming. For example, a special education teacher may be working with 20 students representing grades K through 5, who have learning needs across all curricular areas. Creating a specially tailored packet for each student could consume much of the teacher's time. The "Make It Happen" feature provides some suggestions for getting started with packet work while avoiding the pitfalls.

| **MAKE IT HAPPEN**
|_____ **Packets**

1. Start small. You may want to create packet work for one to five students first and then, as the year progresses, gradually create packets for other students.
2. Limit the focus of activities included in packets. Review students' goals and objectives. Look for similarities. For example, a number of students may be working on developing reading comprehension skills. Identify materials that students could complete independently that work on this area. Find materials at differing levels of difficulty. Arrange these materials in a logical order. Return the packet to each student; identify what his or her specific comprehension needs are; determine the level at which he or she is working; and referring to your collection of materials, select appropriate activities. Add to this collection of materials as the year progresses.

(continued)

Packets *(continued)*

3. Allow students to select activities to include in their packet. To do this you may want to create a set of activities that deal with students' target areas. In one area of the room, display materials for these different target areas. Students are responsible for going to the area matching their goals and selecting activities. New activities could be added to the display once every one or two weeks.

4. Have students check their own work whenever possible. This can lead to student independence and self-directed learning and decrease the burden on the teacher. This may be carried out in several ways.

   a. Divide a student's folder into sections by taping one folder inside another or adding dividers. The activities that the student is to complete could be on white paper and placed in the front section of the folder. Answer keys could be placed in the back section and printed on colored paper. When students have completed an assigned task, they go to the back of their folder, find the corresponding answer sheet, and correct their work.

   b. Or create a three-ring binder with answer sheets. As you develop your collection of materials and select items to include in student folders, make a copy of the activity, write the correct answers on the copy, and place the copy in the binder. Activity answer sheets may be numbered so that students can easily find them in the binder. Activities may also be coded by level and then number. Whatever the system, it should be easy to match the activity to the answer sheet. The binder could be placed in a special place in the room and a marking pencil tied to the binder with a string. The student goes to the binder, finds the corresponding answer sheet, and corrects his or her own work.

5. Have students chart and evaluate their performance. Once they have corrected their work, have them return their papers to their folder, record their performance on a chart stapled to or pasted on the front cover or inside the outside flap, and place the completed work in another section of the folder. To review students' work, you would review their chart and check the completed section of their work.

6. Be sure students know what they may do when their packet work is completed. Moving directly to another activity helps to avoid unwanted disturbances.

Although packets may be motivating for some students, the strict or sole use of packets can lead to boredom and/or may not be developmentally appropriate. If students are required to sit for extended periods of time completing their individual packet work, they may begin to work more slowly because they know that the reward for finishing the work is to be given more work to do. Also, having to work independently for long periods of time can frustrate and lead to the withdrawal of some students. Another related disadvantage is that students may not push or challenge themselves if presented only with paper-and-pencil activities. As with all learning experiences, there is a need for variety and challenge if both students and teachers are to remain motivated and if positive outcomes are to be achieved. Here are some simple ways to overcome some of these drawbacks:

- Limit packet work to a set amount of time each day.
- Allow students to select fun activities to include in their packets.
- Schedule individual conferences with students to discuss their packet work.
- Have students grade each other's work or meet and discuss the work they are doing to add a social, interpersonal component to the activity.
- Write a personal note in the students' packets as a way to let them know that you take their packet work seriously and are monitoring and encouraging their progress.
- Display some of the products of the students' packet work in the classroom.

Projects

Project-based learning affords students opportunities to engage in activities that are of interest to them. Projects may be an appropriate activity when instructional goals include the development of (a) research skills, (b) critical thinking and problem-solving skills, (c) writing and presentation skills, and (for a collaboratively completed project), (d) skills for working effectively with others.

Students of all ages can engage in project learning. Initially, and for younger children, projects may be of short duration and take one or two days to complete. At first, projects may be highly structured by the teacher. As students gain skills in project-based learning, projects may be completed over extended periods of time and require students to do most of the organizing for completion. Implementing project-based learning makes unique demands on teachers. Implementation suggestions are presented in the "Make It Happen" feature.

▎**MAKE IT HAPPEN**

Projects

Materials
1. Ensure materials are readily available to students. Not all materials must be housed on the school campus, but ways to access information must be available. Internet and other information networks can be tapped as well as community libraries and other resources.
2. Provide materials that reflect students' ability levels and interests. At times, energy will need to be invested in locating materials that are appropriate for students (e.g., enlarged print, low-level reading). Planning needs to begin early.
3. Teach students how to locate materials.

Scheduling, Teaching, and Conferencing
1. Provide students with time lines or help them create time lines to guide them to project completion. A time line can list suggested due dates for the various stages of a project. For example, a date may be set for identifying and narrowing their topic, and another date set for securing a minimal number of resources or references. These due dates can serve as benchmarks and help students develop time management skills necessary for carrying out long-term projects successfully.
2. Consider setting aside a certain number of hours each week for project work. Students may also work on the projects at home.
3. Schedule mini-lessons as students work on their projects. Suggestions and strategies for notetaking, for analyzing and synthesizing information, and for writing up results can all assist students in producing a satisfactory final product.
4. Set aside time to conference with students either individually or, for team projects, in teams. During the conference, successes, problems, and conflicts can be discussed and solutions proposed. Conferencing with the students also allows teachers to monitor progress and provide needed encouragement and support.

Modifications
1. Allow final products to take several forms.
2. Adjust project requirements to reflect student needs and challenges. Changing a length requirement is only one way. Modifications include expanding or decreasing the number of sources required, adjusting project sections or components, or tailoring a project to match a student's IEP goals and objectives.

Presentations
1. Determine multiple ways in which students may present their projects to others (e.g., oral presentation, exhibit, videotape recording, photographs, computer software, multimedia).
2. Provide opportunities for students to practice their presentations prior to the main event. This will increase student confidence, improve presentation behavior, and allow opportunities for making adjustments.

To increase authenticity and value for students with severe or multiple disabilities, it may be helpful if projects are completed in community-based settings. The projects may be conducted with the support of nondisabled peers or with natural supports found in community environments. Structuring projects in this way adds meaning for these students. For many of them, time spent reading materials and writing reports may have little long-term value and may not aid them in achieving independence and life skills.

Project-based learning has both advantages and disadvantages. Advantages include (a) enhanced student independence and responsibility for their own learning, (b) expanded curriculum coverage, (c) adjustment of curriculum and expectations to reflect individual needs, (d) expanded opportunities for teachers to work with students individually, and (e) provision of opportunities for students to work together. Disadvantages include: (a) projects may take a great deal of time to complete, (b) some students may have a slow start and not complete the project, (c) some students may become overwhelmed and lost in all the details of completing a project, and (d) some students may be unable to manage a long-term project.

A beginning list of project possibilities is presented in Exhibit 13.2. They are provided only as starting-off points for teachers planning to use projects.

EXHIBIT 13.2

Project-Based Learning: Possible Topics

- Younger students may create a mural of community people, services, and activities. The project may involve the taking and collecting of photographs of neighborhood sites, interviewing members of their family or neighborhood, and collecting artifacts from local businesses and services (e.g., a special set of stamps from the post office, a job application from a local business). Students spend time discussing their findings and integrating that information into a meaningful whole. Speaking and listening skills, reading and writing skills, as well as interpersonal skills, could all be developed through this project.

- Middle school students could be involved in a history and language arts project that challenges them to collect the oral histories of someone significant in their lives and to share that oral history with others. The overall requirements of the project would most likely need to be structured and introduced by the teacher (e.g., definition of an oral history, procedures for gathering an oral history, how to process gathered information, and possible means for presenting that information to others). As the project unfolds, skills in interviewing, transcribing, and analyzing interviews could be taught in small groups as needed. Multiple avenues for presenting the oral histories could be available and left to student choice (e.g., videotaping of the subject; drawings or photographs). Speaking and listening skills, reading and writing skills, presentation skills, as well as interpersonal skills, could all be developed through this project.

- High school students may work on a project that explores community employment opportunities. Again, the structuring of the project would be determined by the teacher, with students making multiple choices along the way. Students could interview people at local businesses, go on mock interviews, secure job application forms, call local businesses advertising openings, and/or arrange for panels of area business representatives to speak to the class about job opportunities. Students may work on a job site as interns during evenings or on weekends. Students who require more assistance may be assigned a job coach and go out to sites to explore job requirements. Students could have multiple ways of presenting their findings and experiences to peers (e.g., write a report of their experiences, show a videotape of the activities they were involved in). Students could develop a World Wide Web site that links local business and employment agencies to the school home page.

Conferences

Conferences—individuals sitting down to discuss a topic, product, or event—are another learning experience or instructional activity. Conferences allow for in-depth exploration and discussion of students' learning, understanding, and experiences, and they help to forge connections between students, teacher, parents, and others.

Peer conferences

During peer conferences, students meet with one another to discuss projects, review work, and provide mutual support. These conferences may also be used to solve problems in the classroom or school community. They can be specifically designed to support students with disabilities. Students with disabilities may conference with nondisabled peers to learn strategies for making friends, for getting along with authority figures in the school and community, and for learning general skills for coping in school and community environments. Through these conferences, students—with and without disabilities—will gain problem-solving skills, enhance their understanding of interpersonal interactions, and expand their repertoire of social skills.

Preparing students for peer conferences is a necessary first step, especially preparing them to work with one another in positive and supportive ways. Suggestions for that preparation include the following:

1. Teach students how to provide constructive feedback through modeling and role-play and have them practice.

2. Teach students how to encourage and support others and have them practice.

3. Teach students how to give suggestions in a positive, sensitive way and have them practice.

4. Ensure students understand that everyone learns in different ways and at different rates and that everyone has strengths and challenges when completing assignments and tasks. This understanding is likely to be especially critical when students with and without disabilities conference with one another.

Student-adult conferences

Students may also conference with adults. From student-adult conferencing, students gain personal insight into themselves as learners and young citizens, and adults learn to see children as individuals with their own unique needs and concerns. The adult may be the classroom teacher, instructional assistant, related service provider (e.g., occupational therapist), administrator, parent, or community individual. The pairs may meet to discuss academic or behavioral concerns, dreams and vocational plans, or personal matters of concern to the student. Sitting down with a student to discuss behaviors exhibited in the classroom or in other settings can increase a teacher's understanding of why a behavior is occurring and what factors may be supporting or encouraging it.

Student participation in IEP meetings is another example of student-adult conferences. As previously discussed, it is important for students to participate in their IEP meetings as soon as it is appropriate for them to do so. Setting goals, benchmarks, and objectives should not occur without input from students—students should play a critical role in setting their goals and structuring their future experiences (Lovitt, Cushing, & Stump, 1994).

Students may also hold conferences with job coaches and community individuals. Conferencing with a job coach can help students enhance their performance on the job and help them develop necessary interpersonal skills for being effective at the work site. Students may conference with community members about trades and professions. Community members may also serve as big brothers or big sisters to students, supporting and encouraging them to continue with their schooling. Sometimes an involved community person can make a great difference in a child's life.

Instructional Games

Board games, word searches, logic problems, and other instructional games are excellent motivators for students while teaching and reinforcing skills. Games also provide authentic situations for development of interpersonal skills. Good sportsmanship, following rules, and turn-taking can all be learned through games. Moreover, students with and without disabilities can play games together.

To be educationally meaningful, games must be connected with curricular goals and objectives. Merely playing a game because students and teachers enjoy it does not guarantee the game is a good use of instructional time. Teachers need to be clear about the purpose of games and how they can be used to support student learning.

Parties, Assemblies, Field Trips, and Extracurricular Activities

Many benefits can be gained by having students participate in event activities. For example, Finn (1989) discusses the role of extracurricular activities in reducing withdrawal from school and also states that involvement may (a) increase students' identification with school, (b) increase their sense of belonging, and (c) allow them opportunities to become attached to school.

At times there may be concerns that certain students with disabilities do not have the skills (e.g., behavior, academic, social) to participate in events and therefore should be excluded. For example, staff may suggest that a student with a behavior disorder be denied permission to go on a class field trip to the mountains for fear the student will not follow the rules, will get into mischief, or may become lost during the scheduled hike. In this situation, it is important for the staff and parents to come up with a plan together to support the student's participation in the activity. It may be that an additional adult, an instructional assistant, or a special education teacher will be asked to go along as a chaperone to ensure the student's participation and safety.

Students may be excluded from other activities because teachers and/or administrators do not believe the activity matches their intellectual abilities. For example, a class may be going to the planetarium. The argument may be made that a student with special needs will not understand the information being presented and thus will not benefit from participation. This becomes a curricular issue. Those involved with the student should meet and discuss what is going to occur on the field trip and whether the excursion might provide an opportunity for the student to work on IEP goals, benchmarks, and objectives such as walking with eyes and head up, listening for certain voices and moving toward them, or trying new things whether he or she thoroughly understands them or not. Then activities can be developed to prepare the student for the trip. Support during the trip (e.g., assigning a peer buddy to check for student understanding of ideas) may also be arranged.

Another consideration, once students have gained access to the activity, is to ensure that they participate in meaningful ways. Consider schoolwide assemblies. Special education students may attend the assembly as a group, only to be seated at the back or side of the room. This seating arrangement may not take into consideration the needs of a child with low vision or the needs of a child who is hard-of-hearing. Preferential seating may be needed so these students can truly benefit from the assembly experience. Many students can learn self-advocacy skills and make these requests themselves.

Having students attend parties and assemblies, participate in extracurricular activities, and go on field trips does not guarantee that they will have a good time or benefit from the experience, however. Care should be taken to foster student interaction during activities so they become members of the group and are not found sitting alone at the back or side of the room or always by the side of an adult.

The inclusion of students with disabilities in these event activities requires planning and collaboration with other faculty and staff. The groundwork must be laid through the creation of many opportunities for students with and without disabilities and their teachers to work together and get to know one another. If students and teachers are comfortable with one another and have learned how to communicate, barriers to students' meaningful inclusion in assemblies, parties, and field trips, and extracurricular learning experiences may be minimized.

Community-Based Learning

Apprenticeships and shadowing are two types of community-based learning experiences that provide students opportunities to work and learn in authentic, community settings. When engaged in community-based activities, students are taught skills within natural contexts. An apprenticeship allows students to learn skills through close contact with an area expert. One example is a student spending time observing and working with a welder in a community manufacturing plant. Shadowing is similar in approach: students shadow, or follow, a person at work. A student who is learning waitressing may shadow a waitress, watching how she interacts with customers, how she takes their orders and asks questions, how she presents orders to the chef, and how she delivers orders to the customers. Through shadowing, the student can observe the skills that she or he will need in order to hold such a position and later can conference about them with job coaches.

Students may also participate in service-learning activities and serve as community volunteers. They may work in hospital settings, retirement homes, the public library, or the police station. As volunteers they can learn secretarial skills (e.g., answering the phone, filing papers), social skills (e.g., working with others, providing support and encouragement to others), and responsibility (e.g., arriving on time, completing required tasks). Opportunities to develop skills and understandings in authentic contexts will most likely result in greater gains for students who experience difficulties in generalizing learnings across people, times, and places.

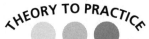

➡ Select two activities that you would like to include in your classroom instruction. Come up with at least two specific examples or situations in which you would use these activities. Identify the advantages and disadvantages of using them. Finally, select one of your examples and develop a lesson plan incorporating that activity. Share your plan with a peer for feedback.

➡ Arrange to observe one of the activity options in practice in a classroom. Describe how the activity was carried out, the actions required of the teacher, and the level of engagement and responsiveness of the students to the activity. Meet with the teacher after the lesson to discuss how she or he felt the activity went. Ask the teacher to describe what she or he did to prepare students for the activity, and what she or he considered to be the greatest positives and drawbacks of the activity for the students. Reflect on this experience and develop a brief handout that describes the experience and the suggestions you have for integrating that particular activity into instructional lessons.

IDENTIFYING APPROPRIATE ACTIVITIES

From this range of options, teachers need to select activities that support and match student needs and goals. In this section we describe two approaches teachers may use to identify appropriate activities: analyzing activity attributes and addressing multiple intelligences of students.

Analyzing Activity Attributes

One approach for identifying appropriate activities for instruction is to analyze the attributes of the activities being considered. Each activity has attributes that influence when and why teachers choose to include it in their instruction. Activity attributes include authenticity, performance demands, alignment with curriculum, grouping arrangements, and material and equipment requirements.

Authenticity

The authenticity of an activity is the degree to which it is representative of what individuals outside school settings are called on to do in their daily lives. Authenticity may be viewed as being on a continuum ranging from high to low. Highly authentic tasks mirror role performances individuals carry out outside school, such as balancing a checkbook, making purchases at a local store, making phone calls, writing letters and notes, or preparing summary reports on the job. Tasks with low levels of authenticity include filling in blanks on a cloze activity, writing the definitions of words, and reading words written on index cards. Low-authenticity tasks in and of themselves are not poor teaching opportunities or experiences—they may play a vital role in students' acquiring and practicing basic skills. But the inclusion of activities that are more authentic in lesson planning is essential if a curricular program is to be well rounded. Moreover, including authentic tasks in the curriculum can be highly motivating for students. Students working on such tasks are less likely to ask, "When will I ever use this?" And the more authentic a task (the closer to actual life role functioning), the more likely it is to be generalizable (able to be transferred or used in different settings and at different times). Tasks that are generalizable help students make connections between what they are learning in school and what they will be required to know and be able to do outside school.

Performance demands

Performance demands are what students are required to do to complete or participate in an activity or task. Performance demands also may be viewed as being on a continuum. High-demand tasks require students to do something actively—act out a role in a play, make an oral presentation to a group, sing a song, solve a complex problem. The "doing" may require physical agility and strength, stamina, or mental power. Low-demand tasks require less of students. Selecting the answer to a multiple-choice question, circling all letters that need to be capitalized in sentences, and writing one- or two-word answers to questions are all low-demand tasks.

Awareness of performance demands allows teachers to modify and adapt learning experiences to reflect student needs. For example, if an activity has high performance demands and requires a student to move about the room and interact with materials, a child with stamina limitations may need extra time, and a child with a physical and/or visual disability may need help to access those materials or the materials may need to be brought to the child. A storyboard, photographs, or other means for communicating ideas may be developed to assist a child who has difficulties communicating orally or who is deaf and does not yet communicate through signing or speech.

Varying the performance demands can keep students interested and motivated. The teacher may intermingle low-demand tasks with tasks demanding greater performance, therefore balancing experiences and allowing students to demonstrate their knowledge in a variety of ways and on a variety of levels.

Alignment with curriculum

To what degree does a learning experience match what has been identified as important in the curriculum? Some learning experiences are highly motivating for both teachers and students but have very little to do with students learning key concepts or target life performances. Such experiences must be carefully screened for instructional intent and their ability to bring about those ends. If they cannot be justified, it may be in the students' best interests to select alternative, more meaningful, learning experiences that directly assist students in achieving goals and objectives more highly aligned with curriculum. Also, the match between an experience and the curriculum should be assessed to ensure that selected experiences maximize students' opportunities to learn and take full advantage of academic learning time.

Grouping arrangements

The way in which students work, whether individually or in groups, is another activity attribute. Consideration of grouping arrangements—individuals working alone, or in dyads, cooperative groups, large groups—helps teachers to structure activities to support students' needs and goal achievement. Sometimes it may be best for students to work individually; at other times a large group may be more appropriate.

Material and equipment requirements

The final activity attribute is the type of materials and equipment the activity requires. When selecting activities to include in lessons, it is helpful to anticipate—while the plan is being developed—what materials and equipment will be needed to carry out the lessons successfuly, and to avoid last-minute searches for materials.

This attribute is especially important for teachers working with individuals with disabilities. For example, planning ahead of time for the reading materials needed is important for a teacher of a student with a visual impairment. Most likely the VI teacher can secure copies of large-print materials but will need some lead time to locate the materials—and a day or two is not likely to be enough. Also, if a great deal of information is to be presented through visual graphs and diagrams, the special education teacher will need time to adapt and modify these materials for students with visual impairments and for other learners experiencing visual-spatial difficulties. Students with academically-based disabilities may require other modifications of materials (e.g., reduced vocabulary demands). Again, consideration of material and equipment needs is a critical part of effective planning and influences the types of activities selected.

Analysis of activity attributes can help teachers select activities that will support student achievement of instructional objectives. Procedures for this analysis and an example of the procedure in action are presented in Exhibit 13.3. Participants in the activity are ninth grade students. All of them have functional reading and writing skills; one student in the group has low vision; another has a physical disability that requires him to write with enlarged letters.

As indicated in the exhibit, the analysis involves four steps and results in the development of three lesson plans. Each of the lesson plans draws from ideas identified in Step 3 and creates activities that address learners' needs and lead to the achievement of the instructional objective(s).

EXHIBIT 13.3

Analyzing Activity Attributes

STEP 1: Specify the instructional objective: Presented a job application and using a personal information card previously developed, students will complete all information requested on the job application with legibility and 100% accuracy.

STEP 2: Using a grid of the attributes, brainstorm what could be done in each attribute area to meet the instructional objective.

ATTRIBUTE	BRAINSTORMING
Authenticity	• teacher could create job applications • teacher or students could secure applications from community employers • teacher could ask students what types of jobs they are interested in and secure applications from representative employers
Performance demands	• allow students to dictate information to be written on the application • require students to type information • require students to handwrite responses • have students complete partially filled-out application forms • have students check teacher-completed forms for accuracy • provide applications in large print to ease writing demands • scan applications into the computer to decrease writing demands • have students transfer information from personal information cards to job application forms
Alignment with curriculum	• functional reading and writing skills: using the phone book; reading a newspaper to locate employment opportunities • daily and community living skills: reading a city map to locate businesses; riding the bus to pick up applications
Grouping arrangements	• students can work individually, in dyads, and in cooperative groups
Material and equipment requirements	• job applications (*see* Authenticity) • paper and pencil, typewriter, and/or computer

STEP 3: Select the ideas that would be most efficacious and meaningful in supporting objective achievement.
Authenticity: teacher will ask students what types of jobs they are interested in and secure applications from representative employers
Performance demands: students will be given partially completed forms
Curriculum alignment: functional reading skills will be addressed by students locating local businesses using the phone book
Grouping arrangement: students will work in dyads, completing one application at a time and then work independently
Material and equipment required: partially completed applications and a pencil; for the student with low vision, an enlarged copy of the application; for the student with a physical disability, a scanned application; phone book; generic job application; overheads; personal information card

STEP 4: Synthesize selected activities to identify lesson activities.

Lesson 1
- discussion of community employers and where students would like to apply for work
- use of phone book to look up names of businesses, phone numbers, and addresses
- student selection of a business at which they would like to apply

Lesson 2
- teacher presents a copy of a generic job application on the overhead projector and walks through the different components and the information requested
- teacher models how to transfer information from the personal information card to the application
- students receive their partially completed application and complete it while working with a peer

(continued)

EXHIBIT 13.3

Analyzing Activity Attributes
(continued)

Lesson 3

• using personal information card, students complete the application for their selected business, with peer and teacher support as needed

Addressing Multiple Intelligences

A second approach to the selection of activities involves the application of the theory of multiple intelligences (Gardner, 1982) to instructional practice and is proposed by Armstrong (1994). Armstrong encourages teachers to consider all types of intelligence when selecting activities and designing lesson plans. His procedure for lesson design emphasizes expanded notions of the activities that may be most appropriate in meeting objectives by addressing seven of the eight intelligences (the eighth intelligence, naturalistic, is not included here). The procedure has seven steps:

1. Identify the objective.

2. Ask questions about how each intelligence will be addressed in the lesson.

3. Consider all the possibilities for including the seven intelligences to meet the objective.

4. Brainstorm ideas about how to include each of the intelligences in the lesson.

5. Select approaches and activities from the brainstormed list.

6. Develop a plan that arranges these ideas in a systematic order.

7. Teach the lesson.

Figure 13.1 presents Armstrong's (1994) graphic and questions for working through steps 1 and 2 of the procedure. Figure 13.2 is an example of how Armstrong's suggestions may be put into practice. Exhibit 13.4 presents a sample lesson plan developed through this approach.

■ FIGURE 13.1

Armstrong's Multiple Intelligences Planning Questions

Source: From *Multiple Intelligences in the Classroom* (p. 58), By T. Armstrong, 1994, Alexandria, VA: Association for Supervision and Curriculum Development. Copyright © 1994 ASCD. Used with permission. All rights reserved.

Logical-Mathematical
How can I bring in numbers, calculations, logic, classifications, or critical thinking skills?

Linguistic
How can I use the spoken or written word?

Spatial
How can I use visual aids, visualization, color, art, or metaphor?

Intrapersonal
How can I evoke personal feelings or memories, or give students choices?

OBJECTIVE

Musical
How can I bring in music or environmental sounds, or set key points in a rhythmic or melodic framework?

Interpersonal
How can I engage students in peer sharing, cooperative learning, or large-group simulation?

Bodily-Kinesthetic
How can I involve the whole body or use hands-on experiences?

FIGURE 13.2
Application of Steps 3, 4, and 5 of Armstrong's Model

Logical-Mathematical
• Students will need to make connections between actions and their consequences when identifying advantages and disadvantages

Linguistic
• Students orally state ideas for how to respond to the situation
• Students orally evaluate these responses and provide recommendations/suggestions
• Student ideas are recorded on the board

Spatial
• Student-generated suggestions, consequences, advantages, and disadvantages are presented in matrix form to illustrate relationships among ideas

Instructional Objective: Given a conflict situation taking place on the playground, students will (a) brainstorm at least 3 possible responses to the situation, (b) identify at least two consequences, 1 advantage, and 1 disadvantage of each proposed response, (c) select and try out one suggestion through role-play, (d) analyze the role play in terms of what was effective/ineffective, and (e) orally state at least 2 suggestions and/or considerations if faced with this conflict situation. Students will develop and perform a rap that includes these suggestions.

Intrapersonal
• Students make choices through brainstorming and self-selection of strategies
• Debriefing requires students to reflect on their own feelings and responses to the situation and proposed solutions

Musical
• Students develop a rap to represent their strategy and to help them remember the strategy when faced with a conflict situation

Interpersonal
• Students engage in role-play
• Students engage in debriefing

Bodily-Kinesthetic
• Students engage in role-play

EXHIBIT 13.4
A Lesson Plan Based on Armstrong's Multiple Intelligences Approach

INSTRUCTIONAL OBJECTIVE
Given a conflict situation taking place on the playground, students will (a) brainstorm at least 3 possible responses to the situation, (b) identify at least two consequences, 1 advantage, and 1 disadvantage of each proposed response, (c) select and try out one suggestion through role-play, (d) analyze the role-play in terms of what was effective/ineffective, and (e) orally state at least 2 suggestions and/or considerations if faced with this conflict situation. Students will develop and perform a rap that includes these suggestions.

ACTIVITIES/SEQUENCE
• Discuss what students like and dislike about recess time.
• Have students identify at least 3 possible problems that can occur during recess.
• Explain that today we are going to work together to come up with a rap about handling conflicts that happen on the playground.
• Describe a conflict situation occurring on the playground.
• Following the description, have students turn to partners and describe what they think happened during the conflict.
• As a group, discuss ideas.
• Returning to pairs, have students brainstorm possible ways to respond to the situation and come up with at least 2 ideas to share with the larger group.
• Call students back to the large group and record their brainstorm ideas on poster paper, forming a web to show relationships among ideas.

(continued)

EXHIBIT 13.4

A Lesson Plan Based on Armstrong's Multiple Intelligences Approach
(continued)

- Have students select 3 ideas they think are most helpful and list those ideas on the consequences, advantages, and disadvantages grid.
- Complete the consequences, advantages, and disadvantages grid for each of the 3 ideas.
- Have students go back into pairs to discuss the 3 ideas and the grid and then select the one they think they would try if they were in this situation, and provide a reason for their choice.
- Back in the large group, student pairs state their choice and reason for that choice.
- Select the most commonly selected response and have two or three students carry out a role-play, creating the situation and trying out the strategy.
- Debrief and revise the strategy as needed.
- As a group, students create a rap to remember the strategy.
- Back in pairs, students come up with two scenarios in which they could apply their rap strategy.

THEORY TO PRACTICE

➡ Interview a teacher to find out how she or he makes decisions about which activities to include in instructional plans. How does her or his selection process compare to the processes proposed in this chapter? What are the advantages and disadvantages of these different approaches?

➡ Think of a lesson or topic that you would like to teach. Define this lesson or topic as an instructional objective. Next, work through the two processes to identify activities that you could use in the lesson. Compare your findings. Which approach seems to provide you the most valuable insight and information needed to plan an effective lesson?

CHAPTER SUMMARY

Chapter 13 describes some of the numerous instructional activities available to teachers for designing lessons and offers suggestions for how to adapt these activities to respond to the range of needs found in classrooms. The chapter describes two procedures for selecting activities to include in lessons and emphasizes elements teachers should consider if they are to design lessons that are engaging and result in student learning.

CHAPTER 14

Teaching Mathematics

Read to find out the following:
- ■ key components of an effective mathematics curriculum
- ■ techniques for teaching mathematics
- ■ strategies for teaching specific skills and concepts
- ■ challenges encountered by students with disabilities when working with mathematics

After a teacher gains awareness of the variety of instructional activities available and has approaches for selecting the most appropriate one for a given goal and/or objective, his or her attention turns to the providing of quality instruction to carry out those activities to support students' achievement of lesson objectives and related IEP goals, benchmarks, and objectives. This chapter addresses strategies and techniques for teaching mathematics. Many of them can be used with students with and without disabilities and some may be adapted to reflect the specific needs of individuals with disabilities.

The opening discussion of the key components of an effective mathematics curriculum is followed by general instructional techniques for teaching math. This material is followed by instructional examples linked with specific skills and concepts (e.g., decimals, patterning). The chapter concludes with a discussion of challenges that mathematics poses to students with disabilities.

KEY COMPONENTS OF THE MATHEMATICS CURRICULUM

All mathematics curricula and instruction, regardless of grade level or level of sophistication, have some components or areas in common that need to be addressed to support students' development of "mathematical power," which the National Council of Teachers of Mathematics (NCTM) defines as

> *an individual's abilities to explore, conjecture and reason logically, as well as the ability to use a variety of mathematical methods effectively to solve nonroutine problems. This notion is based on the recognition of mathematics as more than a collection of concepts and skills to be mastered; it includes methods of investigating and reasoning, means of communication, and notions of context. In addition, for each individual, mathematical power involves the development of personal self-confidence. (National Council of Teachers of Mathematics, 1989, p. 5; hereafter cited as NCTM)*

The mathematics curriculum as framed by NCTM identifies four common areas: (a) mathematics as problem solving, (b) mathematics as communication, (c) mathematics as reasoning, and (d) mathematical connections. Because of their central role in mathematics instruction across the grades, we begin with a discussion of these areas.

Mathematics as Problem Solving

The problem-solving component supports and encourages extensive use of problem-solving activities within mathematics instruction. According to the NCTM (1989),

> Problem solving should be the central focus of the mathematics curriculum. As such, it is a primary goal of all mathematics instruction and an integral part of all mathematical activity. Problem solving is not a distinct topic but a process that should permeate the entire program and provide the context in which concepts and skills can be learned. (p. 23)

According to Reys, Suydam, and Lindquist (1995), "Whenever children are faced with providing a solution to a task they have not mastered, they are solving a problem" (p. 55). This suggests that problem solving involves more than simply finding the answer or solution to a word problem in a textbook. It requires children to (a) rephrase the question they have been given to solve into their own words, (b) critically appraise the information they have been given, (c) formulate hypotheses and select strategies for attacking the problem, (d) put those strategies into place, (e) evaluate those strategies and their outcomes, and (f) determine whether the solution is reasonable.

Problem types

Reys, Suydam, and Lindquist (1995) identify two types of problems students may be asked to solve: routine and nonroutine. *Routine problems* require students to apply their mathematics skills in much the same way in which they learned those skills. For example, "Susan has 2 apples. Sally has 5. How many apples do they have altogether?" The problem can be solved through the development of a simple mathematical equation ($2 + 5 = ?$), thus taking the format of a basic arithmetic fact. In contrast, *nonroutine problems* "often require more thought, since the choice of mathematical procedures to solve them is not as obvious" (Reys, Suydam, & Lindquist, 1995, p. 55). An example of a nonroutine problem is as follows: "Together Susan and Sally have 7 apples. How many different combinations of apples could Susan and Sally each have to make a total of 7 apples?" This problem challenges students to come up with a number of different solutions. Additionally, London (1997) defines nonroutine problems as having the following characteristics:

> The problem requires three steps to complete: problem recognition and orientation, trying something, and persistence.
>
> The problem allows for various solutions and requires students to evaluate a variety of potential strategies.
>
> Every student is able to "solve the problem." Though the quality of solutions will vary, students will be able to confront the problem and generate a solution consistent with their ability and efforts. (p. 36)

Another way to classify problems is to distinguish them between convergent and divergent types (Souviney, 1981). *Convergent problems* are similar to routine problems: the student "decides which operation(s) to apply to the values provided in order to determine the correct answer" (p. 5). Like Reys, Suydam, and Lindquist (1995), Souviney (1981) believes convergent problems limit students' thinking and present problems in overly neat packages, not as they appear in real life. In contrast, *divergent problems,* like nonroutine problems as Reys, Suydam, and Lindquist (1995) define them, require students to identify that there is a problem first and then, working through trial and error, to develop an approach toward a solution that requires both analysis and synthesis. Exhibit 14.1 is a divergent problem proposed by Souviney (1981).

EXHIBIT 14.1

**Jailhouse Blues:
A Divergent Problem**

John Turnkey, the prison warden, decided to free his prisoners for good behavior. The cells were numbered from 1 to 25. Each had a lock that opened when you turned it once and locked when it was turned again, and so on.

One night when the prisoners were sleeping, he quietly turned all the locks once, opening all the cells. He began to worry that he may have freed too many prisoners, so he went back and turned every second lock (2, 4, 6, 8, . . . 24) which locked half the cells. Thinking that there still might be too many prisoners freed, he gave every third lock a turn (3, 6, 9, 12, . . . 24), then every fourth lock (4, 8, 12, . . . 24), fifth (5, 10, 15, 20, 25), sixth (6, 12, 18, 24), seventh, eighth, ninth, tenth, eleventh, and so on, all the way to every twenty-fifth (of course he only turned one lock for every thirteenth and above). Who got out of jail in the morning?

Source: From *Solving Problems Kids Care About* (p. 89), by R. J. Souviney, 1981, Glenview, IL: Good Year Books.

Awareness of these problem types—routine and convergent; nonroutine and divergent—is important to the teaching of problem solving. Teachers need to balance the types of problems students are exposed to. Providing students experiences with only routine problems is not likely to lead to the development of the skills they need to solve nonroutine problems—the types of problems they will encounter in life outside school.

Selecting and writing problems

Selecting and writing problems for students to solve can be a challenging activity for teachers. Souviney (1981) suggests that the following characteristics are reflective of an "ideal problem situation" (p. 5). To meet these characteristics, a problem should

1. *be readily understandable to the student, yet the solution should not be immediately apparent;*
2. *be intrinsically motivating and intellectually stimulating;*
3. *have more than one solution "path";*
4. *require only previously learned arithmetic operations and concepts;*
5. *lend itself to being solved over a reasonable period of time (not a simple computational procedure);*
6. *be somewhat open-ended (solutions should suggest new problems);*
7. *integrate various subject areas—mathematics, science, social studies, fine arts;*
8. *be well defined so you will know when it's solved. (p. 5)*

In addition to providing problems with these characteristics is the challenge to provide students with problems that match their skills and understanding levels, being neither too difficult nor too easy. London (1997) suggests that a problem is of the right level of difficulty when

the student reads the problem, has no idea what the solution is but has a few ideas about how to start, tries something and becomes clearer about the solution, eventually finds a good solution, and, from the processing of the problem, realizes some ways he or she could have improved the process or solution. (p. 36)

Reys, Suydam, and Lindquist's (1995) considerations for selecting and writing story problems are provided in the "Make It Happen" feature.

MAKE IT HAPPEN
Selecting and Writing Problems

Include Problems That
- contain extra or unneeded information
- require students to estimate
- require students to determine the level of accuracy needed
- are directly applicable and/or reflective of problems students will encounter outside school
- require understanding of very large and very small numbers
- reflect students' interests and their community and include their names and the names of local places and attractions
- include reasoning and checking for reasonableness of answers
- do not have a mathematics answer but appear to have one
- require multiple strategies
- include decision making

Develop a Problem-Solving File by
- collect information from newspapers and magazines that can be used as the basis for writing problems
- write problems on your own
- work with others in writing problems or attending workshops that focus on problem-solving strategies and development of problems
- share your problems with others
- have children write their own problems

Source: Adapted from Reys, Suydam, & Lindquist (1995).

Problems may be written to reflect different needs and challenges as well. For students in need of a more functional mathematics curriculum, problem solving could focus on skill areas such as time, money, and measurement. For example, students given a TV schedule could be challenged to come up with at least three different plans for what shows they will watch during two hours of TV viewing each day. This problem is open-ended and nonroutine and relevant to students' lives.

Additionally, rather than solving only textbook and teacher-developed story problems, students may create their own. For this arrangement to be effective, students must be taught the key components of a problem and how to present problems that are comprehensible to others. Students may draw from classroom and personal experiences and thereby increase their overall motivation for developing problem-solving skills because the problems will reflect their lives and interests.

Problem solving strategies

There are numerous problem-solving strategies that may be taught to students. A basic strategy includes these steps:

1. Read the problem.

2. Restate the problem in your own words.

3. Analyze and/or list the information given.

4. Select an approach for solving the problem.

5. Apply the approach.

6. Check the solution.

This strategy, however, cannot always be applied in this step-by-step fashion. For example, students may read a problem, restate the problem, list information, and then select a strategy but as they work through the problem, they may find their approach to be ineffective. At this point, they may need to reread the problem, restate it once again, and reconsider the information given. It may be that some of the information is superfluous or must be manipulated before it can be used to solve the problem. Only after students revisit the problem will they be able to proceed to steps four through six. Because linear problem solving may not always be the best or the most generalizable strategy, teaching numerous approaches to problem solving may be helpful.

Mnemonics can be helpful in supporting student problem-solving skills. FAST DRAW (Mercer, Jordan, & Miller, 1996) is one example of a mnemonic approach to problem solving. This mnemonic is most applicable to routine or convergent problems:

F   *Find* what you are solving for.
    Underline the information that tells what to solve for. The information is usually in the last sentence or in the sentence that poses a question.
A   *Ask* yourself, "What information is given?"
    List information described with numbers as you read it.
S   *Set* up the equation.
    Determine the correct order of the numbers and determine the operation.
    With whole numbers if the answer appears to decrease, the operation is subtraction or division; if the answer appears to increase, the operation is addition or multiplication.
T   *Take* the equation and solve it.
    Solve the problem from memory or use DRAW to solve it.

D   *Discover* the sign.
R   *Read* the problem (i.e., the equation).
A   *Answer* or draw and check (i.e., answer the problem from memory or represent the equation via drawings and check work).
W   *Write* the answer.
    For example, to draw the problem 5×3, draw five horizontal lines to represent the number of groups and draw vertical tallies on each line to represent the number in each group. (Mercer, Jordan, & Miller, 1996, p. 154)

Other problem-solving strategies commonly offered in the literature are listed in Exhibit 14.2. These strategies would not be introduced all at one time but rather over a period of time, possibly an entire academic year or longer. The purpose of presenting these strategies is to provide students with numerous ways to approach and solve problems. Although the strategies listed in the exhibit may be helpful for individuals with disabilities, additional, unique strategies may be needed to support their success in solving problems. The "Make It Happen" feature identifies what else might be done to support student participation in problem-solving activities.

EXHIBIT 14.2

Common Problem-Solving Strategies

Act It Out: Students use themselves or manipulatives to take on roles identified in the problem and act out the problem and its solution.

Make a Drawing or Diagram: Students present problem information in a graphic format to support understanding.

Look for a Pattern: Students look at information to determine whether there is a pattern that will assist them in finding the solution.

Construct a Table: Students organize given information into a table and, by completing the table, arrive at a solution.

Account Systematically for All Possibilities: Students may identify possible solutions for highly complex problems by systematically analyzing solutions and organizing them, then running trials using each solution until a working solution is found.

Guess and Check: Students propose a possible solution and check to see whether it works.

Work Backward: Students start from the solution and work backward to identify needed variables.

Identify Wanted, Given, and Needed Information: Students begin by stating the information they will want to solve the problem, identifying the information they have been given, then identifying additional information they need to solve the problem.

Write an Open Sentence: Students begin by writing an open sentence that they then solve.

Solve a Simpler or Similar Problem: Students reduce the complexity of the problem by using easier numbers or by working through a problem that is similar but not as complex.

Change Your Point of View: Students look at the problem from a new angle.

Source: Reys, Suydam, & Lindquist, 1995.

MAKE IT HAPPEN   **Problem-Solving Supports for Individuals with Disabilities**

Challenge	Possible Supports
Reading level	• Have other students read the problems to the student. • Put the problems on tape. • Put the problems on a computer with a voice output system. • Decrease the vocabulary load of the problems.
Vocabulary	• Highlight key words. • Define key words. • Provide students with a cue card showing key words and their meaning.
Comprehension	• Alter the vocabulary. • Restate the problem in simplified phrasing. • Allow students in pairs to discuss the meaning of the problem and what it is asking. • Provide manipulatives for students to use in modeling the problem.
Motivation	• Write problems that mention students' names. • Write problems that reflect familiar life situations. • Limit the number of problems presented at one time or on one page.
Determination of operation	• Work on problems of a similar type before moving to more complex problems or problem sets requiring mixed operations.

- Have students estimate what their answer will be and then select an operation that will assist them in achieving that solution.
- Have students state the predicted solution in words first and then change those words into an equation.

Relevant and irrelevant information
- Teach a questioning strategy that evaluates each piece of information and its relationship to the problem.
- Have students highlight the information they think is most important.

Arrangements for teaching problem solving

Teachers may present problem solving to students in several ways. One approach is to designate a problem of the week. The problem may be introduced on Monday and students work individually, in pairs, or in small groups during the week, discussing it and coming up with a plan for solving it. Time each day may be devoted to working on the problem, followed by additional instruction during math class. Or, the problem may provide the curricular focus for the week with the teacher conducting mini-lessons on the skills students need to solve it. At the end of the week, students submit their work along with a written explanation of how they arrived at their solution.

Another approach is to designate a problem of the day. The procedure described for a problem of the week may be used for this approach. The problem of the day will be less complex than the problem of the week and will be a problem that students can solve in a reasonable amount of time. It may be presented at the beginning of class as a motivator. Then, after modeling and discussion of a math concept or skill, students return to the problem of the day and apply what they learned during the lesson. The problem of the day may also serve to reinforce students' prior learning and serve as a warm-up activity for the math class. Students may maintain a notebook of mathematical problems they have solved and reflect on this work over time.

Organizing for the teaching of problem solving also calls for consideration of grouping arrangements (e.g., dyads, cooperative learning groups). Souviney (1981) suggests that students work in groups of four to solve problems. In his approach, students assigned to groups of four are presented with a problem or with a list of problems from which they select one to solve. The four students work on the same problem to find a solution. They can seek help outside the group only when all members of the group agree on the question to be asked of the outsider. This constraint forces group members to work with one another and to pool their understanding. Souviney (1981) suggests that at first, groups be given 15 minutes to work on the problem and then return as a class to debrief with a representative from each group describing their problem, their approach, and the progress they made to the whole class.

Burns (1992a, 1992b) suggests a teaching format that involves the class working on a problem as an entire group. The lesson is divided into three sections: Introducing, Exploring, and Summarizing. During *Introducing*, the teacher reviews relevant concepts, presents a problem that is like the problem the class is to solve but is less complex, and then presents it to the students, providing them clues. During *Exploring*, students work in groups and solve the problem with teacher assistance as needed. In *Summarizing*, students debrief and discuss their solutions and problem-solving processes.

Mathematics as Communication

Mathematics as communication focuses on students dialoguing with one another about mathematics and becoming comfortable using mathematical language. According to the NCTM (1989), "Interacting with classmates helps children construct knowledge, learn other ways to think about ideas, and clarify their own thinking" (p. 26). Communicating about mathematical understandings challenges students to analyze, summarize, and evaluate their approaches and solutions as well as to explain and justify the processes and strategies they employ to arrive at a solution.

Specifically, teachers can foster the development of mathematics as communication through the types of instruction they provide. For example, communication about mathematics may be best fostered in group activities that require group problem solving and dialogue. Writing about and drawing responses and then explaining them to peers is one activity that fosters mathematics as communication. Moreover, teacher questioning can lead to development of mathematics as communication. If teachers broaden the types of questions they ask during mathematics instruction, they challenge students not only to think more critically or to reason through their responses, but to develop the mathematical language necessary to express their ideas and understandings.

In their investigation of the questions that teachers ask during mathematics instruction, Hiebert and Wearne (1993) identified four classes of questions: recall, describe strategy, generate problem, and examine underlying features. This taxonomy of questions, presented in Table 14.1, may be used by teachers when analyzing their questioning patterns during mathematics instruction. Each class of question includes multiple question types (first column of the table), each of which is defined in the middle column and illustrated through sample questions in the final column of the table. Students with disabilities may experience difficulty in responding to these different question types and require extensive practice working with them before they are successful. The "Make It Happen" feature offers some suggestions for helping students to develop skills in answering these questions.

TABLE 14.1 CLASSES OF QUESTIONS ASKED BY TEACHER

QUESTION TYPE	DESCRIPTION	EXAMPLE
Recall		
Recall factual information	Recite previously learned or currently available facts	"What number is in the one's place?"
Recall procedures	Prescribe previously learned rule	"What should we do next?"
Recall prior work	Recall a previously discussed topic	"What did we do yesterday?"
Describe strategy		
Describe strategy	Tell how you solved the problem	"How did you find the answer?"
Describe alternative strategy	Describe another way to solve the same problem	"Did anyone do this problem a different way?"
Generate problem		
Generate story	Create a story to match a number sentence	"Who can tell a story about this number sentence?"
Generate problem	Create a problem to fit given constraints	"Can you make up a problem about the distances on this map?"
Examine underlying features		
Explain	Explain why a procedure is chosen or why it works	"Why did you work the problem like that?"
Analysis	Consider the nature of a problem or a solution strategy	"How is this different than the one before?"

From Hiebert and Wearne, "Instructional tasks, classroom discourse, and students' learning in second grade arithmetic," *American Educational Research* 30 (1993): 402. Used by permission.

MAKE IT HAPPEN
Mathematical Question Supports for Students

Recall
- Have students go back and highlight the response in the problem or solutions.
- Provide cards with answers—students select the card they believe is the correct response.
- Provide a checklist of steps for solving the problems—it may be presented in words or pictures.
- Use a notebook as a reference for what was discussed previously.
- Open lessons with a review session.
- Make use of distributed practice (providing repeated opportunities for students to practice skills previously taught).

Describe Strategy
- Have students draw or write with symbols demonstrating how they solved a problem.
- Present steps of the strategy for solving a problem on cards and have the student place the cards in order.
- Have students listen to tape recordings of their peers describing how they solved the problem. Check for understanding.
- Have peers model, using think-alouds, how they approached and solved problems; then have students attempt the problem in the same way.

Generate Problem
- Provide students with partial problems and have them supply the needed information.
- Provide students with a problem frame for which they fill in the information: Harry and Samatha wanted to go to the store to buy _____. They each had $_____ to spend. They wanted to buy a _____ for $_____. Do they have enough money? If so, how much change will they get back? If not, how much more money do they need to buy the _____?
- Have students draw pictures to illustrate a problem.
- Have students work with peers in writing their own problems.

Examine Underlying Features
- For analysis, provide examples of two problems and assist the student in highlighting their similarities and differences.
- Analyze the similarities and differences of problems using a Venn diagram.
- Provide students with strips stating problem characteristics and have students sort those strips into shared features and unique features.

Mathematics journals are being promoted as one means of reinforcing students' understanding of mathematical concepts and procedures and fostering their skills as communicators of mathematics. But the requirement to express understanding through written language may present barriers to the demonstration of mathematical communication and reasoning skills by many students, including those with disabilities. To support these students in their efforts to become writers of mathematics, accommodations and adaptations may be necessary. The "Make It Happen" feature provides some beginning suggestions for supporting student success in writing about mathematics.

MAKE IT HAPPEN
Mathematics Journal Writing

- When introducing writing about mathematics, model the process as a group. Brainstorm and record ideas on the board. Have students select what they consider to be the most important ideas. Translate those ideas into sentences and record them on the board or on an overhead. Students could then write those ideas in their notebooks using the same words or words of their own.
- Write on the board or provide a list of mathematical terms that students may want to use in their writing.
- Provide sentence frames for students. For example, "When solving the problem, the first thing I did was _____ . Second, I _____ ." For more open-ended writings: "The thing I found most difficult about today's math activity was _____." "The thing I found most interesting about the lesson was _____." "The one thing I still do not understand about what we did in math class today is _____ ."
- Allow students to use drawings to explain ideas.
- Have students audiotape their ideas, rather than expressing them in writing. Ideas could also be dictated to a peer, teacher, or assistant in the classroom.
- Allow students to work in pairs to write their responses.
- Encourage students to use the computer for writing their responses.
- Capture mathematics activities using a Polaroid camera or QuickTake camera. Photographs can then be pasted into a journal, and students can add short sentences describing what occurred.
- Videotape mathematics activities. Have students view the tapes, discuss what they see, and then write about their math experience.

Students may also write stories that involve math concepts or write letters to each other explaining a math procedure or new idea they have learned. Books addressing math concepts may be used to help students express their math ideas.

Mathematics as Reasoning

Another key component of the mathematics curriculum is reasoning. Mathematics as reasoning involves students explaining why they believe an answer is correct or reasonable and why they believe their approach was feasible and led to a reasonable solution. At the heart of reasoning is the belief that

> *Students need a great deal of time and many experiences to develop their ability to construct valid arguments in problem settings and evaluate the arguments of others. (NCTM, 1989, p. 81)*

Many of the activities suggested for mathematics as communication also apply here, as long as the communication focuses on answering the question *why* and the justification of the process students used to arrive at a solution. Activities involving mathematics as reasoning require students to reason about things that are happening as well as reason about why they believe they are happening.

Mathematics reasoning presents unique challenges for students with disabilities. They may have difficulties in seeing patterns, in making connections among ideas, and in drawing conclusions or in explaining why things happen. The "Make It Happen" list offers some beginning suggestions for assisting students in developing their reasoning skills.

> **MAKE IT HAPPEN**
>
> ### Development of Reasoning Skills in Mathematics
>
> - Have children predict solutions and support their ideas.
> - Have children estimate and explain their processes for arriving at their estimation.
> - Have students explain their answers and why they believe they are reasonable.
> - Have students illustrate their steps or orally describe their processes for arriving at a solution.
> - Use think-alouds to model the reasoning process.
> - Have students work in pairs, explaining their processes and reasoning to one another.
> - Allow students to create diagrams and drawings that explain their reasoning.

Mathematical Connections

The final key component of the mathematics curriculum is connections—direct links between (a) what students are learning in mathematics instruction and what they are required to do in their daily lives, (b) what students are learning through mathematics instruction and what they are learning in other disciplines, and (c) two or more mathematical topics.

When you are teaching basic geometric shapes, including activities that require students to identify those shapes in their environment, help them to make a connection between the school curriculum and the world around them. When you are teaching the addition, subtraction, multiplication, and division of decimals, topics such as spending money and balancing a checkbook, using credit cards, purchasing insurance, and securing a loan provide links between school and life outside school. Connections may be taught by means of instruction in community-based settings, where students can observe adults using math skills in their day-to-day lives.

Connections may range from very basic (e.g., noticing numbers in the environment) to very complex (e.g., finding relationships between objects in the environment and expressing them algebraically) and will vary depending on the student's age and ability. They may be most critical for students with disabilities because of the difficulties they experience in generalizing understandings to new situations. By making these connections explicit, students will experience greater success in developing concepts.

Connections of the second type—between what is taught in mathematics class and in other courses during the school day—are not always obvious to teachers or students. Both teachers and students may view curriculum as compartmentalized (e.g., English class is for the development of literature appreciation and writing skills). However, a brief survey of all curricular disciplines reveals the presence of mathematical concepts. When completing scientific experiments, students may be asked to measure, draw to scale, compute, and make predictions requiring the manipulation of numbers. Social studies may require students to analyze events according to historical time lines, to apply concepts of longitude and latitude, and to analyze information presented in graphs, tables, and figures. Literature may mention events and actions based on time sequences or use of numbers. For example, *How Big Is A Foot?* (Myller, 1991) is a delightful children's tale about the need for standardized units of measurement. Other literature is available as well for the teaching of mathematical concepts, including the *Tangram Magician* by Ernst and Ernst (1990) and *Eight Hands Round* by Ann Whitford Paul (1991). In *Math and Literature (K–3)* Marilyn Burns (1992a) suggests mathematical activities to be carried out in connection with selected literature. One story in her book is *The Doorbell Rang* by Pat Hutchins. In this story the mother bakes cookies, and just before the children are going to share the cookies, the doorbell rings and in comes a friend who also wants to share the cookies. The doorbell continues to ring, and the children are asked to share the cookies with the new visitors. The arrival of each guest necessitates a new mathematical computation. A World Wide Web site developed by Carol Hurst also lists literature connected with mathematics. The address is *ht.//www.crocker.com/~rebotis/.*

The third type of connection is connections between mathematical topics. For example, when learning basic addition and subtraction facts, students traditionally master addition before moving on to subtraction. Many students who experience this instructional sequence have difficulty in mastering subtraction facts and comment, "I love to add. I hate to subtract." If teaching emphasized connections from the outset, students would see addition and subtraction facts not as separate entities but rather as partners. When learning that $3 + 2 = 5$, they can also learn that $5 - 2 = 3$ and $5 - 3 = 2$. The same strategy can be applied to the teaching of multiplication and division facts. A similar example is the use of addition to explain multiplication—that is, showing that multiplication is repeated addition. Helping students make these connections leads to better conceptual understanding of mathematics.

THEORY TO PRACTICE

➡ Meet with a classroom teacher to learn how she or he incorporates these four key components in her or his mathematics instruction. To what extent does the teacher involve students in all four? What activities and exercises does the teacher use to include them? What accommodations and modifications does the teacher make to ensure the active participation and learning of students with disabilities?

➡ Working with a peer, write a series of problems that you believe would be engaging for students. Be sure to include the different types of problems described in this section. Present your problems to another group to receive feedback. What was most difficult about writing them?

➡ Review the general education mathematics curriculum outcomes for a selected grade level. Create a list of the primary concepts and skills to be covered. For each, come up with at least three connections that could be introduced to students to assist them in seeing the relevance of these mathematics concepts and skills to their daily lives. Select one of your connections and develop a lesson plan for introducing the concept and its connection to a diverse group of learners.

➡ Meet with a teacher who is using journal writing in mathematics. What strategies did the teacher use to introduce mathematical journal writing to students? What strategies is he or she using to support students in expressing their mathematical power through writing? What strategies is he or she using to support students who have difficulties capturing their ideas in writing? If possible, examine copies of students' journal entries. What types of information are they including in their entries? Are students addressing the four key components? If so, how? If not, what could be done to encourage student inclusion of these skills and concepts in their writing?

INSTRUCTIONAL TECHNIQUES

In this section we describe techniques that can be used to teach mathematical concepts and skills. Many of them are useful across grades and student needs.

Concrete, Semiconcrete, and Abstract Representation

Students may understand mathematical concepts and skills best by moving from the *concrete* to the *semiconcrete* and then to the *abstract* stage of representation. In the *concrete stage* students use manipulatives to represent ideas. For example, when adding 2 and 3, students may count out 2 blocks, then 3 blocks, and then count them all to find the sum. The concrete stage is used in all levels of learning—including high school and beyond. In the *semiconcrete stage* students draw representations of the concrete. Instead of taking out blocks to represent the problem, students draw blocks or lines on paper and then count the figures they have drawn to arrive at the sum. Teachers often overlook this stage. In the *abstract stage* students use numbers and symbols to represent ideas: 2 + 3 = 5.

Many teachers provide students time to work at the concrete stage but then rapidly move them to the abstract stage, skipping the semiconcrete stage altogether. One day students could be using manipulatives to solve problems and the next day the manipulatives are not available so the students have to solve problems at the abstract stage. To prevent this segmenting of learning and to foster understanding of the three stages, teachers may find it appropriate for some students to work at all three stages concurrently. Meese (1994) calls this strategy *parallel modeling*. It seems to be most appropriate for older students.

Figure 14.1 is an example of a parallel modeling activity that concurrently incorporates concrete, semiconcrete, and abstract representation. The student first builds the number on a place-value mat using base-10 blocks. Next, on the work paper, the student transfers the work from the mat to a record sheet by drawing the symbolic representation of what was constructed using the manipulatives (lines and dots). Then the student writes the abstract representation of the number in the remaining column of the work paper. In this way, the student makes direct connections and moves smoothly from one stage to another. Figure 14.1 shows the completion of the second problem representing the number 46.

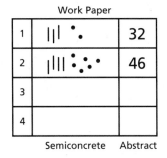

FIGURE 14.1
Three Stages of Mathematical Representation

Miller and Mercer (1993b) used the concrete, semiconcrete, and abstract instructional sequence to teach students with learning disabilities (ages 8 to 11) basic addition facts with sums from 10 to 18 and division facts with quotients from 0 to 9, and the adding of coins to sums of 50 cents. Manipulatives (e.g., checkers, buttons, pennies) were used during the concrete stage. Students made drawings during the semiconcrete stage. During the abstract stage, they were encouraged to solve the problems without using manipulatives or drawings. Findings from the study suggested that this was a successful approach for students learning these particular addition and division skills.

Use of Manipulatives

Currently, manipulatives are strongly encouraged for all levels of mathematics instruction. Manipulatives include fraction bars, base-10 blocks, unifix cubes, counters, geoboards, and rulers—what can serve as manipulatives is limited only by a teacher's imagination. Manipulatives are being encouraged because research indicates that lessons involving the use of manipulatives result in greater mathematical learning than do lessons not including their use (Sowell, 1989).

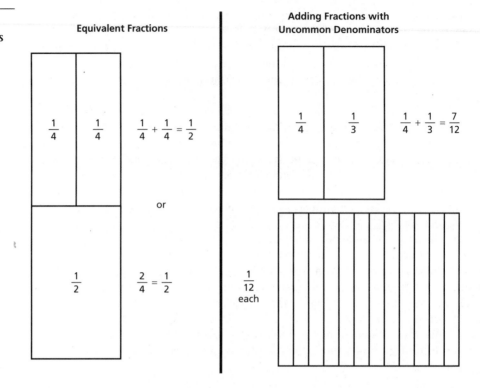

Manipulatives can be used to model problems, to explain theories and operations, and to allow students to see a concept in concrete form before they represent it abstractly. Manipulatives are commonly used to teach basic counting and mathematics facts and operations. They also can be used to teach algebraic concepts, high-level geometry concepts and rules, and probability. Figure 14.2 illustrates how manipulatives can be used to teach the concept of equivalent fractions and the adding of fractions with uncommon denominators. The "Make It Happen" feature offers some suggestions for using manipulatives in the classroom.

▌**MAKE IT HAPPEN**
Using Manipulatives

- Plan how manipulatives will be distributed. Will the set of manipulatives needed for each group be packaged before instruction begins and placed in a bag or container so that each group needs only to pick up a pack of manipulatives for the activity? Will the manipulatives be housed in a common area and will students be responsible for going to that area, counting out and gathering what they need, and then returning to their workstation? Will the teacher pass out and collect the manipulatives? Will groups have specific places for housing their manipulatives? Will groups be responsible for counting their manipulatives before returning them to ensure that none has been lost?
- Allow students to become familiar with the manipulatives before they are required to use them in an activity. For some students, manipulatives will be novel and attractive, and they may become distracted by them if not allowed to explore them first. Allow for free exploration before asking students to use the manipulatives to complete a task to prevent problems during instruction.

- Discuss safety and the use of manipulatives. For smaller children, you may need to discuss how to handle the manipulatives, how to place them on the work surface and not to put them in their mouths, and how to pass them from one person to another. The same may be true for older students who may be using manipulatives with sharp or jagged edges, or manipulatives such as rubber bands that can be used as weapons, and so on. Safety first.
- Model the appropriate use of the manipulatives. This will help students understand how manipulatives can be used to model ideas and assist them in solving problems. Modeling also can decrease the possibility that students will see the manipulatives as toys or "babyish." Modeling can assist students in understanding the important role that manipulatives can play in their development of mathematical understanding.
- Have students use manipulatives when discussing and explaining processes and strategies. The pairing of manipulative use and dialogue about mathematics concepts will serve to reinforce the value of manipulatives.
- Develop manipulatives that can be used by students with physical disabilities and those who experience difficulty handling the manipulatives typically provided in the classroom.

Highlighting and Color Coding

Highlighting and color coding can be used across all areas of mathematics instruction as well as other disciplines. Color coding may be used to call attention to specific information or to the most salient information for a student. For example, plus and minus signs on a sheet of problems may be highlighted or color-coded to draw a student's attention to the operation requested, or key symbols or steps of a procedure may be highlighted or color-coded. Highlighting to box key ideas may be done simply through use of a highlighter or crayons.

Mnemonic Instruction

Mnemonic instruction can help students remember the steps or strategy they are to apply when solving problems. FAST DRAW, described previously, is one mnemonic for mathematics. Another is CAP, which may be used for solving simple algebra equations:

C   *Combine* like terms.
     Combine terms on each side of the equation that have the same variable.
     Combine terms on each side of the equation that do not have a variable.
     Combine terms by doing the computations indicated by the signs.
A   *Ask* yourself, "How can I isolate the variable?"
     Remove nonvariable numbers by changing to 0 (perform the opposite computation). Remove a variable number by changing it to 1 (perform the opposite computation).
P   *Put* the values of the variable in the initial equation and check to see if the equation is balanced (Mercer, Jordan, & Miller, 1996, pp. 154–155).

Demonstration plus Permanent Model Approach

One simple teaching technique that may be used across a variety of mathematics areas is the demonstration plus permanent model developed by Smith and Lovitt (1975). The teacher first models how a problem is to be solved. This example then becomes the permanent model that students refer to when completing similar problems. For example, when a student is working on a sheet of problems, the teacher and student may complete the first problem together, talking through the steps, using thinking-alouds. Once completed, a box can be drawn around the problem and its solution, indicating to the student that it is a model of how the other problems are to be completed. This technique may be applied at higher levels as well. Problems involving multiple steps such as long division, the solutions to algebraic problems, and the development of geometry proofs may be approached through reference to a problem that has already been successfully completed. Steps within the model can be highlighted and directions for the steps can be provided as well.

Use of Calculators

Calculators may serve as critical supports for all students, including those with disabilities. Calculators that talk, that have enlarged numbers, or that have a textured keyboard or braille numbering can all be helpful for students with disabilities. Sheffield and Cruikshank (1996) suggest various uses of calculators in math instruction. Their first suggestion is to introduce the function of each key and how to operate the calculator. Some of their other suggestions are found in the "Make It Happen" feature.

MAKE IT HAPPEN
Using Calculators

Patterns

Students may solve problems quickly and discover patterns in their answers when using a calculator—something that is more labor intensive if each calculation must be completed by hand. For example, students may use the calculator to discover the pattern that is formed when numbers are multiplied by nine. Older students may solve more involved computations in less time on the calculator, thus freeing them to discover patterns.

Operations

Students can use a calculator to solve problems and to discover relationships between operations. For example, when given a story problem involving multiplication, a student may choose to use repeated addition to arrive at the solution. The numbers could be entered into the calculator and, after using both approaches, the findings discussed. Students could also discover easily that addition and subtraction, and multiplication and division, are inverse operations through calculator use. Using a calculator in these situations frees the student to attend to the patterns and operations, rather than becoming distracted, frustrated, or bogged down by the calculations.

Problem Solving and Thinking Skills

By using the calculator, students are free to try multiple approaches to solving a problem without having to stop and do the calculations by hand. For students with disabilities, the calculator removes the need to complete all calculations before learning if their approach is reasonable.

Graphically Display Data

Calculators have capabilities to display algebraic expressions visually that are otherwise difficult or impossible for students to chart and analyze.

Improve Mental Computation and Estimation

Students can quickly and easily check the reasonableness of their mental computations and estimations.

Source: Adapted from Sheffield & Cruikshank (1996).

Use of Computers

Computers and computer software can be used to enhance math instruction. Some suggestions for computer use in mathematics are found in the "Make It Happen" feature. Additional suggestions for the application of computer technology in the classroom are found in Chapter 18 on technological supports.

MAKE IT HAPPEN

Using Computers and Computer Software

Drill and Practice

Multiple mathematics programs are available that provide drill and practice for students. The majority of drill and practice programs include features that make their use functional and practical for the classroom: (a) the types of problems presented can be set to reflect students' skill levels; (b) the rate at which problems are presented can be adjusted to reflect students' abilities; (c) programs provide cues and prompts when students make errors; and (d) programs provide immediate feedback about the correctness of responses and have bookkeeping capabilities that let teachers monitor student performance.

Problem Solving

Mathematics software programs are available that challenge students to solve basic and more complex problems. Some software packages present problems through simulations, adding authenticity to the task. Problem difficulty may be adjusted, feedback is immediate, and cues may be provided to support students in their thinking.

Graphic Capabilities

Software, including spreadsheets and other statistical packages, may be used by students to graph data, analyze trends and patterns in data, and statistically analyze given data sets. Findings can be displayed graphically to allow for visual inspection.

Individualized Instruction

Computer software programs and tasks within programs can be selected and tailored to reflect students' individual needs. Students can also select software to enhance skills they identify as an area of interest or skills they wish to strengthen.

Interpersonal Skills

Computers offer opportunities for students to work together to solve mathematics problems and complete tasks. Students can sit side by side at the computer, dialoguing about their work and thus enhancing their ability to communicate mathematical ideas to others. They can develop skills such as turn-taking, negotiation, consensus, asking questions, providing feedback, and supporting and encouraging others.

One software package especially helpful for teaching computation skills to students with disabilities, particularly physical and learning disabilities, is MathPad (Intellitools, Novato, CA). MathPad walks students through the process of solving computation problems on the computer, aligning numbers to reflect place value and allowing students to show their regrouping skills. Moreover, the software allows students who are not able to use pencil and paper to complete computation problems in the same fashion as their nondisabled peers. (Refer to Chapter 18 for additional information on computer applications.)

➡ Observe a mathematics teacher at work. Which of these techniques did the teacher incorporate into the lesson? How did the teacher include them? What were some of the outcomes associated with their inclusion?

➡ Design a mathematics lesson that includes at least one of the techniques described in this section. When designing the lesson, adapt and modify the technique to respond to the needs of a selected student with disabilities. Present your lesson to a peer for review.

➡ Observe a student with a disability during his or her mathematics class. In what areas does the child appear to experience the most difficulty? The least difficulty? Reviewing these concerns, identify means for reinforcing the student's strengths in mathematics and for using those strengths to address areas in which the child is experiencing the most difficulty. When developing strategies, refer to the suggestions given here. What strategies and approaches would be appropriate for work with this student? Explain your rationale. How would you introduce them to the student and incorporate them in the student's instruction?

TEACHING MATHEMATICAL SKILLS AND CONCEPTS

In this section of the chapter we describe how to teach specific mathematical skills and concepts. Our focus is on eight topics: number sense, estimation, basic facts and operations, measurement, probability and statistics, patterns and functions, fractions, and decimals.

Number Sense

Sheffield and Cruikshank (1996) define number sense as

> *the ability to recognize number relationships, the ability to determine if operations are reasonable, and the ability to interpret numbers used in daily life. (p. 53)*

One concept related to number sense is one-to-one correspondence. Sheffield and Cruikshank (1996) offer the following activity as one means for developing students' understanding of one-to-one correspondence:

> *Collect five small cans for flower pots, such as juice cans . . . Make 15 flowers using pipe cleaners for the stems and construction paper for the petals. Put one to five dots on the outside of each can. Ask the children to match the number of flowers to the number of dots on the can. Let the children count to tell you how many dots and flowers there are. Later, you can increase the numbers of flowers and dots. (p. 104)*

Number sense is reflected in other skills as well, such as classifying, comparing, and counting. Classification activities can be introduced by presenting a set of familiar objects or manipulatives and having students classify them. When presented this task, students may choose to classify the objects in terms of color, size, shape, or some other attribute. The purpose is to challenge students to group objects in a logical way and to explain their system of classification. Comparisons develop understanding of the concepts *more than, less than,* and *equal to,* as well as *long* and *short.* When making comparisons, students arrange objects from shortest to longest, from lightest to heaviest, and so on.

Counting, too, is linked with number sense. Reys, Suydam, and Lindquist (1995) identify two common stages of counting: rote counting and rational counting. Students counting by rote may have an incorrect sequence of numbers (e.g., one, three, four, six) but demonstrate one-to-one correspondence, or they may have the correct number sequence but an incorrect one-to-one correspondence (e.g., skipping an object or assigning more than one number to an object). In rational counting, "the child not only uses one-to-one correspondence in counting, but also is able to answer the question about the number of objects being counted" (Reys, Suydam, & Lindquist, 1995, p. 102). Reys, Suydam, and Lindquist (1995) offer three strategies to help students develop their counting skills: counting on, counting back, and skip counting. In *counting on,* a student begins with a certain number—for example, 12—and *counts on:* 13, 14, 15, and so on. *Counting back* is the opposite. Given a number, the student *counts back:* 12, 11, 10, 9, and so on. In *skip counting,* the student uses *count-bys.* Skip counting by fives is 5, 10, 15, 20, and so on. Skip counting can be forward or backward.

Teachers can take advantage of many "teachable moments" when teaching counting skills. When students are lining up, they can count as they join the line. When supplies are passed out, students can count the objects, applying all three counting strategies. Teachers also may use counting activities as motivators at the start of a math class or as fillers for times when the class is waiting for a guest speaker or is waiting to go to an assembly, to the lunchroom, or to the library, or to be dismissed from class. All students can benefit greatly from practice counting. Skip counting, for instance, can reinforce the relationship between addition and multiplication as well as reinforce multiplication facts.

Estimation

Estimation is an important skill because many times we are required to make an estimate, not to come up with an exact answer. For example, when shopping at the supermarket, we mentally add up the cost of items to arrive at an overall estimate of the total cost of our purchases. Knowing how to make reasonable estimates is a valuable skill to have when we worry that we might arrive at the cash register and find we are short of money.

Estimation is also important because it helps us assess the reasonableness of our answers. For example, when working basic computations, whether using pencil and paper or a calculator, students need to know whether their solutions are reasonable. This can be especially true of students working with calculators. They may tend to believe that whatever the calculator says is true, not realizing that data entry can be fraught with error and lead to erroneous results or that a low battery can greatly reduce accuracy.

One common way to begin developing students' skills in estimation is to have students estimate how many beans, pennies, or marbles are in a jar or how many people are in a particular classroom. The number may be small at first and gradually become larger as students become more adept at estimating. Later, students may be challenged to estimate larger numbers, such as the number of people in the auditorium during a special event.

Students may also be asked to estimate the occurrence of events or the presence of objects in their environment. Hyatt and Brimmer (1997) developed an investigation that motivates students to become investigators while fine-tuning their estimation skills. Students were required to estimate dimensions and quantities first and then to measure or count objects and to compare their findings to their estimates. They measured things like the circumferences of their heads, the number of words in a dictionary starting with a certain letter, the number of times their hearts beat in a week, and the number of dentists in their town.

Basic Facts and Operations

One common approach for teaching basic facts and operations is to use manipulatives, described earlier in this chapter. Cubes, straws, Cuisinaire rods, and base-10 blocks are common manipulatives for teaching basic facts and operations. Figure 14.3 shows how cubes may be used to teach basic facts. Students record each step on a separate record

❚ **FIGURE 14.3**

The Use of Cubes to Teach Basic Math Facts and Operations

Materials: a mat divided into five sections as shown below; individual number cards (0–9); operation signs (+, −, ×, ÷) written on individual cards; and cubes.

Step 1: Using the numbers and operation signs, student sets up the problem on the mat. Student draws the mat onto the record sheet.

2	+	3	=	

Step 2: Student places cubes on the mat to represent the problem. Student draws the cubes onto the record sheet, capturing the work he has completed with the cubes on the record sheet.

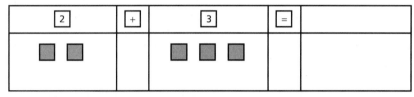

Step 3: Student moves the cubes over to the solution box on the mat, and counts to find the sum. Student records the solution on the record sheet, drawing the cubes and writing the numeral.

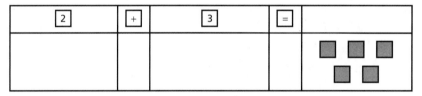

sheet for future review and study. They draw onto the record sheet the representation they created using the manipulatives. In this way, they make connections across all three stages of representation—concrete (creating the problem on the mat using cubes), semiconcrete (drawing the problem onto the record sheet), and abstract (writing the solution in numeral form on the record sheet). The record sheet can be used later for students to dialogue about how they arrived at their solutions. It can also serve as a study sheet for reviewing basic facts.

Mnemonics can also be used to teach basic facts. We described FAST and DRAW earlier. Another mnemonic is SOLVE, proposed by Miller and Mercer (1993a, p. 79):

1. S = See the sign.

2. O = Observe and answer (if unable to answer, keep going).

3. L = Look and draw.

4. V = Verify your answer.

5. E = Enter your answer.

The first step focuses students' attention on the sign and the operation it indicates. In Step 2 the student can simply solve the problem if he or she knows the answer. If the student is not able to respond immediately with the answer, Step 3 encourages the drawing of semiconcrete representations—lines, tallies, or other shapes—and the use of those drawings to find the solution. In Step 4, the student is encouraged to "check the first number and drawings; check the second number and drawings; check the answer and drawings" (Miller & Mercer, 1993a, p. 79). Step 5 reminds the student to record the answer.

Measurement

Burns (1992b) identifies four measurement skills to be taught:

1. **Comparing by matching.** This concept may be taught by giving students a number of objects commonly found in the classroom and asking them to identify which are the longest and the shortest objects, putting them in order. By placing objects side by side, students gradually sequence them according to length. They can record their findings on a chart or, using traced cutouts of the objects, arrange the objects in the proper order.

2. **Comparing objects with nonstandard units.** A common approach is to have students measure things found in the classroom using different measurement tools such as paperclips, rubber bands, and a traced cutout of one hand or foot. Students record their findings on a chart and compare across the measurement tools to determine which is probably the most accurate one for measuring different-sized objects (e.g., paperclips may be good for measuring the length of a book but not as effective for measuring the length of a classroom wall). Students also compare their responses with each other to develop an understanding of the need for standard measurement units.

3. **Comparing objectives with standard units.** This is an expansion of item 2, except this time students use standard units (e.g., inches) when completing measurements. Students compare their measurements for accuracy and discuss the measurement unit most appropriate for measuring the different lengths, weights, areas, and volumes.

4. **Choosing suitable units for specific measurements.** Students are given a list of objects found in their immediate environment as well as other objects (e.g., books, playground equipment, cars, elephants) and are asked to estimate each one's height or weight and to identify the unit that would be most appropriate for its measurement.

Probability and Statistics

Burns (1992b) identifies six concepts to be taught in the area of probability and statistics: (a) collecting data, (b) sampling, (c) organizing and representing data, (d) interpreting data, (e) assigning probabilities, and (f) making inferences. Chamblee (1997) developed an activity for high school students that includes all six steps. This activity required students to predict the population of the United States and of their home state in the near future. Using the World Wide Web, students downloaded census information and displayed this information using scatter plots to identify trends. Next, students used a graphics calculator to determine the "line of best fit" and to model equations for making predictions. This activity not only addressed all six concepts, but included experiences with calculators and computer software.

Exhibit 14.3 presents a nonroutine problem that can be used to develop students' skills in probability and statistics, developed by Burns (1992, p. 71). This activity can be used with elementary and middle school students.

❚ **EXHIBIT 14.3**

**The X-O Problem: A Nonroutine
Problem in Probability and
Statistics**

You need: three cards the same size marked as follows:
         one with an X on both sides
         one with an O on both sides
         one with an X on one side and an O on the other
      paper sack

Play the following game with the materials: Draw one of the three cards at random from the sack and look at what is marked on just one side. Predict what you think is on the other side. Check your prediction. Score a point each time you predict correctly.

   Decide what would be a good strategy for predicting so that you would score the most points possible. Then test your strategy by playing the game 30 times, recording your prediction and outcome each time. How many points did you score? Are you satisfied with your prediction? Try another strategy if you like.

Source: From *About Teaching Mathematics: A K–8 Resource* (p. 71), by M. Burns, 1992, White Plains, NY: Math Solutions Publications.

Patterns and Functions

According to the NCTM (1989),

> *Patterns are everywhere. Children who are encouraged to look for patterns and to express them mathematically begin to understand how mathematics applies to the world in which they live. Identifying and working with a wide variety of patterns help children to develop the ability to classify and organize information. Relating patterns in numbers, geometry, and measurement helps them understand connections among mathematical topics. Such connections foster the kind of mathematical thinking that serves as the foundation for the most abstract ideas studied in later grades. (p. 60)*

Patterning "involves many concepts, such as color and shape identification, direction, orientation, size, and number relationships" (NCTM, 1989, p. 61). One basic instructional sequence in patterning teaches students to predict what will come next, to extend patterns, and to develop their own patterns. Figure 14.4 provides an example of instruction in patterning skills for young children.

❚ **FIGURE 14.4**
Basic Patterning Skills

1. What comes next?
   In this example, the student, through examination of the pattern, is to draw or verbally describe what comes next in the pattern.

   Then the student may be asked to assign letter names to the patterns.

2. Extend a pattern
   In this example, the student is challenged to continue the pattern for the next series or two.

3. Making own patterns
   Students may use a range of manipulatives to develop their own patterns. These patterns could be labeled with letters and recorded in a journal for later sharing with other students. Students could also create games for peers, using patterns they develop.

Fractions

Fractions are a major stumbling block for many students, with or without disabilities. One way to overcome some of the difficulties associated with the teaching of fractions is to introduce the concept of fractions early on, as it naturally arises in the classroom. Dividing materials, snacks, and cutting paper into equal parts presents an opportunity for introducing fractions. When introducing complex fraction operations, relate fractions to life outside school (e.g., buying a Quarter-Pounder at McDonald's), and emphasize how community members use fractions in their jobs (e.g., laying carpet).

One way to introduce fractions to students is to have them make a fraction kit. A fraction kit may be used to teach equivalent fractions, greater and lesser fraction relationships, and basic algorithms involving fractions (the multiplication and division of fractions are generally taught more effectively through different means). Before students use a fraction kit, however, it is important for them to understand what a fraction is, what the numerator and denominator represent, and why pieces must be the same size if given equal values (e.g., when an object is divided into thirds, all three pieces must be the same size because each one will be labeled with the same value). The "Make It Happen" features describe how to make fraction kits and class activities in which students can use fraction kits.

MAKE IT HAPPEN
Making a Fraction Kit

1. Cut strips of paper, each the same size, out of 8 different paper colors. It is easiest to use 8½-by-11-inch paper and cut strips that are 1-by-11 inches.
2. Have students gather one strip in each color.
3. Through modeling and discussion, have students move through the following steps. Discuss the meaning of the numerator and denominator. Students will begin to make comparisons as they cut and label pieces, discovering relationships.

   (a) Fold one strip in half, cut, and label each piece ½.

$\frac{1}{2}$	$\frac{1}{2}$

   (b) Fold another strip into four equal pieces, cut, and label.

   (c) Repeat for eighths, thirds, sixths, fifths, and sevenths.

   Note: The teacher should check to ensure that pieces have been cut appropriately. If the cutting of the pieces is not fairly accurate, the fraction kit will lead to erroneous results. Students may make the kit as a learning experience but then use a teacher-developed or commercially developed kit to solve problems or discover mathematical relationships.

MAKE IT HAPPEN
Using Fraction Kits

Comparison of Fractions

Have students compare fraction pieces by placing them side by side or on top of one another. Students can record these comparisons in a chart to do further analysis once data have been gathered. In this example, students will discover that ½ is larger than ¼, that ½ is larger than ⅓, and that ⅓ is larger than ¼. Then, through either manipulation or deduction, students can determine the sequence from largest to smallest: ½, ⅓, and ¼.

$\frac{1}{2}$		$\frac{1}{2}$		$\frac{1}{4}$
$\frac{1}{4}$		$\frac{1}{3}$		$\frac{1}{3}$

Teaching Equivalent Fractions

Have students compare and put fraction pieces together to create equivalent fractions. Students can record their comparisons and begin to deduce patterns.

$\frac{1}{2}$	
$\frac{1}{4}$	$\frac{1}{4}$

Teaching Addition and Subtraction of Fractions

Starting with fractions with common denominators, students can learn to count how many pieces they have—and thus not be tempted to add the denominators as well as the numerators.

$$\boxed{\frac{1}{4}} + \boxed{\frac{1}{4}} + \boxed{\frac{1}{4}} = \frac{3}{4}$$

Students can also explore the notion of mixed numerals by adding fractions with common denominators and getting a numerator larger than the denominator. Comparison to a whole strip (equaling 1) may be done to determine the final solution written in lowest terms.

$$\boxed{\frac{1}{3}} + \boxed{\frac{1}{3}} + \boxed{\frac{1}{3}} + \boxed{\frac{1}{3}} = \frac{4}{3}$$

$\frac{1}{3}$	$\frac{1}{3}$	$\frac{1}{3}$	$\frac{1}{3}$

1

$$\frac{4}{3} = 1\frac{1}{3}$$

Students can then write out solutions and search for equivalent fractions to write the solution in lowest terms. Additionally, through repeated practice, students may begin to see patterns in how fractions with uncommon denominators may be added. The same activities may be completed for teaching subtraction of fractions. In fact, students may use addition problems to explore subtraction.

Teaching multiplication and division of fractions may be best accomplished by having students memorize procedural steps. For example, to divide mixed numerals (problem: $1\frac{1}{2} \div 2\frac{1}{4}$), the following steps may be taught:

Step 1: Write each mixed numeral as an improper fraction.

$$\frac{3}{2} \div \frac{9}{4}$$

Step 2: Rewrite the problem, using the reciprocal.

$$\frac{3}{2} \times \frac{4}{9}$$

Step 3: Multiply, then reduce.

$$\frac{3}{2} \times \frac{4}{9} = \frac{12}{18} \div \frac{6}{6} = \frac{2}{3}$$

Decimals

Decimals is another area of great difficulty. Again, demonstrating connections between decimals and daily life can help students make the learning of decimals more relevant. Working with money (e.g., opening up a checking account, balancing checkbooks, taking out a loan) requires skills in the use of decimals and may be the most powerful way to introduce and reinforce them. Using manipulatives can also be helpful. For instance, $1.30 represents one whole (a one-dollar bill) and 3 tenths (3 dimes) or 30 hundredths (30 pennies) of one whole (a one-dollar bill). Base-10 blocks may also be used, with flats representing a whole, rods representing tenths, and units representing hundredths. As when base-10 blocks are used to teach renaming in addition and subtraction of whole numbers, students can learn how to trade 10 hundredths for 1 tenth and 10 tenths for 1 whole. Figure 14.5 shows how to solve an addition problem with base-10 blocks.

As with fractions, it may be best to introduce complex decimal problems by means of step strategies. For example, to multiply decimals, students may be taught these two steps:

Step 1: Line up the problem, disregarding the decimal points, and multiply in the usual way.

Step 2: Count the number of digits to the right of the decimal points of the two numbers being multiplied. Looking at the answer, start on the far right of the number and count to the left the same number of digits that you counted in the problem. Write the decimal point in this location.

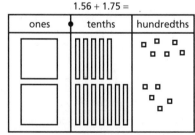

Step 2: *Renaming through trading.* Students add each of the columns on the mat. In this example, students are required to rename two times. The first renaming occurs in the hundredths column. Students trade in 10 hundredths for 1 tenth. Next, they trade in 10 tenths for 1 whole. The figure to the right shows the final result of their work.

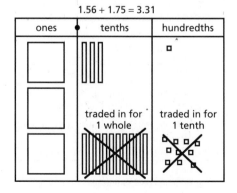

▮ **FIGURE 14.5**
The Use of Base-10 Blocks to Add Decimals

MATHEMATICAL CHALLENGES FOR STUDENTS WITH DISABILITIES

Students with disabilities experience a range of challenges when working in the area of mathematics. Table 14.2 was developed by Mercer (1997) to summarize some of the common difficulties that students with learning disabilities encounter in mathematics curriculum and instruction. The "Make It Happen" feature lists additional challenges that may be common to all students with disabilities and provides recommendations for addressing them.

TABLE 14.2 COMMON DIFFICULTIES THAT AFFECT THE MATH PERFORMANCE OF STUDENTS WITH LEARNING DISABILITIES

LEARNING DIFFICULTY		MATH-RELATED PERFORMANCE
Visual Perception	Figure-ground	loses place on worksheet does not finish problems on a page has difficulty reading multidigit numbers
	Discrimination	has difficulty differentiating between numbers (e.g., *6,9; 2,5;* or *17,71*), coins, the operation symbols, clock hands
	Spatial	has difficulty copying shapes or problems has difficulty writing across paper in a straight line has confusion about before-after concepts (e.g., has difficulty with time or counting) has difficulty relating to directional aspects of math, which can be noted in problems with computations involving up-down (e.g., addition), left-right (regrouping), and aligning numbers puts decimals in the wrong place has difficulty spacing manipulatives into patterns or sets has difficulty using number line has confusion about positive and negative numbers (directional)
Auditory Perception		has difficulty doing oral drills has difficulty doing oral word problems is unable to count on from within a sequence has difficulty writing numbers or assignments from dictation has difficulty learning number patterns
Motor		writes numbers illegibly, slowly, and inaccurately has difficulty writing numbers in small spaces (i.e., writes numbers that are too large)
Memory	Short-term	is unable to retain math facts or new information forgets steps in an algorithm is unable to retain the meaning of symbols
	Long-term	works slowly on mastering facts over time performs poorly on review lessons or mixed probes forgets steps in algorithms
	Sequential	has difficulty telling time does not complete all steps in a multistep computation problem has difficulty solving multistep word problems
Attention		has difficulty maintaining attention to steps in algorithms or problem solving has difficulty sustaining attention to critical instruction (e.g., teacher modeling)
Language	Receptive	has difficulty relating math terms to meaning (e.g., *minus, addend, dividend, regroup, multiplicand,* and *place value*) has difficulty relating words that have multiple meanings (e.g., *carry* and *times*)
	Expressive	does not use the vocabulary of math has difficulty performing oral math drills has difficulty verbalizing steps in solving a word problem or an algorithm

LEARNING DIFFICULTY		MATH-RELATED PERFORMANCE
Reading		does not understand the vocabulary of math word problems
Cognition and Abstract Reasoning		has difficulty converting linguistic and numerical information into math equations and algorithms has difficulty solving word problems is unable to make comparisons of size and quantity has difficulty understanding symbols in math (e.g., >, <, ×, and =) has difficulty understanding the abstract level of mathematical concepts and operations
Metacognition		is unable to identify and select appropriate strategies for solving computation and word problems has difficulty monitoring the problem-solving process in word problems and multistep computations is unable to generalize strategies to other situations
Social and Emotional Factors	Impulsive	makes careless mistakes in computation responds incorrectly and rapidly in oral drills corrects responses frequently when asked to look at or listen to a problem again does not attend to details in solving problems
	Short attention/ Distractibility	does not complete work in assigned time has difficulty doing multistep computation starts a problem and does not finish it but goes on to next problem is off-task
	Passivity/Learned helplessness	omits computation problems omits word problems appears disinterested lacks strategies
	Self-esteem	lacks confidence gives up easily
	Anxiety	becomes so tense during math test that performance is impaired avoids math to reduce anxiety

Source: From *Students with Learning Disabilities*, 5th ed. (pp. 574–575), by C. D. Mercer, 5/e, © 1997. Reprinted by permission of Prentice-Hall, Inc., Upper Saddle River, NJ.

MAKE IT HAPPEN

Overcoming Mathematical Challenges

Challenge	Activity
Has difficulty with number reversals and writing numerals	• Provide multiple opportunities for writing numbers, using several of the strategies offered for overcoming handwriting difficulties. • Follow the guidelines of Baroody and Kaufman (1993) in assessing and remediating numeral-writing difficulties.
Has difficulty memorizing number facts	• Provide time for students to use computer drill and practice software. • Time and chart number fact performance using precision teaching methods. • Teach facts through number families (e.g., 2 + 3 = 3 + 2) rather than having students learn ones, then twos, and so on.

(continued)

Challenge	Activity
Has difficulty memorizing number facts *(continued)*	• Teach relationships between addition, subtraction, multiplication, and division. • Use calculators. • Move on to activities that are eased by memorization of basic facts to provide incentive for memorization (e.g., more complex addition to support memorization of addition facts or to multiplication facts and algorithm). • Move on in the curriculum after multiple attempts to achieve memorization.
Has difficulty completing computation or tasks involving multiple steps	• Provide grid paper to help with overall organization and alignment. • Turn a student's paper sideways for a quick grid. • Use the demonstration plus permanent product approach. • Outline steps in simple-to-understand language. • Put the steps of the operation into a song or rap that students can recite chorally as they work on problems as a group; then move to covert language. • Use computer software as reinforcement.
Becomes overwhelmed when presented with a math worksheet containing many problems or loses his or her place when working on the sheet	• Cut the rows of problems into strips and present the work as strips to be accomplished; once a strip is completed, the student turns it in and receives the next strip of problems. • Fold the paper so that the student does not see the entire sheet of problems but sees just those he or she is working on. • Use a copier to enlarge the problems, and then fold the paper or cut into strips so the student does not become overwhelmed with the amount of information being presented at one time. • Have the student place a sheet of paper over the problems he or she is not working on. • Create a problem window that blocks out all problems the student is not currently working on; the student only works on the problem visible through the window.
Has difficulty copying problems from the board to paper, or from the book to the paper	• Use a copier to reproduce the problems onto paper. • Rather than using the board, write the problems on an overhead transparency. Make a copy of the transparency and allow the student to write responses on that sheet.

Has difficulty writing numbers legibly, takes an extensive time to write numbers on paper, or has great difficulty organizing math problems on paper	• Allow the student to use a computer when completing tasks. The student may enter problems in and then type in the answers, or the worksheet or problem list may be scanned into the computer, and the student writes in responses on the computer. • Provide large enough grid paper for the student to write numbers in the grid when completing problems. • If the child is experiencing fine motor difficulties that result in illegible writing or is taking inordinate amounts of time, allow the student to dictate the answers to someone, or have the child use software to complete the work at the computer. • If problems in this area are due to physical disabilities, develop adaptive keyboarding systems the student may use to respond to math activities and assignments.
Today seems to know facts or understand concepts, but tomorrow will act as though the skills or concepts were never taught	• Provide extensive review at the beginning of each math session. • Incorporate distributed practice (e.g., working on previously taught skills over a period of time as new ideas are introduced) opportunities into instruction. • Provide students with supports such as number fact sheets or grids, strategy outlines, or other tools that serve as reminders of what was taught.
Fails to use mathematical language or does not demonstrate understanding of mathematical terms	• Have students maintain a dictionary of mathematical terms with the definitions as well as drawings of explanations written and drawn by the students themselves. • Have students discuss their processes, findings, and learnings with others. • Teach mathematical terms directly. • Model appropriate use of mathematical terms, and be consistent in use of the terms (e.g., when initially teaching subtraction, attempt to use one way to describe subtraction, rather than mixing several terms such as *take away, subtraction, less than, how many less, minus*).

(continued)

Challenge	Activity
Has difficulty selecting and monitoring use of problem-solving strategies	• Provide self-monitoring charts or grids for students to use when engaged in problem solving. • Require students to debrief following problem-solving activities in order to identify what went well and what could be done differently next time. • Provide students with a simplified menu of possible strategies (e.g., different strategies may be identified by mnemonics or drawings) that they can refer to when engaged in problem solving. • Teach problem-solving strategies specifically; provide multiple opportunities to practice the strategies; and once the strategies are mastered, introduce new strategies. However, only one strategy at a time may be most appropriate for some students.

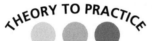

THEORY TO PRACTICE

➡ Select a specific math skill or concept and prepare a mini-unit to present to a group of highly diverse learners. In the unit, be sure to incorporate the four key components of the mathematics curriculum discussed at the beginning of this chapter. Attend to the diverse needs of learners by including adaptations and modifications that will ensure their active participation and learning. Present your mini-unit to a peer for feedback. Revise as needed.

➡ Select a math skill or concept and collect sample activities and materials for teaching it to students. Review the materials, identifying their strengths and weaknesses and their applicability to students with disabilities. Select one of the activities or materials. Conduct an in-depth analysis of how this activity or material could be used in a general education, inclusive classroom. How would the activity or material need to be adjusted to address the range of needs represented in this classroom? What types of accommodations and adaptations would actively include a student with disabilities?

CHAPTER SUMMARY

This chapter introduces the teaching of mathematics to students with disabilities by presenting a discussion of the mathematics curriculum as defined by the National Council of Teachers of Mathematics and used by many school districts as the foundation for the general education mathematics curriculum. Techniques for common curricular strands as well as techniques specific to areas of mathematics curriculum are presented. The chapter concludes with identification of challenges that students with disabilities may encounter and approaches for addressing them.

CHAPTER 15

Emergent Literacy

Read to find out the following:
- what is meant by emergent literacy
- the components of emergent literacy
- the debate over how best to teach reading and writing to students
- strategies and approaches that support student literacy development
- how to involve families in their children's literacy development

Reading and writing skills are essential not only to success in school but also to success in community and life pursuits. Many students with disabilities experience extensive difficulties in developing literacy skills and require intensive and specialized instruction. In this chapter and the next we offer some beginning suggestions for supporting students in their development of reading and writing skills. We present instructional techniques and approaches for teaching general education curriculum with and without modifications, as well as for teaching a functional academics curriculum in reading and writing areas. As teachers of students with different disabilities, readers are likely to require additional strategies for dealing with specific disability issues (e.g., teaching reading and writing to students who are deaf and whose primary language is ASL, not standard English; students with visual impairments). The ideas expressed here, however, will aid all teachers in understanding some of the basic approaches to the teaching of literacy. This chapter focuses on emergent literacy and Chapter 16 focuses on approaches to support continued literacy development.

DEFINING EMERGENT LITERACY

The development of literacy skills begins at a young age. The literacy abilities of infants, toddlers, and young children emerge over time as they observe and approximate the reading and writing behaviors of more proficient readers and writers around them—thus the term *emergent literacy.* Lipson and Wixson (1997) describe emergent literacy as "the *process of becoming literate* as opposed to a series of discrete, specifiable skills that must be developed before learning how to read" (p. 226, original emphasis). Emergent literacy is evident when a young child picks up a book and "reads" it, although she may be holding the book upside down and is truly not able to read any of the words. It is exemplified by a child who scribbles on paper and then reads the message to an adult—the child is imitating how the adults around him use writing as a means to communicate ideas to others. As Valencia (1997) says,

> *Although many of these abilities do not look like adult reading, they are important and legitimate stepping stones in literacy development. Rather than a series of discrete, specific skills that must be developed before children can learn to read,*

emergent reading abilities such as book awareness, concepts of print, understanding stories, phonemic awareness, high frequency sight-word recognition, and sound-symbol correspondence develop simultaneously as children are engaged in literacy activities and instruction. (p. 64)

Therefore, an emergent literacy perspective "identifies children's early years as a period of high activity rather than passive waiting for readiness to unfold" (Lipson & Wixson, 1997, p. 226). Valencia (1997) provides a list of emergent reading behaviors. This list is presented in Exhibit 15.1.

EXHIBIT 15.1

Emergent Reading Behaviors

Book awareness
  Front/back
  Left/right
  Top/bottom
  Title/author
  Where to begin reading
  Pictures/words
  Turn pages in sequence

Concepts of print
  Environmental print
  Understanding that print carries messages
  Match print to voice
  Identify letter, word, sentence

Story sense
  Beginning, middle, end
  Sequence
  Main ideas/concepts
  Makes inferences/conclusions
  Characters
  Problem
  Events
  Resolution

Rereading familiar books
  Refer to pictures, use own oral language to comment or label objects
  Refer to pictures, use own oral language to tell story
  Refer to pictures, use mixture of own language and print to tell story
  Refer to pictures, use language of book (memorized story)
  Refer to print to read, may refuse to read if cannot identify words

Phonemic awareness
  Rhyming
  Initial consonant substitution
  Blending
  Segmenting

Sound/symbol and word identification
  Letter names
  Letter sounds
  Sound/letter associations
  Sight words

Source: "Authentic classroom assessment of early reading: Alternatives to standardized tests," by S. W. Valencia. *Preventing School Failure* 41(2), p. 65, 1997. Reprinted with permission of the Helen Dwight Reid Educational Foundation. Published by Heldref Publications, 1319 Eighteenth St., N.W., Washington, DC. 20036-1802. Copyright © 1997.

Reading instruction viewed from the emergent literacy perspective is different from the more traditional readiness approach to reading. The readiness approach is based on a developmental model that assumes that students must be "ready" to learn to read and that they demonstrate readiness through the performance of certain skills. Readiness skills generally include auditory discrimination (e.g., identifying sounds of letters), visual discrimination (e.g., knowing letters of the alphabet, recognizing shapes), and motor skills (e.g., cutting, running). However, the fact that not all these skills are linked with reading and neither are they all prerequisites to learning how to read (Lipson & Wixson, 1997) calls into question the need to demonstrate them prior to receiving instruction in reading.

The reading readiness approach may be especially controversial when applied to students who are English-language learners—that is, students whose primary language is not English (Peregoy & Boyle, 1997)—and to students with disabilities. Students who are English-language learners may need extensive exposure to the activities that are highlighted in an emergent reading approach (e.g., oral reading of stories, writing of student-generated stories, dialoguing about stories) in order to enhance language development (Anderson & Roit, 1998). And a developmental readiness approach may limit the access of students with disabilities to meaningful literacy instruction. Some students may not be able to name all the letters in the alphabet, some may always have difficulty with auditory discrimination tasks, and some may never demonstrate the physical performance demands sometimes included in readiness checklists, but lacking these skills does not necessarily preclude them from learning to read. However, skills identified as prerequisites to reading readiness can serve as roadblocks to students' participation in meaningful literacy activities and experiences.

The limitations of a readiness approach to reading also apply to the teaching of writing. Traditionally, students participated in writing instruction only after they had developed some facility with reading—in the belief that reading development precedes writing development. The emergent approach differs significantly. As offered by Lipson and Wixson (1997),

> *Although the exact relationship between reading and writing has not been determined, it is clear that reading and writing behaviors emerge simultaneously and that the benefits are reciprocal. (p. 240)*

In an emergent approach, reading and writing are developed simultaneously, each bridging and supporting skill development in the other.

Emergent Reading Behaviors

Exhibit 15.1 identifies a number of behaviors associated with emergent reading. Each of them is briefly described.

Book awareness

At a very young age, children can begin to understand the basic characteristics of books. By engaging in activities in which others read to them, children begin to understand that books have a front and a back and that the reading starts at the front. They become aware that the front of the book generally lists the title of the book and its author. Students, through modeling, learn that reading begins at the top of the page and flows to the bottom of the page and moves from left to right. As they are read to, students become aware of when to turn pages. Children also learn that illustrations provide clues about what is going on in a story.

Print awareness

Print awareness is the students' awareness of print in their surroundings and of how print functions. For example, at very young ages, students are able to read words commonly found in their environment, such as *McDonald's, Cheerios,* and *stop.* This awareness develops as children interpret environmental print. Young children, over time, also learn that print carries meaning. They learn this by watching others write messages or lists and refer to them later (e.g., a parent making a shopping list and referring to it at the store) and by being read to. Children with repeated exposure to reading and writing begin to see individual letters in words and to understand the concept of word and how words are represented on a page. As their skills become more advanced, they begin to differentiate among sentences and notice how sentences are indicated in print (e.g., punctuation and spacing signals).

Story sense

Children who are repeatedly read to begin to understand that stories have a beginning, a middle, and an end. They also begin to retell stories, putting key events in sequence. They may begin to develop a sense of story grammar—realizing that stories have characters, the characters confront a problem, and the characters work to resolve the problem through a series of actions. The ability to discern predictable story elements and make sense of stories serves as a foundation for comprehension when children become independent readers and writers.

Rereading familiar books

As students are read to, they begin to develop a list of favorite books that they will want to have read to them over and over again. At some point, they will begin retelling their favorite stories, eventually using the words of the author, turning the pages of the book as they tell the story. Reading familiar books and rereading favorite books are highly enjoyable pursuits for children and boost their confidence in their ability to interact with books and to be successful readers.

Phonemic awareness

Yopp (1992) defines phonemic awareness as "the understanding that speech is composed of a series of individual sounds" (p. 696). Children with phonemic awareness are able to rhyme words, blend and segment sounds, and identify sounds heard at the beginning, middle, and end of words. Griffith and Olson (1992) point out that

> phonemic awareness is not synonymous with phonics. It is not learning spelling-to-sound correspondences, and it is not sounding out words. It is understanding of the structure of spoken language. (p. 518, original emphasis)

In fact, when teachers work to build phonemic awareness, they generally do not introduce letters, letter names, and the sounds that letters make. As Yopp (1992) explains, written letters and words may be used to teach phonemic awareness to students who know the names of letters, but the introduction of printed letters to students who are not familiar with them may draw students' attention away from the task at hand—working with the sounds of the language. Yopp suggests that oral activities alone be used with younger children to develop phonemic awareness.

Research shows that phonemic awareness is a strong indicator of future reading performance (Yopp, 1992) and that a reciprocal relationship exists between phonemic awareness and learning to read. Yopp (1992) describes this relationship by stating,

> in order to benefit from formal reading instruction, youngsters must have a certain level of phonemic awareness. Reading instruction, in turn, heightens their awareness of language. Thus, phonemic awareness is both a prerequisite for and a consequence of learning to read. (p. 697)

Phonemic awareness "plays a critical role in learning skills requiring the manipulation of phonemes—specifically word recognition and spelling" (Griffith & Olson, 1992, p. 518).

Sound-symbol and word identification

Students, as emergent readers and writers, begin to make associations between the sounds they hear in words (phonemes) and the visual symbols, or letters, used to represent those sounds (graphemes). Teaching the sound-symbol or phoneme-grapheme relationship is generally referred to as teaching phonics. As defined by Stahl (1992), phonics

> merely refers to various approaches designed to teach children about the orthographic code of the language and the relationships of spelling patterns to sound patterns. (p. 618)

Children demonstrate the emergence of sound-symbol connections in their attempts to sound out unfamiliar words and in their invented spelling in early writing.

Understanding the language of books

Lipson and Wixson (1997) add an element to the list of emergent reading behaviors provided by Valencia (1997)—understanding the language of books. As Lipson and Wixson (1997) point out, books use a language that is different from the spoken language students encounter at home, in their communities, and at school. Book language is often more figurative and uses different structures. Part of emergent literacy is learning about and understanding the language used in books.

For some children the distance between the language they find in books and the language they use in daily speech is especially great. Van Keulen, Weddington, and DeBose (1998) identify a discrepancy between the spoken home language of African-American children and the language presented in storybooks or textbooks. They argue that despite this discrepancy, African-American students who come from homes that are print-rich and provide multiple literacy opportunities will have skill levels similar to those of their "White counterparts" (p. 213):

> *The primary differences will most likely be in the language spoken by Black children and the written language in print. This means that Black children may bring different assumptions about the world to the printed page, so teachers must be aware that Black children's interactions with text may be different from White mainstream American English speaking children. These differences are often caused by not having written word–spoken word correspondence, and these differences are what most teachers do not understand. (van Keulen, Weddington, & DeBose, 1998, pp. 231–232)*

As one suggestion for addressing these challenges, van Keulen and colleagues encourage teachers to include in the classroom literature books that reflects the cultures and experiences of all children, including African-American children. Teachers should read stories to students, even at an early age, that include familiar-sounding names, places, and foods. Another suggestion involves the schematic activation of students' prior knowledge through bridging their understandings to information and ideas presented in text. When presented with some texts, students from a variety of cultures may not have the prior experiences and knowledge to call on when they attempt to make meaning from text. They need support and scaffolding to bring meaning to them. As Ladson-Billings (1994) explains,

> *Rather than expecting students to demonstrate prior knowledge and skills, they [teachers] help students develop that knowledge by building bridges and scaffolding for learning. (p. 25)*

Emergent Writing Behaviors

In a manner parallel to the emergence of reading skills, students learn conventions of writing (e.g., writing moves from left to right, from the top of the page to the bottom) and purposes of writing (e.g., writing reminders, communicating with others) by observing proficient writers in their environment. Students move through multiple stages when developing writing skills. These skills are not necessarily linear, however, for students may gain and demonstrate skills at different times and in different ways. Stages in children's writing development as identified by DeFord (1980) are presented in Exhibit 15.2.

EXHIBIT 15.2

Stages of Writing Development

1. Scribbling
2. Differentiation between drawing and writing
3. Concepts of linearity, uniformity, inner complexity, symmetry, placement, left-to-right motion, and top-to-bottom directionality
4. Development of letters and letter-like shapes
5. Combination of letters, possibly with spaces, indicating understanding of units (letters, words, sentences), but may not show letter/sound correspondence
6. Writing known isolated words—developing sound/letter correspondence
7. Writing simple sentences with use of inventive spellings
8. Combining two or more sentences to express complete thoughts
9. Control of punctuation—periods, capitalization, use of upper- and lower-case letters
10. Form of discourse—stories, information material, letters, etc.

Source: From "Young Children and Their Writing," by D. E. DeFord, 1980, *Theory into Practice, 19*(3), p. 162.

This description of emergent reading and writing can be applied both to children developing typically and to children with disabilities. Many students with disabilities, however, will require specific and intensive instructional intervention to gain needed skills. They may require instruction that focuses explicitly on emergent skills. What is common for all students, however, is the importance of engaging in authentic reading and writing experiences at a very early age. Being read to, exploring books, playing with words, and capturing ideas on paper through drawing, scribbling, and invented spelling are critical, early literacy experiences for all learners, although adjustments in these experiences will most likely need to be made for students with sensory impairments (e.g., students who are deaf and those with visual impairments) and for others with significant disabilities.

THEORY TO PRACTICE

➥ Observe a child who is developing reading and writing skills. Referring to the list of emergent reading behaviors (Exhibit 15.1), assess the child's skill development. In which areas does the child demonstrate competence? Which areas are still in an early stage of development? If you were to work with this student to enhance his or her literacy skills, what would you set as possible goals and objectives? Share your ideas with the child's teacher for feedback.

➥ Meet with a primary teacher of reading. What literacy skills and competencies does this teacher identify as the most critical for students to develop at this stage of their reading and writing development? How does he or she describe each of these skills and competencies? How do they manifest themselves in the classroom?

THE DEBATE ON HOW TO TEACH READING AND WRITING

There are many views on how to support early literacy development. Great differences of opinion exist among teachers about what is most important for students to know and do, and for teachers to teach, and what methods teachers should use when presenting skills and information to students.

Recall from Chapter 12 the two broad approaches to teaching: the transmission or traditional model and the constructivist approach. Generally associated with a skills-based approach, the transmission model isolates skills and teaches those skills in a sequential fashion. Students learning to read may work on lists of isolated sight words or may receive direct instruction in phonics skills. Students learning capitalization and punctuation rules may be taught first, through skill drills, that sentences begin with a capital letter and end with an end mark, generally a period.

In contrast, the constructivist model (e.g., Au, 1993; Vygotsky, 1978) and whole language approach (e.g., Graves, 1994) emphasize the teaching of skills within authentic contexts. Students engage in the whole enterprise of reading: they read entire stories and other types of texts, analyze the information read, and receive instruction in skills called for by the authentic context of reading. Likewise, students engage in the whole enterprise of writing: they write stories and other pieces using invented spelling and conventions; the emphasis is on the content of the writing, not the mechanics associated with writing (e.g., spelling, punctuation). Moreover, the constructivist and whole language approaches emphasize the roles of social interaction and dialogue in the construction of skills and understanding. Advocates encourage students to discuss their reading and writing and to seek input and suggestions from others.

The controversy over which approach is more effective in producing capable readers and writers is clouded by the identification of programs as either skill based (sometimes referred to as phonics based) or whole language, despite the variations that exist within both programs, and some teachers who merge the models, creating an eclectic approach to instruction. Moreover, the definition of whole language programs and related instructional strategies and approaches varies from teacher to teacher. As Newman and Church (1990) discuss in their article "Myths of Whole Language," there are many misconceptions about what a whole language approach to reading instruction includes. Here are six myths identified by Newman and Church (1990):

1. *"You don't teach phonics in whole language"* (p. 20).
   In fact, whole language teachers do teach phonics, but they teach it not as a separate, isolated skill but rather in the context of reading text.

2. *"You don't teach spelling or grammar in a whole language classroom"* (p. 21).
   As appropriate, teachers introduce spelling and grammar conventions as the need arises in students' writing.

3. *"Whole language means a literature-based curriculum"* (p. 21).
   Although literature plays an important part in a whole language program, other reading materials (e.g., expository texts) are used as well.

4. *"Whole language is a way of teaching language arts; it doesn't apply to other subject areas"* (p. 21).
   Actually, the philosophy of whole language applies across all curricular areas.

5. *"Whole language teachers deal just with process; the product doesn't matter"* (p. 22).
   There is actually a balance between process and product.

6. *"Whole language won't work for kids with special needs"* (p. 23).
   According to Newman and Church (1990):

   For so many of these children their problems have been exacerbated by the fragmented, right answer skills-based literacy instruction they've been receiving. The instruction, rather than helping them sort out what reading and writing are all about, has interfered with their strategies for making sense, rendering them dependent, cautious learners. Many of these children have stopped believing they can learn. A whole language-based learning environment invites these children to see themselves as learners once again." (p. 23)

Both approaches, skill-based and whole language, have merit for students with disabilities. Some experts argue that a comprehensive whole language approach includes skill-based instruction and therefore is the most appropriate approach for working with all students, including those with disabilities. But drawing from both skill-based and whole language approaches lets teachers achieve the balance important for reaching all students, but especially those with disabilities. At times, students with disabilities can benefit to a significant degree by engagement in whole language–based instruction. Some students may learn writing best when they engage in the entire writing process (e.g., generating ideas, drafting ideas on paper, revising, and editing) rather than working on individual skills. This positive outcome may be partially explained by the difficulty that many students with disabilities face when they attempt to generalize skills. Other students, however, benefit most from a sequential, skill-based approach. Learning skills in isolation and demonstrating fluency in them may help these students apply them later in their own writing. For still other students, it may be best to combine the approaches—involving students in the entire process of writing and participating in skill-based instruction. In this way, students benefit from each approach—developing writing skills through writing and through systematic, skill-based instruction.

We recommend a balanced approach to the teaching of reading and writing. This approach embraces both skill-based and holistic instruction. As offered by Goldenberg (1998):

> A balanced approach is based on an interactive view of reading, which suggests that both skills and meaning are important for literacy development. Instead of exclusively emphasizing letters and sounds or meaning and purpose, a balanced approach involves a mix. It provides children with instruction and learning opportunities that promote both development of phonological processes (i.e., the sounds letters make and how those letters and sounds combine to form words) and attention to authentic communication via the written word—the use of literature, journals, diaries, and other meaningful print forms. Learning about letters and sounds as well as learning about the meaningful and purposeful aspects of literacy complement and reinforce each other. . . . (pp. 4–5)

CREATING A CONTEXT FOR LITERACY LEARNING

The teaching of early literacy skills, whether through a skill-based, holistic, or balanced approach, starts with the development of a learning environment that supports literacy learning by providing numerous opportunities for students to engage in authentic reading and writing experiences. Chapter 11 presents ideas for creating a climate for learning. In addition, specific elements can be introduced to make a classroom a literacy-rich environment.

One beginning point is the creation of a print-rich environment. In such an environment, print is found throughout the room. Classroom objects are labeled (e.g., door, desk) in both print and braille, directions and schedules are written on the board, and bulletin boards display student work. Everywhere students look, they experience print and gain an understanding of how print is used in communication.

Environments conducive to literacy also have inviting reading, writing, and listening centers that provide a variety of materials to encourage students' active engagement in reading, writing, and listening activities. Students may go to the centers to read books, to write stories and poems, to illustrate their work, and to listen to books on tape, and/or they may use a computer to do all of the above (see Chapter 13 for material on setting up and managing learning centers). Centers can be included in middle and high school settings—they are not just limited to elementary classrooms.

A variety of reading materials—tradebooks, magazines, recipes, nonfiction texts, multimedia packages for use on the computer—and writing materials are also available in an environment that fosters literacy. Materials are selected to reflect the diversity of the students, addressing cultural and racial differences, language differences, and differences in ability among the students in the class. Selecting and making multiethnic literature available (literature reflective of the ethnic and cultural groups represented in the classroom) yields multiple benefits. As Au (1993) indicates, the availability of multi-ethnic literature can result in the following positive outcomes: (a) students feel pride about themselves and their people; (b) students respond positively to the literature because they can identify with characters and story events; (c) students realize that their stories and experiences and those of their community are important enough to share with others through written text; (d) students learn about the great diversity of our nation and of the experiences of different people, their cultures, and their beliefs; (e) students gain a more balanced view of our history as a nation by being exposed to a variety of viewpoints on issues and historical events that have shaped our country; and (f) "all students can explore issues of social justice" (Au, 1993, p. 178).

The selection of multicultural materials involves more than finding books and materials that reflect the different cultures in the classroom. Anderson and Roit (1998), in their analysis of the use of multicultural texts in classrooms, caution that some texts representing different cultures may be too complex and difficult for children to understand. These books and materials may discuss aspects of culture in which children have had little experience. Anderson and Roit suggest that in addition to including such books, other, more easily comprehensible books that represent common experiences of the majority of the students in the class also be included in the class library to support literacy development. These materials should be chosen on the basis of how they reflect the diversity of the students in the learning environment.

Another consideration in selecting materials for the classroom is the readability of the texts. As Rhodes and Dudley-Marling (1996) point out, it is important to have *"books that are both readable and challenging for every student in the classroom"* (p. 103, original emphasis), and there should be as many texts available for strong readers as for other readers. Moreover, books and materials should reflect students' interest areas and represent a variety of topics and genres.

Lipson and Wixson (1997), drawing from a number of sources, developed a checklist for evaluating the literacy environment. This checklist, presented in Exhibit 15.3, can be used by teachers to evaluate the extent to which the learning environment in their classrooms supports literacy development.

In My Classroom:	Comments
1. There are many different kinds of books and other print materials	
2. There are many different types of writing materials and tools	
3. Students' work, messages, labels, and stories are displayed	
4. There are messages and/or plans for the current day	
5. Print materials are displayed near objects, pictures, and other center displays	
6. Books or print displays about community, culture, or language are displayed	
7. Print has functional use—sign-ups, charts, etc.	

(continued)

EXHIBIT 15.3

Checklist for Evaluating the Literacy Environment

The Following Areas Are Present in My Room:	Comments
Library—well stocked, accessible, and comfortable	
Writing/publishing center—well stocked and accessible	
Listening/viewing area	
Group meeting place	
Conference area	
Place for sharing, performing, etc.	
Promote Reading and Writing:	**Comments**
Daily opportunities for sustained reading and sustained writing	
Students read for a variety of purposes	
Students write for real audiences and for a variety of authentic purposes	
Students have choices about what to read or write	
Students confer with me and with other students about reading	
I support (scaffold) students during reading and writing	
I teach the fundamentals of writing (conduct mini-lessons, teach conventions, provide spelling instruction)	

Source: From *Assessment and Instruction of Reading and Writing Disability: An Interactive Approach*, 2nd ed. (p. 151), by M. Y. Lipson and K. K. Wixson. Copyright © 1997 by permission Addison Wesley Educational Publishers Inc. Reprinted by permission.

SUPPORTING LITERACY DEVELOPMENT

A number of strategies and approaches are available for supporting the development of literacy skills by students. In this section we provide some suggestions for teachers. Not all of these activities apply equally well to groups of students with specific disabilities. For example, the use of picture books with students with visual impairments and the reading aloud of books to students who are deaf may not be sound educational approaches for these students. Modifications in means of communication, activity presentation, and materials may be necessary for these approaches to be meaningful to them.

Reading Aloud to Students

One of the most important things parents and teachers can do to support student literacy development is to read to children. Reading aloud to children, exposing them to a range of texts, and exploring new lands and new information through text can not only enhance their development of literacy skills but instill a love of reading. Teachers of all grades should read to students. Short stories and novels as well as other materials are appropriate for reading-aloud activities. Teachers may set aside a special time each day or class period to read and may grab the book and read when there are "down times" in the schedule (e.g., when students finish an activity earlier than planned, when students are waiting to line up to attend an assembly or some other event). Reading aloud to students can also be used as a management tool. For example, reading aloud may occur first thing in the morning or at the start of a class period to begin the class on a positive note. Some teachers find it helpful to read to students before and/or after activities such as lunch, recess, assemblies, and other special events. Reading to students before school exit may end the day on a positive note.

Teachers may choose to discuss the story at the conclusion of the reading or as the story is being read. The latter practice is called interactive read-alouds by Barrentine (1996).

> *During interactive read-alouds, teachers pose questions throughout the reading that enhance meaning construction and also show* how *one makes sense of text. Students offer spontaneous comments as the story unfolds. They are also engaged with the reading process information—how stories work, how to monitor one's comprehension, what to think about as a story unfolds. . . . These interactions aim to engage children with strategies for composing meaning and to facilitate their ability to respond to stories. (pp. 36–37, original emphasis)*

The use of interactive read-alouds is different from the oral reading strategy of the teacher reading the text to its conclusion and then opening up the activity to discussion. One criticism of interactive read-alouds is that stopping and discussing can detract from the story and negatively impact student comprehension. Barrentine (1996) counters that, with experience, teachers begin to make judgments about when to expand the dialogue with students and when to return to the story.

Using Picture Books

Picture books offer another way, throughout the grades, to help students develop literacy skills. Through analysis and discussion of picture books, students develop and refine their understanding of story structure, their ability to predict, and their ability to identify relevant facts and details, among other skills. Students may "read" a picture book and then express the story orally in their own words through dictation or writing on their own. They may practice sequencing story events by working with copies of the pictures and arranging them in order. They may develop a sense of the setting by examining the pictures closely for clues about the setting and discussing its impact on story events. They also may develop skills in inferring characters' reactions and emotions through examination of the illustrations and analysis of main events. Picture books can be used with readers and writers of all ages to develop story grammar, to motivate students who are experiencing difficulties in reading and writing, and to build confidence.

Predictable and Pattern Books

Predictable and pattern books, by design, repeat the same words and phrases over and over and thus present excellent opportunities for development of sight word vocabularies and prediction skills. Examples of pattern books include *This Old Man* by Pam Adams, *Where in the World Is Henry?* by Lorna Balian, *The Grouchy Ladybug* by Eric Carle, *10 Bears in My Bed* by Stan Mack, and *Brown Bear, Brown Bear* by Bill Martin.

Bridge, Winograd, and Haley (1983) designed a strategy for using predictable books to enhance students' sight word vocabulary. The authors found that students working with this approach, and with a similar approach using student-generated stories, learned significantly more sight words than did students using a preprimer for reading instruction. The three-step strategy is as follows:

Step 1: Teacher reads and then rereads the book to the children, encouraging them to participate in the reading of the book as soon as they can predict what comes next. Once comfortable with the book, students take turns chorally reading the book. Finally, the students read the book as written on a chart with all picture cues removed.

Step 2: Using the story written on the chart, students are given sentence strips from the story and asked to match their sentence strip to the same sentence found on the chart. The same activity is repeated with individual words from the story.
Step 3: Students chorally read the story. Given individual word cards, students match the words to the words found on the chart.

Predictable and pattern books can also be used for writing and for the concurrent development of spelling and sight word skills. Given the predictable pattern in the book, the students can extend the story or rewrite the story by changing characters or events. For example, if the book has a character meeting new friends around every corner, the student can come up with ideas about new friends the character will meet. The student then uses his or her own ideas when completing a repeating sentence pattern such as "He said good-bye to his friend, and when he turned around the corner,_____." This activity gives the student multiple opportunities to work with key words and reinforces both sight word recognition and spelling.

Shared Reading and the Use of Big Books

Shared reading occurs when a teacher reads a book to students and during that reading, shows students the printed text of the book and its illustrations, much as parents do when young children sit on their laps while being read to (Holdaway, 1979). An integral component of shared reading is the use of big books—books that are large enough that a small group of students, sitting around the teacher, can easily see the text and illustrations.

During shared reading, the teacher moves one hand along under the text to show students how text is read (e.g., from left to right, top to bottom) to assist them in developing book awareness and concepts of print. The teacher may frame individual words to draw students' attention to specific words. Once the story is read, the teacher asks the children to join him or her in rereading the story when they feel they are ready. Predictable books are excellent tools for shared reading because, after a limited number of exposures, students can join in and help read them.

Some students will require preparation for participation in shared reading activities. Anderson and Roit (1998) suggest that teachers working with students who are English-language learners read the selection with them a few days before it is read with other students. This preview gives these students an opportunity to interact with the text and ask questions to clarify its meaning. As a result they are better prepared to participate in the discussion when the book is shared with the class as a whole. According to Anderson and Roit (1998),

> *The focus on meaning will be easier because problems with vocabulary and unfamiliar concepts will have already been addressed. Also, students will be able to clarify any remaining problems, read with more fluency and expression, and discuss what made the text enjoyable or interesting. (p. 46)*

The same strategy can be readily applied to students with disabilities.

Dialogue

One of the basic tenets of the constructivist approach is the social nature of learning: students construct knowledge through their interactions with each other and with more proficient readers and writers. The opportunity to discuss and dialogue with others about stories and students' reading and writing products and activities is a critical component of the development of student reading and writing skills. Rhodes and Dudley-Marling (1996) offer five ways in which teachers and students can work together to dialogue about books:

1. Students in groups read and discuss a piece of literature either while they are reading it or when they are finished.

2. Teachers and students give book talks about what they have read, and they indicate whether they would recommend the book to others.

3. Teachers and students maintain reading logs and refer to the logs for ideas and details when discussing the book with others, or students and teachers exchange reading logs and comment on one another's thoughts and ideas about the text.

4. Students present books to others through drama, multimedia, or other presentation formats.

5. Teachers and students conference about books they have read.

Conferencing (discussed in Chapter 13) can be a powerful approach for engaging students in dialogue about their reading and writing. Conferences may occur between teachers and students or in student groups. The conference may focus on reading and/ or writing activities and provide assessment information a teacher can use for planning. Exhibit 15.4 provides a list of questions a teacher may use during a reading conference with a student.

EXHIBIT 15.4

Reading Conference Questions

What would you like to tell me about what you've read?
Do you have any confusions about what you've read?
What have you been wondering about as you read this?
How did you decide to read this?
What kinds of things have you been wrestling with as you read this? How have you solved the problem(s)?
If you had a chance to talk with this author, what would you talk with him/her about?
What do you plan to read next? Why?
Does this make you think of anything else you've read?
Why do you suppose the author gave this (book, article, etc.) this title?
What parts of this have you especially liked? Disliked?
Do you like this more or less than the last thing you read? Why?
Is there anybody else in our class who you think would enjoy reading this? Why?
Did you skip any parts of what you have read? What? Why?
What is the main thing the author is saying to you?
Why do you suppose the author began this the way s/he did?
Would you like to be one of the people in this? Who? Why?
What other texts by this author have you read? Are the other texts similar in any way to this one?
Does this text remind you of others you have read?

Source: Adapted by permission of Lynn K. Rhodes and Curt Dudley-Marling. *Readers and Writers with a Difference: A Holistic Approach to Teaching Struggling Readers and Writers, 2ed.* (Heinemann, A division of Reed Elsevier, Inc., Portsmouth, NH, 1996).

Predicting

The act of predicting is embedded in many strategies (e.g., shared reading, reciprocal teaching) and can be at the heart of assisting students in making connections between their prior knowledge and experiences and the message of the text being read. Predicting also assists students in becoming actively engaged with the text and monitoring their understanding.

Prediction may be used to introduce new text. For example, a teacher may introduce a new story by discussing and examining the illustrations and, based on that information and students' prior knowledge and experiences, have students predict what the story will be about. These predictions may be written on the board or poster paper and returned to after the passage has been read, to analyze the similarities between the students' predictions and the information presented in text. Older students may scan the text looking for headings and other clues and make predictions about the text based on this information. Predictions may also be made while reading. After reading a segment of text, students may stop to discuss what has happened and, based on that information, predict what will happen next; then they read on to learn whether their predictions come true.

Information on which to base predictions can be developed in the ways described above and through the activation of prior knowledge. After finishing the text, students should examine their predictions to see whether there was a match between them and the events that actually occurred in the text. If their predictions were not borne out, students should analyze how their scenarios would change the story or the author's message. This analysis makes the act of predicting more meaningful and can aid students in interpreting and analyzing the author's message. It should also remove students' concerns about making the wrong prediction because all predictions are valued.

Daily News

A daily news activity gives each child an opportunity to report on something that happened to him or her since the group last met. Children may report on something they did with their families or friends, describe what the family had for dinner, or tell a funny story about a pet. Each piece of news is captured in a sentence that is written by the teacher on the board or poster paper. The teacher uses this activity to draw students' attention to writing conventions, sight words, new vocabulary, letter-sound correspondences, spelling conventions, and other skills and concepts. These will reinforce what has been discussed in the class or be new information for the students.

The Language Experience Approach

The language experience approach (LEA) (Stauffer, 1970) aims at assisting students in developing their reading, writing, and spelling skills concurrently. It is based on the belief that what students have experience in they can talk about, and what they can talk about they can write and then read about. Through this approach, children create their own stories, which they write, read, and share with peers.

LEA begins with students' knowledge, interests, and skills. Students select what they will write about and what they will read. Consequently, the approach is highly responsive to students' prior experiences, cultures, and beliefs and reflects their community. In the beginning, students dictate stories to the teacher or to other adults in the classroom. This may be done individually or in small or large groups. The teacher/adult writes the story down verbatim. This is done in full view of the students so they begin to see how words are represented, that writing moves from left to right, that spaces have meaning, and how capitalization and punctuation are used to indicate stops and starts and to convey other meanings (e.g., commas signal pauses). After dictation, the teacher reads the story to the students and makes the revisions and additions that they suggest. While reading the story, the teacher may point to each word or call attention to key words, phrases, or punctuation. Next, students, individually or chorally, read the story aloud while the teacher points to each word. Students then receive individual copies of the story so they may read the story to themselves and to others for practice reading.

Dictated stories may be used in other ways as well. Students may publish them and create a reading center of class stories that peers can enjoy reading. From their stories, students may select individual words that they want to learn, write those words on cards, study them as sight words and/or spelling words, and use them in other stories. Students may cut up their stories into individual words or sentence strips and use these cutups to rebuild sentences or the story. Students may illustrate their stories as well.

The language-experience approach may also be used with older students who are experiencing difficulties. Sharp (1990) used it with middle school students designated as remedial readers. Sharp's application of LEA began with students dictating stories to the teacher, who keyboarded them into the computer. Each student received a copy of her or his story and practiced reading it for the next week, reading it to the teacher every day. Words that remained unrecognized by the students at the end of the week were put into isolated word lists, which students studied and read to the teacher every day. At the end of the week, unrecognized words were written onto index cards and became cards in the students' word banks. While all this was occurring, students also were dictating new stories and working through the same process with those stories. Additionally, the teacher introduced students to content area materials. Using the materials from the general education content class (e.g., social studies), the teacher read the text aloud to the students; discussions and clarification activities were embedded throughout. Afterward, students dictated everything they could remember about what was read to them and the teacher keyboarded the information into the computer. Each student received a copy of the dictation and the same procedures previously described were repeated.

Sharp (1989) concludes that the language-experience approach has numerous benefits for older students. It motivates students experiencing difficulties with reading and writing. It enhances students' self-esteem. When used in the way described here, LEA forms links across the curriculum, enhances students' vocabulary, and assists students in comprehending and making connections and generalizations concerning content area material. It supports students as they make the transition from narrative to expository text and helps them develop critical reading skills, including the ability to identify relevant information and details. And LEA demonstrates the reciprocity between reading and writing and allows students to engage in the whole enterprise of reading and writing.

Storytelling

Storytelling is another technique that can be a powerful intervention for both reading and writing instruction. As Houston, Goolrick, and Tate (1991) suggest, storytelling can be integrated into the writing process to enhance opportunities for students' creativity and expression. Storytelling "is especially appropriate for learners with exceptionalities because it is a success-oriented, rather than deficit-centered, learning experience that enhances self-esteem" (Houston, Goolrick, & Tate, 1991, p. 41). In a project incorporating storytelling, students selected a story from their family or community that they wanted to share orally. They prepared the story for oral telling to an audience, wrote the story, and refined it to present to another audience. When capturing oral stories in print, children were free to use invented spelling and not to be overly concerned with writing mechanics. Furthermore, the use of nonstandard English expressions was permitted—it was seen as a way to enrich the story being told.

Houston, Goolrick, and Tate (1991) suggest the following steps in using the storytelling project technique with students. First, if possible, have a local storyteller come to the school and tell stories to the students. Second, have the class decide together what story they would like to tell. The story should be about a common event that students experienced as a group. Creating a web of story events is a starting point. Next, have students sequence these events and begin the process of writing the story as a group. When the story is written, students read it chorally.

The same strategy may be applied to individual storytelling. Houston, Goolrick, and Tate (1991) had students interview a family member and then tell that person's story. Students used the notes they had taken during the interview to write the stories. Working in pairs, students helped each other create a story web, sequence ideas, and write the story based on interview notes. Then students edited their work, prepared a final draft, and published the story in both written and oral form (e.g., on tape).

Phonemic Awareness

Yopp (1992) defines phonemic awareness as "the understanding that speech is composed of a series of individual sounds" (p. 696). When teaching for phonemic awareness, teachers engage students in rhyming, blending, and segmenting words, and in identifying sounds in words. Yopp (1992) offers the following guidelines for planning activities to develop phonemic awareness: (a) identify the task you want students to engage in—"match words by sounds, isolate a sound in a word, blend individual sounds to form a word, substitute sounds in a word, or segment a word into its constituent sounds" (p. 699); and (b) select the approach for presenting the skills to students. Yopp suggests that activities be fun and "game-like" and encourage students to experiment with language.

A range of approaches and activities for teaching phonemic awareness skills are suggested in the literature. Griffith and Olson (1992) suggest (a) using literature that allows children to play with sounds in words (e.g., books that use alliteration); (b) engaging students in writing activities; and (c) using clapping and rhythm to teach students to identify words, syllables, and phonemes in words. Yopp (1992) suggests that teachers have children play games and sing songs that play with language. Clay (1979) suggests the use of Elkonian boxes to assist students in hearing the sounds through a visual mode (refer to Clay 1979 to learn more about the use of Elkonian boxes). The "Make It Happen" feature describes some activities for teaching specific phonemic awareness skills.

MAKE IT HAPPEN

Activities for Teaching Phonemic Awareness Skills

Sound-Matching
- Present pictures to students and ask them to identify the pictures that begin with the *s* sound.
- Ask students to name words that begin with a certain letter sound.
- Say two or more words and ask students whether they all begin with a particular sound.

Isolating Sounds
- Say words to students and have them identify the beginning, middle, or end sounds.

Blending
- In order, slowly articulate the isolated sounds that make up a word (/c/-/a/-/t/), and have students blend the sounds together to make the word.

Adding and Substituting Sounds
- Have students sing a song, replacing one of the sounds found throughout the song—for example, "Happy birthday to you" could become "Bappy birthday bo bou" (Yopp, 1992, p. 701).
- Have a sound of the day and have each child pronounce his or her name with that beginning sound.

Segmenting
- Begin by having students isolate and say the first sound in words.
- Have students sing songs that segment the initial sounds from words; for "Pop Goes the Weasel," students could sing, "P-p-p-p-POP goes the weasel!" (Yopp, 1992, pp. 701).
- Play a similar game with students' names: B-b-b-b-b-Ben.

Source: Yopp, H. K. (1992). Developing phonemic awareness in young children. *The Reading Teacher, 45*(9), pp. 696–703.

Phonics

Students should receive instruction in phonics. Phonics instruction helps students learn the relationship between sounds and symbols, or phonemes and graphemes. Phonics, considered by many to be the traditional approach to the teaching of reading, has come under fire with the introduction of whole language approaches. Nevertheless, phonics instruction is the key to the reading and writing success of many students, including those with disabilities. But for some students with disabilities, however, it may not offer much assistance because of a number of factors. For instance, for a child with an auditory processing deficit (a student who has difficulty differentiating sounds), time spent attempting to master sound-symbol correspondences may be instructional time wasted. This student may benefit more from a sight word approach or a literature-based approach. Again, identification of students' strengths and challenges must be the basis from which interventions are selected.

Phonics instruction is significantly different from efforts to increase phonemic awareness. Phonemic awareness is concerned with sounds; phonics is concerned with the grapheme-phoneme (letter-to-sound) relationship. When phonemic awareness is taught, print is not generally involved; students work with the identification and manipulation of sounds (e.g., segmenting). In contrast, in phonics instruction, students learn the sounds that graphemes represent. Phonics is based on print and students' translation of the printed word to sound. Of course, phonics skills are based on phonemic awareness and processing skills. A student who is unable to manipulate sounds is likely to experience difficulties in manipulating sounds in response to letters (graphemes).

Stahl (1992) identifies nine ingredients of exemplary phonics instruction. These nine ingredients are listed in Exhibit 15.5. Stahl (1992) and others, however, suggest that, although the teaching of phonics is important to a reading program, only a limited

---

EXHIBIT 15.5

Ingredients of Exemplary Phonics Instruction

1. "Builds on a child's rich concepts about how print functions" (p. 620).
   As argued by Stahl (1992), "Letter-sound instruction makes no sense to a child who does not have an overall conception of what reading is about, how print functions, what stories are, and so on, and so it must build on a child's concept of the whole process of reading" (p. 620). Stahl suggests that teachers read to students and have students engage in dictated stories and authentic reading and writing experiences. He suggests that an exploratory structure, such as supported by whole language, be used to expose students to phonics initially (in kindergarten), but he believes that students, as they progress in school, benefit from a more systematic study in the area of phonics (beginning in first grade).
2. "Builds on a foundation of phonemic awareness" (p. 621).
3. "Is clear and direct" (p. 621).
   Stahl suggests using written words to help students make connections between letter names and their sounds and to remove some of the confusion. For example, when pictures are used to represent sounds (e.g., the picture of a cat stands for the letter *c*), a student who is unable to segment the sound of *c* from the rest of the word may wrongly conclude that the whole word *cat* represents the sound *c*. Writing the word *cat* and isolating the beginning letter *c* and talking about its sound can help to remove some of this confusion.
4. "Is integrated into a total reading program" (p. 622).
   Phonics instruction is just part of reading instruction, not the sum total of the teaching of reading. As suggested by Stahl (1992), "Phonics instruction, no matter how useful it is, should never dominate reading instruction . . . No more than 25% of the time (and possibly less) should be spent on phonics instruction and practice" (p. 622).
5. "Focuses on reading words, not learning rules" (p. 622).
   Because of all the exceptions in the English language and because of the fact that most readers when encountering unknown words do not resort to rules but rather look to patterns, Stahl (1992) suggests that

(continued)

rules can be taught as supplemental supports but that "children should not be asked to memorize or recite them [rules]. And, when rules are pointed out, they should be discussed as tentative, with exceptions given at the same time as conforming patterns. Finally, only rules with reasonable utility should be used. Teaching children that *ough* has six sounds is a waste of everyone's time" (p. 623).

6. "May include onsets and rimes" (p. 623).

The onset (part of the syllable before the vowel) and rimes (part from the vowel onward) may be used instead of rules to assist students. According to Stahl (1992, p. 623), 500 words can be derived from the following 37 rimes:

-ack	-ain	-ake	-ale	-all	-ame	-an	-ank
-ap	-ash	-at	-ate	-aw	-ay	-eat	-ell
-est	-ice	-ick	-ide	-ight	-ill	-in	-ine
-ing	-ink	-ip	-ir	-ock	-oke	-op	-or
-ore	-uck	-ug	-ump	-unk			

7. "May include invented spelling practice" (p. 623).
8. "Develops independent word recognition strategies, focusing attention on the internal structure of words" (p. 623).

Stahl (1992) lists the following as possible strategies students may apply when encountering unknown words: "sound a word out letter by letter, find a word that shares the same rime as an unknown word, or spell out the word through invented or practiced spelling" (p. 624). Stahl suggests that all of these methods focus the child's attention to the patterns in words.

9. "Develops automatic word recognition skills so that students can devote their attention to comprehension, not words" (p. 624).

Source: Adapted from "Saying the 'p' Word: Nine Guidelines for Exemplary Phonics Instruction," by S. A. Stahl, 1992, *The Reading Teacher, 45*(8), pp. 618–625.

amount of reading instructional time should be spent on the teaching of phonics. Heilman (1998) suggests that

> *The optimum amount of phonics instruction a child should receive is the minimum amount she needs to become an independent reader. To provide less instruction than a child needs would deny her the opportunity to master a skill she must have to progress in independent reading. To subject children to drill they do not need runs the risk of destroying interest in the act of reading. It is easy to turn off a potential learner by requiring that she sit through group drill on sounding letters or complete a series of workbook pages that force her to deal with minute details of word attack when she is already capable of applying these skills in sustained reading. (p. 31)*

Eldredge (1995) comments that 10 minutes of instruction a day may be all that is needed.

The Writing Process

Writing is the act of expressing ideas and thoughts on paper. It involves the careful selection of content and the presentation of that content in ways that are understandable to the reader. Writing instruction, therefore, is more than the teaching of spelling, punctuation, and capitalization rules. One approach for delivering writing instruction is the adoption of the writing process, which can be carried out through writers' workshop (Graves, 1983). The writers' workshop generally involves journal writing, prewriting activities, composing or drafting, revising, editing, writing a final draft, and publishing. Although writing is presented as a process that writers work through when creating a piece, the intent is not to have students move through these steps in lockstep fashion but rather to provide a broad frame through which their understanding of the writing process evolves. As Graves (1994) observed, not all students move through these stages at the same time and in the same order. Exhibit 15.6 presents a list of the common stages of the writing process and a brief description of the strategies and techniques associated with each step.

EXHIBIT 15.6

The Stages of the Writing Process

PREWRITING

PURPOSE	STRATEGIES AND TECHNIQUES
• to motivate • to generate ideas • to identify a topic • to identify purpose and audience • to organize ideas	• brainstorm and web ideas • read literature or other sources to prompt ideas for writing topics • present pictures, videos, artifacts, or other materials that will prompt student interest • allow students to discuss their ideas with others

COMPOSING OR DRAFTING

PURPOSE	STRATEGIES AND TECHNIQUES
• to put ideas down on paper in a first draft, with little or no focus on mechanics	• allow students to dictate their ideas to others • write to an authentic audience • discuss the various purposes of writing • write pieces for identified purposes

RESPONDING

PURPOSE	STRATEGIES AND TECHNIQUES
• to share writing with and receive feedback from others	• have students read and provide comments on each other's writing in pairs, small groups, and large groups • set up individual conferences between the student and teacher to discuss the written piece

REVISING

PURPOSE	STRATEGIES AND TECHNIQUES
• to add and/or delete ideas • to clarify through examples or greater use of descriptive language • to examine organization and the use of examples and supporting details	• arrange peer reviews with peers identifying areas possibly in need of revision • have students select a specific section of their writing to revise

EDITING

PURPOSE	STRATEGIES AND TECHNIQUES
• to refine mechanics and format	• use of checklists for student self-evaluation of work • use of peers to check each other's work • conference between teacher and students to find areas in need of revision • skill-building activities in specific areas of need

POSTWRITING OR PUBLISHING

PURPOSE	STRATEGIES AND TECHNIQUES
• to recognize and acknowledge the finished piece of writing	• illustrate and publish the piece • share finished piece with an authentic audience • place piece in an individual or class portfolio • display students' work throughout the classroom

The writing process, overall, stresses the social context of writing. Students write for an audience, read their work to others and comment, and share their final products with others. The dialogue about writing, which may be a discussion between teachers and students or a peer interaction, has been shown to improve the writing performance of many students, including adolescents with learning disabilities. For example, in their study of teaching adolescents with learning disabilities and those identified as low achievers to write compare-and-contrast essays, Wong, Butler, Ficzere, and Kuperis (1997) found that one of the significant factors contributing to the students' improved writing performance was their engagement in dialogue. In the study, student pairs, with the guidance of a teacher-researcher, critiqued and commented on each other's essays. Students, taking turns, identified ambiguities in their partner's writing and then asked clarifying questions. The pair also discussed the ideas and details included in the compare-and-contrast essays, offering each other suggestions.

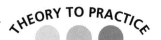

THEORY TO PRACTICE

➡ Observe a reading teacher. What strategies is the teacher using in the classroom? How effective do these strategies appear to be in supporting the students' development of literacy skills? What do you identify as the greatest strength of this teacher's approach to reading instruction?

➡ Observe a special education teacher working with a group of older students developing literacy skills. What strategies and approaches does this teacher use with these students? How do these strategies and approaches support literacy development? How do the students respond to these strategies? What additional strategies and approaches to early literacy development do you think may be effective with this group of students? Why?

➡ Gather writing samples by students at various stages of their writing ability. Analyze the skills demonstrated and those still being developed. Identify at least two strengths and one challenge evident in the writing of each student. Write one objective for each student to support the development of his or her writing skills.

FAMILY ACTIVITIES TO SUPPORT EMERGENT LITERACY

Parents can play a key role in their child's development of literacy skills. Saint-Laurent, Giasson, and Couture (1997) identify multiple strategies that parents can use to engage their children in reading activities that will assist them in developing literacy skills and assist the parents in developing optimal environments in which the children are exposed to enjoyable and meaningful reading experiences. Strategies for parents are presented in the "Make It Happen" feature. These strategies are structured by what the authors consider to be three essential elements for the development of emergent literacy: role models, exploration, and interaction with adults. Parents can serve as role models for reading, they can orchestrate opportunities for their child to explore reading and reading activities, and they can plan opportunities to interact with their child in reading experiences and activities.

MAKE IT HAPPEN
Family Activities That Support Emergent Literacy

Role Models

- Demonstrate the usefulness of reading (e.g., read directions out loud when following a recipe or following instructions to assemble furniture).
- Explain to the child that we read newspapers and other documents when we are looking for information or trying to find a telephone number.
- Explain why we write down messages and grocery lists.
- Show the child that reading can be interesting (e.g., newspapers, magazines, novels).

Exploration

Providing an Environment Rich in Print

- Books should include different types (nonfiction, fairy tales, albums) and a variety of subjects (imaginary and real characters, animals, fruit, insects). The books should be chosen according to several different criteria, including the child's interest, the adult's interest, and vocabulary level. . . .
- Other reading materials that can be used are toy and car catalogues, advertising circulars, newspapers, or any other similar material that allows the child to interact with written language. Finally, puppets can be used to recreate scenes from books or to take on the role of a character in a book.
- Writing material should also be varied and always available. Children should have different types of paper and pencils, as well as magnetic letters and blocks with letters. Magnetic letters and blocks allow children to play with letters, become familiar with these symbols, play at reconstituting words, and learn to form their first name.

Providing Exploration Opportunities

- Sticking magnetic letters to the refrigerator . . . allowing the child to look at a book before going to bed, offering paper and pencils when the parents themselves have something to write, or offering the child a book while parents are reading theirs.

Interaction with Adults

- Read books with the child daily. It is easier to make this a daily activity when it is part of a routine (e.g., when children arrive home from school or day care, after their bath, or before going to bed). Moreover, children usually appreciate the special attention paid to them during this activity.
- Reading stories should not be used as a reward that is withheld to punish the child. The child will probably like being read to very much, so to maintain his or her interest it is essential that it not be associated with any negative situation.
- When the child's attention span and interest is developed enough to follow a story from beginning to end, it is important to read the book rather than recount the story. If the child does not understand certain elements of the text, read it first and then explain it afterwards. If the text is too difficult, use another book for this activity. . . .
- Ask the child to tell the story in his or her own words. In doing so, the child may refer to illustrations, and you can help by asking questions.
- When children are able to tell their favorite story, ask them to reread it (i.e., pretend to read it). At first, the child will find it easier to read one sentence or one page at a time. The child will probably guess or invent some words, which is quite normal.

Source: From "Parents + Children + Reading Activities = Emergent Literacy," 1997, by L. Saint-Laurent, J. Giasson, and C. Couture, *Teaching Exceptional Children, 30* (2), pp. 53, 54, 55.

Siblings may also interact with one another to the benefit of both their reading skills and their enjoyment. Fox and Wright (1997) describe a cross-age reading program, Storymates, in which preteens read to members of their families and to friends. The Storymates program was carried out over a nine-week period and involved a number of activities. These activities are presented in Exhibit 15.7.

EXHIBIT 15.7

Storymates Program Activities

IN SCHOOL

- *Teachers read storybooks aloud to students*
  Through this activity, teachers modeled appropriate oral reading for the students. Stories read aloud were used for group analysis of story structure as well.
- *Students practice reading storybooks with a peer*
  In pairs, students practiced reading the storybooks aloud that they planned to read at home. Each book was read twice. While their peer was reading, their partner rated them on their fluency and wrote comments about one or two positive features of how the story was read. The partner also generated questions and, after the reading, asked the reader to respond to those questions. Additionally, the reader rated his or her own performance.
- *Students examine narrative structure of stories*
  Students presented the narrative structures of the text graphically (e.g., setting, plot, characters, resolution) through mapping, use of story frames, writing of story recipes, and mapping of stories. They also wrote new endings to stories, made predictions, summarized story events, compared character traits and actions, and related activities in order to develop a sense of story structure and comprehension of key story elements and events.
- *Students retell stories read*
  After each story had been read twice in the paired reading-along activity, students wrote a retell of the story.

AT HOME

- *Students read the same stories at home*
  Students read the stories practiced in school to siblings, other family members, and friends.

Source: Fox & Wright (1997).

Using a rubric to score student retells, Fox and Wright (1997) determined that students, after participating in Storymates, were able to write story retells of higher quality. Additionally, teachers reported that students became actively engaged in reading the storybooks, a behavior dramatically different than prior to the program, when students did not engage in reading activities independently or choose reading as an activity option. Analysis of the findings of a project questionnaire indicated that parents perceived a difference in their child's reading performance as a result of the program and a difference in how reading was viewed at home.

THEORY TO PRACTICE

➡ Develop a handout for parents indicating how they can support their children's early literacy development. When developing your handout, take into account the literacy levels of the parents. Share your handout with a peer for feedback.

CHAPTER SUMMARY

This chapter explains what emergent literacy is and what type of learning environment and instructional activities teachers can provide to help students develop early literacy skills. The activities may be used with young as well as older students and may be modified to respond to individual needs.

CHAPTER 16

Supporting Continued Literacy Development

Read to find out the following:
- common challenges that readers and writers may encounter and interventions for addressing those challenges
- instructional approaches for supporting readers
- instructional approaches for supporting writers

Emergent literacy, identified by Valencia (1997) and described in Chapter 15, provides the foundation from which students develop as readers and writers. The instructional techniques and strategies described in Chapter 15 continue to support students in their iteracy development and, when coupled with additional techniques and strategies, help them gain advanced skills to deal with challenging reading and writing activities. Additional techniques and strategies focus on student reading development in (a) word recognition, (b) rate and fluency, (c) vocabulary, and (d) comprehension. In writing, the teaching focus is on (a) spelling, handwriting, capitalization and punctuation, and (b) skills for writing connected text. In this chapter we discuss ways to support student development in these areas and emphasize what teachers can do to address the needs of students who are experiencing significant difficulties in developing their literacy skills.

APPROACHES FOR SUPPORTING READERS

Our discussion of the needs of students who experience significant difficulty in becoming proficient readers is framed by the work of Ciborowski (1995), who wrote an article titled "Using Textbooks with Students Who Cannot Read Them." Ciborowski begins her discussion by differentiating between what good and poor readers bring to the reading experience and how they approach the task of reading for meaning. Exhibit 16.1 summarizes these differences.

GOOD READERS	POOR READERS	EXHIBIT 16.1
		How Good and Poor Readers Differ

Before Reading

GOOD READERS	POOR READERS
• Think about what they already know about a subject	• Begin to read without thinking about the topic
• Know the purpose for which they read	• Do not know why they are reading
• Are motivated or interested to begin reading	• Lack interest and motivation to begin reading
• Having a general sense of how the BIG ideas will fit together	• Have little sense of how the BIG ideas will fit together

During Reading

GOOD READERS	POOR READERS
• Pay simultaneous attention to words and meaning	• Overattend to individual words; miss salience
• Read fluently	• Read slower and at the same rate of speed
• Concentrate well while reading	• Have difficulty concentrating, particularly during silent reading
• Willing to "risk" encountering difficult words and able to grapple with text ambiguities	• Unwilling to "risk"; easily defeated by words and text
• Construct efficient strategies to monitor comprehension	• Unable to construct efficient strategies to monitor comprehension
• Stop to use a "fix-it" strategy when confused	• Seldom use a "fix-it" strategy; plod on ahead, eager to finish
• Reading skills improve	• Reading progress is painfully slow

After Reading

GOOD READERS	POOR READERS
• Understand how the pieces of information fit together	• Do not understand how the pieces of information fit together
• Able to identify what's salient	• May focus on the extraneous, peripheral
• Intereested in reading more	• See reading as distasteful

Source: From "Using textbooks with students who cannot read them," 1995, *Remedial and Special Education 16*(7), 90–101. Copyright 1995 by PRO-ED, Inc. Reprinted by permission.

Analysis of the traits listed in the exhibit reveals how differently these two groups of readers approach reading. By setting a purpose for reading, self-monitoring during reading, and wanting to read more, good readers actively engage with text, enjoy the reading process, and identify meaning-making as the primary purpose for reading. In contrast, students designated as "poor" readers fail to understand the purpose and process for making meaning from text and see reading as a chore to get through. One of the major challenges that teachers of "poor" readers face is how to engage these students in the reading process and support their development of skills and understandings necessary to become good readers. Beginning points for intervention are to apply intensive and systematic instruction in the four broad areas of (a) word identification, (b) rate and fluency, (c) vocabulary, and (d) comprehension.

Word Identification

Word identification skills (also known as word analysis skills) develop from the base of phonemic awareness and phonics skills. Students' ability to recognize words on sight (e.g., when presented a word, they can identify that word in 3 to 4 seconds) and their ability to employ strategies when they encounter unknown words (e.g., they look at the first letter of the unknown word for a beginning sound clue; use context) are components of word identification curriculum. Word identification skills may be clustered into three categories: sight word recognition, word analysis strategies, and orthographic processes (Lipson & Wixson, 1997).

Sight word recognition

Many students with disabilities experience difficulty building a sight word vocabulary and, therefore, lack fluency in reading basic words that they continually encounter in text. Sight words include words such as *the, and,* and *their,* and survival words such as *emergency, exit,* and *poison.* The goal of building sight word recognition is to enhance students' abilities to recognize words automatically that they encounter frequently in text.

There are several techniques for expanding students' sight word recognition. One calls for the identification of words unknown to the student and systematic drill and practice of those words in order to achieve mastery. When this approach is used, students read from a list of basic sight words and the teacher identifies the words students are able to read quickly and those that present difficulties. The teacher generates a list of target words from the list of missed words, and the teacher and/or students write those words on cards, in a personal dictionary, or on a grid. Starting with a small number of those words (e.g., two to five), students read the words on a daily basis, several times during one reading session, and at the conclusion of the session, chart the number of words they have read correctly.

Students refer to their card word file, personal dictionary, or grid when reading and writing stories. Referring to these tools reinforces the reading and spelling of these sight words by increasing the number of opportunities the students have for encountering the words in text.

Picture cards may be used to enhance student sight word recognition. Students write target words on cards and draw pictures that correspond to the words. For survival words, students may take photographs representing the words, mount the photographs on cards, and write the corresponding sight word on the card. These cards are then used for word practice. Students with visual impairments may use senses other than vision and actually touch the place where words are located.

One additional approach to sight word development is the VAKT (Visual-Auditory-Kinesthetic-Tactile) approach. A multisensory approach developed by Fernald (1943) incorporates many of the previous ideas for helping students develop sight word vocabularies while adding a multisensory dimension. Students select words they want to learn and write the words on cards with crayons so that the words have texture. The following strategy is modeled and then repeated by students for each word: (a) say the word, trace the word with two fingers while saying each part of the word, say the word again; (b) write the word without looking at the word card and then compare what was written to the word card; and (c) repeat the first step until the word is written correctly three consecutive times without looking at the prompt card. Students may also draw pictures to go along with the words as visual reminders. Students may maintain a graph to monitor their sight word development over time.

Frequent opportunities to read and encounter targeted sight words in text also foster sight word recognition. One technique is to have students read from predictable or pattern books (see Chapter 15). Another is to have them read the same text several times. These techniques are powerful because they ensure that students confront the same words multiple times during reading. Drawing students' attention to target words as they are encountered in text and in community settings can also reinforce student recognition of those words.

Word analysis strategies

Lipson and Wixson (1997) identify three types of word analysis strategies: contextual analysis, morphemic analysis, and phonic analysis. *Contextual analysis* involves teaching students to use context clues as one approach for decoding unknown words encountered in text. Students are encouraged to skip an unfamiliar word when they come to it, finish reading the sentence that contains the unknown word, and then go back to see whether they can determine what the unknown word is from its context—the meaning of the words surrounding the unknown word.

A direct approach for developing skills in using context clues is the application of the cloze procedure. The cloze procedure requires the reader to supply words that have been deliberately deleted—such as every fifth word, or every adjective, or every verb. The reader is asked to generate words to fill in the blanks. This approach helps students understand that only a limited number of words can be used to fill the blanks in a meaningful way. When attempting to fill in the blanks, students must attend to context clues.

Morphemic analysis involves the breaking down of words into morphemes—"the smallest unit of meaning in our language" (Lipson & Wixson, 1997, p. 28). Morphemes, both free (e.g., *house*) and bound (the last *s* on *houses*), are the smallest meaningful unit in language and are a key to word analysis. The study of morphemes such as prefixes and suffixes, compound words, and contractions can provide valuable clues in identifying unknown words.

Phonic analysis is the final type of word analysis strategies. Recall from Chapter 15 that phonics instruction can help children decode unfamiliar words. When students encounter longer words, they may apply structural analysis and break down words by syllables, and then decode the word syllable by syllable. To support the development of this type of phonic analysis, students may be taught rules of syllabication. Teaching students specific rules (e.g., words, such as *better* and *ladder,* with a vowel and then two consonants followed by a vowel are divided into syllables between the consonants—*bet ter* and *lad der*) can assist them in decoding unfamiliar words. When learning syllabication rules, however, students must be told that there are exceptions to every rule and that rules serve only as guides.

Orthographic processes

This is the final approach for developing word identification skills identified by Lipson and Wixson (1997). Orthographic processes have to do with the appearance of the word. When reading connected text, readers can identify words solely by the way they look. This can also apply to spelling—good spellers many times can tell if a word is spelled right just by looking at it.

Rate and Fluency

Rate (the speed at which words are read) and fluency ("the reader's ability to group words into meaningful phrase units and use expression as they read" (Lipson-Wixson, 1997)) are closely connected with sight word and word identification skills and are linked with comprehension. Without a strong sight word vocabulary or skills for attacking unknown words, students are likely to be dysfluent readers with depressed overall reading rates because they have to stop so often to decode unfamiliar words. Students who read at a low rate of words per minute do not have a rate that allows them to gain a sense of fluency associated with reading, and they may interpret reading to be the task of reading individual words on a page—that is, word calling—rather than reading words to gain meaning. A minimum of approximately 100 correct words per minute seems to be a desirable rate because at this rate students begin to hear the flow of language, begin to focus on the meaning of text, and begin to move away from expending a high percentage of their energy on decoding words when reading.

Fluency influences and is influenced by rate. Students who read with fluency not only read at a reasonable rate but read with expression and phrasing which enhance comprehension. This type of reading is distinct from that of a poor reader who may not only read slowly, but read without fluency—not pausing at the ends of sentences and running sentences and phrases together in patterns that do not support comprehension. For example, read the following passage, pausing at each slash to see how the lack of fluency undermines comprehension:

> The children were / very excited about visiting the planetarium. They had been studying / the stars for / weeks and now had the opportunity / to see how the / stars and constellations appear / in the night sky.

Several techniques are available to support students in their development of reading rate and fluency.

Choral reading

One approach for enhancing reading fluency is choral reading—reading in unison as a group. Choral reading may be done by dyads, by small groups, or by large groups. The teacher or a student may be the reading leader, reading slightly louder than the students and setting the pace of the reading. By hearing the group read the words at an appropriate pace and with fluency, and by participating in that reading to the extent they are able, students begin to expand their sight word vocabularies and develop greater rate and fluency in their reading, and to chunk text into units that aid comprehension.

Neurological impress approach

In the neurological impress approach (Heckelman, 1969), a teacher and student read in unison. The focus is on maintaining an appropriate pace with the student "keeping up" with the teacher, and paying attention to rate and fluency, rather than to individual errors. The teacher sits behind the student, reading slightly louder into his or her ear than the student is reading. As they read, the teacher may move one finger under the words to help the student follow along. The reading does not stop when the student makes an error. Gradually, as rate and fluency increase, the teacher lowers his or her voice and the student becomes the louder of the two readers and begins to set the pace.

Dyad reading

The primary purpose of dyad reading is the improvement of fluency (Eldredge, 1995). The technique is similar to the neurological impress approach. A more capable reader—the lead reader—is paired with a reader who reads more slowly or is unable to read an assigned passage—the assisted reader. While reading together, they share the textbook and sit side by side. The lead reader sets the pace, pointing to each word as it is read. The assisted reader is encouraged to follow and read along to keep pace with the lead reader. The lead reader establishes a pace that promotes rate and fluency, not word calling. Pairs are encouraged to read as much text as possible during the time period allocated.

Repeated readings

Repeated reading (LaBerge & Samuels, 1974) is another technique that allows students multiple opportunities to practice-read a text in order to gain fluency. Passages are read until a student achieves a preset level of fluency and reading rate. Repeated readings may be carried out through tape recording, dyad reading, choral reading, and repeated reading of language-experience stories (Meese, 1994).

Vocabulary

Vocabulary is the collection of words whose meanings an individual understands. Capable readers are familiar with the meanings of many words. Poor readers may have a limited vocabulary. Vocabulary building through instruction is critical for all readers, and especially for those readers experiencing difficulties, because "Readers and writers who do not have adequate knowledge of important words and concepts and/or are unable to determine word meanings will have difficulty successfully comprehending or composing texts" (Lipson & Wixson, 1997, p. 26).

Students' vocabularies may be enhanced in multiple ways. One basic way is to encourage and provide time for students to read and discuss what they are reading. Students can be encouraged to highlight unknown words and discuss the meaning of those words with peers, to use context clues and support materials (e.g., dictionaries) to uncover meaning, and to use new words in their speaking and writing. Other, more explicit approaches are also available.

Individualized dictionaries and card systems

One strategy for assisting students in expanding their vocabularies is the maintenance of individualized dictionaries or card systems. The dictionaries or cards may list words and include pictures of the words, sentences containing the words as used in text, or sentences written by the students to reinforce the meaning of selected words. Students may refer to these dictionaries or cards when reading text, when completing activities, or during fluency-building activities. Word cards can also be organized into a communication book or posted on a communication board for students to use when communicating with others. In this way, students are given specific opportunities to incorporate vocabulary words they are learning in class into their speaking and writing.

Vocabulary sheets

Vocabulary sheets (Stump, Lovitt, Fister, Kemp, Moore, & Schroeder, 1992) offer another means for assisting students in vocabulary development and can be readily applied to the teaching of specialized vocabulary encountered in general education curriculum courses and in the teaching of functional vocabulary. The strategy of using vocabulary sheets draws on precision teaching to monitor student skill development.

On the front of the sheet, words are listed in boxes. Each word is repeated several times to allow for multiple practice opportunities. On the back of the sheet are definitions of the words in the corresponding boxes. The sheets can be used in several ways. Students can work in pairs. One student has the word side of the sheet facing up; the other, the definition side. The student with the word side up says the word and defines it. The other student refers to the vocabulary sheet to check the definition. This paired activity can be timed; students can count how many correct definitions they are able to state in a given time. Students can also use the sheets for individual study. With the word side facing up, the student writes in brief definitions on a blank sheet with empty boxes and when time is up, turns the word sheet over and checks and records the number of correct responses.

Semantic feature analysis

This strategy for supporting students in their vocabulary development begins with the teacher reading the text and identifying *superordinate* concepts (the major ideas presented in the text) and *subordinate* concepts (ideas supporting the major ideas). The teacher then develops a relationship table on which to present the concepts. Figure 16.1 shows a semantic feature analysis relationship table developed by Anders and Bos (1986). Subordinate concepts ("Important vocabulary" in the figure) are listed in the lefthand column of the table; superordinate concepts ("Important ideas") are listed to the right in the remaining space. The table is given to students, who rate how each subordinate term is related to the superordinate concepts. They use a plus sign for a positive relationship, a minus sign for negative relationship, a zero for no relationship, and a question mark when they are unsure of the relationship or when, working as a group, they cannot achieve consensus on the type of relationship that exists.

▐ **FIGURE 16.1**
Semantic Feature Analysis
Relationship Table

The Fourth Amendment

Important ideas

Important vocabulary	Citizen's right to privacy versus	Society needs to keep law and order	Police search *with a* search warrant	Police search without a search warrant	Evidence allowed in court
Search and seizure					
Unreasonable search and seizure					
Probable cause to search					
Your property and possessions					
Absolute privacy					
You give consent					
Hot pursuit					
Moving vehicle					
Stop-and-frisk					
Plain view					
During an arrest					
Evidence					
Exclusionary rule					

Source: From "Semantic Feature Analysis: An Interactive Strategy for Vocabulary Development and Text Comprehension," by P. L. Anders and C. S. Bos, 1986, *Journal of Reading, 29*, p. 613.

Graphic organizers and webs

This set of approaches, similar to semantic feature analysis, provides students visual ways to organize information and understand relationships between concepts. Students can analyze the meaning of words and how words relate to one another through the creation of graphic organizers and webs. For specific information about these approaches, see Chapter 17.

Comprehension

Comprehension is meaning-making, or making sense of information presented in text. Teachers may use many techniques and approaches to systematically and explicitly teach comprehension skills.

One traditional way to teach reading comprehension is to employ the Directed Reading Approach (DRA) (Betts, 1946). Using the DRA, a teacher identifies prereading, during-reading, and postreading activities and arranges them in a specific sequence for each lesson. Activities identified by Lipson and Wixson (1997) include the following:

PREREADING ACTIVITIES	DURING-READING ACTIVITIES	POSTREADING ACTIVITIES
• teacher activates prior knowledge • teacher activates student interest • teacher introduces vocabulary • teacher establishes a purpose for reading	• students read silently • students answer questions related to the purpose set for reading the passage • students answer questions • students orally reread for clarification of meaning	• group discusses the text • group discusses questions provided at the end of the text or by the teacher • teacher provides skill instruction (may or may not be connected to the passage read)

These are the typical steps of the DRA (Betts, 1946):

1. Develop background for student understanding of the text, gain student interest, introduce new vocabulary, and set a purpose for reading.

2. Have students silently read the passage.

3. Have students answer questions to check their comprehension.

4. Have students reread portions of the text to clarify any misconceptions.

5. Have students engage in discussions and extensions of the story or in skill-building activities.

This approach to reading instruction is teacher directed and does not necessarily support students' development of self-monitoring techniques (e.g., setting their own purpose for reading and monitoring for comprehension breakdowns). Also, the DRA may not provide needed instructional supports for students experiencing difficulties in meaning-making—supports such as setting a purpose for reading, asking questions while reading, and checking for understanding.

One way to overcome some of the limitations of the Directed Reading Approach is to apply the Directed-Reading-Thinking Activity (DRTA) approach developed by Stauffer (1969, 1980). This approach is based on students' active engagement in setting a purpose for reading and in monitoring their comprehension by making predictions as they read. Throughout their reading of a passage, students stop and make predictions and, as they read on, check to confirm that their predictions were correct and to modify them based on new information. At the conclusion of their reading, students summarize what they have read and discuss how the process helped them monitor their comprehension.

Both the DRA and the DRTA provide frameworks for the teaching of comprehension. In the remainder of this section we provide information about specific prereading, during-reading, and postreading activities. For some students with disabilities, particularly individuals with sensory impairments, these activities may need to be modified to ensure that they effectively respond to student learning needs.

Prereading activities

The primary purposes of prereading activities are to activate students' prior knowledge and to assist students in setting a purpose for reading. PReP, K-W-L, and previewing are three prereading activities that can be applied across the grades and with a range of students.

PReP. PReP (Prereading Plan) (Langer, 1981) can be used to activate students' prior knowledge before they read text and to help teachers gain a better understanding of what students already know about a topic. This knowledge can help the teacher

> *(1) determine the amount of information a reader has about a specific topic, as well as how the reader has organized this information, (2) become more aware of the language a student uses to express knowledge about a given subject, and (3) make judgments about how much additional background information and vocabulary is needed before students can successfully comprehend the text. (Langer, 1981, p. 154)*

PReP has three phases. During the first phase, the teacher presents a key word or visual that represents the topic to be covered in the text reading. Students brainstorm as many ideas as come to mind when they hear the key word or view the visual and the teacher records their ideas. During the second phase, students determine how their ideas relate to one another and determine the origin of their various ideas. This exploration challenges them to draw associations among ideas. During the final phase, students are challenged to respond to the following question: "Based on our discussion and before we read the text, have you any new ideas about . . ." (p. 154). Analysis of student responses informs teachers if students have much, some, or little prior knowledge and assists teachers in designing appropriate lessons and activities.

K-W-L. K-W-L (Ogle, 1986) is another strategy for activating and bridging the students' prior knowledge to text. K (What We **K**now) is the first step of the strategy. During this step, students brainstorm what they know about a particular topic, the teacher records their ideas, and the students categorize this information. In the second step, W (What We **W**ant to Find Out), students generate questions that they would like answered as a result of reading the text. This activity helps establish a purpose for the reading. The final step, L (What I **L**earned), occurs after the reading of the text. Students identify what they learned from the text, then they return to the questions to see whether they have answers or need to do more reading to find out what they wanted (W). They also may return to what they already knew (K) to assess whether their prior knowledge was correct.

Previewing. Previewing, another prereading activity, builds background knowledge, creates a framework for approaching the material to be read, motivates students to engage with the information, and provides specific information about the passage (Graves, Prenn, & Cooke, 1985). The "Make It Happen" feature describes how teachers can prepare for and implement previewing with students.

❙ **MAKE IT HAPPEN**
Previewing Narrative Text

Preparation for Previewing
- Become totally familiar with the story and its events.
- Determine how you will bridge students' experiences and knowledge to the main theme or topic of the story.
- Prepare a description of the characters, setting, and story events up to the climax of the story.
- Prepare questions or directions to be given to students prior to their reading.
- Prepare all of these steps in writing.

Presenting Previews

- Start by asking questions that will gain students' interest and help them begin the process of connecting what they already know about the topic to the topic presented in the text to be read.
- Conduct a brief discussion of the topic or theme of the story.
- Discuss the characters, setting, and other critical features.
- Discuss story events up to the climax.
- Provide students with a question that they are to answer as a result of reading the passage.

Source: Graves, Prenn, & Cooke (1985).

During-reading activities

During-reading activities also help students develop skills in meaning-making and self-monitoring. This section describes seven strategies teachers may find helpful.

Think-alouds. The use of think-alouds makes the thinking processes involved in completing a task explicit and audible so students can hear and experience them. Teachers can model think-alouds to show students

how they construct meaning, how they decide what's important to pay attention to and learn, how they relate information across sentences and paragraphs, how they deal with difficulties in making sense of the text. (Rhodes & Dudley-Marling, 1996, p. 171)

Here is an example of a partial think-aloud:

The teacher begins by saying:

"OK. My job is to read pages 15 and 16. I am reading this so I can answer the questions on page 16. What's the title of these two pages? Metamorphic rocks. Well, I don't know anything about metamorphic rocks. Maybe it will help if I look at the headings and the pictures."

The teacher then goes on, thinking aloud about what the headings reveal and what the pictures mean and how this information conveys some idea of what the two pages of reading are going to be about. The teacher goes on:

"Now, I have some idea of what the section is about. It's about metamorphic rocks, how they are made, and their properties. I have an idea of what this type of rock looks like and where it is found, but that's all. Maybe before I start reading, I should read the questions at the end of the section. That way I'll have an idea of what I'm supposed to be looking for when I'm reading."

When first using think-alouds, teachers may feel uncomfortable, but with practice the inclusion of think-alouds in instruction will become more natural. Exhibit 16.2 provides a list of ways to incorporate think-alouds into instruction.

EXHIBIT 16.2

**Ways to Use Think-Alouds
in Instruction**

- Use your own background knowledge: "Oh, I've ridden a horse before and I know just what the author means when he says the girl was 'saddle-sore.'"
- Create visual images in your mind: "It's as if I closed my eyes and saw what the author is talking about—(describe the scene)."
- Check predictions: "Hmmm—the author isn't having this character do what I thought he would do next. Remember, I thought he was going to . . ."
- Make an analogy: "This situation is like another one we've read about . . ."
- Adjust reading rate: "I think I'll skim through this section—I don't think it pertains to what we want to find out."
- Determine what's important to understand from the text: "One way I decide what's important is to keep the subtitle of the section I'm reading in mind and think about how what I'm reading is related to the subtitle."
- Determine what's important to understand about the instructional situation: "The social studies teacher always wants people to be able to answer the questions at the end of the chapter, so I think I'll read them first so I know what information to look for."
- Use easier reading material: "I'm not sure I understand what this means and I know it's explained in this book over here, which is easier to read. I'll use the other book to learn what I want to know instead."
- Use sources other than books: "One way to learn about this is to keep reading this book, but the book is very hard to understand. Let's see if the librarian has a film or filmstrip that might help us."
- Reread: "You know, I don't think I was paying much attention when I read that last section. I'd better read it again."
- Read on: "I don't really understand what the author is talking about here. I hope she explains more in the next page or so."

Source: Adapted by permission of Lynn K. Rhodes and Curt Dudley-Marling. *Readers and Writers with a Difference: A Holistic Approach to Teaching Struggling Readers and Writers, 2ed.* (Heinemann, A division of Reed Elsevier, Inc., Portsmouth, NH, 1996).

Questioning. Another common way to support comprehension is through the use of questioning. Teachers and students can prepare questions to be asked prior to reading, during reading, and after reading. Beginning the reading assignment with a provocative question whose answer students are to discover through reading can assist students in setting a purpose for reading and identifying relevant information. Questions can also motivate them to keep reading to find answers.

Students may be taught to generate questions of their own when reading text or they may use teacher-developed questions or questions in the textbook. Wong and Jones (1982) describe a five-step process for assisting students in self-monitoring through the self-generation of questions:

1. Students ask themselves why they are reading or studying the passage.

2. Students find the main idea and underline it.

3. Students formulate a question about the main idea.

4. Students read to find an answer to their question.

5. Students look back and review the questions and the information learned through asking the questions.

Students can be taught to read questions listed in a textbook before they read the material. This strategy is most applicable to the reading of content area materials such as those used in social studies and science.

Mnemonics. Mnemonic devices are another powerful during-reading aid. Englert and Mariage (1990) present the POSSE strategy, which consists of cues to support student comprehension. As students read the text, they gather information in response to these cues:

P = *Predict*
> I predict that . . .
> I'm remembering . . .

O = *Organize*
> I think one category might be . . .

SS = *Search/Summarize*
> I think the main idea is . . .
> My question about the main idea is . . .

E = *Evaluate*
> I think we did (did not) predict this main idea
> (Compare)
> Are there any clarifications?
> I predict the next part will be about . . .

Archer and Gleason (1994) suggest the RCRC strategy for active reading and enhancement of comprehension:

R = Read
> Read a paragraph. Identify important topics and details.

C = Cover
> Use your hand to cover the information read.

R = Recite
> Recite what you learned from reading the information. State topics and details in your own words.

C = Check
> Uncover the material and check your ideas with what was written. Repeat the procedure if you forgot important information.

Additional study skill strategies incorporating mnemonics are provided in Chapter 17.

Multipass. Schumaker, Deshler, Alley, Warner, and Denton (1982) developed Multipass, a strategy for passing through the material multiple times with a different specific purpose each time. Passing through material more than once gives students several opportunities to identify and comprehend important information and ideas. The three passes are described below:

1. *Survey pass.* The purpose of this pass is to discover the main ideas and structure of the passage. Students look at titles and subtitles, pictures and captions, and read the summary paragraph.

2. *Size-up pass.* During this pass, students look for specific information and details without reading the passage in its entirety. They do this by (a) reading the questions at the end of the section; (b) crossing out any questions that they can already answer from the survey pass; (c) looking through the remainder of the passage, cueing into headings and subheadings for hints as to where the answers will be found; (d) stating the answers to the questions in their own words; and (e) restating all the facts and information gained from the passage.

3. *Sort-out pass.* During this final pass, students read the questions again and state the answers in their own words. Students return to the passage to search for answers to the questions they were not able to answer.

Story grammars. Another powerful strategy for supporting comprehension is to apply story grammars before, during, and after reading. Story grammars assist readers in analyzing stories in terms of story elements: characters, setting, problem, resolution of the problem, and ending. These story elements are known collectively as story structure. Analysis of story structure through story grammars can be a highly effective way to help students develop their comprehension skills. Story grammars may come in the form of graphics and visuals or as a series of questions.

Idol (1987) developed and tested the application of a story grammar with students with and without learning disabilities and found that it enhanced reading comprehension for both groups. Figure 16.2 shows the five-part story grammar used in her study. Students can complete the form as they read the story, after reading the story, or as a

▌ **FIGURE 16.2**
Story Grammar

Source: From "Group Story Mapping: A Comprehensive Strategy for Both Skilled and Unskilled Readers," by L. Idol, 1987, *Journal of Learning Disabilities, 20,* p. 199. Copyright 1987 by PRO-ED, Inc. Reprinted by permission.

NAME _____ DATE _____

The Setting
  Characters: Time: Place:

The Problem

The Goal

Action

The Outcome

means to predict story events given advance information about the setting and problem. Story grammars may be completed by students working independently, in dyads, in small groups, or in large groups.

Used in isolation, story grammars may allow for only a one-dimensional understanding of the story or analysis of story elements. For example, students may be able to identify the main characters in the story and include them in their story grammar, but they may be unable to articulate qualities of the characters, the emotions of the characters, or the characters' responses to main events. Therefore, although story grammars provide a foundation for assisting students in comprehending stories, they should be expanded to provide an in-depth analysis of story events and meanings and to reflect story complexity.

Story mapping. Emery (1996) expands on story grammar by helping readers consider the story from the perspectives of the different characters. Emery believes that understanding characters is critical to comprehension because "Character states, such as their desires, feelings, thoughts, and beliefs, are the glue that ties the actions of the story together" (p. 534). To assist students in comprehending stories from the characters' perspective, Emery developed the Story Maps with Character Perspectives (SMCP). The strategy involves the following steps:

1. Students read the entire story.

2. Students list story events, the problem, the events connected with resolving the problem, and the resolution to the problem.

3. Students discuss the perspectives of the characters during the main events of the story.

Students complete a standard story map for steps 1 and 2 and then create an additional chart for step 3. For step 3, students first write in the main events and then consider each event from the perspective of the main characters. Emery (1996) offers teachers a list of generic questions that can be shared with students in order to prompt them as they attempt to understand events from the perspective of the individual characters. Sample questions, slightly modified to be applicable to any story, are presented in Exhibit 16.3.

EXHIBIT 16.3

SMCP Sample Questions

QUESTIONS FOR TEACHERS TO ASK . . .

1. "When students focus on what happened in the story instead of why:"
   - Why did _____ act that way?
   - What was the character thinking when this event took place?
   - What did the character want at this point in the story?
   - How is the character feeling at this point in the story?
2. "When students seem to misinterpret the character's feelings, thoughts, or desires because they are considering only their own perspective:"
   - Is the way the character is feeling the way you would feel in this situation?
   - In what ways is the character different from you?
   - Because the character is different from you, how do you think the character felt at this point in the story?
   - Let's reread some parts of the story that may help us understand why the characters feel differently than you might and would respond differently than you might respond in these situations.

(continued)

EXHIBIT 16.3

SMCP Sample Questions
(continued)

3. "When students' replies seem inadequate because they are focusing only on one particular part of the story instead of the story as a whole:"
   - What else might the character be wanting? be thinking? be feeling?
   - What else has happened in the story up to this point that gives us clues that the character may be feeling this way?
   - What about what the character did and felt when _____ and _____ happened in the story?
   - What does that tell us about what the character may be thinking and feeling now?
4. "When students seem to be considering only one character's perspective or misinterpreting the relationship between characters because they are seeing things from only one point of view:"
   - What about the other character? What was that character thinking/feeling/wanting?
   - When _____ took that action, how did the character think the other character would respond?
   - What was the character thinking about the other character when he/she did that?
   - What did _____ think the other character was thinking/feeling/wanting?

Source: Adapted from "Helping Readers Comprehend Stories from the Characters' Perspective," by D. W. Emery, 1996, *The Reading Teacher, 49*, p. 539.

Shanahan and Shanahan (1997) propose another story mapping approach to help students understand characters' perspectives and develop a more complete conceptualization of the story. Their approach—character perspective charting—is based on their personal experiences using a traditional map to chart a familiar children's story and then remapping the story from a different perspective—identifying a different character as the main character and completing the chart from the perspective of that character. Shanahan and Shanahan found that although they could complete the story map from the perspective of two different characters, the conclusions drawn and the significant themes identified on the two maps were in conflict. Thus they concluded that focusing only on the perspective of the main character and completing story grammars from that perspective only would reduce the reader's ability to understand the complexity of a story.

Character perspective charting works as follows. Students read the entire story. Then they are presented with two charts, each chart labeled with the name of a different main character. Students work through the questions on both charts. The answers to the questions reflect the point of view of the character whose name appears on the chart: Where and when does the story take place? What is the problem facing the main character? What is the main character's goal? What does he or she do to achieve that goal? What happens? How does the main character feel about the outcome? What point does the author make by telling the story from this perspective? Students may answer questions for both characters simultaneously or work with one character at a time. Shanahan and Shanahan (1997) suggest that the following points be discussed during debriefing:

- the thinking strategies students used when analyzing the story
- how the author presented the story—favoring one character over another or building in sympathy for an opposing viewpoint

Shanahan and Shanahan say that character perspective charting works best for stories about two characters who are in conflict.

Reciprocal teaching. As a metacognitive strategy that requires students to read and dialogue about text to construct meaning (Palincsar & Brown, 1984), reciprocal teaching can be a highly effective during-reading intervention. The technique incorporates four strategies: (a) questioning, (b) summarizing, (c) clarifying, and (d) predicting. During reciprocal teaching, students work in cooperative reading groups. At first, the teacher may be a group member, leading and modeling the application of the four strategies. Eventually, however, the responsibility for leading each group is assumed by students in the groups. Each student takes a turn being the "teacher."

The activity begins with students reading a segment of text. Students may read silently, or the group leader or another group member may read the text aloud. Next, the leader asks questions of the group. The questions are used as a starting point for discussing and clarifying the text and the author's message. Students may refer back to the text to answer the questions, and all students may ask questions of the group as the discussion unfolds. Next, the leader does the summarizing or leads the group in summarizing what was read. The leader then assists the group in clarifying what was read. The group may discuss the meaning of individual words, the meanings of phrases, or sections of text that group members found confusing. Finally, the leader makes a prediction about what will occur next and may ask others to make predictions as well. The cycle is then repeated, with a new student in the role of "teacher."

Stump, Wilson, Shirley, and Ung (in press) used reciprocal teaching with sixth grade students in an inclusive classroom. Students worked in book clubs, reading self-selected books representing a range of reading levels. Students read passages from the books independently and in their book clubs, and participated in reciprocal teaching activities. Students completed reading logs targeting clarification and summarization and engaged in the analysis of story grammar features (e.g., character analysis, setting). The study demonstrated the applicability of reciprocal teaching to highly heterogeneous reading groups and the inclusion of students with disabilities in authentic literacy activities with general education peers.

Postreading activities

A number of the strategies previously discussed can be used as postreading activities. For example, after reading, students may map ideas through the use of story grammars or other graphic organizers. Questioning strategies also may be used following the reading of passages. Some other approaches are also available.

Students can dramatize what they have read. This can be a highly effective and engaging postreading activity. Rhodes and Dudley-Marling (1996) offer a number of suggestions for how students can dramatize what they have read: students can select "spontaneous story reenactments, Readers Theatre, role playing, putting on a play, acting out mime, creating a flannel board story" (p. 214). In addition, students may develop a multimedia presentation on the computer or gather (and videotape) a "man on the street" response to main events in the story. Puppets and other creations also can be used to dramatize what was read.

Writing about what was read is another way for students to engage in postreading comprehension building. They can do this writing independently, in dyads, in small groups, or in large groups. Students may write formal responses, may make entries into journals or reading logs, or may present their ideas on a poster or graphic. To increase dialogue among students, students could share works in progress and receive feedback from one another, using an interpreter if one of the students has a hearing impairment.

Rhodes and Dudley-Marling (1996) developed a list of categories to describe students' written responses to literature (see Exhibit 16.4). Teachers may use this classification as one means for structuring writing activities. Students could be asked to use one of these categories when reflecting on a passage or story.

Personal meaning-making: Responses that reveal students are constructing meaning for themselves from their reading of text.

Retelling: Summarizing what has happened in the story, usually in the first part of the story.

Making inferences: Insights regarding the feelings, thoughts, and motives of story characters.

Prediction and validation: Speculation about what is going to happen as the story unfolds.

Expressing wonder or confusion: Questions or wondering about what is happening in the story.

Personal experience: Connections made between something in the book and the reader's life.

Philosophical reflection: The reader's reflections on personal values and convictions that the story stirs.

Characters and plot involvement: Interactions with or reactions to the characters and story elements.

Character interaction: Empathetic involvement with a character.

Character assessment: Judgments about the actions or values of a character measured against the reader's personal standards.

Story evaluation: Personal involvement or reaction to the story as a whole with no rationale (simple evaluation) or specific elements of the story such as location, events, or time (but not character) with rationale.

Literary evaluation or criticism: Acknowledgment of personal literary tastes or connections between the current story and other stories.

Source: From *Readers and Writers with a Difference: A Holistic Approach to Teaching Struggling Readers and Writers,* 2nd ed. (p. 216), by L. K. Rhodes and C. Dudley-Marling, 1996, Portsmouth, NH: Heinemann.

Book groups and discussions are additional postreading activities to support comprehension.

THEORY TO PRACTICE

➡ Meet with a reading teacher to discuss the strategies she or he finds most helpful for assisting students experiencing difficulties in developing reading skills. Combining the information presented here with what you gain from meeting with this teacher, develop a portfolio of reading approaches and strategies that you can apply to the classroom. Include support materials and suggestions in your portfolio.

➡ Observe the teaching of a class involving reading. What are the greatest challenges to students when involved in this activity and lesson? What strategies and approaches does the teacher incorporate into instruction to support student literacy development? What additional approaches may be needed to engage all students activity in the lesson?

APPROACHES FOR SUPPORTING WRITERS

As they do with reading, students move through various stages when learning to write by beginning from a base of early literacy. For some students, the ability to express ideas through print develops through ongoing experiences in writing and through writing for multiple purposes and audiences in numerous genres (e.g., poems, short stories, reports). Other students experience significant difficulties in expressing themselves through writing. There are multiple strategies and techniques that teachers may draw on to support students experiencing difficulties.

One beginning point of intervention is to adapt and/or modify the writing process to include activities and accommodations responsive to students' needs. Strategies for assisting students with disabilities are provided in the "Make It Happen" feature. Other approaches related to spelling, handwriting, and other specific writing skills follow.

▌ **MAKE IT HAPPEN**

Writing Assistance for Students with Disabilities

CHALLENGES	MODIFICATIONS AND ADAPTATIONS
Prewriting • Selecting and making choices when given multiple ideas and options • Recording ideas • Spelling • Generating topics and ideas to write about	• Write brainstorming ideas on an overhead; once finished, make a hard copy or lend the overhead to the student to make ideas readily accessible. • Present students with a hard copy of possible writing topics and have them highlight the one or two they will focus on. • Start with student-generated topics and brainstorm or web specific ideas from those topics. • Provide lists of key words for easy reference either on the board or on a sheet of paper at the students' desks. • Enter key terms to be used in the writing into the computer, sort them according to ideas or alphabetical order, and print out a copy for each student.
Composing or Drafting • Getting ideas down on paper • Organizing ideas on paper • Spelling	• Allow students to dictate ideas to others or make an audiotape for later transcription. • Allow students to use a computer or other adaptive devices to get ideas down on paper. • Provide an outline or graphic for students to complete when organizing ideas. • See ideas above, under "Prewriting" to support student difficulties with spelling.
Responding • Reading other students' work • Understanding peers' writing • Receiving critical feedback from peers	• Have peers read their work to students, who then provide feedback. • Have peers explain their ideas prior to sharing their work for peer feedback. • Identify one or two areas peers are to concentrate on when providing feedback. • Use the 3 to 1 rule: 3 positive comments to 1 negative comment or suggestion for improvement when providing peer feedback. • Identify one or two skill areas students with disabilities are working to improve. Have the peer focus his or her review on those attributes (these skills may be identified either by the teacher or by the students with disabilities). • Provide checklists of things students are to discuss during peer conferences. These checklists may be the same for everyone or specifically tailored to meet individual needs of students, those with and without disabilities. • Have students generate one or two questions they would like their peers to respond to when reading their work.

(continued)

CHALLENGES	MODIFICATIONS AND ADAPTATIONS
Revising • Dealing with extensive revisions • Meeting physical demands of revision	• Have students select one or two things (e.g., including greater detail) to revise and focus energy on those areas. • Use computer word processing programs to ease revision activities. • Have students dictate revisions to a peer or the teacher.
Editing • Spelling, grammar, and other mechanical areas • Organizing the editing process	• Use computer word processing program's spelling and grammar checks. • Use different-color writing tools to indicate editing changes. • Provide a self-editing checklist for students to use when reviewing their work for editing changes. • Have students work in pairs to complete editing tasks. • Provide a writing frame for students.
Postwriting or Publishing • Identifying viable publication options	• Expand choices for publication to include the use of videotapes or photographs or other means, so all students can publish and share their work with others.

Spelling

Students move through various stages when learning to spell. They may begin writing with scribbles and squiggles then, as their awareness develops, gain a sense of letter-sound correspondences and the need for spelling. Lipson and Wixson (1997) identified four developmental stages that students move through when learning to spell:

Pre-phonemic spelling: At this stage, students write letters to represent words, but the letters do not reflect sounds in the words; students have not made attempts at sound-symbol relationship.

Early phonemic spelling: Students begin to demonstrate the phoneme-grapheme relationship in their writing, but this representation is not complete. Students may provide the appropriate first or last letter of a word based on the sound it makes.

Phonetic (and letter name) spelling: Students begin to spell some words phonetically but display another tendency to select letters to represent sounds based on letter names. The example provided by Lipson and Wixson (1997, p. 242) is *lavatr* for *elevator,* drawing from the work of Morris (1981).

Transitional spelling: Students' spellings are more closely reflective of phonetic spellings and are much closer to standard spellings.

Many students with disabilities experience great difficulty with spelling. Use of invented spelling is one way to begin to address this concern, but at some point students will want to know how to spell words correctly and will no longer be satisfied with close approximations. Spelling is the one way that some students who do not speak can communicate *exactly* what they have to say and to show what they know and can do.

Several standard spelling instructional techniques are reported in the literature. Fulk and Stormount-Spurgin (1995) identified 14 strategies for teaching spelling to students with learning disabilities (see Exhibit 16.5).

EXHIBIT 16.5

**Spelling Strategies for Students
with Learning Disabilities**

TEACHER-DIRECTED METHODS

1. *Test-Teach-Test Sequence:* Pretest students on the weekly spelling list and have students study only those words they missed.
2. *Reduced Word Lists:* Pretest subsets of the total spelling list (e.g., introduce 4 words on Monday, rather than all 20 words); students study words missed; and at the end of the week, all introduced words are tested.
3. *Reinforcement:* Provide reinforcement for enhanced spelling performance.
4. *Imitation plus Modeling:* One-on-one, the teacher spells the word as the student writes it and then checks the student's spelling and either reinforces by saying "*yes*" and spelling the word again, or corrects it by stating the word and spelling it correctly.
5. *Analogy Strategy:* The strategy, developed by Englert, Hiebert, and Stewart (1985), is based on the student generating word families (rhyming words) and going through a five-step process working with the rhyming words as aids to learning to spell the target word.
6. *Constant Time Delay:* The first time, students write the word and are immediately presented with a model of the word to check their spelling; the amount of time between students' writing and the presentation of the model is lengthened as students increase the accuracy of their responses.

STUDENT STUDY METHODS

1. *Relevance and Transfer:* Discuss the importance of spelling with students and demonstrate relevance by having students use spelling words in their writing or by selecting their own spelling words.
2. *Error Correction:* Students self-correct their spellings, reinforce themselves for correct spelling, and finally go through the following three steps to correct misspelled words: (a) mark incorrect letters by circling, marking out, or highlighting them; (b) using a correctly spelled model, write the correct letters above the incorrect letters in their own work; and (c) write the correct spelling next to the incorrect spelling.
3. *Systematic Study Procedures:* Three- and five-step procedures that involve saying and writing the word, checking for accuracy, and rewriting the word are offered as suggestions.
4. *Self-Monitoring:* Require students to monitor their spelling performance over time.
5. *Peer Tutoring:* Have students work together on developing and monitoring spelling skills.
6. *Variety in Practice Formats:* Provide multiple ways for students to practice their spelling, including game formats and art activities (e.g., writing spelling words in sand or using finger paints).
7. *Goal Setting/Graphing:* Have students set goals for their spelling accuracy and chart their performance.
8. *Computer Practice:* Use computer software packages to support spelling development and practice.

Source: Fulk & Stormount-Spurgin (1995).

The use of spellcheckers with computer word processing programs and as free-standing tools is one accommodation for students who experience significant difficulties with spelling. Providing students with word reference cards (cards listing words they commonly use in their writing) and copies of vocabulary sheets and common phrases to incorporate during a writing assignment may also be helpful. When students are brainstorming and mapping during the prewriting stage of a writing activity, make copies of this information and disseminate to students. They can use them as a quick reference for the correct spelling of words they want to use in their writing. Standard dictionaries may be helpful as well, but spelling dictionaries (which list only words, not definitions) may be better for some students.

Handwriting

Some students have great difficulty with the physical act of writing. They may have well-developed ideas and the ability to organize them but be unable to produce them in legible form when given paper and pencil. At times, the challenge may reside with difficulties in visual-spatial organization—students are unable to organize their handwriting on the paper and will write letters as if the lines on the paper were not there. For students who experience difficulties of this sort, activities focusing on eye-hand coordination (e.g., coloring, cutting, tracing) can be helpful. Students with visual impairments who are unable to see the lines on the paper may need specially adapted paper (e.g., paper with accentuated lines) if they are going to handwrite responses. Modifications of the means of communication and performance, as described in Chapter 5, can also be of great assistance to these students as they engage in writing activities.

Other students may have physical disabilities (e.g., difficulties with fine motor control) that interfere with their ability to produce written text). For these students, use of pencil grips or adapted pencils or writing tools may be most helpful. For others, the use of computers with enlarged or modified keyboards or with voice recognition systems may be more efficient. Chapter 5 offers additional techniques for assisting students.

Some teachers establish specific handwriting goals. Mercer (1997) offers a list of handwriting objectives for grades K through 6 (see Exhibit 16.6).

EXHIBIT 16.6

Handwriting Objectives for Students in Grades K Through 6 with Learning Disabilities

GRADE LEVEL	OBJECTIVES
Kindergarten	Begins to establish a preference for either left- or right-handedness
	Voluntarily draws, paints, and scribbles
	Develops small-muscle control through the use of materials such as finger paints, clay, weaving fibers, and puzzles
	Uses tools of writing in making letters, writing names, or attempting to write words
	Understands and applies writing readiness vocabulary given orally, such as left/right, top/bottom, beginning/end, large/small, circle, space, around, across, curve, top line, dotted line, and bottom line
	Begins to establish correct writing position of body, arms, hand, paper, and pencil
	Draws familiar objects using the basic strokes of manuscript writing
	Recognizes and legibly writes own name in manuscript letters using uppercase and lowercase letters appropriately
	Uses writing paper that is standard for manuscript writing
Grade 1	Begins manuscript writing using both lowercase and uppercase letters introduced to correlate with the student's reading program
	Writes with correct posture, pencil grip, and paper position; works from left to right; and forms letters in the correct direction
	Copies words neatly from near position
	Writes with firm strokes and demonstrates good spacing between letters, words, and sentences
	Writes manuscript letters independently and with firm strokes
	Writes clear, legible manuscript letters at a rate appropriate for ability
	Arranges work neatly and pleasingly on a page (i.e., uses margins and paragraph indentions and makes clean erasures)
Grade 2	Evaluates writing using a plastic overlay and identifies strengths and weaknesses
	Writes all letters of the alphabet in manuscript from memory
	Recognizes the differences in using manuscript and cursive writing
	Reads simple sentences written in cursive writing on the chalkboard
	Demonstrates physical coordination to proceed to simple cursive writing
Grade 3	Demonstrates ability to decode cursive writing by reading paragraphs of cursive writing both from the chalkboard and from paper
	Identifies cursive lowercase and uppercase letters by matching cursive letters to manuscript letters
	Begins cursive writing with lowercase letters and progresses to uppercase letters as needed

Grade 3 (continued)	Uses writing paper that is standard for cursive writing
	Writes all letters of the cursive alphabet using proper techniques in making each letter
	Recognizes the proper joining of letters to form words
	Writes from memory all letters of the alphabet in cursive form
Grade 4	Slants and joins the letters in a word and controls spacing between letters
	Uses cursive writing for day-to-day use
	Begins to write with a pen *if* pencil writing is smooth, fluent, and neat
	Maintains and uses manuscript writing for special needs, such as preparing charts, maps, and labels
	Writes clear, legible cursive letters at a rate appropriate for ability
Grade 5	Reduces size of writing to "adult" proportions of letters (i.e., one-quarter space for minimum letters, one-half space for intermediate letters, and three-quarters space for tall lowercase and uppercase letters)
	Takes pride in presenting neat work
Grade 6	Customarily presents neat work
	Evaluates own progress in the basic handwriting skills pertaining to size, slant, shape, spacing, and alignment

Source: From *Students with Learning Disabilities*, 5th ed. (p. 467), by C. D. Mercer, 5/e, © 1997. Reprinted by permission of Prentice-Hall, Inc., Upper Saddle River, NJ.

Capitalization and Punctuation

Though receiving decreasing emphasis in the writing curriculum, capitalization and punctuation are essential skills for writers if they are to communicate their ideas to others effectively. Here are some strategies for teaching and supporting the development of skills in these areas:

- Introduce and drill specific skills (e.g., use of a period, comma, and question mark).
- Have students identify how their favorite authors use these conventions in their writing.
- Once a skill has been taught in isolation through drill and practice, require students to apply that skill consistently in their writing.
- As one step in the editing process, highlight when and where punctuation is needed.
- Provide students with cards listing the rules for the use of punctuation. They can refer to the cards when editing.
- Have students work together to edit their writing for capitalization and punctuation.

Writing Connected Text

We present many ideas for supporting students in writing connected text in the discussion of the writing process in Chapter 15 and earlier in this section on writing. Now we offer a few more options for supporting students as they engage in story, journal, paragraph, essay, theme, and report writing.

Zipprich (1995) offers a strategy to support students' writing of narrative text. The strategy—*web making*—is similar to the story grammar developed by Idol (1986). The teacher provides a story web form from which the student writes the story (see Figure 16.3). The student writes her or his ideas in the appropriate sections of the web and then, referring to the web, writes the story in connected text. The web used in Zipprich's study is presented in Figure 16.3.

▌**FIGURE 16.3**
Story Web Form
Source: From "Teaching Web Making as a Guided Planning Tool to Improve Student Narrative Writing," by M. A. Zipprich, 1995, *Remedial and Special Education, 16*(1), p. 6. Copyright 1995 by PRO-ED, Inc. Reprinted by permission.

My Web for Story Writing, by _____   date _____

2. The Setting

Characters
_____
_____
_____
_____

Time (Circle)   Past
                     Present
                     Future

Place
_____
_____

1.   Title
_____

3.   Problem
_____
_____
_____
_____

6.   Goal
_____
_____
_____
_____

4.   Action
_____
_____
_____
_____
_____
_____

5.   Outcome
_____
_____
_____
_____
_____
_____

The use of teacher-provided *writing frames* is another way to support participation in story writing. A writing frame consists of open-ended sentences that students complete by filling in details and supporting information. Here is an example:

The story _____ was about _____ .
           (title)   (description of
                                       main idea/theme)

The main characters in the story were _____ .
                                    (list of main characters)

_____ had a problem. Their problem was
(Names of the main characters)

_____ . They tried to resolve the problem by _____
(description of the
problem)

_____ . They resolved the problem when they
(story events to resolve
the problem)

_____ . The story ended when
(description of the resolution)

_____ .
(description of how the
story ended)

Journal writing offers another support for written language development. One type of journal is a dialogue journal (Gaustad & Messenheimer-Young, 1991). When the teacher reads the journal entry, he writes comments back to the child on what she has written and continues the conversation. The teacher may ask a question about what was written or write about a similar idea or experience that he or she has had. When writing the response, the teacher models correct writing structures and mechanics. For example, if the student misspells a word in her entry, the teacher does not correct the child's spelling but rather incorporates that word in his or her response, thus modeling the correct spelling of the word for the child.

Kluwin (1996) describes a program for using dialogue journals with students who are deaf and with their hearing classmates in general education classes. In this program, general and special education teachers paired general and special education dialogue partners by considering student gender and age, interests, and overall writing ability. The students who were deaf wrote the first journal entry. Journals were then taken to the general education classroom, where they were read and responded to. They were then transported back to the special education classroom and the cycle continued. Kluwin (1996) found that this approach encouraged student writing and reduced the social isolation of students who were deaf.

Writing paragraphs is difficult for some students. Levy and Rosenberg (1990) suggest that these students learn the SLOW CaPS mnemonic strategy for paragraph writing. This strategy can be used to write four types of paragraph: "(a) list or describe, (b) show sequence, (c) compare and/or contrast, and (d) demonstrate cause/effect." Here are the steps (Levy & Rosenberg, 1990, p. 27):

S = show the type of paragraph in the first sentence
L = list the details you want to write about
O = order the details
W = write details in complete sentences and cap off the paragraph with a
    C = concluding
    P = passing or
    S = summary sentence

A paragraph frame may also assist students. A sample paragraph frame is shown in Figure 16.4. In this frame, the topic sentence is supported by the details. Students write notes and key phrases in each area of the frame. These notes and phrases are then written in sentences to form a paragraph containing these essential elements.

Topic Sentence
Supporting Detail
Supporting Detail
Supporting Detail
Concluding Sentence

❚ **FIGURE 16.4**
A Paragraph Frame

The PLEASE strategy (Welch, 1992, p. 122) is another strategy for supporting student paragraph writing. The components of the strategy are listed below:

P = *Pick* a topic
L = *List* your ideas about the topic
E = *Evaluate* your list
A = *Activate* the paragraph with a topic sentence
S = *Supply* supporting sentences
E = *End* with a concluding sentence
    and
    Evaluate your work

Theme and essay writing can be a major stumbling block for some students. Students may find the TOWER mnemonic strategy (Levy & Rosenberg, 1990, p. 27) helpful in theme and essay writing:

T = THINK of the content, and write (a) a title, (b) the major
    areas to be discussed, and (c) the details for each area
O = ORDER major topics and details under each topic
W = WRITE a rough draft
E = use ERROR monitoring strategy (COPS)
    C = Have I capitalized the first word and proper nouns?
    O = Have I made any handwriting, margin, or messy errors?
    P = Have I used end punctuation, commas, and semicolons
        carefully?
    S = Do words look like they are spelled right; can I sound
        them out or use the dictionary?
R = REVISE the rough draft

Wong, Butler, Ficzere, and Kuperis (1997) provide a planning form to support student writing of compare-and-contrast essays (see Figure 16.5). The form incorporates a graphic organizer and provides a process for students to use to plan their essay. In Figure 16.5, the student is writing a compare and contrast essay about concerts. She is comparing rock concerts and school concerts. She begins by brainstorming features of the concerts that can be compared and contrasted. These features are then developed into a thesis statement. The features are further developed, with details listed for each. Finally, each of these features is rated as a similarity or difference. The student next writes a conclusion. Once these ideas are generated and organized on the planning form, the student begins to write the essay, following the sequence of ideas listed in the form.

Working with a middle school English teacher, Graves (1998) discovered that students found that a graphic representing the structure of a five-paragraph essay was helpful for writing essays. The graphic introduced to students is presented in Figure 16.6. As displayed in Figure 16.6, each paragraph of the essay presents unique information. The first paragraph is the introduction and includes the essay theme and the three ideas to be discussed. The next three figures of the graphic represent the three paragraphs that form the body of the essay. Each paragraph presents one of the key ideas presented in the first paragraph and provides three details about the idea. The final figure of the graphic represents the conclusion and those elements needed for a well-developed conclusion. As with the compare/contrast plan, the student generates ideas related to each component included in the graphic first, and then writes the essay based on these ideas, following the organization of the graphic.

Rhodes and Dudley-Marling (1996) developed a data chart that students may use when writing reports (see Figure 16.7). Students write in information to complete the grid and then refer to the grid when writing their essays. The grid assists students in gathering and organizing information.

Name _____   Date _____

COMPARE / CONTRAST PLAN

Topic: *Concerts*

Rock Concerts   Categories   *School Concerts*

Brainstorming for features
Goal   Dress & Demeanor
Content

Thesis sentence (see prompt for help)

In this essay, I am going to compare and contrast rock concerts and school concerts.
I have chosen to write on three features: Goal, Content, and Dress and Demeanor.

Features (Themes)	Ideas (Details)	Sim	Dif
1. *Goal*	a. *both provide entertainment*	✓	
	b. *rock concerts (pay); school concerts (free)*		✓
	c. _____		
2. *Content*	a. *different types of music*		✓
	b. *rock concerts idols, school concerts none*		✓
	c. *both concerts need practice & rehearsals*	✓	
3. *Dress & Demeanour*	a. *correct attire important for rock concerts; not for school concerts*		✓
	b. *rowdy audience in rock concerts, not so in school concerts*		✓
	c. _____		

Conclusion: (see prompt for help)

After comparing and contrasting _____ *rock concerts* _____ and _____ *school concerts* _____ ,
I think I prefer _____ *school concerts* _____ because *they are free, have my kind of music and they*
don't allow rowdy behaviors!

▌ FIGURE 16.5

Planning Form for Compare-and-Contrast Essays

Source: From "Teaching Adolescents with Learning Disabilities and Low Achievers to Plan, Write, and Revise Compare-and-Contrast Essays," by B. Y. L. Wong, D. L. Butler, S. A. Ficzere, & S. Kuperis, 1997, *Learning Disabilities Research and Practice,* *12*(1), p. 5. Reprinted by permission.

▌ **FIGURE 16.6**

Graphic Representation of a Five-Paragraph Essay

Source: From "Instructional Strategies and Techniques for Middle School Students Who Are Learning English," by A. Graves (1998). In R. M. Gersten and R. T. Jiménez (Eds.), Promoting learning for culturally and linguistically diverse students (p. 177). Belmont, CA: Wadsworth. Reprinted by permission.

▌ **FIGURE 16.7**

Data Chart for Report Writing

Source: From *Readers and Writers with a Difference: A Holistic Approach to Teaching Struggling Readers and Writers*, 2nd ed. (p. 265), by L. K. Rhodes and C. Dudley-Marling, 1996, Portsmouth, NH: Heinemann.

	What is the habitat of _____?	What eats _____?	What does _____ eat?	What does _____ look like?	How does _____ harm/ help man?
Me					
Source #1					
Source #2					
Summary					

All of these techniques can be used as prewriting activities to support student writing of connected text. They may also be adapted to respond to the unique learning needs of particular students.

THEORY TO PRACTICE

➡ Meet with a teacher to discuss the strategies she or he finds most helpful for assisting students experiencing difficulties in developing writing skills. Combining the information presented here with what you gain from meeting with this teacher, develop a portfolio of writing approaches and strategies that you can apply to the classroom. Include support materials and suggestions in your portfolio.

➡ Observe the teaching of a class involving writing. What are the greatest challenges for students while participating in this activity and lesson? What strategies and approaches does the teacher incorporate into instruction to support all writers? What additional approaches would you include to engage all students in the activity?

CHAPTER SUMMARY

This chapter explores a variety of ways to support individual students experiencing difficulties in developing reading and writing skills. Reading skills are presented in terms of word identification, rate and fluency, vocabulary, and comprehension (prereading, during-reading, and postreading activities). Writing approaches are presented in terms of spelling, handwriting, capitalization and punctuation, and writing connected text.

CHAPTER 17

Teaching Learning Strategies, Study Skills, and Life Skills

Read to find out the following:
- how to teach students learning strategies for approaching a range of tasks
- how to teach students study skills that they can apply across all curricular options
- how to teach students life skills that will enhance their independence and lifestyles

In this chapter we introduce techniques for teaching learning strategies, study skills, and life skills to students with disabilities. The first two sections on learning strategies and study skills can serve as powerful means to modify general education curriculum in order to make it more accessible for students' active learning and participation. These techniques, as well as those suggested for the teaching of life skills, may be adapted and modified for use across multiple curricular areas.

LEARNING STRATEGIES

As highlighted in Chapter 3 on general education curriculum with and without modifications, one way to modify general education curriculum is by teaching learning strategies. Learning strategies help students learn how to learn; how to approach tasks in systematic ways through the application of strategies. As reported by Mercer (1997), drawing from the work of Deshler, Schumaker, and others at the University of Kansas, students move through eight stages when learning, applying, and generalizing learning strategies to the challenges they encounter in and outside school. In the first stage, *pretest and make commitments,* students are provided with an overview of the strategy they will be learning, the purpose for the strategy, and how the strategy can assist them in responding to tasks they will encounter in and outside school. Discussion of the strategies students are currently using and why these strategies are failing to bring about desired results serves to emphasize to them their need for a new, more effective strategy. At this stage, it is critical that students commit themselves to learning and applying the strategy if the overall process is to be beneficial.

In the second stage, *describe the strategy,* the "when and why" of applying the strategy are discussed, followed by a step-by-step presentation of the strategy. This presentation includes a mechanism to help students remember the strategy. The mechanism may be a simple mnemonic or a list of steps to memorize. In the third stage, *model the strategy,* the teacher uses think-alouds and demonstrates how students can self-monitor as they move through the strategy. At this stage, students become involved in carrying out the strategy.

In the fourth and fifth stages, *verbal elaboration and rehearsal* and *controlled practice and feedback,* students are provided opportunities for controlled practice, all the while receiving feedback from the teacher. During the fourth stage, students state the purpose of the strategy first and when and why they could use it; then they engage in verbal rehearsal and vocalize the mnemonic or steps of the strategy. This verbalization must occur until students can state the steps of the strategy automatically and without hesitation. During the fifth stage, students verbalize and perform the strategy while working on control materials (e.g., materials written at the students' reading level to prevent low reading skills from interfering with mastery of the strategy). At this stage, the teacher may continue to model the strategy as students follow along, gradually turning more and more responsibility over to them.

In the sixth stage, *advanced practice and feedback,* students apply the strategy to grade-appropriate materials. The role of the teacher has faded and students have assumed responsibility for both using the strategy and providing feedback to peers as they use the strategy. The seventh stage, *confirm acquisition and make generalization commitments,* confirms that students have indeed mastered the strategy and are able to apply it to grade-appropriate materials and activities.

In the eighth stage, *generalization,* the teacher assists the students in deciding how and when to apply the strategy to multiple situations. The ability to generalize rests on students' understandings of the strategy, of the rationale behind the strategy, and of how the strategy can help them in various tasks and activities. During this stage, students are taught how to adapt the strategy to changing situations.

This description of the stages of strategy acquisition highlights several important features of strategy instruction: (a) students require time, dedication, and repeated opportunities for practice in order to learn and use the strategies; (b) teachers cannot assume that one or two introductions to a new strategy will result in student ownership of that strategy; (c) if strategy instruction is to be worthwhile, students need to be committed to learning and applying a strategy; and (d) students must be taught how to generalize a strategy if they are to maximize their learning.

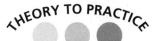

THEORY TO PRACTICE

➡ Secure copies of one of the strategies proposed by the Kansas group by requesting either the *Strategies Intervention Model* or *Learning Strategies Curriculum* from Coordinator of Training, Center for Research on Learning, 3061 Robert Dole Human Development Center, The University of Kansas, Lawrence, KS 66045-2342. Analyze the steps required for student acquisition and generalization. How and why would you incorporate this learning strategy into your curriculum?

STUDY SKILLS

Study skills are designed to assist students in mastering materials and completing tasks and, therefore, are different from learning strategies, whose primary purpose is to assist students in learning how to learn. In this section we examine some study skill strategies useful for teachers and students.

Listening Skills

Developing and applying good listening skills can be highly challenging for students with disabilities, especially for students with visual impairments. Rivera and Smith (1997, p. 399) suggest some things that teachers can do to assist students in developing listening skills:

1. asking questions and then calling on a student—this heightens the "level of concern" . . .

2. using a variety of media (e.g., overhead projector, chalkboard, computer and projection panel, manipulatives) to keep lessons interesting and presentations diverse

3. providing a short amount of information followed by a check for understanding . . .

4. asking students to summarize newly presented content on paper or with a neighbor (i.e., have students think about the information, summarize the information, pair with a partner, and share the information that was just presented)

5. using transitional words (e.g., "I am going to provide three important points. First, . . .")

6. telling students there will be a quiz following the activity

7. providing an outline of the information presented and having students fill in the blanks

Exhibit 17.1 presents additional strategies to build listening skills.

EXHIBIT 17.1

Strategies to Build Listening Skills

- Arrange the room to limit distractions. Take into consideration students' proximity to the teacher and others when they engage in activities. For instance, a student who has difficulties attending may do better when sitting closer to the speaker.
- Vary your voice when speaking. Modulate your voice from loud to soft and speak with expression.
- Move about the room when speaking to encourage students to "follow you" and your message.
- Encourage students to take notes on key ideas. Jot key ideas down on the overhead, chalkboard, or poster paper as a reminder.
- Chunk or cluster information presented. Gauge your audience's attention span and speak for that duration. Follow with brief breaks to provide time for students to talk with one another about the information.
- Maintain students' attention through phrases and prompts such as "Listen closely" and "This next piece of information is very important."
- Have students self-monitor their listening. At the conclusion of directions or verbal presentations of information, have students evaluate their listening using symbols (smiley faces, neutral faces, frowns) for younger students and ratings (1 = was really attending, 2 = attended for the most part, 3 = failed to maintain attention) for older students. Students may also maintain a self-recording list of tallies for each time they find themselves listening during a session or each time they find themselves "drifting off" during a presentation. Students could chart their performance over time and discuss strategies they can employ next time to assist them in enhancing their listening skills.
- Play listening games. For instance, have students raise their hands whenever they hear a certain word or phrase during a fun language activity.
- Discuss listening skills with students. Students may not be aware of the importance of listening and may not have strategies for assisting themselves in listening (e.g., keeping eyes on the speaker, taking notes, doodling, self-questioning). Have students practice and reflect on these skills.

Notetaking

Notetaking skills are generally required in middle school and high school where a great deal of information is presented auditorally, as through lectures and presentations. Students with disabilities, as well as many of their peers, experience multiple challenges when faced with the task of notetaking. Exhibit 17.2 describes some notetaking formats teachers can introduce to students. Teachers can model these different formats and ask students to select the one they find most helpful. Teachers may also introduce one format at the beginning of the year and reinforce its use throughout the year.

1. *Four-fold.* Students either fold or are given paper divided into the following four sections. Appropriate information is written in each section.

EXHIBIT 17.2

Notetaking Formats

NAME: DATE: TOPIC: OBJECTIVE:	PERSONAL RELEVANCE: (Why this information is important to me.)
MAIN IDEAS:	SUPPORTING DETAILS:

2. *Index cards.* During lectures, students are instructed to write key words on one side of the cards and their definitions on the other side. The cards can be used for review and study.
3. *Slotted outline.* The teacher creates a slotted outline and leaves spaces for students to fill in with key words and ideas. As the lecture unfolds, students read the outline and provide missing information.
4. *Notetaking outline.* This can be a two-column notetaking system as presented below.

MAIN IDEAS	SUPPORTING DETAILS

5. *Use of cooperative notes.* Students are assigned to groups, and the responsibility for notetaking rotates among group members. The first student takes notes for the first five minutes; then the notetaking paper is passed to the next student, who takes notes for the next five minutes, and so forth.
6. *Use of graphic outlines,* such as web and maps (these are explained in an upcoming section).

Source: Adapted from Fister & Kemp (1995), pp. 55–58.

Besides presenting a variety of notetaking formats, teachers may introduce a mnemonic to assist students when taking notes. A mnemonic referred to as LITES (Fister & Kemp, 1995, p. 56), works as follows:

Listen to the teacher and look at what he or she is saying aloud and writing.

Identify key vocabulary, important concepts, and examples/nonexamples that the teacher is using or saying aloud.

Take down (write down) the key vocabulary, concepts, and examples.

Evaluate what has been taken down. Ask yourself questions like: Could I explain this to someone? Could I give more examples? If not, put a question mark in the left margin and use your strategy for asking a question or asking for a clarification.

Save your notes by dating them, coding chapters or topics, and putting them in a folder or notebook.

Teachers may also modify notetaking responsibilities for a number of students. Possibilities include:

1. Have a peer or paraprofessional serve as a notetaker for a student. Have the peer place a sheet of carbon paper between two pages of writing paper so that the notes are automatically "copied" and can be given to the student immediately following the lecture.

2. Provide students with an outline of lecture notes. The outline may be complete and students follow it during the lecture. A partial outline that requires students to write in key words or phrases or to circle or highlight key information as it is discussed may be used. A bare-bones outline, a third option, provides the overall frame being used during the lecture and students add all needed content.

3. Allow students to record ideas by using a computer during the lecture. Some students may be able to capture ideas by means of a computer keyboard (modified or unmodified) better than through the use of pencil and paper.

4. Allow students to audiotape or videotape the lecture. Students can review the tape and capture key ideas by starting and stopping the audiotape or videotape and recording their own ideas, either through written text or the use of technology (e.g., computer word processing program, audiotape recorder).

Content Enhancements That Aid Comprehension

Various content enhancements are available to teachers and have been used successfully with special education students attending general education classes. Common enhancers identified through a meta-analysis conducted by Hudson, Lignugaris-Kraft, and Miller (1993) include advance organizers, graphic organizers, study guides, mnemonic devices, peer-mediated learning, audio recordings, and computer-assisted instruction.

Advance organizers

Advance organizers can help students get ready for learning by establishing a purpose for learning (Mayer, 1979). Advance organizers may take the form of an outline or web that highlights the important information to be learned and discussed. By beginning a lesson or an activity by referring to an advance organizer, students can gain an understanding of what they will be learning and the key ideas they will be encountering.

An advance organizer may be less formal as well. An advance organizer may be a simple statement at the beginning of a lesson that tells students what they will be learning during the lesson. For example, a lesson may open with the following advance organizer: "Today, we are going to learn more about the life cycle of a butterfly." In some classrooms, it is essential that the advance organizer also indicate behavioral and social expectations. For example, the following information may be added to the previous advance organizer: "We will be working in groups and sharing supplies when we build our individual dioramas. When working in groups, we will use our inside voices, we will share materials appropriately, and we will assist each other in cleaning up our workspace when we are finished." Inclusion of these behavior/social expectations in the advance organizer is an example of proactive classroom management—the teacher is letting the students know, up front, what the expectations are for the day. Of course, more specific directions and modeling are provided as the lesson unfolds; the advance organizer provides only a beginning frame for the lesson.

Graphic organizers

Graphic organizers are another means for assisting students in understanding the content presented. Used in numerous ways and presented in multiple formats, graphic organizers have been found to be effective in helping students organize information, make connections between facts and concepts, and recall previously presented information (Horton, Lovitt, & Bergerud, 1990). They may be generated by the teacher and presented to students, generated through teacher-student interaction as a lesson unfolds, or generated by students at the completion of a lesson as a way to analyze and synthesize important information explored during the lesson. Or, teachers may find it helpful to provide partially completed graphic organizers that students complete as they participate in the lesson as a whole group while the teacher completes a copy on the overhead projector. Students may work in cooperative groups, either completing one copy of the organizer as a group, or completing it individually. In peer work, students may work with a partner to fill in the missing information. Individually, they may refer to a textbook or other media to complete the organizer.

One common form of a graphic organizer is a web, or semantic map. It is a visual display illustrating relationships among key information and concepts. According to

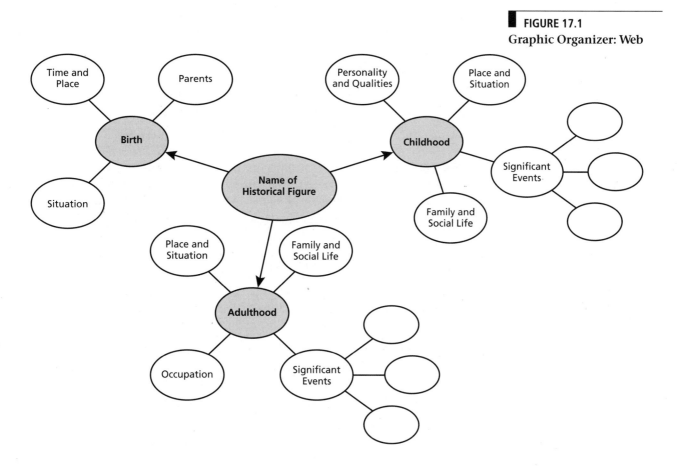

Scanlon, Duran, Reyes, and Gallego (1992), "Mapping procedures are intended to help students comprehend and recall concepts by drawing relationships among them" (p. 142). Figure 17.1 shows a web that students may create when studying the life and times of a historical figure.

Webbing and mapping may be very effective for a number of students, including those with and without disabilities. But Scanlon, Duran, Reyes, and Gallego (1992) found that some students with learning disabilities did not fully benefit from the approach because of their difficulties in identifying important details and in understanding and inferring the relationships among key ideas. To overcome these challenges, they suggest that teachers use interactive semantic mapping, which has a built-in collaborative component. When engaged in an interactive semantic mapping activity, students work together in a group to create a collaborative map. The activity consists of five steps:

1. The teacher presents the topic, students brainstorm what they know about the topic, and this information is recorded and discussed. In this process, students are drawing on prior knowledge and experiences to make predictions about what they will be learning about the topic and to report to others what they already know about it.

2. Students search the text to find out what topic clues the author presents. The teacher can prompt students to look for headings or bold words and to consider graphics and other visuals to discern what the author is talking about. As students discover these clues, they are recorded next to the brainstorm list.

3. With the assistance of the teacher, students develop the map. They begin by placing the topic in the center of the map. Then they skim the brainstorm and

clue lists to come up with ideas that go together. Once they have determined these, they come up with a label for each of these subtopics and record them on the map, drawing lines from the topic to the subtopics. They then can record on the map specific ideas or information related to the subtopic. They continue to do this until they believe they have captured all necessary information. As the process unfolds, additional lines are drawn to show relationships.

4. Students read the information included in the map. As they are reading, they are instructed to "justify and confirm or modify their predicted relationships, adding or deleting ideas from their map as they judge necessary" (Scanlon, Duran, Reyes, & Gallego, 1992, p. 145). Students may make notes as they read and think about the similarities between the knowledge they generated and included in their map and the information presented in the text.

5. The group reviews the map and discusses any modifications that anyone wants to make, providing justification for those changes. Students may also consult outside sources to check the accuracy of the information generated in the map but not discussed in the text.

This activity involving interactive semantic mapping draws on students' prior knowledge and experience, helps them—through comparison and contrast—to bridge this information to information provided in the text, and encourages them to dialogue and learn from one another. Reyes and Bos (1998) suggest the use of interactive semantic mapping and charting techniques with students who are English-language learners.

Graphic organizers also may be diagrams that students label. Elementary-age students may be given a diagram on which they are to label the primary components of a tree. High school science students may be given a diagram of a cell or a worm on which they are to label primary organs and explain their functions. This type of graphic organizer assists many students in organizing important information, in seeing relationships, and in making the work visual.

Another form of graphic organizer is a flow chart. Flow charts can be used to describe relationships among important details and facts. Figure 17.2 provides an example of this type of graphic organizer.

▌**FIGURE 17.2**
Graphic Organizer:
Flow Chart

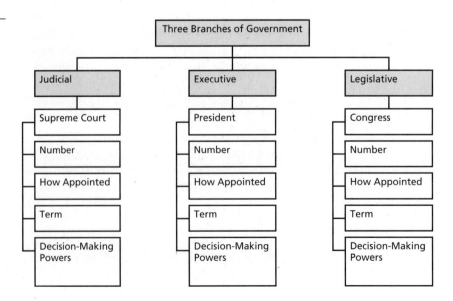

PLANETS OF THE SOLAR SYSTEM

PLANET	SIZE	DISTANCE FROM THE SUN	TEMPERATURE	OTHER FACTS
Mercury				
Venus				
Earth				
Mars				
Jupiter				
Saturn				
Uranus				
Neptune				
Pluto				

▮ **FIGURE 17.3**
Graphic Organizer: Table

Tables, too, can be graphic organizers. Figure 17.3 presents a graphic organizer in table format. Students add information to the table and then use it for purposes such as (a) comparing and contrasting information, (b) developing oral and/or written reports about the planets, and (c) creating posters of planet facts.

Students may refer to graphic organizers in preparation for tests and quizzes. They may be used in small groups for peer tutoring and reviewing information. They also may be used as informal tests: the teacher presents students with either a blank or a partially filled-in organizer to complete.

Study guides

Study guides are another form of content enhancer. Study guides may simply be outlines of important information to be covered, completed by the teacher or students, and referred to in preparation for quizzes and examinations. Study guides come in various forms: (a) a series of questions, (b) sentences including blanks supported by word banks, (c) a series of multiple choice items, and (d) lists of words and definitions for matching.

Study guides can vary greatly in sophistication. The format can be adapted to reflect student needs. If a guide is a series of questions, the questions may be factual—that is, answers are found directly in the text—or they may require inference or application of outside information to arrive at an answer. To support questions, page numbers or page and paragraph numbers indicating the page on which the answer or pertinent information is located can be listed for students who have difficulty locating key information in text. When study guides require students to provide words to fill in blanks, key terminology may be listed in a word bank, page prompts may be provided, or students may be left on their own to find the missing words (Horton & Lovitt, 1989).

Exhibit 17.3 provides one example of a study guide. This guide provides page and paragraph prompts. Its format may be appropriate for students experiencing difficulty with reading and gaining meaning from the text, possibly students with disabilities included in a general education classroom, or even students who are new to the topic. The "Make It Happen" feature suggests ways to use study guides before, during, and following instruction.

EXHIBIT 17.3	p. 11, paragraph 4 1. What is a basic definition of the Internet?
Example of a Study Guide with Page and Paragraph Prompts	p. 11, paragraph 4 2. What is the relationship between the Internet and the World Wide Web?
	p. 12, paragraph 1 3. What are some different ways people refer to the World Wide Web?
	p. 13, paragraph 1 4. Why is the way in which the Internet is designed considered to be radical?
	p. 14, paragraph 6 5. Define each of the four facts about the Internet presented on page 14.

MAKE IT HAPPEN
Using Study Guides

Before Instruction
- Students can read the questions and/or items included in the study guide to set a purpose for reading.
- Students may skim of the study guide and make predictions about what they will be learning.
- After opening a new unit using a K-W-L activity, students can skim the study guide, and referring back to the K-W-L ideas, tentatively answer those questions for which they believe they already have the information and then highlight the items on the K-W-L list that they believe will be answered through the activity.

During Instruction
- Teachers can fill in a partially completed or blank study guide on the overhead projector as the lesson unfolds, while students complete their individual copies of the study guide at their seats.
- Students may work in pairs, cooperative groups, or independently, reading text and completing the study guide as they encounter the needed information.

Following Instruction
- Students may return to earlier predictions as indicated in the study guide to compare what they originally predicted they would learn to what they did learn.
- Students may return to their K-W-L list and check, using the study guide, that the information they listed under K (know) was indeed correct and then, returning to W (Want to know), answer questions listed.
- Students may work in pairs or individually to use the study guide as a test preparation tool. In pairs, students may ask each other questions on the guide and check for the accuracy and completeness of their peer's responses. When working individually, students may work their way through the study guide covering an answer, reading the question, providing the answer, and uncovering the answer to check for accuracy.
- Students may share their study guide with their parents and recruit their help in preparing for an upcoming quiz.

Mnemonic devices

Mnemonic devices are another type of content enhancer. A mnemonic device for remembering the names of the nine planets is: **My very educated mother just served us nine pizzas** (M = Mercury, V = Venus, E = Earth, M = Mars, J = Jupiter, S = Saturn, U = Uranus, N = Neptune, and P = Pluto).

Several study strategies rely on mnemonics. For example, the RIDER strategy (Clark, Deshler, Schumaker, Alley, & Warner, 1984) is designed to assist students in self-questioning and visualizing to make meaning of text. The RIDER strategy is as follows:

R = **R**ead the first sentence.
I = **I**magine a picture in your mind.
D = **D**escribe the image.
E = **E**valuate the image for completeness.
R = **R**epeat the steps with each subsequent sentence.

Peer-mediated learning

Another way to enhance student content understanding is to have students work in peer-mediated learning arrangements. These include dyads and cooperative learning. These approaches were discussed in Chapter 11.

Audio recordings

The use of books and other materials on audiotape can enhance the content in areas such as social studies and science, as well as literature. For many students with disabilities, books on tape open up a new avenue for gaining information from text. Although the use of audio recordings is common in schools, empirical support for the use of books on tape is limited (Hudson, Lignugaris-Kraft, & Miller, 1993). If books on tape are used, ensure that the student has a copy of the text in order to follow along when listening to the tape, that the student stops periodically to take notes about what has been read or to think about ideas presented so far, and that the student uses the tape-book combination as an opportunity to listen *and* to enhance reading skills.

Computer-assisted instruction

Computers offer multiple avenues for assisting students in reading and gaining information from text. Descriptions of these applications and approaches are presented in Chapter 18.

Time Management

Time management is concerned with how students organize and use their time to complete tasks and activities. It includes the ability to schedule time for completing homework, for carrying out chores and responsibilities around the house and on the job, and for engaging in leisure and recreational activities. Some students with disabilities may need assistance in learning how to manage their time. They may not begin assignments on time, may waste time in nonproductive activities when attempting to begin or complete work, and may not know how to organize their work space in order to enhance productivity. The "Make It Happen" feature provides some beginning teacher suggestions for aiding students in developing time management skills.

▌**MAKE IT HAPPEN**
Time Management

- Assist students in developing a schedule for their various activities. Include school, family, work, and community responsibilities and activities to aid students in developing a balanced schedule.
- Teach students how to record and maintain records of school assignments, and family, work, and community responsibilities. Use of a planner or an assignment notebook may be helpful.
- Assist students in developing self-management and self-monitoring skills in order to evaluate their own performance. Students may record when they begin and end work on an assignment, the actual number of minutes they spend on a given activity, or the time they spend in getting organized for a new activity or in searching for needed materials. Keeping charts and examining them can help students see ways in which they can enhance their overall efficiency and have more time for activities they enjoy.
- Help students plan, organize, and set up a study area. Adequate lighting, a comfortable chair, and necessary support materials (e.g., technology, reference materials, art supplies) should be considered.

Test-Taking Skills

Many teachers administer unit quizzes or tests to assess understanding of presented information. Tests and quizzes present major hurdles for many students with and without disabilities. Students may understand information presented in class but "freeze" and therefore be unable to demonstrate their knowledge when given a test paper. Some of these problems may be linked with the test itself. The format, including the wording of items and directions and the type of responses required (e.g., short answer responses, multiple choice responses), may be what is causing the difficulty—not the content of the test. If that is the case, then there is a need for modification of the test to allow for a meaningful assessment of student understanding.

According to Polloway, Bursuck, Jayanthi, Epstein, and Nelson (1996), test modifications generally occur in the following areas:

> test preparation (e.g., providing study guides), test construction (e.g., including fewer questions), test administration (e.g., providing extra time), test sites (e.g., testing in a distraction-free site), and test feedback (e.g., providing individual feedback). (p. 141)

The selection of these adaptations may be based on how helpful they are in assisting students in being successful in the testing situation, the ease with which the adaptations can be made (e.g., time demands), the fairness of the adaptations for students not working with the adapted test, and students' preferences for test adaptations (Polloway, Bursuck, Jayanthi, Epstein, & Nelson, 1996).

Weimer, Cappotelli, and DiCamillo (1994), through the development of a self-advocacy program for middle school students with disabilities, devised the menu of test modifications shown in Exhibit 17.4. Students checked the modifications they thought would be helpful for an upcoming test and presented the menu card to their teacher for consideration. Salend (1995) offers several suggestions teachers may consider when designing and administering tests. Some of those suggestions are listed in Exhibit 17.5.

1. Flexible scheduling or setting
   ✓ extended time
   ___ several sessions day/days
   ___ individually separate location
   ✓ small group, separate location
   ___ special lighting
   ___ adaptive or special furniture
   ___ special acoustics
   ___ location with minimal distractions
2. Revised test format
   ___ braille edition
   ___ large print type
   ___ increase space between items
   ___ reduce number of items
   ___ increase size of bubble
   ___ passages with one sentence per line
   ___ arrange answer choices; vertical format
   ___ omit questions which can't be revised

3. Revised test directions
   ✓ read directions to student
   ___ reread directions for each page
   ✓ simplify language of directions/questions
   ___ highlight verbs in directions/questions
   ___ provide additional examples
   ✓ questions read to student in content areas
4. Use of aids
   ___ visual magnification devices
   ___ auditory amplification devices
   ___ auditory tape questions
   ___ masks or markers to maintain place
   ___ use of calculator
   ___ use of computer
5. Other
   ___ _____
   ___ _____
   ___ _____

EXHIBIT 17.4

Test Modifications Checklist for Middle School Students

Source: From "Self-Advocacy: A Working Proposal for Adolescents with Special Needs," by B. B. Weimer, M. Cappotelli, and J. DiCamillo, 1994, *Intervention in School and Clinic, 30*(1), p. 49. Used with permission.

---

1. Test items should reflect both what was taught and how it was taught during instruction. For example, if students used a certain procedure to respond to problems, they should be able to use that same procedure when responding to test items. The terminology used on the test or quiz should be the same terminology that was used in class so as to decrease the possibility of misinterpretation.
2. Tests should focus on the most important content.
3. Test items should be legible, provide adequate space for responding, and be presented in a logical order.
4. Prompts or cues for how to respond to items may be provided. For example, highlighting key words in directions and printing important terms or directions in boldface can focus students' attention on the most important aspects of the items.
5. Tests should allow for adaptations in response modes. Write key terminology on the test paper or board for reference in order to assist students who experience spelling difficulties. Allow students to dictate responses if they have difficulties in written language or have a disability such as low vision or a physical disability. And support the use of adaptive and supportive equipment (e.g., computers, communication boards) for responding to test items.
6. The following format modifications can be helpful to students: (a) providing fewer choices in multiple choice items, (b) limiting the number of items included in matching tasks, (c) presenting both columns of a matching task on the same sheet of paper, (d) having equal numbers of items in both matching columns, (e) providing a word bank for sentence completion items, (f) listing key terms or ideas to include in an essay, (g) providing a framework or outline for the writing of essay questions, and (h) matching the reading level of the test to students' reading levels.

EXHIBIT 17.5

Test Preparation and Administration Considerations

Source: Adapted from Salend (1995).

Homework and Completing Assignments

Selecting, assigning, completing, and submitting homework can be a demanding undertaking for students, parents, and teachers. At times, parents may feel that they must become their child's teacher in order for homework to be completed. The child does not come home prepared with knowledge of how to complete the task or with understanding of the content demands presented in the task. The amount of homework assigned and associated due dates can also turn homework time into a family battle of wills.

In one of their studies investigating homework practices and outcomes, Jayanthi, Nelson, Sawyer, Bursuck, and Epstein (1995) interviewed high school students to discover their homework preferences. Students identified the following teacher behaviors related to homework as helpful:

- Assigning homework at the beginning to middle of class;
- Allowing students to begin homework in class;
- Assigning small amounts of homework;
- Explaining the homework assignment carefully;
- Helping students with their homework (e.g., where to find answers in text);
- Checking homework and giving immediate feedback to students;
- Establishing a set routine for assigning homework from the beginning of the year (Polloway, Bursuck, Jayanthi, Epstein, & Nelson, 1996, pp. 135–136)

Although all of those suggestions may be applied to students with disabilities, these students also encounter some unique situations pertaining to homework. For example, students with disabilities may be pulled out of a class to receive specialized services (e.g., to work with a speech-language pathologist or physical therapist) and thus miss homework assignments given and started in class. Should those students be held accountable for that classwork? If that work is considered homework, students with disabilities who were pulled out of class are likely to have *more* homework but receive *less* guidance in its completion than their nondisabled peers who were given class time to start the assignments. If the children are held accountable for classwork missed, they may feel that their workload is doubled since they must complete their classwork as well as the work required by the specialist. Communication among teachers, specialists, the child, and the parents can be helpful in addressing and resolving these issues.

Providing time for students with disabilities to complete their homework during resource time or during after-school programs can assist students in completing and turning in work. Additional homework management suggestions are offered by Jayanthi, Bursuck, Epstein, and Polloway (1997) in the "Make It Happen" feature.

MAKE IT HAPPEN
Managing Homework

Teachers
- Provide computer-generated progress reports on student homework performance to parents. These reports should include descriptive comments about homework performance.
- Communicate using written modes of communication (e.g., progress reports, notes, letters, forms). Use brightly colored paper to grab attention and prevent misplacement.
- At the beginning of the semester, give parents information regarding course assignments for the semester, homework adaptations available in the classroom, and policy on missed assignments and extra credit homework.

Administrators
- Use homework hotlines or answering machines so that students and parents can call and gain access to homework information.
- Change teacher schedules and office locations to facilitate communication among teachers. Clear communication among teachers should result in clear communication between home and school.
- Develop schoolwide or districtwide policies on homework and home-school communication.

- Encourage students to use an assignment notebook for recording assignments. Assignment notebooks can serve as a communication vehicle between home and school.

Parents
- Call teachers early in the morning so that they can return the call later on in the day.
- Communicate expectations regarding homework and communication to both teachers and students.
- Make every attempt to attend face-to-face meetings.
- Check with children about homework each night.
- Establish consequences when children do not complete their homework, and follow through with those consequences.

Students
- Take responsibility for completing and submitting homework on time (e.g., keep track of homework; ask the teacher if you do not understand; ask parents for help).
- Act as a contact between home and school (e.g., tell parents about homework requirements; give teacher notes from parents; hand-deliver teacher letters to parents).
- Maintain an assignment book, and have the book available both during and after school.

Source: From "Strategies for Successful Homework," by M. Jayanthi, W. Bursuck, M. H. Epstein, and E. A. Polloway, 1997, *Teaching Exceptional Children, 30* (1), pp. 6–7.

THEORY TO PRACTICE

➡ Observe a teacher presenting a lesson in a content area (e.g., social studies, science). What study skills did this teacher incorporate in his or her lesson? How did students respond to each study skill? What level of competence did they demonstrate in the skill? What other study skills could the teacher have included in the lesson to support students in actively participating and gaining from the lesson? What suggestions do you have for the inclusion of study skills in this teacher's curriculum?

➡ Select one of the study skills discussed in this section, and design a mini-unit for introducing the skill to students. Determine when and how you would embed the teaching of this study skill into the existing curriculum. Present your mini-unit to a peer for feedback.

LIFE SKILLS

The life skills curriculum is a viable curricular addition or modification to the general education curriculum (see Chapter 4). Functional academics, daily and community living skills, and transition education constitute the three principal areas of this curriculum.

Functional Academics

The functional academics curriculum focuses on practical academic skills and fundamental knowledge to assist individuals with major life activities. Functional academic skills include handling money, writing personal information (e.g., name, address, signature), and reading survival and emergency words (e.g., *emergency exit, poison*).

Many of the instructional approaches presented in Chapters 11 through 15 can be applied to the teaching of functional academics. Additional approaches and strategies for teaching functional mathematics and reading are listed in Exhibit 17.6.

EXHIBIT 17.6 **Teaching Functional Mathematics and Reading**	Time	• Use digital clocks. • Teach students how to use an appointment book to manage their time. • Develop schedules for students that include clock faces as reminders. • Use a time clock and have students punch in and out and calculate work time.
	Basic Facts and Computation	• Use calculators. • Use calculators with enlarged display and speech output if needed. • Use manipulatives. • Provide a checklist or outline of required steps. • Provide strategy instruction associated with memorization of basic facts.
	Money	• Implement a token economy system in the classroom. • Have students hypothetically apply for a job and, working with their salary, rent an apartment, budget money for purchases, write checks, use credit cards, take out loans, and pay their taxes. • Teach use of special locations/cues for different coins and bills in purse/wallet • Teach use of calculators to total purchases. • Teach the strategy of rounding to the nearest dollar when making purchases. • Have students create money envelopes that contain money for specific needs (e.g., bus fare, movie money).
	Sight Words	• Drill and practice with a set of words. • Chart sight word growth over time. • Label objects in the classroom, home, and work environments.
	Comprehension	• Use materials students will encounter in the community, on the job, and in their personal lives (e.g., medications, directions for operating appliances). • Provide material on tape and assist students in developing skills in how to obtain materials on tape. • Break down material into steps and add illustrations and photographs as necessary to increase understanding. • Work on building student reading fluency. • Use computer software that provides screen reading of content to students.
	Writing	• Teach students how to word-process to produce text. • Identify key words and phrases and focus on student acquisition. • Provide students with reminder sheets (e.g., typed copy of personal information that they can refer to when completing job applications). • Buy word stamps and signature stamps to limit the amount of writing needed. • Focus on the type of writing students will be required to do after they exit school.

Daily and Community Living Skills

Some of the instructional activities presented in Chapter 13 and the general instructional strategies presented in Chapters 11 and 12 apply to the teaching of daily and community living skills. In this section we offer some specific instructional examples for teaching in this curricular area and explain how these strategies may be generalized and applied to other areas as well.

Career and vocational education

The teaching of career and vocational education skills should begin when a child enters school and continue throughout the child's school career. Many of the instructional activities presented in Chapter 13 can be used to teach these skills. Additionally, Table 4.1 (in Chapter 4), phases of career education identified by Razeghi (1998), provides suggestions for instructional activities during the four phases of career education: career awareness, career orientation, career exploration, and career preparation.

Home and family

Home and family skills emphasize personal care skills such as eating, brushing teeth, doing laundry, and cooking. The teaching of personal care, however, goes beyond the mechanics of teaching an individual how to eat, brush teeth, and get dressed as independently as possible. As Kimm, Falvey, Bishop, and Rosenberg (1995) indicate,

> *Personal care skills involve the total physical well-being of individuals, including an understanding of the need for task performance as well as an awareness of the choice and options involved. (p. 209)*

For example,

> *Learning to eat independently includes not only the specific mechanical skills of eating, but also the ability to make choices about what and when to eat, to develop good nutritional habits, and to understand social norms associated with eating. Foods should be chosen in accordance with student preference, family food and cultural norms, nutritional value, texture, and specific eating goals (e.g., peanut butter can be used to encourage tongue lateralization). (Kimm, Falvey, Bishop, & Rosenberg, 1995, p. 211)*

When teaching these skills and having students practice them in authentic situations, teachers and other care providers must ensure the dignity of the individual. For example, if eating skills are to be taught in the cafeteria, care must be taken not to expose the child to public ridicule or teasing. Teachers should ensure that the environment provides a meaningful experience in which the child is able to develop skills. When possible, a general education peer may also assist as a natural support, augmented by the use of materials the individual will be using when performing the task being learned. Learning how to use a cafeteria tray as part of learning how to feed oneself and to eat independently in the cafeteria are other reasons for and considerations teaching skills in authentic settings. The student may develop appropriate eating skills more readily when in this natural environment because of peer modeling and because of motivational factors present in a natural environment. Nevertheless, care must be taken to safeguard the dignity of the individual as instruction occurs.

Here are some general principles for teaching home and family curriculum: (a) teach for generalization; (b) teach skills and provide students opportunities to practice skills in authentic contexts; (c) incorporate natural supports (e.g., coworkers, parents, siblings) in the teaching of these skills; (d) teach the skills that are most important for a child's independence and quality of life; and (e) respect the privacy and dignity of the individual, especially when teaching skills in public places.

Leisure pursuits

Leisure skills may be introduced through physical education and adapted physical education provided at the school and through participation in clubs and extracurricular activities. Schools need to adopt an open-door policy for all activities—welcoming all students and encouraging everyone to participate—and teachers and related support staff need to be encouraged to recruit all individuals, especially those who are hesitant to participate in those activities. To support this open-door policy, coaches and faculty sponsors of sporting events and clubs may benefit from an orientation relating to the needs of individuals with disabilities and may learn what can be done to include them meaningfully in activities, with follow-up support by special education staff for their efforts. Additionally, peers may be recruited as natural supports to assist students as they participate in activities.

As for participation in community activities, teachers can assist parents in supporting their child's involvement. Connecting parents with area agencies and organizations (e.g., Parks and Recreation, Boys-and-Girls Clubs) and with activities for their child and for the family is a beginning step. Johnson, Bullock, and Ashton-Schaeffer's program (1997) is one example.

Johnson, Bullock, and Ashton-Schaeffer (1997) developed the Family Link in Leisure Education program. Students and their parents met with a project staff to learn of available leisure activities that would help students gain skills as a consequence of participation. Project activities included assessment of student needs and goals and, on the basis of this information, provided (a) assistance to parents and students in identifying leisure activities of interest and value to the individual student and (b) guidance in how to gain the most from participation in these activities. As a result of this curricular intervention, families participated more in leisure activities and became familiar with activities available in their community, and the students expanded their participation in leisure activities and developed self-determination and self-selection skills as well.

Community involvement

Community involvement skills may be developed through student participation in a general education social studies curriculum, with and without modifications, as well as in leisure activities. Course content focusing on awareness of what makes up a community (e.g., workers, businesses, neighbors) and individuals' rights and responsibilities as citizens (e.g., voting, obeying laws) can provide a foundation for exploring community involvement opportunities. Adaptations and modifications of the general education curriculum addressed in Chapters 3 and 15 and in the sections in this chapter on learning strategies and study skills can be used to teach these skills and understandings.

Additionally, students may participate in service activities that the school orchestrates. They may serve as volunteers in district schools (e.g., working as tutors for younger students, assisting with special projects occurring at a school site); in community organizations (e.g., helping to wrap gifts at a holiday toy fund drive, visiting the elderly); and in community businesses (e.g., gaining work experience through volunteer work). Such activities give students opportunities to meet and interact with individuals in the community. Additionally, involvement in leisure activities can assist students in increasing their level of community involvement.

Physical/emotional health

Physical and emotional health curriculum targets skills such as participating in exercise programs, seeking medical help as needed, managing drug regimens, and participating in needed mental health services. Using schedules; providing photographs depicting a sequence of tasks to be completed; and teaching students how to use public transportation, access community resources, and participate in leisure activities all are instructional supports for students as they gain skills and competency in this curricular area.

Safety issues and mobility skills are also covered in this curriculum. Pattavina, Bergstrom, Marchand-Martella, and Martella (1992) describe a program they developed to teach a student with severe cognitive delays how to cross the street safely. Simulated crossing situations created by staff were captured in photographs, many of which included the student. These photographs served as the primary instructional tool for the program. Instruction was carried out through four steps:

1. Verbal rehearsal. The student was shown the photographs and asked whether it was time to cross the street. The student was to respond *yes* or *no* following evaluation of the photographed situation and to provide an explanation for his or her answer.

2. Crosswalking at a major intersection with assistance of the teacher. The teacher and student waited at the intersection. The teacher asked the student whether it was OK to cross, asked for a justification of the response, and then, together, they crossed when it was safe.

3. Crossing independently, with the teacher standing 2 to 3 feet away.

4. Crossing other streets in the community.

Self-determination

Self-determination curriculum focuses on the ability to make choices, to self-select, to self-monitor, and to self-advocate. One powerful tool for teaching and assisting students in maintaining and generalizing these skills is self-management. Whether behavioral, social, emotional, or academic goals are targeted, the development of self-management skills can assist students immensely in making decisions and acting on those decisions in a self-advocating way. Self-management allows students to take charge of their learning and behavior and empowers them by providing means for them to monitor and analyze their behavior and for developing new responses to old challenges.

Self-management programs for students take various forms. Here, we present the instructional plan proposed by Carter (1993) because of its completeness and simplicity. This plan is presented in Exhibit 17.7 and involves nine steps. Notice that along with the listing of the steps, Carter includes a self-management plan example for a student, Geoff.

EXHIBIT 17.7

A Self-Management Plan

Student _____ Geoff _____   Teacher _____ Mr. Sherman _____

School _____ Lane Middle School _____   Date _____ 10-31-92 _____

STEP 1: SELECT A TARGET BEHAVIOR
  (a) Identify the target behavior.
    Geoff talks without raising his hand and does not wait to be recognized by the teacher during structured class time. Geoff talks to himself and to peers in a voice loud enough to be heard by the teacher standing 2 feet or more away from Geoff.
  (b) Identify the replacement behavior.
    During structured class times, Geoff will raise his hand without talking and wait to be recognized by the teacher before talking.

STEP 2: DEFINE THE TARGET BEHAVIOR
  Write a clear description of the behavior (include conditions under which it is acceptable and unacceptable).
    Given a structured class setting with teacher-directed instructional activity, Geoff will raise his hand and wait to be called on before talking 9 out of 10 times. Geoff may talk without raising his hand during unstructured, noninstructional times and during class discussion.

STEP 3: DESIGN THE DATA RECORDING PROCEDURES
  (a) Identify the type of data to be recorded.
    Geoff will make a plus mark (+) on his data sheet if he raises his hand and waits to be called on before talking during each 5-minute interval for 9 intervals. If he talks without raising his hand, Geoff will mark a minus (−).
  (b) Identify when the data will be recorded.
    Geoff will self-record during his third period English class.
  (c) Describe the data recording form.
    Geoff will use a 5 x 8 index card with 5 rows of 9 squares each, one row for each day of the week. At the end of each row will be a box marked "Total" in which Geoff will record the total number of pluses earned that day.

STEP 4: TEACH THE STUDENT TO USE THE RECORDING FORM
  Briefly describe the instruction and practice.
    The teacher will review the data recording form with Geoff, showing him where and how to self-record. The teacher will role play with Geoff the use of a timer and will model examples and nonexamples of appropriate hand raising.

(continued)

EXHIBIT 17.7

A Self-Management Plan
(continued)

STEP 5: CHOOSE A STRATEGY FOR ENSURING ACCURACY

Geoff will match his self-recording form with the teacher's record at the end of each English period.

STEP 6: ESTABLISH GOAL AND CONTINGENCIES

(a) Determine how the student will be involved in setting the goal.

Geoff will meet with the teacher and discuss his goal and then will share the goal with his parents.

(b) Determine whether or not the goal will be made public.

No

(c) Determine the reinforcement for meeting the goal.

Each day that Geoff meets his performance goal, the teacher will buy Geoff a soda from the soda machine.

STEP 7: REVIEW GOAL AND STUDENT PERFORMANCE

(a) Determine how often the student and teacher will review performance.

Geoff and the teacher will meet one time per week before school to review his progress and make new goals.

(b) Identify when and how the plan will be modified if the goal is met or is not met.

If Geoff has not met his performance goal for 3 consecutive days, the teacher will schedule an extra meeting with Geoff. If Geoff meets his goal for 3 consecutive days, the teacher and Geoff will modify his goal at their next meeting.

STEP 8: PLAN FOR REDUCING SELF-RECORDING PROCEDURES

Geoff will match with the teacher's record daily, then 3 days per week, and eventually 1 day per week (picked randomly).

STEP 9: PLAN FOR GENERALIZATION AND MAINTENANCE

Geoff will self-record initially in English only. When he can successfully self-record, accurately match the teacher's record, and has met his performance goal in English for 2 weeks, he will begin self-recording in math and then social studies. When Geoff has met his performance goal for 3 weeks, self-recording will be eliminated and Geoff will earn the reinforcer for maintaining his performance goals.

Source: From "Self-Management: Education's Ultimate Goal," by J. F. Carter, 1993, *Teaching Exceptional Children, 25*(3), p. 32. Reprinted with permission.

Self-management is only one means for teaching self-determination skills. Other interventions include the gradual introduction of choice into the curriculum. Discussions and role-playing of various choices and having students maintain journals that included discussion of the choices they made, how they felt about the choices, outcomes of those choices, and what they would do next time if presented with a similar choice, are starting points for teaching students about choices. Discussions, role-plays, and simulations can all provide students opportunities to try out new skills and alternative ways for communicating their needs and desires to others. Once they demonstrate competence in these self-advocacy skills, they can apply them in authentic situations, debriefing with others about the outcomes of their efforts.

A critical component of the teaching of a self-determination curriculum is the active involvement and ongoing support of the students' parents and caregivers. Parents and caregivers must provide opportunities for students to practice their newly developed skills in family and community situations in order to support the generalization of those skills. Moreover, parents and caregivers must believe in the student's ability to make choices and to carry out those choices in a responsible manner.

Social skills

As indicated in Chapter 4, the social skills curriculum assists students in their development of interpersonal skills (e.g., getting along with others, being a friend, exhibiting appropriate behavior in social situations). Friendship and a sense of belonging are key social skills students need to be successful in and outside school. Brolin's *Life Centered*

Career Education: A Competency Based Approach (1991) lists activities for assisting students in making and maintaining friendships (see Exhibit 17.8).

Domain: Personal-Social Skills
Competency: 13. Maintaining Good Interpersonal Skills
Subcompetency: 58. Make and Maintain Friendships

EXHIBIT 17.8

Activities to Assist Students in Making and Maintaining Friendships

OBJECTIVES	ACTIVITIES/STRATEGIES	ADULT/PEER ROLES
a. Identify necessary components of a friendship.	• Students describe their interpretation of friendship. • Students role-play persons demonstrating friendship. • Students discuss the behavioral aspects of a friendship. • Students list on chalkboard the behavioral/attitudinal characteristics involved in friendship (e.g., openness, sincerity, understanding, love, friendly behavior, etc.). • Class creates a display on the bulletin board illustrating people engaged in friendly activities.	• Parents identify the similar aspects of friendships and family memberships. • Parents assist the student in identifying essential components of a friendship and assist the student in developing them. • Youth workers discuss the need for friendship in people's lives.
b. List personal considerations in choosing a friend.	• Students conduct values clarification exercises on expectations for a friend. • Students identify and describe their friends at various times in their life. • Students conduct shared interests-values clarification exercise in which they are combined in pairs with similar interests. • Class discusses the equality of friends so that no person is superior in the relationship. • Students discuss choosing friends based on a person's personal qualities.	• Parents assist in identifying interests that could be shared with a friend. • Parents discuss their choice of friends. • Two people who have been friends for long periods of time discuss their relationship with the class.
c. List rights and responsibilities important in personal friendships.	• Students role-play problem situations in which they must respond to a friend's dilemma. • Students discuss the responsibilities of friendship. • Students list on chalkboard the privileges of friendship.	• Parents assist the student in deciding the limitations in helping friends. • Parents emphasize the shared rights and responsibilities of friendships and family life.
d. List activities that can be shared with friends.	• Students discuss what they share with friends (sports, social events, study, etc.). • Class creates a bulletin board illustrating activities that people share. • Students discuss the value of having a variety of friends (e.g., broadens the base of experience, allows for less reliance on one particular person, etc.).	• Parents encourage the student to engage in peer activities (e.g., recreational, study, hobby, etc.). • Recreation personnel discuss the effects of shared experiences on friendships and community facilities and programs.

Source: From *Life Centered Career Education: A Competency Based Approach*, 3rd ed. (pp. 84–85), edited by D. E. Brolin, 1991, Reston, VA: Council for Exceptional Children. Reprinted with permission.

Another way to encourage the development of friendships between individuals with and without disabilities is through natural supports. As students interact and work together toward common goals, there are opportunities for discovering shared interests and for the development of friendships. Peers (with and without disabilities) can serve as natural supports for students with disabilities included in general education settings and experiences. They can provide students assistance in physical tasks, can assist them when working in cooperative groups, and can assist them in meeting IEP goals, benchmarks, and objectives. If general education peers are allowed opportunities to serve as natural supports for students with disabilities, rather than having those needs met solely through support personnel and/or teachers, students will have an opportunity to interact with one another, to begin to know one another, and possibly to develop friendships.

Another approach to assist students in forming friendships is to have the student develop a circle of support map (see Figure 17.4). As discussed by Miner and Bates (1997), circle of support maps, first discussed by Pearpoint and Forest (1992), are a form of person-centered planning. To make a circle of support map, students (or teachers and parents, if needed) draw four concentric circles. In the center circle goes the name of the person making the map—Matthew, in Figure 17.4. In the next circle, Matthew writes in the names of individuals close to him. These individuals may include family members, relatives, and/or close friends. In the third circle, working outward, Matthew lists individuals with whom he comes in contact through daily activities. In the fourth circle, he lists individuals who are paid to support and interact with him. Matthew's circle of support map indicates that he has limited interactions with others. He does not list any friends in his map, and, except for his brother, all the individuals identified are adults. This map suggests a need to provide Matthew enhanced opportunities to interact with peers.

❙ **FIGURE 17.4**
Circle of Support Map

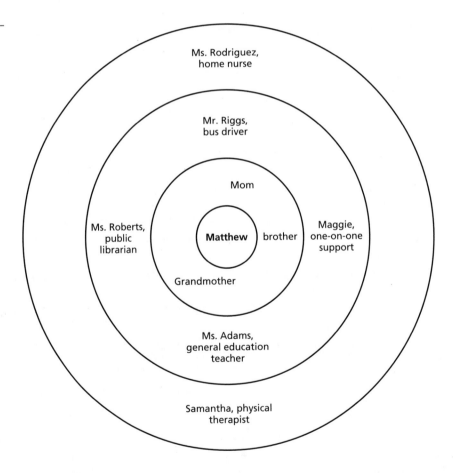

Developing friendships, as well as other social skills, may be taught through multiple techniques drawn from cognitive approaches (which emphasize thinking processes for working through situations and forming solutions or responses), behavioral approaches (which emphasize the analysis of stimulus and response and the use of reinforcement), and cognitive-behavioral approaches (which combine features of both cognitive and behavioral approaches). Descriptions of several approaches for teaching a range of social skills are presented in Exhibit 17.9.

EXHIBIT 17.9

Approaches for Teaching
Social Skills

APPROACH	DEFINITION	APPLICATION
Role-playing	students assume role of characters and act out situations	• for teaching students specific social skills responses (e.g., how to greet another person; how to ask questions appropriately) • for helping students develop alternative responses to challenging situations (e.g., playing out a scenario of a conflict on the playground and coming up with possible responses to the situation)
Coaching	trainer provides specific verbal feedback and suggestions in authentic situations as events unfold	• for teaching students on-the-job skills • for teaching students appropriate behavior in restaurants, shopping malls, grocery stores, and other public places
Discussion	students and teachers talk about issues	• for exploring new situations students may encounter • for evaluating a range of responses to a specific situation
Retelling stories	students and teachers share experiences	• for aiding students in learning from one another and from one another's experiences • for developing an understanding that many conflicts and challenging situations are not new—that others have experienced and survived similar situations
Modeling	*live modeling:* individuals assume actual roles and play out a situation *symbolic modeling:* videotapes are used to present situations	• for teaching a variety of skills for how to respond to various social situations such as resolving conflict, complimenting a peer, providing assistance, and engaging in conversations with authority figures • for teaching interviewing skills and other vocationally related skills
Group contingencies	predetermined reinforcement is provided when specified members or all members of a group achieve a set criterion of performance	• for ensuring participation of all members during cooperative learning by means of a group contingency, such as all members must contribute at least five ideas to the group project
Peer pairing	students work together to respond to challenging situations	• for creating opportunities for students to share ideas with peers and to support their peers when in challenging situations • for providing role models of appropriate behavior by pairing a student experiencing difficulty with a student who has a greater degree of success in the social skills domain
Dispensing reinforcement	reinforcement is provided when desired behavior is displayed	• for assisting students in engaging in appropriate behavior (e.g., reinforcing a student for raising a hand before speaking)
Adult-mediated prompting	adult prompts child in socially appropriate behavior as needed during authentic situations	• for providing on-the-spot assistance to students experiencing difficulties (e.g., providing prompts on how to ask questions or when to ask questions when working in cooperative groups)
Social praise	student engaged in appropriate behavior is praised	• for catching students "doing it right" (e.g., praising a student for helping another student)
Behavioral rehearsal and feedback	students are provided with opportunities to try out behaviors	• for assisting students in developing new responses to situations (e.g., providing opportunities for students to practice saying *no* to peers when they do not want to engage in a suggested activity)

Source: Adapted from Rivera & Smith (1997).

Transition Education

As discussed in Chapter 4, students move through a number of transitions during their school careers. This section provides a few suggestions for assisting students in making those transitions successfully.

From one school level to another

One transition that all students experience is the transition from one level of schooling to another. Such transitions, from home/preschool to kindergarten, from elementary school to middle/junior high, and from middle/junior high to high school, can be traumatic unless students know what to expect in the new learning environment. The "Make It Happen" feature suggests ways for teachers, students, and parents to help make these transitions successful and rewarding for students with disabilities.

MAKE IT HAPPEN   **Successful Transitions from One School Level to Another**

- *Hold IEP meetings at the new site*
  - meet the new teachers and administrators
  - become familiar with the layout of the building
  - find the location(s) of the student's classroom(s)
- *Visit the new site*
  - go as a group on a field trip to the new school
  - make an appointment for a student to visit the school individually
  - arrange for the student to spend half a day at the new school
- *Hold an orientation for new students and their parents*
  - provide a map of the school and tours of the campus
  - provide copies of the school handbook that addresses curricular/ extracurricular options and includes course descriptions
  - provide copies of the school policy on discipline and grading
  - introduce faculty, staff, and administrators to the group and allow for questions
- *Toward the end of the year, modify classroom experiences to reflect what occurs at the new site*
  - provide more opportunities for students to make choices
  - provide students with more privileges paired with increased responsibility for their own learning
- *Identify and teach skills students will need at the new site*
  - teach needed study skills, self-management skills, and prosocial skills

---

From special education environments to other learning environments

One approach for preparing and assisting students in making this type of transition is to use a classroom inventory to learn about the new learning environment into which the student will be transitioning. Fuchs, Fernstrom, Scott, Fuchs, and Vandermeer (1994) provide an inventory that teachers may find helpful when transitioning elementary-age children from special education classrooms into general education classrooms (see Exhibit 17.10). The inventory is completed by the special education teacher after an observation in the targeted general education setting. Similar inventories may be used when students are transitioning into business and community-based environments.

EXHIBIT 17.10

**Classroom Ecological Inventory
for Transitioning Schoolchildren
into General Education Settings**

Special Education Teacher _____ Grade _____ Date _____

Regular Education Teacher _____ Number of Students in Regular Class _____

Student _____

PART 1: CLASSROOM OBSERVATION

Physical Environment
Directions: Please circle or provide the appropriate answer.

1. Is there an area for small groups?	Yes	No
2. Are partitions used in the room?	Yes	No
3. Is there a computer in the classroom?	Yes	No

4. Where is the student's desk located? (for example, front of room, back, middle, away from other students, etc.) _____

Teacher/Student Behavior
Directions for #1–#4: Please circle the appropriate answer.

1. How much movement or activity is tolerated by the teacher?	Much	Average	Little	Unclear
2. How much talking among students is tolerated?	Much	Average	Little	Unclear
3. Does the teacher use praise?	Much	Average	Little	Unclear
4. Was subject taught to the entire group or to small groups?		Entire	Small	

Directions for #5–#7: Please provide an appropriate answer.

5. During the observation, where did the teacher spend most of the time? (for example, at the board, at teacher's desk, at student's desk) _____

6. What teaching methods did you observe while in the classroom? (for example, teacher modeled the lesson, asked students to work at board, helped small groups, helped individual students) _____

7. How did the teacher interact with students who appeared to be low achieving or slower than their classmates? (for example, helped them individually, talked to them in the large group) _____

Posted Classroom Rules
If classroom rules are posted, what are they?

SPECIAL EDUCATION	REGULAR EDUCATION
_____	_____
_____	_____
_____	_____

Is there any other pertinent information you observed about this classroom that would be helpful in reintegrating the student? (for example, crowded classroom)

_____

_____

(continued)

EXHIBIT 17.10

**Classroom Ecological Inventory
for Transitioning Schoolchildren
into General Education Settings**
(continued)

PART 2: TEACHER INTERVIEW

	SPECIAL EDUCATION	REGULAR EDUCATION

Classroom Rules

1. During class are there important rules? (Yes or No)

2. If yes, how are they communicated? (for example, written or oral)

3. If class rules are *not* posted, what are they?

4. If a rule is broken, what happens? What is the typical consequence?

5. Who enforces the rules? (teacher, aide, students)

Teacher Behavior

1. a. Is homework assigned? (Yes or No)

   b. If so, indicate approximate amount (minutes) of homework, and

   c. the frequency with which it is given.

Directions for #2–#4: Using a 3-point scale (1 = Often, 2 = Sometimes, 3 = Never), rate each item according to frequency of occurrence in class. Place an asterisk (*) in the righthand margin to indicate important differences between the special and regular education classrooms.

	SPECIAL ED	REGULAR ED			SPECIAL ED	REGULAR ED
2. Assignments in Class				3. Tests		
a. Students are given assignments:				a. Tests are		
• that are the same for all	___	___		• presented orally	___	___
• that differ in amount or type	___	___		• copied from board	___	___
• to complete in school at a specified time	___	___		• timed	___	___
• that, if unfinished in school, are assigned as homework	___	___		• based on study guides given to students prior to test	___	___
				• administered by resource teacher	___	___
b. Evaluation of assignment:				b. Grades are:		
• teacher evaluation	___	___		• percentages (example, 75%)	___	___
• student self-evaluation	___	___		• letter grades (example, B+)	___	___
• peer evaluation	___	___		• both	___	___

	SPECIAL ED	REGULAR ED			SPECIAL ED	REGULAR ED
4. Academic/Social Rewards				5. To what extent do each of the following contribute to an overall grade? *Estimate the percentage for each so that the total sums to 100%.*		
a. Classroom rewards or reinforcement include:						
• material rewards (example, stars)	_____	_____		• homework	_____	_____
b. Classroom punishment includes:				• daily work	_____	_____
• time out	_____	_____		• tests	_____	_____
• loss of activity-related privileges (example, loss of free time)	_____	_____		• class participation	_____	_____
• teacher ignoring	_____	_____		6. Please list skills that have been taught since the beginning of the school year (Regular Education Teacher Only):		
• reprimands	_____	_____				
• poorer grade, loss of star, etc.	_____	_____				
• extra work	_____	_____		Skill	Will Reteach Later? (Yes or No)	
• staying after school	_____	_____				
• physical punishment (example, paddling)	_____	_____		_____	_____	

Source: From "Classroom Ecological Inventory," by Dr. D. Fuchs, P. Fernstrom, S. Scott, L. Fuchs, and L. Vandermeer, 1994, *Teaching Exceptional Children, 26*(3), p. 11. Reprinted with permission.

Some students will continue to move between educational environments and will not necessarily transition out of one and into another. They may participate in general and special education environments. For example, a student with a physical disability may spend most of the day in a general education setting but receive physical therapy by a specialist outside that environment. In this case, teachers, parents, and the student must communicate about the goals and expectations of these different experiences and how they will ensure that there are maximum benefits from both environments and that the student's goals are not hindered in any way as a result of that participation.

From school to young adult roles and responsibilities

Another difficult transition for many individuals with disabilities is the transition from high school to work and from high school to postsecondary education. Cobb and Hasazi (1987) and Rojewski (1992) specify exemplary practices associated with effective transition programs. These practices include (a) creating Individualized Transition Plans that include residential, vocational, and postsecondary educational options and goals for independent living; (b) placing students in mainstream settings; (c) providing students paid work experiences during high school; (d) encouraging parent, consumer, and family involvement in transition planning; (e) providing an occupational planning and placement curriculum; (f) coordinating services across agencies; and (g) gathering outcome data for program evaluation purposes. Cobb and Hasazi (1987) include one additional component: flexible scheduling for school personnel involved in the programs to allow them to be responsive to the changing needs of students in the field and to professional development and enhancement opportunities. These elements can be put into place during a student's high school career to ensure a smoother transition to post–high school experiences.

Bishop, Amate, and Villalobos (1995) identify seven standards they believe must be included in transition service programs for students with disabilities. These seven standards are listed in Exhibit 17.11 and may be part of high school, as well as elementary and middle school experiences, because curriculum at all levels can and should include vocational and career components (Wehman, 1996).

EXHIBIT 17.11

Standards for Successful Transition Programs

1. *Chronological age appropriate.* Skills, activities, and environments must reflect those typical for peers without disabilities of the same chronological age.
2. *Functional/critical skills.* These include skills or activities that are required or expected of peers without disabilities. They are essential to the student's performance and participation in a variety of community environments.
3. *Cultural/linguistic sensitivity.* Activities must reflect an awareness and appreciation of the skills, values, customs, and heritage that are important in the individual's culture/linguistic/religious background.
4. *Natural environments.* Teaching and participation in activities should take place in environments where they would naturally occur (as opposed to pretend grocery stores, for example).
5. *Zero inferences.* Once a student has acquired a skill, inferences would not be made concerning the student's performance of similar skills at a different time or in a different environment. Instruction must occur across a variety of natural environments, persons, cues, and materials, instead of inferring generalization.
6. *Physical and social integration.* Instruction and participation should include
   a. Presence of same-age peers without disabilities
   b. Ongoing interactions with peers without disabilities in natural environments
   c. A ratio of people with and without disabilities that reflects natural proportions
   d. Equal access to community facilities
   e. Qualified, appropriate personnel to provide the necessary training and support
7. *Student preferences.* Activities and curricula must emphasize student preferences and ongoing choice-making opportunities. Although all students may not be able to communicate preferences verbally, teachers and parents must work together to ascertain such preferences (e.g., examining behavior patterns, affect, eye contact, attention span, and attendance).

Source: From "Postsecondary Conditions," by K. D. Bishop, S. L. Amate, and P. J. Villalobos, 1995, in *Inclusive and Heterogeneous Schooling: Assessment, Curriculum, and Instruction* (pp. 370–371), edited by M. A. Falvey, Baltimore: Paul H. Brookes.

The transition of students with disabilities to college and other postsecondary educational institutions is receiving increased attention as more and more students with disabilities are choosing this option upon exit from high school. Plans must be made early if students plan to go on to postsecondary education because admission requirements generally are linked directly to course selection during high school (e.g., some colleges require three years of mathematics, others two). Therefore, teachers, students, and parents must work together when planning a student's curriculum so that curricular choices do not delay or prohibit a student's participation in postsecondary educational opportunities. Kravets (1996) offers suggestions for planning the transition to college for individuals with attention deficit hyperactivity disorders:

1. Assess emotional/social readiness and academic readiness.

2. Prioritize what is most important in selecting a school (e.g., small class sizes, availability of tutoring and readers, advising supports).

3. Decide whether to disclose the individual's disability on application materials.

4. Make arrangements for and complete necessary testing for admission.

5. Ask individuals for letters of recommendation that describe the individual's strengths, challenges, and major accomplishments.

6. Prepare students for interviews by school personnel.

7. Tour campuses of interest and talk with students and others to learn more about the school.

8. Select the school based on a match between the individual's needs and offerings and supports available at the school.

9. If the person is not admitted, develop a plan for enhancing the individual's academic record to increase the likelihood of acceptance at a future date (e.g., enrollment in junior and/or community college to raise grade-point average).

Once on campus, students may experience personal and unique challenges. Suggestions for addressing these challenges include (a) self-advocating for special needs and accommodations by talking with professors; (b) registering with the disability student services on campus to gain access to needed services and modifications; (c) enrolling and participating in tutoring and support group programs available at the school; and (d) becoming involved in the social life of the campus to form friendships and a social network that can be called on to provide help in overcoming barriers.

The transitions from high school to post–high school experiences are generally mediated by a transition coordinator. The many jobs and responsibilities of a transition coordinator are listed in Exhibit 17.12.

EXHIBIT 17.12

The Roles and Responsibilities of Transition Coordinators

What Does a Transition Coordinator Do?

1. Intraschool Linkage
   a. Disseminate transition information to teachers/administrators
   b. Present inservice training
   c. Assist families, parents, and students to access transition services
   d. Facilitate communication between special and vocational education teachers
   e. Serve as a liaison between vocational school and special education teachers to monitor student progress
   f. Serve as a liaison to identify appropriate accommodations
   g. Serve as a liaison to screen for student placement
   h. Facilitate appropriate referrals to school-based programs
   i. Assist school staff in interpreting assessment results and recommending appropriate placements
   j. Assist school staff in understanding strengths and weaknesses and modifications
   k. Assist vocational teachers in adapting curriculum
   l. Provide technical assistance to school staff
2. Interagency/Business Linkages
   a. Identify, establish, maintain linkages with community agencies and businesses
   b. Educate adult services about agencies, school programs/procedures
   c. Write cooperative agreements
   d. Facilitate referrals to other agencies

   e. Lead interagency transition meetings
   f. Initiate and maintain collaboration between and among different local education agencies
   g. Link students with postsecondary special support coordinators
3. Assessment and Career Counseling
   a. Identify and refer students for vocational assessment within the school
   b. Identify and refer students for vocational assessments at regional centers
   c. Facilitate implementation of recommendations of reports by communicating and interpreting results with parents, and teachers, others
   d. Coordinate the development of career awareness and explore activities as part of the career counseling process
   e. Collaborate with guidance for student participation in career fairs and job fairs
4. Transition Planning
   a. Identify transition services provided by community agencies
   b. Attend/participate in team and IEP meetings
   c. Assist in planning and placement decisions
   d. Identify appropriate assistive technology
   e. Monitor adherence to federal laws
   f. Oversee the development of postsecondary employment or training plans

(continued)

EXHIBIT 17.12

**The Roles and Responsibilities
of Transition Coordinators**
(continued)

5. Education and Community Training
    a. Promote self-advocacy activities and curriculum
    b. Train special education teachers and employers to understand the need for self-advocacy
    c. Prepare students for self-advocacy
    d. Coordinate school and community work-based learning opportunities (job shadowing, mentorship, internship, cooperative education, student apprenticeship)
    e. Identify job placements
    f. Develop community-based training sites and school-based training
    g. Provide technical support/assistance to employers and supervisors
    h. Implement job support services for work adjustment and success
    i. Identify/coordinate transportation options
    j. Manage/coordinate job coaches
    k. Monitor and coordinate job coaching activities
    l. Coordinate community-based instruction
    m. Coordinate teaching of daily living skills
    n. Examine/identify postsecondary training and education options
    o. Conduct various tours of employment/vocational training/education options

6. Family Support and Resource
    a. Inform parents/families of community resources—understanding services
    b. Develop and provide parent training
    c. Promote understanding of laws, eligibility requirements, availability of services
    d. Assist students/families in understanding the system and accessing services
    e. Mediate between schools and families
    f. Counsel and communicate with parents regarding parent/student changing roles

7. Public Relations
    a. Disseminate information (videos, print material) to employers, parents (variety of audiences)
    b. Write newspaper articles, public service announcements, presentations
    c. Provide awareness events/presentations to employers, teachers, parents, students, and service organizations
    d. Develop business partnerships (guest speakers, field trips, equipment, mentorship programs, etc.)
    e. Promote work-based learning opportunities with businesses, and recruit businesses
    f. Serve on a variety of community committees: Mayor's Committee for Persons with Disabilities, CSBS (disability services), employment network, Tech Prep, regional transition committees, postsecondary committee, business/school alliance
    g. Coordinate/sponsor transition fairs

8. Program Development
    a. Develop process in transition planning
    b. Develop system guidelines, programs, and procedures
    c. Develop and revise procedures and forms
    d. Develop and manipulate transition curriculum
    e. Collaborate with agencies for program development
    f. Propose new ideas for grant development
    g. Write grants for supplemental services

9. Program Evaluation
    a. Carry out school and community needs assessment
    b. Identify gaps in transition services
    c. Devise evaluation forms
    d. Conduct follow-up study on students who exit the program
    e. Analyze and use information gained from evaluations
    f. Complete annual reports

Source: From "Transition Coordinators," by S. B. Asselin, M. Todd-Allen, and S. deFur, 1998, *Teaching Exceptional Children 30*(3), p. 14. Reprinted with permission.

In addition to the role of a transition coordinator, students may be assigned a job coach to facilitate their transition to the workplace. The role of job coaches is changing, however, as greater emphasis is placed on the use of natural supports. Exhibit 17.13 compares the roles of job coaches and employment consultants and/or employers who have a natural supports orientation. Regardless of the specific approach, the primary purpose is to support the individual on the job.

EXHIBIT 17.13

Job Coaches' Responsibilities and the Introduction of Natural Supports

STRATEGY	TRADITIONAL JOB COACH	EMPLOYMENT CONSULTANT/ NATURAL SUPPORTS
Finding jobs	Jobs found by seeking high turnover jobs, cold calls, etc. Potential job site supports not examined.	Personal connections used to identify opportunities for job and social supports.
Job matching	Focus on person-task match.	Focus on person-task-environment match.
Adaptations/ modifications	Job coach determines and generates accommodations.	Employers and coworkers involved in developing accommodations. Supported employee involved as much as possible.
Job training and support	Job coach provides direct training and support until fading occurs.	Employment consultant supports worksite personnel to provide training and support, and facilitates social relationships as needed.
General work-site support	Job coach focuses on person with disabilities.	Employment specialist looks at overall work environment as it impacts supported employee.

Source: From Natural Supports: Reconceptualizing Job Coach Roles, Pat Rogan, David Hagner, Steven Murphy, 1993, Journal of The Association for Persons with Severe Handicaps 18(4) pp. 275–281. Reprinting and title adaptation by permission.

THEORY TO PRACTICE

➡ Select one area of the life skills curriculum to infuse into an existing general education curriculum. Design a plan for its infusion, including (a) the purpose for including the area in the curriculum, (b) student and teacher benefits, and (c) activities and related instructional approaches. Present your plan to a general education teacher for feedback.

CHAPTER SUMMARY

This chapter explores instructional approaches for the teaching of learning strategies, study skills, and life skills. Many of the strategies presented in previous chapters in Section 3 on instruction can be applied to teach these skills as well.

CHAPTER 18

Technology in the Interactive Curriculum

by Vicki Casella and Loretta Giorcelli

Each decade brings great expectations that new technologies will radically alter the way teaching and learning take place. Educators were excited by the instructional prospects of the film technology in the 1920s. When television made major inroads into the American home in the 1950s, parents and teachers alike were thrilled by the possibilities this technology offered for teaching and learning. The 1980s brought computers to the forefront. The world sat up and took notice of this micro revolution while much ado was made about the promise and potential of this technology. In the 1990s, as information technology became a dominating force, educators again found themselves raising expectations about the impact technology would have on them, their students, and the entire educational process. To this point, despite the potential, few would dispute that only modest benefits have been realized through the use of the technology and overall the "revolution" in education so far remains just a "promise." Now, entering the next century, the challenge of fully utilizing technologies to support student learning is even more imperative.

Where technology *is* making a major difference is in the education of students with special needs. As authors describe in earlier chapters, curriculum and communication have become accessible to a whole population of individuals who traditionally have been shut out of one or both. Students with little or no use of their hands now type or "talk" information into word processors, and printers spew out their ideas. Students who are nonspeaking have found a "voice" through microtechnology and now have equal opportunity to interact with their peers and to give oral reports when required. Students who need a little more practice to achieve mastery or who need the material presented in a different manner have unlimited opportunity through computer use to interact with the information. They may receive corrective feedback when they make mistakes, benefit from tutoring prompting provided through computer software, and create and problem solve in varieties of situations brought to them through computer technology. Selected software programs also reward them for a job well done. The potential and the promise are still there for *everyone*. There are, however, major barriers that must be overcome if the potential and promise are to be realized.

IDENTIFYING AND OVERCOMING BARRIERS TO TECHNOLOGY

Equipment

When computers first came on the education scene, getting the equipment into the classroom was a major objective. Computer companies, realizing the potential market, lowered prices and offered education discounts, as well as sponsored give-away programs, and in general made tremendous efforts to get the equipment into the hands of children and teachers. School districts, wanting to jump on the bandwagon, allocated millions of dollars to the purchase of machines. Parents, anxious that their children become computer literate, raised money and made contributions themselves to increase the number of computers available to their children in school. Frequently the focus was on the number of machines rather than on the quality; thus, the life span of much of the equipment was limited, and much of it ended up in storage rooms or closets in a short amount of time. Even the most advanced computers become outdated.

The equipment is constantly evolving with progressively more power, more graphics capability, enhanced color, stereophonic digitized sound, digital video imaging, and greater speed and storage capacity. One of the most important advances has been in the ease of use. Graphic user interface design and user-friendly operating systems have eliminated the need for extensive training in the operation of the equipment, and the focus has shifted from how to operate the equipment to how the equipment can best be used. Classroom teachers realize that the real promise of the new technology lies not in the machinery but in its integration into the educational curriculum.

Software

The key to curriculum integration is the evaluation and selection of educational software. Initially teachers looked for software that would extend rather than expand their teaching. Drill and practice programs offering little more than electronic worksheets were the most commonly used programs in classrooms. Using this type of software did not require the teacher to learn any new information or to alter teaching practices in any way. At the end of an activity, instead of working on a ditto sheet, all children went to the computer and let it generate problems for them to solve. Gradually as teachers gained more confidence and as the quality of the educational software improved, there was a move to use more intricate, sophisticated programs. Tutorial programs offered students another "teacher" to introduce new material. Educational games engaged students for extended periods of time as they sought to "survive" difficult situations or earn game points. Problem-solving software forced students to think of multiple solutions to problems. Personal productivity software made the writing process more engaging as editing, incorporating graphics, and publishing changed the face of students' work. CD-ROM-based encyclopedias and dictionaries provided electronic research material at the click of a button, and now the information superhighway, the Internet, brings the world into the classroom.

Revision of Curriculum

Although some of the uses of technology fit into the traditional curriculum, revision must occur if the technology is to have a major impact on educational outcomes. This is an area of concern that must be addressed by administrators, teachers, students, and parents. Schools cannot continue to do business as usual when the business is constantly changing and evolving into something entirely different. A perfect example of how the business is changing occurred in a third grade classroom recently when a young student came into class one morning and told the teacher that the book the class had read the day before was wrong. When questioned further, he offered that the book had stated that people in Holland grew tulips but none of the three people in Amsterdam whom he had "talked" to the night before grew tulips. His session on the Internet had given him all the proof he needed to show that the materials used in the class were outdated and that the teacher needed, as he eloquently stated, "to get with it." The teacher took advantage of the situation and gave the class an assignment that required students to get on the Internet, find a school in Holland, and ask the students there to share some of their parents' occupations. Once the students had gathered that information, they surveyed each other and the class next door and compared the information they collected. The results of the analysis of data were put into a database and sent by electronic mail to the class in Holland. This on-the-spot revision of the curriculum put the students in charge of their own learning, expanded their communication ability, encouraged them to use technology in a real-life experience, and changed the activity from one of recalling rote facts to one of gathering, analyzing, comparing, and reporting data. This is one example of how standard curriculum objectives can still be addressed, and the delivery system revised to reflect the power of technology to enhance learning. All curriculum goals and objectives must be examined in the context of a technology-rich environment, and subsequent changes must be made to reflect the skills and knowledge base that students will need in this environment. Other areas to be considered in the revision process include assessment and evaluation practices, presentation of information, curriculum content, and student performance.

Training

Lack of training is a major barrier to realizing the potential and promise of technology. Until recently, most preservice teacher training programs did not offer instruction in the use of technology to realize curriculum goals and objectives. Currently, although most training programs require some competency in the use of computers, the emphasis is on the operational side, not the functional or curriculum side of computer use. The same is true of many inservice programs. It is important for teachers to learn to use computers in ways that relate to their teaching, the specific goals and objectives of the educational program, and the needs of their students. Learning to operate the machine, however, is the simplest task. Training programs must move beyond the operation of the equipment and address the use of technology *in curriculum delivery*—a topic that encompasses the criteria for the selection of appropriate equipment and software, effective teaching strategies that promote integration of technology in the learning process, creative student-centered learning opportunities around the use of the computer, and evaluation procedures that take into account the expanded learning experiences of students. The focus needs to be directed toward integrating the various aspects involving technology into all the courses taken by students at the preservice level or teachers at the inservice level. For example, if a person is taking a class on teaching reading and associated instructional materials, the appropriate software and hardware should be introduced as readily as the latest best-selling storybook, novel, or textbook.

Access

There is a pervasive feeling that technology will broaden the gap between socioeconomic groups, and there is some evidence that gender must be an access concern as well. In education, care must be taken that everyone has equal access to equipment and software. This is particularly true for students with special needs. There have been instances when students in special day classes were actually prohibited from using the computer lab. The reason given was that they didn't know how to use it and would destroy it. In actuality, computer technology can be the equalizing factor for some of these students. They are able to perform tasks and engage successfully in curriculum materials that were unavailable to them before the advent of microtechnology. Not only should students have equal access to computers in labs or in the classroom, but when a student's only access to the curriculum is through technology, dedicated equipment should be provided for that individual. For example, if students with a physical disability cannot produce written work using traditional writing tools, they should have full access to equipment, assistive input devices, and software to accomplish the task (as described in Chapter 5).

Where the equipment is located in the school is another access consideration. Some administrators prefer to place all computers in a lab and have a teacher or technician schedule classes to use the equipment. This arrangement limits access and prevents the classroom teacher from integrating the technology on a regular basis into the curriculum. The best scenario is for a school to have a well-equipped computer classroom and for each classroom to have at least one computer. The computer classroom is the perfect place to teach the operational level of computer use: keyboarding, a word processing program, scanning, a desktop publishing program, and printing. The classroom, however, is where the functional use of the computer must take place—where students learn how to write, to organize, to problem-solve, to read, and to compute. If technology is to be integrated into the curriculum, students need access to the computer in the classroom.

TEACHING WITH TECHNOLOGY

Breaking the Failure Cycle

Frequently, the use of the computer to do traditional tasks improves student performance. Many of the students with special needs faced failure with traditional materials, but when the same information was presented on the computer, they were able to perform. For example, a group of students at high risk for school dropout/failure were assigned to work with a teacher on using the computer to write. The instructor started by having the students play a simulation game that required reading at the third grade level. The text on each screen consisted of three or four sentences displayed under a graphic representing the situation. When asked to read the information from the screen, several of the students indicated they couldn't read, but as the game progressed, they were giving appropriate input prior to having the screen read to them. When this was brought to their attention, they discussed what was happening and decided that their perception of reading meant going over a chapter independently and then answering the questions at the end. None of them had been successful doing that task, but all were successful at reading the material presented on the computer. The teacher later modified the text in the traditional textbooks to present only small segments at a time, giving students the opportunity to discuss what they had read and then formulate answers to questions based on the reading. All were successful. The computer did not play a role in the modification of the material, but it gave the instructor a chance to observe the students being successful and to determine what was necessary to ensure that there was carryover to traditional materials. The major task was to break the cycle of failure these students had established, and the computer was the tool. The students had not experienced failure using that as a tool and were not afraid to take the risk.

Software Selection

Students at risk in the education system are extremely diverse. They come from different cultural backgrounds, bring different experiences into the classroom, speak a variety of languages, and have different abilities and special needs. Regardless of these differences, students who experience problems in school share one or more of the following characteristics: (a) reduced self-image as a learner, (b) irregular achievement profile in school subjects, (c) inadequate skills and knowledge in one or more content areas, and (d) problems with organization, sequencing, predicting and testing, selecting, and synthesizing information. A major task for the teacher is to provide opportunities for these students to reclaim and maintain some control over their own learning processes. This requires the selection of materials that offer structured content but are flexible enough to allow for different learning styles, strengths, and needs. Technology can assist if software is selected carefully and attention is paid to the various options built into software programs. The type of software program (e.g., drill and practice, tutorial, simulation, problem solving, educational game) determines which options are viable, but some features play a major role in the success of many students:

- *Ability to control the speed at which material is presented.* This parameter may be part of a teacher- or a student-controlled function. Students' learning is enhanced when students have more control of the situation, so software that allows them to control the display of the information is preferable. For example, if the software program has multiple pages of text and/or graphics and the students control the display, the students may click through some pages more quickly than others, based on the difficulty of the text.

- *Ability to control the size of the display.* The size of text and graphics is an important variable for some students. A feature to enlarge or reduce text and graphics is built into some software programs and is a standard option (Closeview™) in the system software for the Macintosh computer.
- *Ability to control response wait time.* Students who are experiencing difficulty should not have the added pressure of having to give a timed response. Although timing might be appropriate in some situations, skill development and knowledge acquisition should be the focus in most instructional sessions. Allowing the student complete control over the pacing of the presentation is a major consideration in software selection.
- *Feedback that is supportive, not simply judgmental.* When a student is practicing new skills or acquiring new information, judgmental feedback (e.g., "right answer," "wrong answer") alone is not meaningful. Programs that provide more information or that prompt the student to think through the problem are far more beneficial to learning.
- *Ability to select level of difficulty.* Students, in consultation with teachers, should be able to determine where, along a continuum, to begin their practice. If an assessment feature is built into the computer program and placement on a particular level is based on performance on the assessment, the student and/or teacher should have the final decision about the appropriateness of the placement.
- *Carefully controlled reading level.* The amount and level of reading required to operate a software program should be relevant to the task and to the ability level of the student. Reading the instructions or the content of the problem should not pose a barrier for the student.
- *Design that does not detract from the content.* Cute graphics and animation add to the "bells and whistles" effects of a program but can sometimes interfere with the learning that should be taking place. Screen displays should be attractive; graphics and animation should be used with discretion; and audio signals should be included when appropriate (always with the option of turning them off). None of these features should be so distracting that the student is attending to them rather than to the content of the program.
- *Control for presentation and record-keeping capability.* Drill and practice programs should have some record-keeping capacity, including number of problems worked, number correct, error analysis, and level of difficulty. Controls for presentation should include teacher or student options that allow for control of the frequency and type of reinforcement, number of problems presented, number of trials per problem, display features, and control of speed of presentation and response time.
- *Allowance for more than one correct answer or way to solve the problem.* Problem-solving programs should encourage students to explore various options to resolve a situation, to compare and contrast different responses, to build on their responses from one situation to the next, and to use additional, nontechnological references and support to complete an assignment.
- *Multiple presentation formats.* Tutorial programs should use the technology to present information in a variety of formats rather than use a textbook approach. They should incorporate features that are not possible in other materials, including branching instructional routines, multiple reading levels, graphics and animation if appropriate, and a selection of practice exercises.
- *Educational support prompts.* Discovery programs should have built-in support features that make it obvious to students "what" they have discovered. For example,

when a young student presses the letter *A* and a picture of an airplane comes on the screen, little learning takes place unless the student knows the name of the letter, the name of the object, and the fact that pressing that letter caused the picture to appear.

There are numerous other features that teachers want and look for in programs. All teachers have a shopping list for what they value in educational materials, and software selection is no different in that respect.

Use of Technology to Meet Educational Requirements

Even the best software cannot compensate for poor teaching or a weak curriculum, nor does it work equally well for all students. In order to be effective, the software must be selected and used to help students overcome the barriers they face to mastering the curriculum goals and objectives set for them. For example, learning the alphabetical sequence of letters is a reading readiness skill emphasized in the preschool/primary curriculum. One popular way to reinforce this skill is to have students complete a picture by connecting dots that are labeled with the letters of the alphabet and then to color the finished product. Naturally this task is a major obstacle for students who are unable to see the dots, who have severe motor problems, or whose hand-eye coordination is limited. Software programs such as *Dot-to-Dot* from SchoolZone Publishing Co. (Grand Haven, MI) can help students with these special circumstances master this curriculum objective by providing exactly the same practice other students can get by using conventional materials. The computer monitor becomes an electronic worksheet, displaying dots labeled with letters of the alphabet. To connect the dots, the student uses only the number or letter keys or an alternative input device such as an expanded keyboard. When the task is completed, the computer displays the finished picture in full color, accompanied by animations. The computer, in this example, provides the teacher with an alternative delivery system.

Other tools to help older students meet educational requirements are word processors that have built-in speech capabilities. Frequently students are required to write an assignment, proof it, edit it, and then publish the final copy. This is a difficult assignment for a large percentage of the school population, regardless of grade, age, or ability level. Talking word processors can make the editing process possible for students with visual impairments and less difficult for those students who cannot detect their own errors when they reread their own texts. Hearing their writing read back to them gives some students the support they need to find their errors and make corrections. *Write: OutLoud* from Don Johnston Incorporated (Wauconda, IL) is a talking word processor that goes one step further and includes a talking spellcheck routine. This has proved to be one of the most effective editing tools available for students who need to improve their spelling skills. In addition to providing a list of suggested words, *Write:OutLoud* will read the list to help the student narrow the selection.

Ultimately, if software is chosen with selection criteria such as (a) the individual needs of the students, (b) the established curriculum, and (c) the teaching style of the teacher, and then, if the software is used effectively by the teacher with the student, it becomes a viable instructional tool. Some examples of how technology can be used to meet educational requirements are described below.

Educational requirement: automaticity in recall of basic facts

The most common use of computers in education is to provide additional drill and practice on content the classroom teacher has already taught. Drill and practice software programs can very effectively meet the needs of students who require extensive repetition before they can master a particular concept or skill. Research indicates that students will spend twice as much time on repetitive drill presented on the computer than on pencil and paper tasks. Critics of drill and practice programs frequently refer to them as nothing more than electronic flash cards, but for students who cannot access standard writing tools, such programs can make the difference between simply being exposed to educational concepts and actually mastering them. Again, a major consideration is *how* the programs are used in the educational situation.

Educational requirement: development of problem-solving strategies

Once children have been identified as special learners, educators often focus their instructional programming on the mastery of academic information through teaching strategies such as repetition, using alternative teaching materials, and reducing the level of expectation. Doing this to the exclusion of other aspects of the child's cognitive development can diminish tremendous learning potential. Software programs that allow students to explore different approaches to solving a problem, analyze the strategies being used to reach the solution, and promote the attitude of risk taking are especially important to a total curriculum. A popular software program used in elementary through high school grades that encourages these skills is *The Factory* and *The Super Factory* from Sunburst Communications (Pleasantville, NY). Students design factories, create products, and issue challenges to their friends while learning to solve problems by thinking ahead, developing insights into spatial relationships, using visual planning strategies, and learning to break problems down into parts. In *The Super Factory* this all takes place in a three-dimensional world as students construct products out of cubes, analyze and identify sequences, and discover the concepts of rotation and rotational symmetry. Little keyboard use is required, so concept mastery is the program's focus rather than keyboarding skills. The programs work with the Personal Touch Window™, which further reduces distracters and allows learners to touch the options on the screen to make choices.

Educational requirement: social interaction with others

Isolation that students with special needs often experience does not result in an effective teaching and/or learning situation. The computer can provide an avenue for integrating students with special needs with the larger student population. Perhaps the most exciting learning with computers is reflected not in increased academic performance but rather in the quality of interactions resulting from computer use with groups of children. The standard configuration for computers in classes to date is one computer per classroom rather than one computer per child. At the elementary level especially, this is an advantage because the situation fosters improved communication skills and increased strategies for establishing social interaction. Tom Snyder Productions (Watertown, MA) created the *Decisions, Decisions*™ series specifically for the one-computer classroom. In this series students take on roles such as president of a country, mayor, or advertising executive as they face a different set of challenges in various situations.

Another Tom Snyder series for younger children is *Choices, Choices*™. These programs focus on everyday situations faced by children and when used by a skillful teacher can teach critical social skills and responsibilities as they help students enhance their communication strategies. For example, in *Choices, Choices: On the Playground,* the new kid at school doesn't fit in, so students explore and discuss the situation and their reaction to it. Various options are open to them. Do they ignore him, do they help him, do they invite him to join in, or do they make fun of him? Students can talk about and develop communication skills as they learn about cause-and-effect relationships in the context of discussing their own feelings, behaviors and responsibilities. In addition, problem-solving and/or simulation software such as *The Magic School Bus*™ series from Scholastic Inc. (New York, NY) lends itself to group situations more readily than do ditto sheets and workbook assignments. Providing a role for each participant in the group can allow the student with special needs to make use of his or her strengths and as a result can develop self-esteem for the student and new respect from other group members.

The latest tool used by educators to foster social interaction extends beyond the classroom and reaches into cyberspace. The Internet is seen by many to be one of the most far-reaching electronic handshakes known. Students are no longer limited to individuals in their school, community, state, or country; they literally have access to interact with people from all over the globe. This tool forces teachers to take on different roles in their jobs as educators, for they are not necessarily the students' primary source of information any longer. If students want to know about events in another country, they can simply log on to the Internet, locate a World Wide Web site, and interact with someone living the event. The power of this communication tool was demonstrated during an upheaval in the former Soviet Union. A group of hearing-impaired students in Australia had been in communication with a group of schoolchildren in Moscow over a period of time. During the coup attempt, the newspapers and radio and TV stations were shut down, but the phone lines remained open. The teachers from the Russian school joined their students to interact directly with the hearing-impaired students because they were desperate for information about the events taking place in their own country. The hearing-impaired students had access to the news and relayed the information back to the school in Moscow. Their former social interactions suddenly became a vital link for these electronic penpals and the outside world.

As the use of the Internet becomes more established in educational programs, teachers will need to examine their roles within the context of this information explosion. Traditionally teachers were able to have some reasonable control over the information their students were receiving, but with all the advances in technology and the availability of hundreds of commercial TV channels, students are being bombarded with information. Teachers will need to take on the responsibility of helping them access the information, classify it, critically evaluate it, and then internalize and generalize material selected. This role is made more difficult by teachers themselves not having the expertise necessary to use the Internet effectively and not having the skills to manage the quantity of data available.

Using Technology to Enhance Instruction

Technology may also be used to enhance instructional practices in the classroom. Examples of how this enhancement may occur are described below.

Instructional need: presentation of material in developmental sequence

Once a curriculum goal has been set, it is the teachers' responsibility to determine how to separate it into manageable objectives as they present it to their students. But the size of these segments may or may not match the learning needs of each student in the class. Some may be able to master the material when it is presented in large conceptual units, but others may need minute, step-by-step instructions. Excellent software tools are available in some curriculum areas to accommodate these individual differences in learning. The value these programs can have is illustrated in the situation where a child consistently makes computational errors in math whenever regrouping to the next column or columns is required. In this case, the teacher often bases an instructional intervention on the assumption that the child has not mastered basic math facts, which is not accurate. This cycle will persist until the specific errors the child is making are analyzed and this can take up significant time for the teacher. Carefully selected programs can provide detailed information on the errors the student makes so that the teaching intervention can be focused on the specific problem areas rather than on the entire process of "basic math facts."

Instructional need: varying rates of presenting material

To maintain student motivation and increase performance, it is critical that the teacher realize when the student has mastered a given concept and is ready to move on to the next level. Computer software programs such as the *Brick by Brick: Reading*® and *Brick by*

Brick: Math® series from Hartley (San Diego, CA) make this easy for both student and teacher. The Instructional Management System available for these programs allows the educator to customize the curriculum to meet the needs of individual students. By providing detailed reports on the progress of all students, the program allows teachers to identify students having difficulty with content and those doing well. The reading programs provide performance information in the areas of vocabulary, usage, and comprehension. In the mathematics programs information is provided in numeration, operations, geometry, and measurement. Pre- and posttests help determine placement and mastery of content, and in the math series branching tutorials help students review basics they might have missed through traditional instruction. Some of the most powerful features of the *Brick by Brick: Math®* program are (a) help screens; (b) instructive, corrective feedback; (c) an on-line calculator; and (d) optional digitized audio, which provides clear, precise instructions and help. The management system features automatic, multilevel, diagnostic placement for individual students based on their performance. All these features free teachers from some of the tedious details of record keeping and allow them to focus on instruction and meeting the needs of their diverse student population.

Instructional need: interactions with out-of-school situations

Computers and software are not the only technology-related instructional materials making a difference in how instruction is being delivered. Educational videotapes and videodisks can enhance instruction by bringing real-life situations and environments to the classroom. Videotapes add realistic pictures, action, and sound to enliven curriculum teaching and learning situations. With the increased ease of use of videocameras, the greater portability of the cameras, and the reduction in videotape cost, this medium is becoming more available to teachers. Videodisk technology differs from videotape in that the images are permanently burned into a laser disc and are indexed so that a single frame or one sequence out of thousands can be accessed instantly. A teacher who wants a segment of the video to illustrate a point need not fast-forward or fast-reverse a tape; instead, the teacher enters the number of the frame into the videodisk player, and the video is displayed. Hofmeister and Thorkildsen (1987), two pioneers in interactive technology, clarify a major difference between videodisk and videotape technology: videodisk systems allow "both a massive storage capacity and fast random-access facility to combined instructional functions of videotape players and film and slide projectors" (p. 191). Students can interact with instruction in this format in many ways. So far this new medium has only begun to penetrate educational programs. Specific applications of this technology pertaining to persons with disabilities have included assessment, academics, and social skills (Hofmeister & Thorkildsen, 1987). The entry of CD-ROM technology into the educational scene has greatly impacted the use of videodisk systems and may prove to displace them as the system of choice.

Instructional need: alternative presentation and assessment tools

In addition to interactive videodisk technology there are some exciting new materials available for classroom presentations and assessment. New interactive multimedia production and presentation tools are currently making a tremendous impact on the educational scene. CD-ROM equipment previously was considered optional peripherals for computers but now has become part of the standard package, and CD-ROM-based material for education is rapidly expanding. Students in the early primary grades can easily learn to use the new authoring tools to create slide shows incorporating text, sound, graphics, and live video. Where written reports have traditionally been the standard, more and more students are putting together multimedia presentations to demonstrate their mastery of information. *Kid Pix® Studio,* a product Brøderbund (Novato, CA) advertised for users from pre-kindergarden to grade 12, makes putting together a multimedia presentation child's play. Students have painting tools, scaleable construction tools, over 100 video clips, songs, and sound effects, 14 different fonts, and animation tools, all of which can be used to create productions that integrate animation, video, special effects, photos, music, and sound. Students can begin their electronic portfolio as early as kindergarten. Scholastic Inc. actually produces *Electronic Portfolio,* a software system to assist teachers in creating, managing, and showcasing multimedia student portfolios.

SOFTWARE FOR CURRICULUM SUBJECT AREAS

Another major consideration in using computer technology is how the teacher can enhance instruction in each curriculum area through the careful selection of educational software. Some excellent programs are available for the different curriculum areas. Skillfully applied, they become valuable assets for the classroom teacher. When evaluating educational software programs, teachers need to remember the diversity of their students' needs and select programs that will aid in meeting those needs while implementing the students' individual instructional plans.

Written Language Skills

One of the most promising uses for computers in the curriculum for all learners is in language arts. Every major educational journal has published research and descriptive articles on using word processing programs to improve students' reading and writing skills, including students who have been identified for special education services. This application of computer technology may well be the most important reason to have computers in the schools. Teachers are enthusiastically reporting that students approach the task of writing with a more positive attitude. They are willing, and in some instances eager, to edit what they have written. They write more, and they express themselves more clearly than with pencil and paper.

Standard features of word processing programs

There are a variety of word processing programs that have standard features such as word wrap, use of different fonts, ability to change size of fonts, line-spacing options, spellcheck, and alignment choices. Most will allow users to specify what style of type they want to include: **bold,** *italic,* underlined, outlined, and shadow. Popular word processing programs in elementary schools are *The Student Writing Center* from The Learning Company, *AppleWorks* and *ClarisWorks* from Claris, Inc. (Cupertino, CA) and *Microsoft Works* from Microsoft, Inc. (Redmond, WA). These programs have the standard features of word processing programs, are easy to use, and have extensive published supportive materials for classroom use. Many middle and high school programs have chosen to use integrated software programs such as *ClarisWorks* and *Microsoft Works* because they contain data management, spreadsheet, communication and graphics programs as well as a word processor. *The Student Writing Center* from Learning Company (Cambridge, MA) is popular with language arts teachers who require their students to generate a bibliography with their written reports. *The Bibliography Maker* in it allows users simply to type in source information, and the program accurately formats each new entry alphabetically.

Assistive writing tools

Some word processing programs were developed specifically for use with students with special needs. Many students who do not have identified special needs also benefit from the use of these programs. *IntelliTalk,* a very simple word processing program from Intellitools (Novato, CA), defines ease of use as it adds speech and different-color text to students' writing. *Write:OutLoud* from Don Johnston, Incorporated is another talking word processor, and the computer not only speaks the text that has been generated but it also reads the menu items that are displayed as icons at the top of the screen. One of the problems with most other talking programs is that the computer will speak the text that has been entered and will perform a spellcheck on the data, but the spellchecker is silent. Children who have difficulty spelling will most likely have difficulty determining which of the displayed choices in the spellcheck routine are correct. This is avoided in *Write:OutLoud,* for each component is designed to provide the maximum support for writers through speech output and icon-based program commands. Another particularly useful feature of the spellcheck routine is that the unfamiliar word is displayed in context, so the user has the additional support of the sentence being displayed and the option to have the sentence read again in isolation.

One of the most powerful assistive writing tools available for students with special needs is *Co:Writer,* an intelligent word prediction program from Don Johnston, Incorporated. *Co:Writer* works in conjunction with word processing programs to increase typing speed and decrease frustration and fatigue. The user simply types in a letter and *Co:Writer* gives logical word choices that fit the sentence. Word predictions are based on subject-verb agreement, grammar rules, word relationships, proper names, frequency, and user preference.

Word processing for primary students

Some of the most exciting programs are greatly impacting the writing produced by students in the primary grades. *Kid Works 2* from Davidson and Associates (Torrance, CA) combines word processing, a paint program, and voice, all in one writing tool for students up to grade 4. Children can create their own story and hear the computer read it back to them. They can illustrate their work with a clever drawing program complete with sound effects. If children want to use "electronic rubber stamps," they are part of the effects in the drawing program. While they are writing, they can use icons to illustrate their story, or they can write text and then have the computer change the words into pictures. Simply by clicking on one icon, all the words that have a picture associated with them in the program become pictures. From the "dust buster" that vacuums the screen clean to the spraycan that sprays graffiti-like marks, the icons "make sense" to the children.

Creative Writer from Microsoft is another excellent program to stimulate students to write. This program is far more than a simple word processing program. It's full of graphics, colorful patterns, zany ideas for stories, powerful text tools, and sounds that students can use to write a letter, tell a story, create a newspaper, and/or design a card or a banner. Clever pop-up "help" balloons reduce the learning curve for *Creative Writer,* and icon menus offer some options usually found only in expensive, desktop publishing programs. *Creative Writer* will help students produce some very professional-looking finished documents in full color.

Teachers from kindergarten to grade 5 are finding that *Storybook Weaver* from MECC (Minneapolis, MN) is a tremendous addition to their writing program. *Storybook Weaver* allows students to create a background, add graphics and sound, and then write a story. The process of thinking through the story, selecting the appropriate background, and then choosing graphics to illustrate a point is a learning process in and of itself. Students who do not like to draw or who have difficulty with pencil and paper can produce professional-looking illustrated stories using this program.

Readiness Skills

Computers are being used successfully with very young children to assist in developing reading and math readiness skills and to encourage the use of critical thinking skills.

There are numerous programs available in math readiness. Some of the skills to be developed at this stage are matching, counting, number recognition, patterning, shapes, discrimination, and simple problem solving. It is important to look for programs that allow children to explore without penalty, develop basic levels of understanding, practice new skills, test out hypotheses, and receive positive corrective feedback and encouragement. Edmark (Redmond, WA) incorporated many of these principles in the six different activities of *Millie's Math House™*. This program also provides spoken directions and feedback so that reading ability is not a factor in mastering the content. There are exploratory exercises in sequencing, shape recognition, sizing, recognizing and completing patterns, and counting. The animated graphics are colorful, add to the understanding of the content, and are appropriate for the young child target audience.

There is a profusion of reading readiness programs. Some of the most popular with children are the CD-ROM-based *Living Books* series from Brøderbund. This series has multiple titles including *Just Grandma and Me, The Tortoise and the Hare, The New Kid on the Block,* and *Arthur's Teacher Trouble.* Each title is based on stories and books of proven literary value and appeal to children. The exact text from the book is displayed on the screen and is read to the student as each page is turned. There are many child-controlled options on each page. A simple point and click of the mouse will offer music, sound effects, and animated graphics.

Discovery-based and problem-solving programs such as *Thinkin' Things Collection 1, 2* and *3, The Treehouse™, The Playroom™,* and *The Backyard™* from Edmark (Redmond, WA) allow children to explore possibilities, learn classification principles, and develop expertise in following directions. It is important for all learners to experience success and be encouraged to take risks to test out a hypothesis they might have. Problem-solving and discovery programs facilitate these curriculum objectives.

Science

Due to physical limitations, problems with hand-eye coordination, or a visual impairment, many youngsters are excluded from science classes or projects involving gathering data or conducting experiments. *The Science Toolkit* from Brøderbund has made many scientific experiments and observations accessible to special learners. *The Science Toolkit* includes the software, a user's manual and experiment guide, an interface box for the computer, a temperature probe, and a light probe. Students from elementary through high school can take part in scientific experiments while using the computer in much the same way scientists use it to collect and interpret data.

Sammy's Science House (Edmark) introduces young students to the exciting world of scientific discovery. Teaching science in the early primary classes sometimes takes a backseat to other curriculum areas such as reading and math, and when asked to explain why, many teachers respond that they "don't have the right materials" or "don't really feel comfortable teaching science" or "feel that science will be taught in the higher grades and right now we need to concentrate on reading and writing." These are very narrow viewpoints and easily discounted when children can enter *Sammy's Science House* and experience the wonder that comes with making discoveries about their environment; design, plan, and construct machinery; investigate seasonal impact on plants and animals; manipulate weather variables and see the results of their decisions; categorize plants, animals, birds, and minerals; and actually make a movie and critique the results. There are literally thousands of things that can be done with this program, and the *Curriculum Connections* activities that come as part of the documentation illustrate the tip of the possibilities iceberg. *Sammy's Science House* can be integrated into art, creative dramatics, language arts, mathematics, music, physical education, problem solving, science, and social studies. In addition, there are reproducible activity sheets and reproducible pages of *Science House* characters to use on the bulletin board.

CD-ROM technology provides multimedia exposure to science in programs such as *A.D.A.M.® Essentials* and *A.D.A.M.® The Inside Story™* (A.D.A.M. Company: Atlanta, GA). Middle and high school students can use *Essentials* to explore human anatomy and learn how the various systems work. *Essentials* helps students identify over 3,600 anatomic structures, prompts exploration of the 12 major body systems, encourages understanding of the inner workings of complex systems through the use of animated graphics, and assists in vocabulary development with audio identification of various structures. *Inside Story* provides much of the same information found in *Essentials,* but does so at a less complex level so that it is appropriate for younger students.

The Voyages of the Mimi from Sunburst (Pleasantville, NY) are excellent tools that promote multimedia interdisciplinary study. The first voyage of the *Mimi* uses a story of a scientific expedition to study whales as its main theme, and the second voyage takes students on an archaeological expedition in search of a lost Mayan city. Both programs use videotapes, videodisks, software, student support books, teaching guides, and instructional support material.

Social Studies and Geography

One curriculum goal in social studies requires students to gather and retain massive amounts of information about various countries. Traditionally this has meant that students must memorize the names of states, capitals, important cities, and natural formations and be able to list, label, or locate them on a map. Rote memorization of this material out of context is difficult for most students, and the retention rate is abysmal. Technology, in the form of cleverly designed software, can diminish many of the problems associated with listing, labeling, and locating the sites on a map outline as well as generate enthusiasm for the study of geography, history, and cultures. Brøderbund's Carmen Sandiego series has been a major factor in engaging students in the study of geography and history. *Where in the USA Is Carmen Sandiego?* (grades 4–12) encourages students to gather data about all 50 states and the District of Columbia from the computer screen and from the *Fodor Travel Guide of the United States* as they chase Carmen Sandiego and her V.I.L.E. henchmen to recover stolen treasures. Students analyze clues related to history, geography, economy, and culture to determine their travel direction. *Where in the World Is Carmen Sandiego?* (grades 4–12) pushes beyond the U.S. borders and entices students to explore dozens of the world's greatest cities and cultures. The most difficult of the Carmen Sandiego series takes students on an adventure into the cosmos. *Where in Space Is Carmen Sandiego?* (grades 6–12) incorporates mythology behind the constellations, facts and features of 32 locations in the solar system, and the current science of planetary exploration. Digitized NASA photographs and the VAL 9000 database introduce students to real-life scientific images and to the functional use of a data management system. For junior players (pre-kindergarten through grade 3) Brøderbund offers *Carmen Sandiego Junior Detective Edition,* which does not require reading but does require memory, strategy, and matching ability. Seven regions of the world are explored in terms of agricultural products, geographical features, landmarks, and cultural events, among other things. The learning of facts, figures, history, and geographical locations becomes like a game in this series, and as a result, the students are more involved in the learning, gather information across the disciplines, and retain more of the information they encounter.

Students who experience difficulty looking up information in an atlas will find using *Maps 'N' Facts*™ from Brøderbund an excellent alternative. This software provides not only a comprehensive world atlas but a vast database of information about the different regions and specific countries. Once students have learned where the different countries, states, or cities are located, they can move on to *ZipZapMap!,* a computer game from National Geographic (Washington, DC) in which the task is to place major geographic features in their correct location on an outline map.

Math

Most math curricula cover everything from the mastery of basic math facts through advanced algebra and calculus to high-level problem-solving skills. Numerous software programs address readiness and computation skills, but relatively few high-quality programs support the development of math problem-solving skills.

Computation

The majority of computation programs are in the form of drill and practice. One of the most popular of all these is from Davidson and Associates. *New Math Blaster Plus!* provides four learning activities in which the student can practice more than 750 math facts in addition, subtraction, multiplication, division, fractions, decimals, and percents. The program has record-keeping capabilities, will print out Certificates of Excellence, and has graphic reinforcements in all activities. Perhaps the best feature of *New Math Blaster Plus!* is the editor, which allows the teacher or student to enter problems that become part of the four activities. Milliken (St. Louis, MO) produces one of the most widely used drill and practice software programs for math. *Math Sequences* has many user options that make it suitable for a wide range of ages and abilities. The program automatically adjusts for the difficulty level depending on the performance of the user. The series covers everything from readiness to equations and can be used from first to twelfth grades.

Algebra

Traditional software programs for algebra have been drill and practice with little branching capabilities, but many students find *AlgeBlaster* and *AlgeBlaster Plus!* from Davidson and Associates a challenging, fun way to practice concepts presented in class. Teachers like the editor function, which allows them to enter their own problems in concert with their curriculum. Sensei™ moved one step further with *Algebra,* which incorporates explorations and tutorials with the standard drill. This program is especially helpful for students who have difficulty visualizing abstract concepts. In the exploration function, students can see situations animated as they experiment with different possibilities and discover relationships. LOGAL™ Software (Cambridge, MA) adds another dimension to the study of algebra with the *Tangible Math Series. Algebra Animator,* according to the developers and numerous middle and high school teachers, allows "students to use dynamic environments to construct objects, conduct experiments, and collect and analyze data in order to discover what happens when objects are set in motion. They can make predictions, test conjectures, and even develop their own theorems based on the results of numerous observations" (Rosin & Shenkerman, 1994, p. iii). This outstanding software program engages students, provides a powerful teaching tool for the teacher, and can serve to break the invisible "algebra barrier" many students feel they have to overcome in order to comprehend the language and concepts involved in this discipline.

Geometry

There are numerous geometry and higher math software programs and Internet web sites to support student learning. Softouch Software (Nepean, ON, CAN) has a "visual" series for functions, geometry, quadratics and trigonometry. Tutorials provide a text explanation, related formulas and graphic representations of fundamental concepts in geometry. Ventura Educational Systems (Grover Beach, CA) offers Geometry Concepts and Coordinate Geometry to help students master difficult concepts by providing interactive tutorials and learning games.

The Math Forum (http://www.forum.swarthmore.edu), an interactive web site sponsored by Swarthmore College, is an excellent resource for students and teachers. Their "Problem of the Week" project encourages students to solve geometry problems and to submit them to the web site for viewing by others. The site has a HELP section for teachers and students as well as a Recognitions and Awards feature.

PRACTICAL GUIDELINES FOR SELECTING SOFTWARE

After computers were introduced into the educational system, it did not take long for educators to realize that technology, in and of itself, was not going to make the radical changes promised in the media. Serious issues were raised about equity in access, the role of technology in the classroom, training of teachers, the interface of technology with existing curriculum goals and objectives, and the changes that technology would facilitate in the development of new and effective teaching strategies and instructional material. Slowly the industry and the education community came to realize that bigger and better machines were not going to provide the answer to these questions, but that many of them could be addressed through the development of academically sound, challenging, interactive software programs. This set the stage for the role of the teacher in this process. Once again teachers were faced with the need to evaluate, assess, and select educational materials that would complement their curriculum.

Selection guides, checklists, and evaluation criteria abound in the technology literature. These are helpful in determining some of the aspects of software, but the most critical elements in software evaluation and selection are frequently ignored in these reviews. What is important is how effective the software will be in enhancing the learning of the students and how it can be used to facilitate the acquisition of information or expand the thought processes involved in solving a problem. Frequently the answers to these questions are found not in the software program itself but in the clever way a teacher uses it to reach curriculum goals. The following practical suggestions regarding software selection reflect the thinking and experience of educators who are first of all excellent teachers and, secondarily, respected users of technology:

- Never follow the advice of a teacher who consistently "puts down" students, especially students with special needs. Anyone who cannot understand that students come to school with varying abilities cannot be trusted to select educational material that can be used by the diverse population in schools today.
- Always ask clever, creative teachers what they are using in their classrooms. If it works for them, it might work for you. If you have problems, you have a ready resource available to help you resolve the difficulties.
- Talk to students who use technology and see what they enjoy using at home and in school.
- Always ask for a preview privilege when ordering software. Many companies will allow you a 30-day preview. During that time period, use the software with your students to see how they respond. Evaluate it in terms of your curriculum goals and objectives.
- Visit as many classrooms as possible where computers are being used and check out their programs. This strategy will also give you an opportunity to see how the teacher and students are using the software.
- Make a list of software you have heard about, and then ask different selected teachers about those specific programs.
- Read reviews written by people you respect in the field.
- Call the software company representatives and talk to them.
- Know what curriculum goal or objective you want the software to help address before you make any decisions or contacts about it at all.

Those are just a few guidelines to use in the selection of software. Every educator must decide which are important and which will work in her or his environment. The important point to remember is that ultimately all instructional materials—from textbooks to technology—are just tools and, like all other tools, can work magic in the hands of a master.

CHAPTER SUMMARY

This chapter introduces teachers to the fascinating realm of uses of computers and other related technology to meet curricular needs of students with disabilities and special needs. It explains some operational and curriculum barriers to computer use, along with ways teachers might avoid or overcome them and move on to the use of computers in functional ways in their instruction. The chapter covers strategies for teaching with technology to break the failure cycles of students who have learning difficulties, to meet individual needs through modification of options such as speed of presentation and size of image on screen, to use the computer to meet educational requirements of identifying and meeting unique needs of individuals, and generally to enhance instruction. Finally, the chapter identifies specific software and other technological materials and explains their uses in meeting needs of students with special needs. Vignettes and very practical, stimulating suggestions highlight the chapter.

CHAPTER 19

Application Activities Organized by Chapter

In this chapter we present an application activity for each of the previous eighteen chapters. The application activities challenge you to analyze, synthesize, and evaluate information from the text, and then combine that information with class and field experiences to respond to the kinds of questions, issues, problems, and dilemmas that educators face. The application activities may be completed individually, by small groups, or by a large group. You can present your final responses in multiple formats—oral presentations, posters or other visual displays, written reports or handouts, or other ways as appropriate.

CHAPTER 1

Return to the scenes of special education at the beginning of this chapter and identify the services, modifications, and other supports that are in place to support the students' success in the described learning environments. Next, identify the type of plan that you believe each student has. Using the information provided, attempt to specify at least one goal and one objective that you believe each student has worked on in the past, is currently working toward, and will be working on in the future. Who do you think was or is involved in the development, implementation, and evaluation of these individualized plans? What do you identify as the LRE for each student? If you were a member of a team, what would your suggestions be for future interventions and supports for these students?

CHAPTER 2

Meet with a special education teacher to talk about the curriculum options in which his or her students are involved and the types of IEP goals and objectives developed for these students. From this information, create a profile or a composite of an actual child enrolled in this program. Develop a course of study form for the student, using the format presented in Exhibit 2.10. Additionally, specify the standards, goals, and outcomes for each area of the child's curriculum and their sources. From this profile and analysis, what other curricular areas and goals, outcomes, and standards do you identify as priorities for this student? How would you go about including them in the student's course of study?

CHAPTER 3

Observe in a general education classroom, attending to the following:

1. the curricular area(s) being addressed

2. the structure of the curriculum

3. modification and adaptations made in the curriculum to allow for access by students with and without disabilities

How successful is the teacher in presenting this curriculum to the range of students in the classroom? If students with disabilities are included in the classroom (or are to be included), how do they fare (or would they fare) in this environment? What recommendations and suggestions do you have for the teacher to modify the curriculum more effectively in order to reach more students in the classroom? What specific curricular modification procedures would you use and why?

CHAPTER 4

Imagine you are a special education teacher for a group of middle school students who exhibit a range of disabilities. Although the students are included in various general education classrooms and participate in the general education curriculum with and without modifications, you are concerned that they are in need of curricular augmentation in the form of life skills instruction. You do not want to remove the students from their general education experiences to participate in this curriculum but you believe they could benefit from a focus on functional academics, daily and community living skills, and transition education. Select one or two skills from each of the three areas of the life skills curriculum and indicate how you, as a special education teacher, would work with the general education teacher to incorporate these skills, understandings, and knowledge into existing general education experiences. Present your plan to a general education teacher for feedback.

CHAPTER 5

Curriculum in modified means of communication and performance represents curricular areas that can apply to all individuals with disabilities. Review the five components of this curricular area and explain how these areas apply to students with mild to moderate disabilities (e.g., learning disabilities, mild cognitive impairment), students with moderate to severe disabilities (e.g., severe cognitive impairment), and students with low incidence disabilities (e.g., physical and health disabilities, deaf or hard-of-hearing, visual impairments). What unique and collaborative roles do you believe general and special education teachers and related service providers should have in order to implement the development, implementation, and evaluation of curriculum interventions in the area of modified means of communication and performance? How would these curricular needs be identified and included in a child's individualized plan or program? How would you integrate these curricular needs with the other three curricular options—general education, general education with modifications, and life skills? What mechanisms would you put into place to ensure these curricular needs are addressed in the general education classroom and in other settings in which students with disabilities are participants? How would you encourage general educator/family/paraprofessional aide participation in the delivery and support of this curriculum for individuals with disabilities?

CHAPTER 6

andContact a local school or special education office to obtain information and forms related to its prereferral and referral procedures. Using this material and information from this textbook and other sources, develop a handbook for parents that describes the prereferral and referral process, including IEP development.

CHAPTER 7

Imagine you have been asked to serve as an outside consultant for a district's special education program. Your job is to evaluate the district's current policies and programs related to special education eligibility, annual reviews and reevaluations, and program evaluation procedures. Develop an evaluation plan that includes the following components:

- Purpose of the evaluation and its subcomponents
- How information will be used
- Questions to be addressed
- Information sources, including informants, to be accessed
- How information will be analyzed

Your plan must reflect the special education law (the IDEA Amendments of 1997) and demonstrate understanding of the basic procedures related to each activity (e.g., prereferral, referral, annual reviews, reevaluations, and program evaluation). Also, the plan must address the adoption of assessment methods and tools for use in decision making.

CHAPTER 8

Develop a case study of a student referred for eligibility testing. First, complete a referral form to clarify the areas of concern. Next, develop an assessment plan that includes questions to be asked as well as assessment methods and tools to be used in data gathering. Review selected tools for their properties, analyzing them in terms of the ADS model. Additionally, examine the manuals of selected instruments to determine exactly what developers claim is being tested and how, and how this information will be used to respond to generated questions. Develop those instruments not commercially available but included in your plan (e.g., interviews, checklists). Present your case study to a peer for review. Justify your assessment plan and tool selection. After the presentation and peer review, reflect by making changes to your plan to reflect new insights and to respond to questions raised by your peer. Finally, reflect on how this process would be carried out when you are actually working with this student. What recommendations and suggestions do you have for individuals involved in the assessment process?

CHAPTER 9

Meet with a school psychologist or diagnostician to discuss the interpretation of their testing findings for a selected student. With parental permission, have the school psychologist or diagnostician "walk you through" the tests given and give you their interpretation. Reflect on the experience. What are some things you will remember when you serve on a team charged with gathering and assessing student performance data to determine eligibility and/or continuance in special education programs?

CHAPTER 10

With parental permission, secure a copy of a student's IEP with all identifying information removed. Analyze the IEP goals, benchmarks, and objectives by asking the following questions:

1. To what extent do the goals, benchmarks, and objectives reflect information identified through assessment and provided in the present levels of performance? What, if any, important information is missing?

2. To what extent do the goals, benchmarks, and objectives reflect district, state, and/or national standards, outcomes, and goals? What adjustments do you suggest be made to align the student's goals and objectives more closely with these frameworks?

3. What types of benchmarks and objectives are provided? Are they challenging student thinking and skill performance on a variety of levels (e.g., knowledge, evaluation, performance)? Do they reflect a range of curricular options? What revisions and/or additions would you make to the list of benchmarks and objectives?

4. Do the benchmarks and objectives address the student's participation in authentic activities in natural settings and/or in general education settings? If they do, do they meet the indicators of best practice outlined by Hunt et al. (1986; 1994)? What modifications or revisions do you suggest?

5. To what extent have these goals, benchmarks, and objectives been modified to address the student's unique learning styles and needs?

CHAPTER 11

Reflecting on the information gained in the curriculum and assessment sections of this book (Sections 1 and 2), and integrating it with the information presented in this chapter, consider the needs of an individual with a disability who is to be included in a general education classroom. Given this person's curricular and instructional needs as identified through assessment, specify how you would address the factors presented in this chapter for creating a context conducive to and supportive of learning. Develop a plan for ensuring that these factors are in place in this general education classroom.

CHAPTER 12

Challenge yourself to move through the entire sequence presented in this chapter, culminating in the writing of a lesson plan for a selected student (either real or hypothetical). First, select an objective from the student's IEP. Next, develop this IEP objective into a series of instructional objectives. Then, write a lesson plan to reflect the first instructional objective. Present your plan to a peer for evaluation. Together discuss how your lesson plan reflects either the transmission or the constructivist model. Identify how your plan takes into consideration the curricular needs of the student as identified through assessment and the factors associated with a supportive context for learning. Revise your plan as needed.

CHAPTER 13

Look through curricular materials and select a topic on which you would like to present a lesson. Identify some activities that you might use to teach this material to students. To identify the activities you will include in your lesson, work through both of the chapter's strategies for selecting instructional activities. Compare and contrast the conclusions you reach using each strategy. Finally, select the activities you believe will best convey the lesson and write a lesson plan that includes them. Present your lesson plan to a peer for feedback, or if possible, teach your lesson to a group of students. Reflect on the experience.

CHAPTER 14

Observe a teacher teaching a mathematics class. What strategies did the teacher use when presenting ideas to students? What types of activities were the students engaged in? What did the teacher do to include all students in active participation and learning? Which of the four key components of mathematics were addressed in the lesson? How were they addressed? If any were missing, what could be done to include them? Reflect on the lesson. What do you identify as its greatest strengths and weaknesses? If you were to teach this lesson to a group of students, what changes would you make? Explain *why* you would make them.

CHAPTER 15

Design a plan for supporting a student's continued early literacy development. First, design methods to assess the child's current literacy skills, incorporating a range of approaches (e.g., interviews, observation). Next, implement your assessment plan to identify the student's skills and areas needing development or strengthening. Then, develop an instructional plan for addressing those areas. Share your information with the student's teacher for feedback. If possible, work with the student, implementing your instructional plan.

CHAPTER 16

With the assistance of a general education classroom teacher, identify a student who is experiencing difficulties in reading and/or writing, or both. Meet with the student's teacher to discuss the types of difficulties the child is experiencing and the interventions the teacher has introduced to help this student enhance his or her reading and writing skills. Next, observe the child during a language arts activity. Note the types of difficulties and successes you observe. Also, note the extent to which the child engages in the activities. Then meet with the student to discuss his or her reading and/or writing performance. Ask the student to discuss the activity you observed in order to gain some understanding of the student's perception of his or her ability and willingness to participate in language arts activities. Following analysis and synthesis of your information, imagine you are the student's teacher. What could you do to support this student's success in this general education environment? Develop a plan for addressing this student's needs and, if possible, implement the plan with the student.

CHAPTER 17

Imagine that you are working with a student with a disability who is included in a general education science class (either a real or hypothetical student). The general education teacher welcomed the student to the classroom but is not making any curricular or instructional modifications to include learning strategies, study skills, and life skills. Considering the student's needs (if the student is a hypothetical one, you determine what the child's needs are), identify the learning strategies, study skills, and the life skills curriculum and instructional approaches you would like to see infused into this general education classroom to better support this student with disabilities. Select one area and develop a plan for introducing it and your instructional approaches to the classroom teacher. Share your ideas with a peer or general education teacher for feedback.

CHAPTER 18

Working in a team, gather samples of educational software available for students in a specific curriculum area. Evaluate this software in terms of its application for students with disabilities and its ability to support student development of understanding, skills, and knowledge as they are specified in national, state, and district curricula, as well as in student IEP goals and objectives. How could you use your selected software with students? What accommodations and/or modifications would be necessary? How would you set up instruction in the classroom to incorporate the use of this computer software?

REFERENCES

Anders, P. L., & Bos, C. S. (1986). Semantic feature analysis: An interactive strategy for vocabulary development and text comprehension. *Journal of Reading, 29,* 610–616.

Anderson, V., & Roit, M. (1998). Reading as a gateway to language proficiency for language-minority students in elementary grades. In R. M. Gersten & R. T. Jiménez (Eds.), *Promoting learning for culturally and linguistically diverse students* (pp. 42–56). Belmont, CA: Wadsworth.

Anderson, W., Chitwood, S., & Hayden, D. (1990). *Negotiating the special education maze: A guide for parents and teachers.* Rockville, MD: Woodbine House.

Archer, A., & Gleason, M. (1994). *Skills for school success: Teacher guide.* North Billerica, MA: Curriculum Associates.

Armstrong, T. (1994). *Multiple intelligences in the classroom.* Alexandria, VA: Association for Supervision and Curriculum Development.

Asselin, S. B., Todd-Allen, M., & deFur, S. (1998). Transition coordinators: Define yourselves. *Teaching Exceptional Children, 30*(3), 11–15.

Association of Educational Therapists. (1982). 1482 Ventura Boulevard, Suite 207, Sherman Oaks, CA 91403.

Au, K. H. (1993). *Literacy instruction in multicultural settings.* Fort Worth: Harcourt Brace College Publishers.

Bandura, A. (1982). Self-efficacy mechanism in human agency. *American Psychologist, 37*(2), 122–147.

Barrage, N. C., & Erin, J. N. (1992). *Visual handicaps and learning* (3rd ed.). Austin, TX: PRO-ED.

Barrentine, S. J. (1996). Engaging with reading through interactive read-aloud. *The Reading Teacher, 50*(1), 36–43.

Battish, V., Solomon, D., & Delucchi, K. (1993). Interaction processes and student outcomes in cooperative learning groups. *The Elementary School Journal, 94*(1), 19–32.

Batzle, J. (1992). *Portfolio assessment and evaluation: Developing and using portfolios in the classroom.* Cypress, CA: Creative Teaching Press.

Beakley, B. A., & Yoder, S. L. (1998). Middle schoolers learn community skills. *Teaching Exceptional Children, 30*(3), 16–21.

Beery, K. R. (1989). *The Developmental Test of Visual-Motor Integration, Third Revision.* Austin, TX: PRO-ED.

Bereiter, C., & Englemann, S. (1966). *Teaching disadvantaged children in the preschool.* Englewood Cliffs, NJ: Prentice-Hall.

Betts, E. A. (1946). *Foundations of reading instruction.* New York: American Books.

Bigge, J. (1988). *Curriculum based instruction for special education students.* Mountain View, CA: Mayfield.

Bigge, J. (1991). *Teaching individuals with physical and multiple disabilities* (3rd ed.). New York: Merrill.

Bishop, K. D., Amate, S. L., & Villalobos, P. J. (1995). Postsecondary considerations. In M. A. Falvey (Ed.), *Inclusive and heterogeneous schooling: Assessment, curriculum, and instruction* (pp. 363–393). Baltimore: Paul H. Brookes.

Bos, C. S., & Vaughn, S. (1994). *Strategies for teaching students with learning and behavior problems* (3rd ed.). Boston: Allyn and Bacon.

Boschee, F., & Baron, M. A. (1993). *Outcome-based education: Developing programs through strategic planning.* Lancaster, PA: Technomic Publishing.

Bracey, G. W. (1983). On the compelling need to go beyond minimum competency. *Phi Delta Kappan, 64*(10), 712–717.

Bridge, C. A., Winograd, P. N., & Haley, D. (1983). Using predictable materials vs. preprimers to teach beginning sight words. *The Reading Teacher, 36*(9), 854–890.

Brigance Systems. Albert Brigance. North Billerica, MA: Curriculum Associates, Inc.

Brolin, D. E. (Ed.). (1991). *Life centered career education: A competency based approach* (3rd ed.). Reston, VA: Council for Exceptional Children.

Brooks, J. G., & Brooks, M. G. (1993). *In search of understanding: The case of constructivist classrooms.* Alexandria, VA: Association for Supervision and Curriculum Development.

Browder, D. M., & Snell, M. E. (1993). Functional academics. In M. E. Snell (Ed.), (4th ed.), *Instruction of students with severe disabilities* (pp. 442–475). New York, NY: Merrill.

Brown, V. L., Cronin, M. E., & McEntire, E. (1994). *Test of Mathematical Abilities, Second Edition.* Austin, TX: PRO-ED.

Bruininks, R. H. (1978). *Bruininks-Oseretsky test of motor proficiency.* Circle Pines, MN: American Guidance Service.

Burke, L. J. (1996). Using strategies and services for success in college. *Attention!, 3*(2), 23–27.

Burns, M. (1992a). *Math and literature (K–3).* White Plains, NY: Math Solutions Publications.

Burns, M. (1992b). *About teaching mathematics: A K–8 resource.* White Plains, NY: Math Solutions Publications.

Butler, K. A. (1986). *Learning and teaching style: In theory and practice.* Columbia, CT: Learner's Dimension.

Butterworth, J., Hagner, D., Kiernan, W. E., & Schalock, R. L. (1996). Natural supports in the workplace: Defining an agenda for research and practice. *JASH, 21*(3), 103–113.

Buzolich, M. J., & Higginbotham, K. J. (1985). *Analyzing and facilitating the communicative competence of augmentative system users.* Short course presented at the Annual Convention of the American Speech-Language-Hearing Association, Washington, DC.

California Department of Education. (1978a). Steps in devising differential standards. In *Developing proficiency standards for pupils in special education programs: Workshop outline and agenda.* Sacramento: Author.

California Department of Education. (1978b). *Developing proficiency standards for pupils in special education programs.* Sacremento, CA: Author.

California Department of Education. (1992). *History–social science: K–12 goals and curriculum standards.* Sacramento: Author.

California Department of Education. (1996). *California special education programs: A composite of laws* (18th ed.). Sacramento: Author.

Campione, J. C. (1989). Assisted assessment: A taxonomy of approaches and an outline of strengths and weaknesses. *Journal of Learning Disabilities, 22,* 151–165.

Campione, J. C., & Brown, A. L. (1987). Linking dynamic assessment with school achievement. In C. S. Lidz (Ed.), *Dynamic assessment.* New York: Guilford Publications.

Carbo, M., Dunn, R., & Dunn, K. (1986). *Teaching students to read through their individual learning styles.* Needham Heights, MA: Allyn and Bacon.

Carter, J. F. (1993). Self-management: Education's ultimate goal. *Teaching Exceptional Children, 25*(3), 28–32.

Cawelti, G. (1993). *Challenges and achievements of American education.* Alexandria, VA: Association for Supervision and Curriculum Development.

Chamblee, G. (1997). Predicting year 2000 populations of California and the United States. *The California Mathematics Council CommuniCator, 22*(4), 56–57.

Chandler, L. K. (1993). Steps in preparing for transition: Preschool to kindergarten. *Teaching Exceptional Children, 25*(4), 52–54.

Chittenden, E. (1991). Authentic assessment, evaluation and documentation of student performance. In V. Perrone (Ed.), *Expanding student assessment* (pp. 23–31). Alexandria: Association for Supervision and Curriculum Development.

Choate, J. S., Enright, B. E., Miller, L. J., Poteet, J. A., & Rakes, T. A. (1995). *Curriculum-based assessment and programming* (3rd ed.). Boston: Allyn and Bacon.

Ciborowski, J. (1995). Using textbooks with students who cannot read them. *Remedial and Special Education, 16,* 90–101.

Clark, F. L., Deshler, D. D., Schumaker, J. B., Alley, G. R., & Warner, M. M. (1984). Visual imagery and self-questioning: Strategies to improve comprehension of written material. *Journal of Learning Disabilities, 17,* 145–149.

Clark, G. M. (1994). Is a functional curriculum approach compatible with an inclusive education model? *Teaching Exceptional Children, 26*(2), 36–39.

Clark, S. N., & Clark, D. C. (1994). *Restructuring the middle school: Implications for school leaders.* Albany: State University of New York Press.

Clay, M. M. (1979). *The early detection of reading difficulties* (3rd ed.). Hong Kong: Heinemann.

Clay, M. (1993). *An observation survey of early literacy achievement.* Portsmouth: Heinemann.

Cobb, B., & Hasazi, S. B. (1987). School-aged transition services: Options for adolescents with mild handicaps. *Career Development of Exceptional Individuals, 10,* 15–23.

Cochran, L., Feng, H., Cartledge, G., & Hamilton, S. (1993). The effects of cross-age tutoring on the academic achievement, social behaviors, and self-perceptions of low-achieving African-American males with behavioral disorders. *Behavioral Disorders, 18*(4), 292–302.

College Board Publications. (1983). *Academic preparation for college: What students need to know and be able to do.* Princeton, NJ: Author.

Collett, D. J. (1990). Learning-to-learn needs for adult basic education. In R. M. Smith and Associates, *Learning to learn across the life span.* San Francisco: Jossey-Bass.

Compton, C. (1996). *A guide to 100 tests for special education.* Palo Alto: Globe Fearon.

Conderman, G., & Katsiyannis, A. (1995). Section 504 accommodation plans. *Intervention in School and Clinic, 31*(1), 42–45.

Conejo Valley School District (May, 1994). *Kid friendly math rubric.* Thousand Oaks, CA.

Connolly, A. J. (1988). *KeyMath-Revised: A Diagnostic Inventory of Essential Mathematics.* Circle Pines, MN: American Guidance Service.

Corn, A. L. (1980). *Development and assessment of an in-service training program for teachers of the visually handicapped: Optical aids in the classroom.* Unpublished doctoral dissertation, Teachers College, Columbia University.

Corn, A. L., & Koenig, A. J (Eds.). (1996). *Foundations of low vision: Clinical and functional perspectives.* New York: American Foundation for the Blind.

Copple, C. E., Kane, M., Matheson, N. S., Meltzer, A. S., Packer, A., & White, T. G. (1993). SCANS in the schools: Teaching the SCANS competencies. In *Secretary's commission on achieving necessary skills (SCANS)* (pp. 7–53). Washington, D.C.: U.S. Department of Labor.

Council for Exceptional Children (The). (1995). *What every special educator must know: The international standards for the preparation and certification of special education teachers.* Reston, VA: (Author).

Cowan, C., & Shepler, R. (1990). Techniques for teaching young children to use low vision devices. *Journal of Vision Impairment and Blindness, 84*(9), 419–421.

Cronin, M. E., & Patton, J. R. (1993). *Life skills instruction for all students with special needs: A practical guide for integrating real-life content into the curriculum.* Austin, TX: PRO-ED.

Crystal, D. (1992). *An encyclopedic dictionary of language and languages.* Cambridge, MA: Blackwell Publishers.

Curry, B., & Temple, T. (1992). *Using curriculum frameworks for systemic reform.* Alexandria, VA: Association for Supervision and Curriculum Development.

DeFord, D. E. (1980). Young children and their writing. *Theory into Practice, 19*(3), 157–163.

Delpit, L. (1995). *Other people's children: Cultural conflict in the classroom.* New York: New Press.

DePaepe, P., Reichle, J., Doss, S., & Shriner, C. L. (1994). A preliminary evaluation of written individualized habilitation objectives and their correspondence with direct implementation. *Journal of the Association for Persons with Severe Handicaps, 19*(2), 94–104.

DiBella-McCarthy, H., McDaniel, E. A., & Miller, R. (1995). How efficacious are you? *Teaching Exceptional Children, 27*(3), 68–72.

Disability Research Systems, Inc. (1992). *Addressing unique educational needs of individuals with disabilities: An outcome-based approach (emotional impairment)*. Lansing, MI: Author.

Disability Research Systems, Inc. (1996). *Addressing unique educational needs of individuals with disabilities (AUEN), Version 3.0*. Lansing, MI: Author. Level 1: *Educational performance expectations for achieving full independence in major life roles*. Level 2: *Educational performance expectations for achieving functional independence in major life roles*. Level 3: *Educational performance expectations for achieving supported independence in major life roles*. Level 4: *Educational performance for participation in major life activities*.

Disability Research Systems, Inc., & State of Michigan Dept. of Education. (1994). *Addressing unique educational needs of individuals with disabilities—An outcome-based approach*. Lansing, MI: Author.

Donahue, K. (1996, Winter). Reading method rooted in phonics and skills draws strong results for students with learning disabilities. *Counterpoint, 17*(2), 1, 4–5.

Dunlap, G., Kern, L., dePerczel, M., Clarke, S., Wilson, D., Childs, K. E., White, R., & Falk, G. D. (1993). Functional analysis of classroom variables for students with emotional and behavioral disorders. *Behavioral Disorders, 18,* 275–291.

Dunn, L. M., & Dunn, L. M. (1981). *Peabody Picture Vocabulary Test-Revised*. Circle Pines, MN: American Guidance Service.

Dykman, A. (1994–1995). Fighting words: Across the nation outcome-based education is embroiled in controversy. *Vocational Education Journal, 79,* 36–39.

Eisner, E. W. (1995). Standards for American schools: Help or hindrance? *Phi Delta Kappan, 76*(10), 758–764.

Eldredge, J. L. (1995). *Teaching decoding in holistic classrooms*. Englewood Cliffs, NJ: Prentice-Hall.

Elliott, S. N. (1994). *Creating meaningful performance assessments: Fundamental concepts*. Reston, VA: Council for Exceptional Children.

Emery, D. W. (1996). Helping readers comprehend stories from the characters' perspectives. *The Reading Teacher, 49*(7), 534–541.

Englemann, S. (1996, Summer). *Direct instruction*. Unpublished paper. University of Oregon.

Englert, C. S., Hiebert, E. H., & Stewart, S. R. (1985). Spelling unfamiliar words by an analogy strategy. *The Journal of Special Education, 19,* 291–306.

Englert, C. S., & Mariage, T. (1990). Send for the POSSE: Structuring the comprehension dialogue. *Academic Therapy, 25*(4), 473–487.

Eresh, J. T. (1990, April). *Portfolio assessment as a means of self-directed learning*. Paper presented at the meeting of the American Educational Research Association, Boston.

Ernst, L. C., & Ernst, L. (1990). *The tangram magician*. New York: Harry N. Abrams, Inc.

Espinola, O., & Croft, D. (1992). *Solutions: Access technologies for people who are blind*. Boston: National Braille Press.

Esterson, M., & Bluth, L. F. (1987). *Related services for handicapped children*. Boston: College-Hill Press.

Evans, S., Evans, W., & Gable, R. (1989). An ecological survey of student behavior. *Teaching Exceptional Children, 21*(4), 12–17.

Falvey, M. A. (1989). *Community-based curriculum: Instructional strategies for students with severe handicaps* (2nd ed.). Baltimore: Paul H. Brookes.

Falvey, M. A. (Ed.). (1995). *Inclusive and heterogeneous schooling: Assessment, curriculum, and instruction*. Baltimore: Paul H. Brookes.

Falvey, M. A., Gage, S. T., & Eshilian, L. (1995). Secondary curriculum and instruction. In M. A. Falvey (Ed.), *Inclusive and heterogeneous schooling: Assessment, curriculum, and instruction* (pp. 341–362). Baltimore: Paul H. Brookes.

Falvey, M. A., & Grenot-Scheyer, M. (1995). Instructional strategies. In M. A. Falvey (Ed.), *Inclusive and heterogeneous schooling: Assessment, curriculum, and instruction* (pp. 131–158). Baltimore: Paul H. Brookes.

Falvey, M. A., & Rosenberg, R. L. (1995). Developing and fostering friendships. In M. A. Falvey (Ed.), *Inclusive and heterogeneous schooling: Assessment, curriculum, and instruction* (pp. 267–283). Baltimore: Paul H. Brookes.

Federal Regulations for Individuals with Disabilities Education Act (IDEA) Amendments of 1997. *Federal Register* (34 CFR § 300), Wednesday, October 22, 1997. Federal Regulations are available from: Government Printing Office, Superintendent of Documents, P.O. Box 371954, Pittsburgh, PA 15250-7954, Phone (202) 512-1800. (Requests must include the month, day, year of the *Federal Register.*)

Fernald, G. M. (1943). *Remedial techniques in basic school subjects.* New York: McGraw-Hill.

Feuer, M. J., & Fulton, K. (1993). The many faces of performance assessment. *Phi Delta Kappan, 74,* 478.

Finn, J. D. (1989). Withdrawing from school. *Review of Educational Research, 59,* 117–142.

Fister, S. L., & Kemp, K. A. (1995). *TGIF: But what will I do on Monday?* Longmont, CO: Sopris West.

Fitzpatrick, K. A. (1991). Restructuring to achieve outcomes of significance for all students. *Educational Leadership, 48*(8), 18–22.

Florida Commission on Education Reform and Accountability. (1994). *Florida's system of school improvement and accountability (Blueprint 2000).* Tallahassee, Florida: (Author).

Florida Department of Education and Disability Research System, Inc. (1995a). *Performance assessment system for students with disabilities—Functional supported expectations.* Lansing, Michigan and Tallahassee, Florida: State of Florida Department of Education.

Florida Department of Education and Disability Research System, Inc. (1995b). *Performance assessment system for students with disabilities—Goal 3 student performance standards.* Lansing, Michigan and Tallahassee, Florida: State of Florida Department of Education.

Ford, A., Davern, L., & Schnoor, R. (1992). Inclusive education: "Making sense" of the curriculum. In S. Stainback & W. Stainback (Eds.), *Curriculum considerations in inclusive classrooms: Facilitating learning for all students* (pp. 37–61). Baltimore: Paul H. Brookes.

Ford, A., Schnorr, R., Meyer, L., Davern, L., Black, J., & Dempsey, P. (1989). *The Syracuse community-referenced curriculum guide for students with moderate and severe disabilities.* Baltimore: Paul H. Brookes.

Foster-Johnson, L., & Dunlap, G. (1993). Using functional assessment to develop effective, individualized interventions for challenging behaviors. *Teaching Exceptional Children, 25*(3), 44–50.

Fox, B. J., & Wright, M. (1997). Connecting school and home literacy experiences through cross-age reading. *The Reading Teacher, 50*(5), 396–403.

Fuchs, D., Fernstrom, P., Scott, S., Fuchs, L., & Vandermeer, L. (1994). Classroom ecological inventory: A process for mainstreaming. *Teaching Exceptional Children, 26*(3), 11–15.

Fuchs, L. S., & Deno, S. L. (1992). Effects of curriculum within curriculum-based measurement. *Exceptional Children, 58*(3), 232–243.

Fulk, B. M., & Montgomery-Grymes, D. J. (1994). Strategies to improve student motivation. *Intervention in School and Clinic, 30*(1), 28–33.

Fulk, B. M., & Stormount-Spurgin, M. (1995). Fourteen spelling strategies for students with learning disabilities. *Intervention in School and Clinic, 31*(1), 16–20.

Fullan, M. (1993). Innovation, reform, and restructuring strategies. In G. Cawelti (Ed.), *Challenges and achievements of American education.* Alexandria, VA: Association for Supervision and Curriculum Development.

Gage, S. T., & Falvey, M. A. (1995). Assessment strategies to develop appropriate curricula and educational programs. In M. A. Falvey (Ed.), *Inclusive and heterogeneous schooling: Assessment, curriculum, and instruction* (pp. 59–110). Baltimore: Paul H. Brookes.

Galvin, J. C., & Scherer, M. J. (1996). *Evaluating, selecting and using appropriate assistive technology.* Gaithersburg, MD: Aspen Pub.

Gandal, M. (1995). Why we need academic standards. *Educational Leadership, 53*(1), 84–86.

Garber, S. W., Garber, M. D., & Spizman, R. F. (1990). *Is your child hyperactive? inattentive? impulsive? distractible? Helping the ADD/hyperactive child.* New York: Villard Books.

Gardner, H. (1983). *Frames of mind: The theory of multiple intelligences.* New York: Basic Books.

Gartner, A. J., & Riessman, F. (1994). Tutoring helps those who give, those who receive. *Educational Leadership, 52*(3), 58–60.

Gaustad, G. M., & Messenheimer-Young, T. (1991). Dialogue journals for students with learning disabilities. *Teaching Exceptional Children, 23*(3), 28–31.

Gearheart, C., & Gearheart, B. (1990). *Introduction to special education assessment: Principles and practices.* Denver: Love Publishing.

George, N. L., & Lewis, T. J. (1991). EASE: Exit assistance for special educators—Helping students make the transition. *Teaching Exceptional Children, 23*(2), 34–39.

Giangreco, M. F. (1997). Persistent questions about curriculum for students with severe disabilities. *Physical Disabilities: Education and Related Services, 15*(2), 53–56.

Giangreco, M. F., & Putnam, J. (1991). Supporting the education of students with severe disabilities in regular education environments. In L. H. Meyer, C. A. Peck, & L. Brown (Eds.), *Critical Issues in the Lives of People with Severe Disabilities* (pp. 245–270). Baltimore: Paul H. Brookes.

Gibson, S., & Dembo, M. H. (1984). Teacher efficacy: A construct validation. *Journal of Educational Psychology, 76*(4), 569–582.

Goldenberg, C. (1998). A balanced approach to early Spanish literacy instruction. In R. M. Gersten & R. T. Jimenez (Eds.), *Promoting learning for culturally and linguistically diverse students* (pp. 3–25). Belmont, CA: Wadsworth.

Goldstein, A. P., & McGinnis, E. (1997). *Skillstreaming the adolescent: New strategies and perspectives for teaching prosocial skills* (rev. ed.). Champaign, IL: Research Press.

Gollnick, D. M., & Chinn, P. C. (1990). *Multicultural education in a pluralistic society.* New York: Merrill.

Good, T. L., & Brophy, J. E. (1991). *Looking in classrooms* (5th ed.). New York: HarperCollins.

Graden, J. L. (1989). Redefining "prereferral": Intervention as intervention assistance: Collaboration between general and special education. *Exceptional Children, 56*(3), 227–231.

Graves, A. (1998). Instructional strategies and techniques for middle school students who are learning English. In R. M. Gersten & R. T. Jimenez (Eds.), *Promoting learning for culturally and linguistically diverse students* (pp. 167–186). Belmont, CA: Wadsworth.

Graves, D. H. (1983). *Writing: Teachers and children at work.* Portsmouth, NH: Heinemann.

Graves, D. H. (1994). *A fresh look at writing.* Concord, Ontario: Heinemann.

Graves, M. F., Prenn, M. C., & Cooke, C. L. (1985). The coming attraction: Previewing short stories. *Journal of Reading, 28*(7), 594–600.

Griffith, P. L., & Olson, M. W. (1992). Phonemic awareness helps beginning readers break the code. *The Reading Teacher, 45*(7), 516–523.

Gronlund, N. E. (1995). *How to write and use instructional objectives* (5th ed.). Englewood Cliffs, NJ: Prentice-Hall.

Guild, P. (1994). The culture/learning style connection. *Educational Leadership, 51*(8), 16–21.

Gurganus, S., Janas, M., & Schmitt, L. (1995). Science instruction: What special education teachers need to know and what roles they need to play. *Teaching Exceptional Children, 27*(4), 7–9.

Haberman, M. (1991). The pedagogy of poverty versus good teaching. *Phi Delta Kappan, 73*, 290–294.

Hammill, D. D., & Larsen, S. C. (1988). *Test of Written Language-Second Edition* (TOWL-2). Austin, TX: PRO-ED.

Hammill, D. D., & Newcomer, P. L. (1997). *Test of Language Development-Intermediate, Third Edition.* Austin, TX: PRO-ED.

Hamre-Nietupski, S., McDonald, J., & Nietupski, J. (1994). Enhancing participation of a student with multiple disabilities in regular education. *Teaching Exceptional Children, 26*(3), 60–63.

Hardman, M. L., Drew, C. J., & Egan, M. W. (1996). *Human exceptionality: Society, school and family.* (5th ed.). Boston: Allyn & Bacon.

Hart, D. (1994). *Authentic assessment: A handbook for educators.* Menlo Park, CA: Addison-Wesley.

Hatlen, P. (1996, Spring). The core curriculum for blind and visually impaired students including those with additional disorders. *Review, 28*(1), 25–32.

Hazekamp, J., & Huebner, K. M. (Eds.). (1989). *Program planning and evaluation for blind and visually impaired students: National guidelines for educational excellence.* New York: American Foundation for the Blind.

Hazel, S., & Schumaker, J. (1987). *Social skills and learning disabilities: Current issues and recommendations for future research.* Paper presented at the National Conference on Learning Disabilities, National Institutes of Health, Bethesda, MD.

Heckelman, R. (1969). The neurological impress method of remedial reading instruction. *Academic Therapy, 4,* 277–282.

Heilman, A. W. (1998). *Phonics in proper perspective* (8th ed.). Upper Saddle River, NJ: Merrill.

Heinze, T. (1986). Communication skills. In G. T. Scholl (Ed.), *Foundations of education for blind and visually handicapped children and youth: Theory and practice* (pp. 301–314). New York: American Foundation for the Blind.

Herman, J. L., Aschbacher, P. R., & Winters, L. (1992). *A practical guide to alternative assessment.* Alexandria, VA: Association for Supervision and Curriculum Development.

Herrnstein, R. J., & Murray, C. (1994). *The bell curve: Intelligence and class structure in American life.* New York: Free Press.

Heward, W. L., Gardner, R., III, Cavanaugh, R. A., Courson, F. H., Grossi, T. A., & Barbetta, P. M. (1996). Everyone participates in this class: Using response cards to increase active student response. *Teaching Exceptional Children, 28*(2), 5–10.

Hiebert, J., & Wearne, D. (1993). Instructional tasks, classroom discourse, and students' learning in second-grade arithmetic. *American Educational Research Journal, 30,* 393–425.

Hill, E., & Ponder, P. (1976). *O & M techniques: A guide for the practitioner.* New York, NY: American Foundation for the Blind.

Hofmeister, A., & Thorkildsen, R. (1987). Interactive videodisc and exceptional individuals. In J. Lindsey (Ed.), *Computers and exceptional individuals* (pp. 189–205). Columbus, OH: Merrill.

Holbrook, M. C. (1996). *Children with visual impairment.* Bethesda, MD: Woodbine House.

Holdaway, D. (1979). *Foundations of literacy.* Sydney, Australia: Ashton Scholastic.

Horton, S. V., & Lovitt, T. C. (1989). Using study guides with three classifications of secondary students. *Journal of Special Education, 22,* 447–462.

Horton, S. V., Lovitt, T. C., & Bergerud, D. (1990). The effectiveness of graphic organizers for three classifications of secondary students in content area classes. *Journal of Learning Disabilities, 23,* 12–29.

Hourcade, J. J., Parette, H. P., Jr., & Huer, M. B. (1997). Family and cultural alert! Considerations in assistive technology assessment. *Teaching Exceptional Children, 30*(1), 40–44.

Houston, G., Goolrick, R., & Tate, R. (1991). Storytelling as a stage in process writing: A whole language model. *Teaching Exceptional Children, 23*(2), 40–43.

Howell, K. W., Fox, S. L., & Morehead, M. K. (1993). *Curriculum-based evaluation: Teaching and decision making* (2nd ed.). Pacific Grove, CA: Brooks/Cole.

Hoy, C., & Gregg, N. (1994). *Assessment: The special educator's role.* Pacific Grove, CA: Brooks/Cole.

Hudson, P., Lignugaris-Kraft, B., & Miller, T. (1993). Using content enhancements to improve the performance of adolescents with learning disabilities in content classes. *Learning Disabilities Research and Practice, 8*(2), 106–126.

Hunt, P., & Farron-Davis, F. (1992). A preliminary investigation of IEP quality and content associated with placement in general education versus special education class. *Journal of the Association for Persons with Severe Handicaps, 17*(4), 247–253.

Hunt, P., Fearon-Davis, F., Beckstead, S., Curtis, D., & Goetz, L. (1994). Evaluating the effects of placement of students with severe disabilities in general education versus special classes. *Journal of the Association for Persons with Severe Handicaps, 19*(3), 200–214.

Hunt, P., Goetz, L., & Anderson, J. (1986). The quality of IEP objectives associated with placement on integrated versus segregated school sites. *Journal of the Association for Persons with Severe Handicaps, 11*(2), 125–130.

Hunter, M. (1995). Mastery teaching. In J. H. Block, S. T. Everson, & T. R. Guskey (Eds.), *School improvement programs* (pp. 181–204). New York: Scholastic, Inc.

Hyatt, C., & Brimmer, M. (1997). Estimation and investigation. *California Mathematics Council CommunicaCator, 22*(3), 50–51.

Idol, L. (1987). Group story mapping: A comprehension strategy for both skilled and unskilled readers. *Journal of Learning Disabilities, 20*(4), 196–204.

Idol, L., & West, J. F. (1987). Consultation in special education (Part II): Training and practice. *Journal of Learning Disabilities, 20*(8), 474–497.

Irwin, P. A., & Mitchell, J. N. (1983). A procedure for assessing the richness of retellings. *Journal of Reading, 26*(5), 391–396.

Jacobs, H. H. (1991, October). Planning for curriculum integration. *Educational Leadership, 49*(2), 27–28.

Jayanthi, M., Bursuck, W., Epstein, M. H., & Polloway, E. A. (1997). Strategies for successful homework. *Teaching Exceptional Children, 30*(1), 4–7.

Jayanthi, M., Nelson, J. S., Sawyer, V., Bursuck, W. D., & Epstein, M. H. (1995). Homework-communication problems among parents, classroom teachers and special education teachers: An exploratory study. *Remedial and Special Education, 16*(2), 102–116.

Jefferson County Schools. (1983). *Senior high study skills booklet.* Golden, CO: Author.

Jenkins, J. R., Jewell, M., Leicester, N., O'Connor, R. E., Jenkins, L. M., & Troutner, N. M. (1994). Accommodations for individual differences without classroom ability groups: An experiment in school restructuring. *Exceptional Children, 60,* 344–358.

Johnson, D. E., Bullock, C. C., & Ashton-Schaeffer, C. (1997). Families and leisure: A context for learning. *Teaching Exceptional Children, 30*(2), 30–34.

Johnson, D. W., Johnson, R. T., & Holubec, E. J. (1994). *The new circles of learning: Cooperation in the classroom and school.* Alexandria, VA: Association for Supervision and Curriculum Development.

Joint Committee on Standards for Educational Evaluation. (1994). *The program evaluation standards* (2nd ed.). Thousand Oaks, CA: Sage Publications.

Kagan, S. (1989–1990). The structural approach to cooperative learning. *Educational Leadership, 47*(4), 12–15.

Kaufman, A. S., & Kaufman, N. L. (1985). *Kaufman Test of Educational Achievement.* Circle Pines, MN: American Guidance Service.

Kimm, C. H., Falvey, M. A., Bishop, K. D., & Rosenberg, R. L. (1995). Motor and personal care skills. In M. A. Falvey (Ed.), *Inclusive and heterogeneous schooling: Assessment, curriculum, and instruction* (pp. 187–228). Baltimore: Paul H. Brookes.

King-Sears, M. E. (1994). *Curriculum-based assessment in special education.* San Diego: Singular Publishing Group.

Kline, L. W. (1995). A baker's dozen: Effective instructional strategies. In R. W. Cole (Ed.), *Educating everybody's children: Diverse teaching strategies for diverse learners* (pp. 21–46). Alexandria, VA: Association for Supervision and Curriculum Development.

Kluwin, T. N. (1996). Getting hearing and deaf students to write to each other through dialogue journals. *Teaching Exceptional Children, 28*(2), 50–53.

Knapp, M. S., & Shields, P. M. (Eds.). (1992). *Better schooling for the children of poverty: Alternatives to conventional wisdom.* Berkeley, CA: McCutchan.

Kniep, W. M., & Martin-Kniep, G. O. (1995). Designing schools and curriculum for the 21st century. In J. A. Bean (Ed.), *Toward a coherent curriculum: The 1995 ASCD Yearbook* (pp. 87–100). Alexandria, VA: Association for Supervision and Curriculum Development.

Koenig, A. J. (1996). Selection of learning and literacy media for children and youth with low vision. In A. L. Corn & A. J. Koenig (Eds.), *Foundations of low vision: Clinical and functional perspectives* (pp. 246–279). New York: American Foundation for the Blind Press.

Koenig, A. J., & Rex, E. J. (1996). Instruction of literacy skills to children and youth with low vision. In A. L. Corn and A. T. Koenig (Eds.), *Foundations of low vision: Clinical and functional perspectives* (pp. 280–305). New York: American Foundation for the Blind Press.

Kravets, M. (1996). Key steps to selecting a college for students with ADD. *Attention!, 3*(2), 8–21.

LaBerge, D., & Samuels, S. I. (1974). Toward a theory of automatic information processing in reading. *Cognitive Psychology, 6,* 293–323.

Ladson-Billings, G. (1994). *The dreamkeepers: Successful teachers of African-American children.* San Francisco: Jossey-Bass.

Langer, J. A. (1981). From theory to practice: A prereading plan. *Journal of Reading, 25*(21), 152–156.

Larsen, C., & Hammill, D. (1994). *Test of Written Spelling-2.* Austin, TX: PRO-ED.

Lerner, J. (1997). *Learning disabilities: Theories, diagnosis, and teaching strategies* (7th ed.). Boston: Houghton Mifflin Company.

Levack, N. (1991). *Low vision: A resource guide with adaptations for students with visual impairments.* Austin, TX: Texas School for the Blind and Visually Impaired.

Levy, N. R., & Rosenberg, M. S. (1990). Strategies for improving the written expression of students with learning disabilities. *Learning Disabilities Forum, 16*(1), 23–30.

Light, L., Dumlao, C. M., & Stecker, P. M. (1993). Video résumé: An application of technology for persons with severe disabilities. *Teaching Exceptional Children, 25*(3), 58–61.

Lim, L. H. F., & Browder, D. M. (1994). Multicultural life skills assessment of individuals with severe disabilities. *Journal of the Association for Persons with Severe Handicaps, 19*(2), 130–138.

Lindsley, O. R. (1990). Precision teaching: By teachers for children. *Teaching Exceptional Children, 22*(3), 10–15.

Lipson, M. Y., & Wixson, K. K. (1997). *Assessment and instruction of reading and writing disability: An interactive approach* (2nd ed.). New York: Addison Wesley Longman.

London, R. (1997). The role of technology in solving nonroutine problems. *California Mathematics Council CommunicaCator, 22*(3), 36–38.

Lovitt, T. C., Cushing, S. S., & Stump, C. S. (1994). High school students rate their IEPs: Low opinions and lack of ownership. *Intervention in School and Clinic, 30*(1), 34–37.

Lowenbraun, S., & Thompson, M. D. (1994). Hearing impairments. In H. G. Haring, L. McCormick, & T. G. Haring, *Exceptional Children and Youth* (6th ed.) (pp. 381–410). New York: Macmillan.

Loyd, R. J., & Brolin, D. E. (1997). *Life centered career education: Modified curriculum for individuals with moderate disabilities.* Reston, VA: Council for Exceptional Children.

Lutfiyya, Z. M. (1988, September). Other than clients: Reflections on relationships between people with disabilities and typical people. *Newsletter of the Association for Persons with Severe Handicaps, 14*(9), 3–5.

Madison Metropolitan School District, Department of Integrated Student Services. (1994, January). *Goals for areas function—Career/vocational/transition.* Madison, WI: Author.

Mangold, P. N. (1985). *Teaching the braille slate and stylus: A manual for mastery.* Castro Valley, CA: Exceptional Teaching Aids.

Markwardt, F. C. (1989). *Peabody Individual Achievement Test-Revised.* Circle Pines, MN: American Guidance Service.

Martin, J. E., & Marshall, L. H. (1995). Choicemaker: A comprehensive self-determination transition program. *Intervention in School and Clinic, 30*(3), 147–156.

Marzano, R. J. (1992). *A different kind of classroom: Teaching with dimensions of learning.* Alexandria, VA: Association for Supervision and Curriculum Development.

Marzano, R. J., & Kendall, J. S. (1995). The McREL database: A tool for constructing local standards. *Educational Leadership, 52*(6), 42–49.

Marzano, R. J., Pickering, D., & McTighe, J. (1993). *Assessing student outcomes: Performance assessment using the dimensions of learning model.* Alexandria, VA: Association for Supervision and Curriculum Development.

Mayer, R. (1979). Can advance organizers influence meaningful learning? *Review of Educational Research, 49,* 371–383.

McCarney, S. B., & Wunderlich, K. C. (Eds.). (1993). *The prereferral intervention manual.* Columbia, CT: Hawthorne.

McDaniel, E. A., & DiBella-McCarthy, H. (1989). Enhancing teacher efficacy in special education. *Teaching Exceptional Children, 21*(4), 32–38.

McLaughlin, M. J., & Hopfengardner-Warren, S. H. (1992). *Issues and options in restructuring schools and special education programs.* College Park, MD: Center for Policy Options in Special Education, Institute for the Study of Exceptional Children and Youth, University of Maryland.

McLoughlin, J. A., & Lewis, R. B. (1994). *Assessing special students* (4th ed.). New York: Merrill.

Meese, R. L. (1994). *Teaching learners with mild disabilities: Integrating research and practice.* Pacific Grove, CA: Brooks/Cole.

Meltzer, L., & Reid, D. K. (1994). New directions in the assessment of students with special needs: The shift toward a constructivist perspective. *Journal of Special Education 28,* 338–355.

Mercer, C. D. (1997). *Students with learning disabilities* (5th ed.). Upper Saddle River, NJ: Prentice-Hall.

Mercer, C. D., Jordan, L., & Miller, S. P. (1996). Constructivistic math instruction for diverse learners. *Learning Disabilities Research and Practice, 11,* 147–156.

Merrell, K. W. (1994). *Assessment of behavioral, social, and emotional problems.* New York: Longman.

Meyer, L. H., Reichle, J., McQuarter, R., Cole, D., Vandercook, T., Evans, I., Neel, R., & Kishi, G. (1985). *Assessment of social competence (ASC): A scale of social competence functions.* Minneapolis: University of Minnesota Consortium, Institute for the Education of Severely Handicapped Learners.

Miller, D. R. (1994). On your own: A functional skills activity for adolescents with mild disabilities. *Teaching Exceptional Children, 26*(3), 29–32.

Miller, S. P., & Mercer, C. D. (1993a). Mnemonics: Enhancing the math performance of students with learning disabilities. *Intervention in School and Clinic, 29*(2), 78–82.

Miller, S. P., & Mercer. C. D. (1993b). Using data to learn about concrete-semiconcrete-abstract instruction for students with math disabilities. *Learning Disabilities Research and Practice, 8*(2), 89–96.

Miner, C. A., & Bates, P. E. (1997). Person-centered transition planning. *Teaching Exceptional Children, 30*(1), 66–69.

Mitchell, R. (1992). *Testing for learning: How new approaches to evaluation can improve American schools.* New York: Free Press.

Monson, M. P., & Monson, R. J. (1993). Who creates curriculum: New roles for teachers. *Educational Leadership, 51*(2), 19–21.

Morgan, D. P., & Jenson, W. R. (1988). *Teaching behaviorally disordered students: Preferred practices.* Columbus, OH: Merrill.

Morris, D. (1981). Concept of word: A developmental phenomenon in the beginning reading and writing process. *Language Arts, 58,* 659–668.

Myller, R. (1962). *How big is a foot?* New York: Dell Publishing.

National Assessment Governing Board. (1991, October). *The levels of mathematics achievement.* Washington, DC: Author.

National Assessment Governing Board. (1996). *Science framework for the 1996 national assessment of educational progress.* Washington, DC: Author.

National Council for the Social Studies. (1994). *Curriculum standards for social studies.* Washington, DC: Author.

National Council of Teachers of Mathematics. (1989). *Curriculum and evaluation standards for school mathematics.* Reston, VA: Author.

Newman, J. M., & Church, S. M. (1990). Myths of whole language. *The Reading Teacher, 44*(1), 20–26.

Nieto, S. (1996). *Affirming diversity: The sociopolitical context of multicultural education* (2nd ed.). New York: Longman.

Ogle, D. M. (1986). K-W-L: A teaching model that develops active reading of expository text. *The Reading Teacher, 39*(6), 564–570.

Olsen, K. R. (1993). Who's afraid of O.B.E.? *Education Week, 13*(15), 25–28.

Olsen, K. R., & Massanari, C. B. (1991, October). *Special education program evaluation: What should states consider.* Lexington: Mid-South Regional Resource Center, Interdisciplinary Human Development Institute, University of Kentucky.

Olson, M. R. (1981). *Guidelines and games for teaching efficient braille reading.* New York: American Foundation for the Blind.

Overton, T. (1996). *Assessment in special education: An applied approach* (2nd ed.). New York: Merrill.

Palincsar, A. S., & Brown, A. L. (1984). Reciprocal teaching of comprehension-fostering and comprehension monitoring activities. *Cognition and Instruction, 1,* 117–175.

Pate, P. E., McGinnis, K., & Homestead, E. (1995). Creating coherence through curriculum integration. In J. A. Beane (Ed.), *Toward a coherent curriculum: The 1995 ASCD Yearbook* (pp. 62–70). Alexandria, VA: Association for Supervision and Curriculum Development.

Pattavina, S., Bergstrom, T., Marchand-Martella, N. E., & Martella, R. C. (1992). Moving On: Learning to cross streets independently. *Teaching Exceptional Children, 25*(1), 32–35.

Patton, J. M. (1998). The disproportionate representation of African Americans in special education: Looking behind the curtain for understanding and solutions. *The Journal of Special Education, 32*(1), 25–31.

Paul, A. W. (1991). *Eight hands round.* New York: Collins Publishers.

Paulson, F. L., Paulson, P. R., & Meyer, C. A. (1991). What makes a portfolio a portfolio? *Educational Leadership, 48*(5), 60–63.

Pearpoint, J., & Forest, M. (1992). Kick'em out or keep'em in: Exclusion or inclusion. In J. Pearpoint, M. Forest, & J. Snow (Eds.), *The inclusion papers: Strategies to make inclusion work* (pp. 80–88). Toronto: Inclusion Press. (ERIC Document Reproduction Service No. ED 359 677)

Pearpoint, J., O'Brien, J., & Forest, M. (1992). *PATH: Planning alternative tomorrows with hope.* Toronto: Inclusion Press.

Peregoy, S. F., & Boyle, O. F. (1997). *Reading, writing, and learning in ESL* (2nd ed.). New York: Longman.

Polloway, E. A., Bursuck, W. D., Jayanthi, M., Epstein, M. H., & Nelson, J. A. (1996). Treatment acceptability: Determining appropriate interventions within inclusive classrooms. *Intervention in School and Clinic, 31*(3), 133–144.

Posner, G. J. (1992). *Analyzing the curriculum.* New York: McGraw-Hill.

Poteet, J. A., Choate, J. S., & Stewart, S. C. (1993). Performance assessment and special education: Practices and prospects. *Focus on Exceptional Children, 26*(1), 1–20.

Powers, L. E. (1994). *Take charge.* Lebanon, NH: Dartmouth Medical School.

Powers, L. E., Sowers, J., Turner, A., Nesbitt, M., Knowles, E., & Ellison, R. (1996). Take charge: A model for promoting self-determination among adolescents with challenges. In L. E. Powers, G. H. S. Singer & J. Sowers (Eds.), *On the road to autonomy: Promoting self-competence for children and youth with disabilities* (pp. 291–322). Baltimore: Paul H. Brookes Publishing Co.

Powers, L. E., Wilson, R., Matuszewski, J., Phillips, A., Rein, C., Schumacher, D., & Gensert, J. (1996). Facilitating adolescent self-determination: What does it take? In D. J. Sands & M. L. Wehmeyer, *Self-determination across the life span: Independence and choice for people with disabilities* (pp. 257–284). Baltimore, MD: Paul H. Brookes Publishing Co.

Prentke Romich Company. (1996, Spring/Summer). *Current expressions.* Wooster, OH: Author, pp. 1–2.

Provus, M. (1971). *Discrepancy evaluation.* Berkeley, CA: McCutchan.

Psychological Corporation. (1992). *Wechsler Individual Achievement Test.* San Antonio: Harcourt Brace.

Public Laws (Current). Public Laws are Available from: (1) Senate Document Room, US Senate, Hart Senate Office Building, B-04 Washington, DC 20510, Phone: (202) 224-3121 (Requests must include the title and number of the law; and, if by mail, a self-addressed mailing label). (2) Website: www.ed.gov/offices/OSERS/IDEA; Choose "The Law"
Public Law 93-112. The Rehabilitation Act of 1973 as Amended, Section 504.
Public Law 101-336. Americans with Disabilities Act of 1990 (ADA).
Public Law 105-17. Individuals with Disabilities Education Act; (IDEA) Amendments of 1997.
Public Law 103-227. Goals 2000: The Educate America Act.

Ravitch, D. (1995). *National standards in American education.* Washington, DC: Brookings Institution Press.

Razeghi, J. A. (1998). A first step toward solving the problem of special education dropouts: Infusing career education into the curriculum. *Intervention in School and Clinic, 33*(3), 148–156.

Redmond, N. B., Bennett, C., Wiggert, J., & McLean, B. (1993). Using functional assessment to support a student with severe disabilities in the community. *Teaching Exceptional Children, 25*(3), 51–52.

Reid, R., & Katisyannis, A. (1995). Attention-deficit/hyperactivity disorders and Section 504. *Remedial and Special Education, 16*(1), 44–52.

Reyes, E. L., & Bos, C. S. (1998). Interactive semantic mapping and charting: Enhancing content area learning for language-minority students. In R. M. Gersten & R. T. Jimenez (Eds.), *Promoting learning for culturally and linguistically diverse students* (pp. 133–150). Belmont, CA: Wadsworth.

Reys, R. E., Suydam, M. N., & Lindquist, M. M. (1995). *Helping children learn mathematics* (4th ed.). Boston: Allyn and Bacon.

Rhodes, L. K., & Dudley-Marling, C. (1996). *Readers and writers with a difference: A holistic approach to teaching struggling readers and writers* (2nd ed.). Portsmouth, NH: Heinemann.

Rivera, B. D., & Rogers-Adkinson, D. (1997). Culturally sensitive interventions: Social skills training with children and parents from culturally and linguistically diverse backgrounds. *Intervention in School and Clinic, 33*(2), 75–80.

Rivera, D. P., & Smith, D. D. (1997). *Teaching students with learning and behavior problems* (3rd ed.). Boston: Allyn and Bacon.

Rojewski, J. W. (1992). Key components of model transition services for students with learning disabilities. *Learning Disability Quarterly, 15,* 135–150.

Rosenshine, B., & Stevens, R. (1986). Teaching functions. In M. C. Wittrock (Ed.), *Handbook of research on teaching* (3rd ed., pp. 376–391). New York: Macmillan.

Rosin, M., & Shenkerman, E. (1994). *Software Documentation.* LOGAL Software Inc.: Cambridge, Mass.

Ryan, S., & Paterna, L. (1997). Junior high can be inclusive: Using natural supports and cooperative learning. *Teaching Exceptional Children, 30*(2), 36–41.

Ryle, G. (1949). *The concept of mind.* New York: Barnes & Noble.

Saint-Laurent, L., Giasson, J., & Couture, C. (1997). Parents + children + reading activities = emergent literacy. *Teaching Exceptional Children, 30*(2), 52–56.

Salend, S. J. (1995). Modifying tests for diverse learners. *Intervention in School and Clinic, 31*(2), 84–90.

Scanlon, D. J., Duran, G. Z., Reyes, E. I., & Gallego, M. A. (1992). Interactive semantic mapping: An interactive approach to enhancing LD students' content area comprehension. *Learning Disabilities Research and Practice, 7,* 142–146.

Scholl, G. T. (1986). What does it mean to be blind? Definitions, terminology, and prevalence. In G. T. Scholl (Ed.), *Foundations of education for blind and visually handicapped children and youth* (pp. 23–33). New York: American Foundation for the Blind.

Schrag, J. (1991, October). *America 2000 and students with disabilities.* Presentation at the 2nd annual meeting of the U.S. Office of Special Education Programs, Technical Assistance and Dissemination Projects. Washington, DC: Office of Special Education Programs.

Schrumpf, F., Crawford, D. K., & Bodine, R. J. (1997). *Peer mediation: Conflict resolution in schools.* Champaign, IL: Research Press.

Schumaker, J. B., Deshler, A. D., Allen, G. R., Warner, M. M., & Denton, P. H. (1982). Multipass: A learning strategy for improving reading comprehension. *Learning Disability Quarterly, 5,* 295–304.

Schwartz, A. (1996). *Choices in deafness.* Bethesda, MD: Woodbine House.

Secretary's Commission on Achieving Necessary Skills. (1991). *What work requires of schools.* Washington, DC: U.S. Department of Labor.

Secretary's Commission on Achieving Necessary Skills. (1993). *Teaching the SCANS competencies.* Washington, DC: U.S. Department of Labor.

Serna, L. A., & Lau-Smith, J. (1995). Learning with purpose: Self-determination skills for students who are at risk for school and community failure. *Intervention in School and Clinic, 30*(13), 142–146.

Shanahan, T., & Shanahan, S. (1997). Character perspective charting: Helping children to develop a more complete conception of story. *The Reading Teacher, 50,* 668–677.

Sharp, S. J. (1990). Using content subject matter with LEA in middle school. *Journal of Reading, 33,* 108–112.

Sheffield, L. J., & Cruikshank, D. R. (1996). *Teaching and learning elementary and middle school mathematics* (3rd ed.). Englewood Cliffs, NJ: Merrill.

Shinn, M. R., & Hubbard, D. D. (1992). Curriculum-based measurement and problem solving assessment: Basic procedures and outcomes. *Focus on Exceptional Children, 24*(5), 1–20.

Shriner, J. G., Ysseldyke, J. E., Thurlow, M. L., & Honetschlager, D. (1994). "All" means "all"—Including students with disabilities. *Educational Leadership, 51*(6), 38–42.

Silberman, R. K. (1996). Children with visual impairments. In E. Meyer (Ed.), *Exceptional children in today's schools* (3rd ed.) (pp. 351–398). Denver: Love Publishing Company.

Silberman, R. K., & Sowell, V. (1998). Educating students who have visual impairments with learning disabilities. In S. Z. Sacks & R. K. Silberman (Eds.), *Educating students who have visual impairments and other disabilities* (pp. 161–186). Baltimore: Paul H. Brookes Publishing Co.

Simpson, R. L., Ormsbee, C. K., & Myles, B. S. (1997). General and special educators' perceptions of preassessment-related activities and team members. *Exceptionality, 7*(3), 157–167.

Singham, M. (1995). Race and intelligence: What are the issues? *Phi Delta Kappan, 77,* 271–278.

Smith, D. D., & Lovitt, T. C. (1975). The use of modeling techniques to influence the acquisition of computational arithmetic skills in learning-disabled children. In E. Ramp & G. Semb (Eds.), *Behavior Analysis: Areas of research and application.* Englewood Cliffs, NJ: Prentice-Hall.

Snell, M. (Ed.). (1993). *Instruction of students with severe disabilities.* New York: Merrill.

Souviney, R. J. (1981). *Solving problems kids care about.* Glenview, IL: Scott, Foresman and Company.

Sowell, E. J. (1989). Effects of manipulative materials in mathematics instruction. *Journal for Research in Mathematics Education, 20,* 498–505.

Spady, W. (1991). *Seven models of outcome defined OBE curriculum design and delivery.* Santa Cruz, CA: High Success Program on Outcome-Based Education.

Spady, W. (1994). *Outcome-based education: Critical issues and answers.* Arlington, VA: American Association of School Administrators.

Spady, W. (1995). Outcome-based education: From instructional reform to paradigm restructuring. In J. H. Block, S. T. Everson, & T. R. Guskey (Eds.), *School improvement programs: A handbook for educational leaders.* New York: Scholastic.

Spady, W., Marshall, K., & Rogers, S. (1994) Light, not heat, on OBE. *The American School Board, 181*(11), pp. 29–33.

Spady, W. G. (1994a). Choosing outcomes of significance. *Educational Leadership, 51*(6), 18–22.

Spady, W. G. (1994b). *Outcome-based education: Critical issues and answers.* Arlington, VA: American Association of School Administrators.

Spady, W. G. (1994c). It's time to take a close look at outcome-based education. *Communiqué, 20*(6), 16–18.

Spady, W. G., & Marshall, K. J. (1991). Beyond traditional outcome-based education. *Educational Leadership, 49*(2), 67–72.

Stahl, S. A. (1992). Saying the "p" word: Nine guidelines for exemplary phonics instruction. *The Reading Teacher, 45*(8), 618–625.

Stainback, S., & Stainback, W. (Eds.). (1992). *Curriculum considerations in inclusive classrooms: Facilitating learning for all students.* Baltimore: Paul H. Brookes.

Stauffer, R. (1969). *Teaching reading as a thinking process.* New York: Harper & Row.

Stauffer, R. (1980). *Directing the reading-thinking process.* New York: Harper & Row.

Stauffer, R. G. (1970). *The language-experience approach to the teaching of reading.* New York: Harper & Row.

Steffy, B. E. (1993a). Top-down–bottom-up: Systematic change in Kentucky. *Educational Leadership, 51*(1), 42–44.

Steffy, B. E. (1993b). *The Kentucky education reform.* Lancaster, PA: Technomic Publishing Co., Inc.

Stenmark, J. K. (1989). *Assessment alternatives in mathematics: An overview of assessment techniques that promote learning.* Berkeley, CA: EQUALS.

Stump, C. S. (1992). *Special education: The high school experience.* Unpublished doctoral dissertation, University of Washington.

Stump, C. S. (1995). *Contextualized assessment and the assessment dimension system.* Unpublished manuscript. San Francisco State University.

Stump, C. S. (1998). *Data-based decision making.* Unpublished manuscript, San Francisco State University.

Stump, C. S., Lovitt, T. C., Fister, S., Kemp, K., Moore, R., & Schroeder, B. (1992). Vocabulary intervention for secondary-level youth. *Learning Disability Quarterly, 15,* 207–222.

Stump, C. S., Wilson, C., Shirley, R., & Ung, E. (1999). Literacy and the collaborative classroom: Building supportive contexts for all students. In A. Watson & L. R. Giorcelli (Eds.), *Accepting the literacy challenge* (pp. 230–260). New York: Scholastic.

Swicegood, P. (1994). Portfolio-based assessment practices. *Intervention in School and Clinic, 30*(1), 6–15.

Taylor, R. L., Sternberg, L., & Richards, S. B. (1995). *Exceptional children: Integrating research and teaching* (2nd ed.). San Diego: Singular Publishing Group.

Thurlow, M. L., Ysseldyke, J. E., & Anderson, C. L. (1995). *High school graduation requirements: What's happening for students with disabilities?* Minneapolis: University of Minnesota, National Center on Educational Outcomes.

Toronto Board of Education. (no date). Elementary mathematics examples. *Benchmarks: Standards of student achievement.* Toronto: Author.

Turnbull, A. P., & Turnbull, H. R. (1990). *Families, professionals, and exceptionality: A special partnership* (2nd ed.). Columbus, OH: Merrill.

Turnbull, A. P., Turnbull, H. R., Shank, M., & Leal, D. (1995). *Exceptional lives: Special education in today's schools.* Columbus, OH: Merrill.

Valencia, S. (1990). A portfolio to classroom reading assessment: The whys, whats, and hows. *Reading Teacher, 43,* 338–340.

Valencia, S. W. (1997). Authentic classroom assessment of early reading: Alternatives to standardized tests. *Preventing School Failure, 41*(2), 63–70.

van Keulen, J. E., Weddington, G. R., & DeBose, C. E. (1998). *Speech, language, learning and the African American child.* Boston, MA: Allyn and Bacon.

Venn, J. (1994). *Assessment of students with special needs.* New York: Merrill.

Vygotsky, L. S. (1978). *Mind in society.* M. Cole et al., eds., Cambridge, MA: Harvard University Press.

Wagner, T. (1995). What's school really for, anyway? And who should decide? *Phi Delta Kappan, 76*(5), 393–399.

Waldron, M., Diebold, T., & Rose, S. (1985). Hearing impaired students in regular classrooms: A cognitive model for educational services. *Exceptional Children, 52*(1), 39–43.

Walker, H. M., Colvin, G., & Ramsey, E. (1995). *Antisocial behavior in school: Strategies and best practices.* Pacific Grove, CA: Brooks/Cole.

Walker, H. M., McConnell, S., Holmes, D., Todis, B., Walker, J., & Golden, N. (1993). *The Walker social skills curriculum: The ACCEPTS program* (a curriculum for children's effective peer and teacher skills). Austin, TX: PRO-ED.

Wechsler, D. (1991). *Wechsler Intelligence Scale for Children-Third Edition: Manual.* San Antonio: Psychological Corporation.

Wehman, P. (1996). *Life beyond the classroom: Transition strategies for young people with disabilities.* (2nd ed.). Baltimore: Paul H. Brookes Publishing Co.

Wehmeyer, M. L., & Meltzer, C. A. (1995). How self-determined are people with mental retardation? The national consumer survey. *Journal of Mental Retardation, 33,* 111–119.

Weimer, B. B., Cappotelli, M., & DiCamillo, J. (1994). Self-advocacy: A working proposal for adolescents with special needs. *Intervention in School and Clinic, 30*(1), 47–52.

Welch, M. (1992). The PLEASE strategy: A metacognitive learning strategy for improving the paragraph writing of students with mild learning disabilities. *Learning Disability Quarterly, 15,* 119–128.

Wechsler, D. (1991). *Wechsler Intelligence Scale for Children, Third Edition* (WISC-III). San Antonio: The Psychological Corporation.

Wesson, C. L., & King, R. P. (1996). Portfolio assessment and special education students. *Teaching Exceptional Children, 28*(2), 44–48.

West, R. P., Young, K. R., & Spooner, F. (1990). Precision teaching: An introduction. *Teaching Exceptional Children, 22*(3), 4–9.

Westling, D. L., & Fox, L. (1995). *Teaching students with severe disabilities.* Englewood Cliffs, NJ: Prentice-Hall.

White, O. R. (1986). Precision teaching—Precision learning. *Exceptional Children, 52,* 522–534.

Wiederholt, L. J., & Bryant, B. R. (1992). *Gray Oral Reading Tests-Third Edition.* Austin, TX: PRO-ED.

Wilkinson, G. S. (1993). *Wide Range Achievement Test-Revised (WRAT3).* Wilmington, DE: Jastak Associates.

Williams, W. B., Sternach, G., Wolfe, S., & Stranger, C. (1993). *Lifespace access profile: Assistive technology assessment and planning for individuals with severe or multiple disabilities.* Sebastopol, CA: Lifespace Access.

Wolf, D. P. (1989). Portfolio assessment: Sampling student work. *Educational Leadership, 46*(7), 35–39.

Wong, B., & Jones, W. (1982). Increasing metacomprehension in learning disabled and normally achieving students through self-questioning training. *Learning Disability Quarterly, 5,* 228–240.

Wong, B. Y. L., Butler, D. L., Ficzere, S. A., & Kuperis, S. (1997). Teaching adolescents with learning disabilities and low achievers to plan, write, and revise compare-and-contrast essays. *Learning Disabilities Research and Practice, 12*(1), 2–15.

Wood, P., & Lazarus, B. (1991). Overview of educational issues that impact learners with emotional impairments. *Addressing unique educational needs of individuals with disabilities: An outcome based approach (emotional impairment).* Lansing, MI: Disability Research Systems.

Woodcock, R. W. (1987). *Woodcock Reading Mastery Tests-Revised.* Circle Pines, MN: American Guidance Service.

Woodcock, R. W., & Johnson, M. B. (1990). *Woodcock-Johnson Psycho-Educational Battery-Revised: Tests of Achievement: Standard and Supplemental Batteries: Examiners Manual.* Dallas: DLM Teaching Resources.

Yopp, H. K. (1992). Developing phonemic awareness in young children. *The Reading Teacher, 45*(9), 696–703.

Ysseldyke, J. E., & Thurlow, M. L. (1993). *Self-study guide to the development of educational outcomes and indicators.* Minneapolis: University of Minnesota, National Center on Educational Outcomes.

Ysseldyke, J. E., Thurlow, M. L., & Gilman, C. J. (January, 1993). *Educational outcomes and indicators for students completing school.* Minneapolis, MN: University of Minnesota, National Center on Educational Outcomes.

Zessoules, R., & Gardner, H. (1991). Authentic assessment: Beyond the buzzword and into the classroom. In V. Perrone (Ed.), *Expanding student assessment* (pp. 47–71). Alexandria, VA: Association for Supervision and Curriculum Development.

Zimmerman, G. J. (1996). Optics and low vision devices. In A. L. Corn and A. J. Koenig (Eds.), *Foundations of low vision: Clinical and functional perspectives* (pp. 115–143). New York: American Foundation for the Blind.

Zipprich, M. A. (1995). Teaching web making as a guided planning tool to improve student narrative writing. *Remedial and Special Education, 16*(1), 3–15.

INDEX